fundamentals of CHARACTER DESIGN

How to create engaging characters for illustration, animation & visual development

3dtotalPublishing

fundamentals of CHARACTER DESIGN

How to create engaging characters for illustration, animation & visual development

3dtotalPublishing

3dtotalPublishing

Correspondence: publishing@3dtotal.com
Website: store.3dtotal.com

First published in the United Kingdom, 2020, by 3dtotal Publishing.

Reprinted in 2026 by 3dtotal Publishing.

Address: 3dtotal.com Ltd,
6 Sansome Street, Worcester,
WR1 1UH, United Kingdom.

Soft cover ISBN: 978-1-912843-18-3
Printed and bound in China by
C&C Offset Printing Co., Ltd

Visit store.3dtotal.com for a complete list of available book titles.

Managing Director: Tom Greenway
Studio Manager: Simon Morse
Lead Designer: Fiona Tarbet
Lead Editor: Samantha Rigby
Editor: Marisa Lewis
Editor: Philippa Barker
Designer: Matthew Lewis
Editorial Assistant: Tilly Barnett

Cover images © Individual artists as listed throughout the book

MIX
Paper | Supporting responsible forestry
FSC® C008047

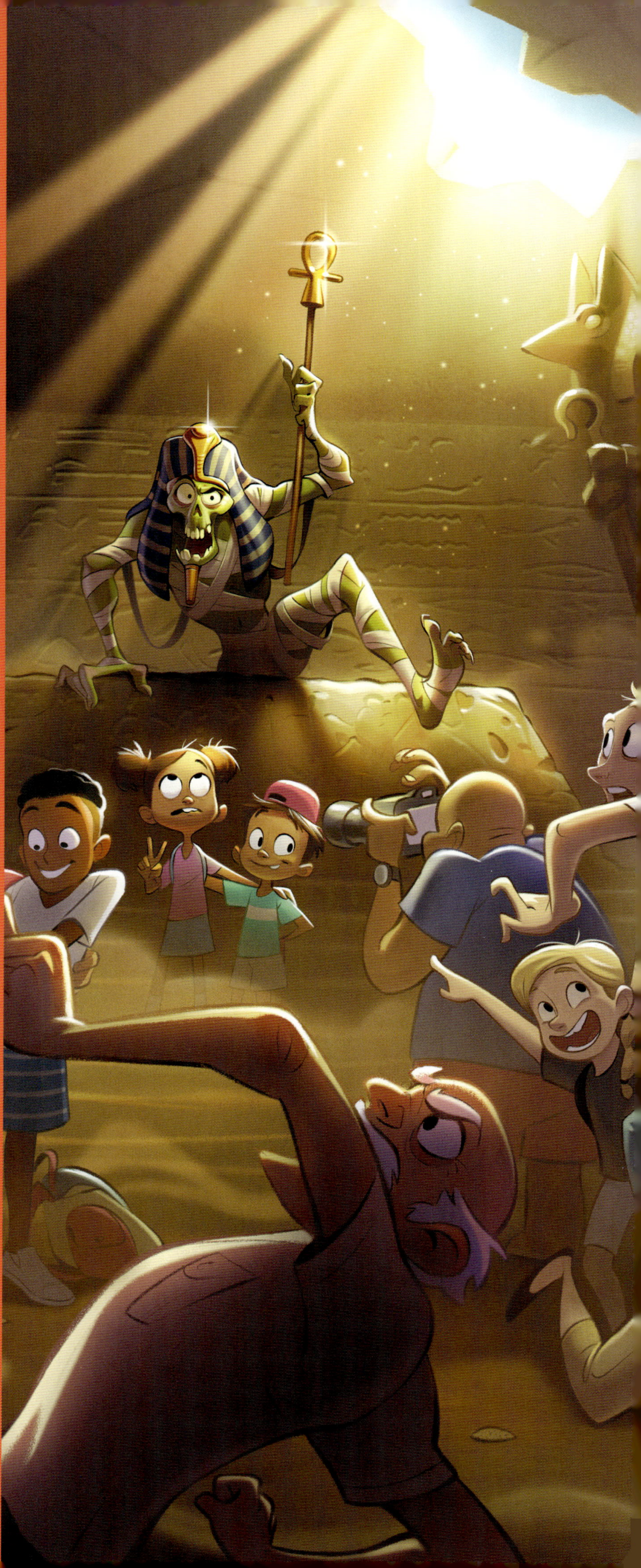

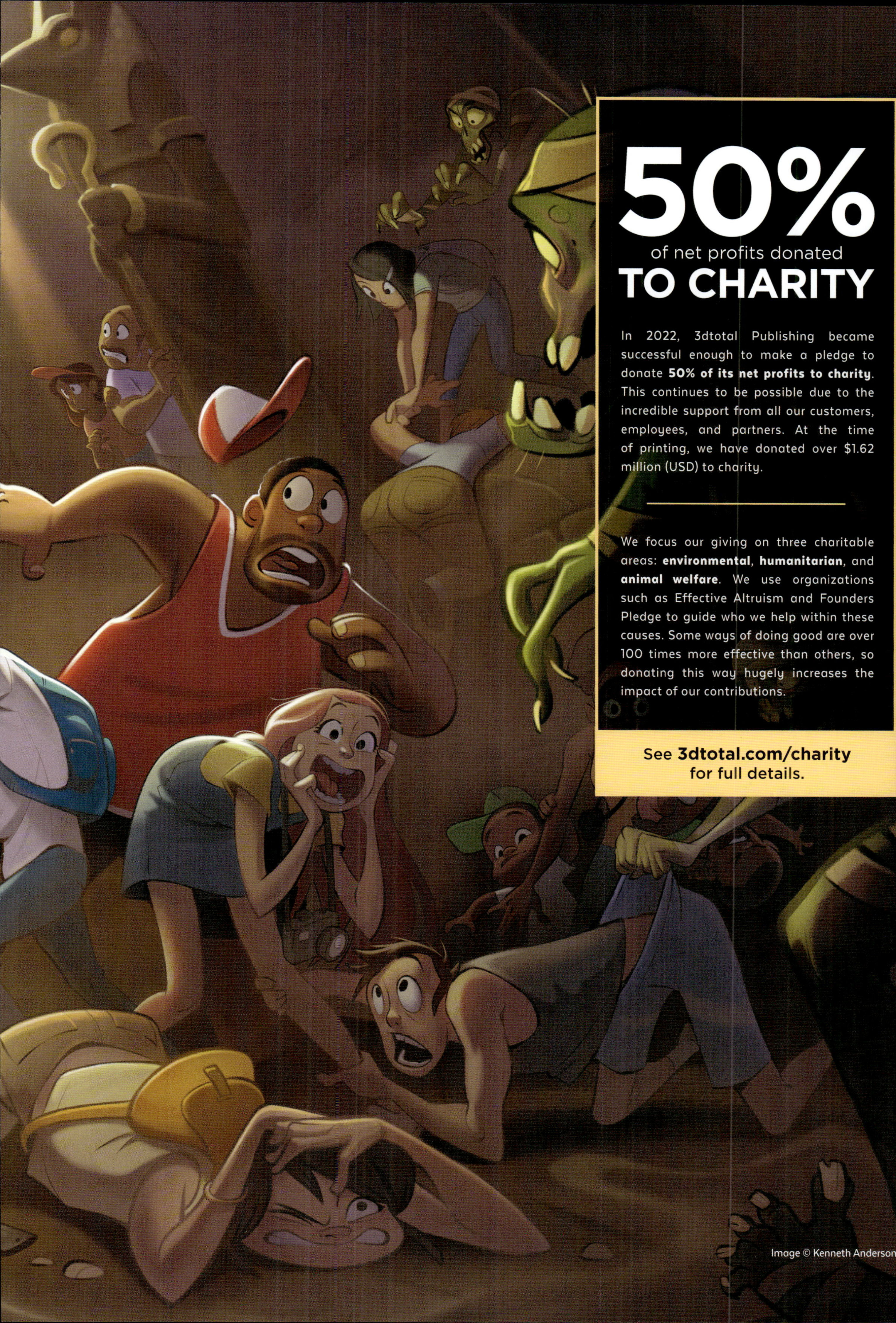

Image © Kenneth Anderson

CONTENTS

INTRODUCTION 8

HOW TO USE THIS BOOK 9

WHAT IS CHARACTER DESIGN? 10

- OVERVIEW 12
- ESTABLISHING THE STORY 18
- TELLING THE STORY 24

RESEARCH & IDEATION 34

- WHY IS RESEARCH IMPORTANT? 36
- HOW CAN YOU RESEARCH? 44
- IDEATION 48

KEY DESIGN PRINCIPLES 52

- SHAPE LANGUAGE 54
- COLOR & VALUE 60
- LIGHTING 66
- BALANCE & CONTRAST 70
- SCALE 76
- REPETITION 78
- RHYTHM 80
- TANGENTS 82

FIGURE BASICS 84

- ANATOMY OVERVIEW 86
- CONSTRUCTION & BASIC SHAPES 90
- DIFFERENT BODY TYPES 94
- EXAGGERATION OF FORM 98

POSE, MOVEMENT & GESTURE 106

- LINES OF ACTION & MOVEMENT 108
- HOW TO CONSTRUCT UPWARD FROM GESTURE 114
- EXAGGERATION OF GESTURE 120
- POSES LIBRARY 128

THE FACE 152

- CONSTRUCTING THE FACE & HEAD 154
- EXAGGERATING SHAPES 162
- EXPRESSIONS 166
- EXAGGERATING EXPRESSIONS 170
- EXPRESSIONS LIBRARY 174

AGE 190
COMMUNICATING AGE 192
BABY CHARACTERS 197
CHILD CHARACTERS 198
TEEN CHARACTERS 200
ADULT CHARACTERS 202
ELDERLY CHARACTERS 204
CASE STUDY: THE LIBRARIAN 206

ACCESSORIES 210
OVERVIEW 212
COSTUME LIBRARY 216
HAIRSTYLES LIBRARY 224
PROPS LIBRARY 232

PUTTING IT ALL TOGETHER 240
CREATING ENGAGING CHARACTERS 242
HERO VERSUS VILLAIN 244

WORKING WITH MULTIPLE CHARACTERS 250
OVERVIEW 252
TWO CHARACTERS 256
MAIN CHARACTER & SIDEKICK 260
CLASSROOM 264
BUS-STOP QUEUE 268
FAMILY DINNER 272
MUSIC BAND 276
CROWD 280
SPORTS TEAM 284

WORKING IN CHARACTER DESIGN 288
KEY CONSIDERATIONS 290
PRESENTATION 294
STYLE 296

IDEAS GRID 298

CONTRIBUTORS 302

INDEX 306

INTRODUCTION

Character design forms the backbone of so many stories that we know and love. From TV shows and animated films to video games and illustrated books, much of the media we find iconic and memorable is made so by brilliant character design. Creating fictional characters that are unique, fun, and appealing is an art form, and the most successful designs have the power to live on through decades and generations.

In this book, professional artists from across the creative industries will introduce the core tenets and essential skills of character design. They will share insightful breakdowns of subjects such as shapes, proportions, exaggeration, poses, expressions, costumes, and props – all vital ingredients in creating characters that tell a story and capture the viewer's imagination. We hope this book enriches your understanding of your favorite character designs and inspires you to create unique characters and stories of your own.

Marisa Lewis

Editor, 3dtotal Publishing

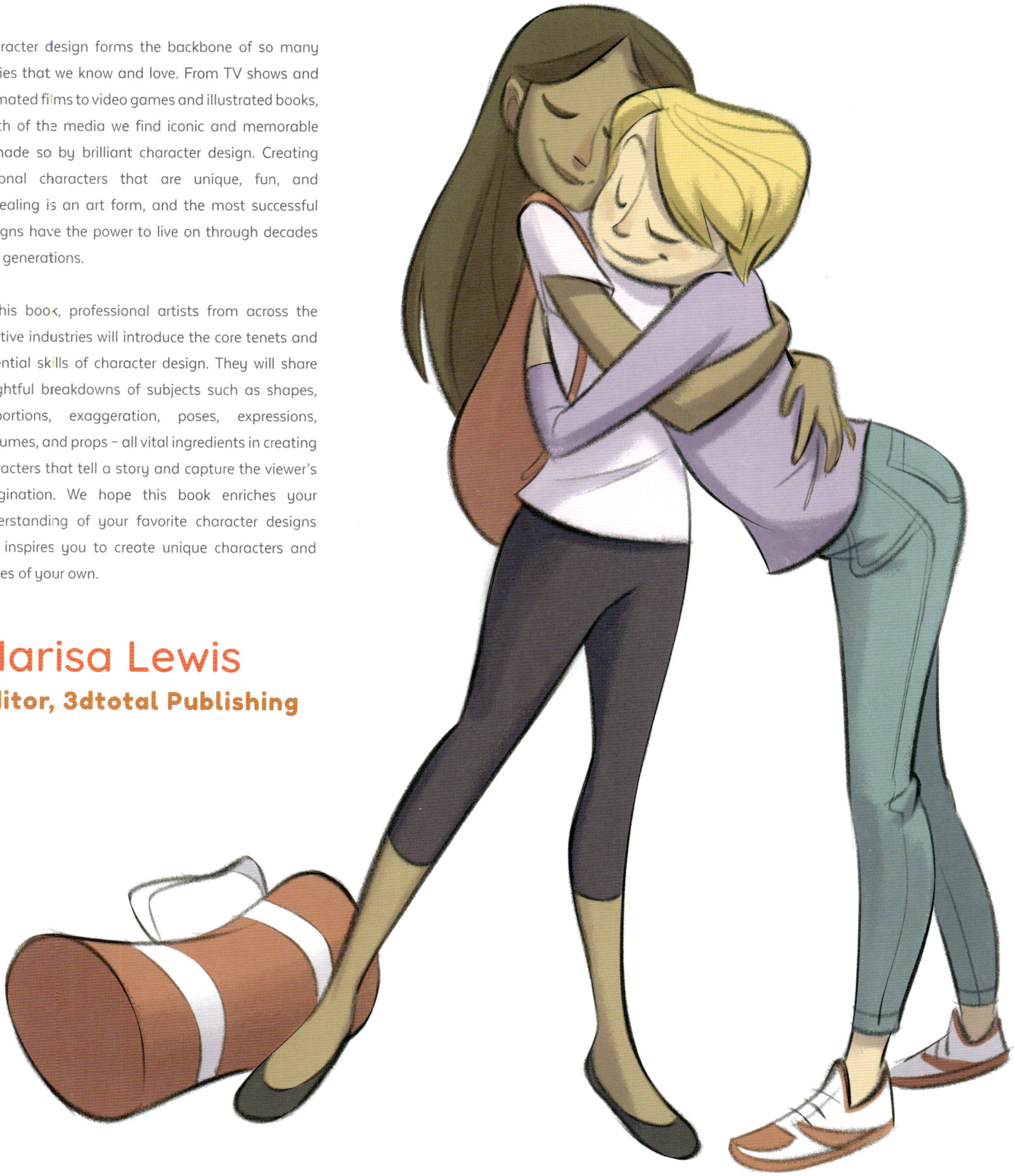

Image by Kenneth Anderson

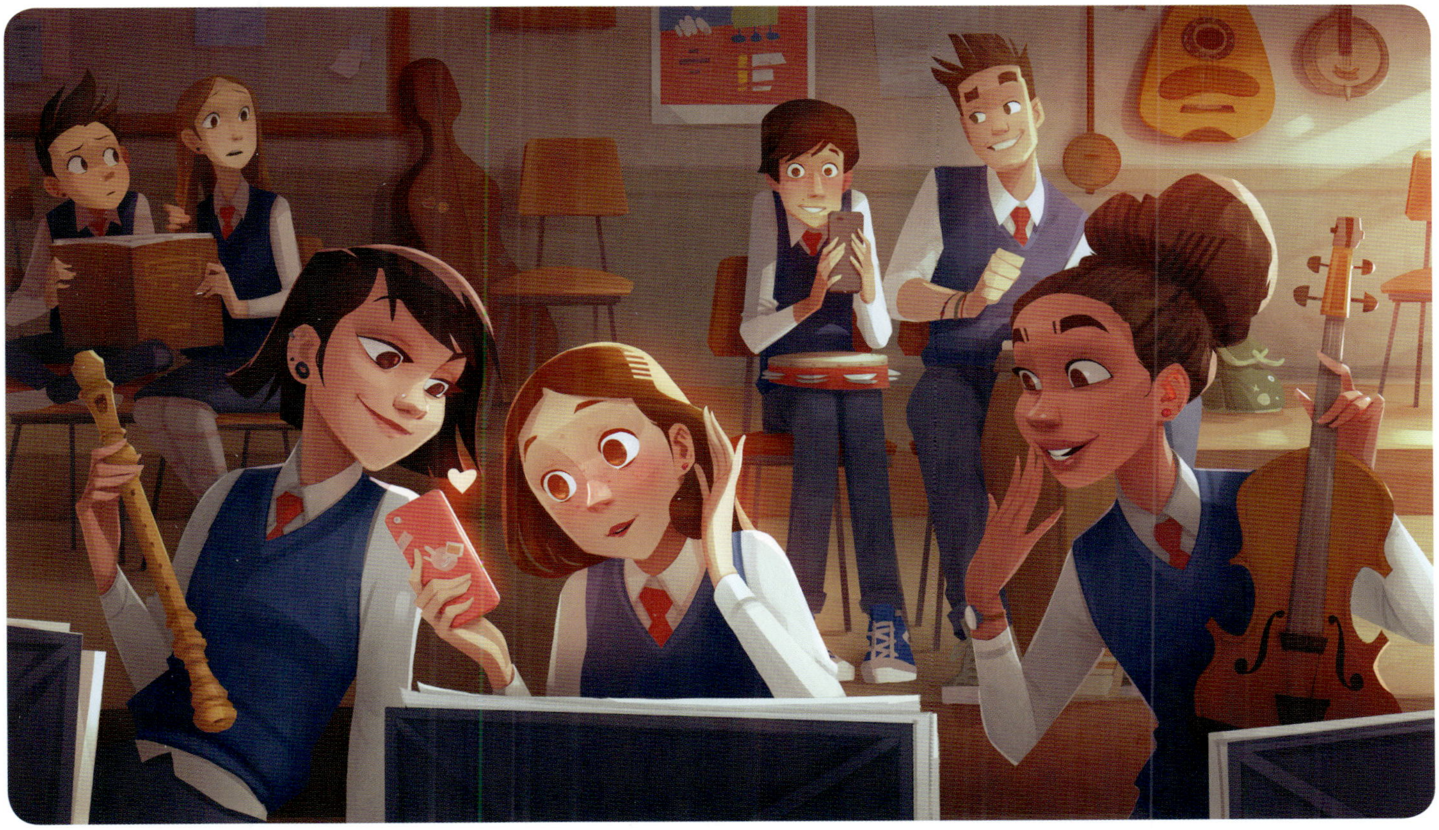

HOW TO USE THIS BOOK

It is strongly recommended to follow the book in order, starting with the **What is character design?** chapter (page 10), which talks about the background of character design and the many places in which it can be found. Following this, **Research & ideation** (page 34) offers an overview of how designs are born from research, study, and exploration, and why these are so important for creating any kind of character.

The **Key design principles** chapter (page 52) investigates how fundamental art theories such as shape, color, scale, and contrast are used in character design. The ideas and terminology covered in this chapter are applied throughout the rest of the book.

The **Figure basics** (page 84), **Pose, movement & gesture** (page 106), and **The face** (page 152) chapters explore the different features and proportions of the body and face, and how these can be stylized and exaggerated to create fun, distinctive characters full of life and personality.

The **Age** chapter (page 190) shows how to represent different stages of youth and adulthood in your designs, to help you create characters that physically grow and change throughout their stories.

The **Accessories** chapter (page 210) covers a wealth of other features, such as clothing, hair, and props, that can help make your characters rounded and engaging. **Putting it all together** (page 240) shows how to apply everything you have learned in the previous chapters to create quality character designs.

Throughout the book, you will find "libraries" of subjects such as poses, facial expressions, costumes, and accessories, showing how multiple artists interpret different emotions, themes, and props, to help you generate ideas for your own characters. Each of these talented contributors then creates a project in the **Working with multiple characters** chapter (page 250), showing how they depict character interaction in a dynamic narrative scene, ranging from depicting pairs of characters to entire rooms full of them!

The **Working in character design** chapter (page 288) offers insights into the demands of taking on professional projects for different types of media, and how these will influence your ideas and work processes as a character designer.

Finally, the **Ideas grid** (page 298) closes the book with fun mix-and-match exercises that can help you find inspiration for a new character, or jump-start a new avenue of research.

Look out for colored boxes as you read – they contain extra tips, tricks, and information related to the current topic.

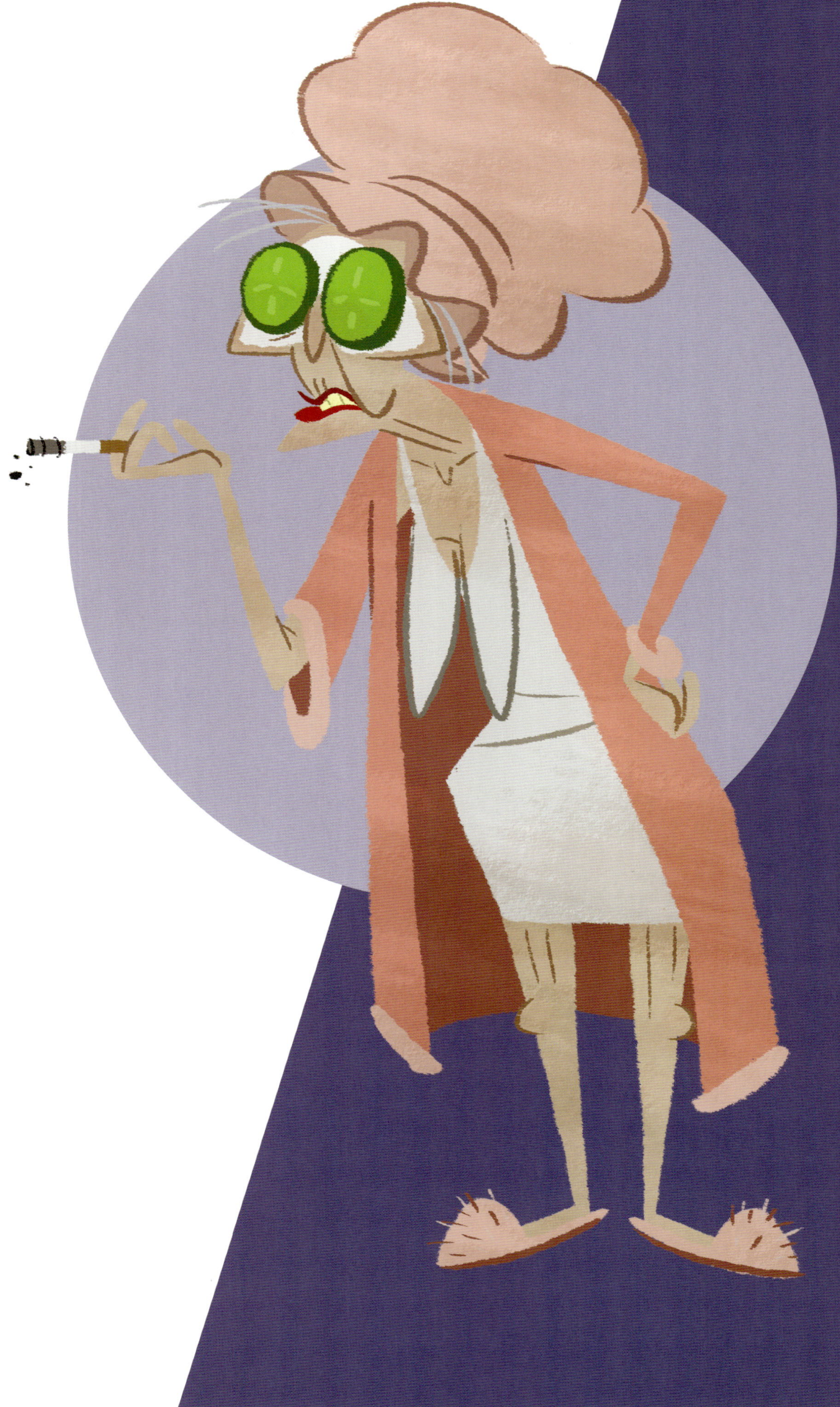

Image by Dom "Scruffy" Murphy

WHAT IS CHARACTER DESIGN?

OVERVIEW
PAGE 12

ESTABLISHING THE STORY
PAGE 18

TELLING THE STORY
PAGE 24

OVERVIEW

Dom "Scruffy" Murphy

Great stories capture our attention and stick with us for years, becoming ingrained in our minds. But where would these stories be without characters to drive them forward? That is where character design comes into play. At the heart of every great story you will find great characters. Whether they are fraught with peril on a dangerous quest or simply living out their lives as best they can, each will play an integral part in **driving their respective story** forward. You can find these characters in movies, TV shows, games, and the pages of your favorite books, but none would exist without character design. It is the character designer's job to breathe life into the characters inhabiting these stories. Without this, the stories would be dull and lifeless.

A character designer has to take into account all of the different projects they may find themselves working on. Here is an example of a design created with a 2D TV-show pipeline in mind, emphasizing clean lines and multiple stylized angles of the character.

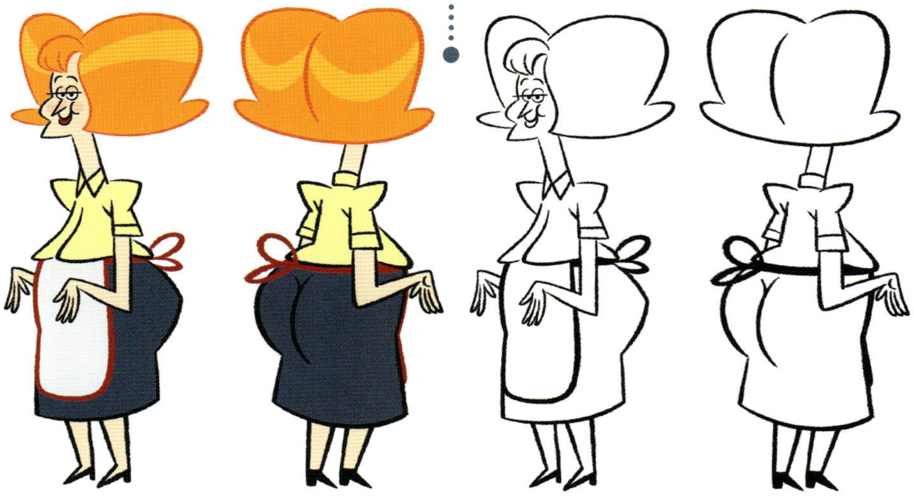

Here is a kid character designed for a 1980s mystery TV show. His appearance and outfit help set the tone of the show. You can easily imagine this character trying to solve a mystery.

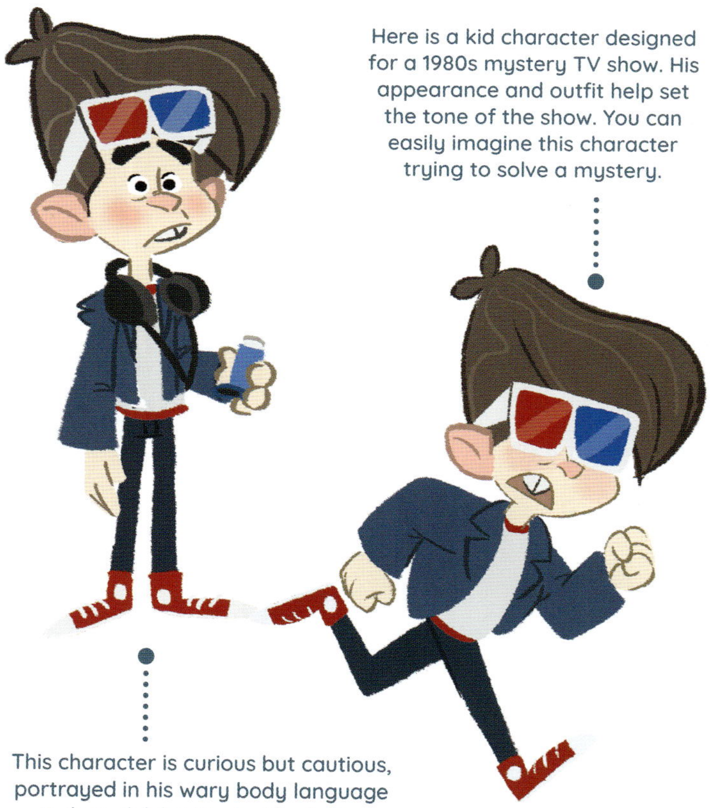

This character is curious but cautious, portrayed in his wary body language and youthful attitude. His design reflects both his personality and the adventurous tone of the show.

A character designed to portray historical figure Edgar Allan Poe in a friendly show.

Creating a recognizable caricature with exaggeration helps set the comical tone.

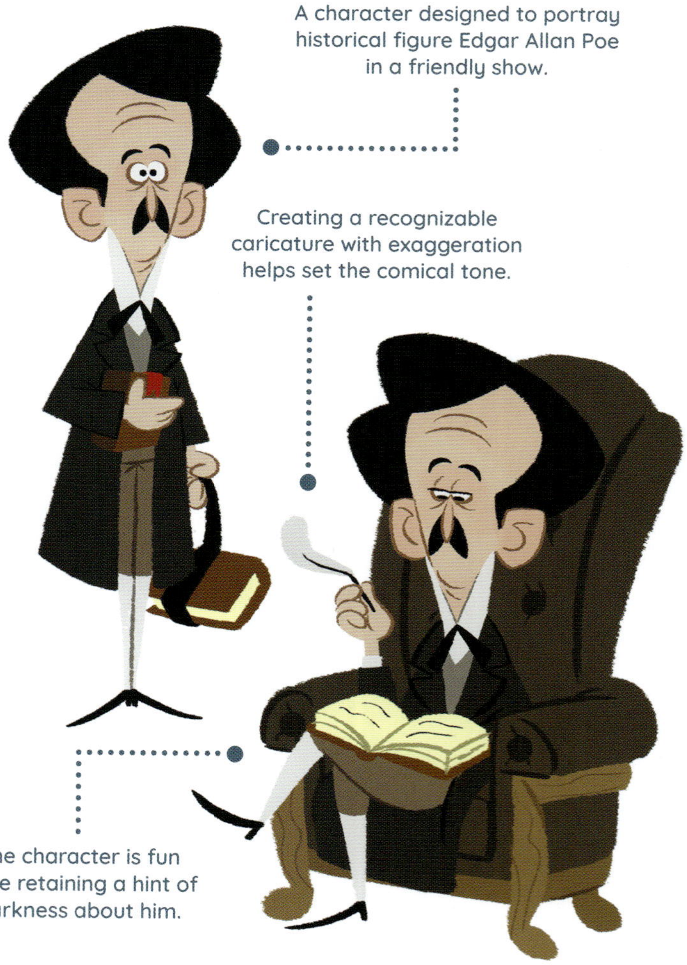

The character is fun while retaining a hint of darkness about him.

KEY STYLES

You can't talk about character design without mentioning those who have gone before. After all, we stand on the shoulders of giants. Over the years, character design throughout the entertainment industry has changed and evolved in many ways. For example, we can observe the transition from Disney's early "musical years" – focusing on realism over style and movement, and when artists "drew as they pleased" – to the days of the studio when it hired illustrators such as Ronald Searle and Gerald Scarfe to define the look and direction of its productions.

Across the world, character design changes with the country and culture. From the Western influences of Disney and Pixar, to the continental style of the French and European industries, to that of Japanese anime, each place has its own unique take on characters and how those characters tell a story. In the West, Disney is a giant and has a huge influence all of its own. When you think of Western animation, and North American animation in particular, Disney is front and center. Many others were born from that style, Pixar being one example. Pixar is heavily influenced by the Disney style of character design, but emphasizes shape and simplification more, due to its use of CG in animation. The studio uses shape as a foundation and driving force to great effect, much like the classic UPA (United Productions of America) cartoons of the 1940s to the 1970s.

Heading over to Europe and the French animation industry, it's a different situation entirely. With films in the style of Sylvain Chomet and others in the region, the French industry showcases an illustrative style that pushes the boundaries of what can be achieved in the art form. This leads to anime and the Eastern influence on character design and animation as a whole, which is impossible to discuss without mentioning Hayao Miyazaki and Studio Ghibli, an artist and studio whose influences on modern animation can be seen right across the globe.

Ultimately, the people and cultures behind character design influence a character as much as the story for which they are intended.

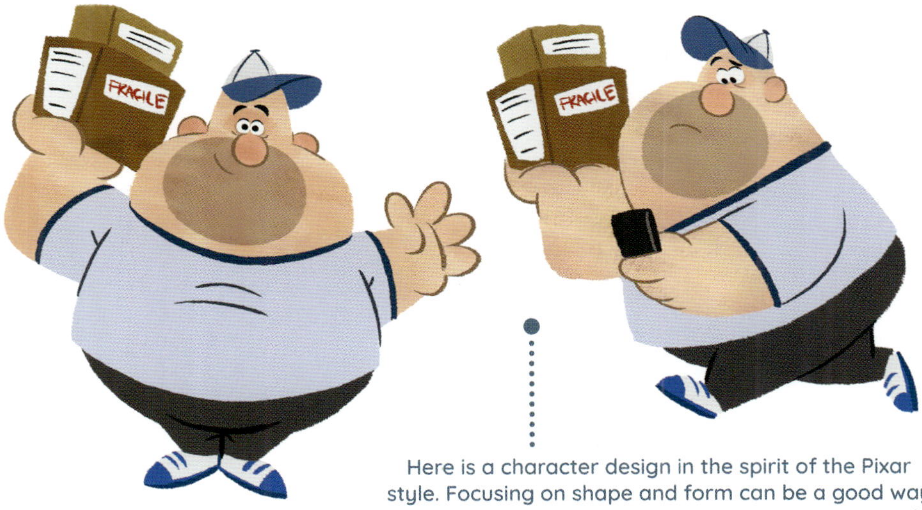

Here is a character design in the spirit of the Pixar style. Focusing on shape and form can be a good way to portray personality without having to say a word.

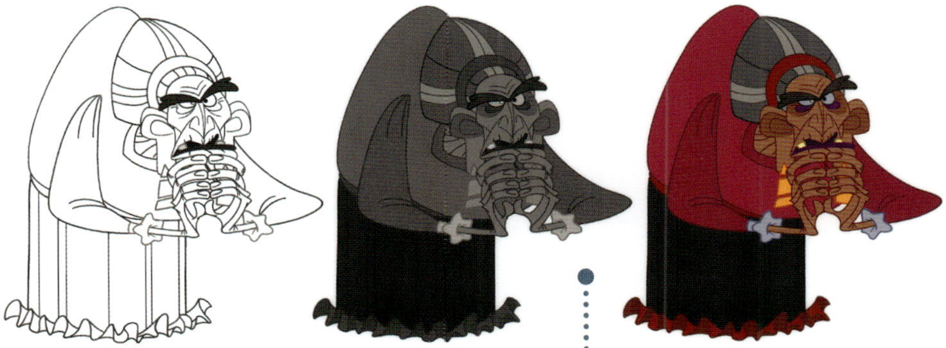

The French style of character design can be heavily stylized. Taking inspiration from comics and classic film, the graphic style succeeds in portraying character and personality in a broad range of story settings.

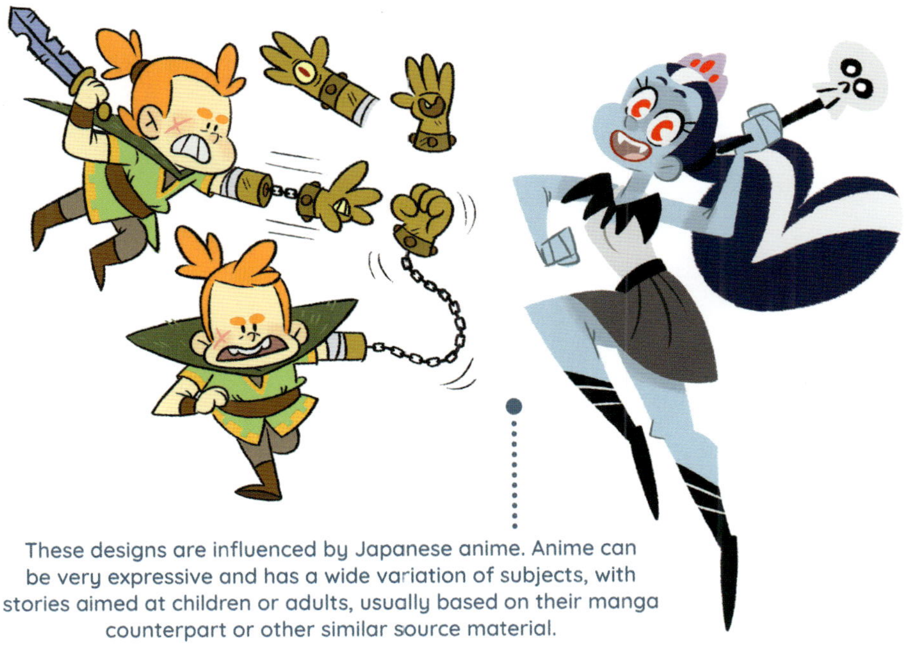

These designs are influenced by Japanese anime. Anime can be very expressive and has a wide variation of subjects, with stories aimed at children or adults, usually based on their manga counterpart or other similar source material.

MEMORABLE DESIGNS

Good character design can make or break a project, story, or production. On the one hand, if the characters are lacking in some way, the whole project can suffer because of it. On the other hand, a good character design that has all the basics covered, from appealing design to personality, can uplift a story and make a great story even better. These are the ones that stick with you, that capture your heart, not just because they catch your eye or look good on paper or screen, but because they are relatable. You can see yourself or people you know in them, become invested in their journey, and want to know more.

Take Woody from *Toy Story*, for example. Woody is not just memorable because his design stands out and is unique. His warm character and personality enhance his overall design, so much so that you're able to suspend disbelief for an hour or two and believe that a toy can walk and talk, plus relate to and feel his love for his owner, Andy, and his rival-turned-friend, Buzz Lightyear. Good characters are not just vehicles that move a story from point A to point B; they do all that and make pit stops along the way that flesh out the story and world they inhabit, remaining with their audience for years to come.

The Western genre is great for creating memorable characters. In a sea of generic cowboys, one that stands out will stick with you. Take this design - is he a villain or a character that inhabits the gray area of the moral code? One thing's for sure - he looks like he's not to be messed with!

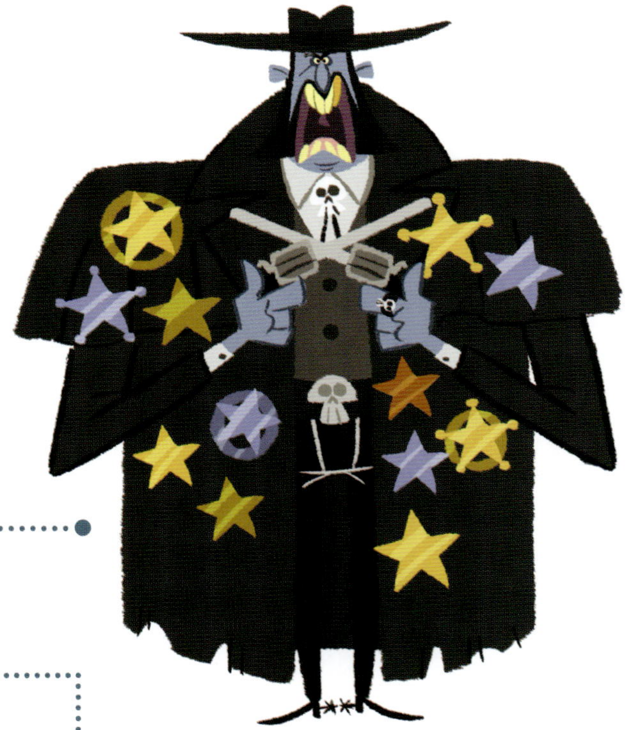

Exploring different versions of the same character can help in finding their voice. Expressions created in one version might influence another and progress the character's development.

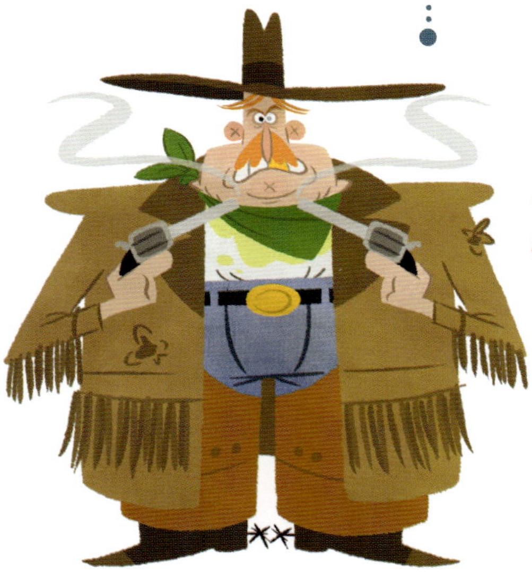

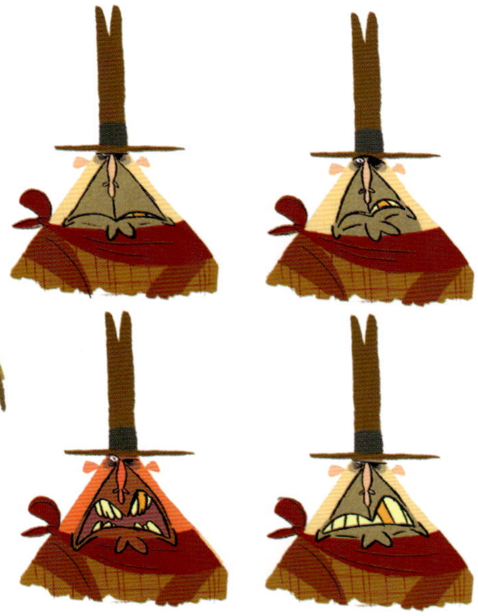

Shapes can help greatly when designing a character. For example, using unconventional shapes can yield interesting characters you might not discover using more stereotypical means.

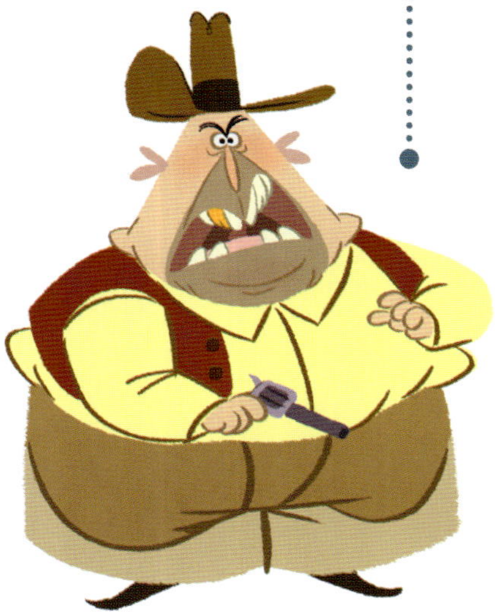

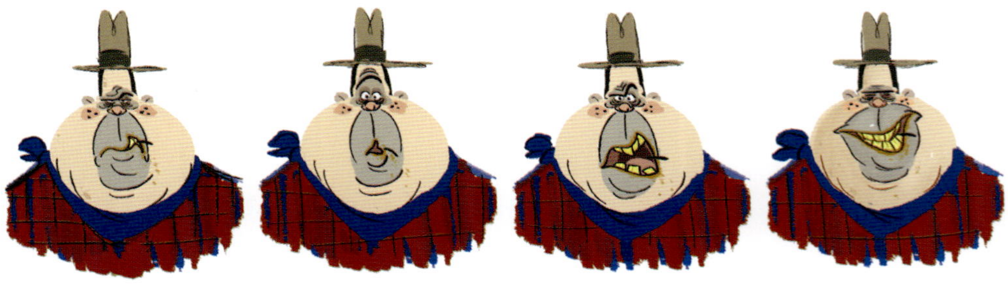

One of the best ways to create memorable characters is to break the norm and go completely outside the box, especially with a well-known genre like Westerns. Showing your audience something different will make it more likely the character will stick with them.

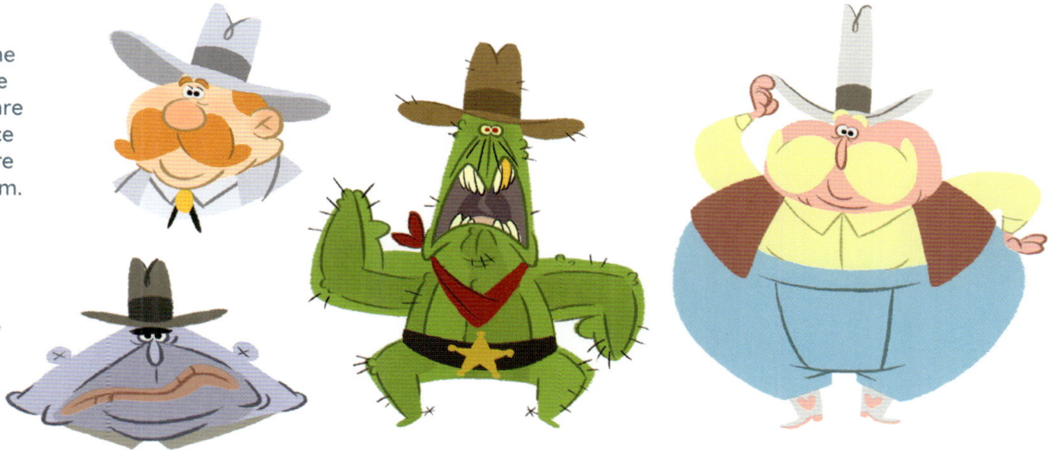

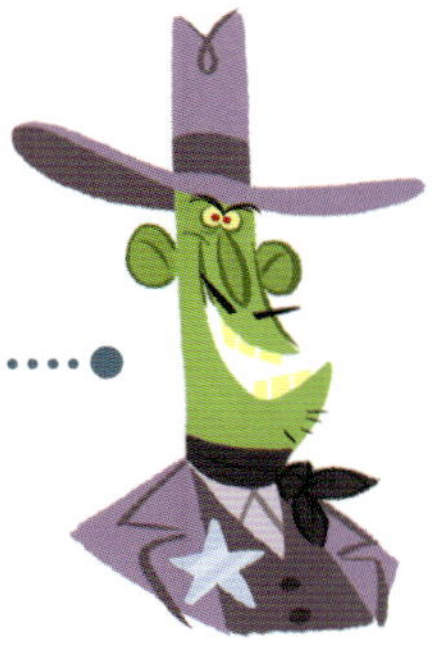

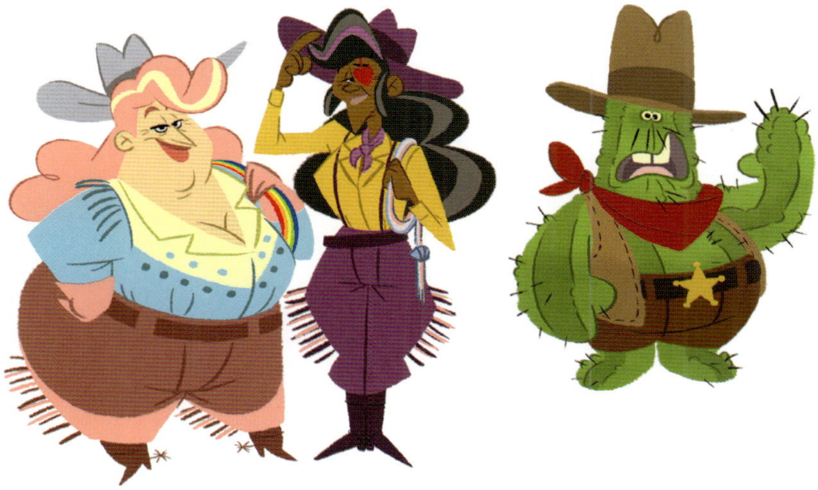

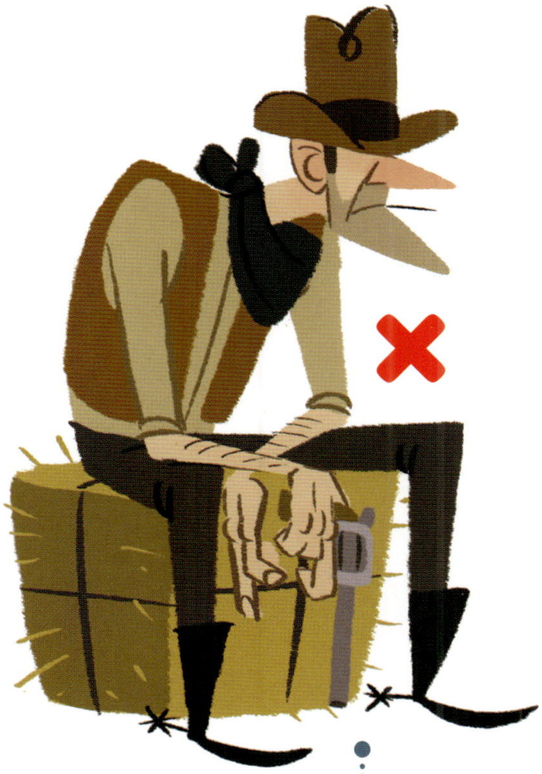

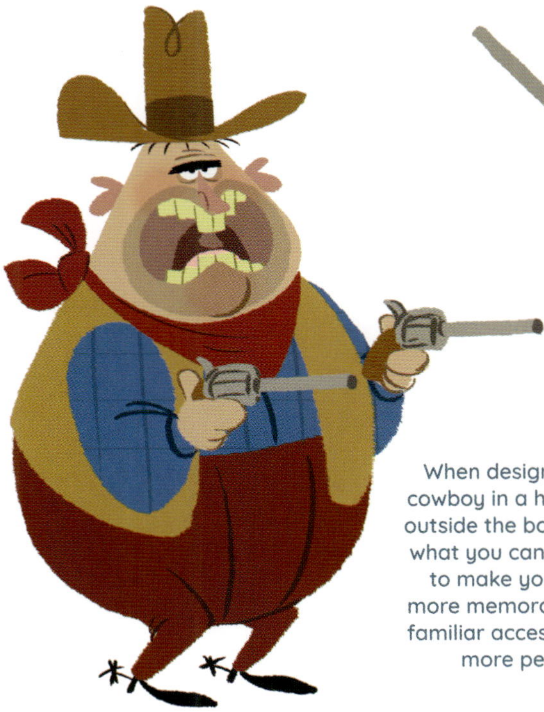

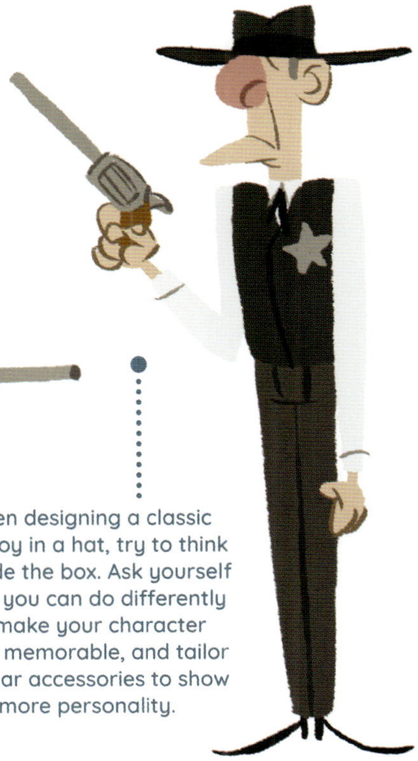

Try to avoid generic and stereotypical designs where possible. There is nothing wrong with them, and sometimes a story might call for such characters, but if you want your character to be memorable, you need them to stand out from the crowd.

When designing a classic cowboy in a hat, try to think outside the box. Ask yourself what you can do differently to make your character more memorable, and tailor familiar accessories to show more personality.

WHAT IS THE STORY?

The two key components to keep in mind when designing a character are: *what is the story, and how do I help to tell it with this character?*

You first need to figure out where the character fits into the story and what impact the story has on them. Does it affect their appearance? Their personality? Multiple factors will help to flesh out and breathe life into the character, giving them a mind of their own. It's not enough to simply design a character for a story; you have to make them believable, and convince the audience that the character inhabits their story's world, that they are a product of it. The best characters are ones that completely fit into the world and surroundings of their story. They have a foundation and grounding in that world, a purpose in it that has helped make them who they are and, in turn, gives them weight in driving the story forward. That is what will make them believable and memorable.

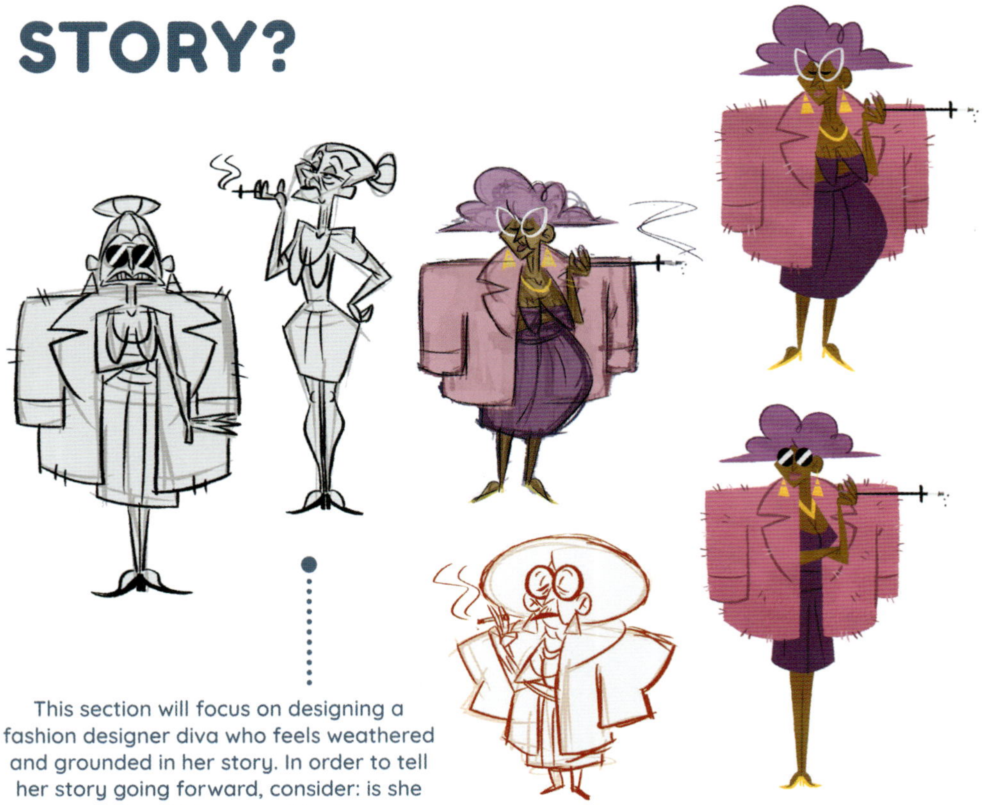

This section will focus on designing a fashion designer diva who feels weathered and grounded in her story. In order to tell her story going forward, consider: is she young and ambitious, or older in years and more world-weary?

Having decided the fashion designer will be older in years, you can begin to narrow down what direction her character will take.

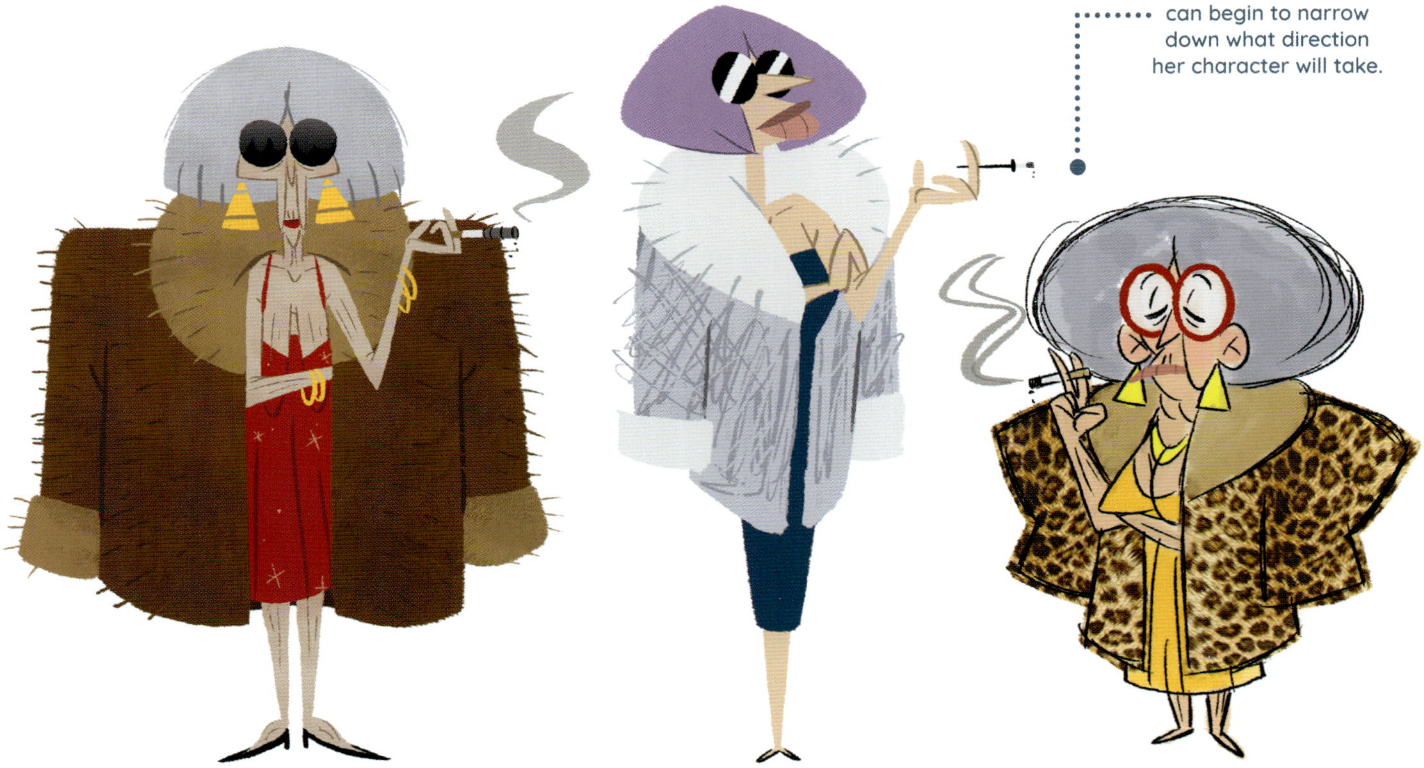

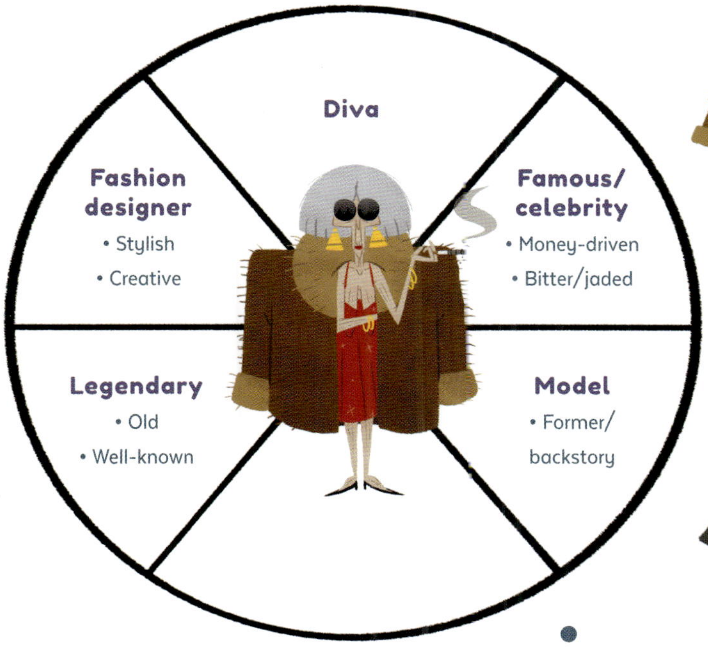

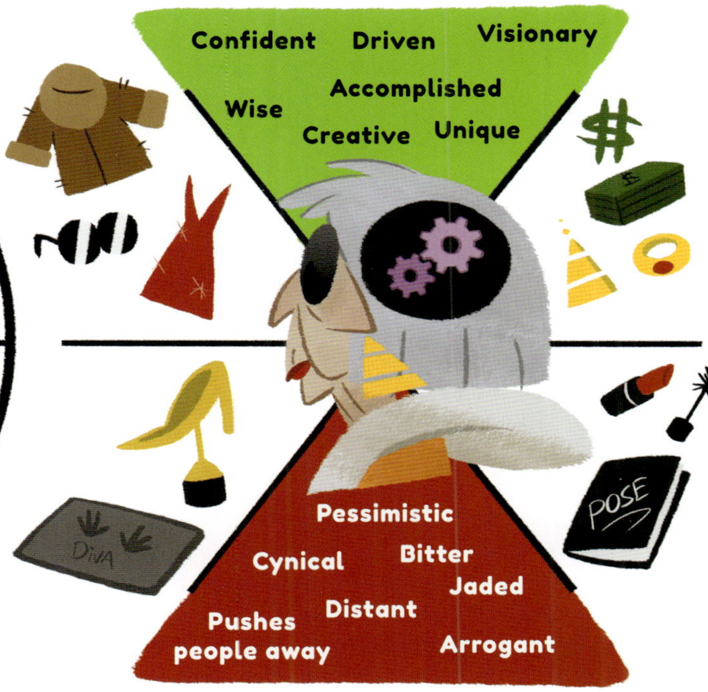

A good way to get to know the character you are creating is to use mind maps to explore their personality. This helps you see where the character is coming from, where they are heading, and what makes them tick.

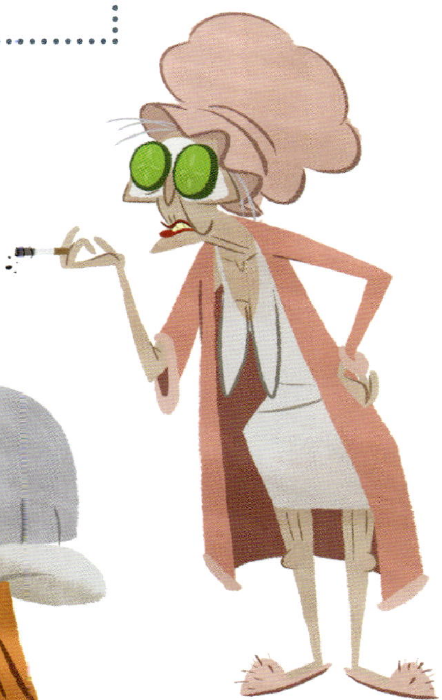

Once you have pinned down the direction of the character, you can begin to flesh them out and breathe life into them, keeping in mind how they might act in different situations.

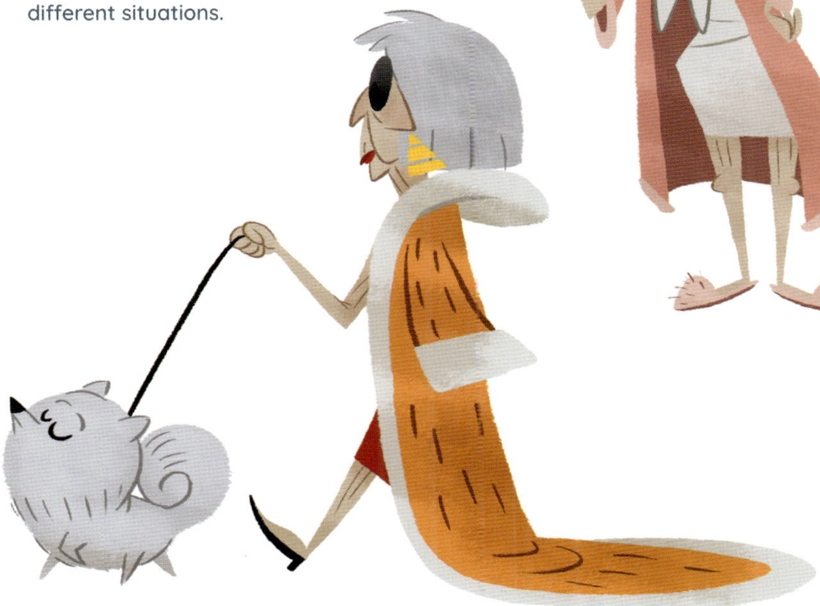

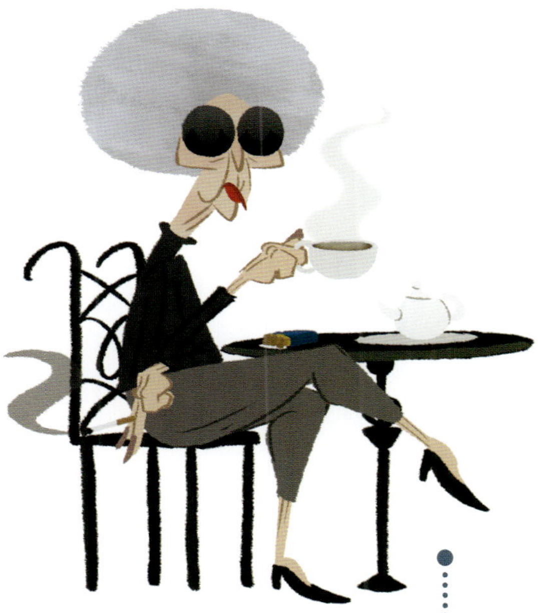

After going through this process, you should have a character that feels grounded in the story, and who is capable of driving it forward.

ESTABLISHING THE STORY

Dom "Scruffy" Murphy

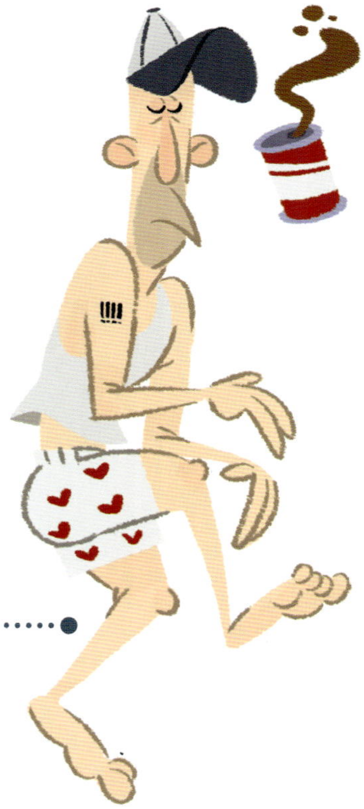

BUILDING A CHARACTER

When building a character, here are some useful questions to keep in mind.

Who are they?

Where does this character fit in relation to the story? Are they good, bad, or indifferent? Are they a driving force in the story, or just a bystander?

How do they feel?

How does this character feel about the events, situation, or circumstances they find themselves in throughout the story, or prior to it? Knowing this can really help in fleshing out their backstory and, in turn, the character themselves. Also, what do they like and dislike? Giving consideration to these details can greatly help you discover their personality and flesh them out as a character.

What are they doing?

Establishing what a character is or will be doing throughout a story, or prior to it, can be the difference between making them a captivating character and one that could be easily forgotten or dismissed.

When are they?

This could mean multiple things in the creation of the character. Literally, when they appear in the story's timeline progression is one of the main factors in shaping the character. Figuratively, "when" they are in their own personal progression, growth, and story arc greatly impacts how a character is formed and their forward projection. Also, when are they in the sense of time period? Present, medieval, futuristic?

Where are they?

Where are they currently, in all you have planned out for them? Are they near the end of their story or just beginning? Also, what is their physical environment? All these things need to be taken into account when creating a character.

This character is designed to be a space-port worker for a comical sci-fi project. He is a character conflicted in his emotions, which is portrayed in his design and personality. There are sci-fi elements to his design, but also details that keep him grounded back to Earth.

He prefers objects and items from back home to those of the space port where he works, as shown by his baseball hat and fondness for home comforts.

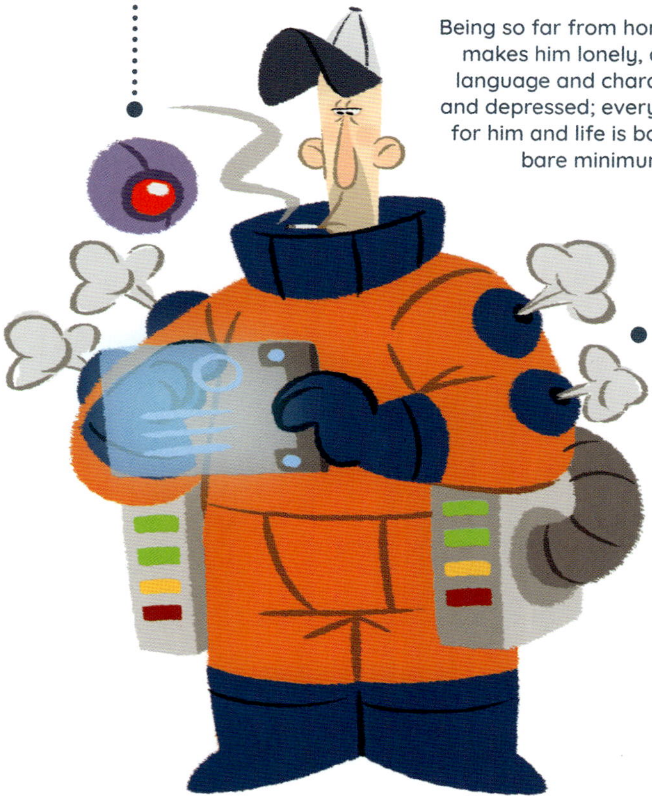

Being so far from home with no human contact makes him lonely, as portrayed in his body language and characteristics. He is subdued and depressed; everything has become routine for him and life is boring, so he only does the bare minimum with little effort.

- **Lazy**
- **Lonely**
- **Reserved**
- **Depressed**
- **No motivation**
- **Indifferent**

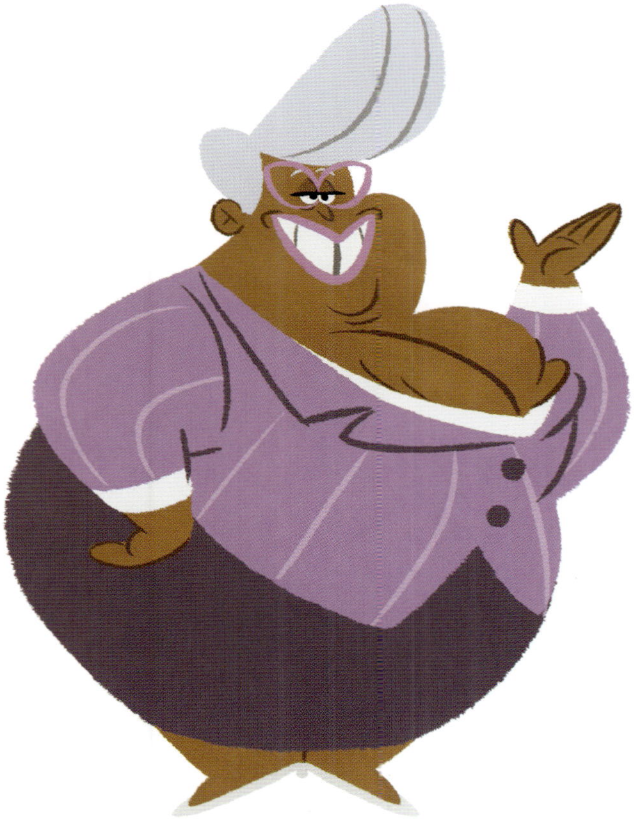

This character is a business executive ghost, shown through her ghostly appearance and business fashion sense. Choosing to include her business past in her design helps to convey her character.

- **Innovative**
- **Confident**
- **Decisive**
- **Leader**
- **Business-minded**
- **Smart**

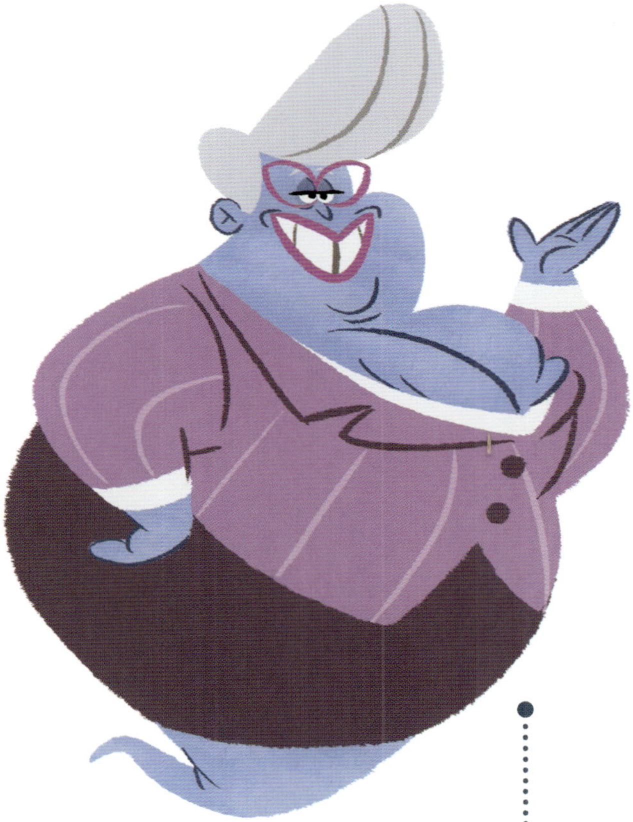

Her confidence and self-assurance are portrayed through her design and body language. She's larger than life, even in death!

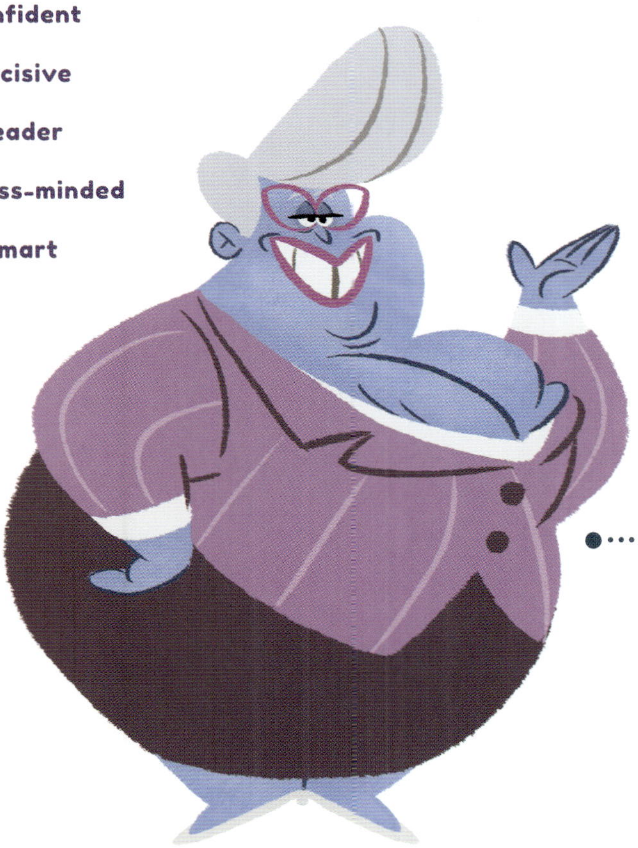

Color can help to tell a character's story. Her ghostly appearance has a blue skin tone, different to that of her previous human form.

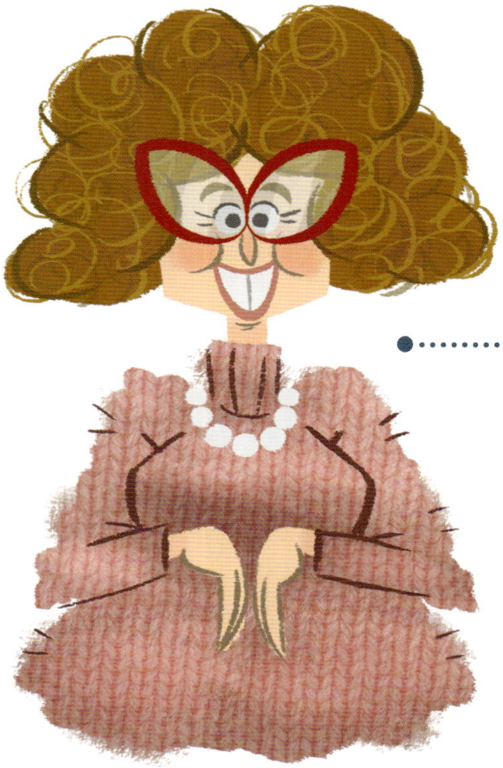

This character is designed as an eccentric aunt for a TV sitcom-type project, her oddball appearance reflecting her kooky personality and character.

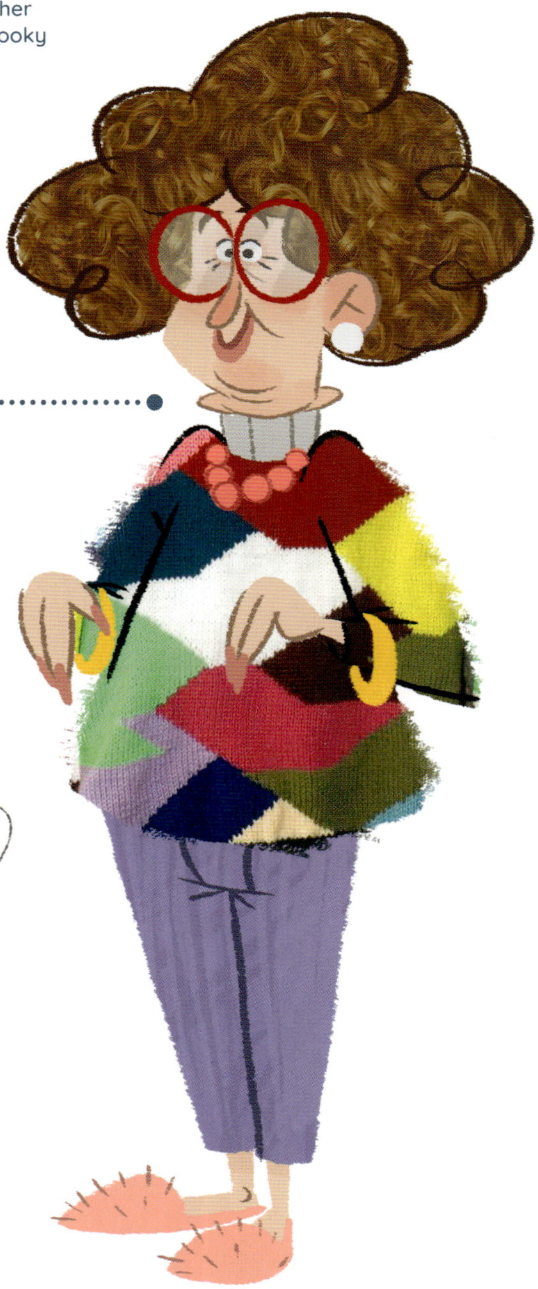

Her eccentric personality is portrayed through her colorful clothing and quirky fashion sense.

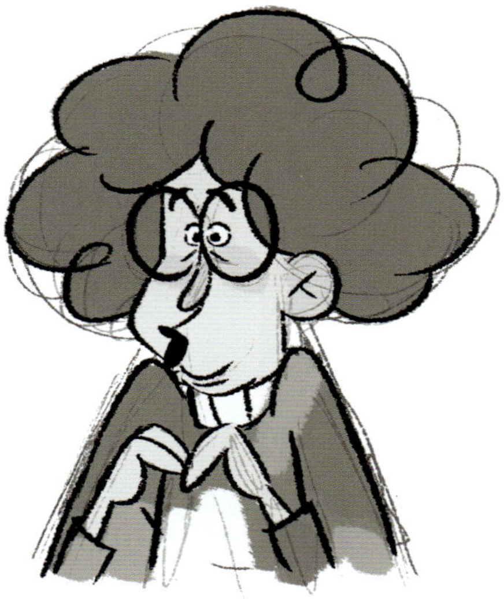

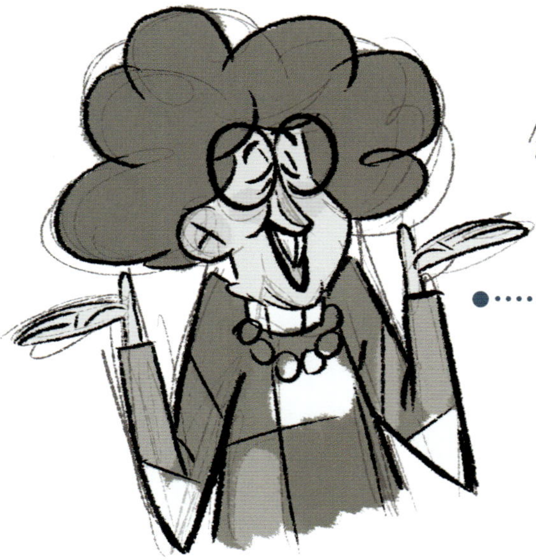

It would be important to keep in mind her energetic personality when designing how she acts and moves.

- **Eccentric**
- **Energetic**
- **Offbeat dress sense**
- **Awkward**
- **Funny**
- **Optimistic**

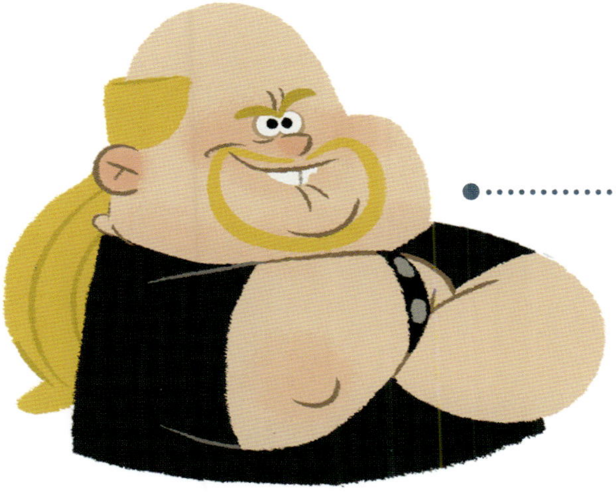

This character is a huge rock-band fan, shown in his intense personality and rocker appearance.

- **Passionate**
- **Loyal**
- **Dreamer**
- **Lives in the past**
- **Doesn't like change**
- **Good heart**

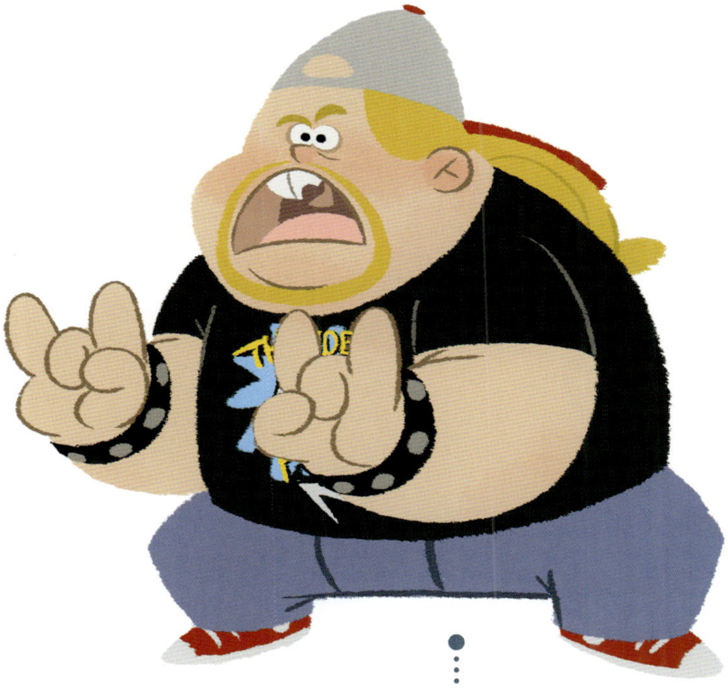

Though middle-aged, he is young at heart, which is portrayed in how he acts.

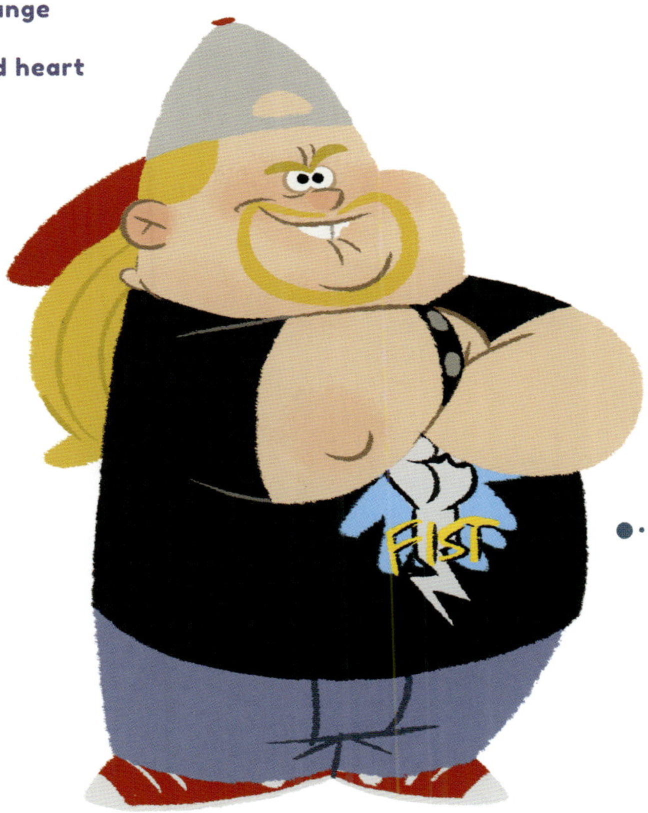

Clothes are used to help convey his character and story; in this case, a rock-band t-shirt.

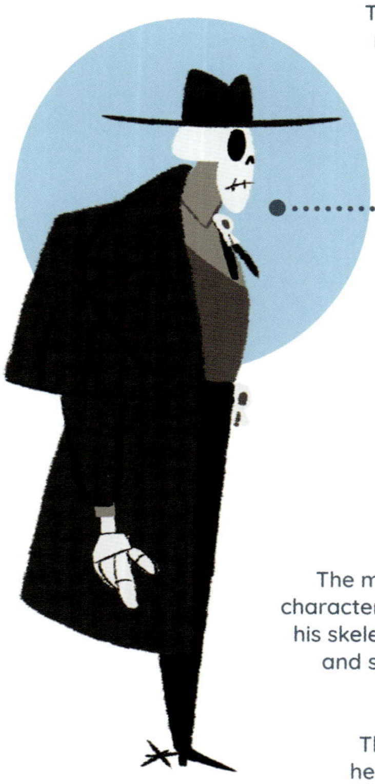

This character is designed to be a mysterious wanderer, capturing the audience's attention.

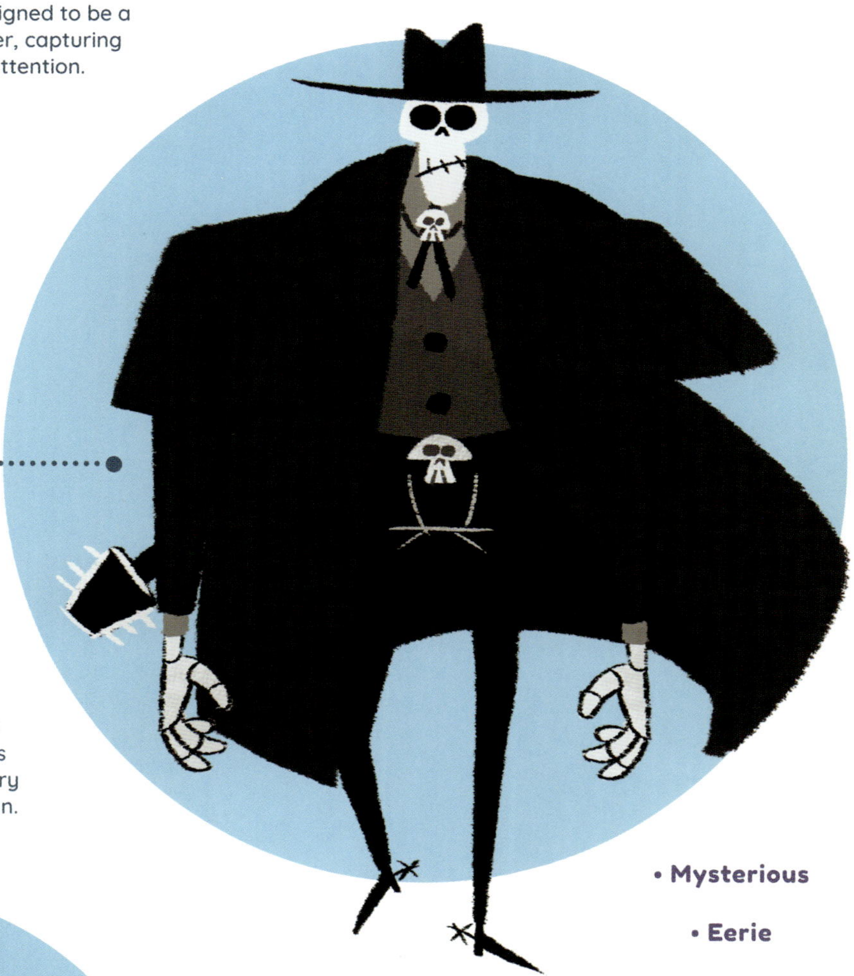

The mystery of this character is underlined by his skeletal appearance and spooky outfit.

The guitar and music he plays help to set his purpose and tell his story as a wandering musician.

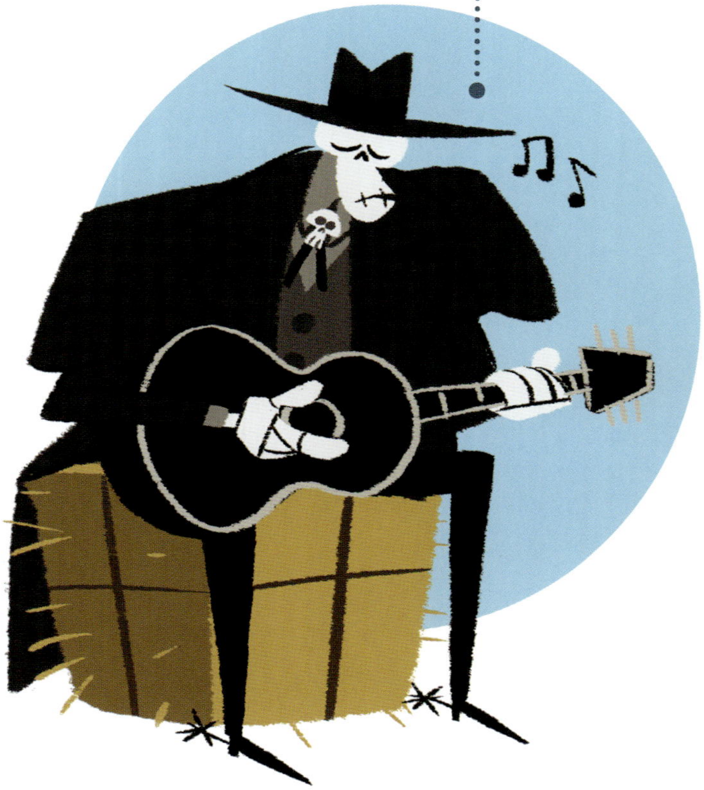

- **Mysterious**
- **Eerie**
- **Folk legend**
- **Mythical**
- **Wandering loner**

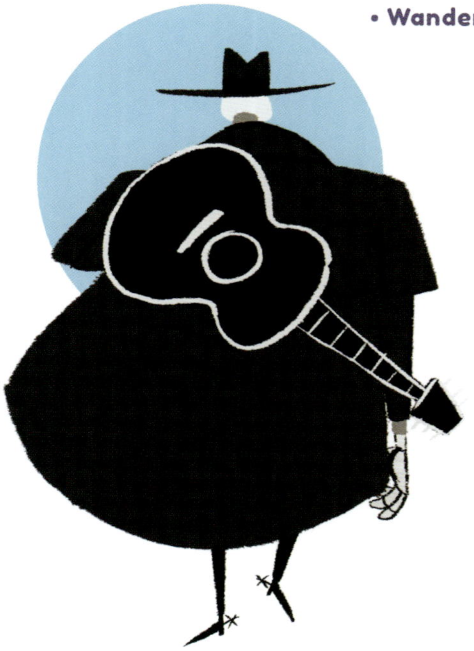

This character is a hard-working little office employee, clutching a briefcase and office plant that suggest his role.

His shy personality is portrayed in his reserved manner and how he handles himself.

- **Shy**
- **Unadventurous**
- **Square**
- **Reserved**
- **Odd**
- **Hard worker**

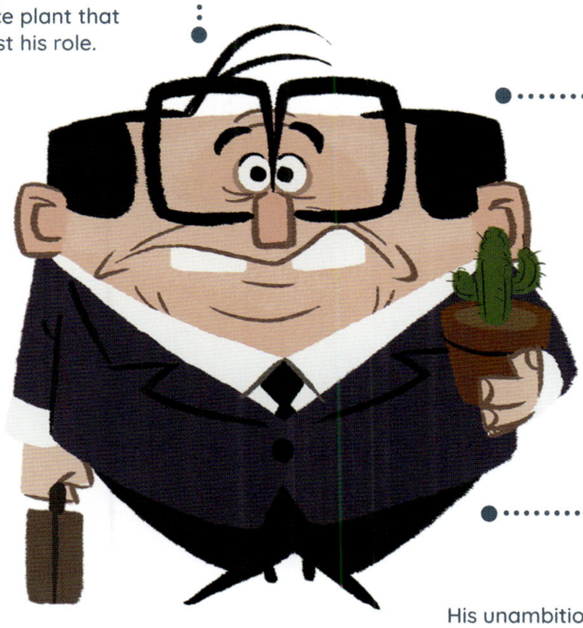

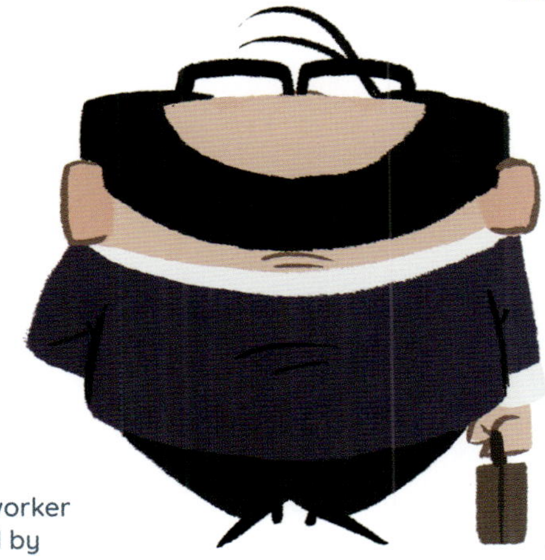

His unambitious office-worker character is conveyed by his dull outfit and square characteristics.

This character is a loyal scout leader.

Pushing this character further would yield better results, producing a character that tells a more captivating story.

The design is generic, boring, and doesn't tell much of a story.

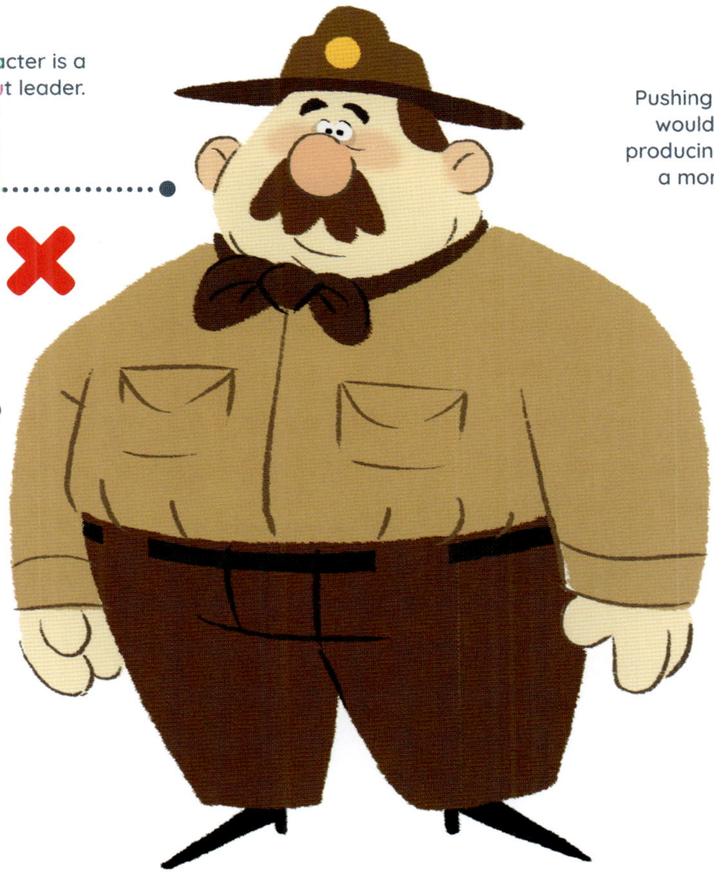

- **What is this character's personality?**
- **How can his appearance tell more of a story?**
- **What props or accessories could be added?**

TELLING THE STORY

Dom "Scruffy" Murphy

When telling a story, keeping the **tone** of the project in mind is key. For example, designing characters that are too scary and dark in tone for a young audience might not be appropriate and could result in the failure of a project. It's important to consider your **target audience** (be it adults, teens, or children) when setting out to design a character. Simplification and exaggeration, as we have seen, are key tools for conveying a character's personality, and these feed into most of the areas explored in this book. We have also seen how costumes, accessories, and poses can tell the viewer about a character's story and role.

For the most part, sticking to humorous, friendly, simple designs is the way to go when designing for a young audience. As you move to a teen audience, you can incorporate a darker and more eerie tone, and more visual complexity. However, that's not to say all designs need to remain within the niche of their audience and should stick to a particular tone or style. The ones that don't are often the ones that are remembered. Adults, for example, can enjoy cute designs, and kids can appreciate spooky ones.

It's a character designer's job to assess each brief and know which direction to take. A show aimed at an adult audience might benefit from simpler, friendlier designs to get its comical story across, whereas a show aimed at children might benefit from darker designs that reflect stories and situations with a heavier tone. Knowing how to thoughtfully approach designs for different situations and narratives can result in a project that remains with audiences for years to come.

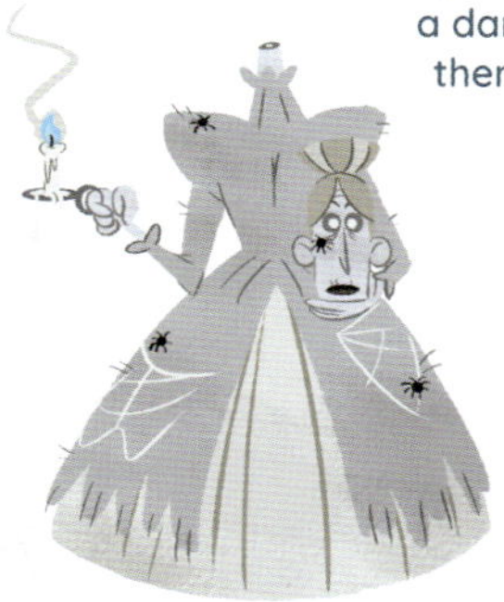

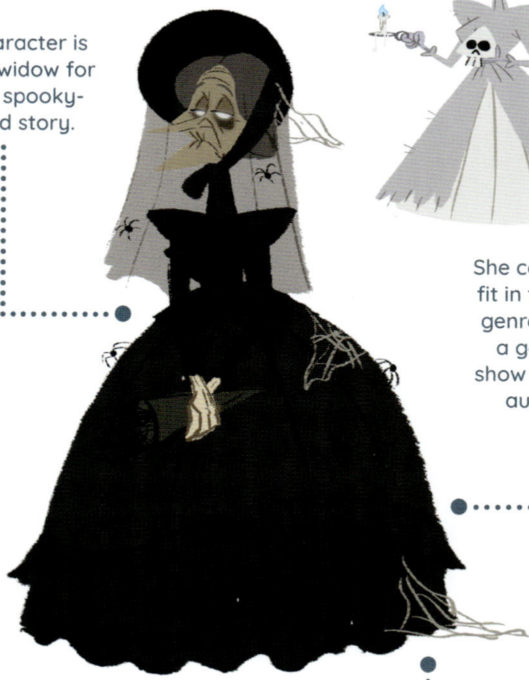

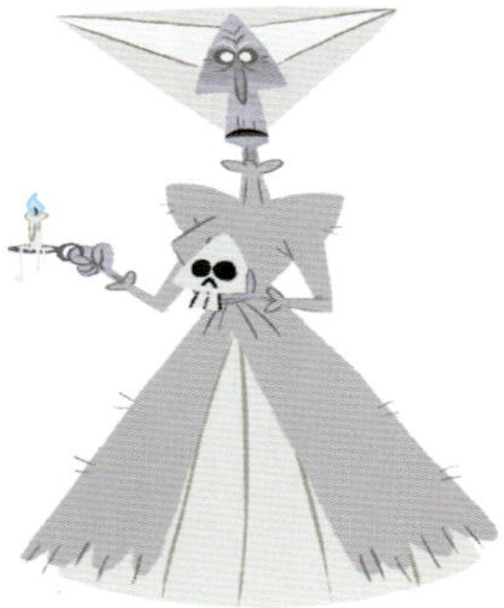

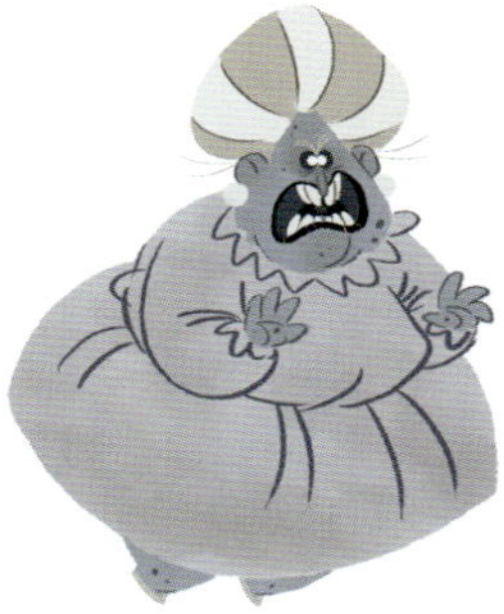

This character is a ghost widow for a dark, spooky-themed story.

She could easily fit in the horror genre, or even a gothic TV show for a teen audience.

A few alternative takes on this character were explored before settling on this design, as shown in the smaller thumbnails here.

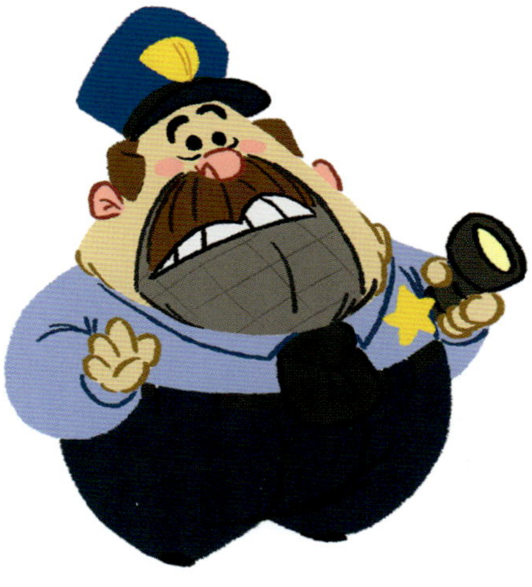

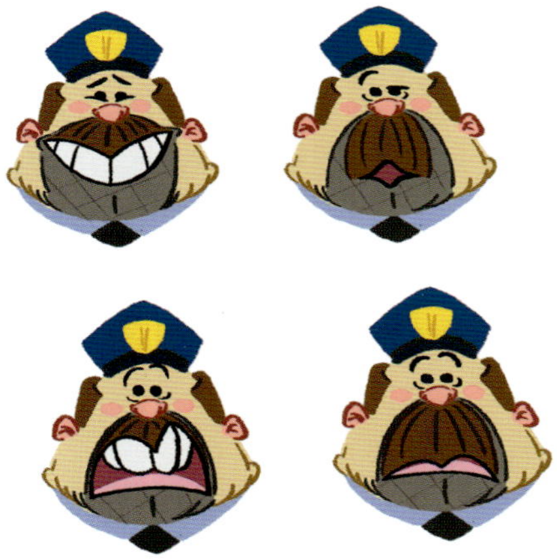

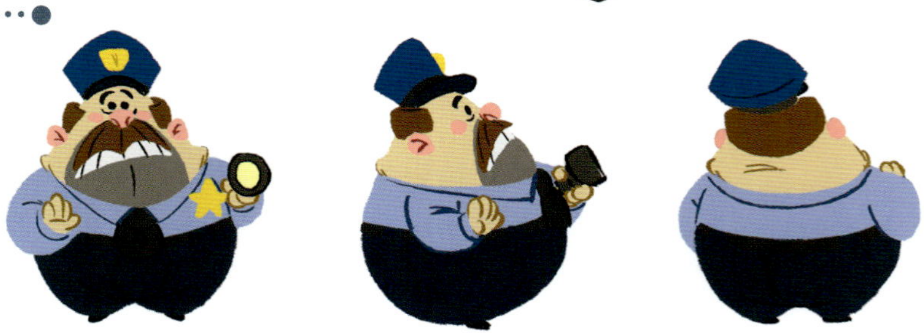

Designing for a pre-school audience brings its own set of challenges. If the target audience will be a young age group, aim for fun designs, shapes, and colors to capture and retain their attention.

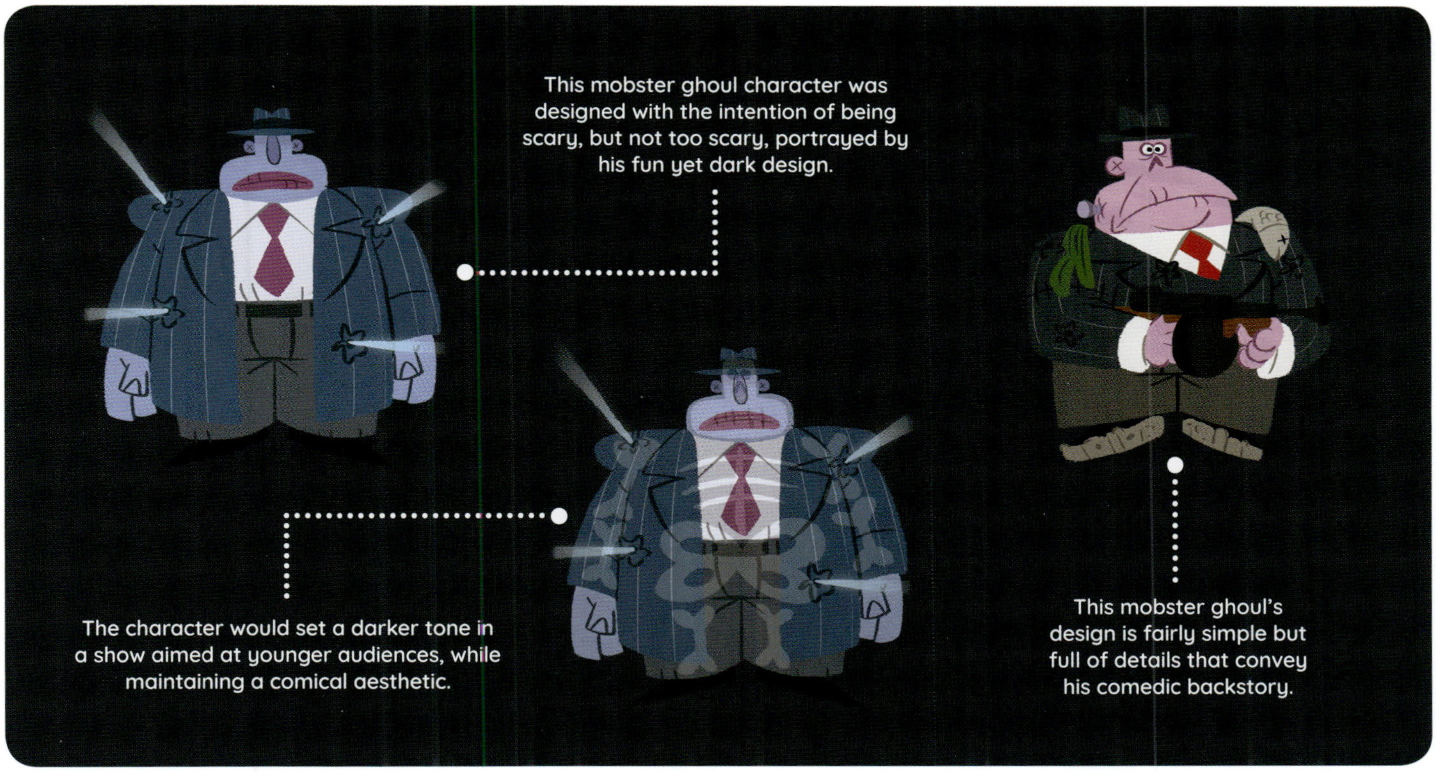
This mobster ghoul character was designed with the intention of being scary, but not too scary, portrayed by his fun yet dark design.
The character would set a darker tone in a show aimed at younger audiences, while maintaining a comical aesthetic.
This mobster ghoul's design is fairly simple but full of details that convey his comedic backstory.

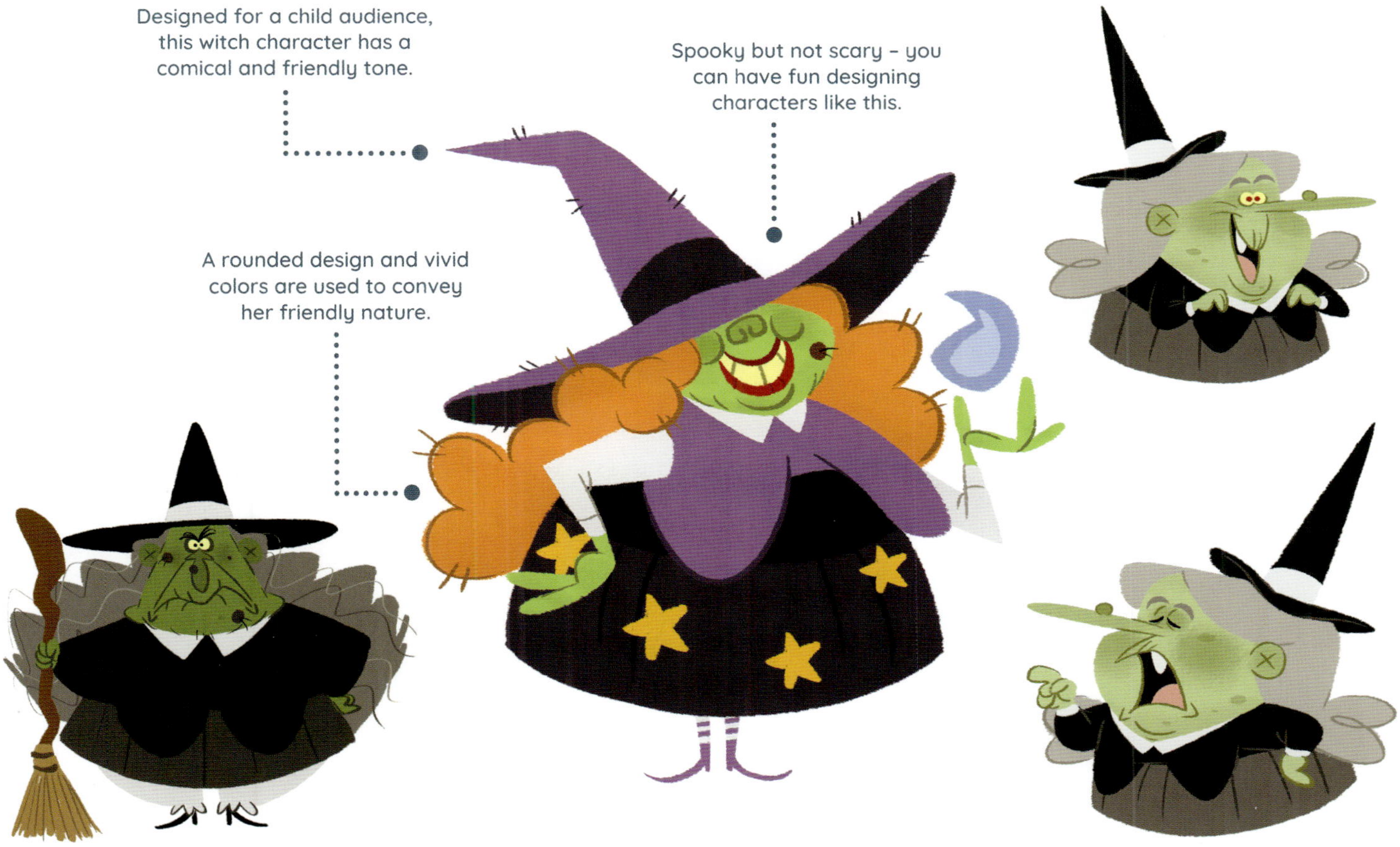
Designed for a child audience, this witch character has a comical and friendly tone.
Spooky but not scary – you can have fun designing characters like this.
A rounded design and vivid colors are used to convey her friendly nature.

When designing a character that will ultimately be translated into a three-dimensional sculpt, exploring shape and form from an early design stage will help greatly throughout production.

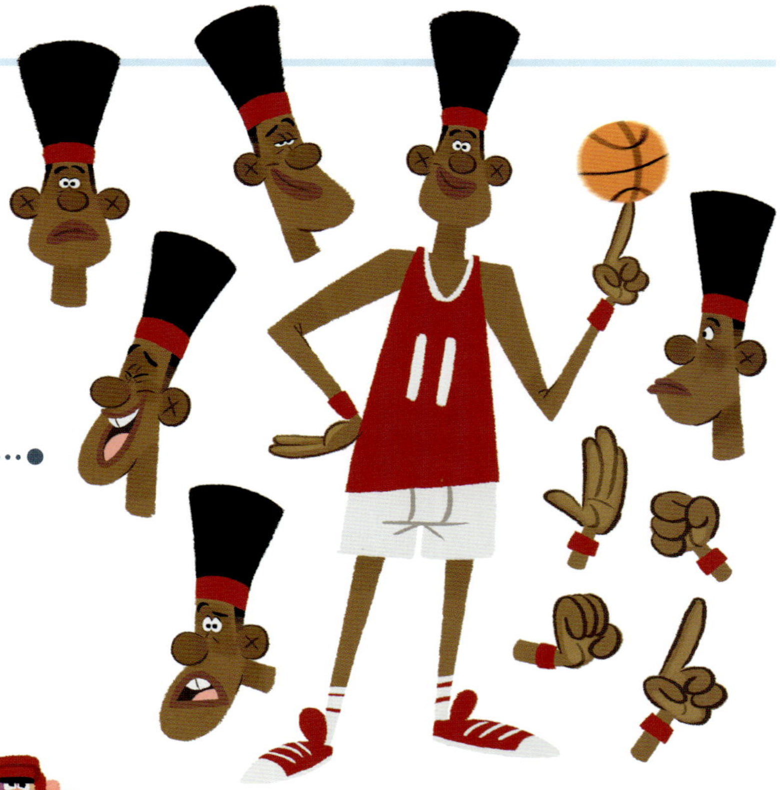

These boxer characters are designed for a sports project.

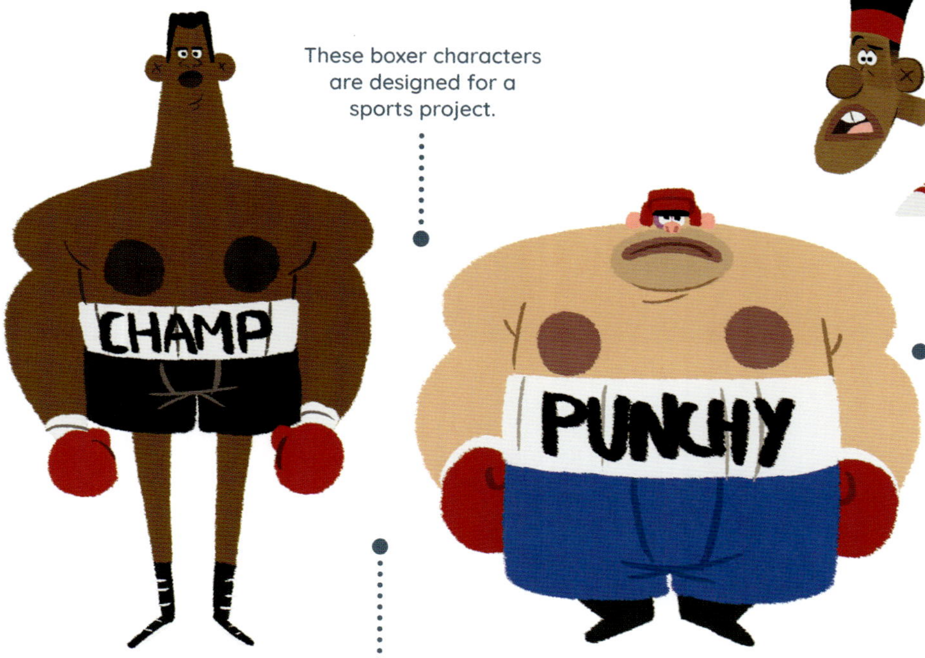

These designs have been created with the purpose of being used to their full extent in exaggerated animation.

They portray sportiness with an entertaining tone and boldly simplified visuals.

This character would benefit from a softer and friendlier approach.

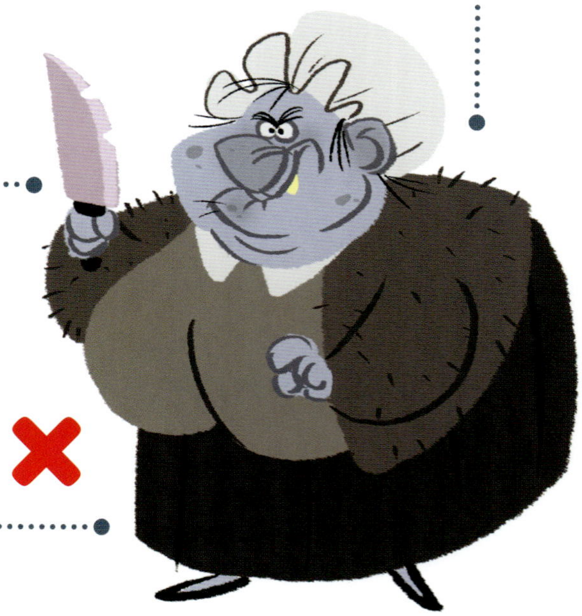

This character was designed to be in a children's TV show based on nursery rhymes, but fails to meet the tone. While nursery rhymes can sometimes be dark in nature, this design pushes that too far.

What's on paper will not always match the intended tone. It's up to you to know how to approach it.

SIMPLIFICATION

Simplification plays an integral part in character design. Often, the simpler you make a character, the more impactful their design becomes. When designing for a show or project, the art direction might require a more streamlined stylized look, which is where simplification comes into play the most. When you are trying to get the point of your character across in the most basic way possible, you are condensing that character down to their primary, core characteristics, using as little detail and nuance as possible. In this "less is more" approach, what you *do* choose to include makes all the difference.

Take a look at your character and ask yourself, "What makes them *them*?" Take those essential characteristics and amplify them as much as you can, in the simplest way possible. One tool that can help you do this is shape. You can be strict and abide by the rules of the shape, or simply use it as a guideline or underlying structure without being tied down by it. Head shapes are a great example of this. For the most part, "how to" books or even art teachers will tell you there is only one way to draw a head: a combination of a ball and a jaw shape. There is nothing wrong with that, but it closes the doors of experimentation, even if you just want to draw "realistic" work. If you look at people's heads and body shapes in real life, none are the same. If you stick to one way of drawing them, your results will keep looking the same. Mix up your simplification by using different shapes, and don't be afraid to exaggerate the proportions. There is no right or wrong way, and experimentation is the key to variation.

The simpler you keep the shapes of your character, the more you can play around with a design, finding fun ways to incorporate shapes and squash or stretch them to create gestures and emotions. If you look at the Viking character to the top right of this page, for example, you will notice that omitting his face and opting for eyes in his helmet streamlines his body with his beard. This results in a more stylized look, gives the character a mysterious, intimidating presence, and creates interesting new ways for him to emote.

There is no better way to practice simplification than by sketching people from life. Go out into the world and look at the people around you. Find what makes them *them*, and reduce that down until you can get their personality and character across using as little detail as possible. Done right, simplification can make a good design even better, and is one of the best tools at a designer's disposal when creating memorable characters.

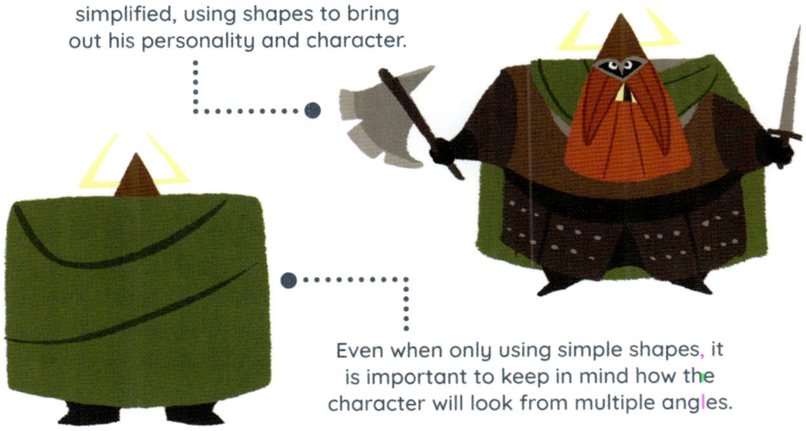

Here is a Viking that has been simplified, using shapes to bring out his personality and character.

Even when only using simple shapes, it is important to keep in mind how the character will look from multiple angles.

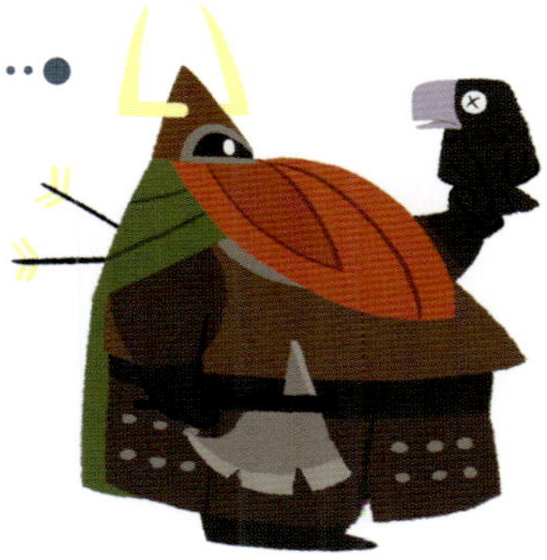

The use of square and sharp shapes portrays his strong, bulky nature, as well as his more dangerous and physically imposing side.

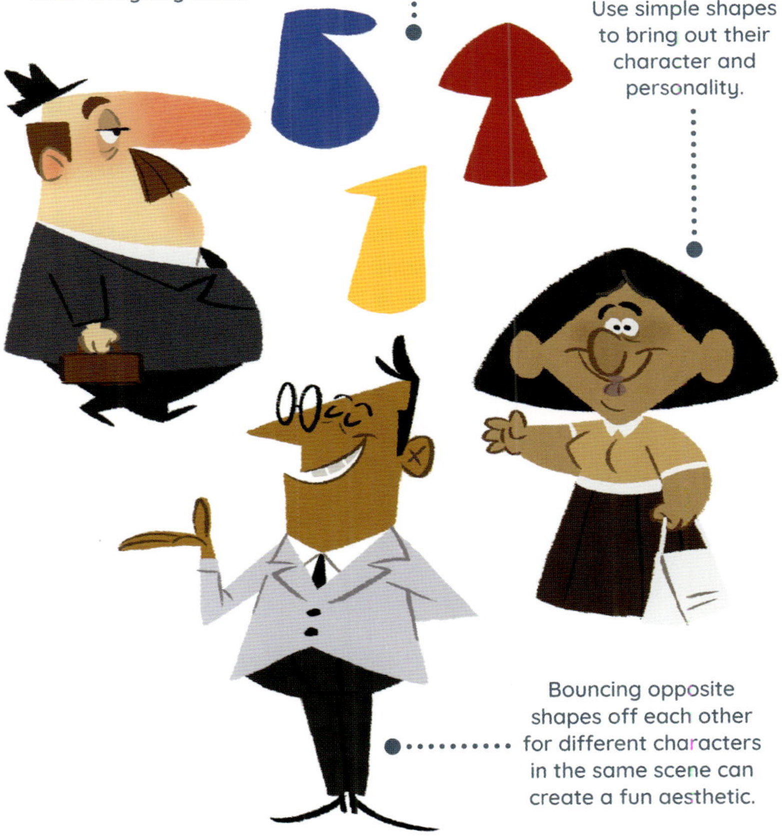

One of the best ways to simplify characters is to keep one shape in mind when designing them.

Use simple shapes to bring out their character and personality.

Bouncing opposite shapes off each other for different characters in the same scene can create a fun aesthetic.

Using simpler shapes can help give a project a more artistic feel.

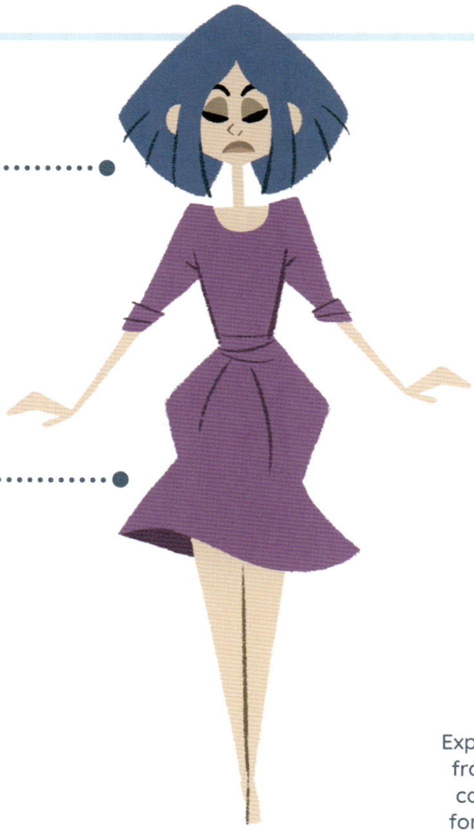

The simple design of this mysterious girl creates an air of intrigue that can be taken in any direction.

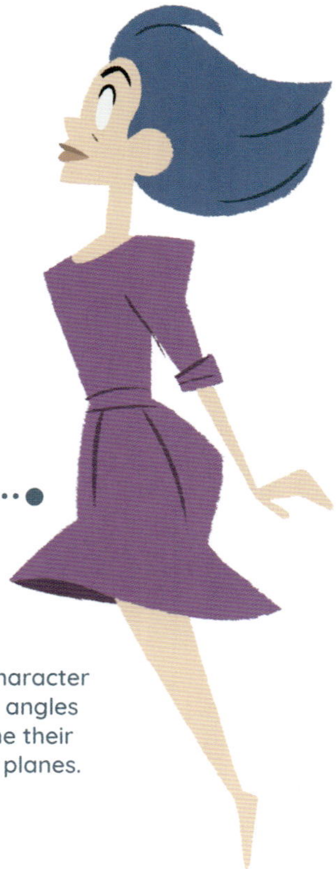

Exploring the character from different angles can help define their form in simple planes.

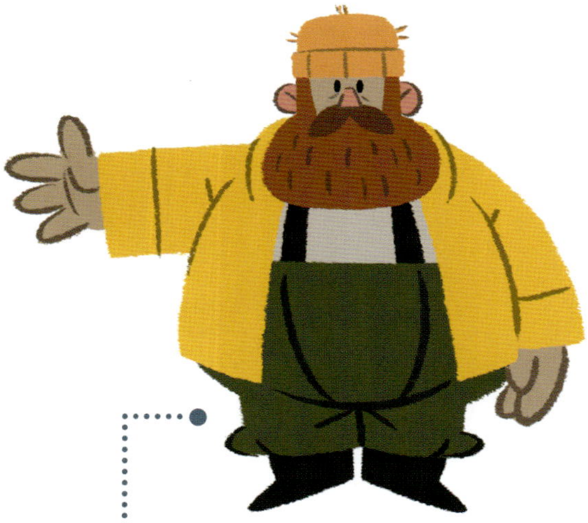

This fisherman has been simplified, from his overall shape to his expressions, while retaining his ability to convey emotion.

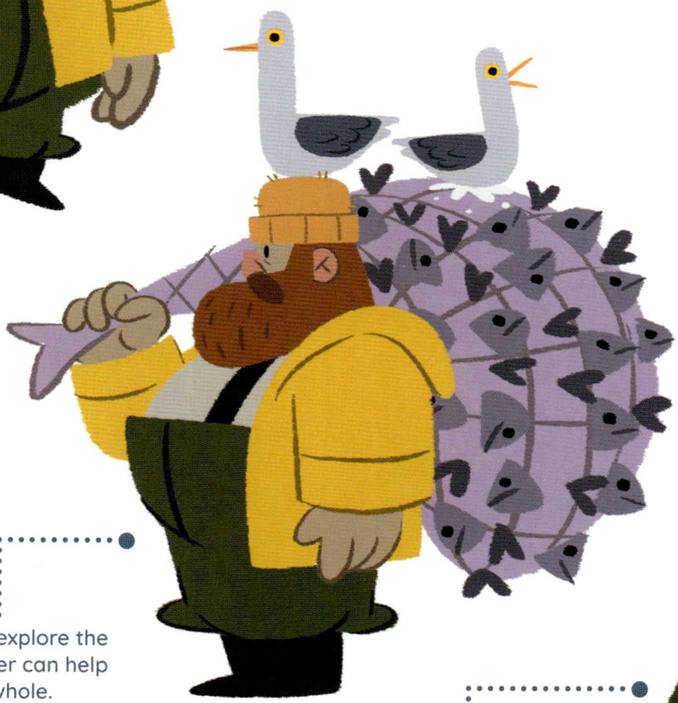

Using simple shapes to explore the world around a character can help define them as a whole.

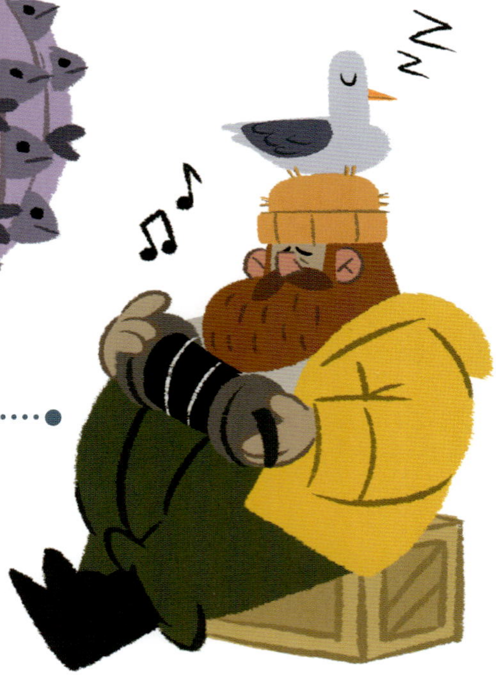

Different situations can help realize how the character fits into their world and how to simplify other objects they interact with.

One of the best ways to achieve a simple, effective shape in your design is through the use of silhouettes.

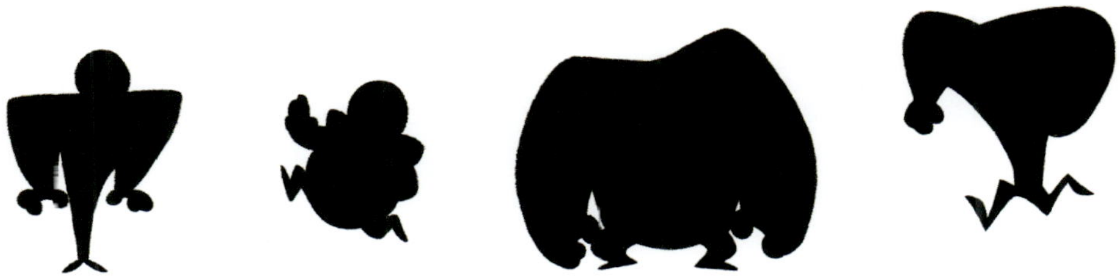

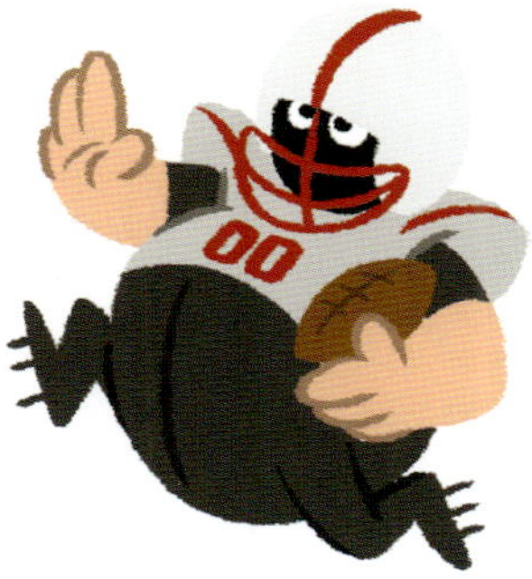

These American footballers have bold, fun shapes without using much detail.

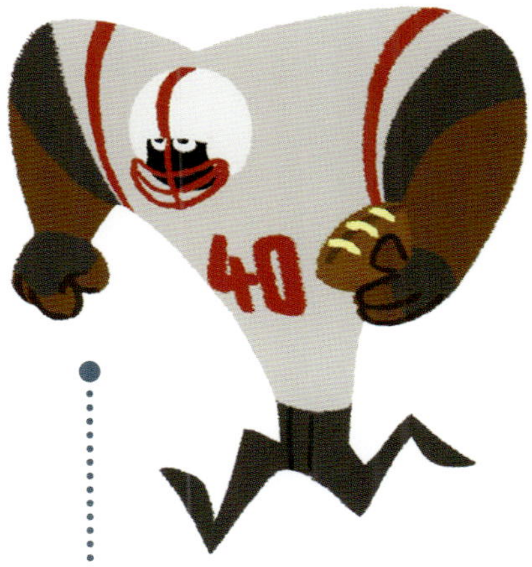

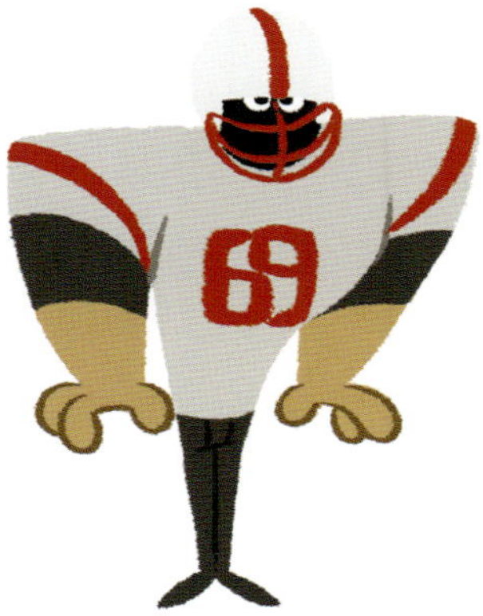

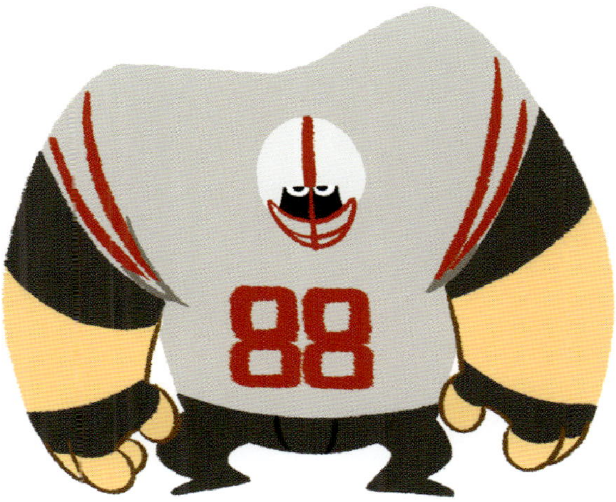

These heavily simplified, exaggerated forms help achieve an overall look and theme for the project.

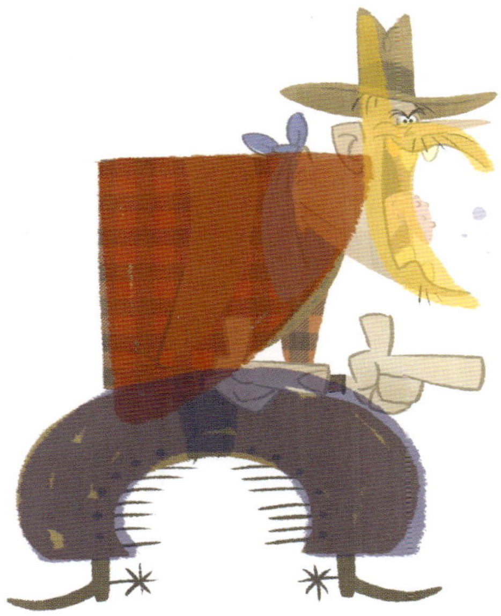

Sometimes pushing a shape too far doesn't work.

This cowboy might work while static on paper, but he may not work so well in an animation project.

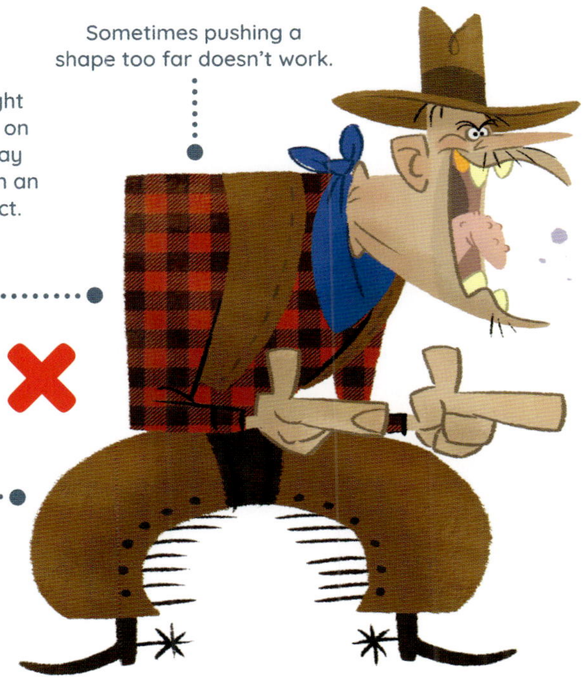

Keep in mind the intended purpose of the design on a project-by-project basis. What works well for one project might not work at all for another.

Bottom images © Dom "Scruffy" Murphy

Above all else, one of the most effective ways to apply simplistic shape in your designs is to get out in the world and study real people.

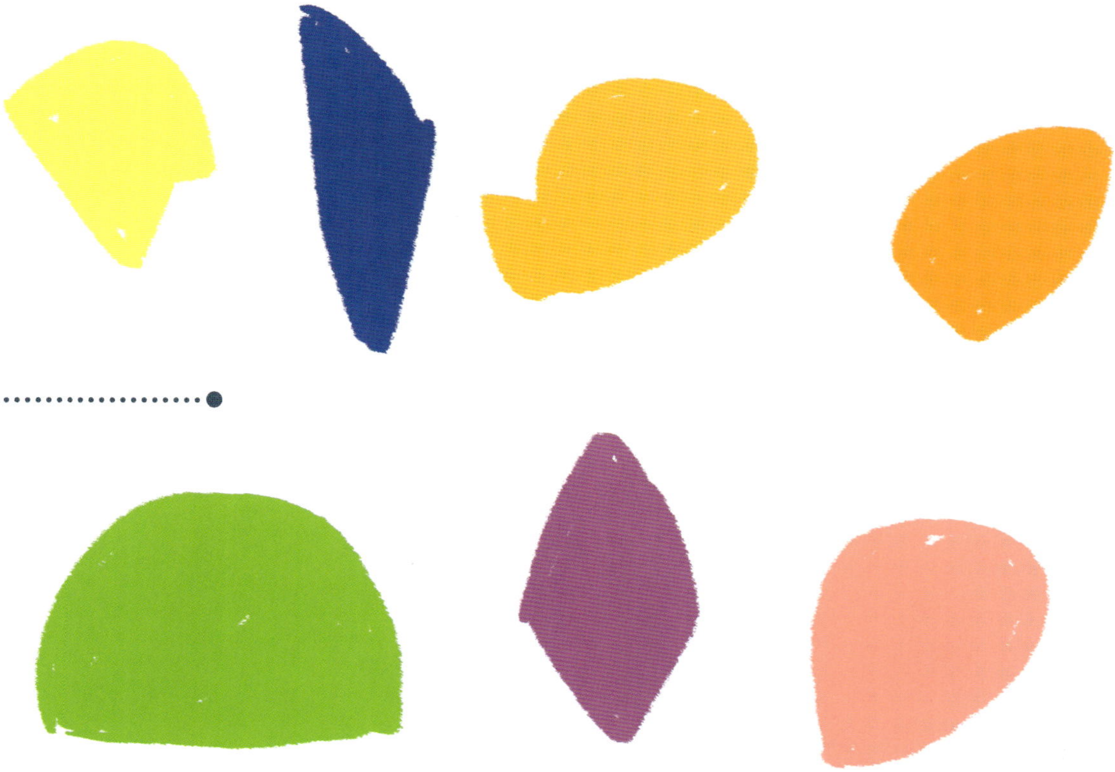

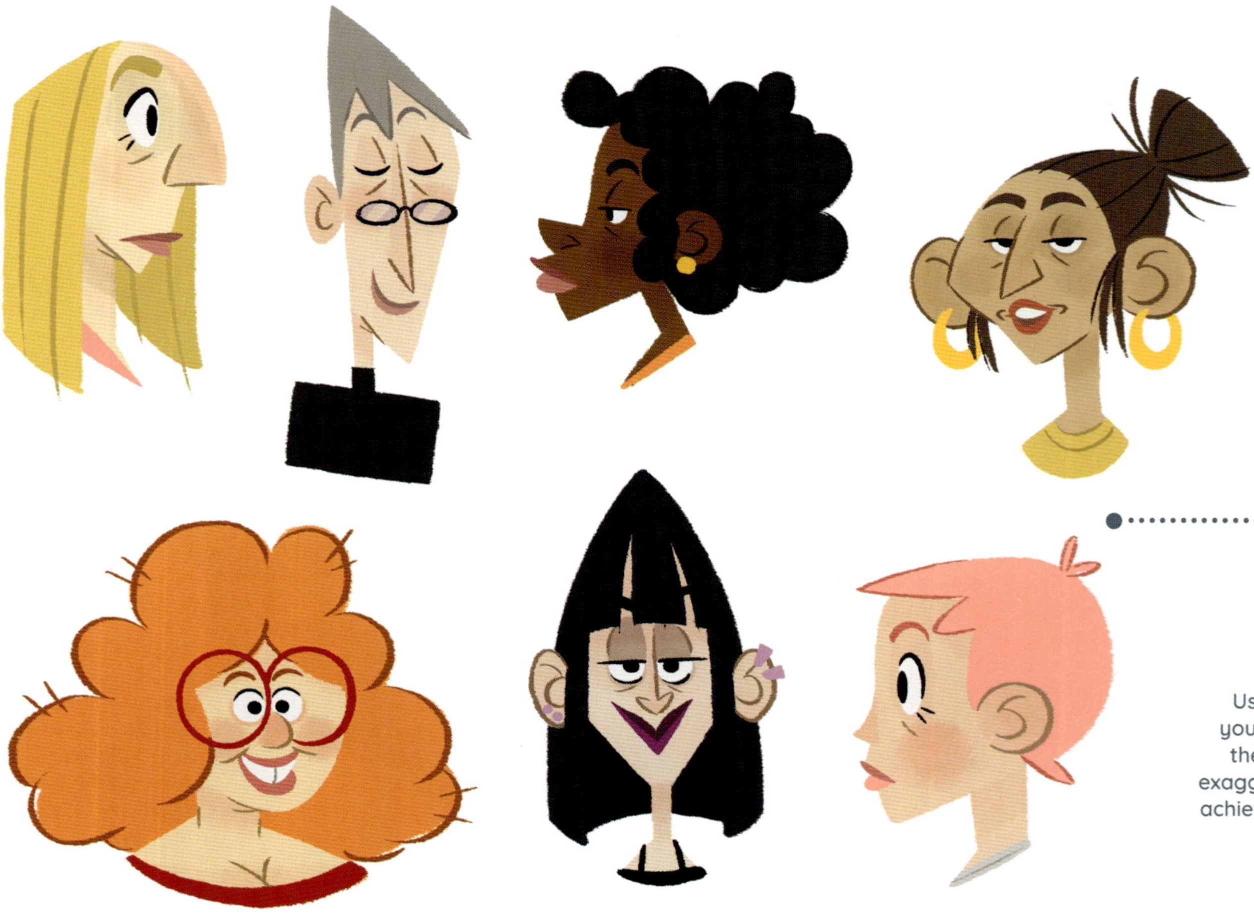

Use the shapes you see, breaking them down and exaggerating them to achieve great results.

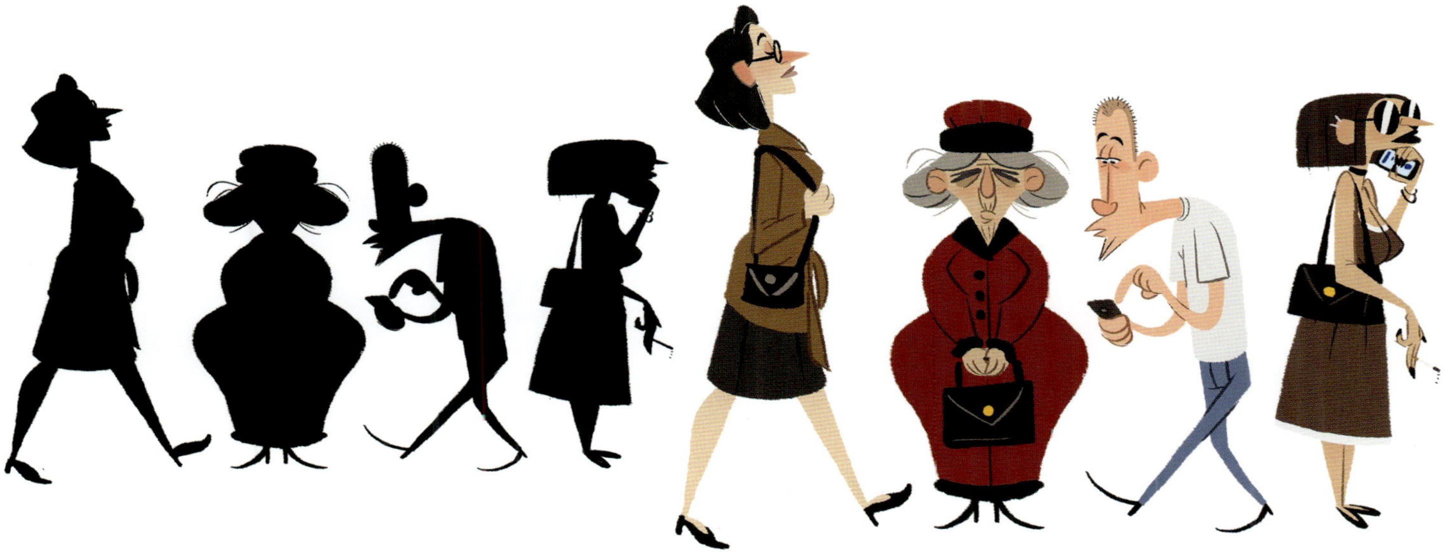

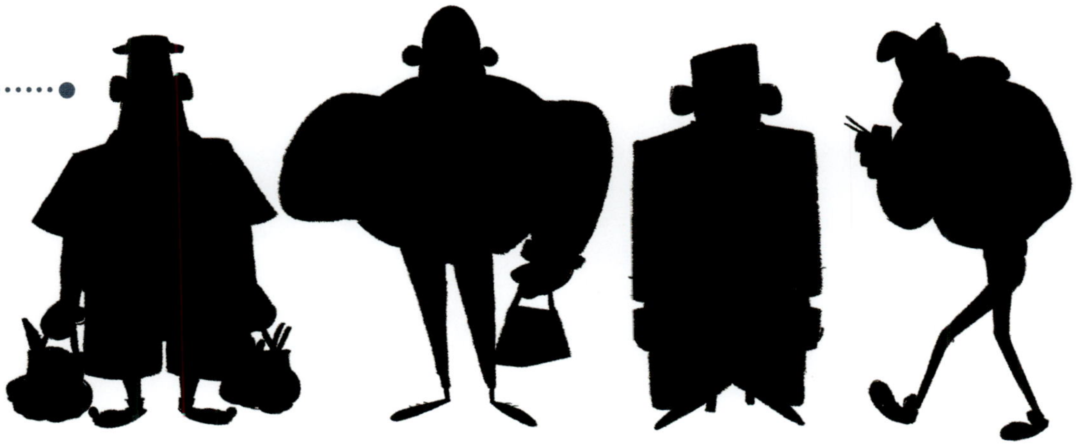

Studying the shapes around you will teach you what shape combinations work well together, and how to reduce a complex concept down to its essentials.

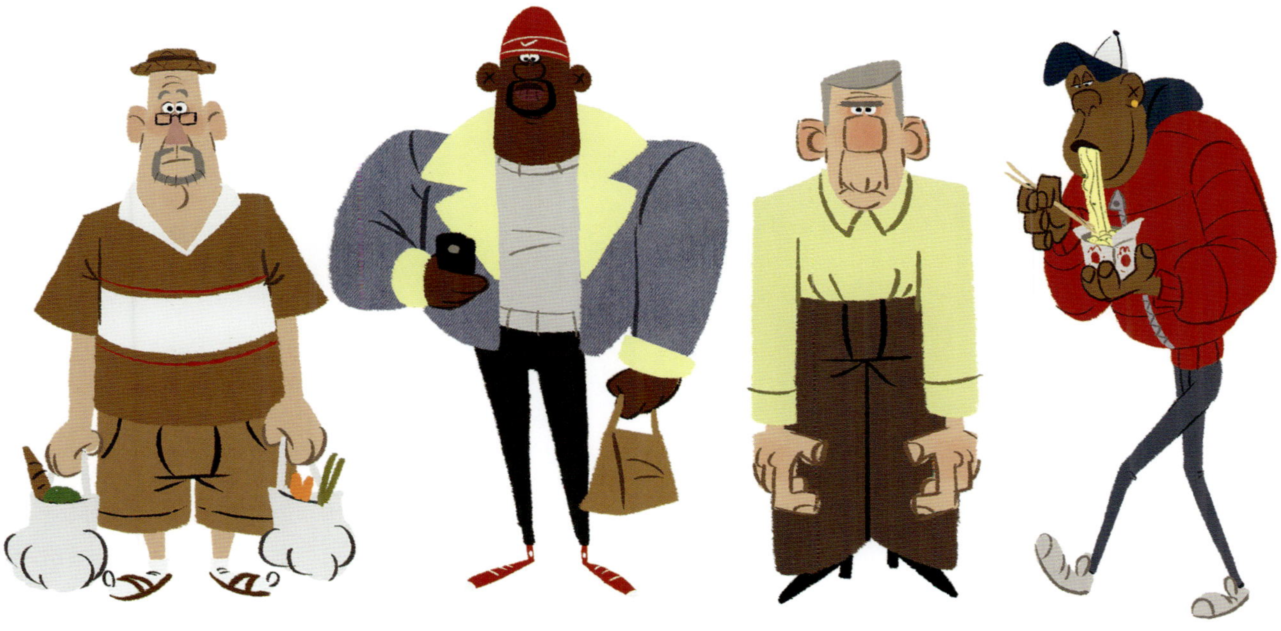

EXAGGERATION

Another key part of character design is exaggeration. When used effectively, it can make a character stand out, and can even bring out more personality that wasn't there before, making a good design even better. Knowing what to exaggerate and what to leave alone is one of the important parts of a character designer's job – if not *the* most important. Push too much and you can ruin a character. Don't exaggerate enough and you run the risk of missing good design opportunities to establish a memorable character.

One guideline to follow is, "If something is worth doing, it's worth overdoing." If a nose is big, make it bigger. If the ears are big, make them bigger. Exaggeration can be used as a tool to make the shapes and proportions of your characters play off one another more effectively. For example, if a character is small, exaggerate this and maybe contrast them with a character who is considerably larger. If you have a lineup of characters in a project, try to exaggerate each one in their own way, so that they stand out from one another.

When using exaggeration as a design tool, you always need to keep in mind how it will serve the story, or help the character tell a story of their own. Take the elderly character on the right with a mobility scooter, for example; to avoid the generic design of an old man with a scooter, we can push his features further. To give the impression that he has a spark of youth left, and is maybe a former racer, we can change the design of the scooter and how he holds himself in it. When exaggerating the man himself, we can take the shapes of his face and squash or stretch them to make them more memorable; exaggerating his hunched posture, too, gives his overall shape a more streamlined and pleasing look.

When designing the soul singer on the opposite page, the first attempt was not a good fit for the intended story – it's too simple and too exaggerated. In order to squeeze as much emotion and personality out of the design as possible, we can revise the design with more shapes, keeping in mind that the level of exaggeration should be enough for the story without detracting from it. As a designer, it is your job to know what to do to accomplish a memorable character that serves the story or tells it well.

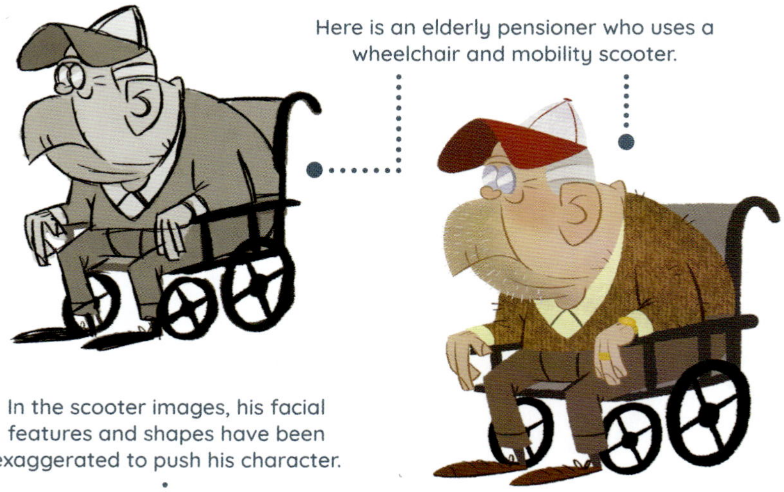

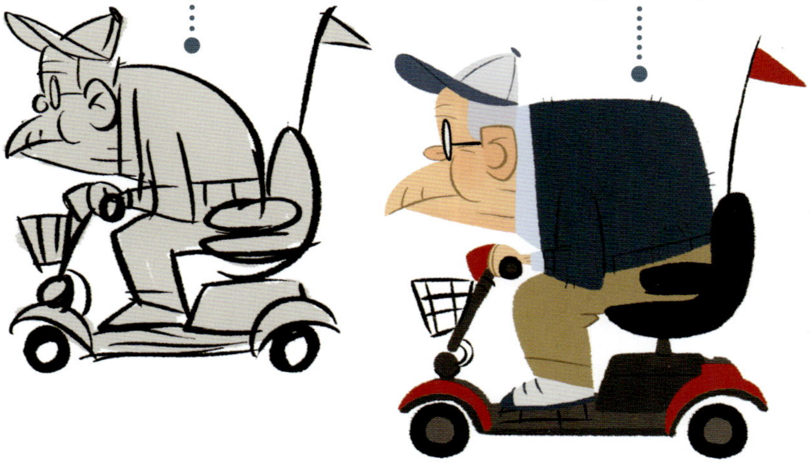

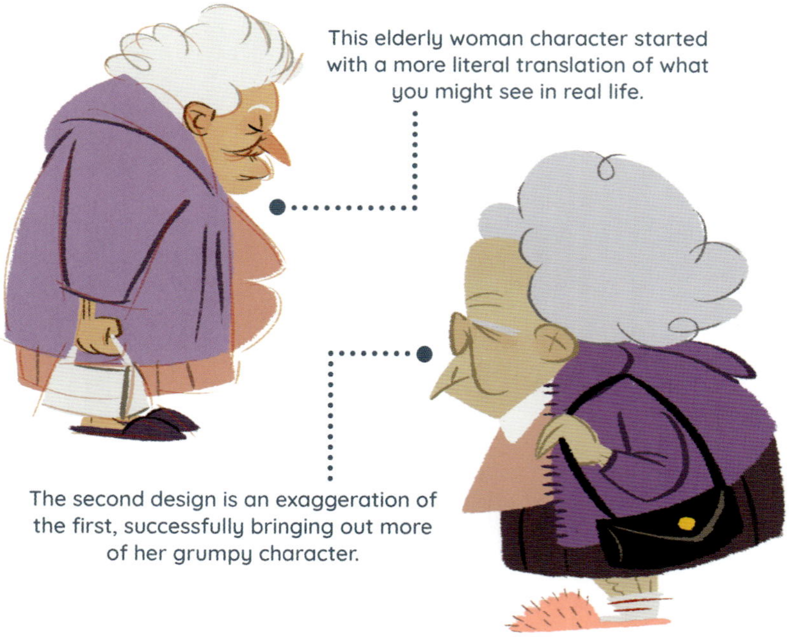

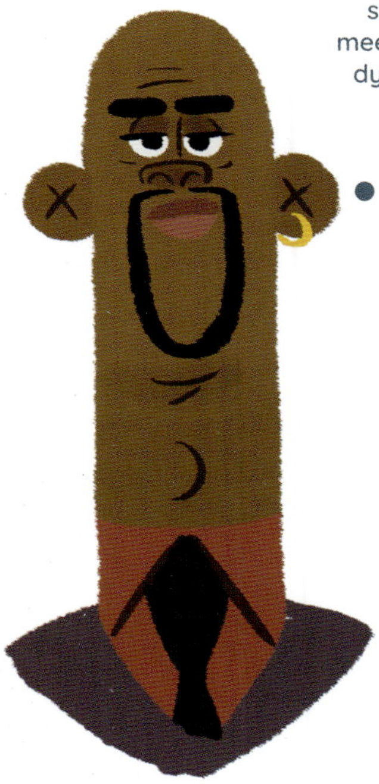

This soul singer character started with a simpler shape, but this didn't meet the aim of making a dynamic, suave design.

In the new designs, his shapes and expressions have been exaggerated.

You can achieve more interesting expressions and poses with the new design that the initial design couldn't fulfill.

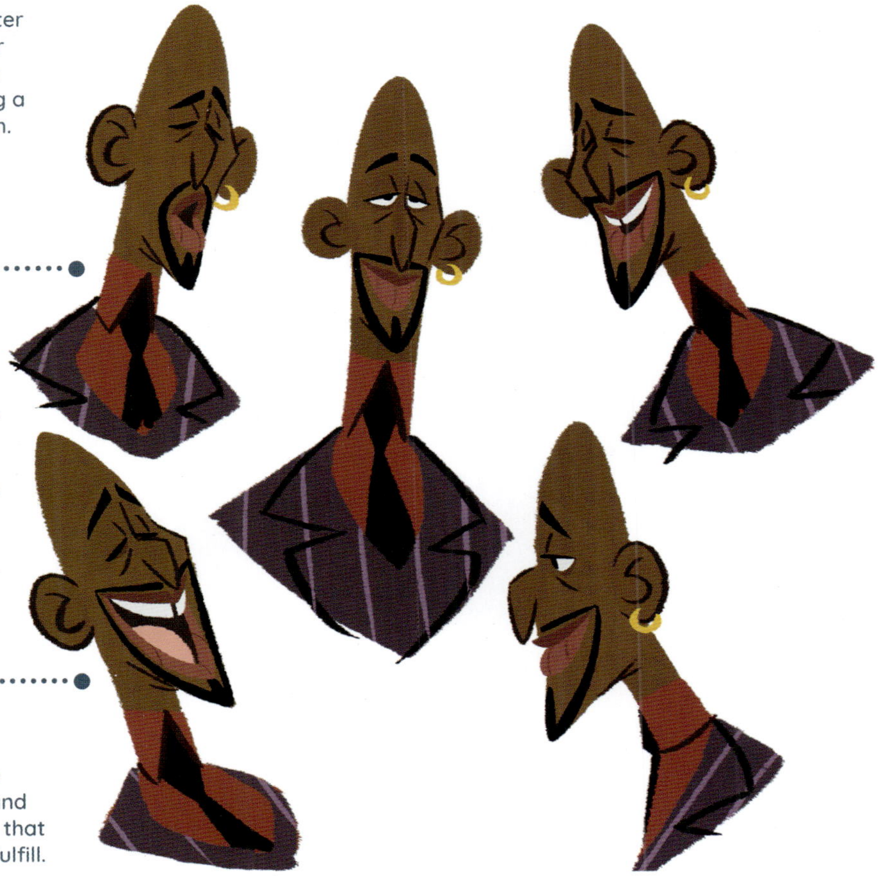

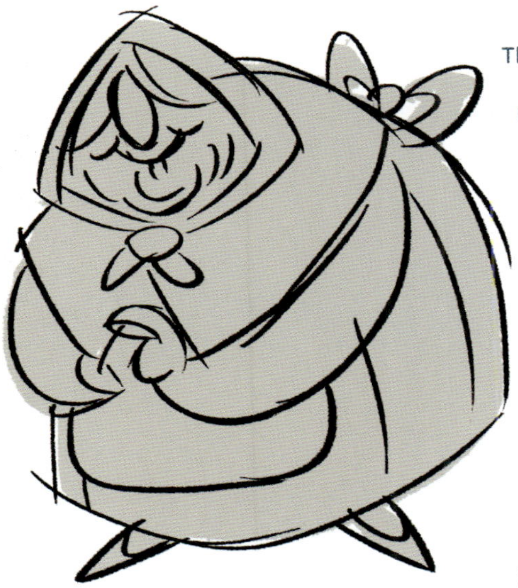

The shapes of this grandmother could be simplified and exaggerated to bring out her soft, motherly character.

Her facial structure has been changed and exaggerated to emphasize her old age, but also simplified so it works better.

Her feet were removed to emphasize and exaggerate her rounded body shape, which works better as a whole.

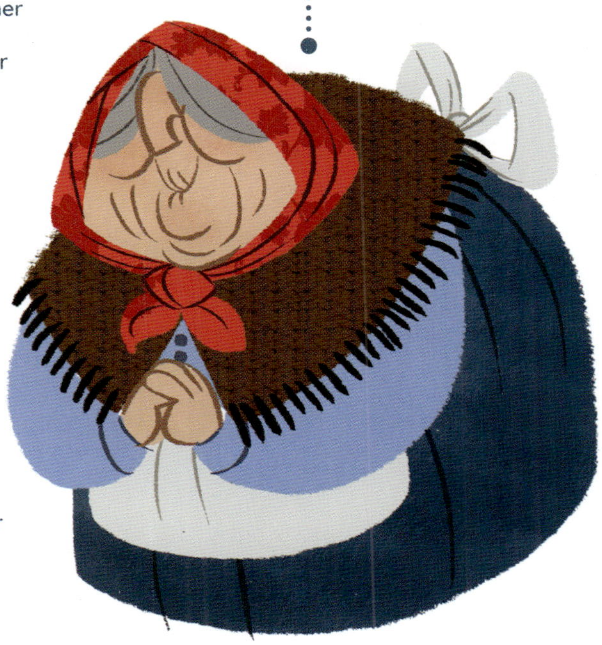

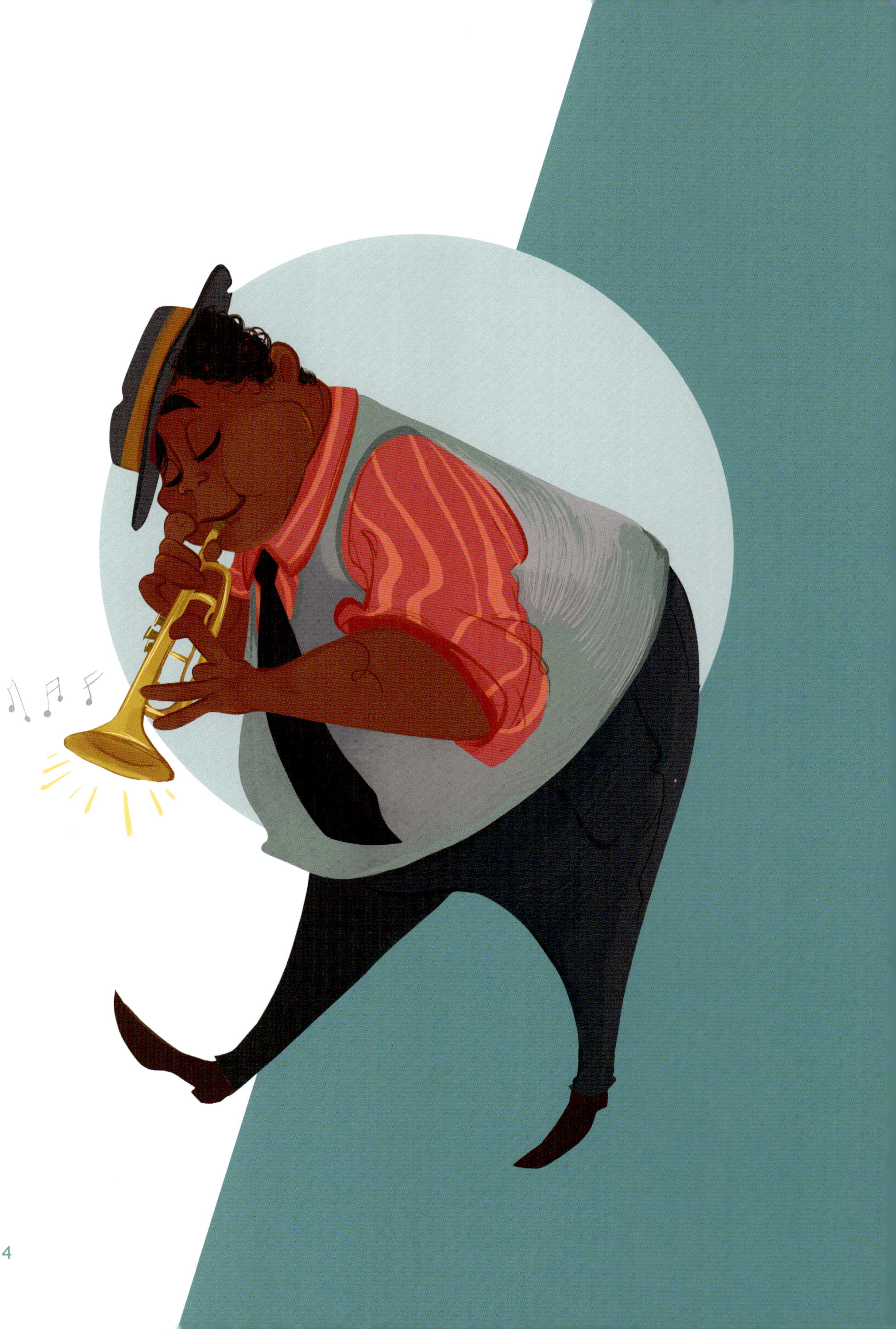

Image © Vanessa Morales

RESEARCH & IDEATION

WHY IS RESEARCH IMPORTANT?
PAGE 36

HOW CAN YOU RESEARCH?
PAGE 44

IDEATION
PAGE 48

WHY IS RESEARCH IMPORTANT?

Vanessa Morales

Character design is the cornerstone of some of the greatest creations we know and enjoy. From TV series to movies, character design exists all around us. It lives in the gardener watering the plants, the girl taking her dog for a walk, or within your own reflection in the mirror. The existence of life implies emotion, action, and purpose, which are transferred into design to create the characters we know and love. Everybody has different characteristics that make them recognizable. We can often infer who someone is and what they do from their appearance, without us even asking. That makes them a character!

A character is not only designed to look good – its main objective is to speak for itself. Not all characters come with a written storyline, so their story needs to be told through their appearance rather than with words. But when characters are designed without doing enough research and using enough references, they are less likely to stand out or make an impression on the viewer. Even if they are telling an incredible story, a character that lacks **believability** will detract from the whole experience. The human eye can pinpoint almost immediately when something doesn't feel right, because we know instinctively how the human body works. Regardless of the artist's style, a character needs some basis in reality to be appealing. Of course, this doesn't mean that there is a fixed model or template on how to stylize a character, but even with the most unique styles or abstractions, there should be a structure that makes the design recognizable.

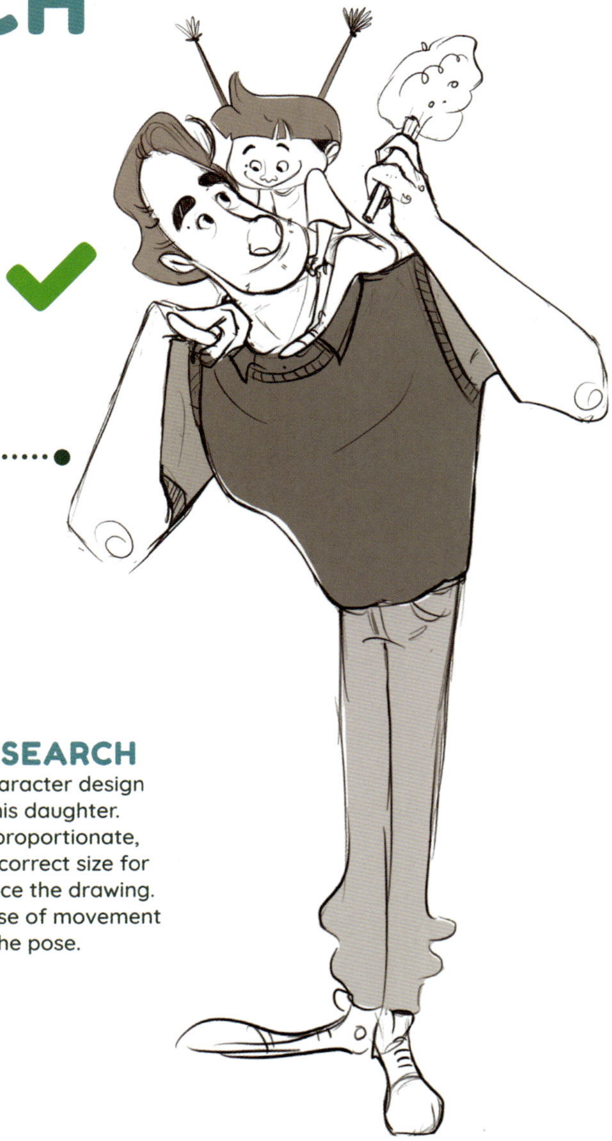

ANATOMY RESEARCH
The concept for this character design is a father carrying his daughter. He doesn't appear disproportionate, and his daughter is the correct size for her age and helps balance the drawing. There is a believable sense of movement and strength in the pose.

When you are given a task, it helps to **ask questions** that will inform the details. What do you need to do? How are you going to approach it, and why? This will help structure your process before you begin. As an artist, you will often have a brief to follow, but sometimes the brief can be ambiguous or tricky. There may be conflicting voices and opinions that will distract you from your goal, so it's important to know and trust the source of your **references**, so you don't go off track. Whether your references are found firsthand or through books and the internet, you can use them to create a stronger depiction of your character's personality and appearance.

Research can take up a considerable amount of time, but the more you dive into possible references for your character, the **richer** and more believable they will become. This is especially important when approaching a character in a historical setting or a subject you aren't familiar with, but you should approach *every* new design this way – even if you have researched a topic before, it's best to have fresh, accurate information in front of you.

Research is one of the most important steps of the design process and one that is often overlooked. Most of the time, people rush through it, thinking this will save time, but the reality is usually the opposite. A lot of artists have the misguided belief that researching shows a lack of creativity and is considered cheating, but this is simply not the case. Research and references will help ground your characters in the real world and take your creativity to new levels.

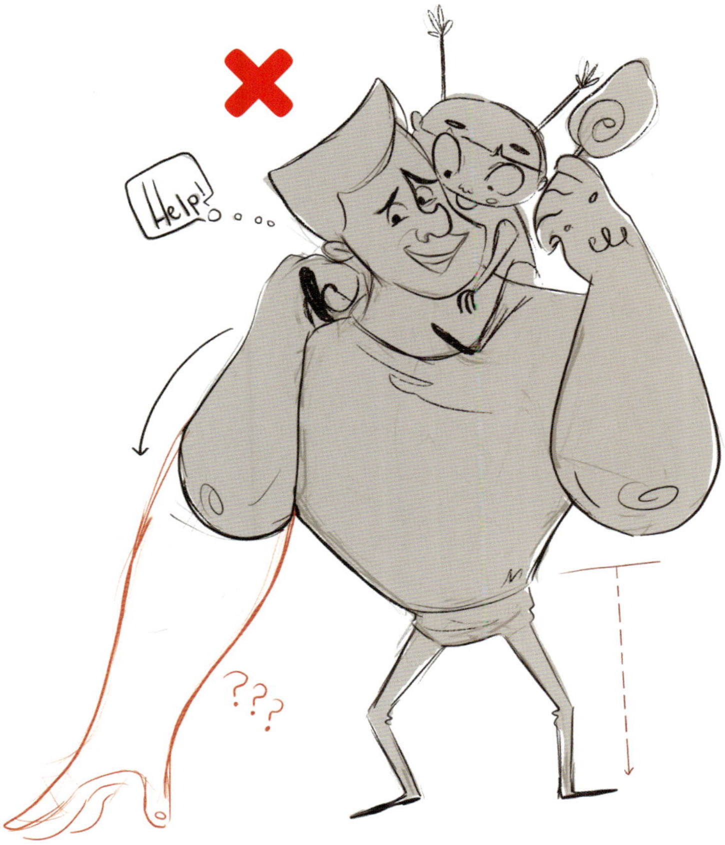

NO ANATOMY RESEARCH

This image shows the same concept as the opposite page, but lacks the correct proportions. The small, skinny legs are too exaggerated, and look incorrect when contrasted with the size of the arms and head. When it comes to stylization, small legs and a big upper body can work, but in this case there is no balance, so it does not work well.

CULTURAL RESEARCH

This sumo wrestler, or rikishi, is ready to fight. He is wearing a belt called a mawashi and his hair is tied up in a traditional bun. These accurate details help relate the design to real life.

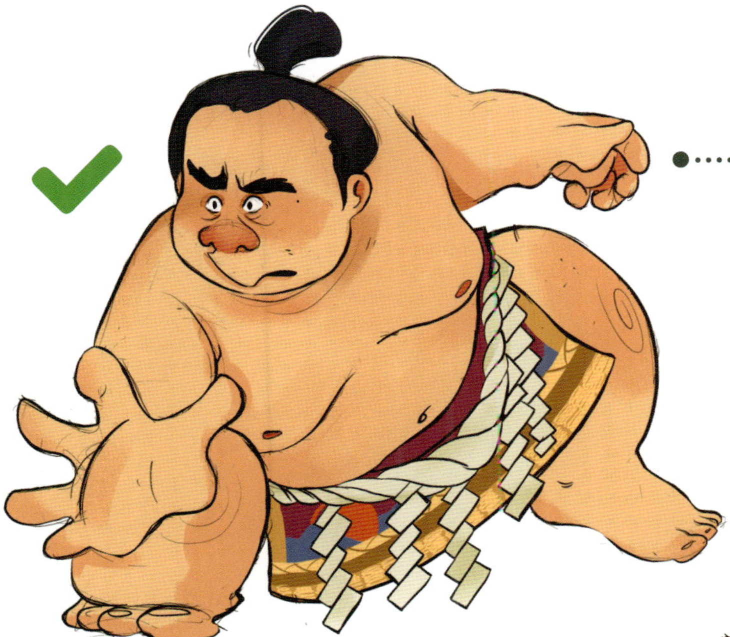

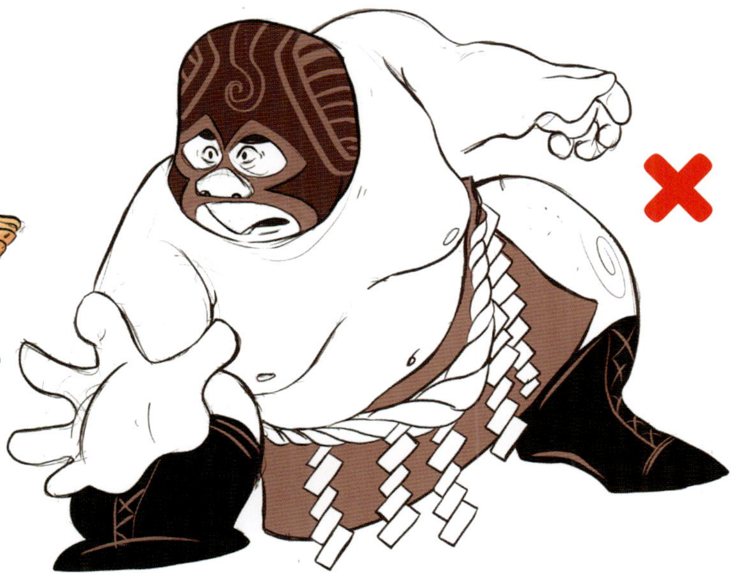

NO CULTURAL RESEARCH

With the addition of one or two inaccurate details, the sumo wrestler loses his identity. Is he a sumo or lucha libre wrestler? If we're aiming to show a traditional sumo wrestler, we need to pay attention to the correct details.

QUEEN OF THE CITY

PERSONALITY
- Kind
- Loyal
- Strong

SOCIAL STATUS
- Believed to be a human-goddess
- Has a jaguar pet/friend

MAYA CULTURE

This design will be of a young girl from the ancient Maya culture. A mind map can be used to organize ideas in order to find keywords that are going to lead the research.

APPEARANCE

ANATOMY
- Young, in her 20s
- Black hair
- Tall
- Medium-brown skin

CLOTHING
- One-piece fabric dress
- Jade jewelry
- Bracelets
- Earrings

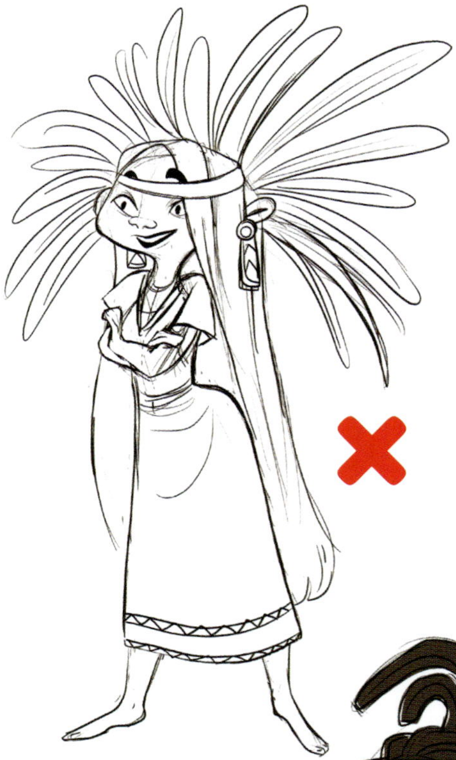

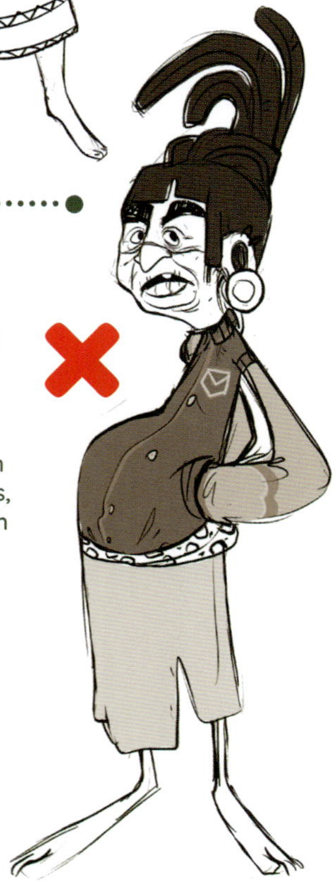

INACCURATE DETAILS
The character above is from a pre-Hispanic setting, but the details are Aztec, not Maya – they belong to another culture and place. The design on the right has some correct features, but the modern blazer does not match the ancient Maya character we are trying to portray.

ACCURATE DETAILS
The character shows details and features from the Maya culture. Her accessories and the animal she has as a pet give us clues to her personality.

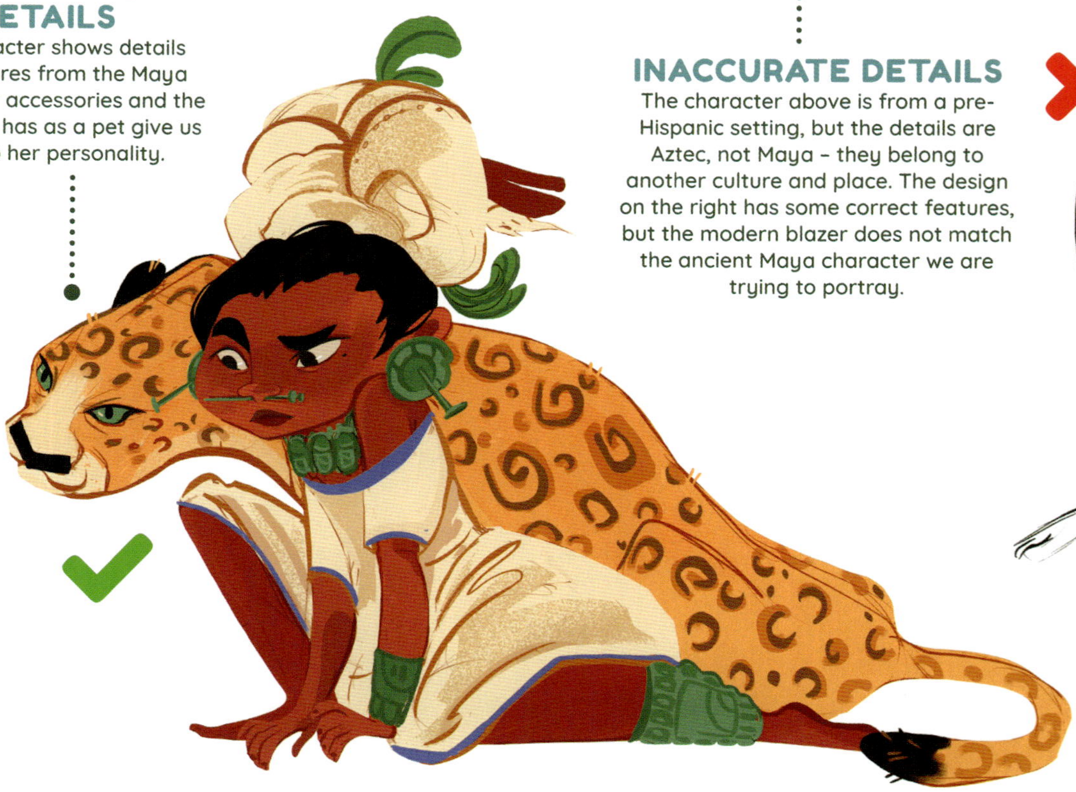

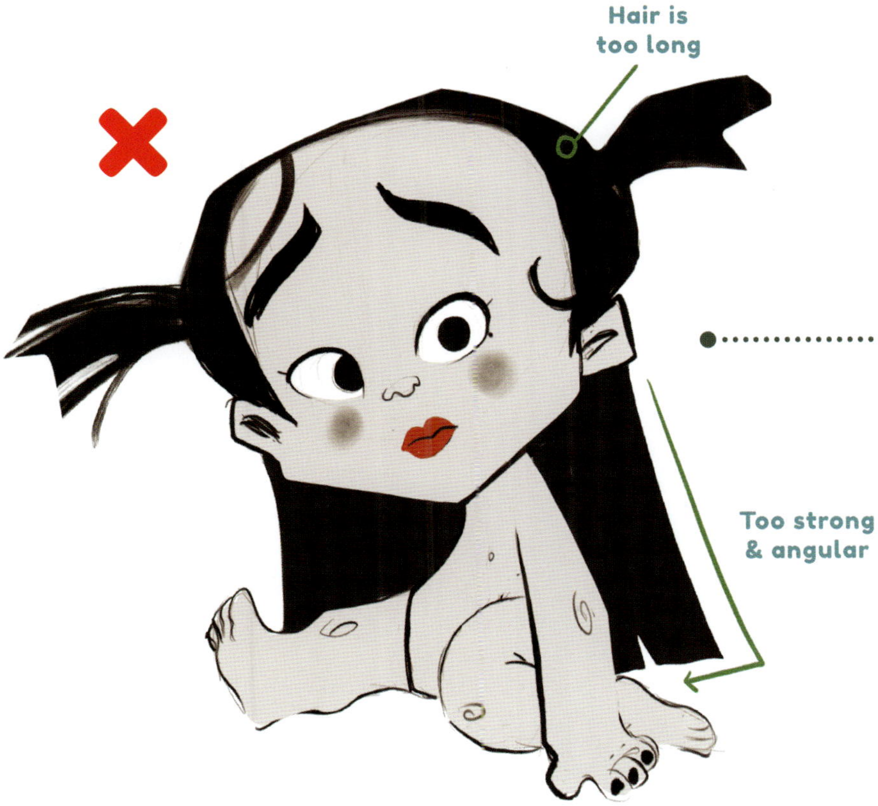

UNSUITABLE SHAPES

Both of the characters on this page are young babies, but the use of straight or rounded lines makes a huge difference in how their designs come across. From what we instinctively know of babies, an angular, long-haired baby feels wrong. More research could help as a reminder of a baby's features.

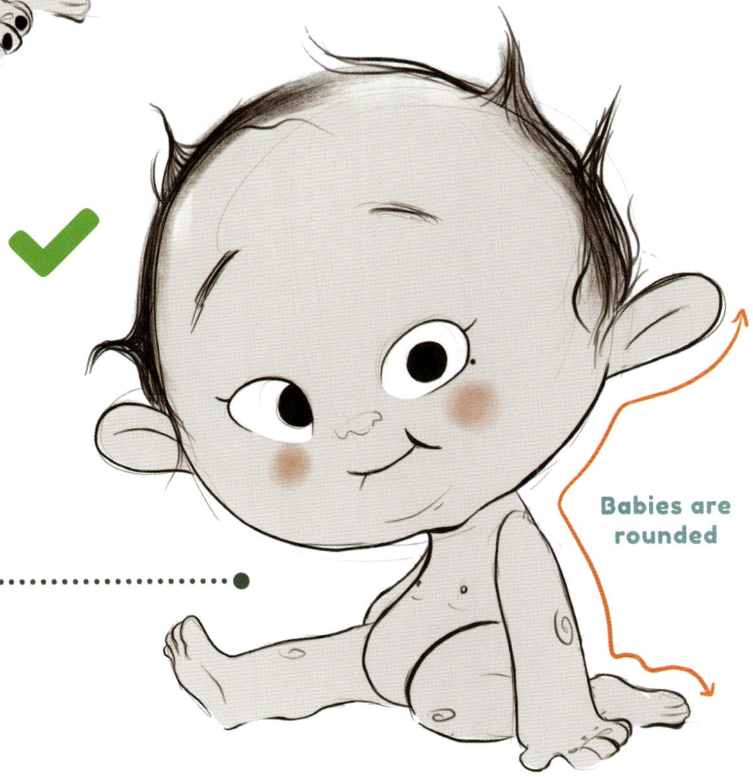

SUITABLE SHAPES

As you will learn on page 197, a human baby has round shapes and little hair. Without these features, the design loses its identity. This doesn't mean that you can't include unusual details to create something new, but if your goal is an accurate depiction, respect your references and use common sense to apply them.

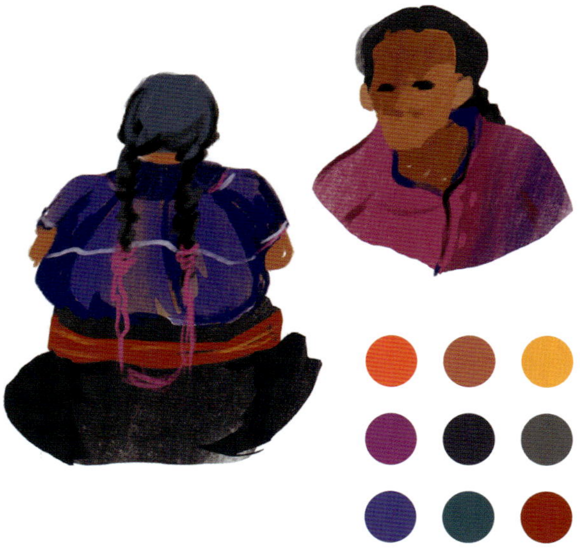

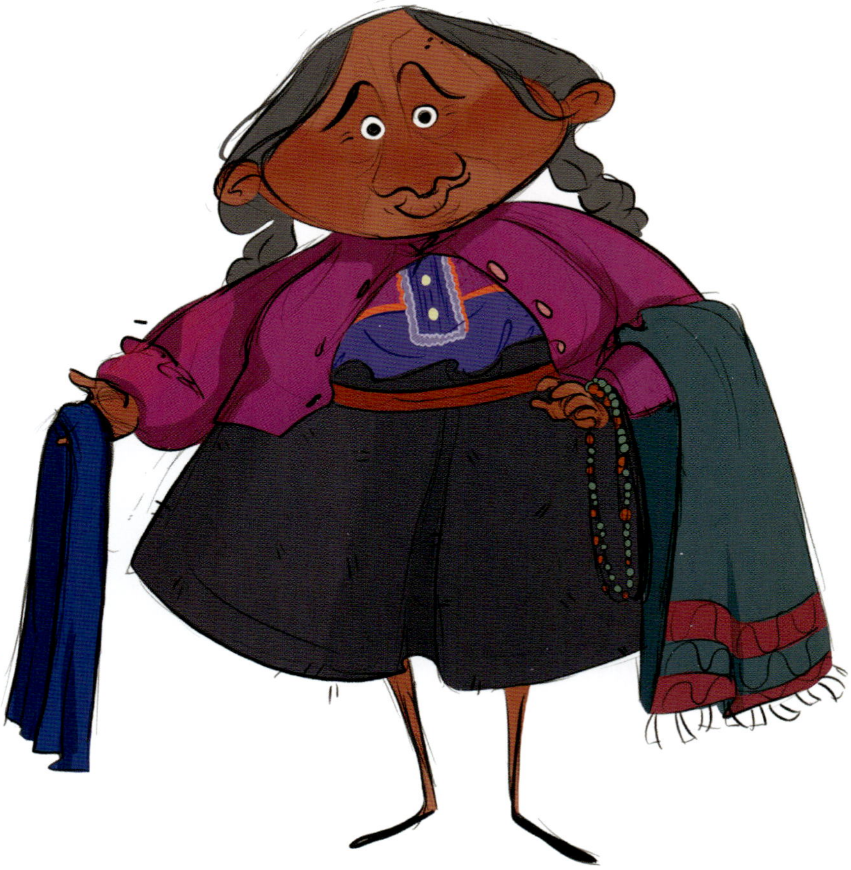

This character has a color palette based on real-life reference. Often, the color choices of your characters are going to speak for them. In this case, the colors reflect the character's origin and culture.

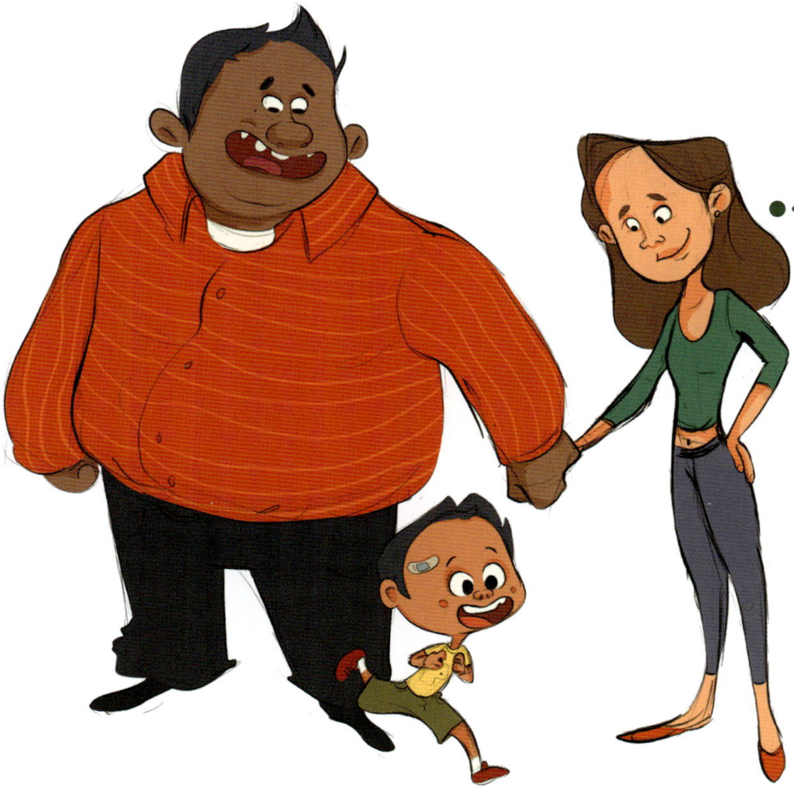

These characters' shapes are accentuated using contrast. The man is a strong character, but his roundness makes him friendly rather than intimidating. The woman's shape is based on a triangle; even with rounded sides, she feels lightweight and angular. The little boy is a combination of the two adults.

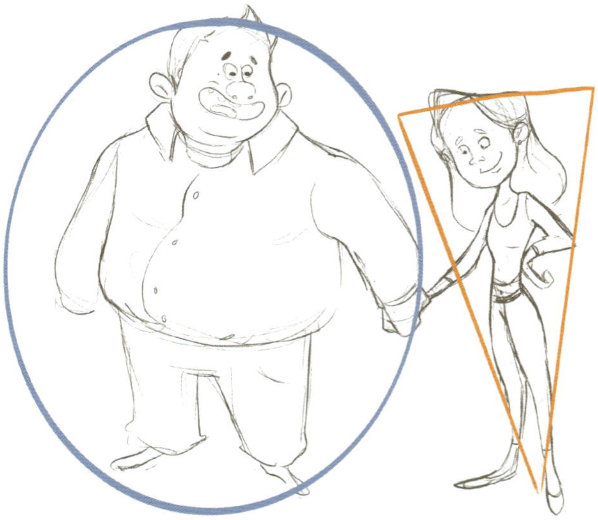

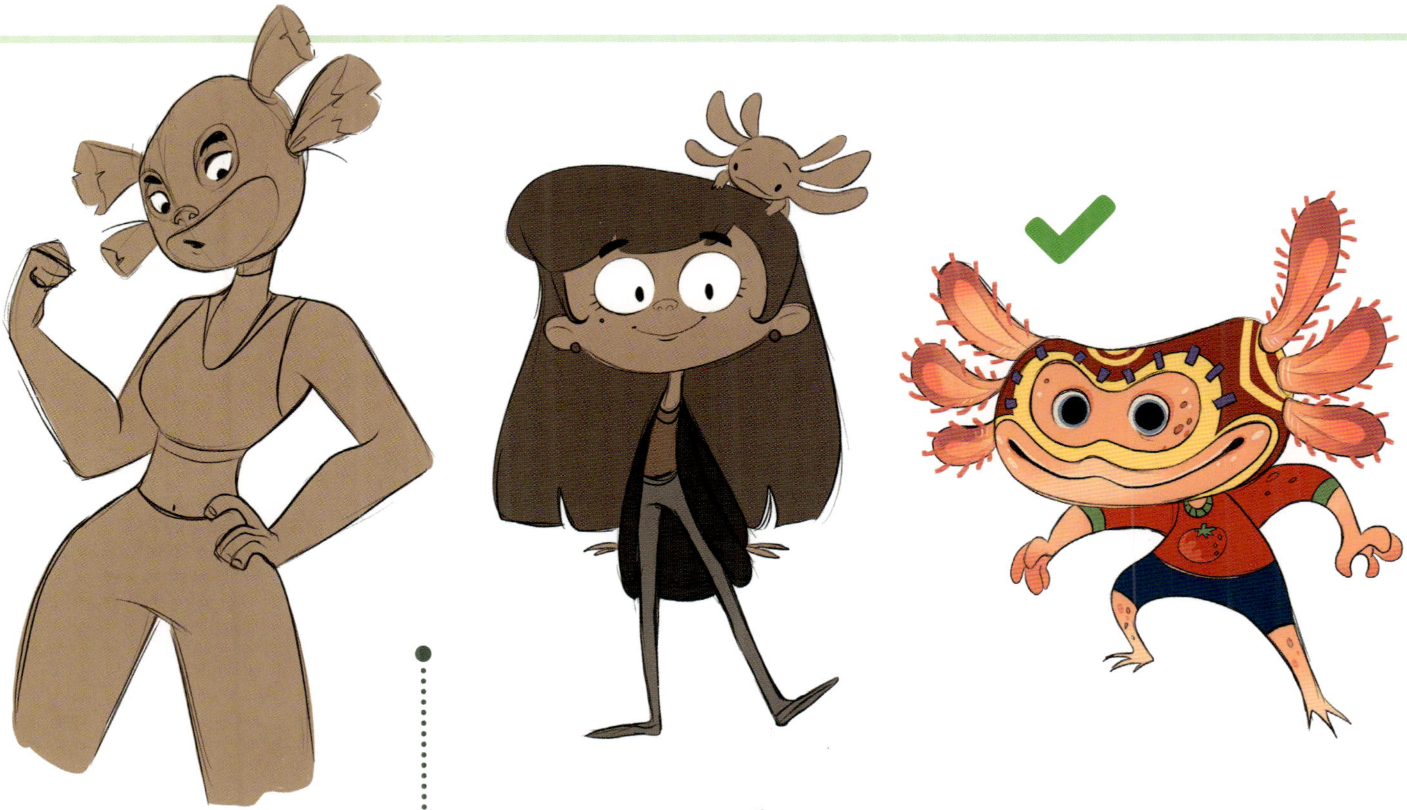

You can use almost anything as inspiration for your characters, such as animals or inanimate objects. These characters were all inspired by three words: wrestler, girl, and axolotl.

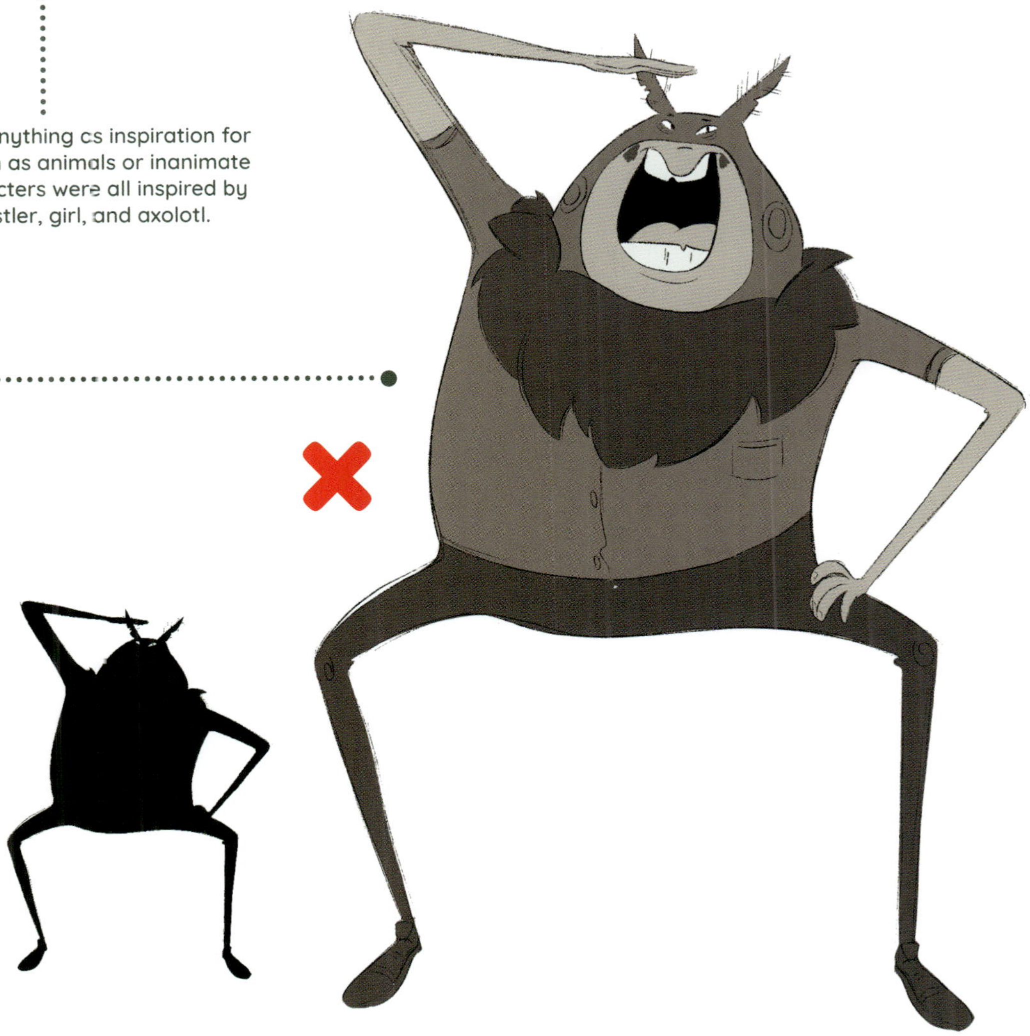

This character was very fun to draw, but no research was put into his design. The aim was to create a "cockroach man," but this is a poor depiction that lacks detail and information. The proportions are not right, and while the silhouette is readable, it's unclear how it relates to an insect.

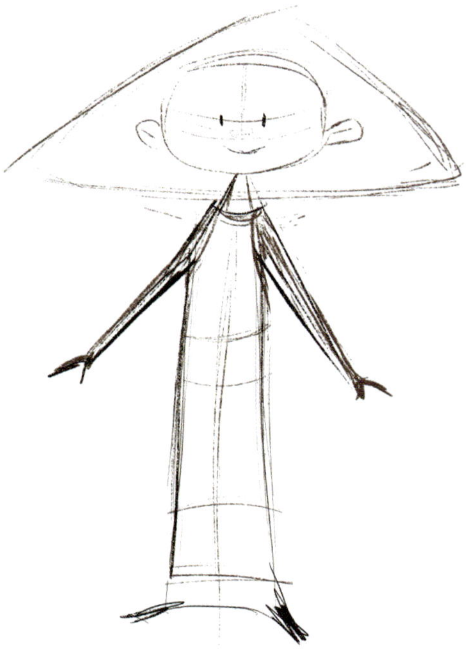

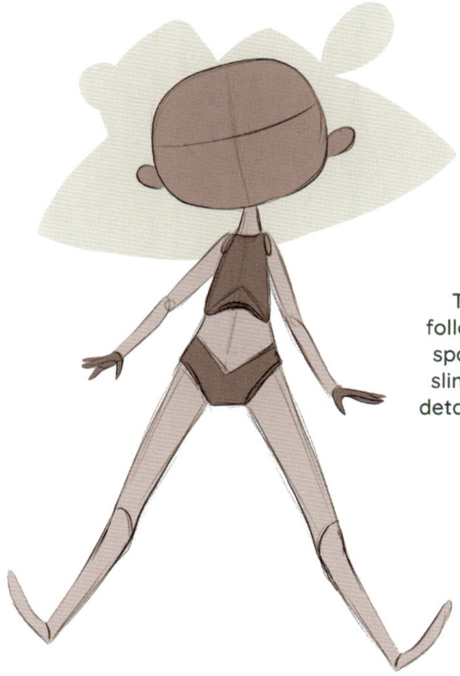

The construction of this character follows the general shape of the ace of spades, with large, pointed hair and a slim body. Her clothes, hair, and other details reflect the same shape, to tie the whole design together.

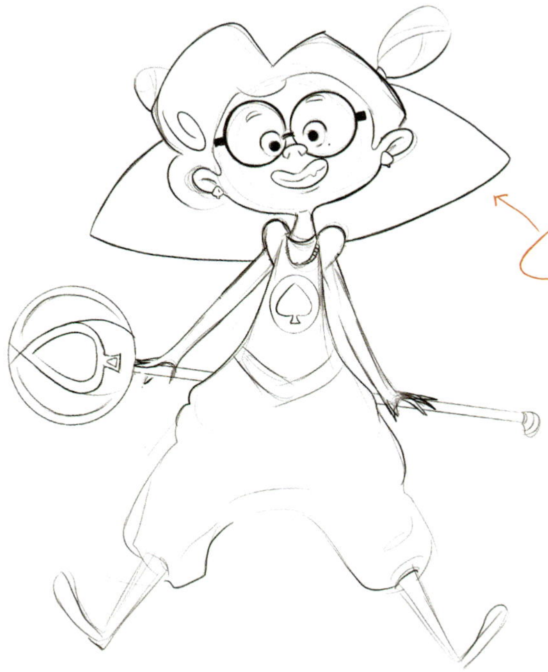

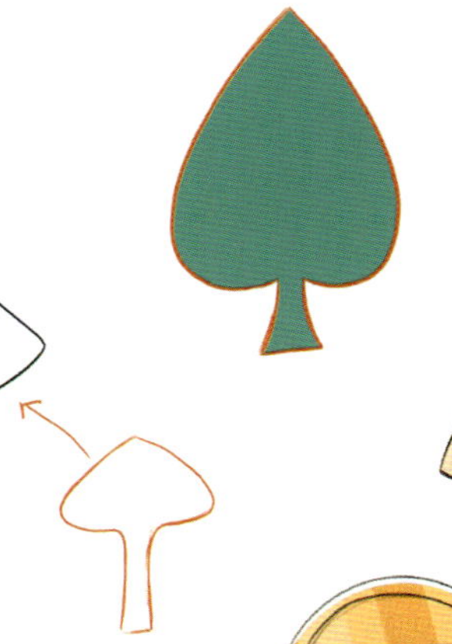

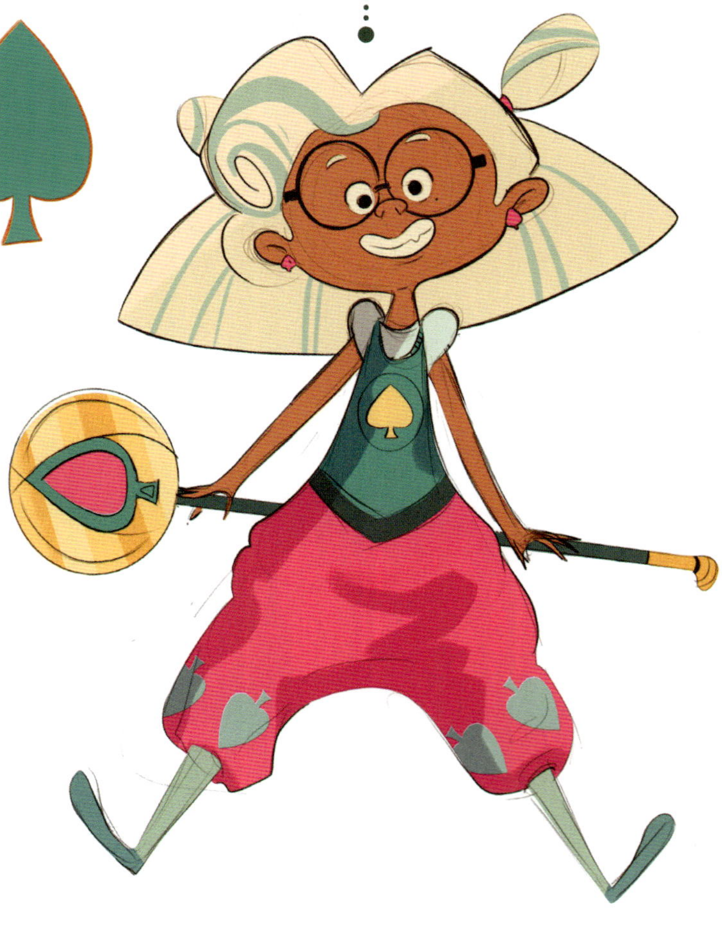

AVOID THE OBVIOUS

When designing a character, it's important to not use the first idea that comes to mind. Your initial instinct is often to depict a shallow interpretation of the subject, and settling on this first design will hold you back. Creating thumbnails - multiple small, quick sketches - will help you get the most obvious ideas out of your system, and help you avoid falling into clichés, stereotypes, and overused designs. Of course, this doesn't mean your character has to be unrecognizable and far off-topic - going to the opposite extreme isn't what you want, either! Try to find a balance between the design being authentic and being recognizable, as this is what will make your characters appealing.

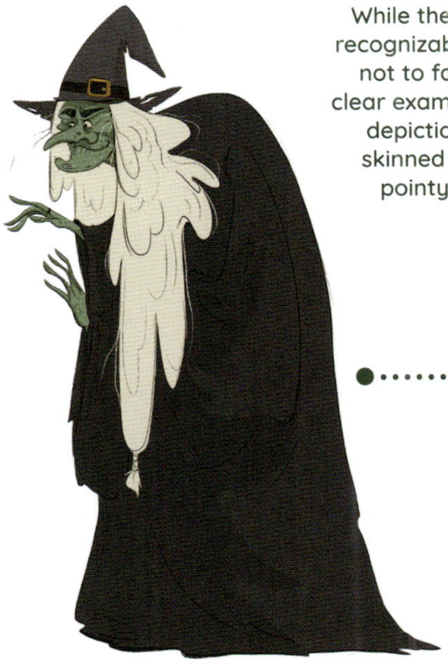

While the character needs to be recognizable, it's always important not to fall into clichés. This is a clear example of the most common depiction of a witch: a green-skinned old woman with a big, pointy nose and white hair.

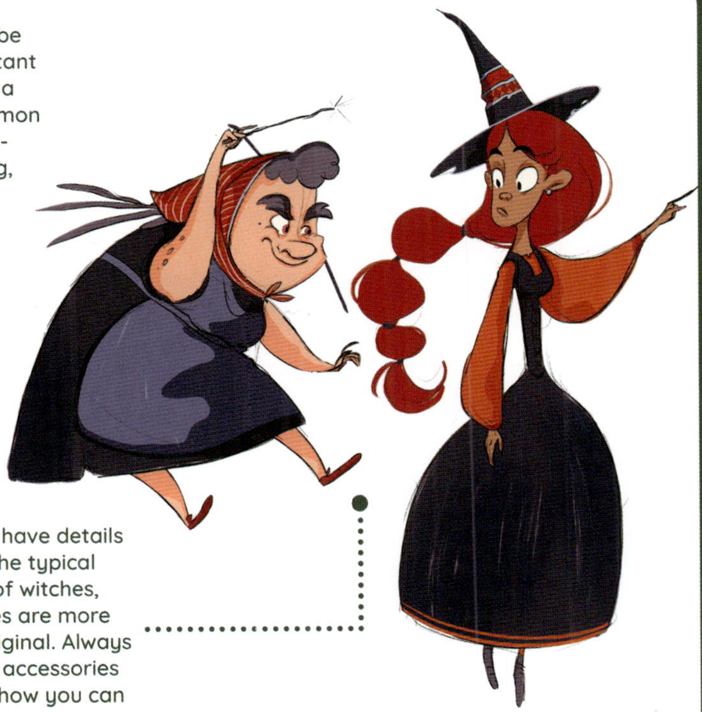

These characters have details that relate to the typical interpretation of witches, but their features are more humanized and original. Always play around with accessories and props to see how you can enhance a design.

This witch lineup was created with the words "magic" and "school" in mind. Accessories such as robes and big hats indicate that they are magical characters, but each of them has their own distinct appearance and personality.

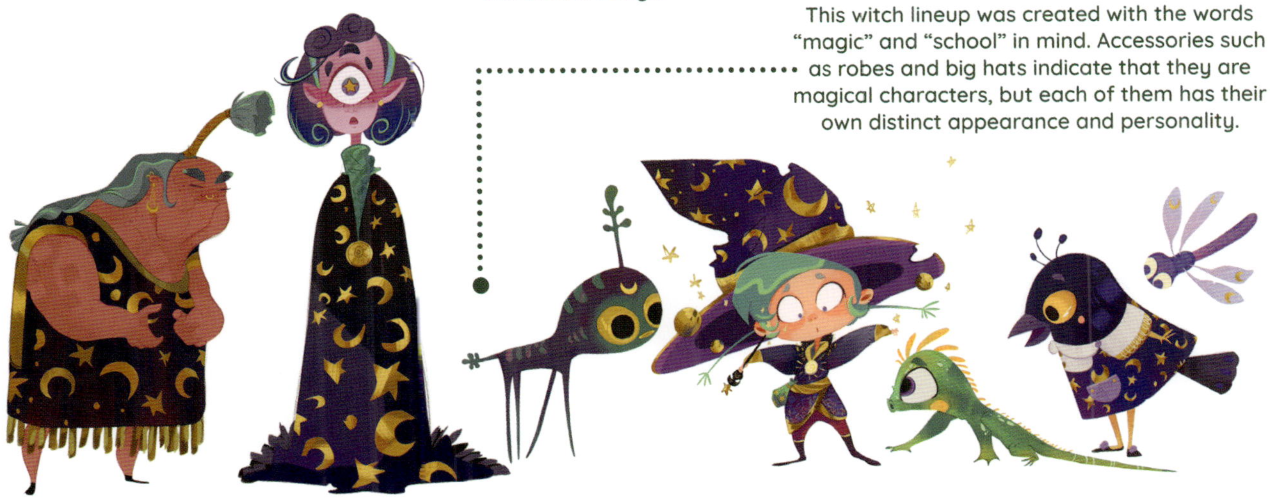

HOW CAN YOU RESEARCH?

Vanessa Morales

Once you have figured out the direction to take your character, you can begin the deeper research. Even if you've been given a brief, there is always room for you to have your own ideas and interpretations. There is no one way to approach and use references in your design process, but there are some tools that can help with the process. For example, you can create a visual library with key words on a **mind map**, allowing you to expand the spectrum of features you want to include or avoid.

Collecting references firsthand allows you to experience a subject in its environment, so try looking at regular people around you from whom you can derive your character. A lot of animation teams do this when they start to develop a story. You can go outside to **sketch life in motion**, or use the internet to "travel" to a different time and place. Combine **photographs** with real-life research and save useful information for future projects. Don't just view the images as a whole, but study and **analyze** their successful and unsuccessful features. Every detail you analyze and interpret will tell you something.

There are many things you can use to expand your visual library: magazines, books, photographs, documentaries, and research texts. Make a **moodboard** – a collage of relevant references – from all these resources and consult it while you work. Look at other artists' work to see what has been done before, so you can learn and expand on it. Really try to understand the "answers" the artists gave to the questions about their characters. This will help you find your own solutions and see what possibilities are out there for your own design.

When you study your moodboard, you're filling up your "creative tank." Ask yourself questions about what you are trying to say, because all the information you find through your research – whether shape language, color, structure, texture, or detail – could lead you toward potential designs.

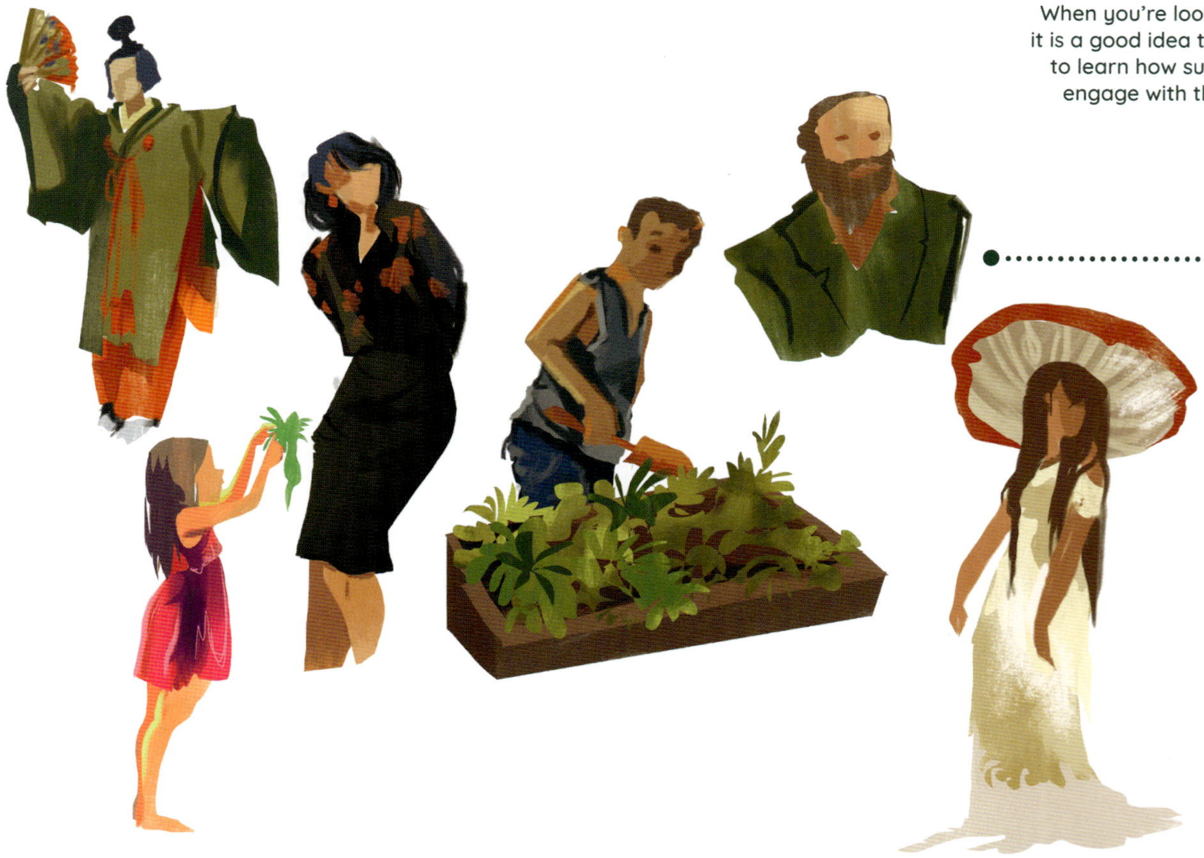

When you're looking for references, it is a good idea to study from photos to learn how subjects behave and engage with their environment.

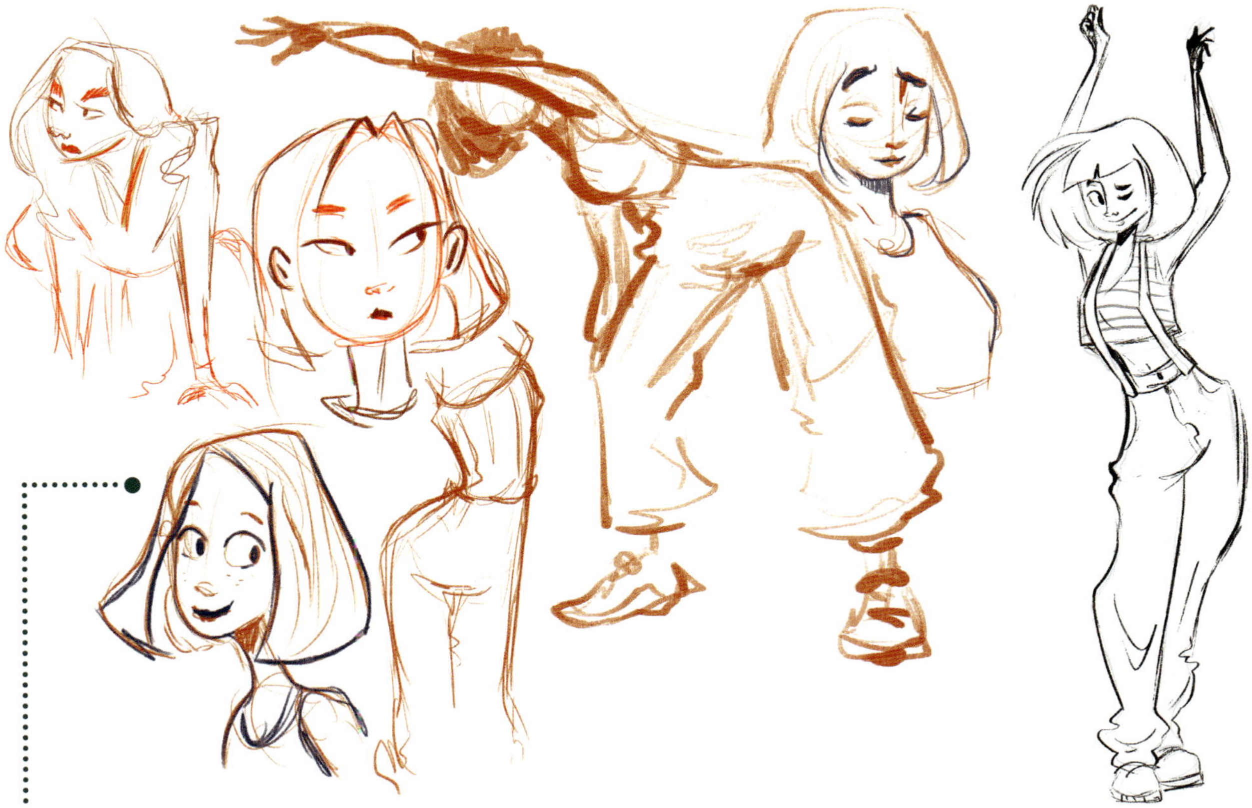

Try to observe and capture movement, so you understand how people respond to the "cause and effect" law. This study was made by observing a music video.

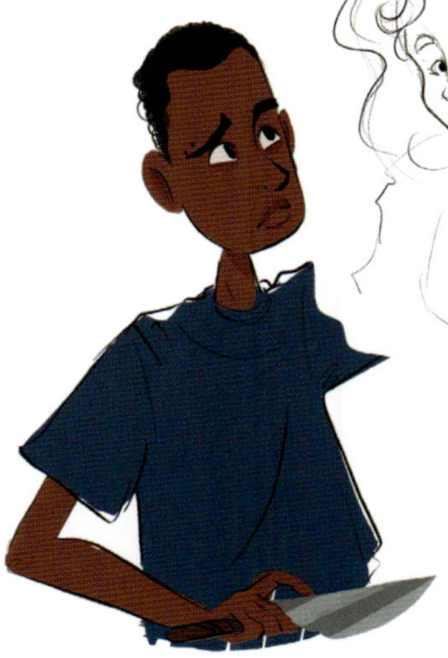

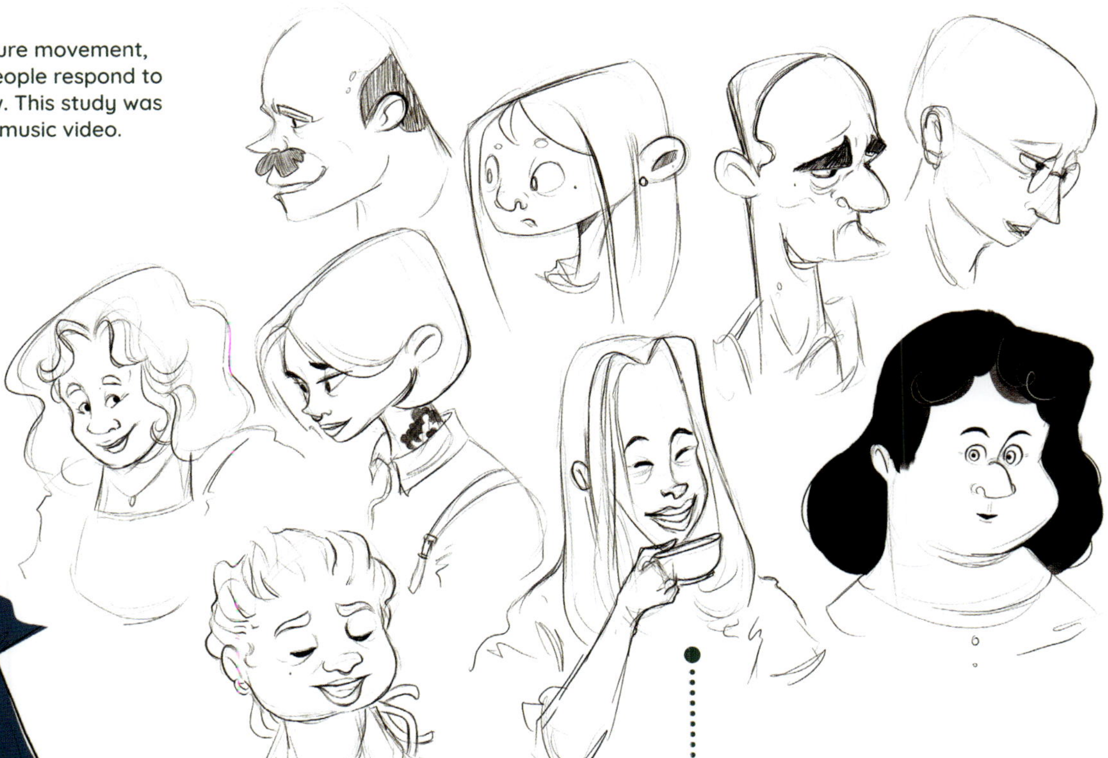

The face is one of the main sources of information for a character, so try to sketch faces from real life and capture their natural expressions. These sketches were made in a busy cafeteria.

This set of characters is inspired by the cafeteria studies on the previous page. Even if you only take a few ideas or don't use 100% of a sketch, life studies can be a valuable base for your final ideas.

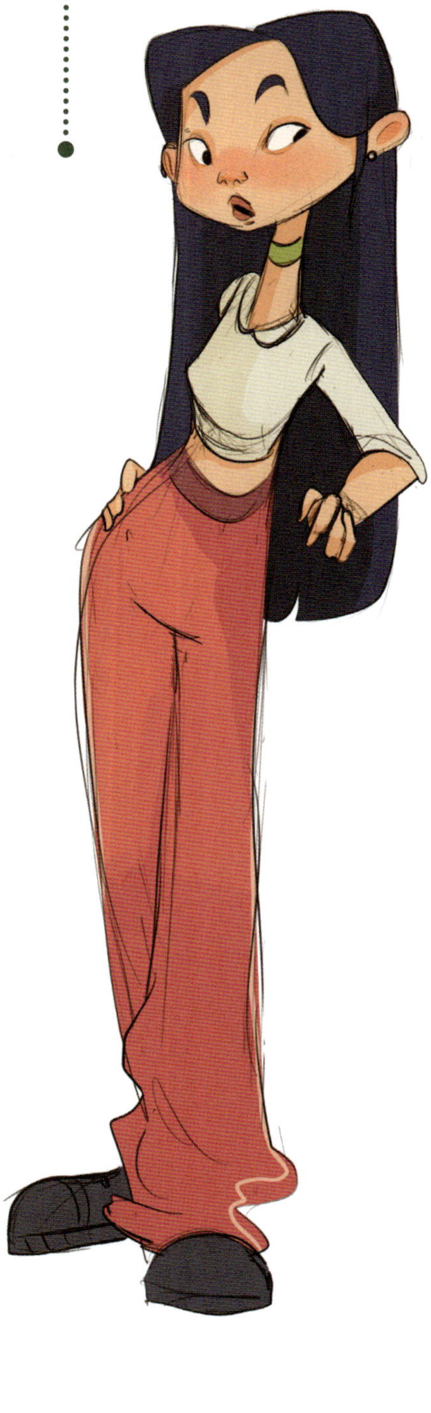

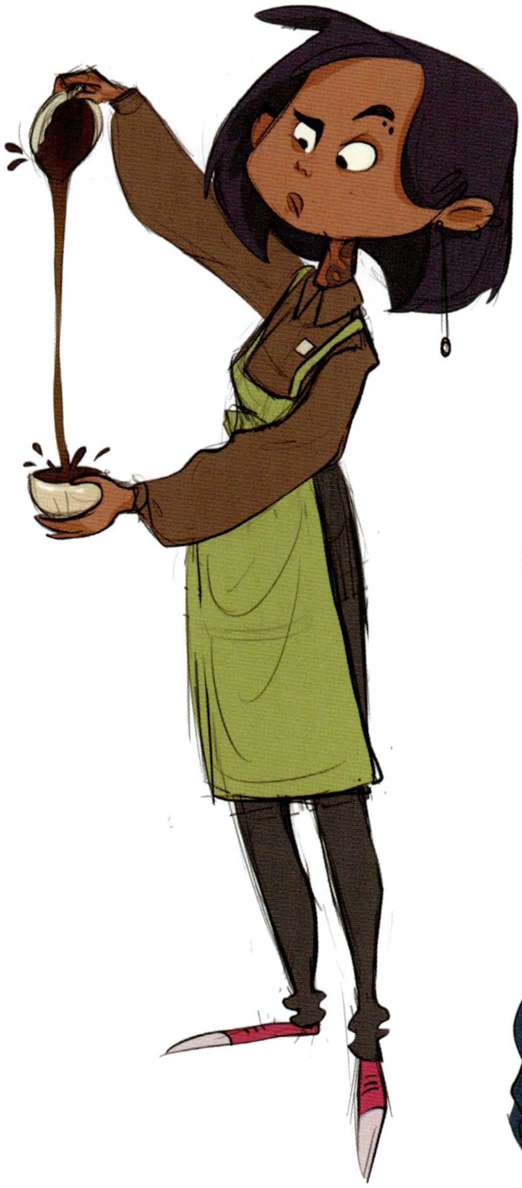

This barista is quite true to the real-life reference, but with some added piercings to give her an extra edge!

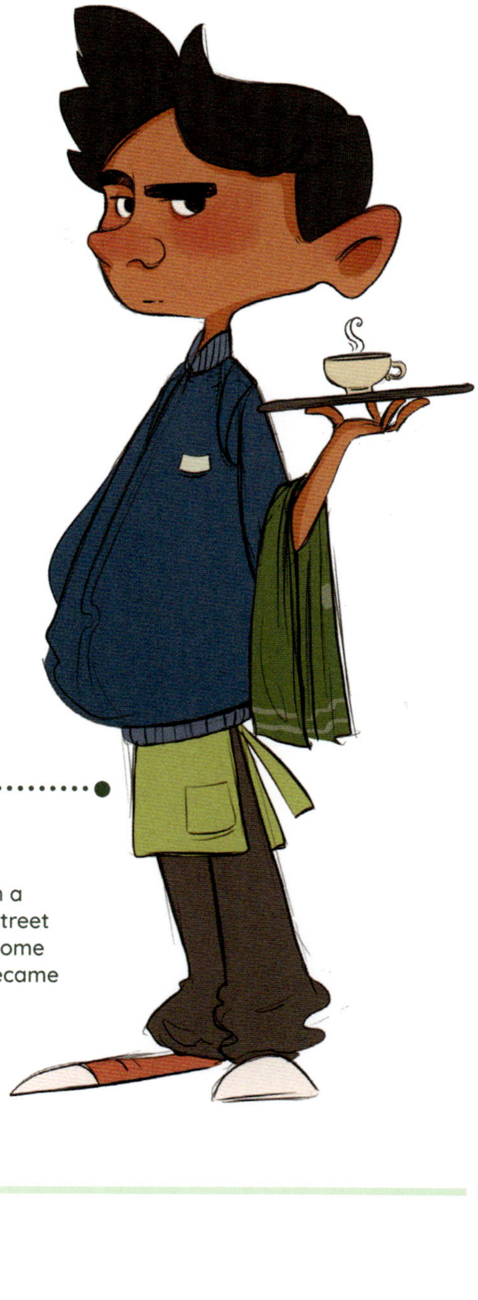

This character is based on a slightly grumpy boy on the street outside the cafeteria. With some props and adjustments, he became a fictional waiter.

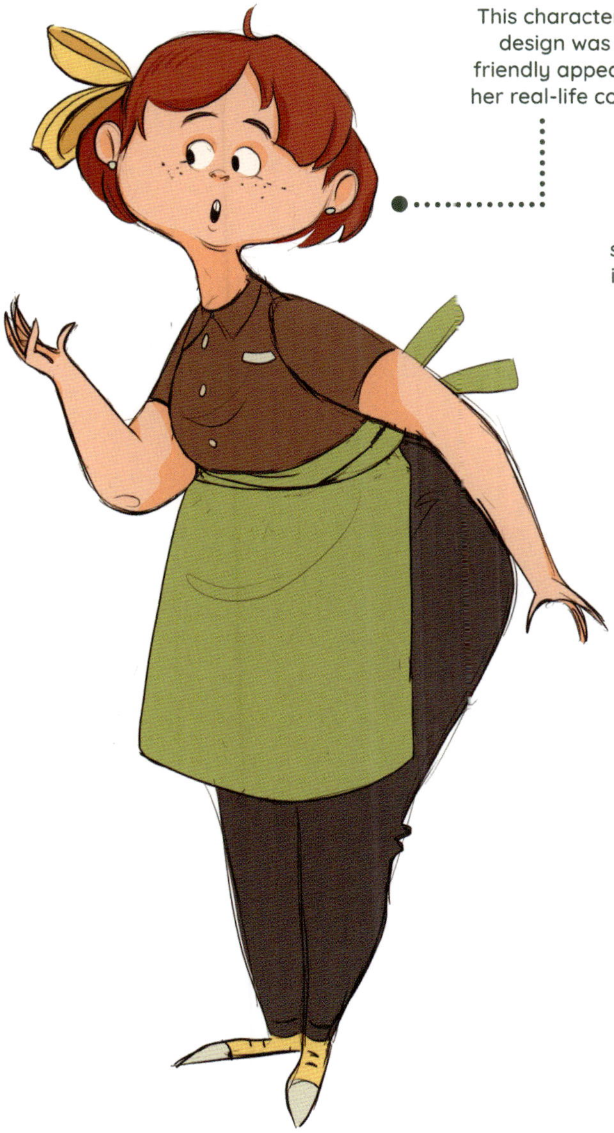

This character's rounded, endearing design was inspired by the kind, friendly appearance and behavior of her real-life coffee-shop counterpart.

This elderly man was inspired by two real-world people, and adds some interesting age variation to the inhabitants of this fictional cafeteria.

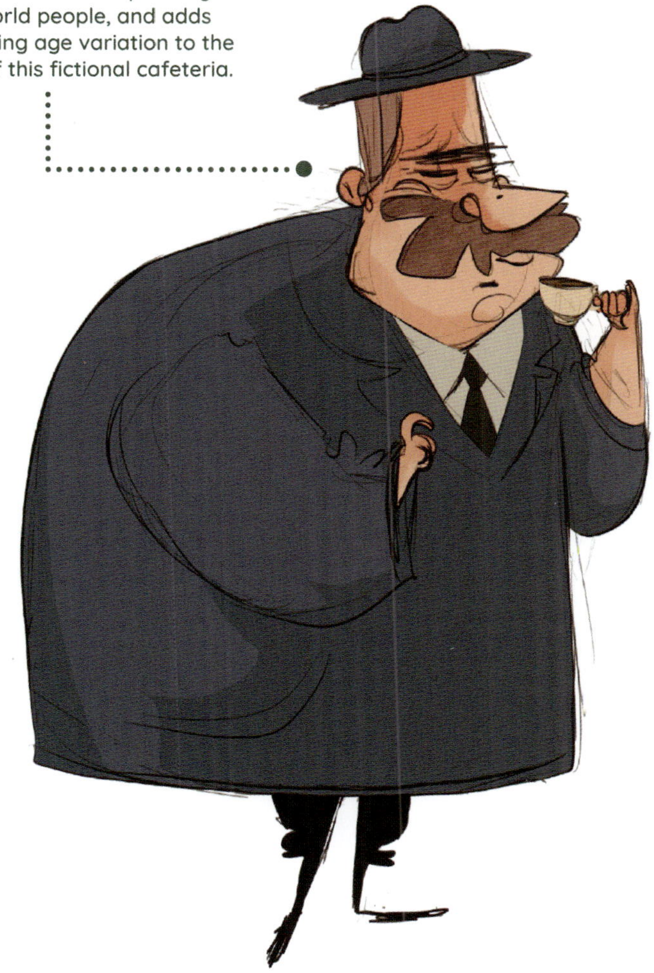

BUT BEWARE!

If you're in doubt about something, go back to your moodboard and see how that problem has been solved in someone else's artwork, for example. What choice did that artist make? Is it similar to yours? Check if these solutions can be applied to your own work, but be careful not to directly reference that design. Do not just copy an existing character – try to use different images as inspiration without repeating the exact same characteristics. Borrow from different sources to make something new. Think of it like creating your own recipe – using one or two ingredients from existing recipes to make a new dish.

It's important to be honest and ethical about your work, and to respect how you use your sources. When you are out in the real world gathering firsthand references, respect people's personal space and try not to be invasive. The same applies when using others' work as reference, whether it's an artist's personal concept or a photographer's copyrighted photo – take them as inspiration but don't duplicate them.

IDEATION

Vanessa Morales

Every artist approaches the design process a little differently, but let's look at one example project now. This is a very simplified and streamlined process – in reality, the process is not always this linear.

1. Key words

This character will be male and based on the words "street," "jazz," and "trumpeter," giving a starting point for a mind map of words and ideas to include in the research phase. Asking "Who is this character?" will help you develop a backstory. This will inform whether the character is old, tall, cheerful or shy, what kind of trumpet he plays and how he plays it, and even if he's human or animal.

2. Research

Now you can begin researching, finding images online that relate to the keywords and analyzing them. Sometimes, if you are really unfamiliar with a topic, it's useful to watch documentaries or interviews with experts to get a better understanding of the subject. Through this research, you will be able to identify the elements that would make the character recognizable and true to the concept.

This street jazz musician is going to be based in modern New Orleans, so you can begin researching clothing and instruments, as well as street musicians and how they interact with their public. It's always helpful to research different types of people to "play" the role of your character. When I think of jazz and trumpets, I think of Louis Armstrong, so I look into his music and find photographs to include on my moodboard of references.

Focus on the main features and key words that will lead you through the research process. A mind map is helpful for working out what features and elements of the character need more attention.

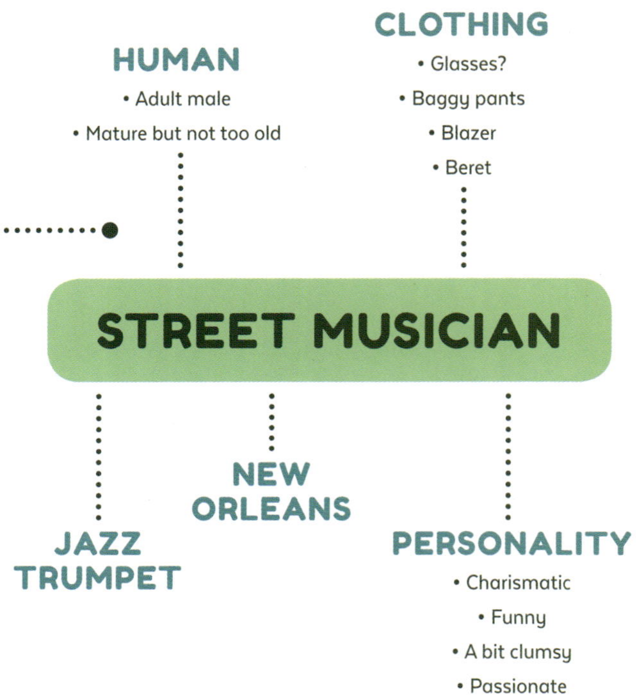

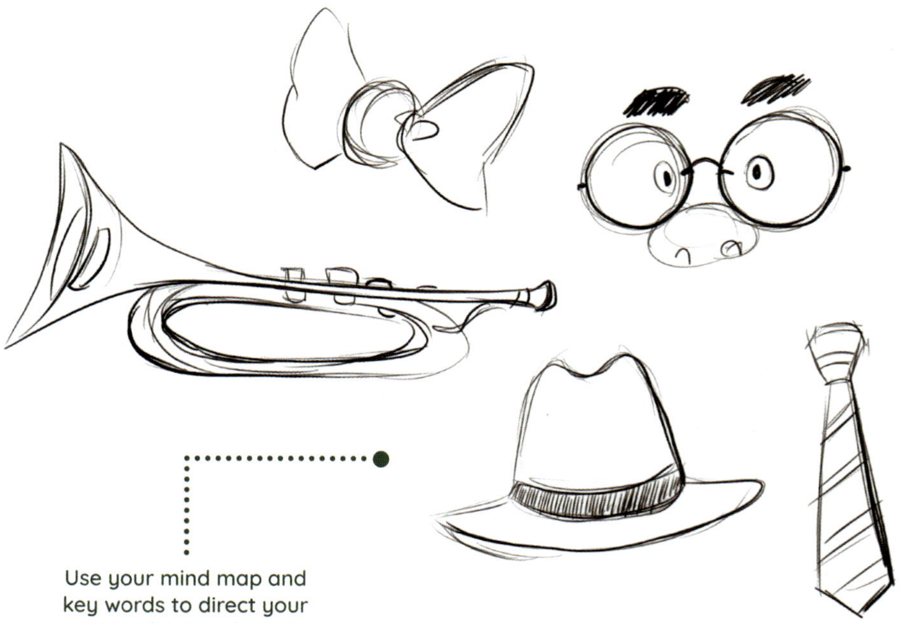

Use your mind map and key words to direct your research into relevant features, people, details, and accessories.

3. Thumbnails

At this stage you can use your references to make some rough sketches and thumbnails. Every artist has their own thumbnailing method, such as line sketches or silhouettes (shown right and bottom right). Use a mix both of methods you are comfortable with and new methods that might yield interesting results. Keep in mind any "actors" you found in your research who could perform this role - Louis Armstrong, in this case - as their physicality can influence this stage.

Creating multiple thumbnails will help you find the character you want to develop further.

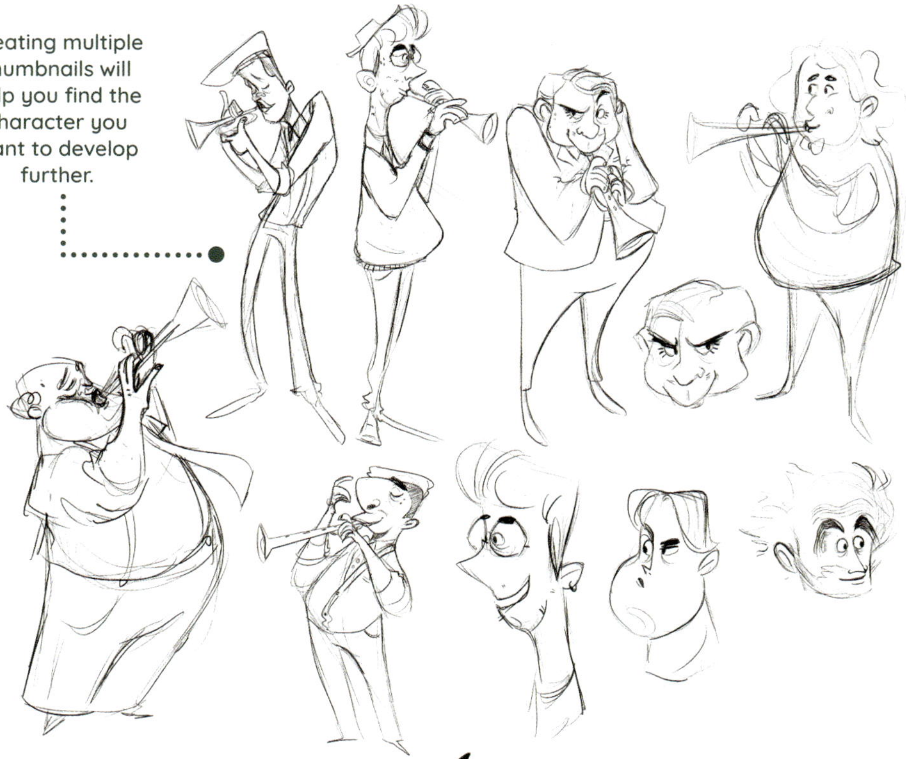

4. Expressions & poses

Now that you have decided on the character's key elements, you need to convey their sense of life and attitude through posing, acting, and expressions (shown below). I like to check my moodboard to remind myself *who* the character is. This street-jazz trumpet player needs to have charisma, be passionate about music, and have fun while playing. He would probably smile and dance while playing, and exaggerate his movements.

Focus on poses and expressions that are relevant to the character - in this case, dancing, playing, and enjoying the music.

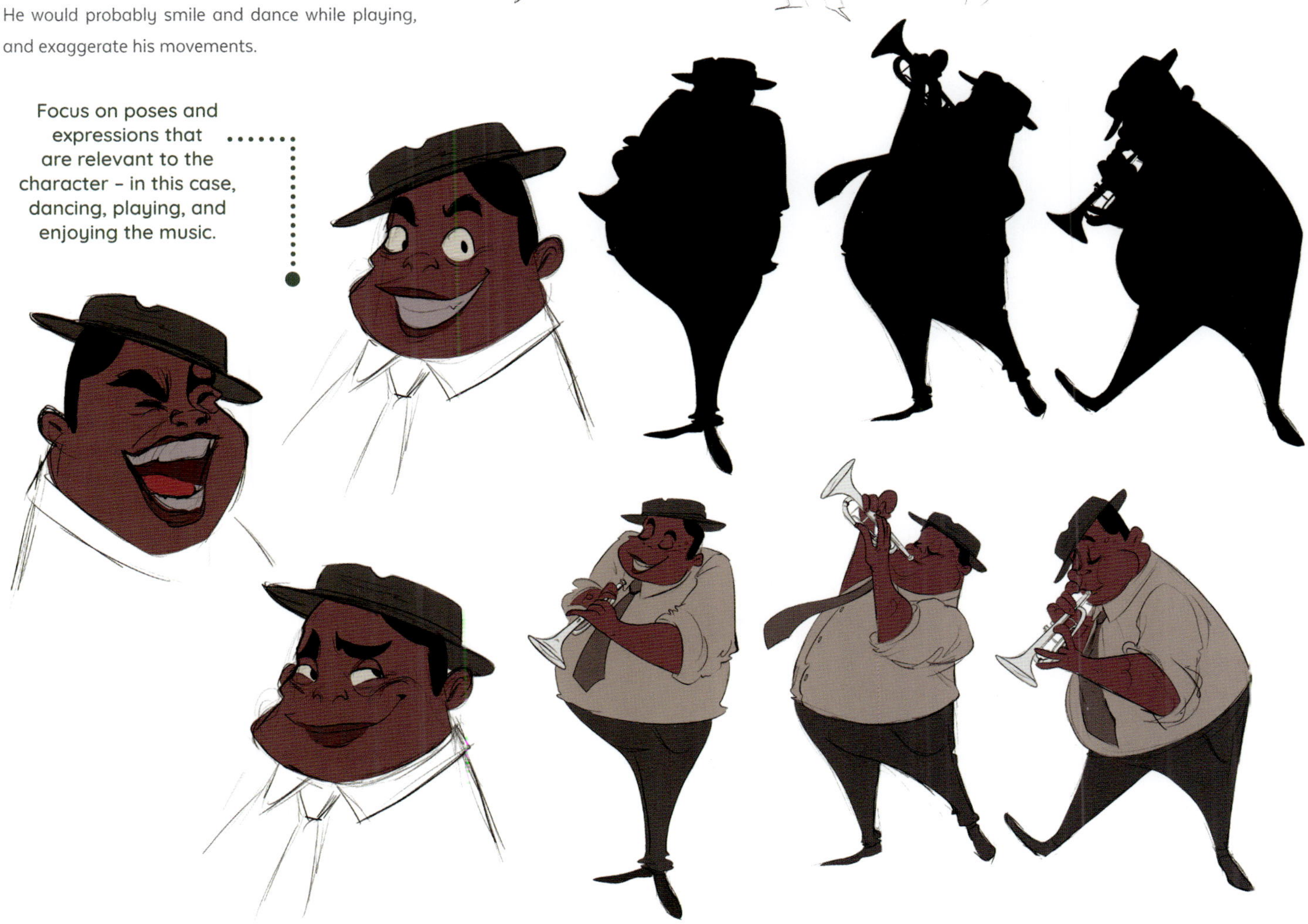

5. Color palettes

When choosing a color palette, it's important to look at your references again. This character is a fun, enthusiastic musician, which needs to be shown through his color palette. A vibrant shirt with a pattern would suit him well. Try to create different color schemes on a rough copy of your character, then compare the results and choose the palette that suits your character the best. You can learn more about color on page 60.

6. Final design

After experimenting with pose, expression, color, and other details such as pattern and costume, you will come to your final design. At this point, check that the character has truly come to life. Did you fulfill the original brief and offer a relatable interpretation for the viewer? Are the details clear and is the character easy to read? Do you understand their story in just one glance? Does the character reflect the research you carried out? Taking a step back to review these questions will help ensure your character is engaging and memorable for the audience.

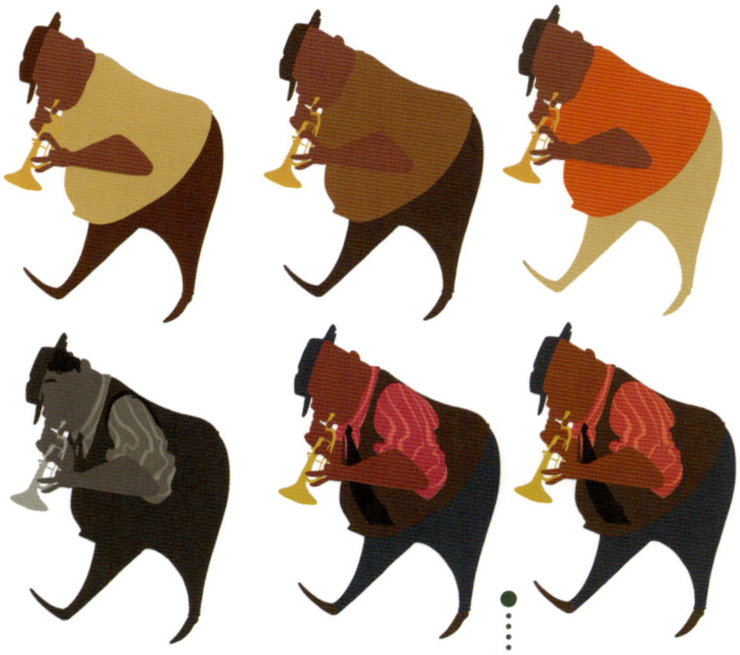

The trumpeter's color scheme needs to showcase details such as his instrument and costume, and express his joy in the music.

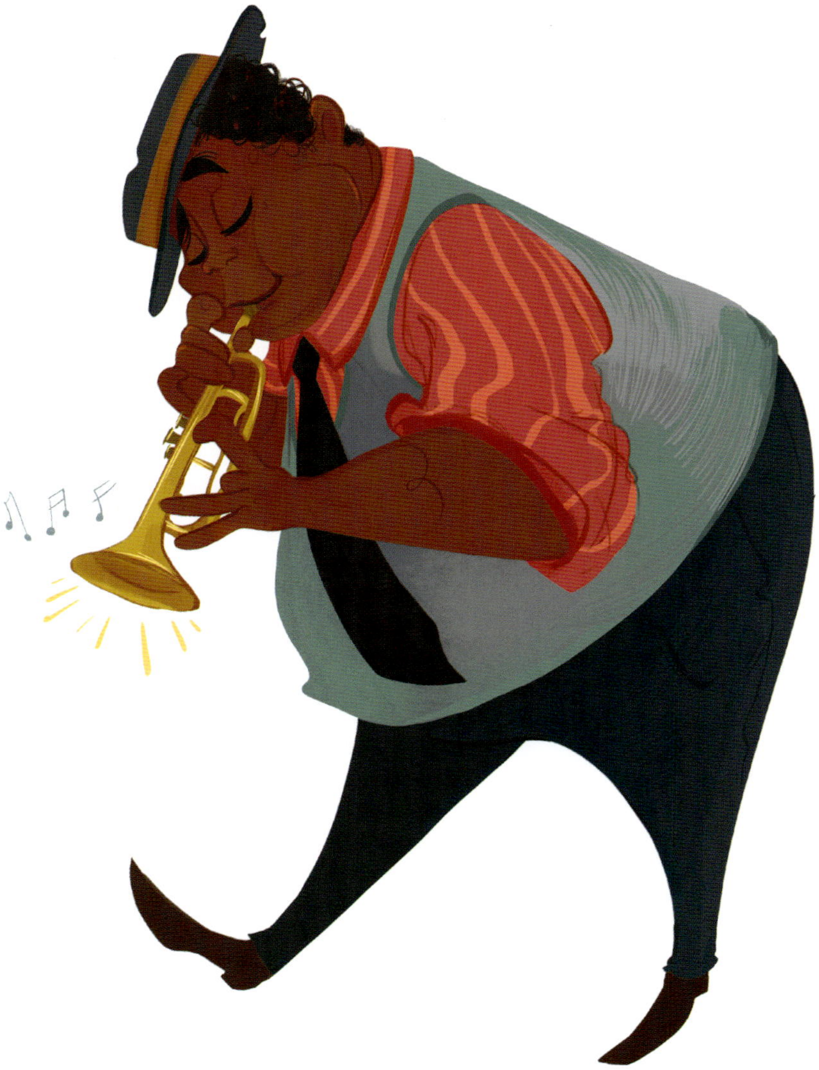

Following an ideation process such as this one will help make your characters richer and more relatable.

INSPIRATION

Inspiration can be found anywhere, and through the process of creating characters, our influences can increase greatly. You learn to find characters in almost anything you see, like a bottle, a random shape, a song, or a word you come across. Any stimulus your brain receives can help influence a potential character design. One way to help encourage this process is to take different shapes and try to find the characters within them. There's a phenomenon called "pareidolia," where we search for faces and patterns within inanimate objects and environments - for example, finding a face in a pattern on your bathroom wall! Use this natural phenomenon to help find potential characters all around you.

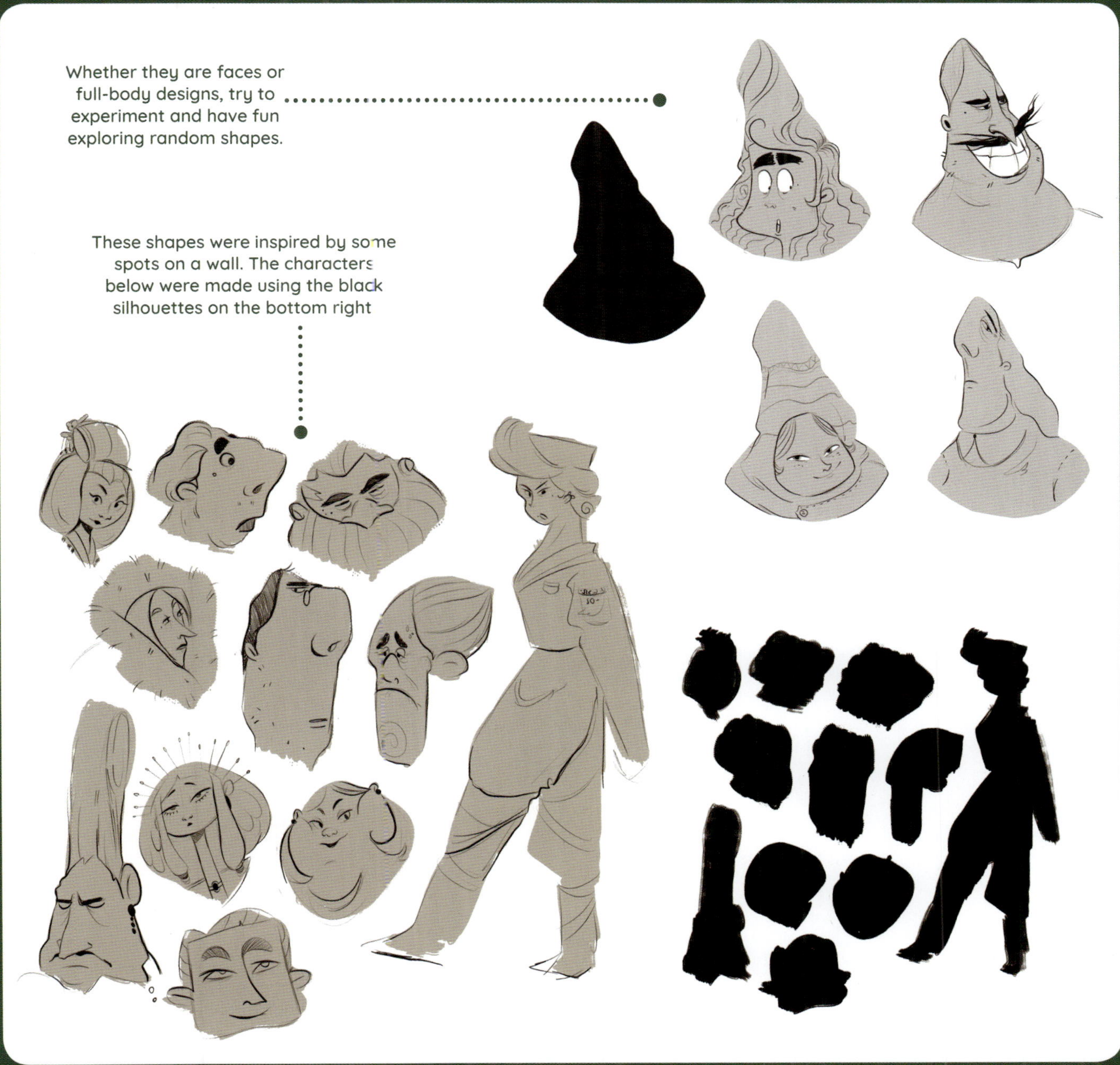

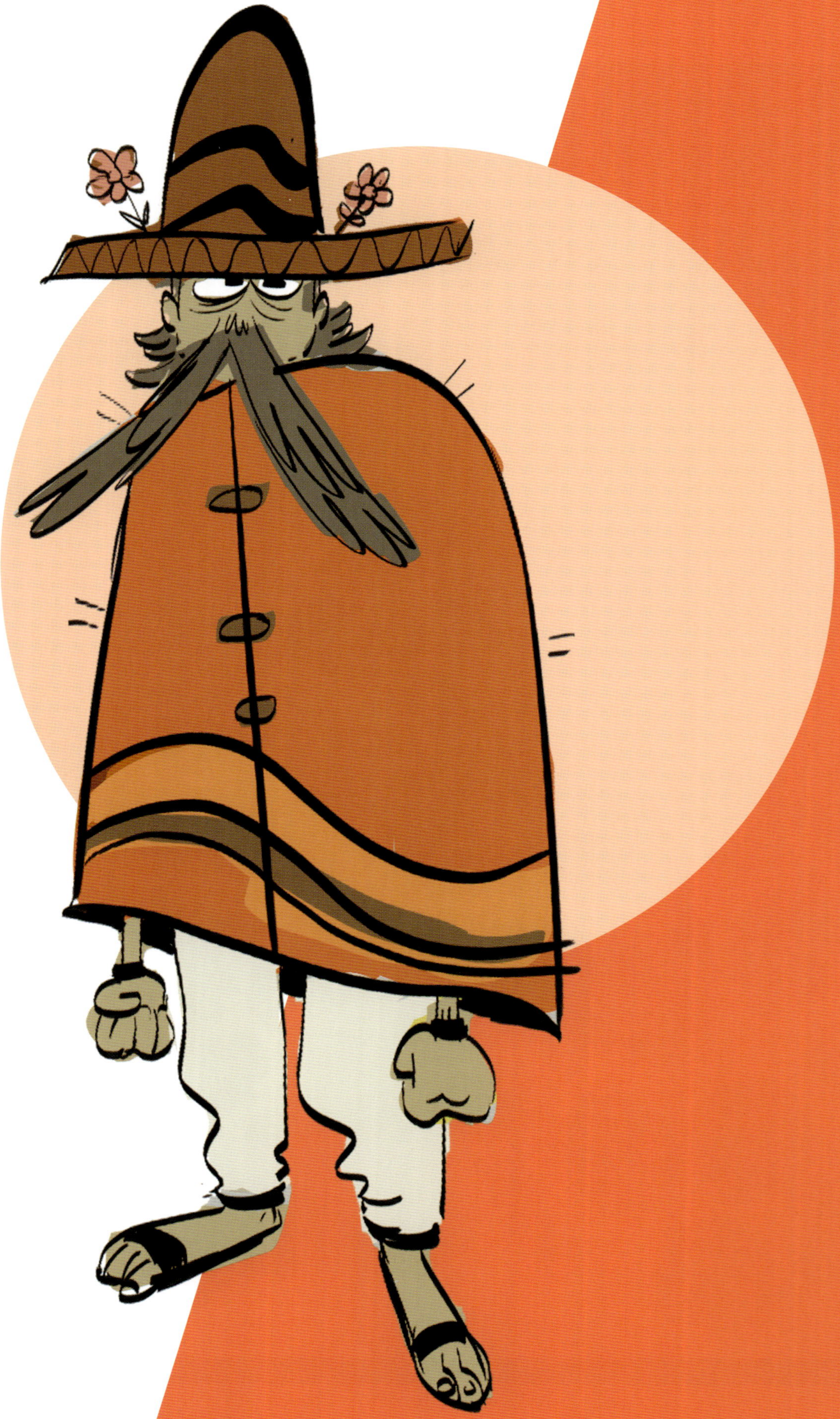

Image by Stephanie Garcia Rizo

KEY DESIGN PRINCIPLES

SHAPE LANGUAGE
PAGE 54

COLOR & VALUE
PAGE 60

LIGHTING
PAGE 66

BALANCE & CONTRAST
PAGE 70

SCALE
PAGE 76

REPETITION
PAGE 78

RHYTHM
PAGE 80

TANGENTS
PAGE 82

SHAPE LANGUAGE

Stephanie Garcia Rizo

As a character designer, it's important to understand the shapes you are using in your designs, and what effects they can create. Shape language can help you (and the audience) to figure out who a character is, and can be used to emphasize their personality.

Shape language centers around three basic shapes: the circle, triangle, and square. Each shape conveys different emotions and personalities, and can be used to tell a story and create an iconic design. Once shape is established, additional details like color, value, and light can then be utilized to improve the character's look.

The circle

Circles convey constant movement, life, and energy, and create a sense of completion, connection, and simplicity. Using round shapes in a design can create feelings of innocence and vulnerability, or show that the character is approachable, friendly, and safe.

The triangle

Triangles convey energy, excitement, and danger. They can be used to create a feeling of anger, tension, and movement. Triangles and sharp angles are often used in creating villainous characters, but they can also be used to symbolize strength and confidence.

The square

Square shapes can represent sturdy, steadfast, heavy, and, some might say, boring personality traits. They don't symbolize anything flashy or exciting. Squares can be used to make a character appear stubborn, strong, grounded, and confident.

Here are some quick thumbnail sketches based on a circle. Circles can be stacked in many different ways to create a variety of unique designs and personalities.

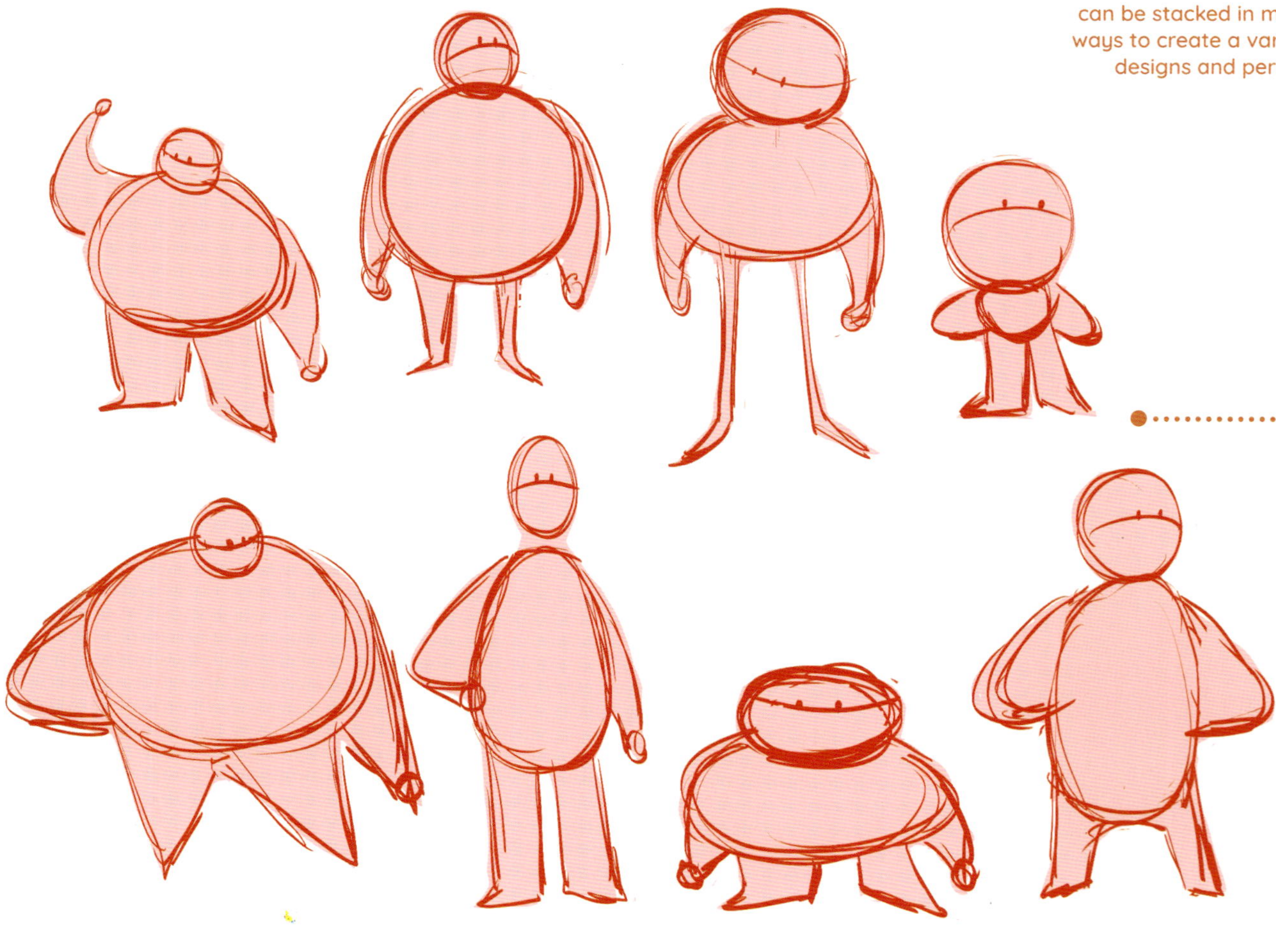

These thumbnail sketches use a triangle for a base. The triangle is such a dynamic shape, it already lends these small designs a lot of energy and visual interest.

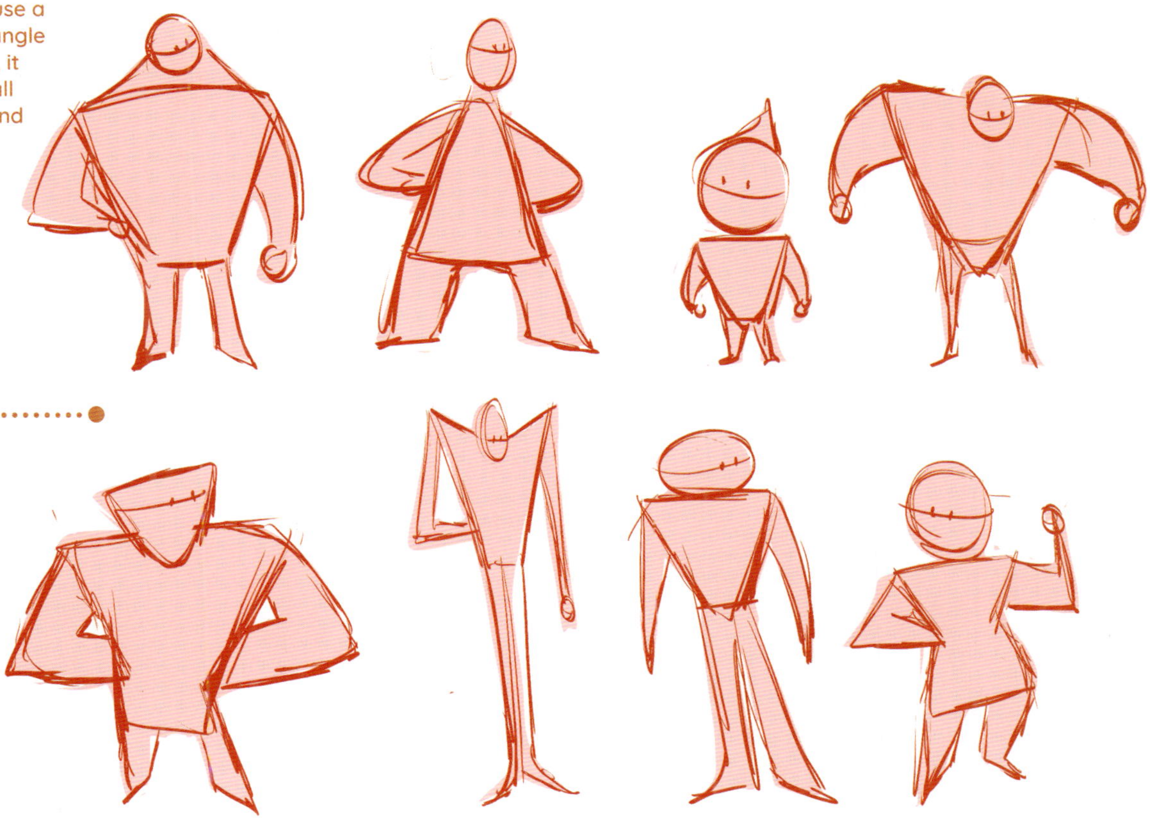

These thumbnails are based on a square. Just like the other shapes, the square can be pushed and stretched to create more interesting variations.

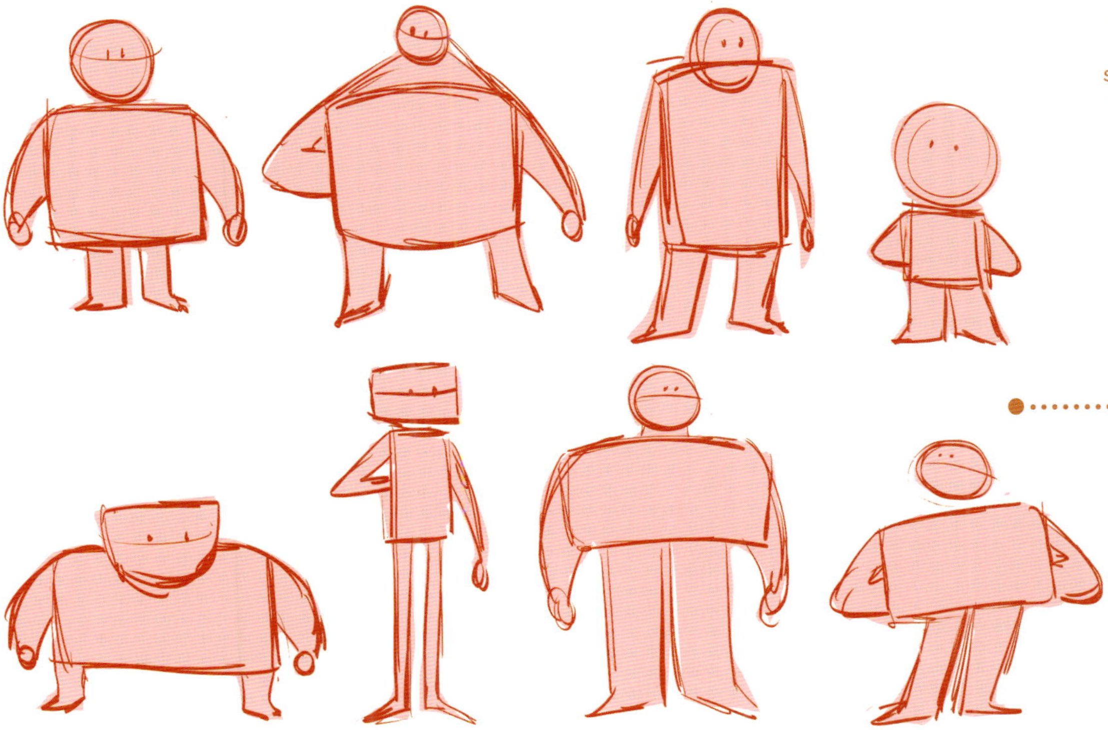

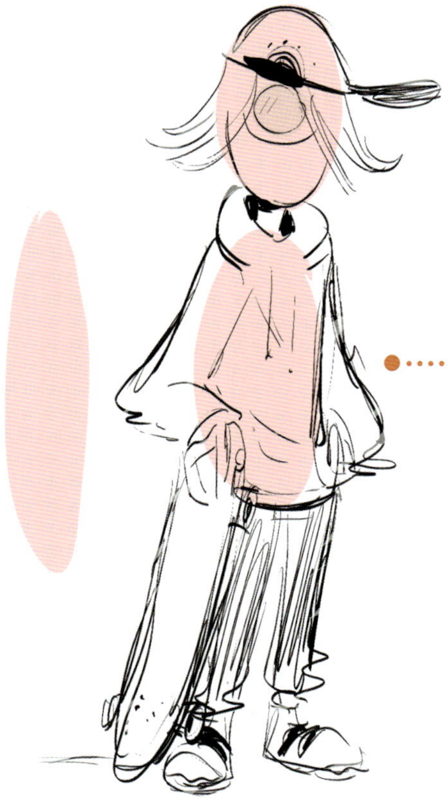

This skater's overall shape is an oval, with ovals in his head and body. This gives him a feeling of calmness and approachability.

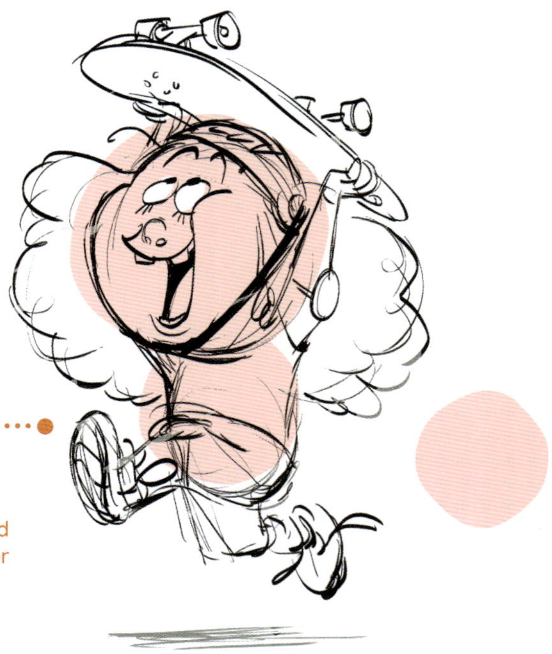

This skater girl is designed with circles, expressing her energy, movement, and innocence.

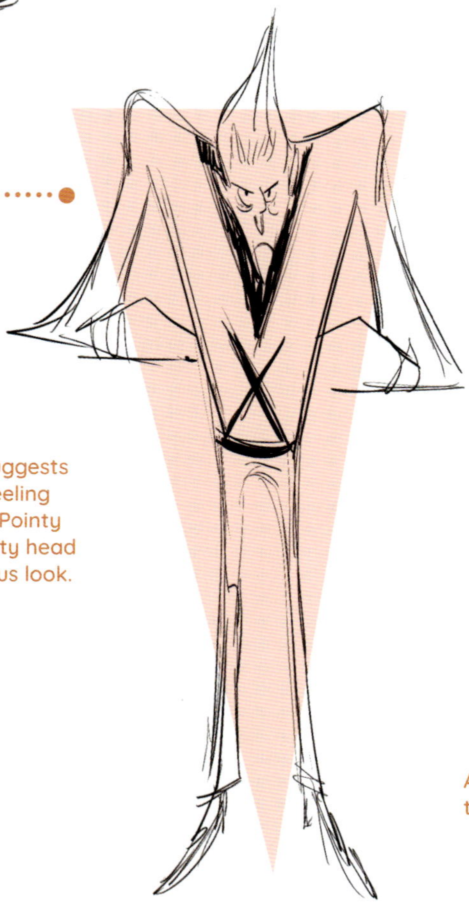

A narrow triangle suggests this character is feeling anger and tension. Pointy shoulders and a pointy head emphasize a villainous look.

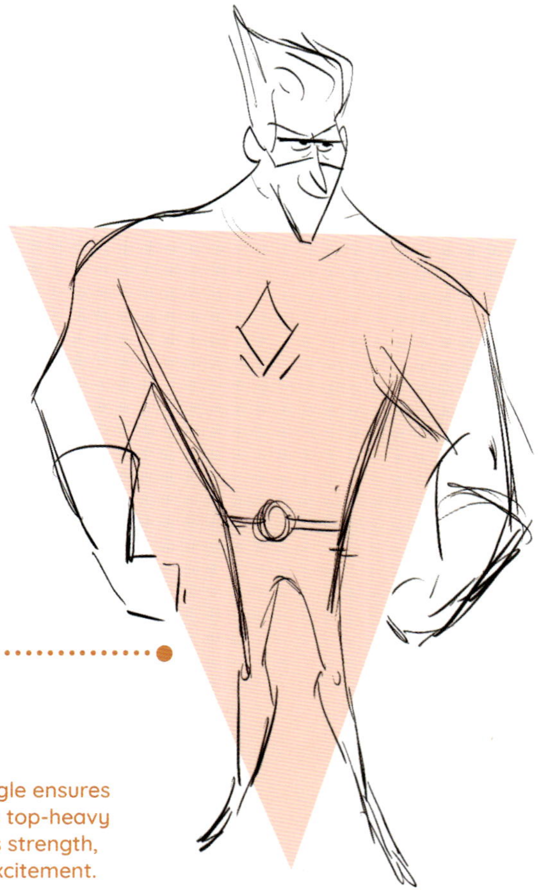

A broader triangle ensures this superhero's top-heavy shape conveys strength, energy, and excitement.

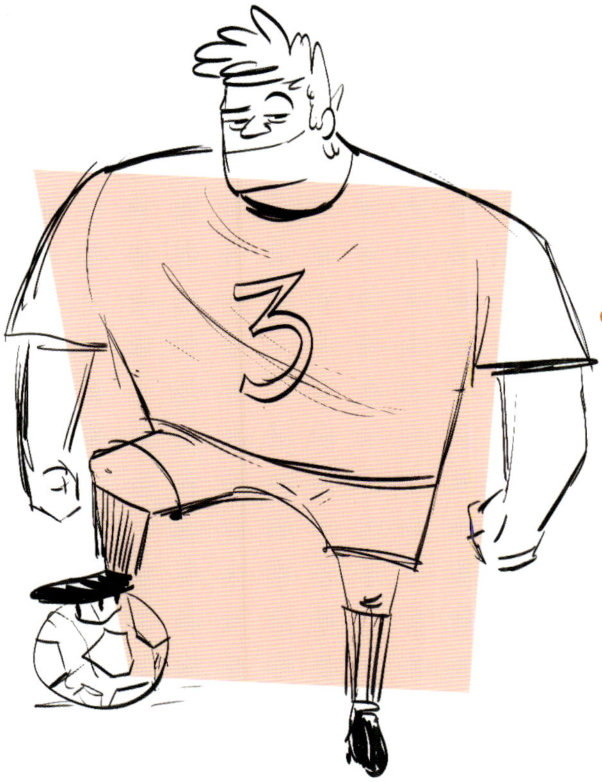

This football player's body shape is square, his broad shoulders and square face conveying his grounded, strong, and confident character.

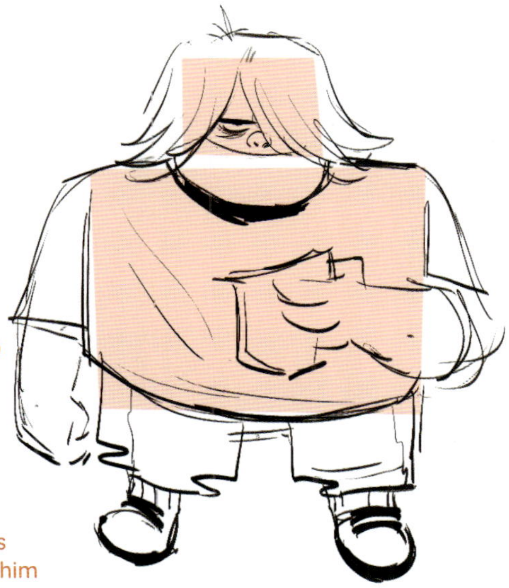

The squares used here emphasize this character's bullying personality, making him feel stubborn, heavy, and obtuse.

This character is made up of both a circle and square, creating a diverse personality. While he has a burly, stubborn body type, his round face creates a sense of kindness.

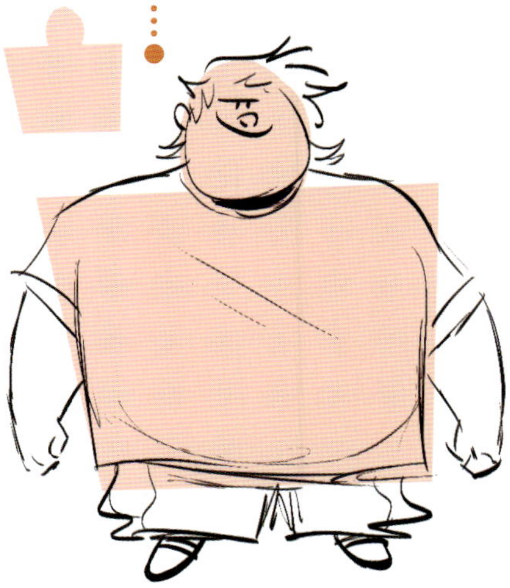

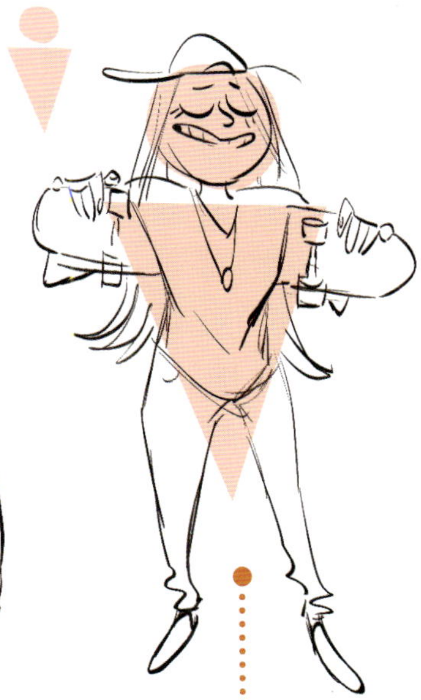

This skater's design is made up of a triangle and a circle. The triangle conveys her confidence and energy, while her round face suggests a softer personality, creating a pleasing balance.

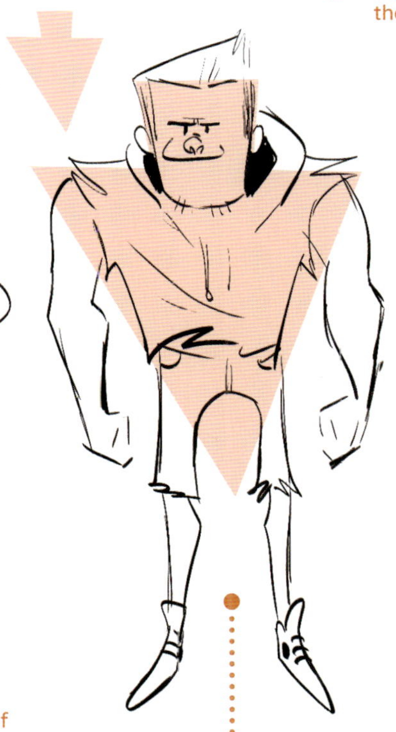

This character is a combination of a square and triangle, suggesting a character that is tense, stubborn, and energetic. His square face furthers the idea that he has c hot-headed personality and is a troublemaker.

This character has a circular head, creating a feeling of approachability. This is combined with a rectangular body, suggesting a grounded rather than lively persona.

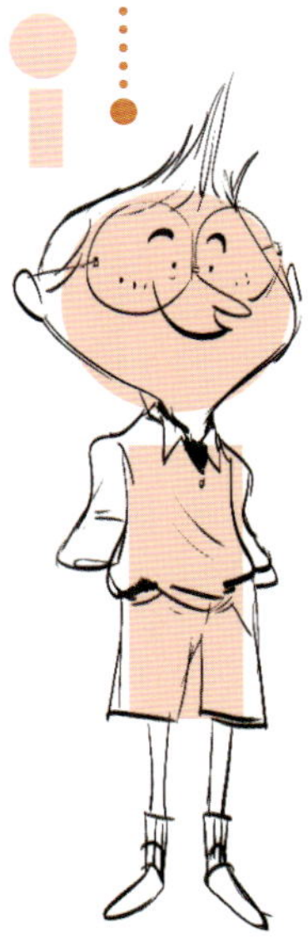

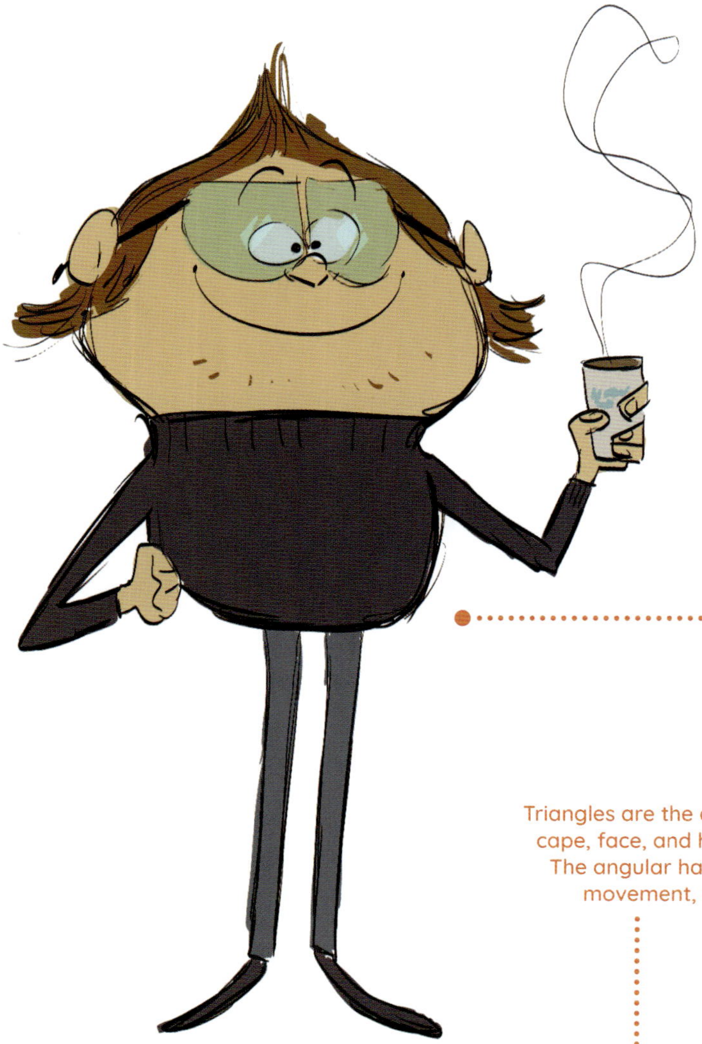

Circles were used to create this upbeat, energetic coffee-drinker. Repeating the circular shapes in both the body and head helps to emphasize his soft, endearing character. When using repeated shapes, remember to change their size to create a more dynamic design.

Triangles are the overall shapes in this design, repeated in the cape, face, and hair to create a feeling of evil and mischief. The angular hair provides the character with energy and movement, while his pointed teeth convey danger.

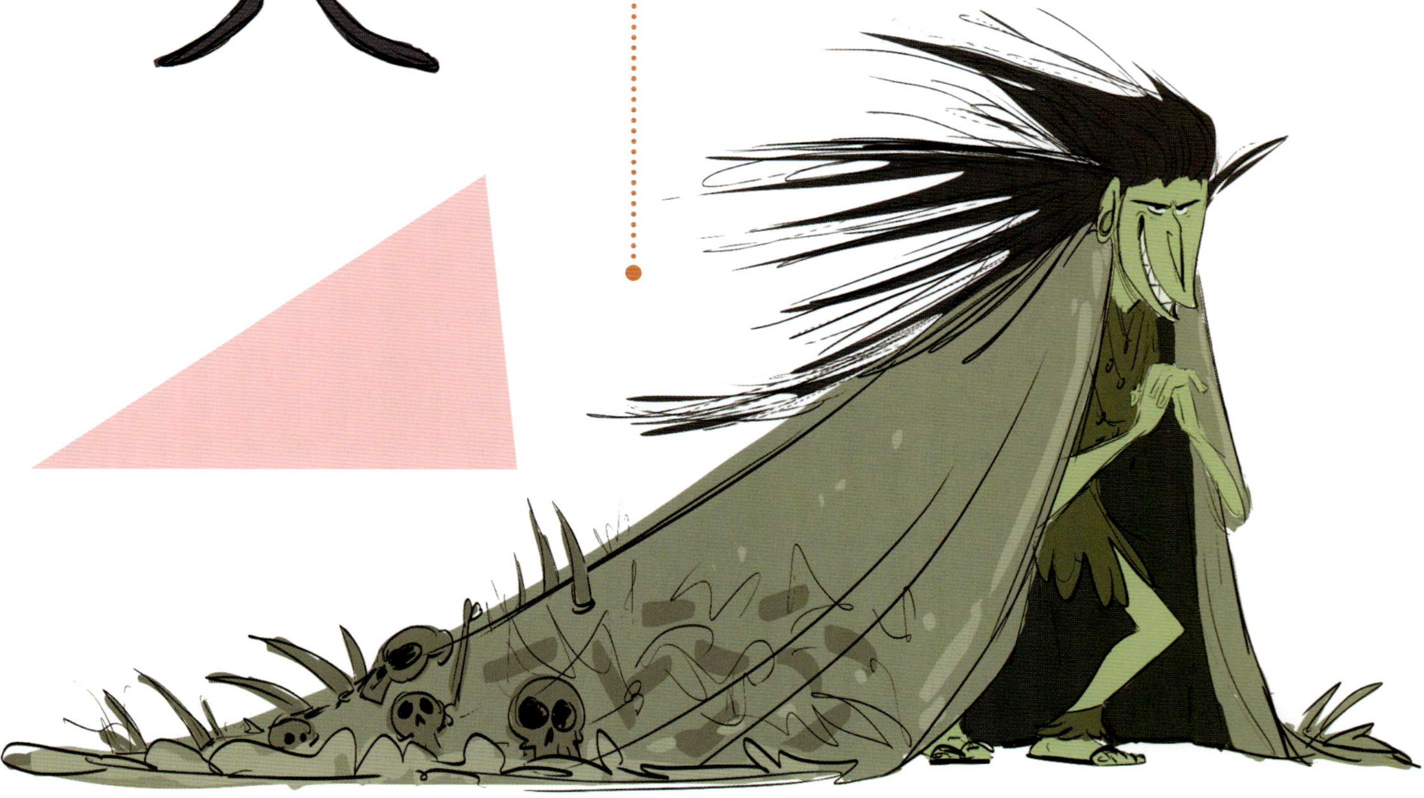

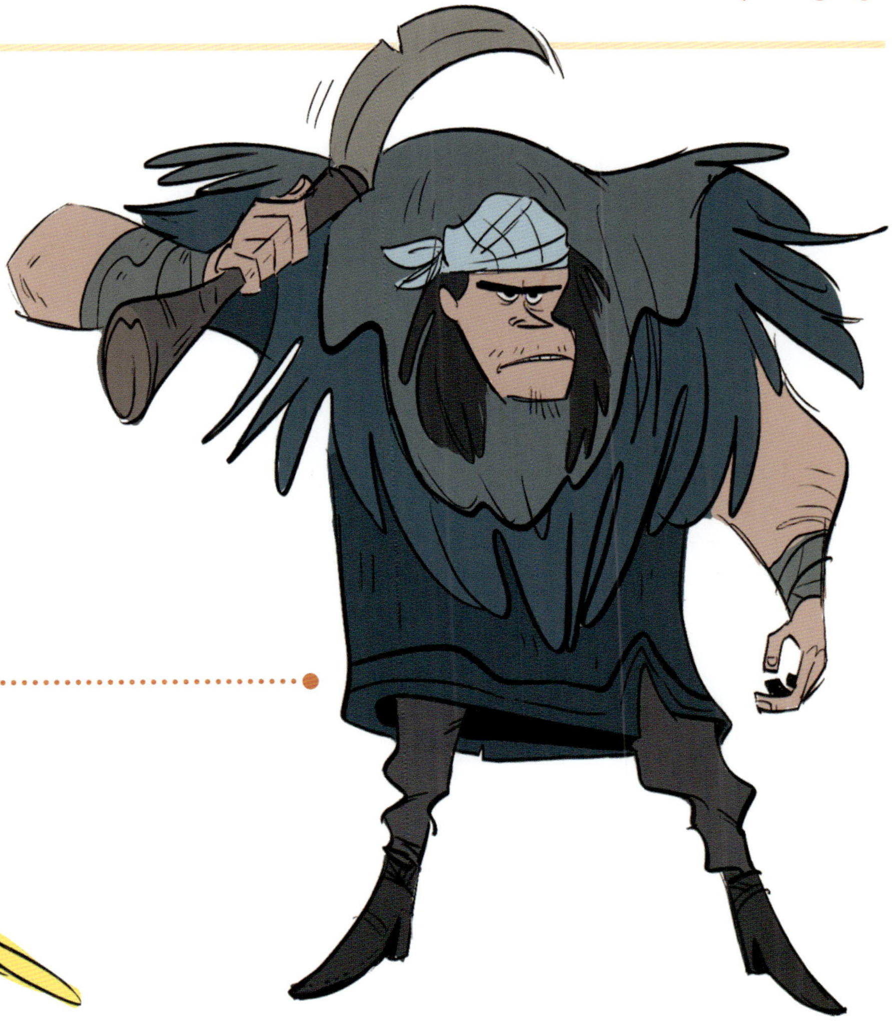

Rectangles and squarish shapes make this pirate henchman feel formidable and heavyset. These shapes are even reflected in his strong jaw and scowling brow. The curved blade adds a dynamic contrasting shape with his blocky, oblong body.

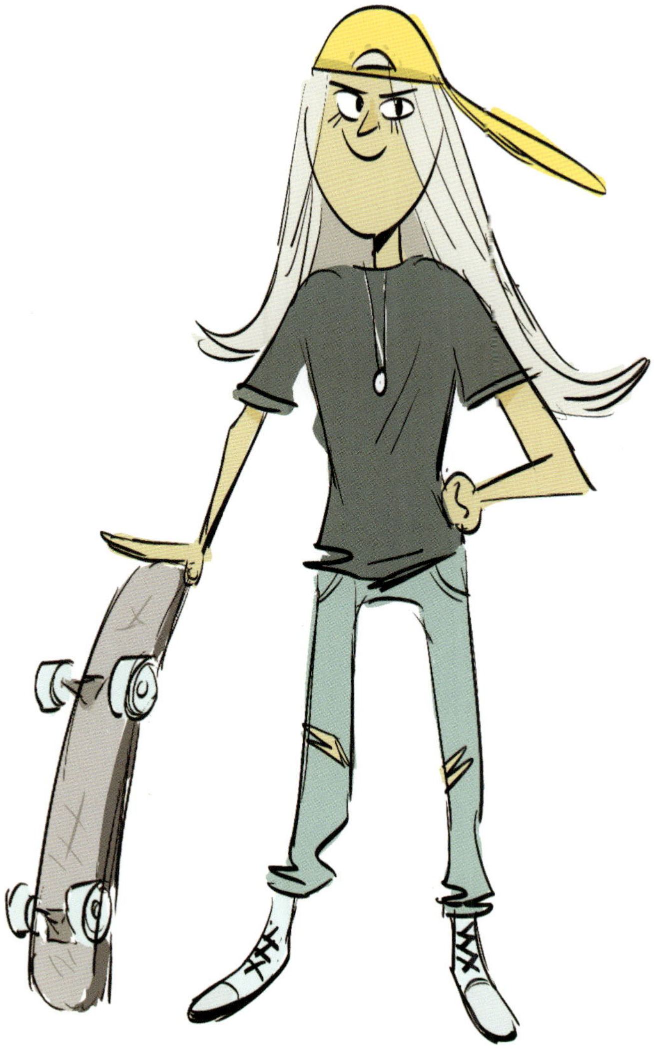

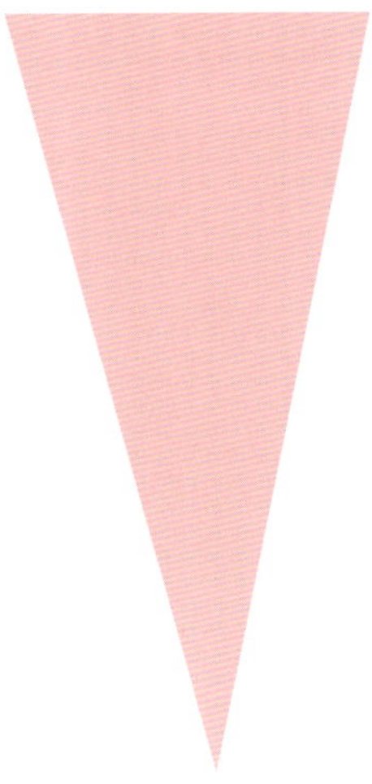

As you saw on page 57, combining different shapes creates a more diverse and complex character. This skater girl design pairs a circle and a triangle. Using an upside-down triangle gives her broader shoulders and helps to emphasize her confidence and energy. Her circular face creates contrast and a balance with her more angular limbs.

COLOR & VALUE

Stephanie Garcia Rizo

How can you use color and value to enhance the design of a character? While there are no strict rules, there are ways to use color wisely to further a character's story, and to emphasize what you wish to convey through their design. As discussed on page 50, once you have sketched and explored a variety of different designs for a character, the next stage is to test multiple color palettes to see which one works best. Avoid using only one level of **value (lightness or darkness)**, as the audience won't know where to focus on the design. Explore combinations of light and dark colors. It's usual to want the audience to focus on the subject's eyes, face, and hands, as these often express most of a character's emotion, so choosing values carefully for these areas will enhance the impact of your design.

Try different **combinations of hues**, too. An "analogous" color palette uses hues that are similar, such as red and orange, and will create a very different effect than a "complementary" color palette, which uses hues that are opposites, such as red and green. A bright, bold accent color can help make focal points stand out. It is not enough to make a character look pretty or to add fancy effects. Always ask yourself *why* you are choosing those colors, and how each hue can help your character to look or feel a certain way. As shown on this page, colors can be used to evoke certain psychological or cultural assocations in the viewer.

Red

Red often symbolizes love, confidence, energy, strength, and power. It can be used to express passion, anger, heat, and danger. It is commonly used as an intense accent color in areas of a design that need to draw the viewer's attention. It can be an overwhelming color if it's overused.

Orange

Orange can symbolize health and creativity. It feels energetic, friendly, inviting, and wholesome. In design, orange is another very intense color, often used as an accent to draw attention to specific areas. Like red, it's a potent color that can become overwhelming.

Purple

Purple is a luxurious color that can be used to evoke feelings of nobility, creativity, magic, and mystery. It can lend the subject an unusual, mystical, regal, or opulent quality, especially in costumes or lighting.

Yellow

Yellow can symbolize hope, courage, sunshine, warmth, energy, and sometimes even danger. Emotionally, it brings cheerfulness, happiness, and high energy. Using pure yellow in a design can create strong contrast or vivid accents, such as in clothing details or accents around the face.

Green

Green can symbolize nature, growth, stability, wealth, relaxation, and well-being. Light greens can be used to create a harmonious, organic feeling, while dark greens can represent envy, sickness, and mystery.

Blue

Blue represents calmness, responsibility, reliability, and spirituality. Emotionally, blue is typically associated with sadness, cold, or depression, but blue can also feel like magic, hopefulness, or strength, depending on the tone and context.

White

White can symbolize purity, hope, energy, cleanliness, and health. It can evoke a feeling of hope, forgiveness, simplicity, emptiness, and strength. Using pure white in a character's costume is a bold visual choice, and can be a useful neutral base for other accents and colorful accessories.

Black

Black is a bold, versatile color that can symbolize power, strength, sophistication, death, night, rebellion, sadness, and mystery. Black can help your design feel intense and bold, and is useful for creating high-contrast accents in costumes and props.

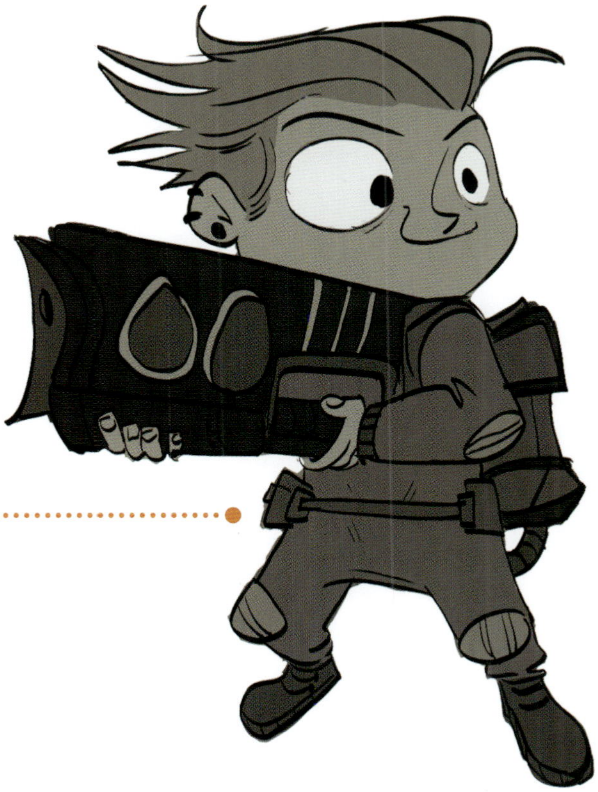

When applying color, it can be helpful to create a black-and-white value layer so you can identify the areas of higher contrast in the design. These are where the audience's eyes will focus. For this character, we want the viewer to focus on the face and space-gun prop, so these areas have the most intense values: the character's light eyes and the dark shape of the gun.

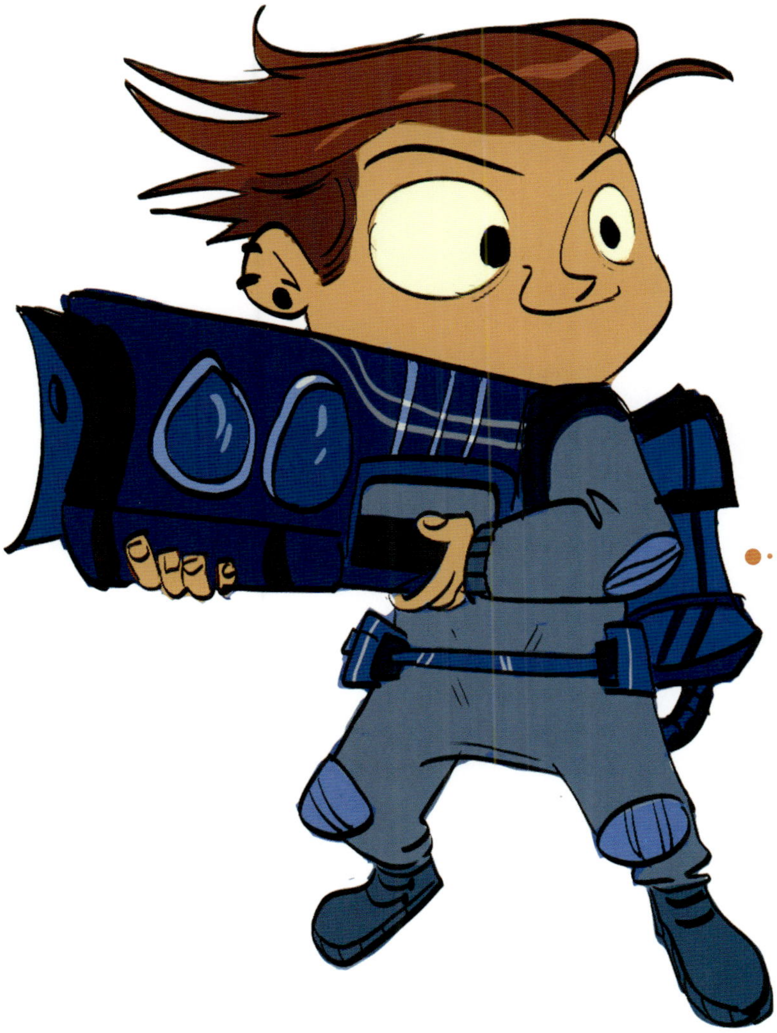

DIRECTING FOCUS

A character's hand and body gestures will reinforce your use of color further and help guide the audience's focus. The same goes for shapes (page 54) and textures (page 72).

Once you have a value layer, you can then apply color to the design. Adding a more vibrant blue with lighter accents to the prop creates contrast, while the other areas are a fairly monochromatic blue, which helps make the character's face stand out.

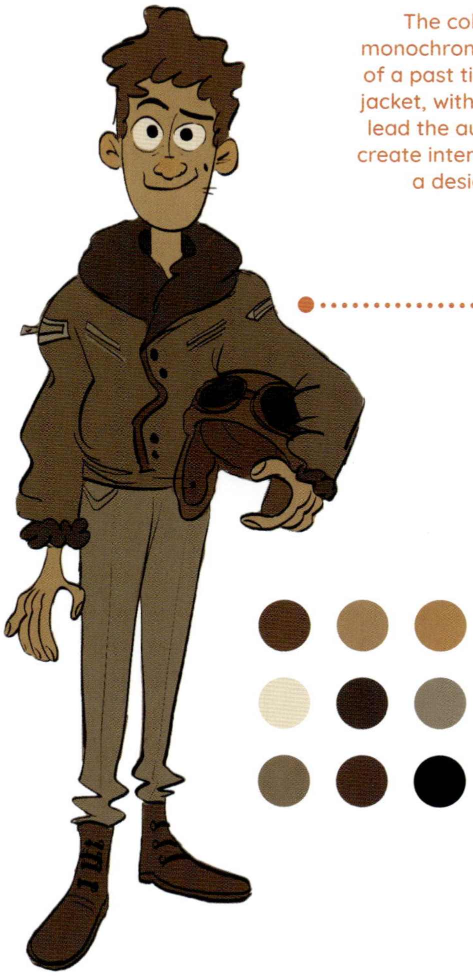

The color palette of this pilot character is monochromatic brown and tan, creating a feeling of a past time, such as the 1940s. The character's jacket, with its pale accents and dark collar, helps lead the audience's eye toward his face. You can create interest by using a pattern of values across a design, such as dark, light, dark, light.

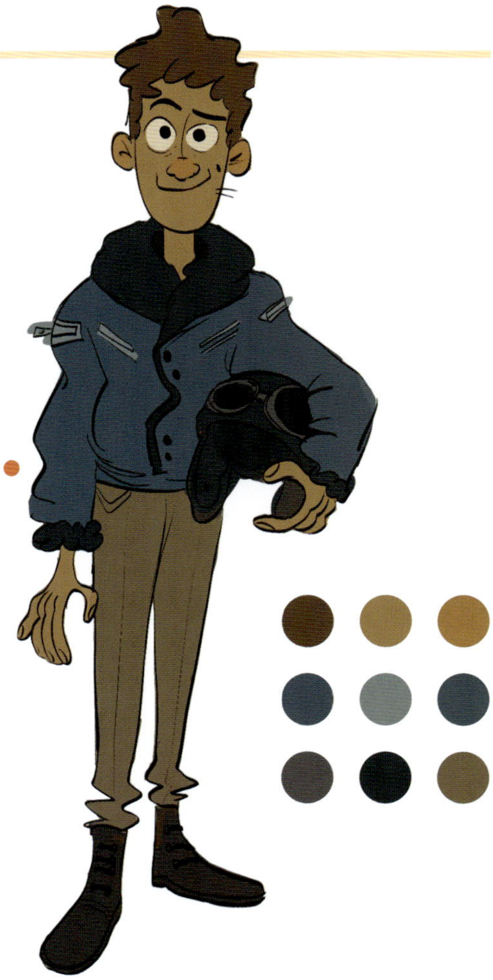

This color palette has a cooler hue. The calm, formal blue of his jacket suggests that the pilot is of a higher rank.

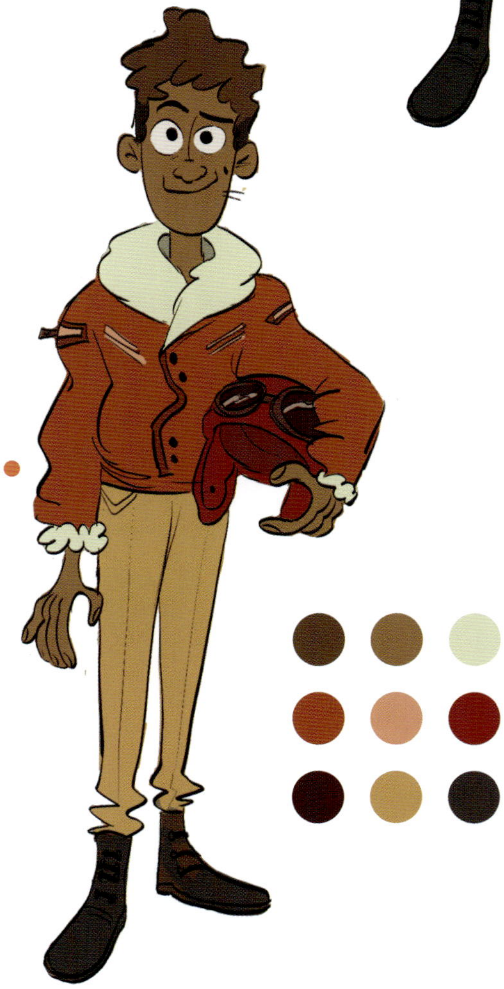

The oranges and reds in this warm palette help suggest where the pilot is based. Perhaps he works in a much warmer location, like a canyon or desert region. Red and orange can also represent power, so here they could suggest he is a confident pilot with years of experience under his belt.

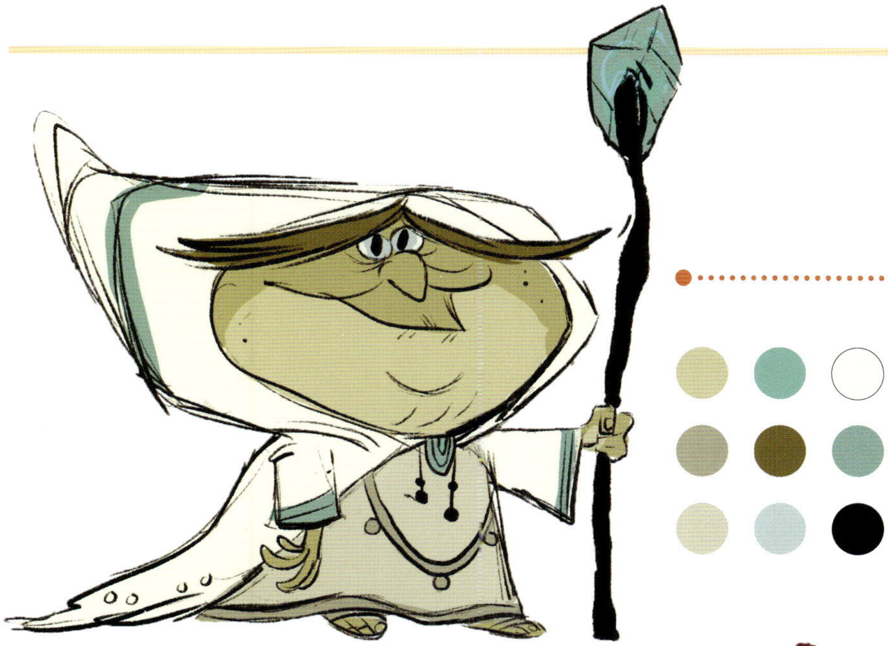

A color palette consisting of neutral colors can suggest this wizard is peaceful and helpful. White and blue represent calmness and a positive tendency, so perhaps he's a magical healer with enlightening wisdom. Adding similar colors to the wizard's staff and clothes helps lead the eye around the design.

This color palette is more vibrant and balanced. It could convey that the wizard is neither good nor bad. Perhaps he would help a passing villager, but there's a catch! Using a vibrant pink and red can convey danger, power, and intensity, giving him an unpredictable edge.

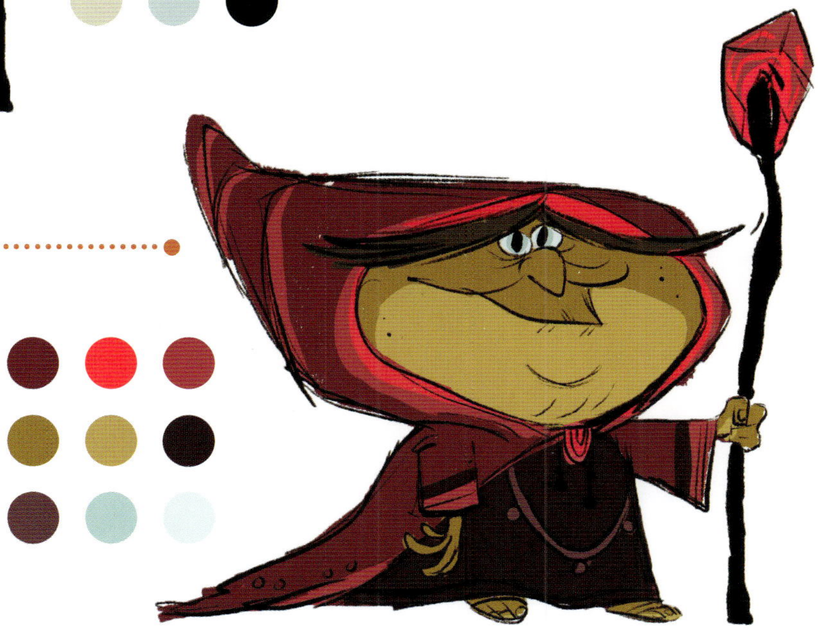

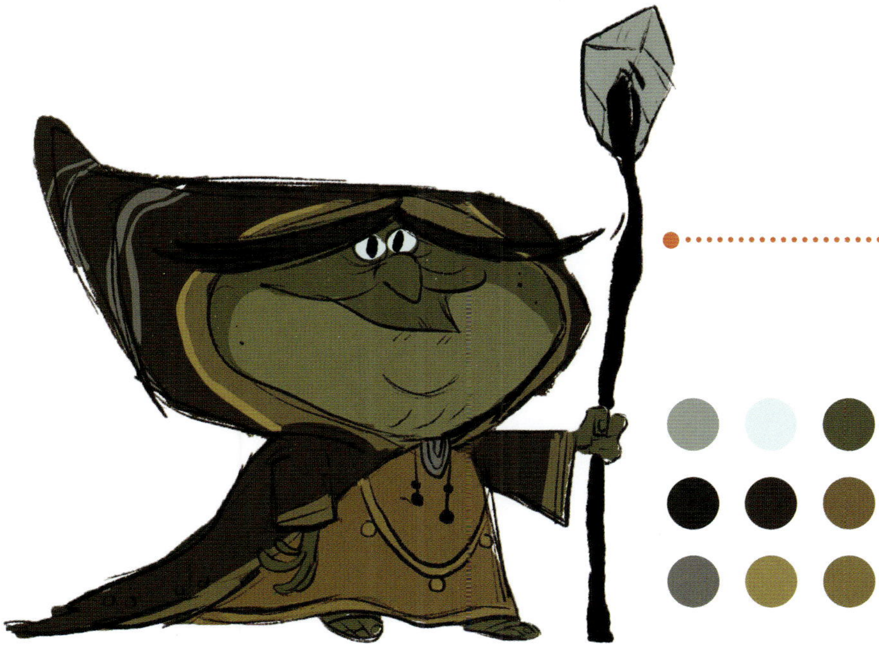

A duller color palette, though hard to read, can emphasize the character's mystery. Where did he come from? Perhaps a swamp or river, or a roadside cave on the lookout for passing villagers to cast spells on. Making his eyes the most vibrant part of the design ensures the audience remains focused on his face.

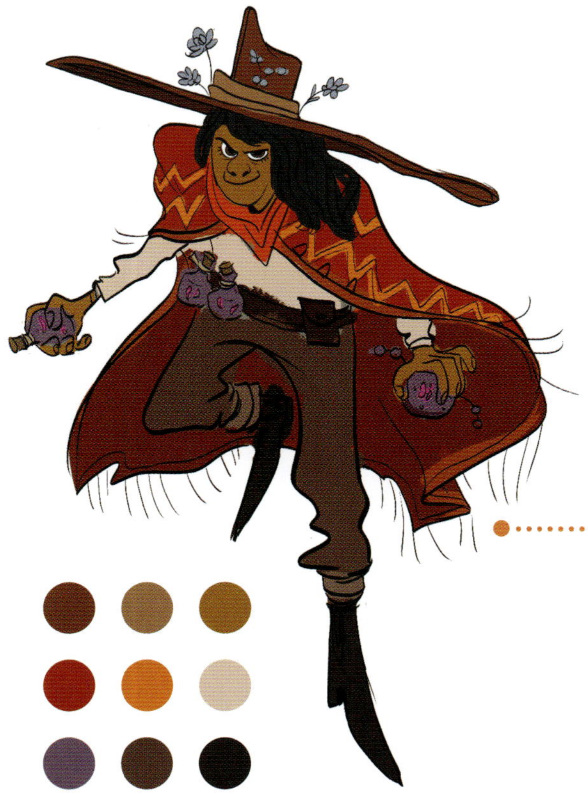

Warm color palettes have a red base. When using more than two or three colors, try adding red to them to create dynamism. This bandit has a few bright accents, still with a reddish touch to them. Even the purple, though usually found on the cool spectrum, has a warm tone to unify the design. These accents help lead the eye around the whole design.

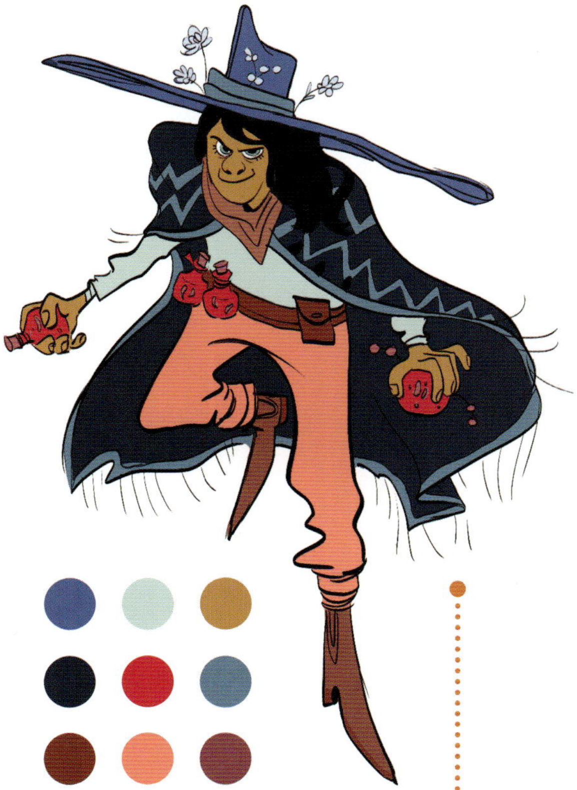

Cool color palettes have a blue base. This palette includes colors that would usually fall into the "warm" category, but adding a tint of blue cools them down. The pale green, brown, pink, and purple work together to help the design feel unified.

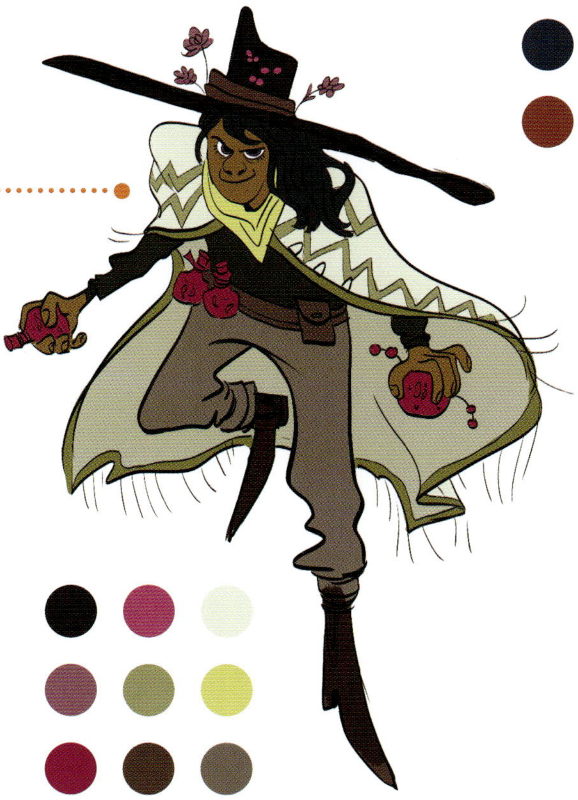

A low-value color palette can make a character appear mysterious. By using mostly low-value colors, the more vibrant areas of the character stand out as focal points, and make her feel confident and assured. The use of purple is eye-catching and keeps the viewer engaged.

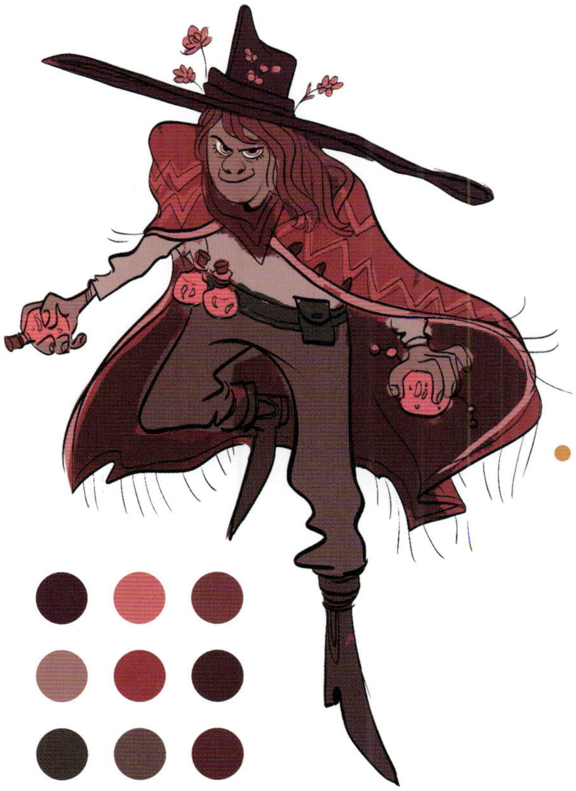

Using a range of values can really make a character pop, even if the colors themselves are quite monochrome. Though her colors are mainly purple and pink, this character appears energetic, powerful, and even chaotic. Her design looks focused, appealing, and dynamic.

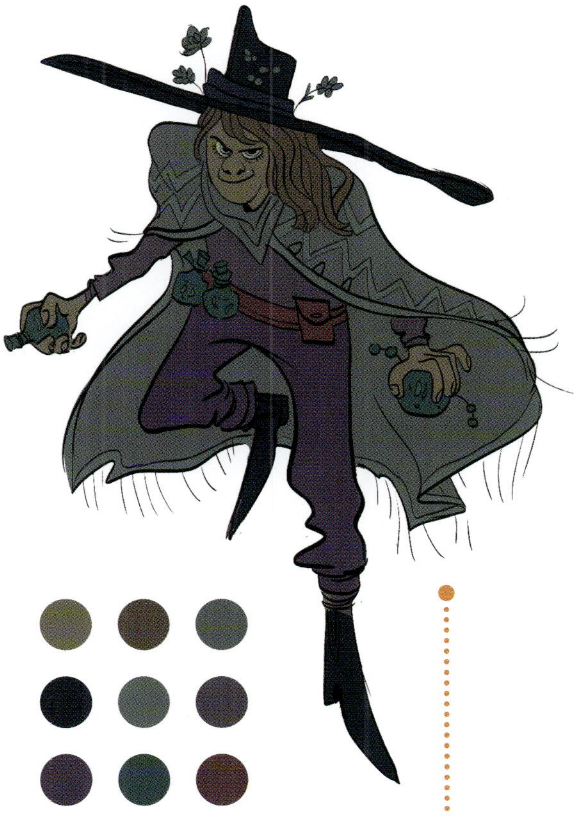

A desaturated palette can detract from a character design, making it appear muddy and obscuring important details. The design loses its appeal as it's hard to know what to focus on. Though there are more than two colors in this palette, they are so dark and desaturated that the result is bland, almost lifeless. Depending on the story or theme of the character you're creating, a desaturated palette can either strengthen or weaken a design.

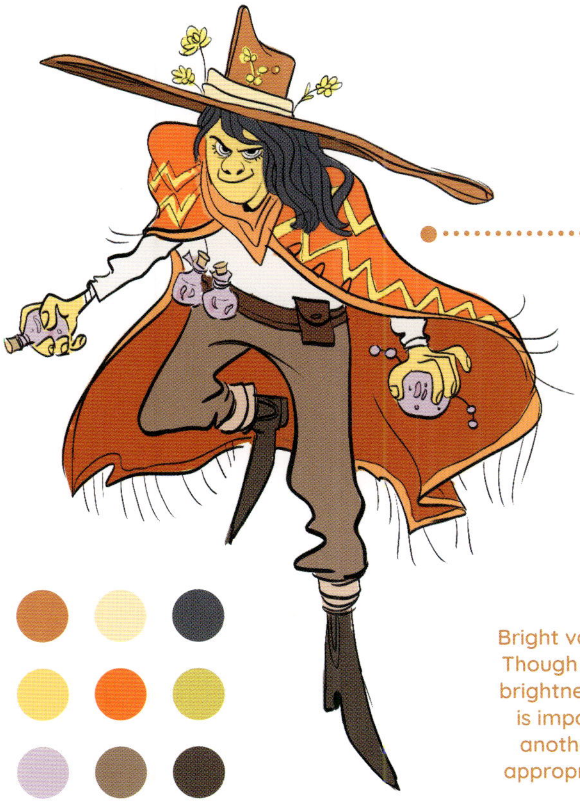

Bright values can create a very high-energy character. Though there are different colors in this palette, their brightness makes it hard for the eye to focus on what is important. All the colors are competing with one another for the viewer's attention. Whether this is appropriate all comes down to the story you want to tell through your character.

LIGHTING
Stephanie Garcia Rizo

Lighting a character well can improve the overall look of a design. As much as color can tell a story, lighting a character creates story too, emphasizing the character's mood and emotion as well as the atmosphere or setting they find themselves in. As you have learned so far, when creating a character, story comes first. What story are you trying to tell through the character? What lighting decisions could help convey their personality and situation? Lighting a design will give it more dimension and life.

The light can come from a range of different angles, including from the foreground, from above, from above-left or above-right, from behind, from below, and from the side. The **light source** itself could be the sun or moon, a light bulb or lamp, a reflection, or an open flame like a fire or candle. Each lighting choice will convey a different **atmosphere**, **emotion**, and **mood**. For example, a bright spotlight will create a very different mood to a dim, candlelit scene. Just like colors have warm and cool palettes, lighting can also be warm or cool, enhancing certain color palettes and the emotions they convey.

While lighting a character can be fun, avoid adding too much light and shadow, as they can distract from the **focal points** of the design. There are scenarios that will call for extreme lighting, but their suitability depends on the story and mood you are trying to convey to the audience.

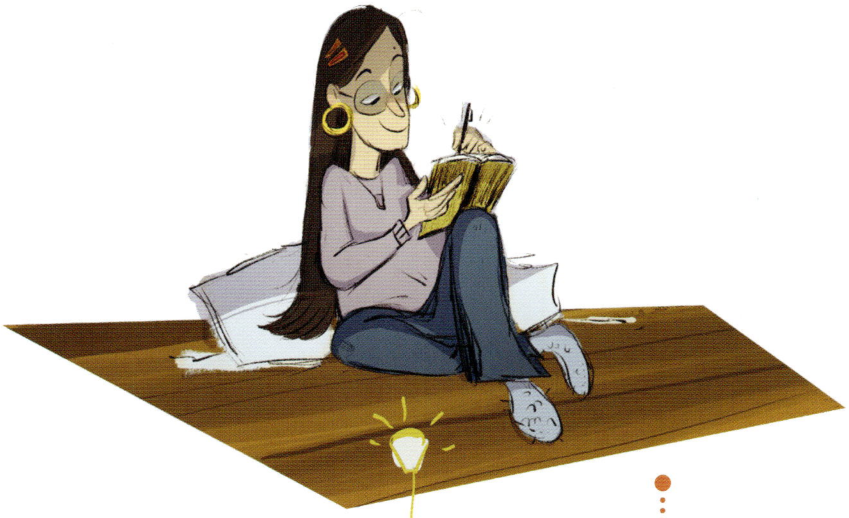

Foreground

This character is lit from the foreground by a light source around her level. Perhaps she is writing in her diary in front of a window or lamp, using the light to see the pages of her notebook. The areas of her body closest to the light are brightest, while the areas farther away and farther up are dimmer.

Above

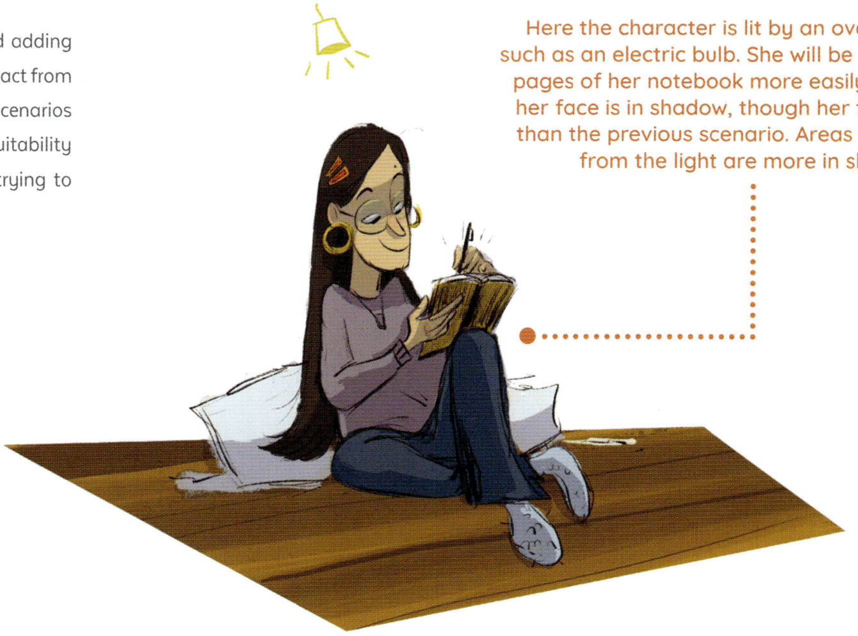

Here the character is lit by an overhead light, such as an electric bulb. She will be able to see the pages of her notebook more easily now. Part of her face is in shadow, though her face is lighter than the previous scenario. Areas farther away from the light are more in shadow.

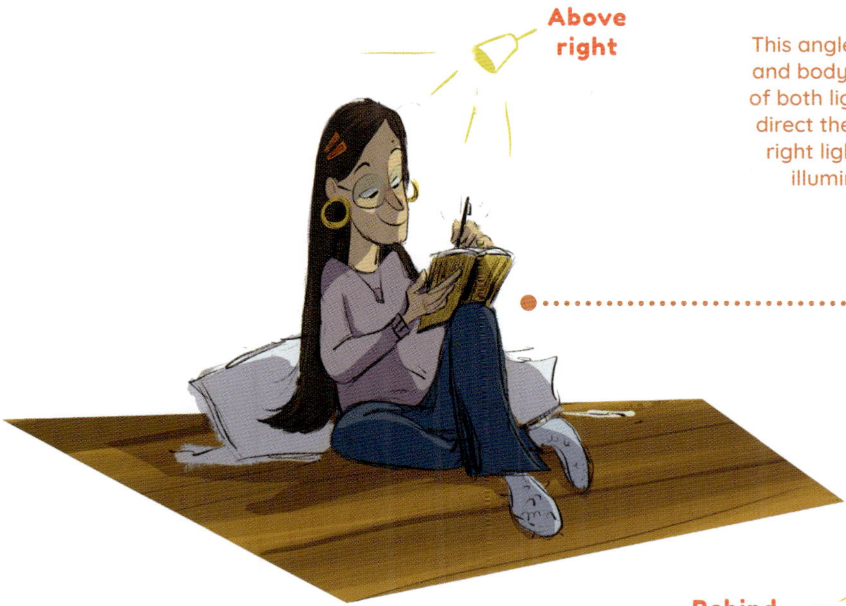

This angle shines light on the character's face, neck, and body, emphasizing those areas. Including zones of both light and dark helps to balance a design and direct the audience's gaze. An above-left or above-right light source is a good all-purpose option for illuminating the important parts of a design.

Lighting from behind casts the front side of the character in shadow. Her color palette is now cooler in tone, with the shadows creating more of an ambient, low-lit feeling. This scenario is less suitable for clearly illuminating character details, but is useful for creating atmosphere or drama.

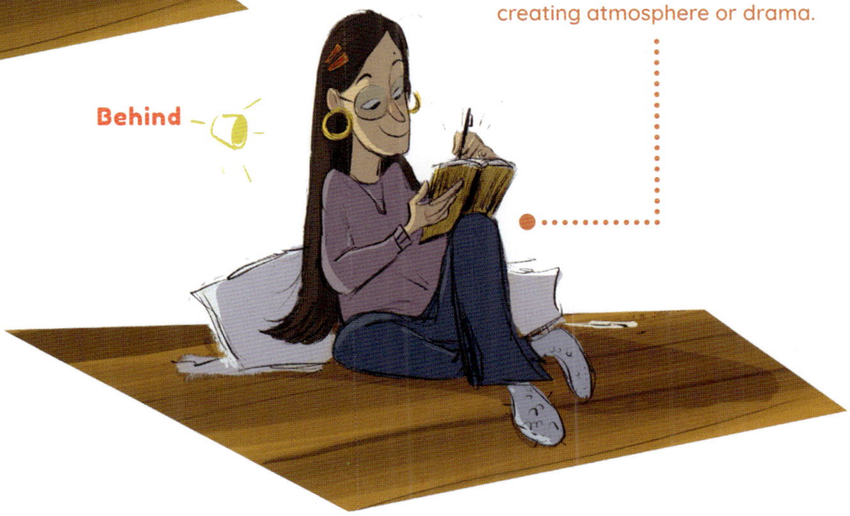

Here the character is lit from the side, lighting the pages of her notebook as she writes. This can be good for focusing the audience's attention on a certain side or part of the design, by putting the less important side in shadow. Again, like lighting from behind, this option may conceal some character details, so make sure you choose the appropriate situation for it.

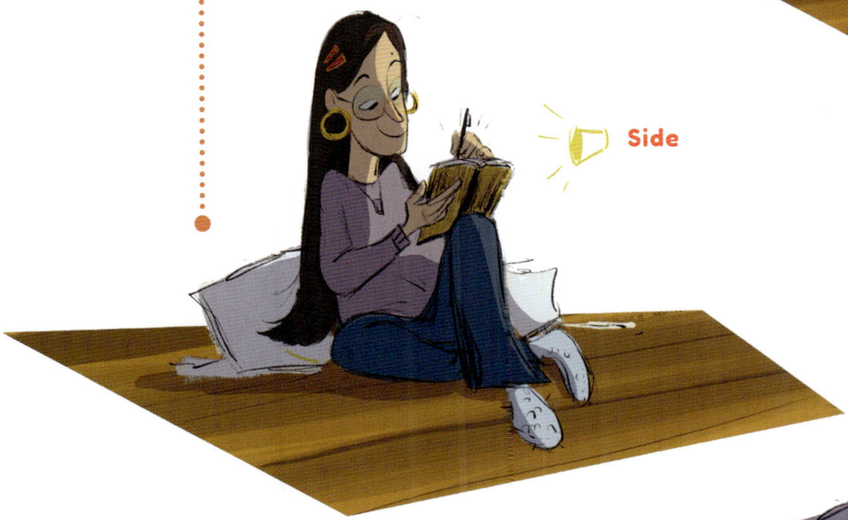

Another less-used lighting scenario is lighting a character from underneath, as if they're lit with a torch from below. This can create a spooky, dramatic, or startling effect, casting stark shadows and making the subject look eerie or unfamiliar.

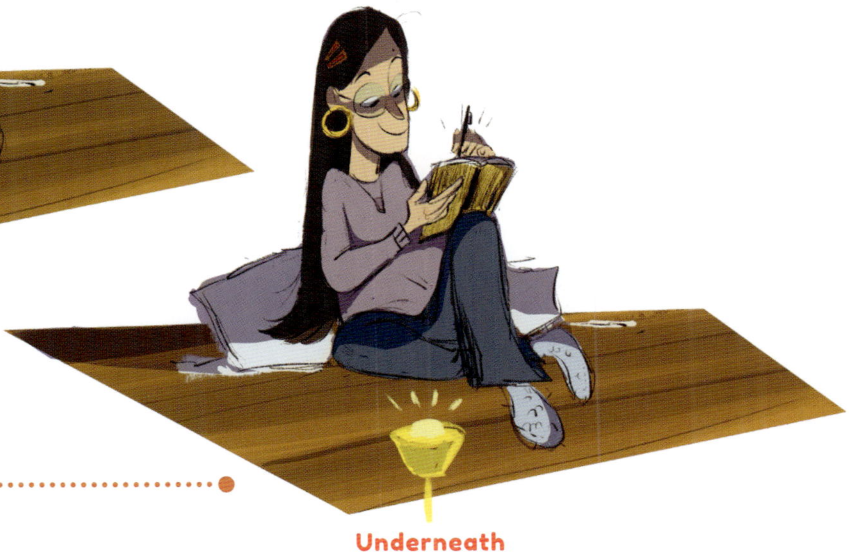

This raccoon wizard is using his magical powers, with a fiery light source that creates a feeling of energy, danger, and excitement. The light coming from the fireball casts a shadow behind the character and gives his color palette a warm, vibrant, and high-contrast glow. The fireball also tells the audience more of the wizard's story, showcasing his magical powers and perhaps slightly dangerous personality.

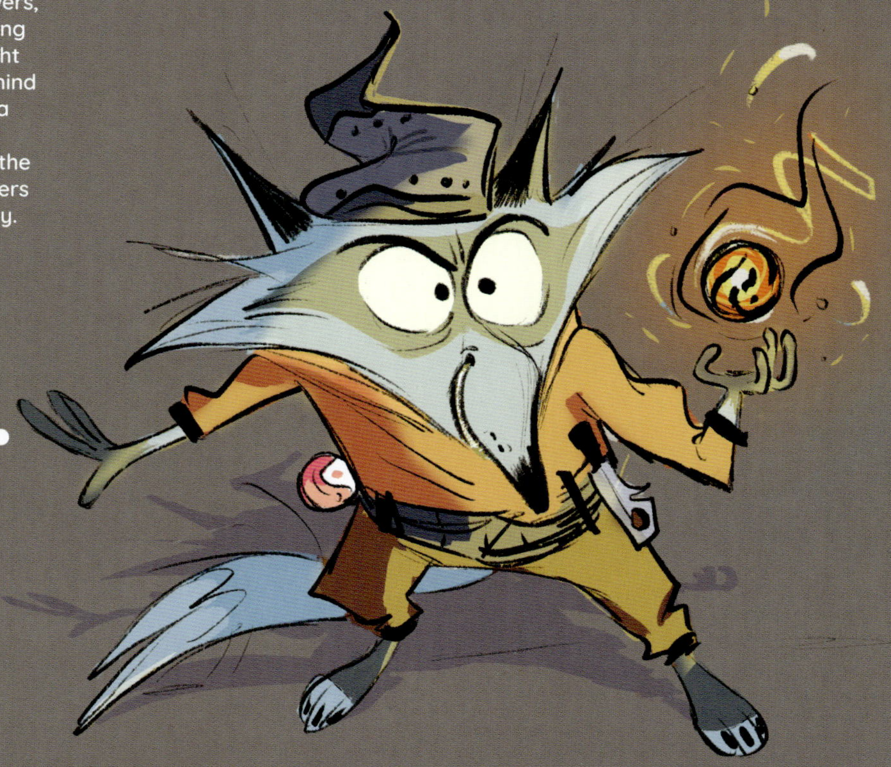

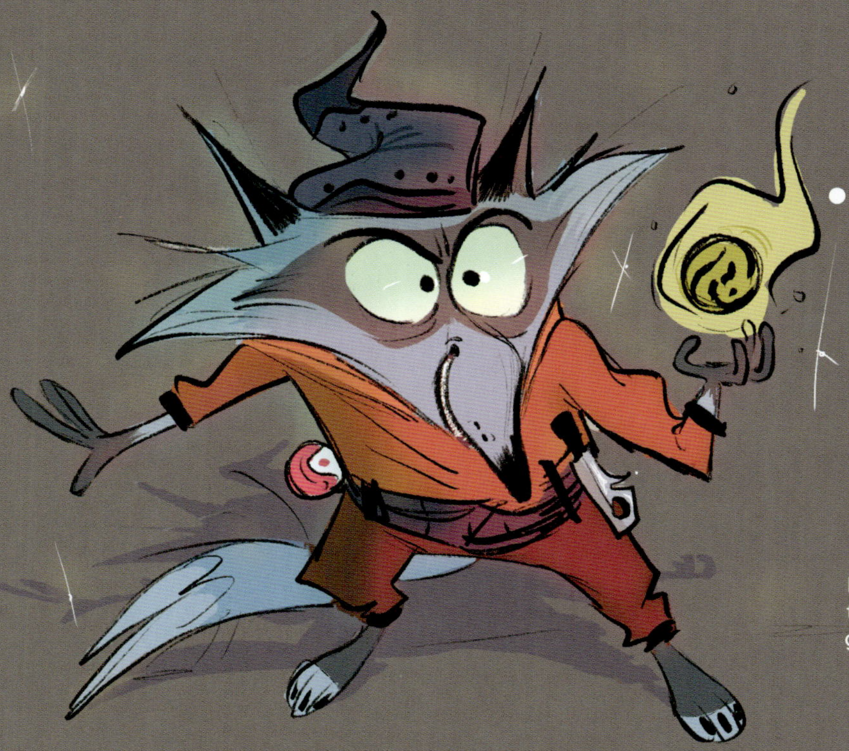

When creating a soft, hazy look, it's important to maintain a balance between the soft and bright qualities of the light. Hazy, misty, or eerie lighting is great for lighting characters and scenes that require a magical or otherworldly mood. This type of lighting could also be used to convey candlelight or a similar soft, gentle light source.

This vibrant neon-pink fireball has much higher saturation, casting a powerful glow that adds to the character's magical nature, as pink and purple can be used to convey a mysterious quality. When using a colored light source, such as a neon or colored bulb, keep in mind that the color of the light will affect the color palette of the character.

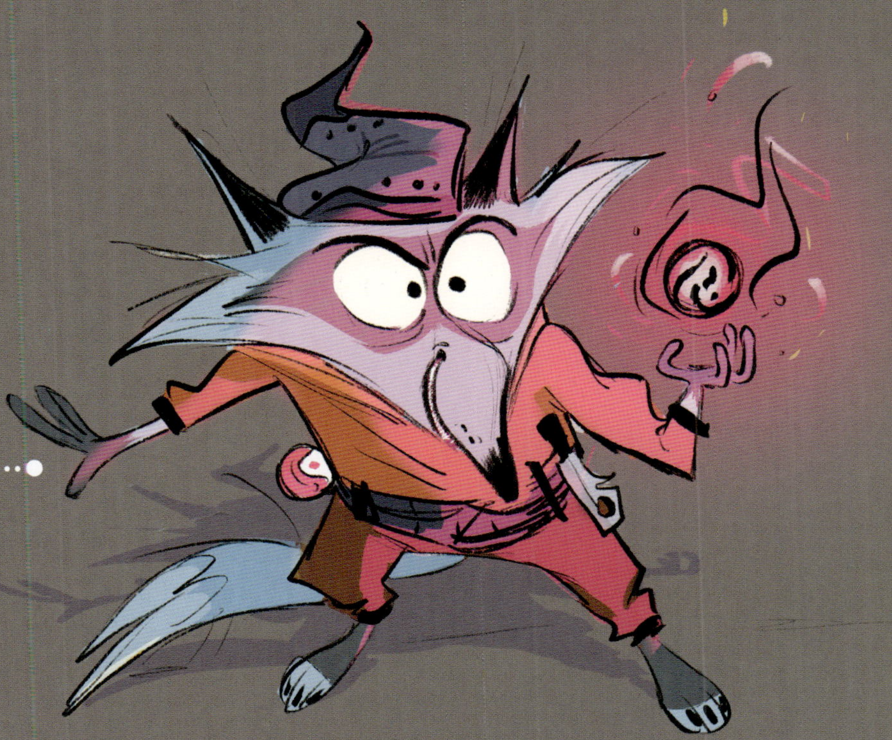

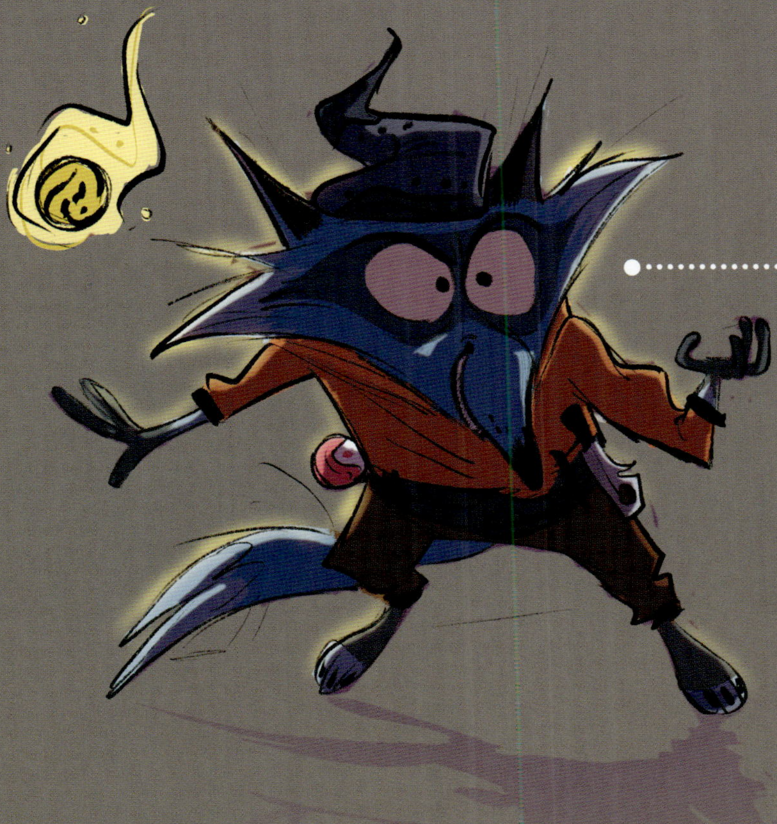

A dramatic, backlit lighting scenario casts dark shadows and creates a mysterious, uneasy feeling. A light source coming from behind the character creates a glow around his contours, while his front is cast in shadow. This type of backlighting can sometimes have a light source so bright that you can barely see the character's silhouette at all! This type of light could be cast by a spotlight, floodlight, or similar intense directional light source.

BALANCE & CONTRAST

Stephanie Garcia Rizo

The key to a successful design is combining the elements you have learned about so far – shape language, color, value, lighting – and finding an effective balance and contrast between them. This section of the chapter will explore the different ways you can enhance your designs with contrasts such as straight versus curved, symmetry versus asymmetry, and simple versus complex.

STRAIGHT VERSUS CURVED

Straight lines can be used to lead the eye quickly through the design, while curved lines help slow down the viewer's gaze and focus it on the more interesting or important areas. When we create characters, we have to make sure that they are not just still and static – even if they are standing still, their designs should be appealing and dynamic. This is where straight lines and curves come together to create gesture and flow, as shown in these three examples.

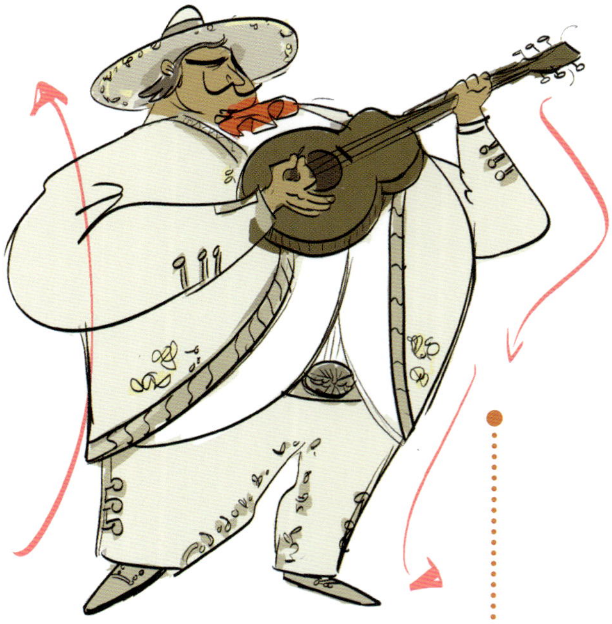

Mariachis already have a lot of lively patterns in their costumes, but we can create even more movement and energy by using a combination of curved and straight gestures. The straight gesture of this character's back pushes up toward his head and hat, where the curves slow the viewer down, before directing the audience's gaze over his guitar and down to his feet.

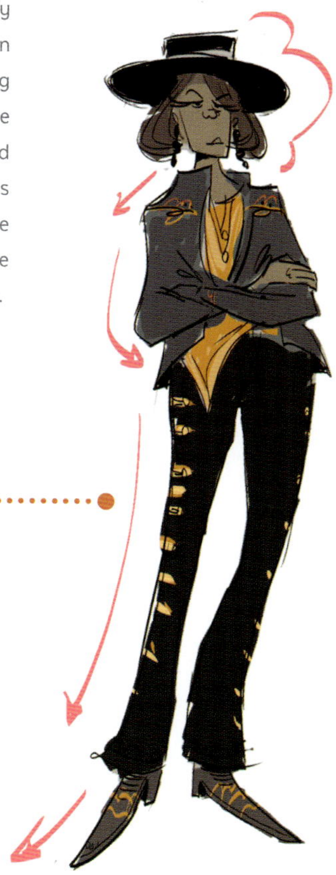

This mariachi exhibits a strong balance between straight and curved lines. Her hat and hair create curves around her head, drawing the viewer's attention there, before guiding the eye straight down to her arms and the rest of her design.

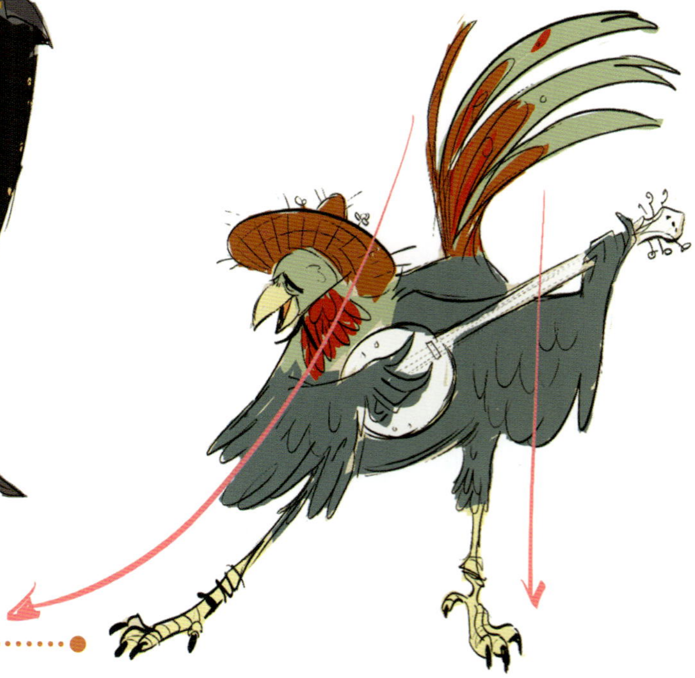

This mariachi rooster shows the strongest contrast between curved and straight. One leg is standing tall and straight, while the rest of his body pushes down toward his face to emphasize his expression and the enthusiasm of his pose. His feathers create curves that balance out the straight gesture and lead the viewer's eye toward his banjo.

SYMMETRY VERSUS ASYMMETRY

Symmetry and asymmetry can be used to make your designs feel more grounded or more energetic. As with anything else, you need a balance of both to create an effective character, but it's generally a good idea to explore more asymmetry as it is more dynamic and interesting. Just by tilting a character's head or hips, you create an action that helps the audience invest. You can make your character stand out further with asymmetrical props or costume elements, or physical details such as a facial mole, different-sized eyes, or crooked ears. However, symmetry has many uses, and a symmetrical design or pose can help make a character feel stubborn or still.

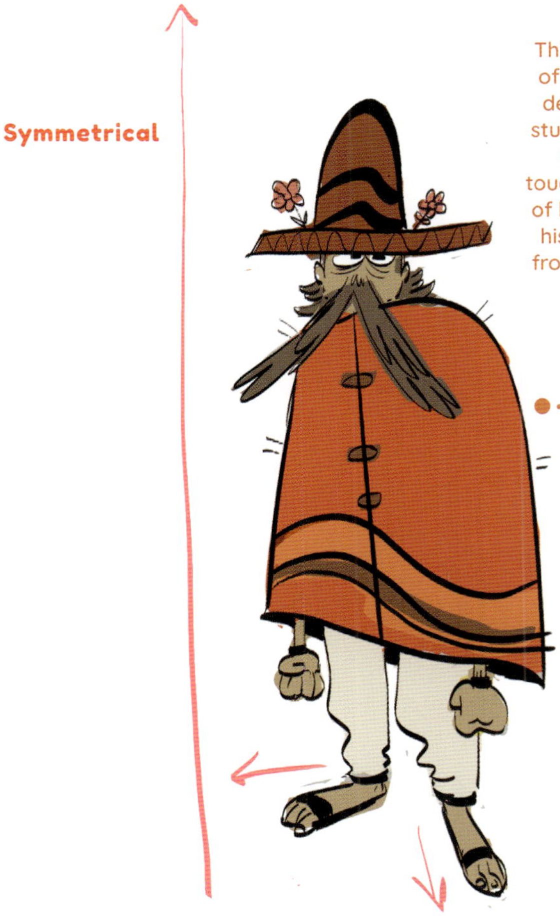

This bandit is an example of a largely symmetrical design. He feels steady, stubborn, and mysterious. Small asymmetrical touches like the positioning of his feet and the hem of his coat keep the design from feeling totally static.

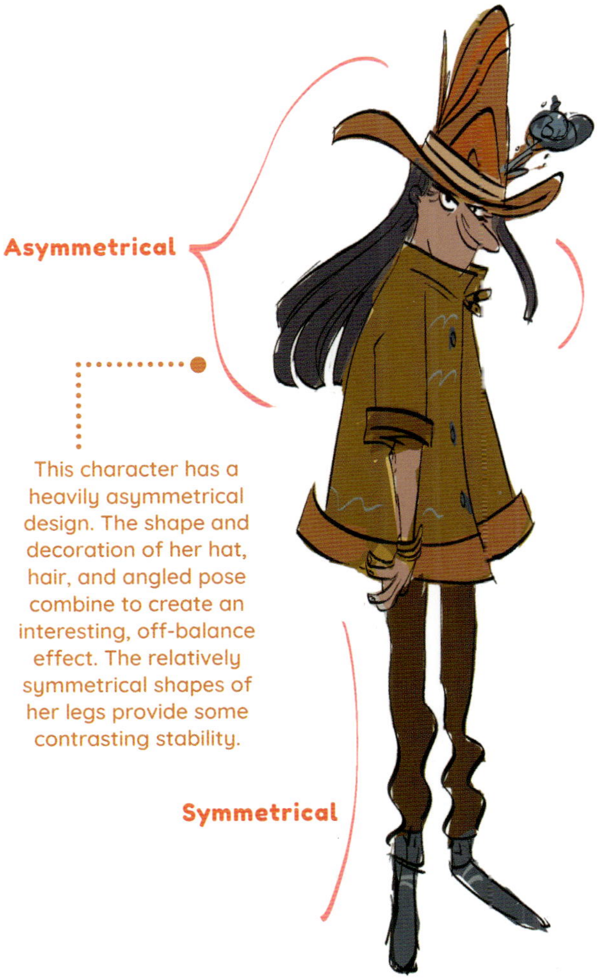

This character has a heavily asymmetrical design. The shape and decoration of her hat, hair, and angled pose combine to create an interesting, off-balance effect. The relatively symmetrical shapes of her legs provide some contrasting stability.

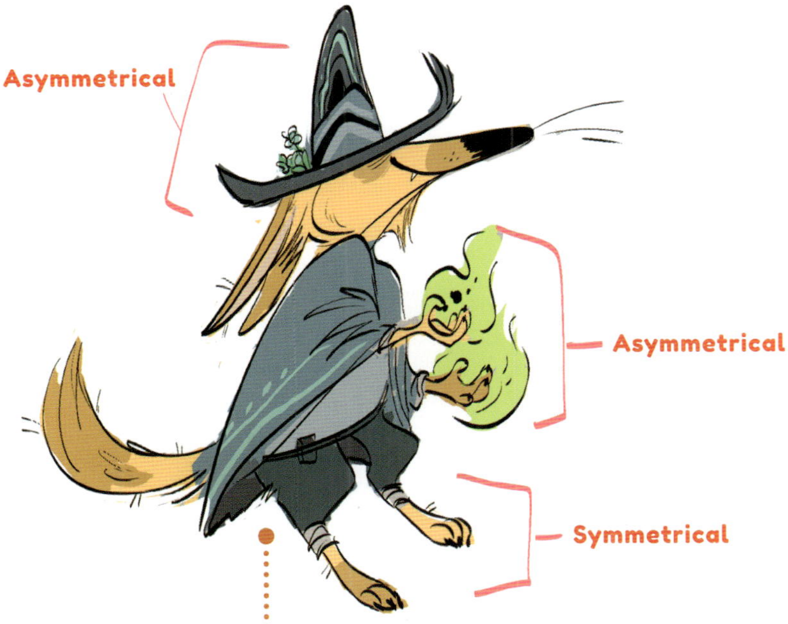

This coyote character shows a balance of symmetry and asymmetry. His hat has a flower only on one side, as well as a dynamic pattern. His hands are in an asymmetrical pose, moving in opposite directions, while the stance of his feet is quite symmetrical in comparison. This contrast helps to focus the viewer on the key focal areas of his head and hands.

LINE WEIGHT & TEXTURE

As you discover your drawing style, you will find there are many different ways to express a character with line weight and texture. The thickness or thinness of a line – its weight – can create the impression of a character feeling heavy or light. Line weight can communicate different types of energy, whether calm and steady or wild and erratic. Adding textures or patterns to a character's hair, fur, skin, or clothing can also enhance their personality and tell their story. As always, you must find a careful balance of these elements – too many lines and too much texture can weaken a design instead of helping the audience know where to look. Like other types of contrast, the key to success is knowing where to apply more or less intensity or detail.

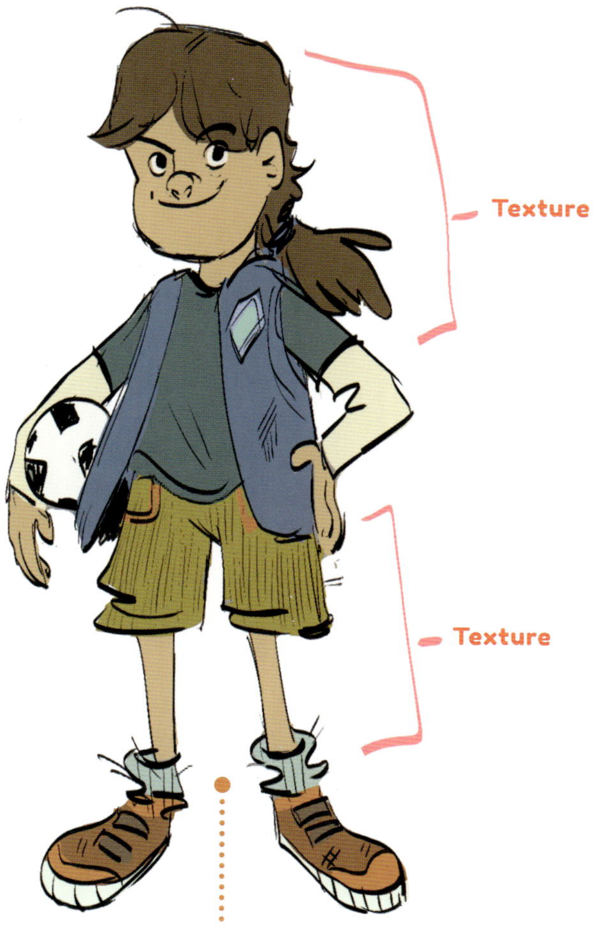

There are several areas of this sporty character that use texture to convey her personality. Her hair is slightly frizzy to show how active she is. Her shorts are lightly patterned and her socks are scruffy and loose, creating interesting details that lead the viewer around the whole design.

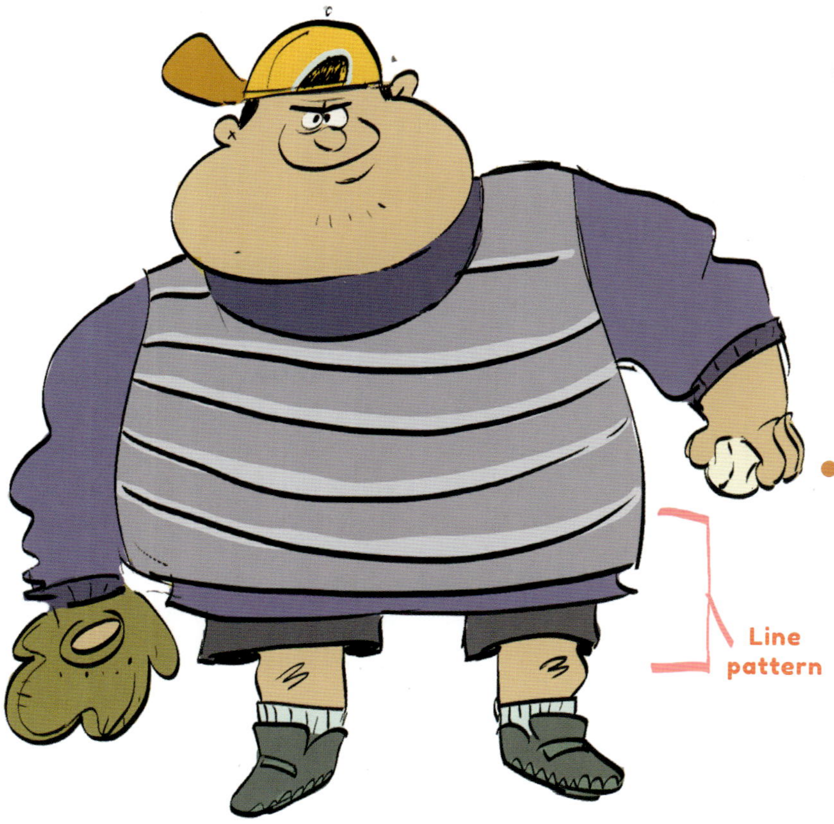

Line weight is used to convey this character's personality and shape. In order to emphasize his broad shape, the striped pattern on his shirt uses thicker strokes than other areas of his design. This creates a more dynamic drawing when contrasted with the plain undershirt and thinner lines elsewhere.

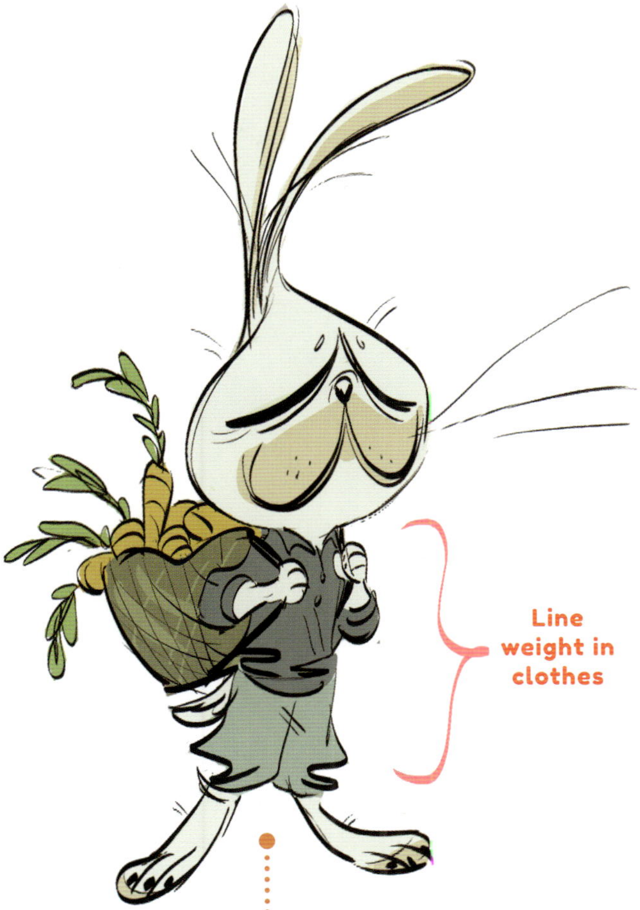

This design combines line weight and texture to tell this rabbit farmer's story. Heavy, drooping strokes emphasize his tired, melancholy features. Loose, varied lines add interest to his baggy clothes, and his basket of carrots creates an area of texture and pattern that adds variation to the design.

LINEWORK & MARK-MAKING

When choosing a visual style or drawing technique for your character design, your decision should come down to the story. How does this style of linework support your design? The lines and marks you make, whether complex or simple, can create energy and emotion in your design.

This character is a middle-school kid playing a trumpet. Even though he's standing still, the linework is not constant or static; instead, it gives a feeling of energy and movement. Textures and marks are drawn throughout the character to guide the viewer's eye, such as the swirl marks in his hair and the rough strokes of his bushy eyebrows, which help focus attention on his head and face.

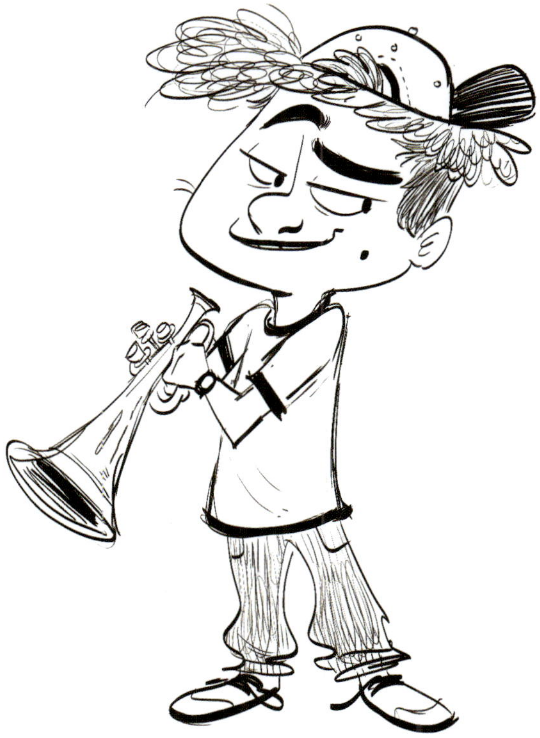

SIMPLE VERSUS COMPLEX

A strong design needs to find harmony between simplicity and complexity. Simple areas help the viewer's eye to move quickly to the next area of detail – usually a more complex focal point such as the face or an important prop. Too much detail can become confusing or distracting, and too little detail can leave a design feeling bland or unfinished. Creating a balance between these two qualities will result in a much more interesting and appealing character.

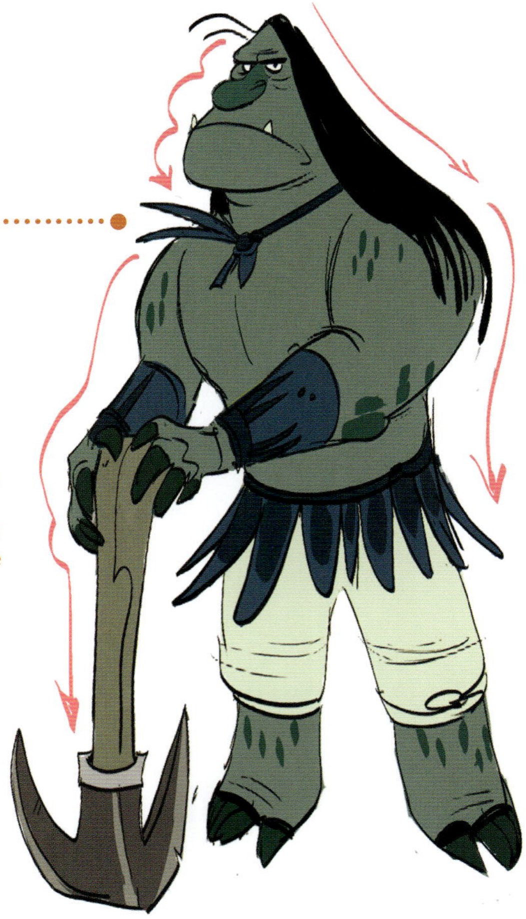

The face is the most complex area of this ogre warrior's design. His long, slick hair and smooth upper body are simple in comparison, leading the viewer down to the more important details of his costume and weapons.

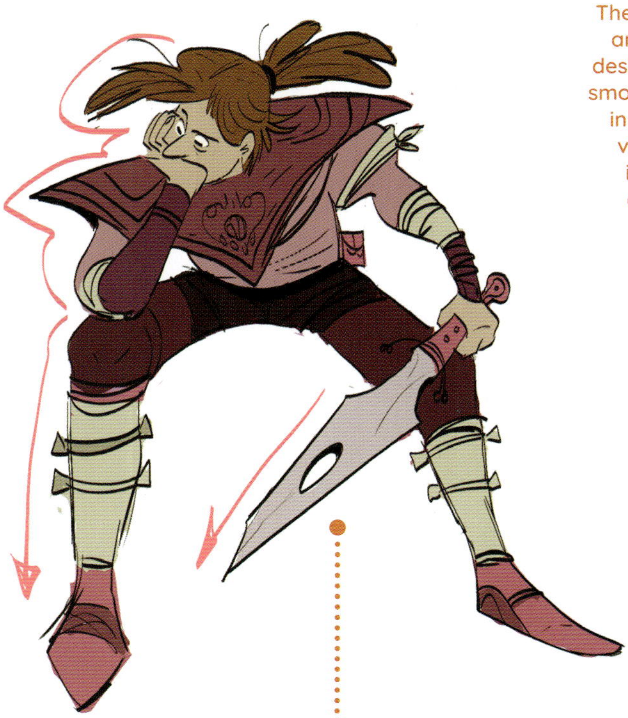

This warrior's design is more complex. Her shoulder armor, hair, weapon, and posture show some dynamic and unusual shapes, but these are balanced out by the relative simplicity of the rest of her costume.

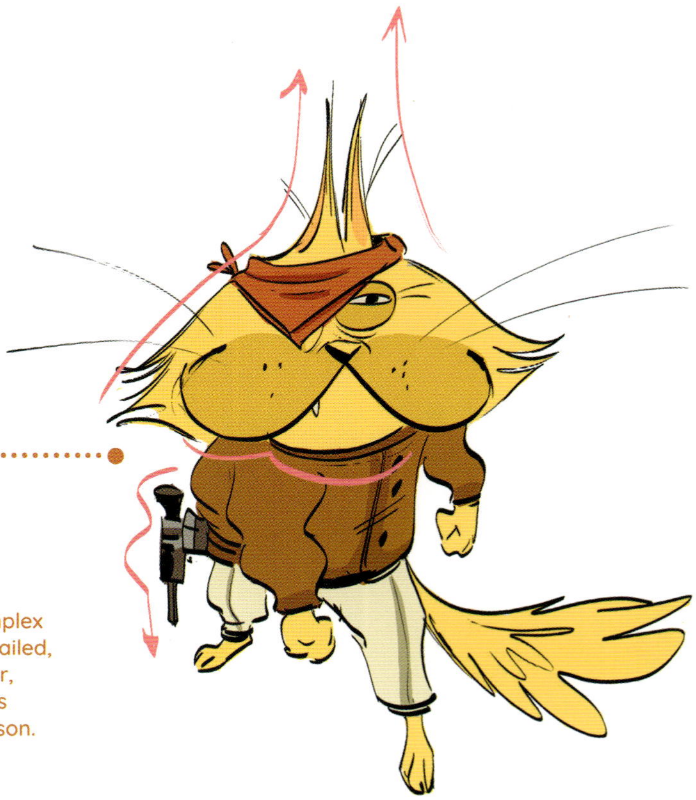

This space-bandit cat exhibits a good mix of complex and simple areas. His face, tail, and props are detailed, drawing attention to his expression, scruffy fur, and bandit accessories. The rest of his clothes and body are quite clean and simple in comparison.

POSITIVE & NEGATIVE SPACE

In art, "positive space" is the space occupied by your subject, while "negative space" is the blank space around it. Negative space may seem to be empty, but it can be a powerful visual presence that forms distinct shapes of its own. In an action pose, for example, creating clear negative shapes around or within the gaps of the character's limbs will ensure that their pose is legible, even from a distance or at a glance. Understanding positive and negative space is the key to creating characters with appealing shapes, memorable silhouettes, and clear poses.

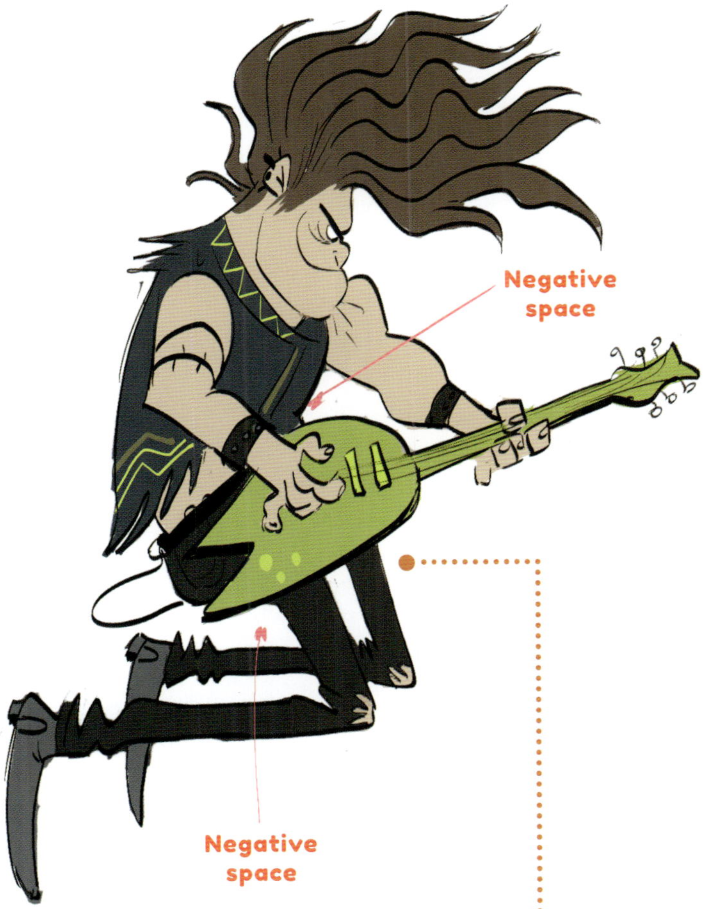

This musician features some extreme motion and several overlapping elements that are enhanced by negative space. His extended arm and jumping legs create distinct negative space shapes, ensuring that his silhouette is clear and fully understandable.

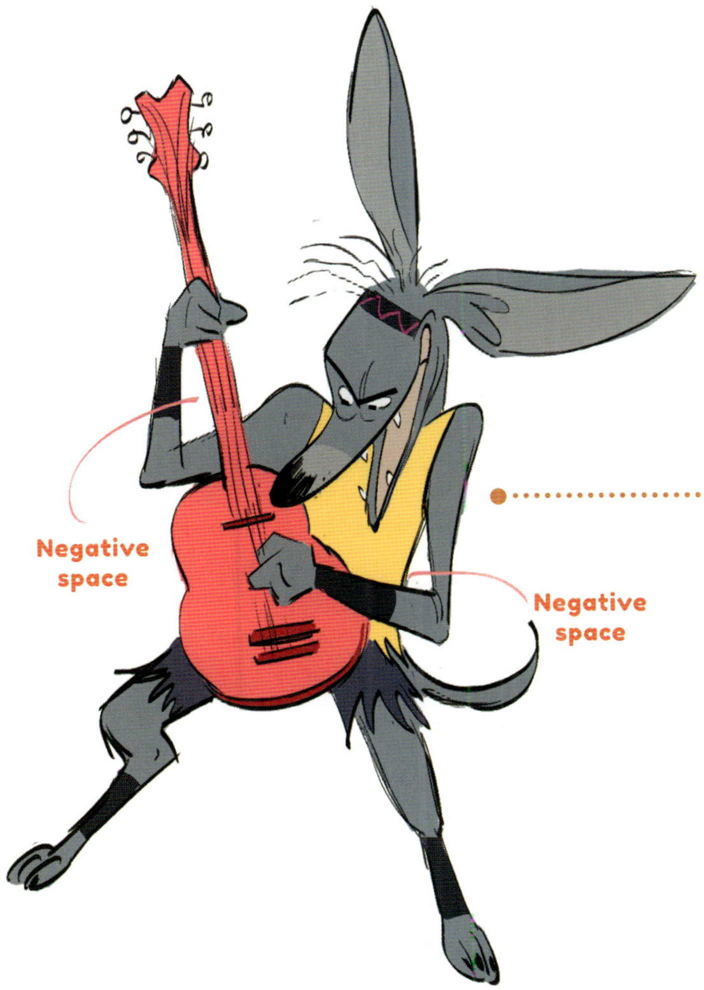

This Mexican rock 'n' roll dog has big ears and a raised guitar that form a positive silhouette, while the negative spaces inside his arms keep the pose readable and punchy. There are even positive/negative shapes within his design, where his open mouth forms a distinct shape against the backdrop of his shirt.

SCALE

Stephanie Garcia Rizo

There are many ways you can convey size and scale in character design. You can use different props or background elements to help the viewer understand how big or small your character is. Sometimes the audience can tell whether a design is big or small because of who or what the character is – for example, if they're a rabbit or a basketball player – but this becomes more complicated if you want to portray a large version of something that's usually small, or vice versa. This is why providing details and clues to indicate a character's scale is important.

Including large or small **props** with your design is a great scale indicator, and also part of storytelling, helping the audience to understand the character's personality and role as well as their size. You can also scale parts of a character's body differently to create interesting proportions and show more about their personality, as shown on page 98, such as giving them a small head or big, strong arms.

Scale can also be used to evoke particular **emotions** in the viewer. If you show a big, formidable-looking character being a soft, lovable giant through his interactions with a smaller character, you have used to scale to play with the viewer's expectations. Perhaps a character is small in size, but is also aggressive or destructive. Scale can even provide opportunities for humor. Our goal as designers is to do everything we can to help tell the character's story to the audience, and scale is just one of the many visual tools available to us.

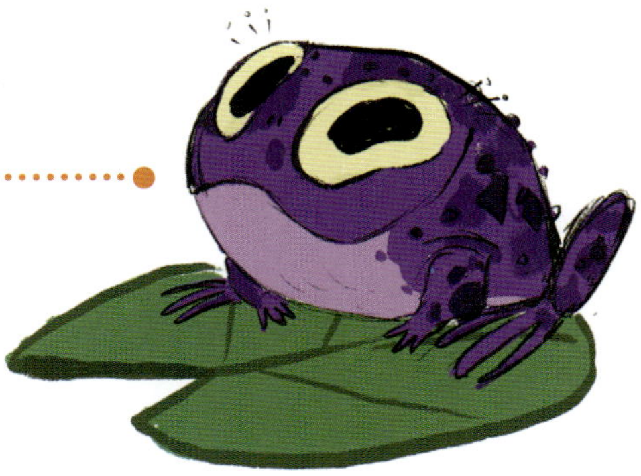

You can tell that this mischievous frog character is small. It has a small body and big eyes, and is sitting on a leaf, which all help to convey its proportions. This character would be a little jumpy, as life is dangerous for a small frog, and its design helps to show this combination of vulnerability and alertness.

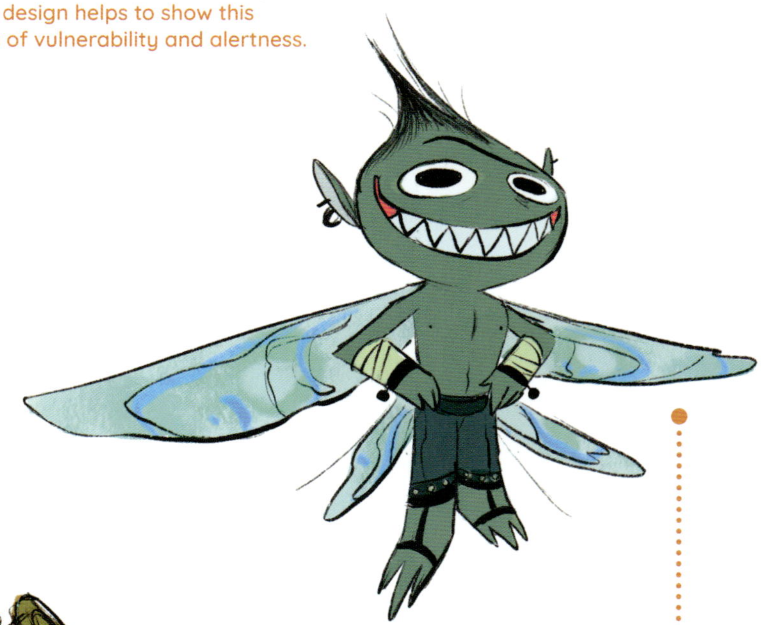

This vicious-looking fairy is another design that comes across as small. His proportions are somewhat childlike, with a big head and small torso, to immediately convey his smaller stature to the viewer. His dragonfly wings and tiny garments confirm the initial impression of his size.

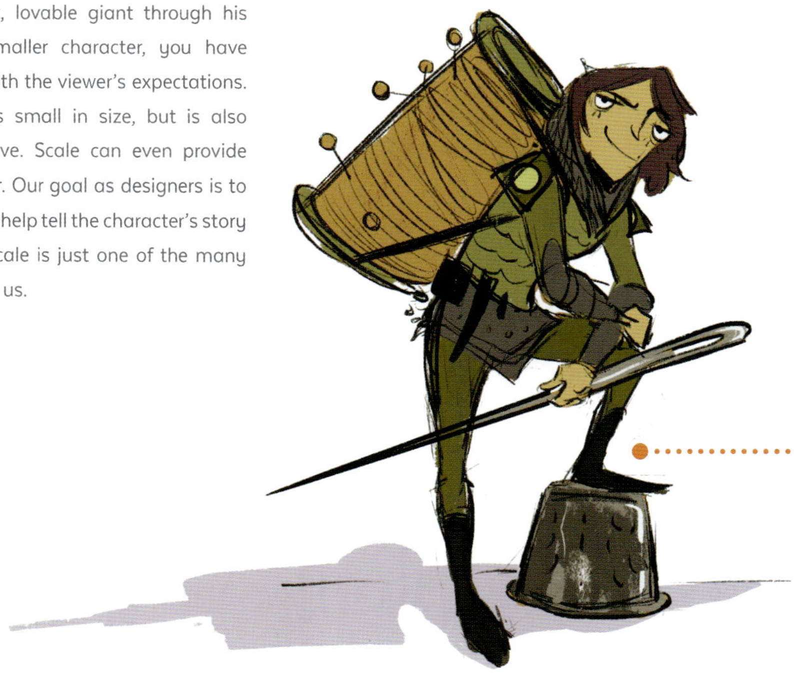

We can tell from the props that this is a small, Thumbelina-like character. She's holding a sewing needle, wearing a spool of thread on her back, and resting her foot on a thimble. All these props emphasize her size and suggest her role as a tiny scavenger or adventurer.

This dragon character feels large – perhaps a few feet taller than a human would be. The design has a long neck and heavy bottom, with small horns and wings that add a bit of humor and make the rest of the body seem larger in comparison.

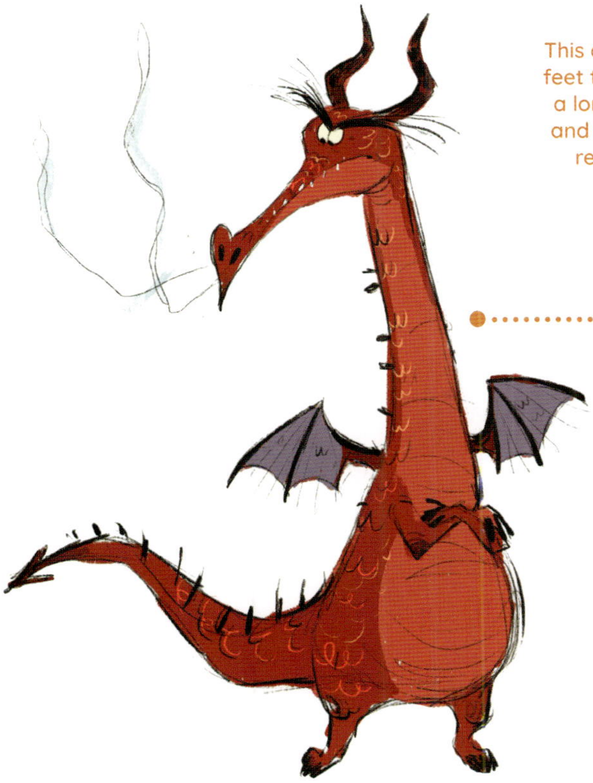

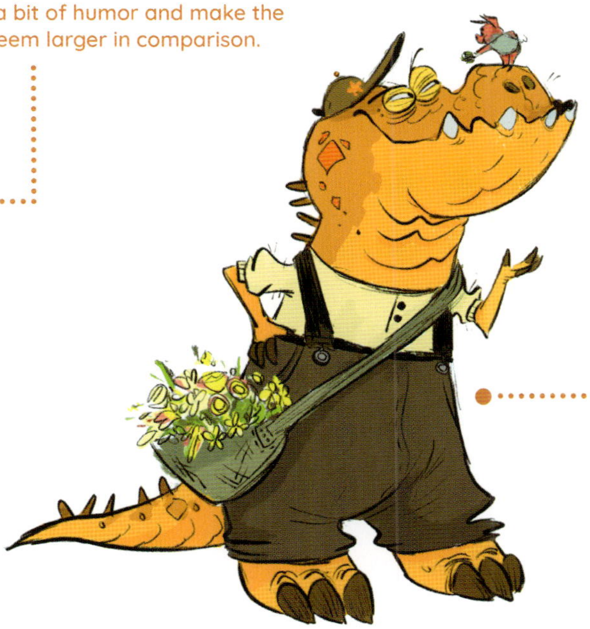

This dinosaur florist feels large, not just because he's a dinosaur, but because he has a customer standing on his nose – a little pig paying for his flowers! This contrast in size helps convey how soft and kind the character is – even though he's a big dinosaur, he's a gentle giant.

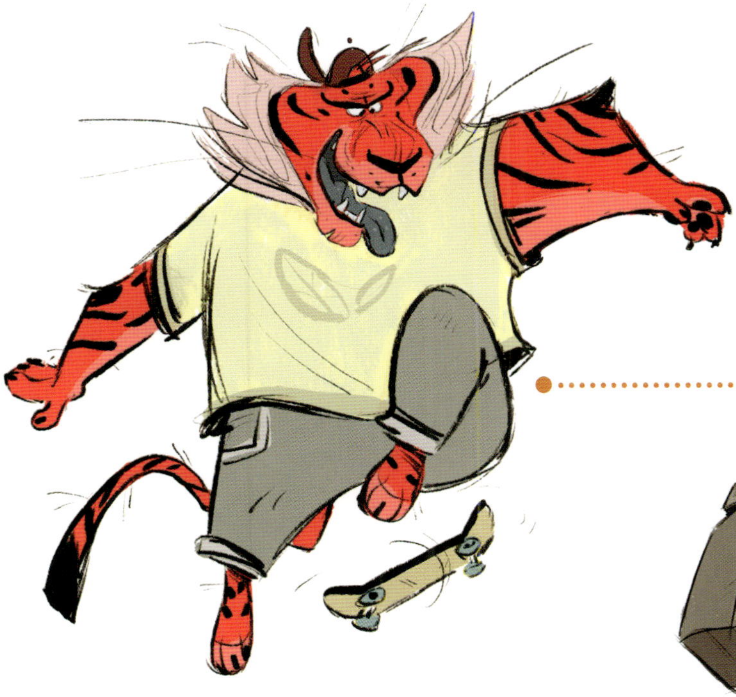

This skateboarding tiger's large size is emphasized by his small skateboard, creating a fun and asymmetrical design. The relative smallness of his skateboard and hat makes the design more entertaining, and suggests that he's a laid-back, funny character.

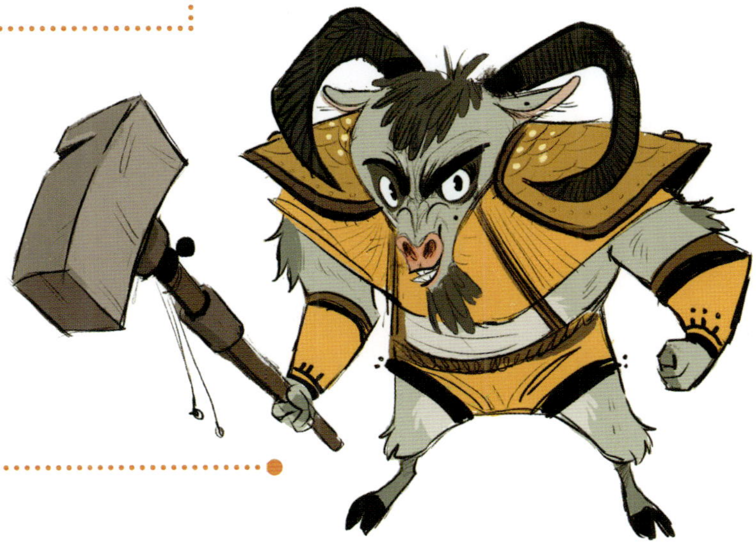

This warrior is carrying a large prop, but still feels large himself, due to his broad physique and heavy equipment. The higher level of detail on the face and body show that this is a design with more surface area and size to play with.

REPETITION

Stephanie Garcia Rizo

Repetition can help you create designs that feel consistent. Using similar shape language, colors, or details throughout a design makes it feel cohesive, rather than adding lots of elements that feel like they do not belong together. When used poorly, repetition can weaken a character design and make it feel stagnant – for example, using too much of the same texture or color. When used well, it can create visual impact and flow that make a design look more dynamic and considered. Whether the repetition is in shape, body language, color, or texture, it should help tell who the character is.

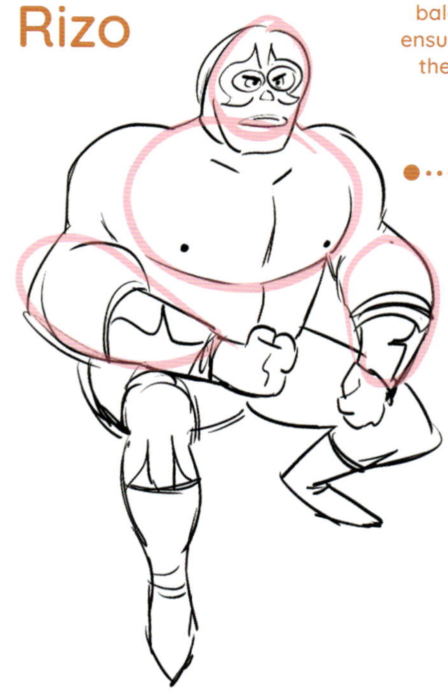

In this example, oval and circle shapes repeat themselves throughout the design at different sizes. Repeating these shapes creates a balanced design, while the variety of sizes ensures that the design stays interesting and the character's personality is maintained.

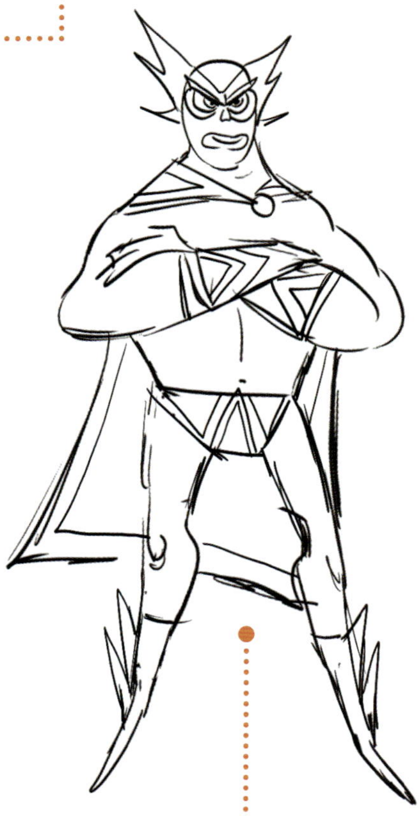

Triangles are repeated throughout the costume of this luchador. The character feels well-balanced because the triangles around his head, the focal point, are larger than the triangles across the rest of the design. Not only is his costume triangular, but his whole body creates a triangle shape!

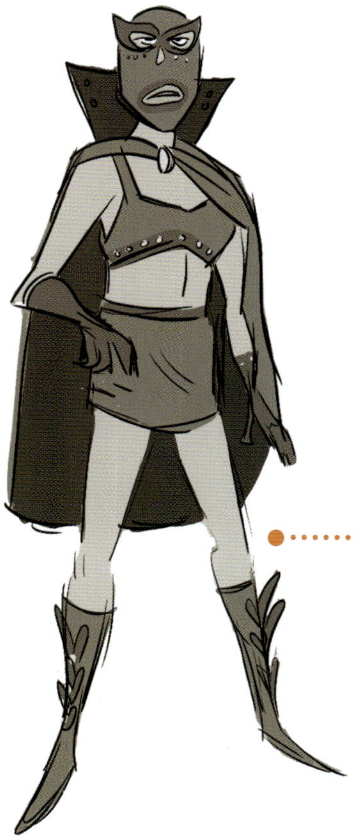

In this example, a range of values are used to maintain variety, but they are repeated throughout the character's whole costume. This unifies her design while keeping it interesting and appealing.

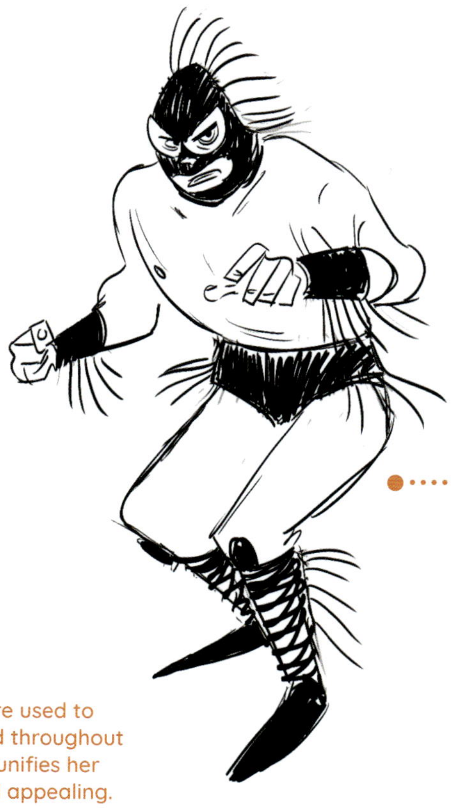

This design shows repetition of texture and value. This wrestler's costume has black fringes on it, creating movement and appeal in his design. If he was wearing a full suit in this style, it would be too much, but it works well as he's wearing very little. These dark, textured details help draw attention to his face, hands, and feet – the key areas of the design.

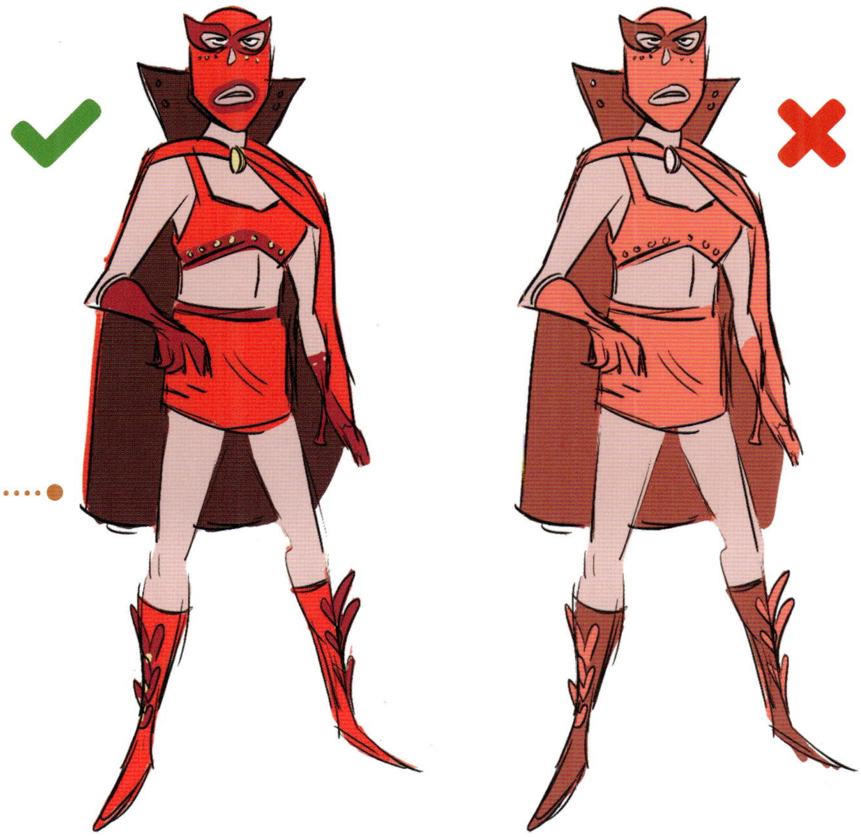

Here are examples of strong and weak color repetition. The version on the left shows balance and variety in its use of red tones, but the version on the right is too repetitive. Too many areas of her costume use the same color, making it harder for the viewer to distinguish important areas, such as her hands and face.

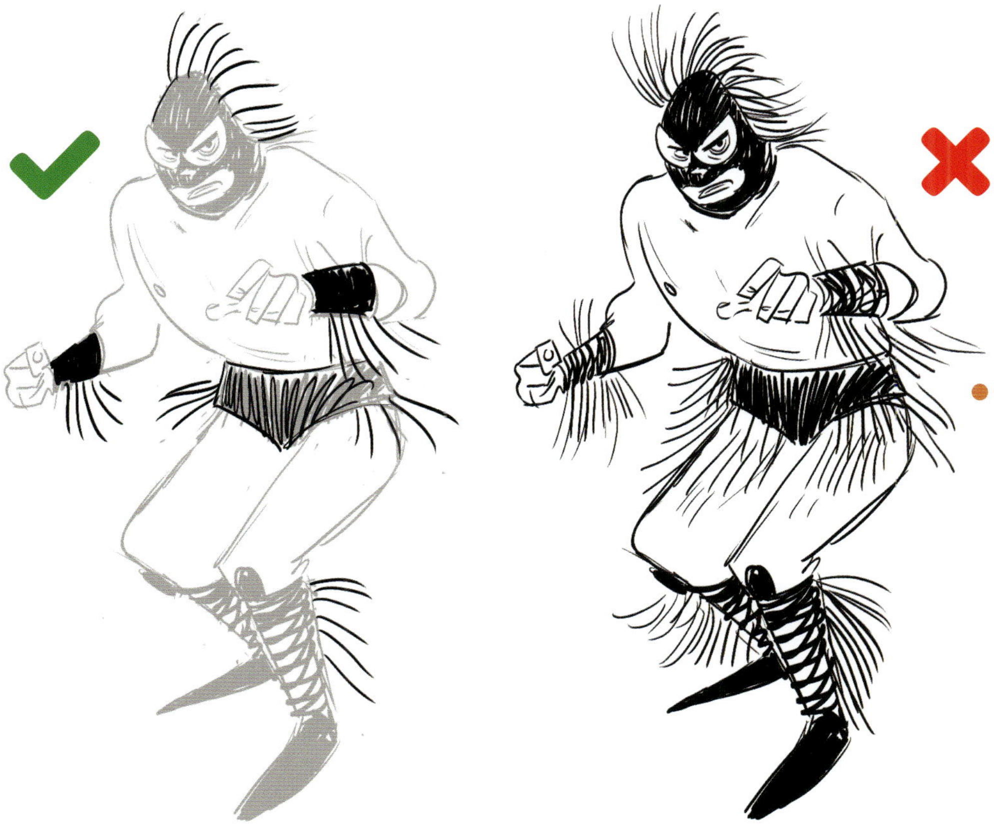

Here's another example of repetition used poorly. The costume on the right is far too distracting; there's so much texture that the viewer isn't sure exactly where to look. The version on the left is more balanced and less messy, helping to focus the viewer's attention on the key areas.

RHYTHM

Stephanie Garcia Rizo

A good character design has rhythm written all over it. Clear visual rhythm gives your characters life and energy, and strengthens your designs by making them easy to read in action and directing the viewer's eye to the most important areas. Whether rhythm is found in the energy of a straight line against a curve, the repetition of a color or shape, or a strong line of action in a pose, it's important to understand how to create it in your designs. Rhythm feeds into storytelling and posing, whether you want your character to look sad, energetic, excited, or bored. You may often find yourself breaking the rules of anatomy to make these design decisions, but creating a character is about more than how good your design looks while standing in one pose. The character needs to live and breathe, to walk and talk, and that is where rhythm comes into play. If a character's rhythm doesn't express who they are, you must try to understand why.

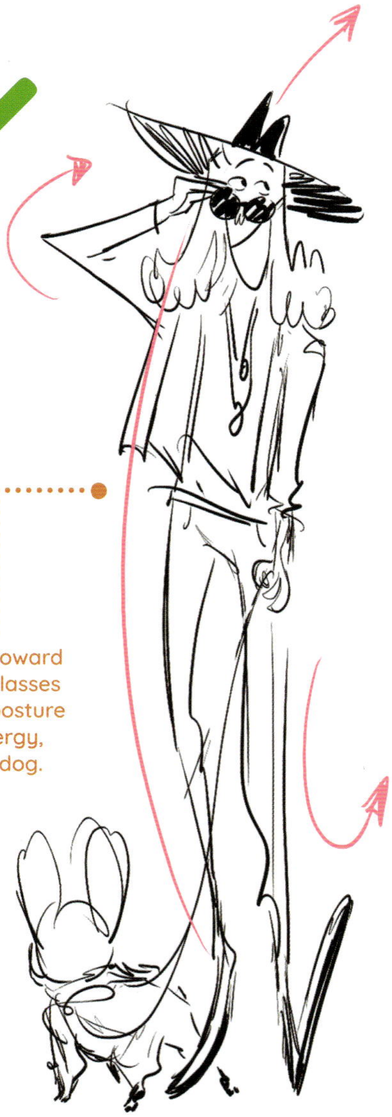

The rhythm in this gesture sketch flows up toward the character's face. The arm holding her glasses leads us toward her face, and the way her posture leans to the right gives her pose more energy, like she's having a good time walking her dog.

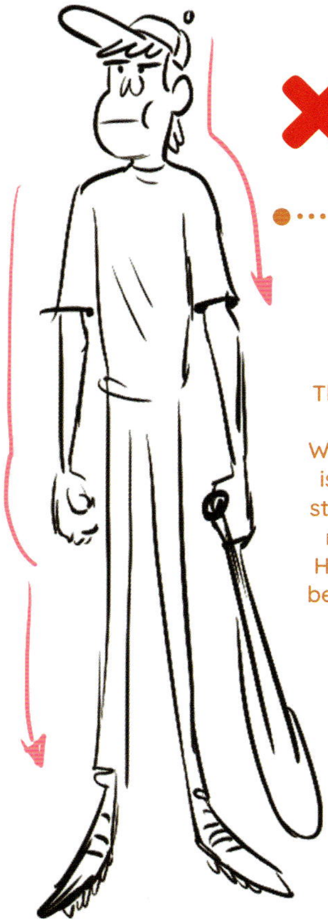

This is an example of a sketch with a weaker rhythm. We can see that this character is a baseball player, but he's standing still and we don't see much energy or dynamism. His arms and feet flow a little better, but overall, he is a very flat and static character.

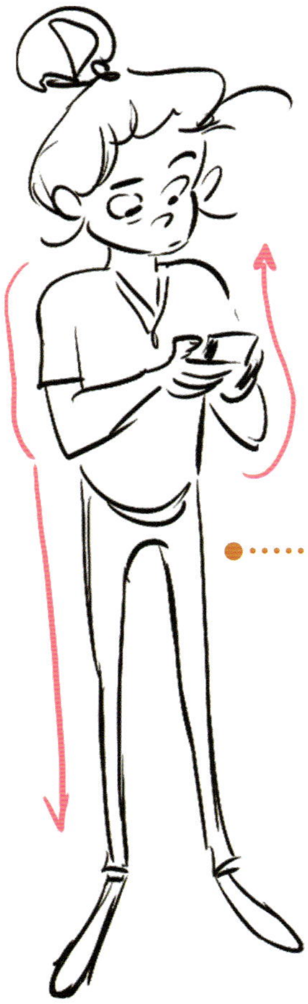

Here is another example of a character with a weak rhythm. Even though we can see that she is texting, it's hard for the audience to discern her mood or energy. Emphasizing the posture, emotion, and action of the character would make a much stronger impression.

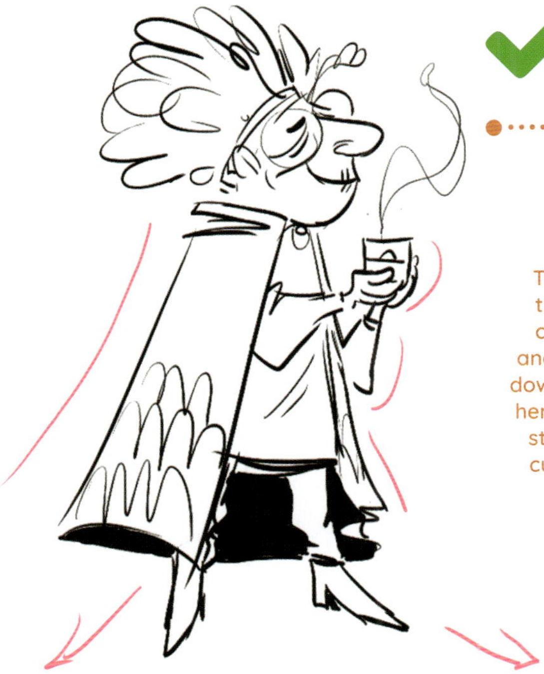

This woman is standing still, but there is still rhythm in her pose, created by contrasting straight and curved lines. The rhythm flows down and out from her feet, making her feel grounded, flowing over the straight line of her cloak and the curves of how she holds the cup.

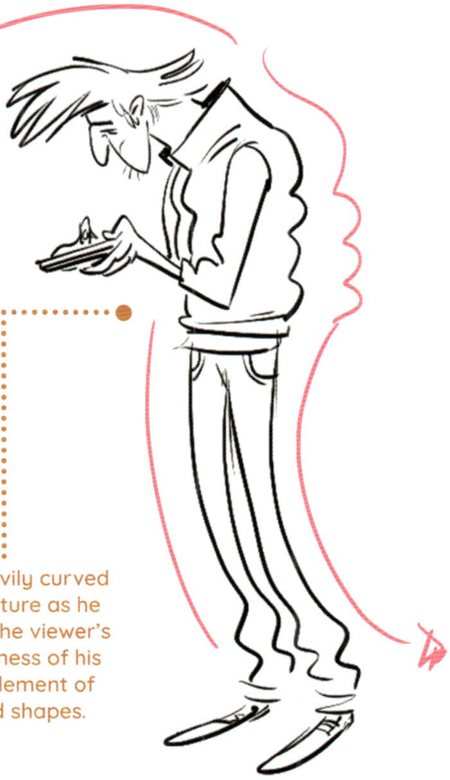

The rhythm in this sketch is heavily curved to capture this man's poor posture as he leans over his phone, focusing the viewer's attention there too. The sloppiness of his jacket and trousers adds an element of interest that also uses curved shapes.

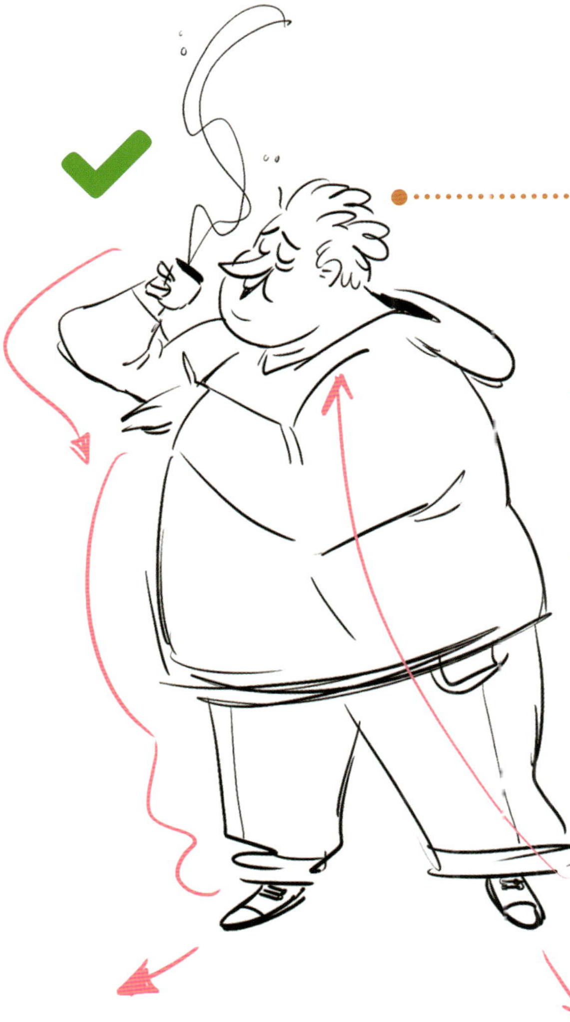

This character is holding a cup up to his face, creating an angle that contrasts with the curve of his stomach and the straight line of action that flows up his leg and spine. These rhythms and details all help direct the viewer's eye to the character's face and expression.

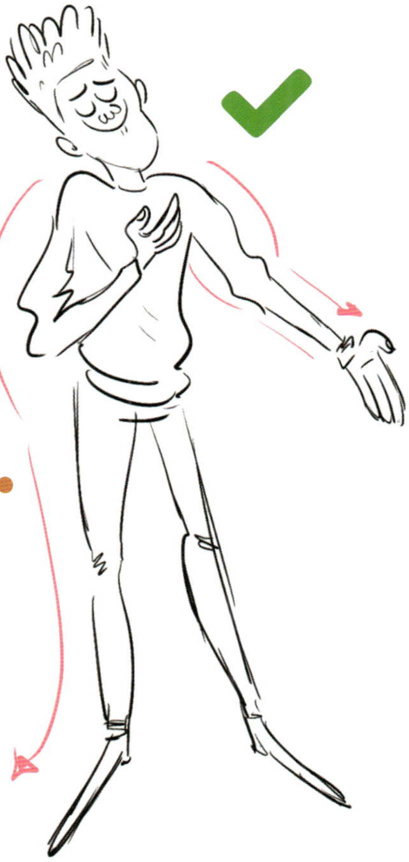

This character's posture is strengthened by the contrasting straight and curved rhythms of his hand and arm. Even his sweater helps to guide the viewer up to his face and down to his extended hand. Straight away, the audience can tell that he's politely letting someone pass by or lending a helping hand.

TANGENTS

Stephanie Garcia Rizo

Tangents occur when lines or characters touch in a way that's confusing or awkward. Sometimes they are created by clothes, props, or even the placement of the character in a scenario. If lines or objects touch or intersect in a way that undermines the clarity of the image, it leaves the audience wondering what something is or what a character is supposed to be doing. You can spot tangents and avoid them by planning your characters as silhouettes, or just by stepping back from your image to check that the characters and props are interacting clearly with each other. In some ways, it's like creating rhythm – making sure there's a clear flow and pattern to the drawing, so that the character or action is conveyed effectively to the viewer.

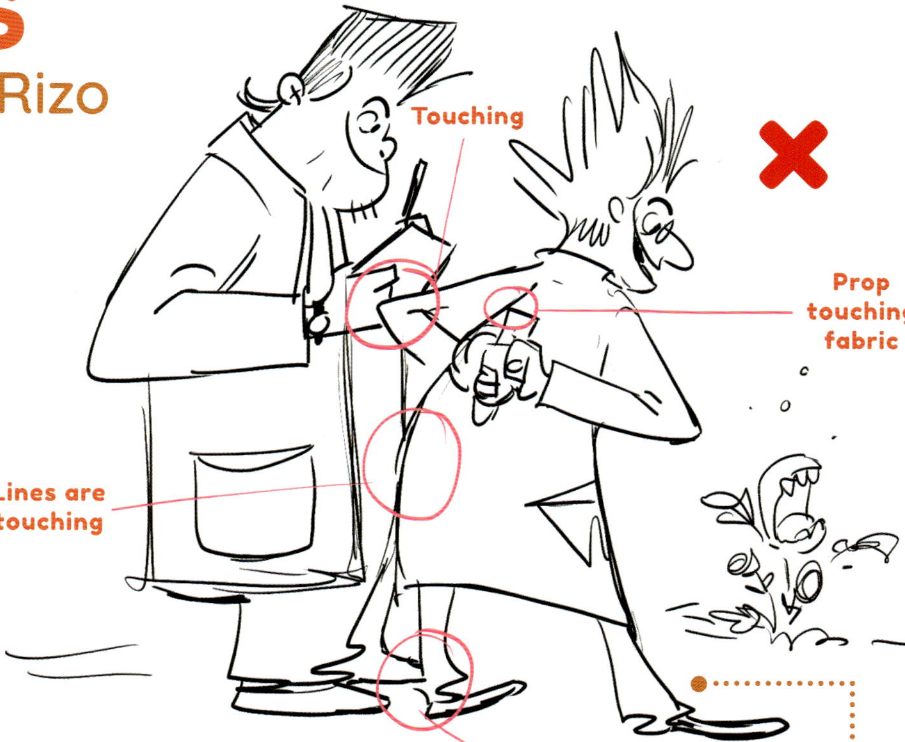

There are multiple places in this drawing where lines create tangents. The scientist on the right is holding a prop that precisely touches the line of his back – as does the cuff of his left sleeve. The characters' feet and clothes touch just enough to confuse the depth of the scene.

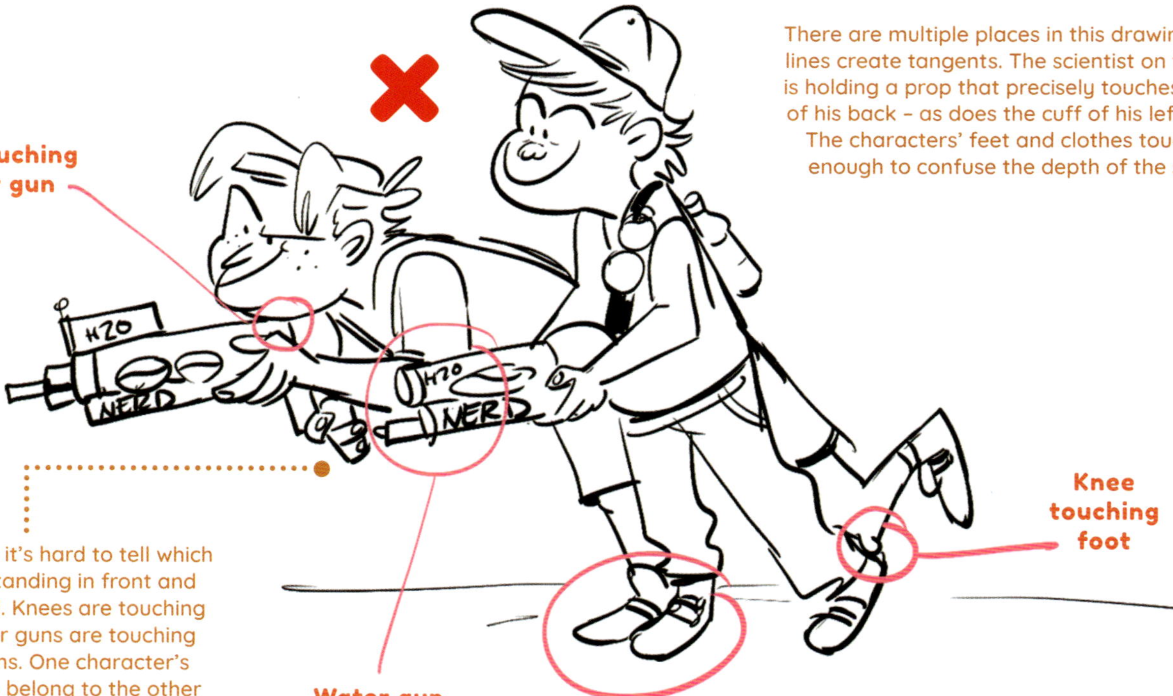

In this example, it's hard to tell which character is standing in front and which is behind. Knees are touching feet and water guns are touching chins and arms. One character's leg appears to belong to the other character at first glance. When two characters are next to each other, it's important that their overall silhouette still reads clearly.

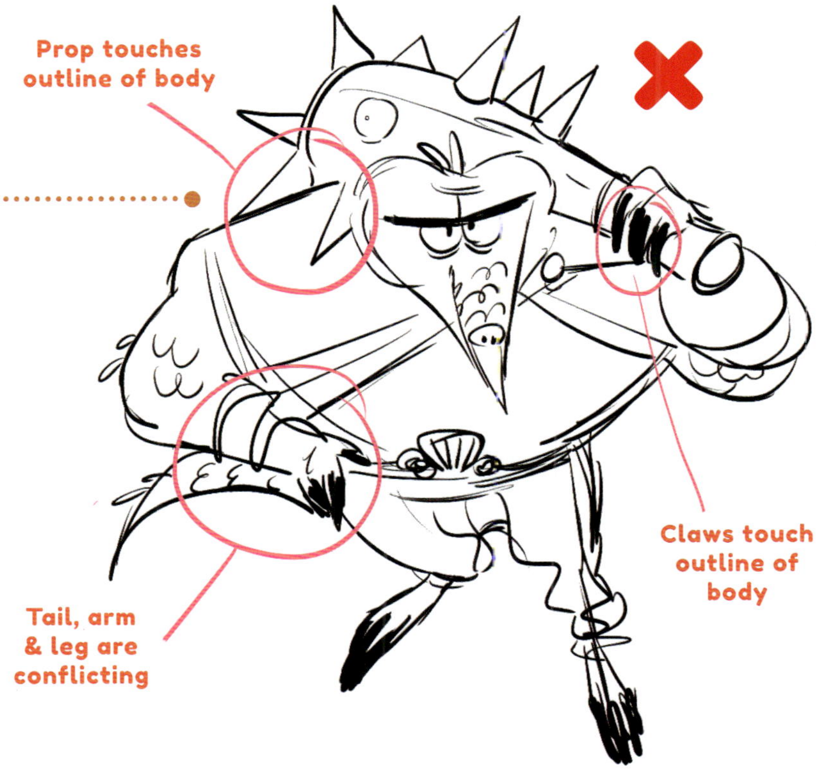

There are three tangents in this image. The spiky club confuses the character's silhouette because it sits flush against his shoulder. The claws on his hands intersect awkwardly with the lines of his leg and shoulder, not quite overlapping enough to be clear. The line of his tail conflicts with his arm and leg, making that area difficult to interpret.

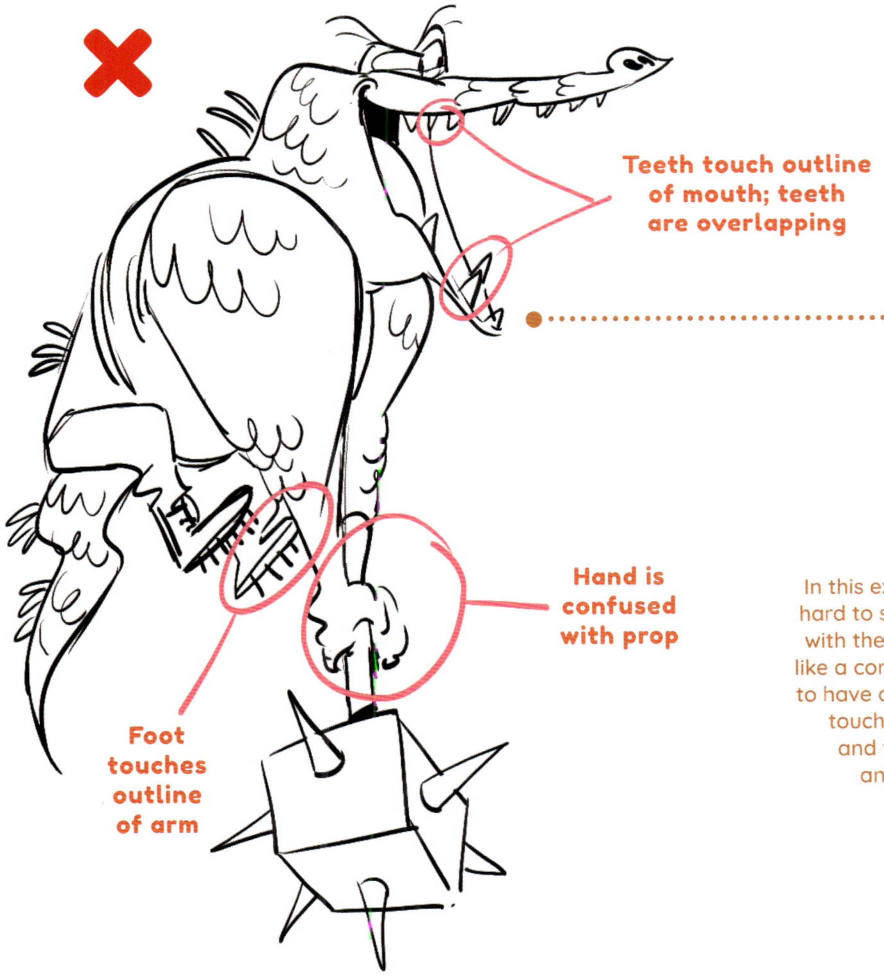

In this example, the tensions of the pose are hard to see. The handle of the weapon aligns with the character's arm in a way that looks like a comical mistake – at a glance, he seems to have a club for a hand! The toe of one foot touches the line of the foreground arm, and the teeth conflict with each other and with the outline of the mouth.

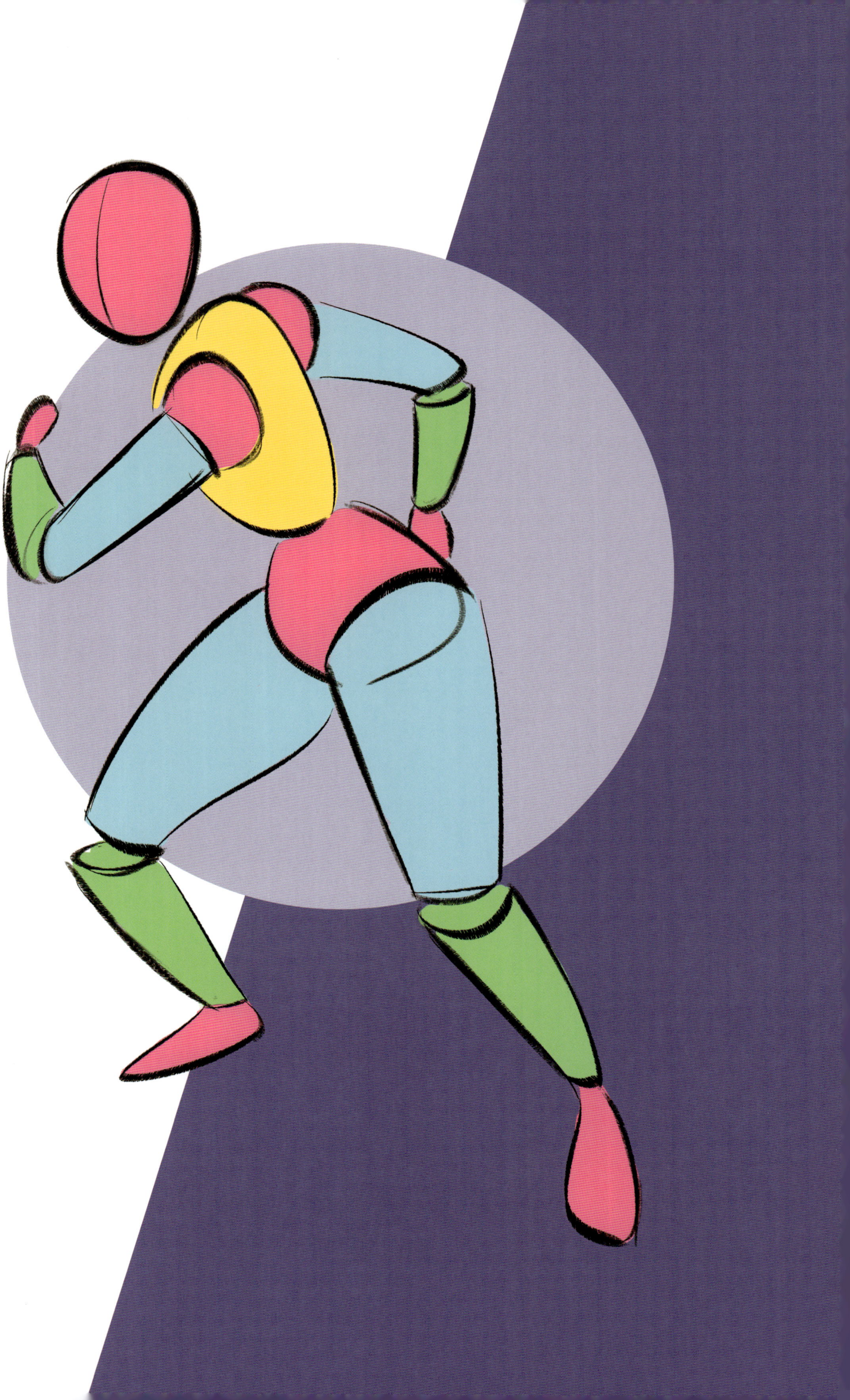

Image by Kenneth Anderson

FIGURE BASICS

ANATOMY OVERVIEW
PAGE 86

CONSTRUCTION & BASIC SHAPES
PAGE 90

DIFFERENT BODY TYPES
PAGE 94

EXAGGERATION OF FORM
PAGE 98

ANATOMY OVERVIEW

Kenneth Anderson

Human anatomy is one of the fundamental building blocks of all character design, with human characters being abundant in cartoons, games, illustrated books, and comics. Even when designing animal characters, there is a good chance they will be anthropomorphized or take some cues from human anatomy. Why is this? As human beings, we relate best to characters that also appear human or can express themselves in a human-like manner. Therefore, designing characters would prove difficult without a strong knowledge of human anatomy.

Every human body is different and there is no universal rule that applies to one and all, yet that has not stopped people idealizing the human form throughout history. The Ancient Egyptians used standardized proportions of eighteen fists, from a figure's hairline to the bottom of their feet, in their depictions of people. Polykleitos' *Doryphoros* sculpture is an example of Ancient Greek idealized human proportions from the high Classical period, the sculpture's head being a ratio of 1:7 to the body. Leonardo da Vinci's *Vitruvian Man* presents a later idealized form, showcasing da Vinci's belief in the mathematical nature of human proportion. In more modern examples, the anatomist and artist Paul Richer suggested an average height of seven and a half heads for an adult, while the artists Andrew Loomis and George Bridgman suggested eight.

Keep in mind that these ideals are based on particular cultures from distinct periods in history. In truth, there are a range of head-to-body ratios that look and feel right for realistic human anatomy. As a character designer, you can play with these ideas without feeling bound by them – use them as guides and not laws. The key is to think in terms of the size of the head in proportion to the rest of the figure, knowing that natural human proportions will fit, on average, into a particular range. This chapter will show you some simple foundations of human anatomy and how it is applied to character design.

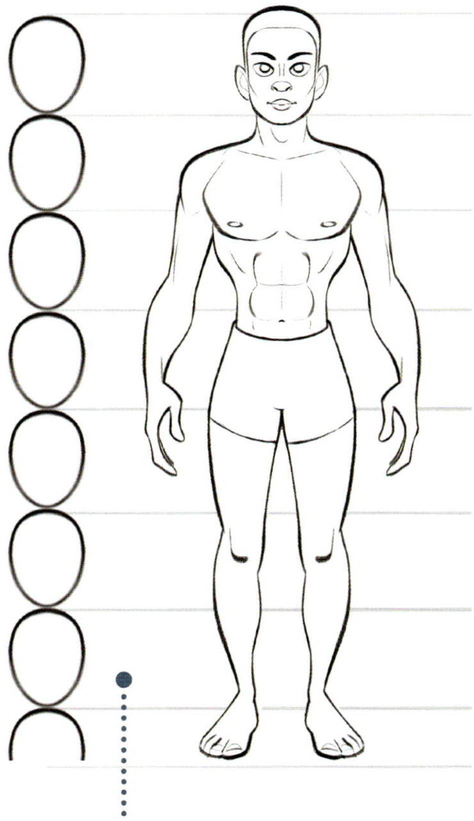

This "archetypal" male has a height of seven and a half heads. Note his wider shoulder-to-hip ratio compared to the female figure.

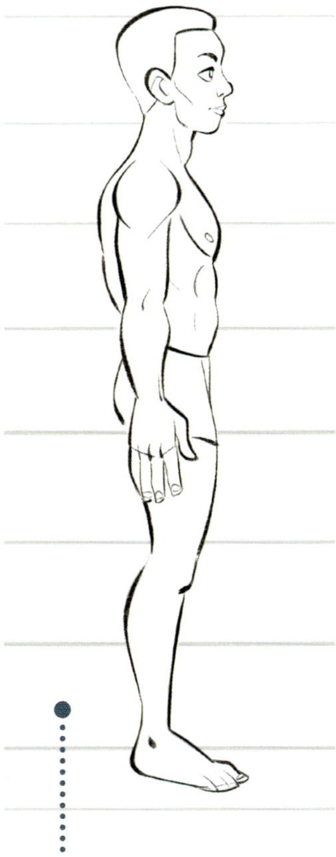

When turning a character in space, keeping the established head-to-body ratio in mind can help maintain consistency.

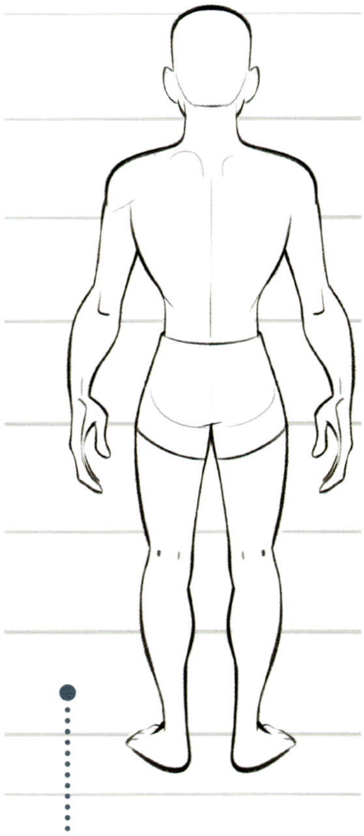

The width of the latissimus dorsi (the large wing-shaped muscles on the back) is pronounced here and adds to the width of the shoulders.

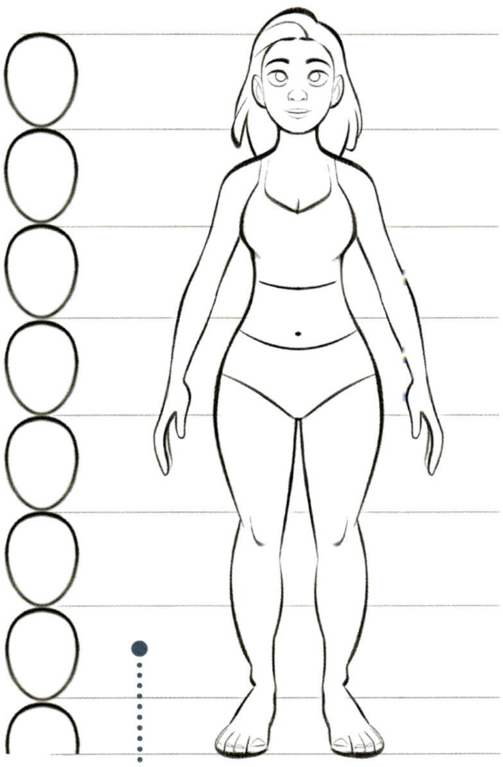

This "archetypal" female is also seven and a half heads in height. Note how the heads are slightly smaller than the male heads to account for average size differences between the male and female body.

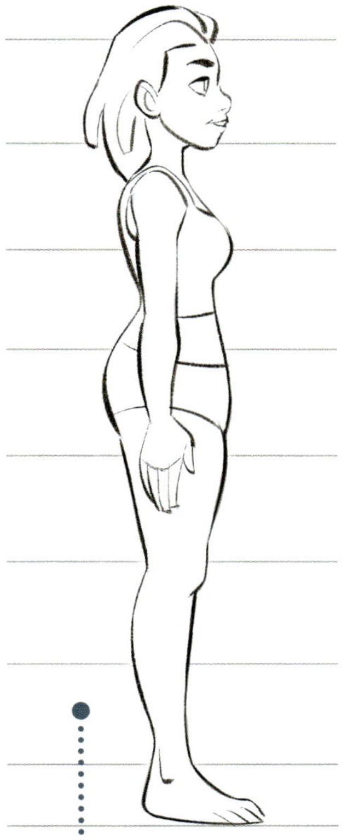

With a side view, the differences in archetypal male and female anatomy become more apparent.

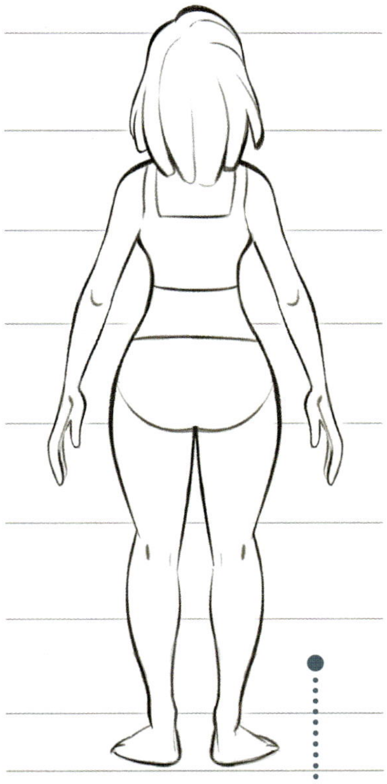

While there are differences in male and female anatomy, it is clear there are also major similarities.

Human variables

What other variables can come into play? A good rule to remember is that the younger the character, the fewer "head-heights" they will have. This is because as people grow, the size of the body increases in relation to the head. Besides the obvious anatomical differences, a male body will generally tend toward more muscle mass, while a female body will likely have a higher natural fat percentage.

Hip-to-shoulder ratio is another key factor to keep in mind, with men tending toward broad shoulders and thinner hips, and women tending toward wider hips and thinner shoulders. It is also true that, on average, men are taller than women. And don't forget that some people do not fall into the typical categories - those with restricted growth, for example, will be shorter and differently proportioned.

Bone, muscle & fat

Human anatomy is complex, so it can be helpful to simplify the figure by thinking about it in three parts. First, the skeleton, which gives the body structure. Second, the muscles, which allow the body to move as well as change its shape. And finally, body fat, which serves its own purpose but also alters the shape of the body, depending on the amount and distribution.

As a rule, bones do not bend or squash, while muscles can stretch and bulge depending on whether they are flexed or not, and fat can only respond to the actions of the skeleton and muscles underneath it. Key anatomical landmarks such as the elbows, knees, rib cage, and spine can all help, alongside the major muscle groups, in defining the overall shape of a character.

The skeleton

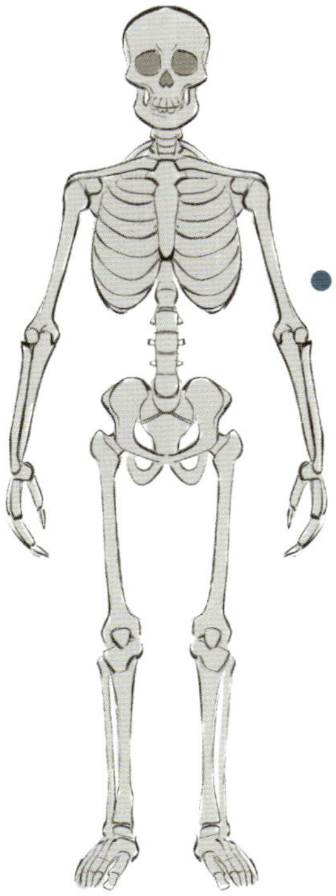

The human skeleton is very complex. It's a good idea to copy it from reference as practice.

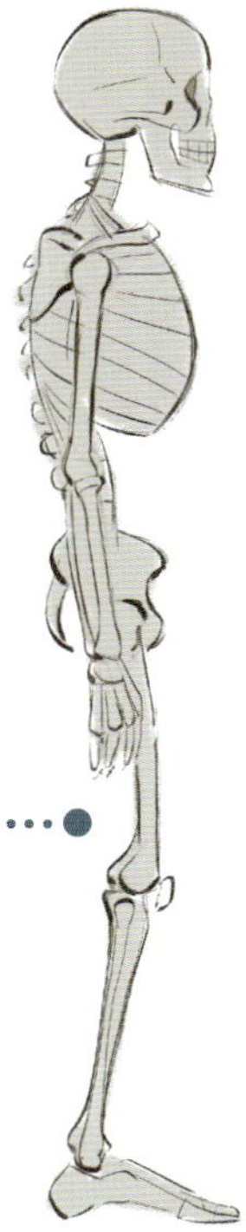

Note how the skeleton forms the foundation of the structure of the human body.

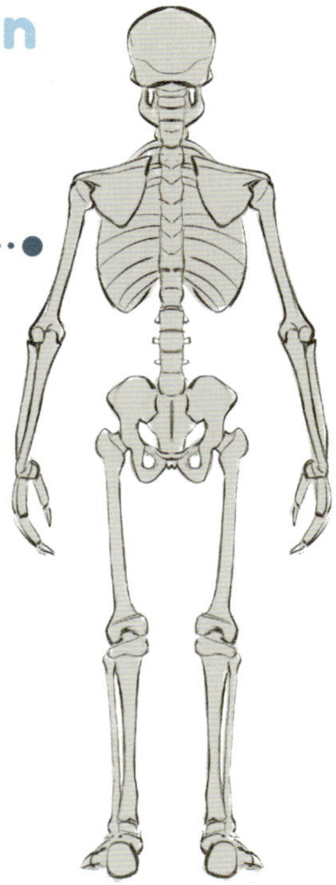

Look at key points on the skeleton, such as the spine and rib cage. Some of these areas are still noticeable even when overlaid with muscles and skin.

Muscle structure

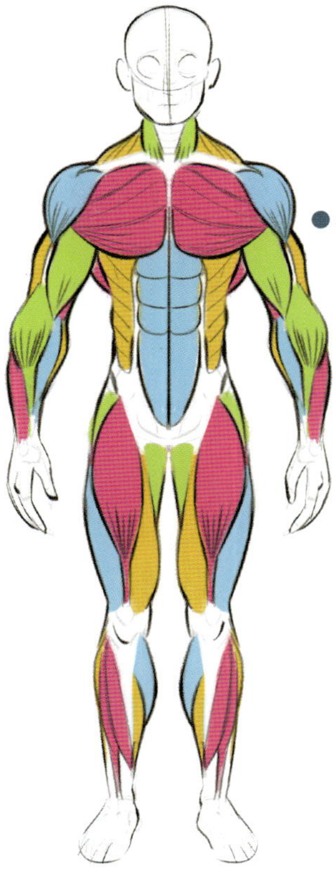

Just like the skeleton, the muscles in the body are complex. Try breaking them down into larger overall masses. They are exaggerated here for clarity.

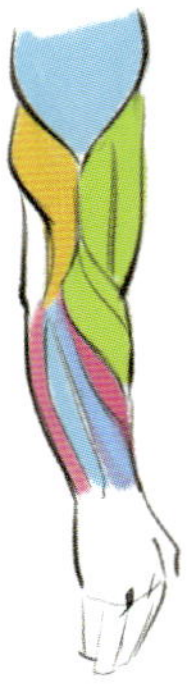

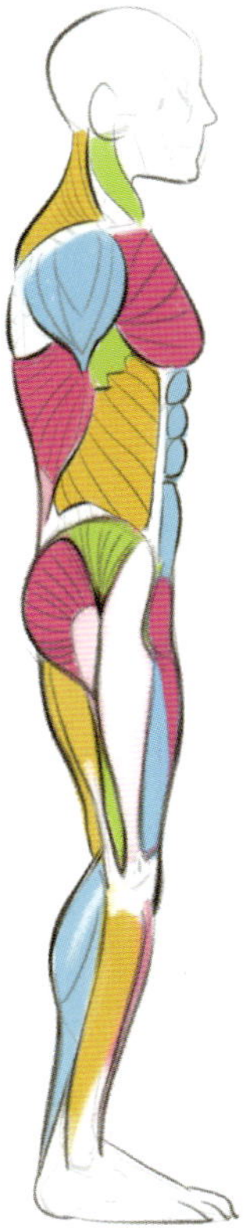

The effect the muscles have in altering the shape of the body is most apparent from the side view. Note how they create the feeling of "straights versus curves" (see more on page 70) in the legs and arms.

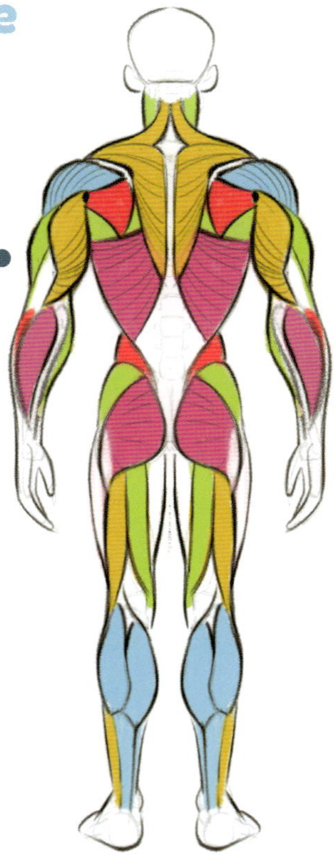

Notice the complexity of the back muscles, even in this simplified diagram. A good understanding of what's happening underneath the skin will really help when it comes to stylizing a character.

Body fat

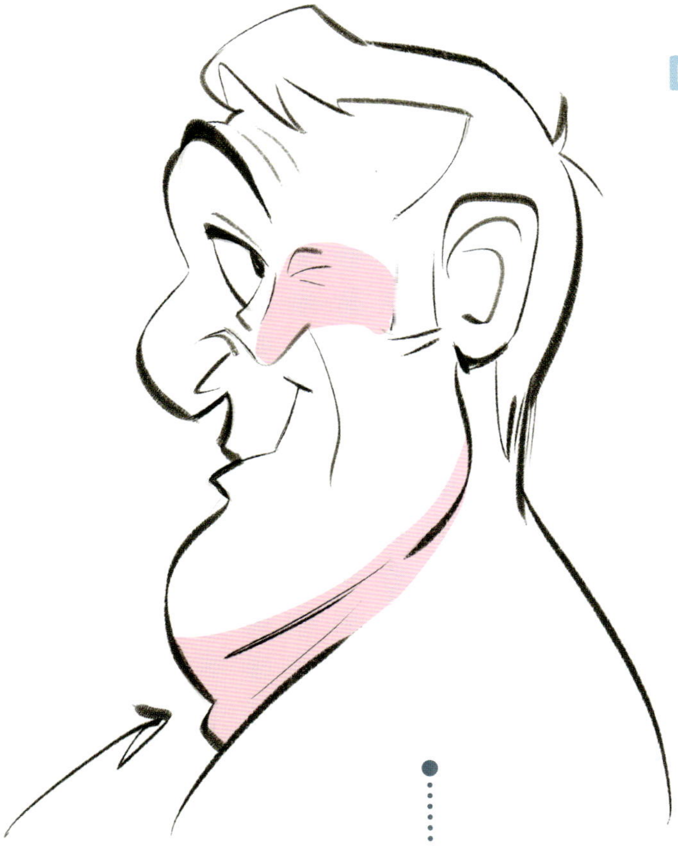

Underlying fat deposits can change the shape of a character. Here they affect the area of the chin and neck.

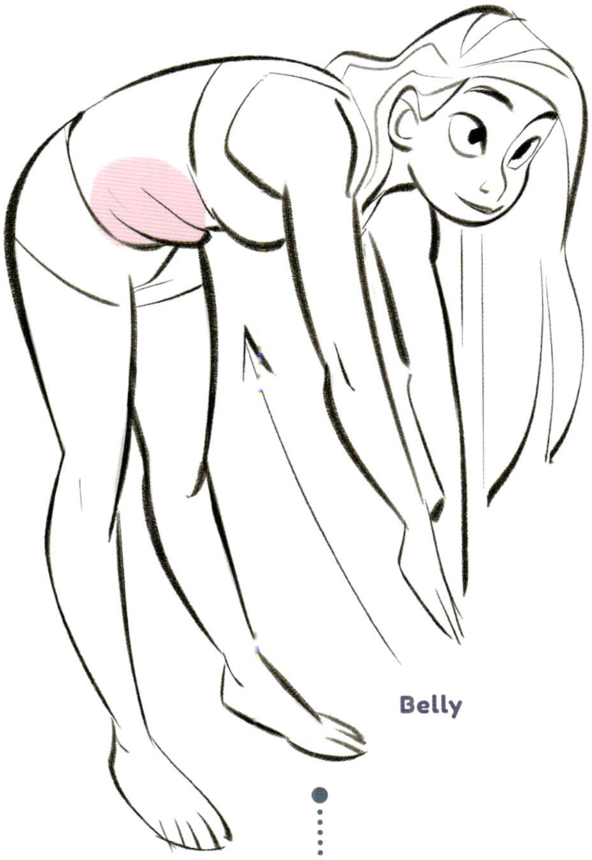

Even a little bit of body fat can affect shape, especially when it reacts to the movement of the body.

USE REFERENCE

Reference is essential when designing realistic characters with accurate anatomy. The human body is so complex, it can be difficult to memorize all the details. Over time and with lots of practice, knowledge of anatomy will become second nature, and the need for reference will become less as you shift your reference from the real world to your memory. But it's always good to refer back to reference to refresh and fix bad drawing habits!

Remember, there is no shame in using reference. In fact, it should be encouraged, particularly if you find yourself stuck with a particular point of weakness in your abilities. Reference can be particularly useful for the more intricate parts of a character, such as the hands, feet, and face. Style will influence your interpretation of anatomy – the more cartoon-like you go, the less realism you need to worry about. That said, even the most stylized, rubber-hose-armed character must adhere to some rules to look human!

The best references are anatomy books, photographs, observation, life drawing, and a good mirror! But do not rely on your own body for reference too much – expand your reference pool for a wide variety of human anatomy.

CONSTRUCTION & BASIC SHAPES

Kenneth Anderson

The human figure is complex, and distilling it into a strong character design is no easy task – especially when you want to stylize the anatomy in the process. This is why knowledge of anatomy is essential to a character designer – trying to learn anatomy while simultaneously stylizing it will not yield good results. It's hard to stylize something without fully understanding it first.

Thankfully there are tried-and-tested methods to make the process easier. It helps to break the figure down into basic simple shapes first to create a foundation upon which to draw. With any design process, a "general to specific" approach works best: going from the macro "big picture" to the micro "small picture." Getting bogged down in anatomy details before establishing a strong foundation of gesture, pose, and underlying body mass can be very counter-productive.

Looking at the human figure, it naturally breaks down into simpler masses: the head, chest, pelvis, shoulders, arms, and legs. The arms and legs can be broken down further still, into upper and lower limbs, plus the hands and feet. Playing with the proportions and shapes of these main elements can easily create a variety of different character body types without worrying about the complexities of anatomical details. Just remember the overall big picture first!

Breaking up the body also allows you to experiment with one of the fundamentals of good design: contrast. What happens if you make the chest small and the legs really long? Or sketch a large body and small legs? Avoid pushing too far, though. Imagine a character with a tiny body and a head three times the size. It may have good size contrast, but does it work as a human character? Does it feel right? It might work in very particular design scenarios, but probably not in most cases. This is why a good knowledge of anatomy and a general understanding of human proportion is essential – it helps you to recognize when you have pushed a character beyond its breaking point.

You can also use curves, angles, and straight lines to your advantage. Combining these can create volume and rhythm in anatomy, and can simulate the natural "straight versus curved" shapes found throughout the human body and in nature. You are no longer simply experimenting with the proportion of body parts, but building on a strong foundation, using shape and design language to push anatomy further toward visual appeal.

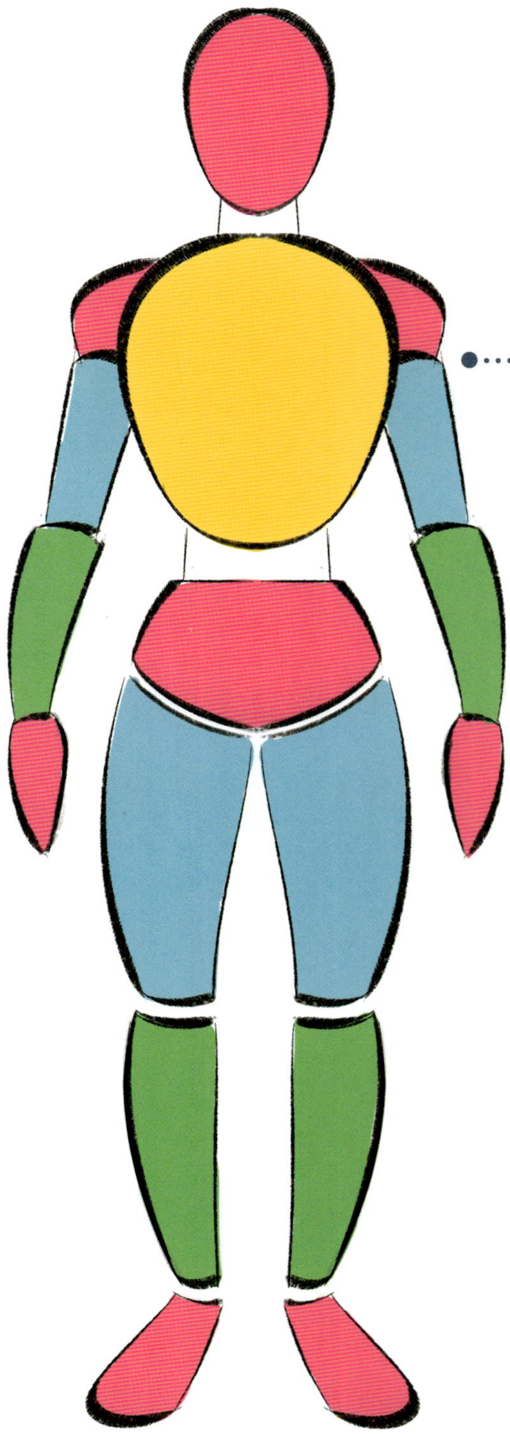

The human body naturally breaks down into these basic shapes.

Simplified male figures

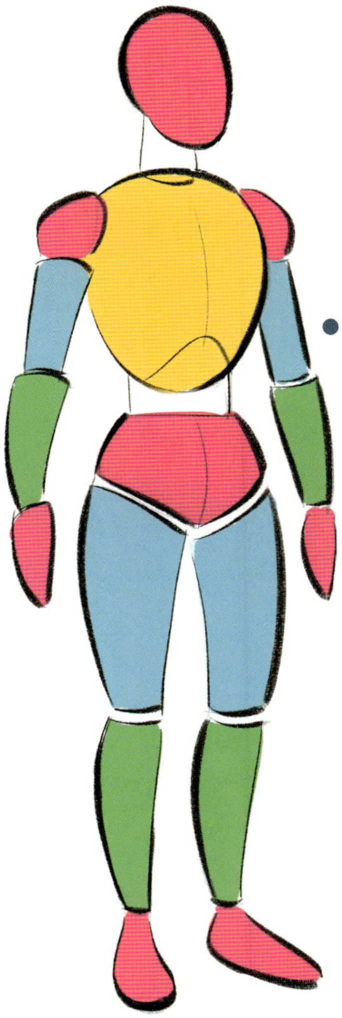

Simplifying a character like this can help you turn complex anatomy in space, especially in three-quarter views.

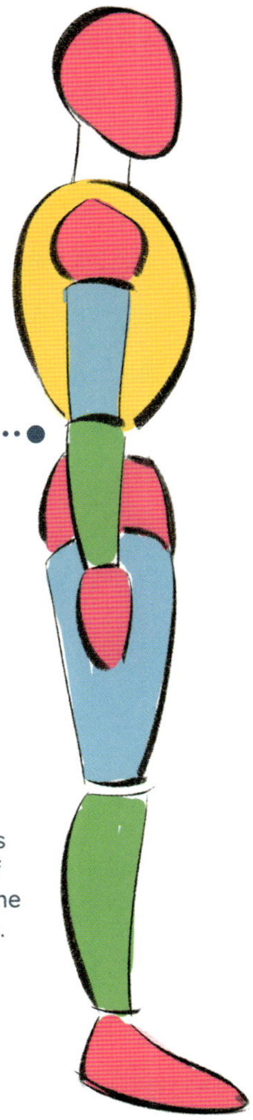

Note how the basic shapes simplify the complexity of the anatomy, made up of the skeleton, muscles, and fat.

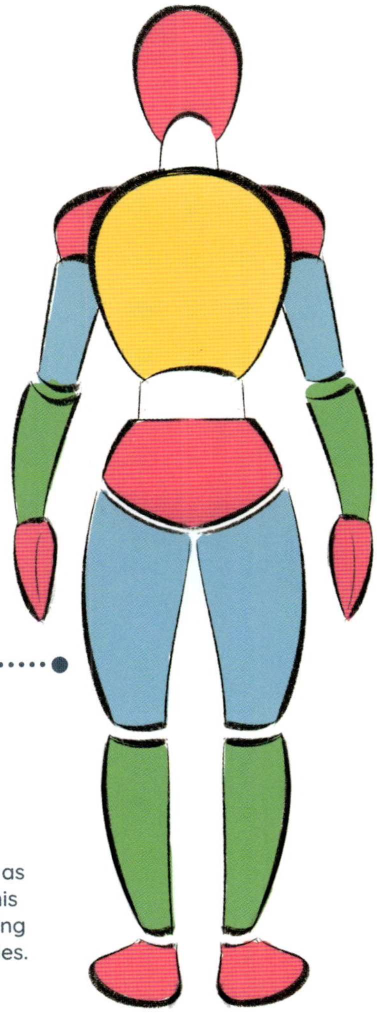

Think of these shapes as three-dimensional. This will help when visualizing anatomy from all angles.

Simplified female figures

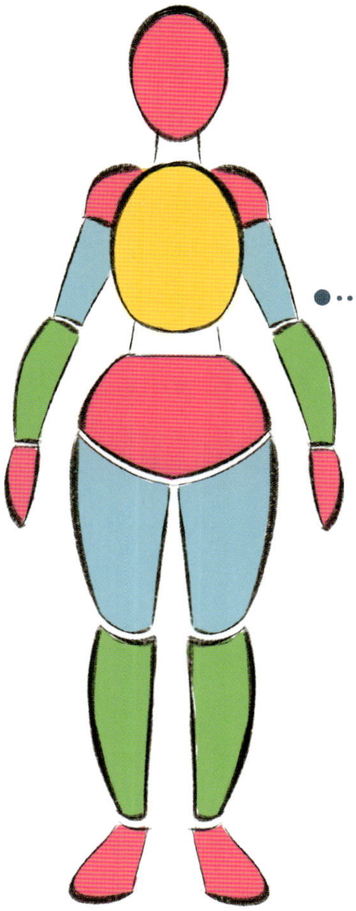

In general, the basic shapes that make up female anatomy will differ in proportion to those of a male, though they are essentially the same.

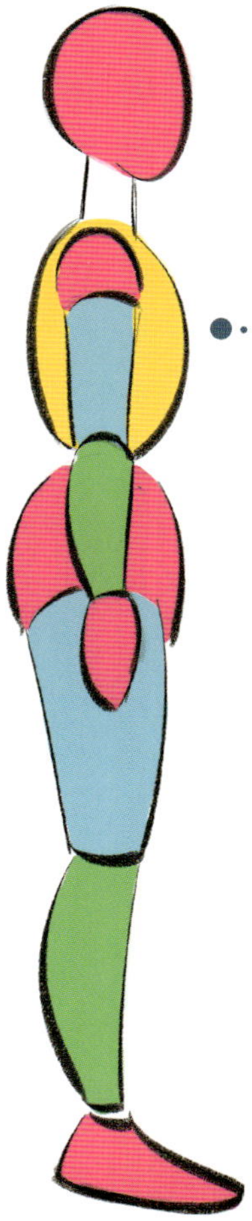

When breaking a character down like this, don't become too distracted by details such as the shape of the female chest. That can easily be drawn on top afterward.

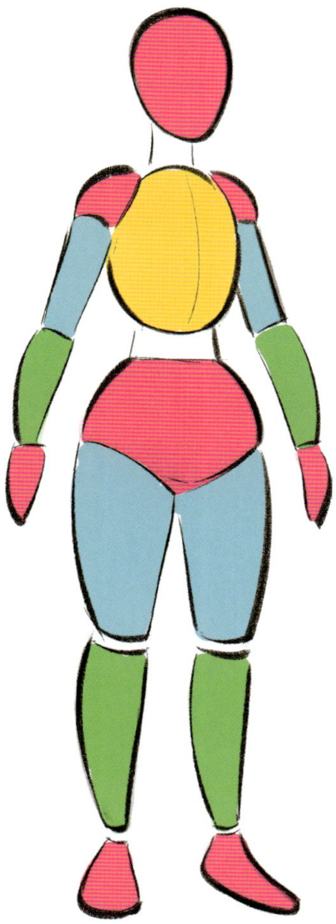

See how these shapes turn slightly differently from the male character, mainly in the chest and hips, which are more rounded here.

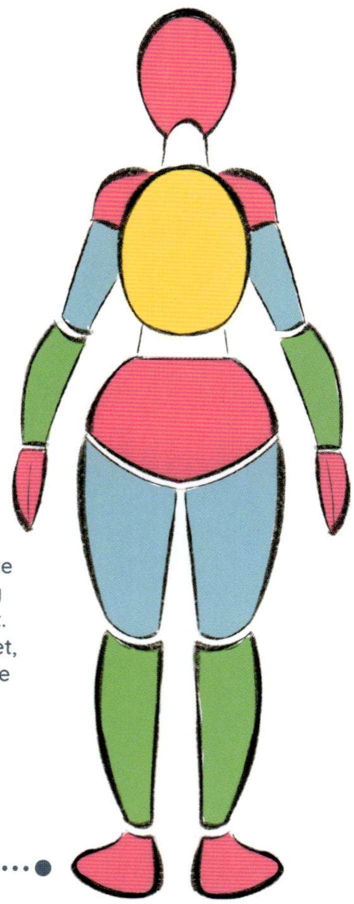

The shapes and silhouette from the back generally mirror those of the front. The exception is in the feet, where you can clearly see the angles of the heels.

Simplified figures in action

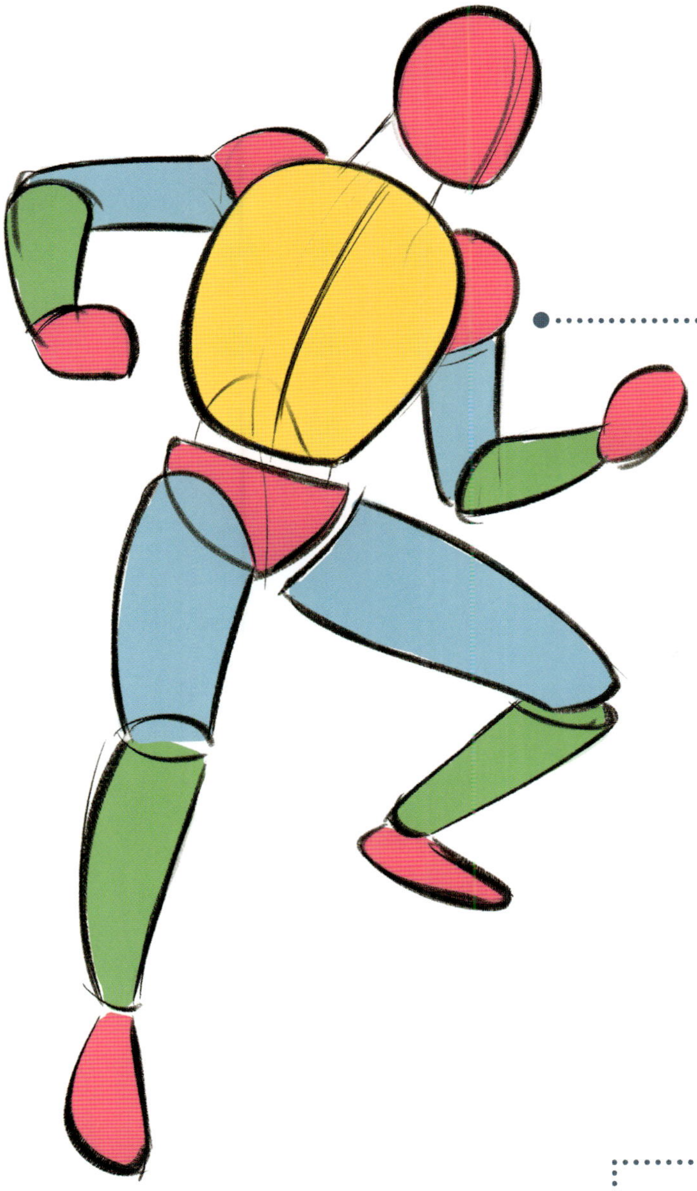

Using these basic shapes can help when constructing a character in an action pose. The simplicity allows you to focus on the movement and gesture.

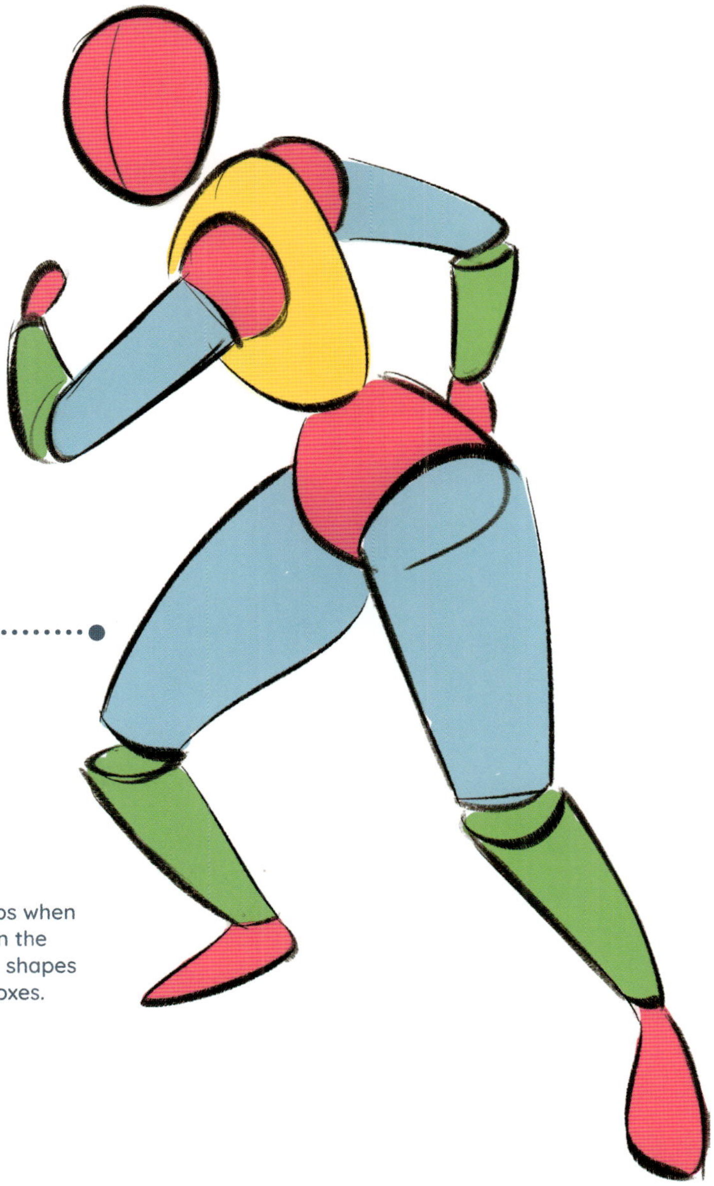

Using basic shapes also helps when drawing foreshortening in the anatomy. Think of the basic shapes as tubes, spheres, and boxes.

DIFFERENT BODY TYPES
Kenneth Anderson

Human bodies come in all shapes and sizes. Take a look at people in the street and you will see a variety of different body types – this is great reference for character designers! There are many reasons why you might want to experiment with character body types and push them in all directions. It may suit a particular story or character, for example. The main reason, however, is visual interest: contrast is what makes things interesting. If you only draw classical or archetypal body types, all your characters will look the same and will soon become boring.

You can also borrow ideas from elsewhere to expand the way you think about body types. A common (though controversial) concept, often discussed in the world of bodybuilding, is that of "somatotypes" – generalized body types that have a certain set of characteristics. These are: the ectomorph, characterized by their tall height, long and thin limbs, low body fat level, and thinner shoulders; the mesomorph, with broad shoulders, a larger chest, more muscle mass, and low body fat; and the endomorph, characterized by larger limbs, a wider waist, high muscle mass, but also more body fat.

While these categories might be questionable from a scientific point of view, they can be useful for character designers as a way to think about different body types when drawing. The key thing to take away from this are the three fundamental factors that dictate how the human body looks: the length, thickness, and proportions of the skeleton; the size of the muscles; and the amount of overall body fat. Considering these three elements, you can create almost any human body type imaginable.

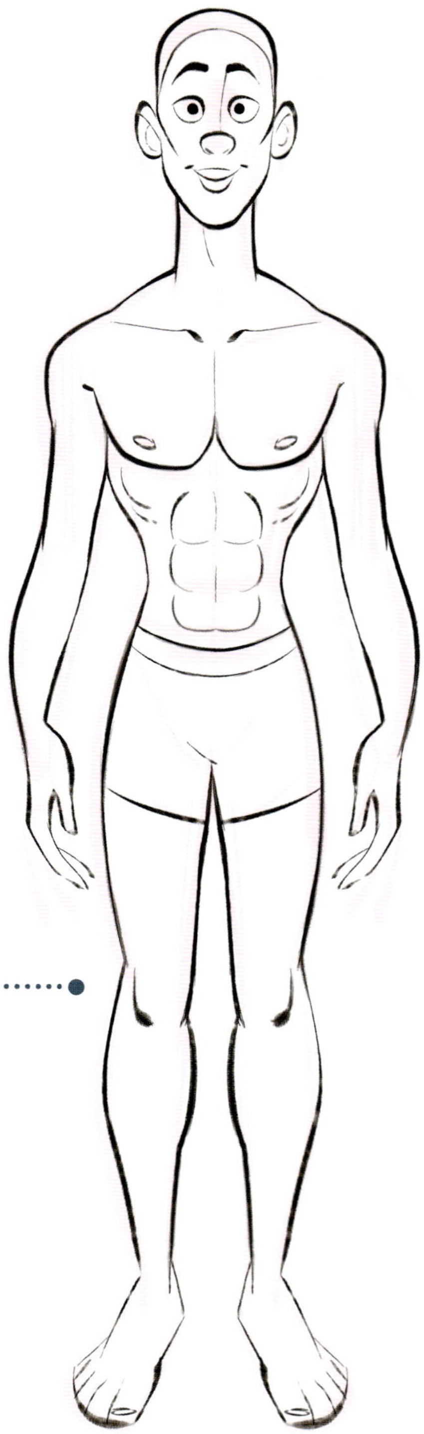

The **ectomorph** is the stereotypical skinny character, with low fat, lean muscles, and small joints.

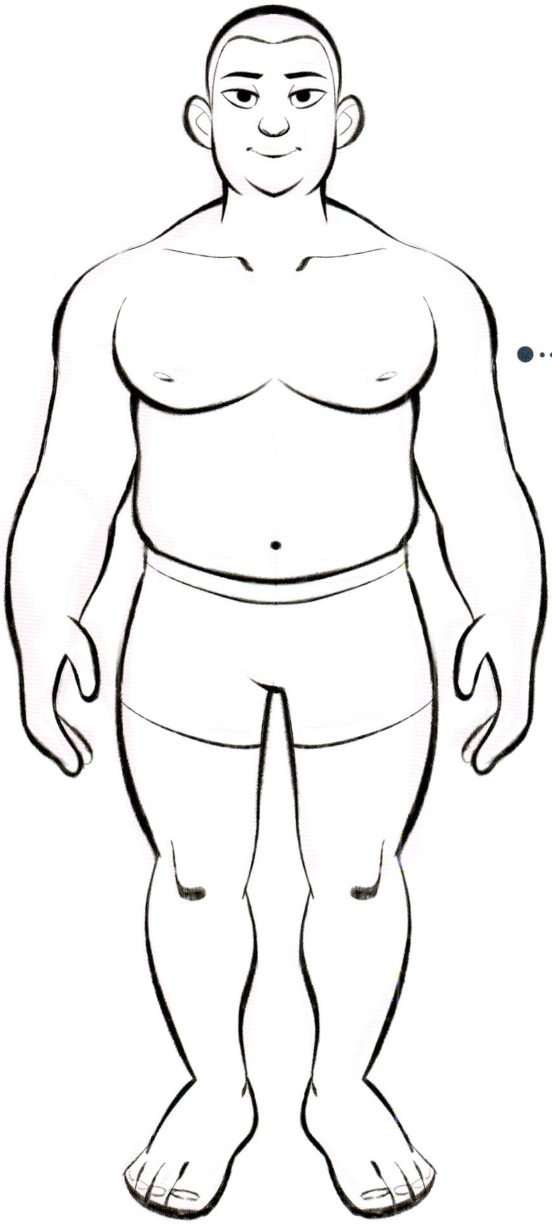

Generally shorter than the other types, the **endomorph** can be muscular but tends toward storing body fat, giving them a rounder, softer body type.

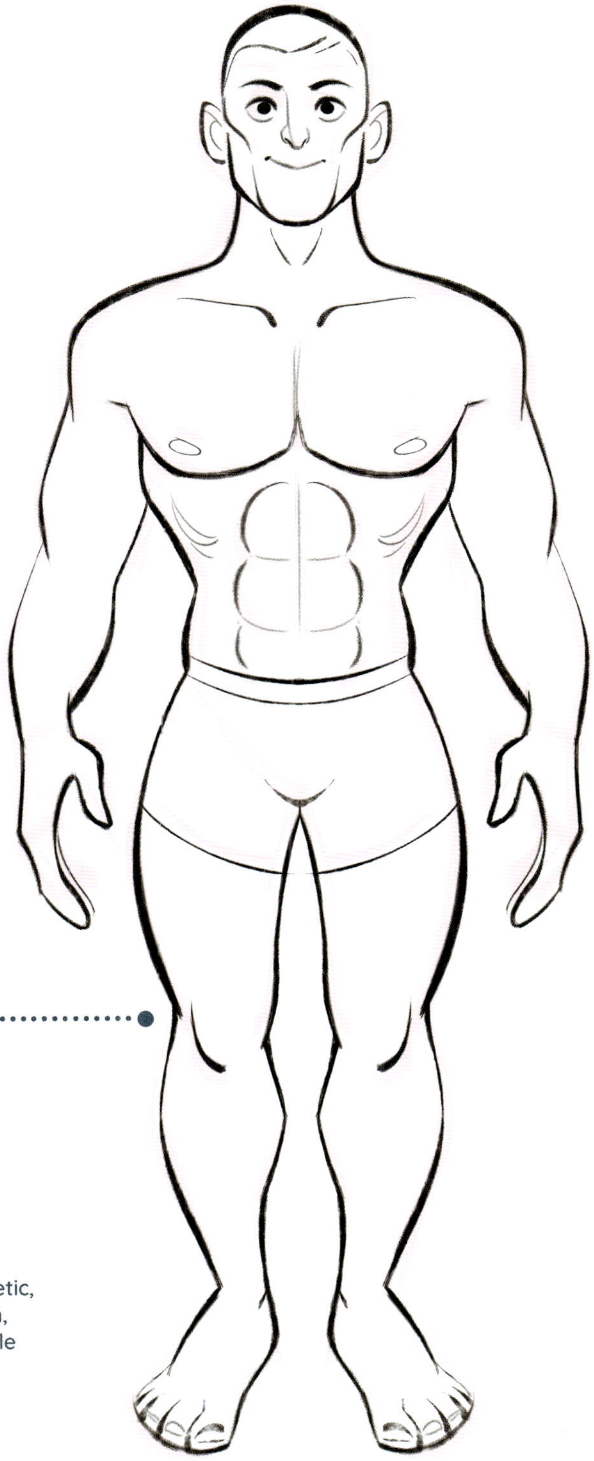

The **mesomorph** is athletic, well-muscled, and lean, with the archetypal male shoulder-to-hip ratio.

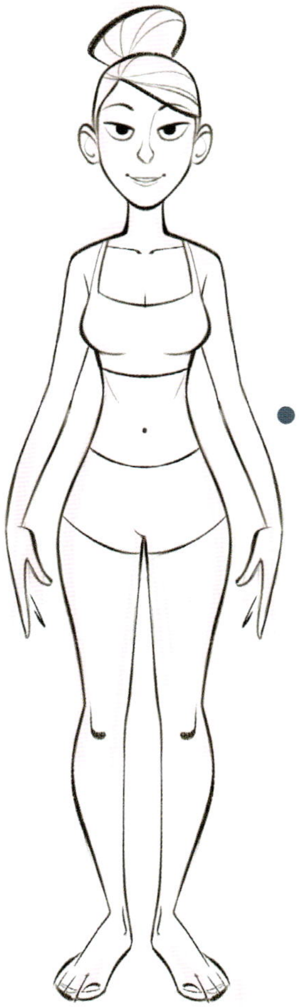

A character with very low body weight can have a more prominent bone structure and won't have much definition based on their body fat or muscles.

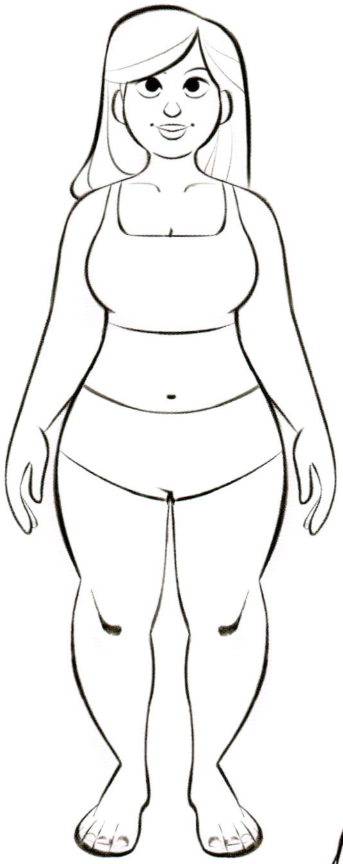

A fuller female figure will often have a more emphasized hip-to-shoulder ratio – but keep in mind that different people store fat differently.

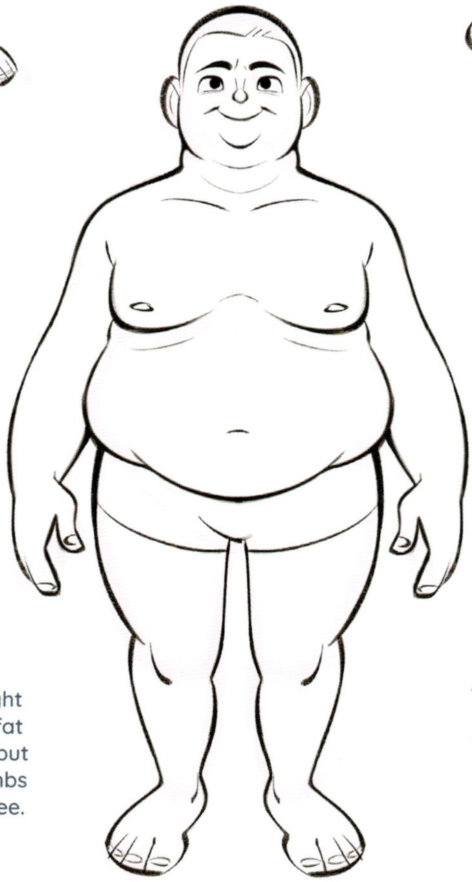

A man who is overweight will likely store excess fat around his midsection, but it will also affect the limbs and face to some degree.

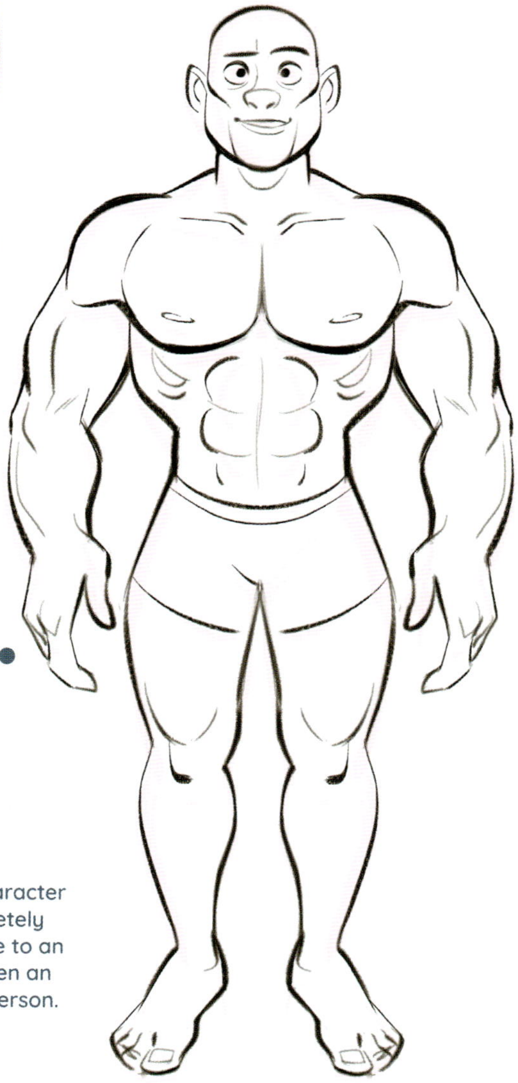

A well-muscled character creates a completely different silhouette to an overweight or even an average-bodied person.

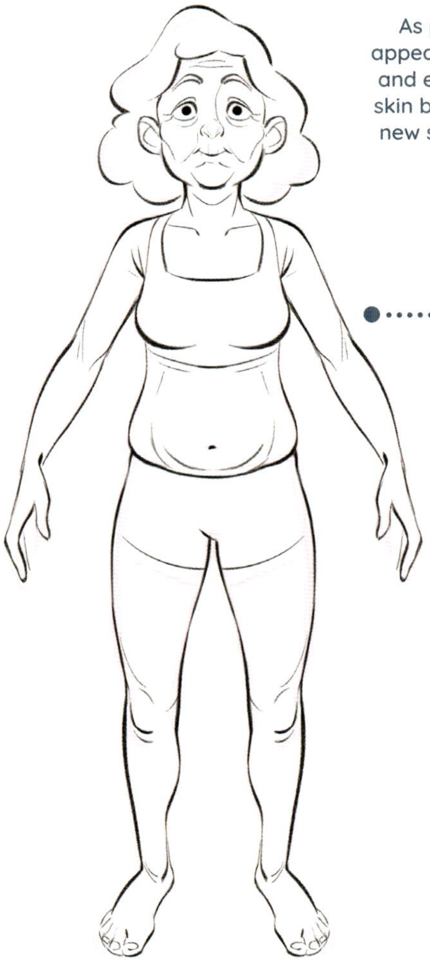

As people age they tend to appear shorter, though the nose and ears continue to grow. The skin becomes less taut, creating new shapes. Learn more about age on page 190.

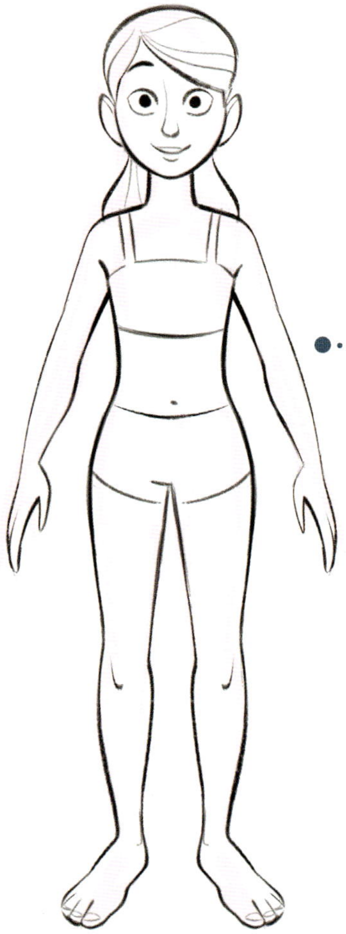

A typical teen often looks like they don't quite fit in their body yet. Their head-heights are somewhere between those of a typical child and an adult.

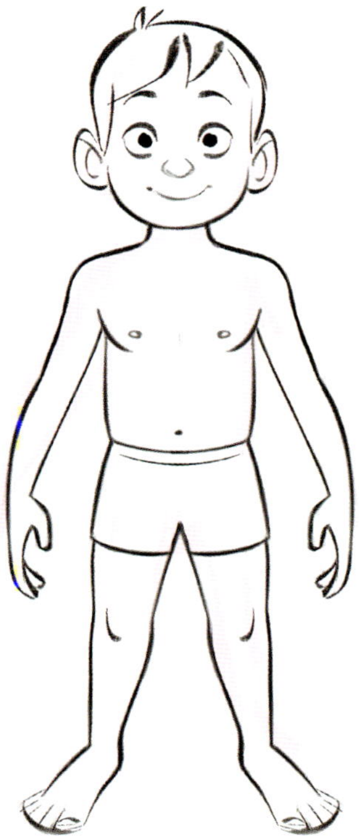

A child will have a lower head-to-body ratio. Note the head size feels a bit larger in comparison to the body.

EXAGGERATION OF FORM

Kenneth Anderson

As a character designer, you have the power to make design choices that make statements and convey ideas. One way to do this is through exaggeration and contrast. Depending on the style, which will set the limits of design, exaggerating design choices can create a visually interesting character. You can begin exploring exaggeration by adding symbolic meaning to your designs through "shape language."

Shape language is grounded in the scientific phenomenon of "contour bias." Contour bias is a human preference toward rounded forms, while angular forms activate an area of the brain linked to fear response. Is it any wonder character designs for preschoolers tend to be rounded and soft, or that "evil" characters often exhibit more angular, triangular design choices? Ultimately, this means you have the power to influence an audience's perception of a design, and therefore a character, on a subconscious level by exaggerating shapes. By emphasizing a character's appearance according to these biases, pushing their forms and proportions to become extremely blocky, or sharp, or round, you can highlight specific qualities of their personality.

A good example of where shape has been used to convey personality is the character of Carl Fredricksen from Pixar's *Up*. His whole design is boxy and square – from his body shape, to his head shape, to the shape of his glasses. He's a square, both in design and personality! Contrast his design with that of Russell, his unexpected sidekick, who is rounded and soft. This is a perfect example of shape language in action. Look at the characters in DreamWorks' *Madagascar* – their shapes are exaggerated and stylized to create memorable designs. Alex the lion is instantly recognizable due to his geometric and perfectly manicured mane.

Nevertheless, a character's form cannot fully convey their personality. A designer can use subconscious cues to generate a feeling in the audience, but a character's personality is ultimately revealed through their acting and performance. You cannot rely on shape language to tell the whole story, but it's a useful tool in your toolbox.

Square design language can encourage the idea of a character as an immovable object, or can hint at their strength.

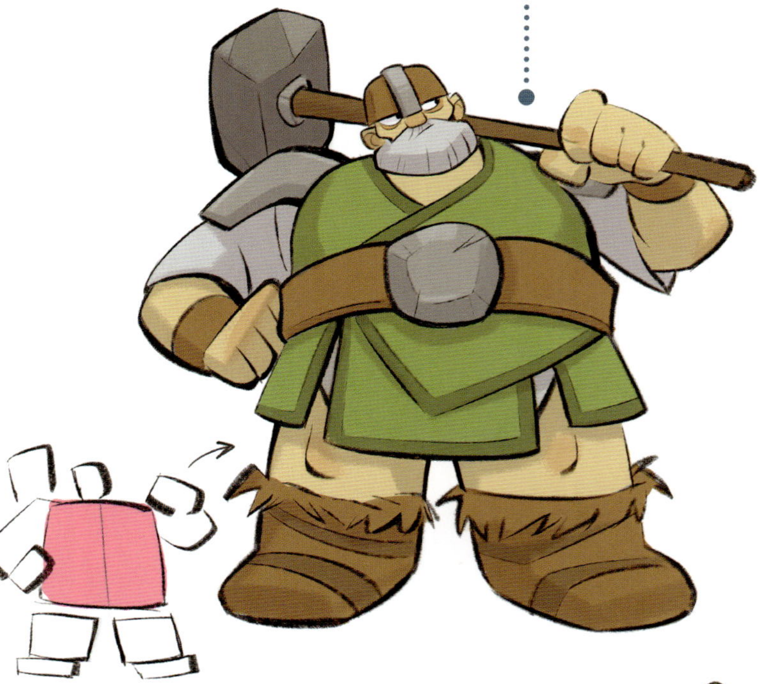

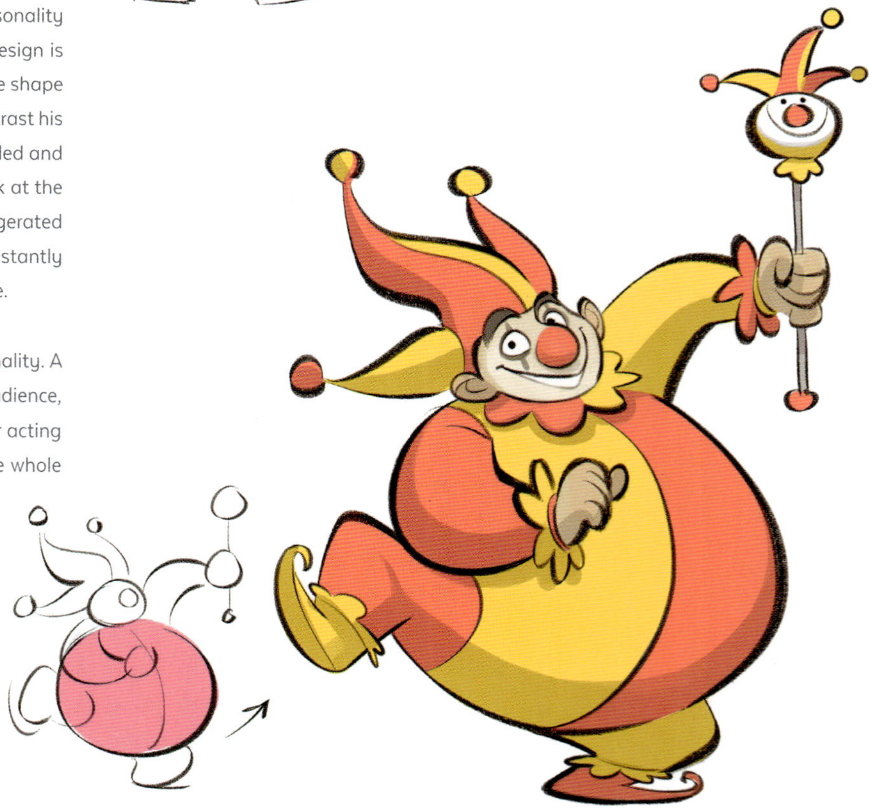

A character with exaggerated circular design language can feel jovial and unthreatening.

Emphasizing triangles in a design can take advantage of contour bias and subconsciously convey an idea of threat, or in this case, perhaps distrust.

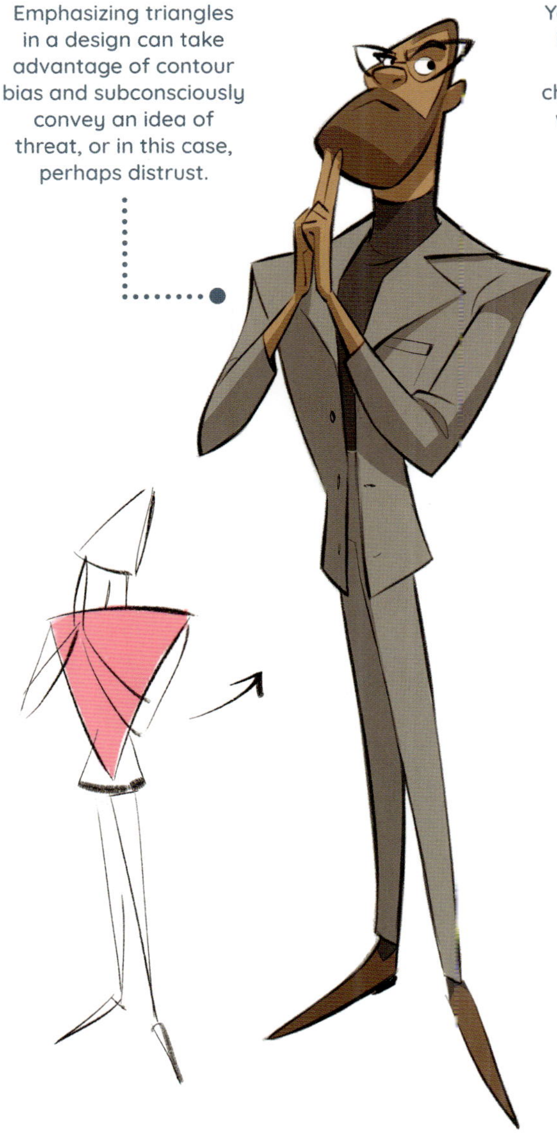

You can combine shapes, but it's best to exaggerate one more dominant type. This character makes a statement with his large, rounded, yet boxy body shape.

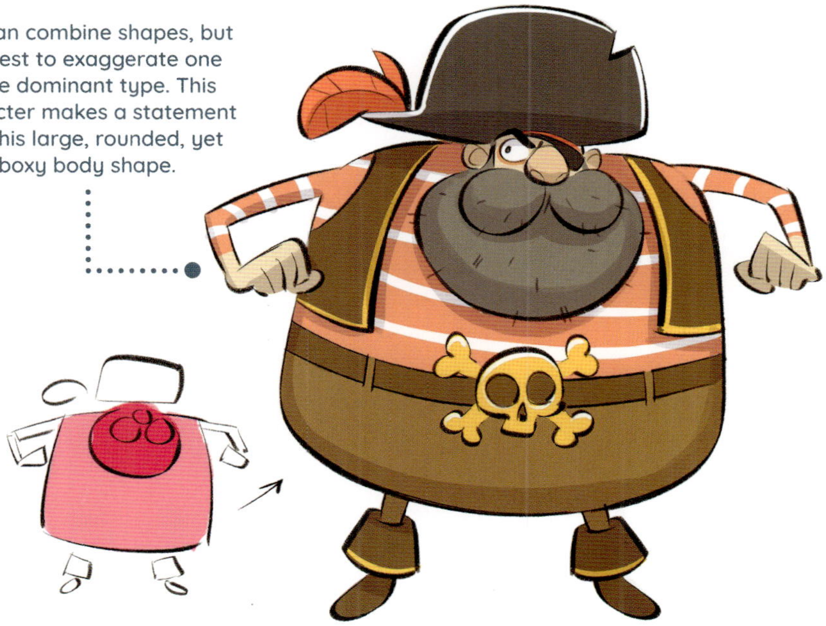

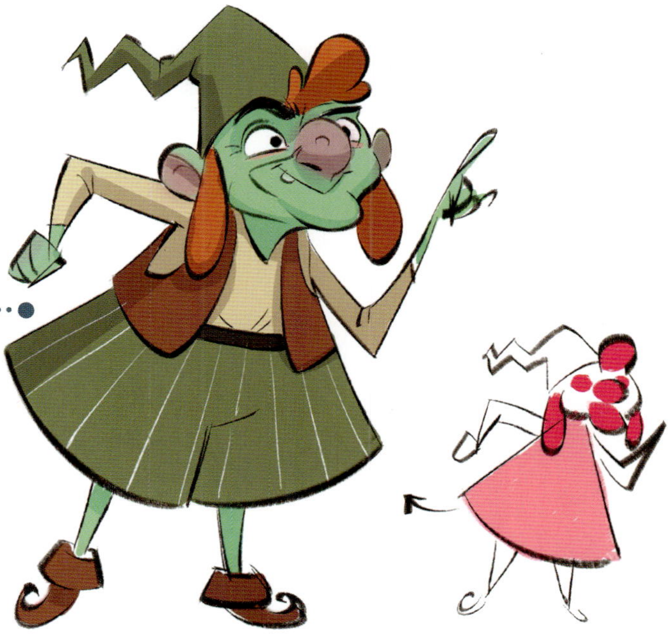

Again, note that one shape, the triangle, is dominant, while the circular forms are smaller and secondary.

SQUASH & STRETCH

"Squash and stretch" is a useful animation principle to keep in mind while designing characters. The human body naturally squashes and stretches as it moves, compressing and expanding areas depending on an action, such as in the belly area or the muscles in the arms or face. Take advantage of this and exaggerate it. Bringing the squash and stretch principle into your work can add believability to a design and suggest a character is flesh and blood, has form, and is not just a drawing or a three-dimensional model. If a character's masses never distort, they will start to look wooden and lifeless.

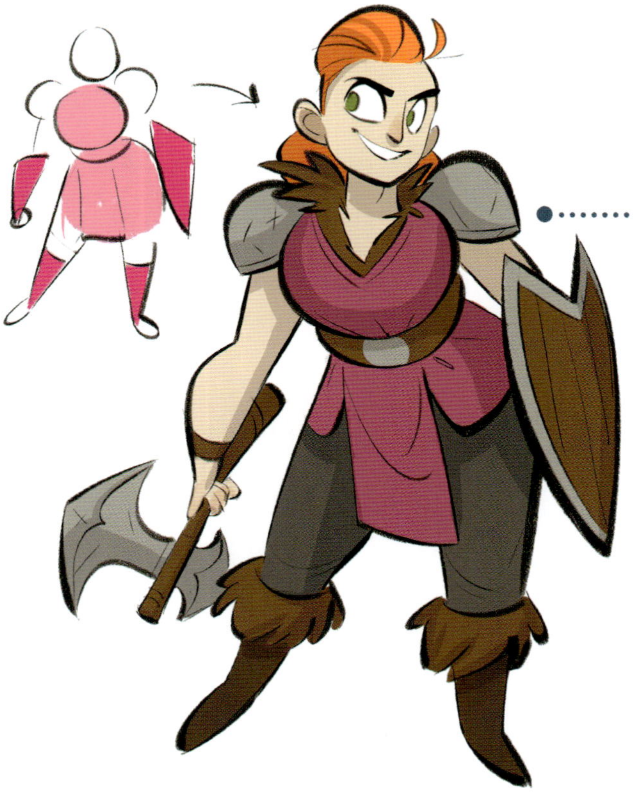

The dominant forms here are rounded, which could suggest an amicable character. The triangular forms found in her weapons and limbs might hint at her more dangerous side!

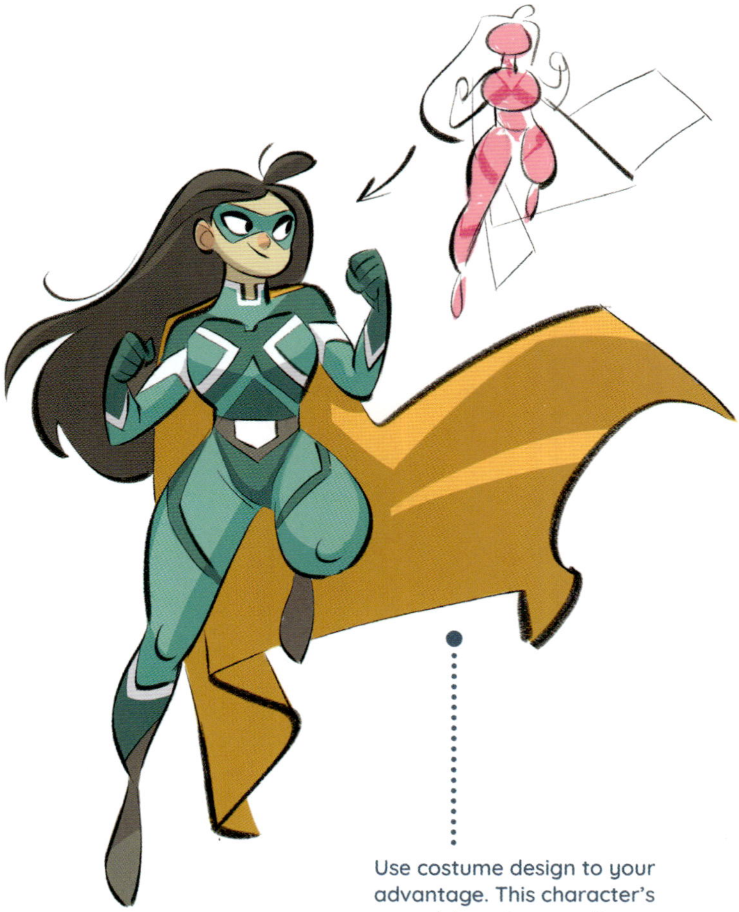

Use costume design to your advantage. This character's squarish costume patterns and angular cape contrast with her rounded anatomy.

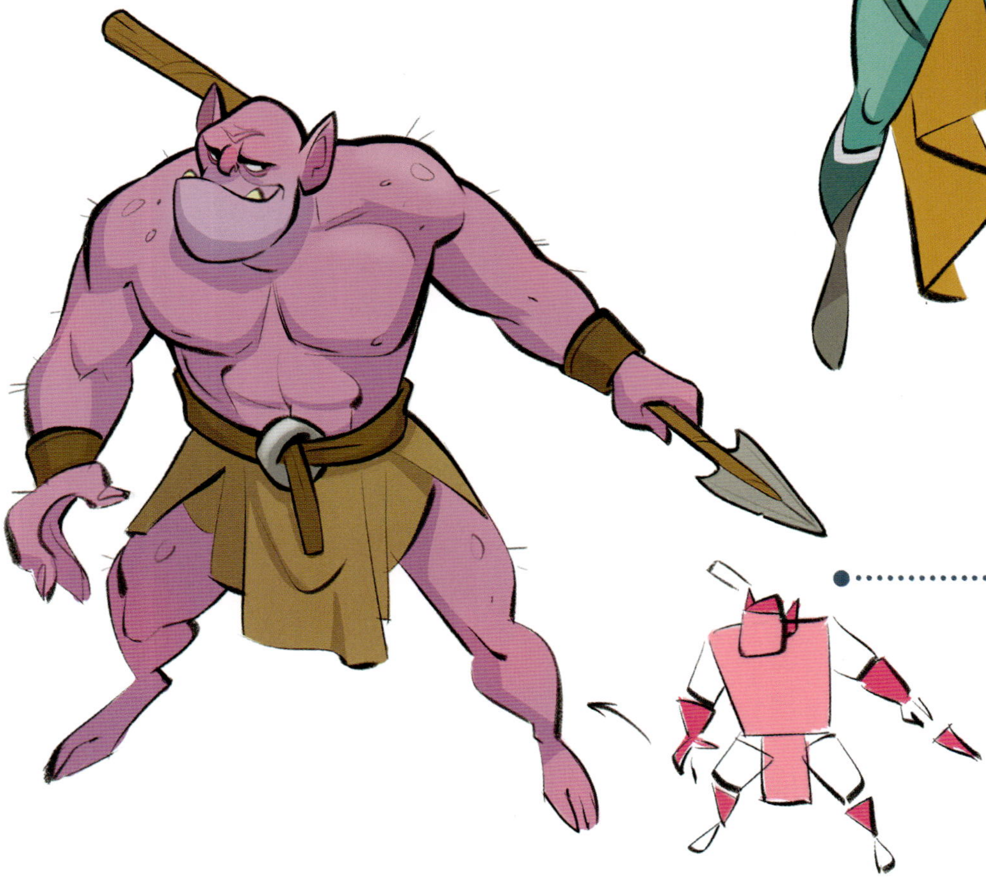

This character looks strong and sturdy due to his squarish body, while the secondary triangular shapes give him a bit of an edge.

When combining more than two shapes, take care to balance them effectively. Experiment with proportion, scale, and dominance of forms to achieve such balance in a design.

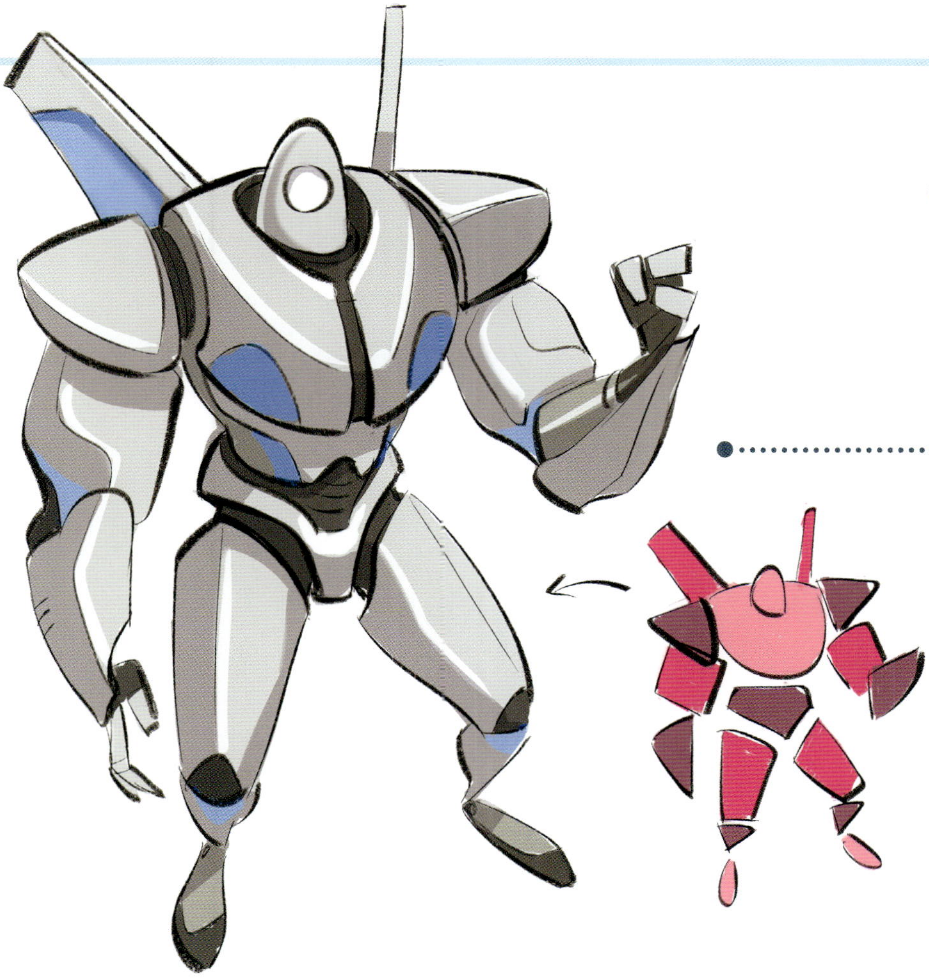

If this character was meant to inspire fear in an audience, it might help to choose less rounded shapes! Instead, it reads more comically, which would work well for a fun kids' TV show.

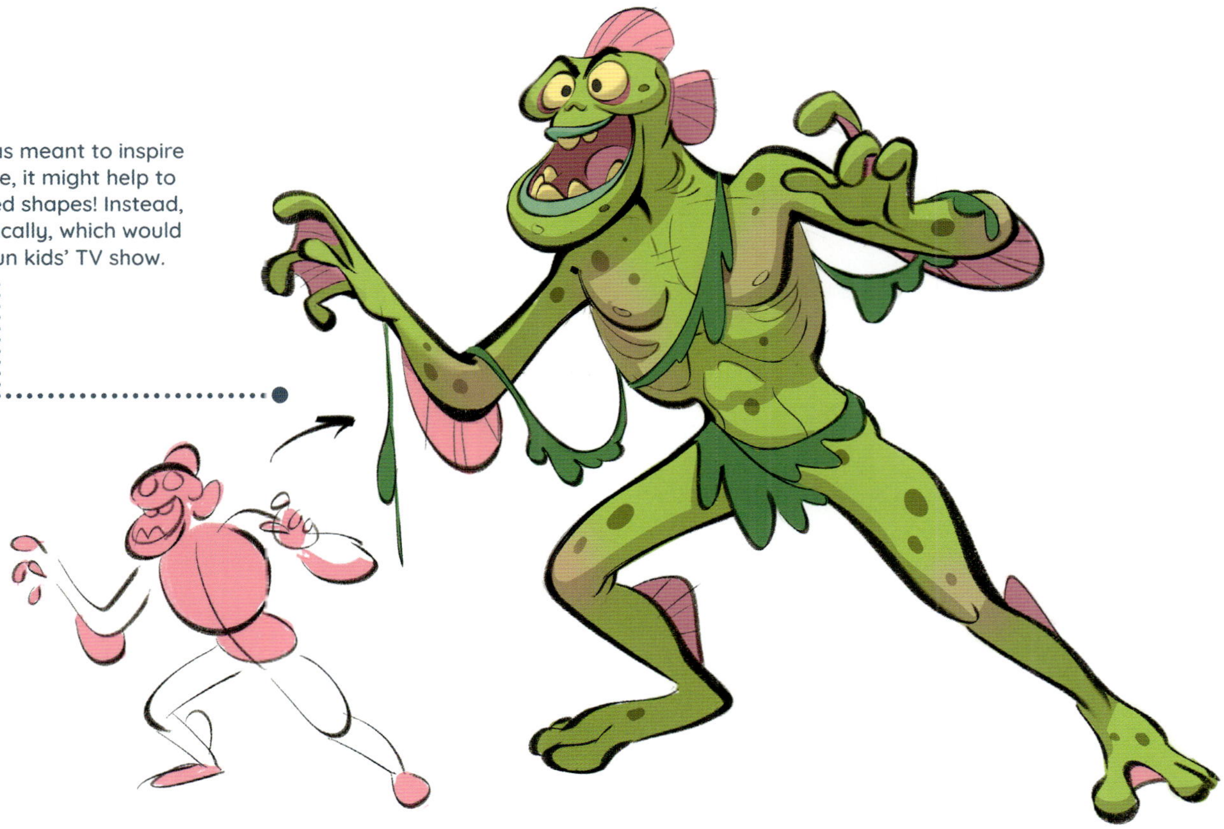

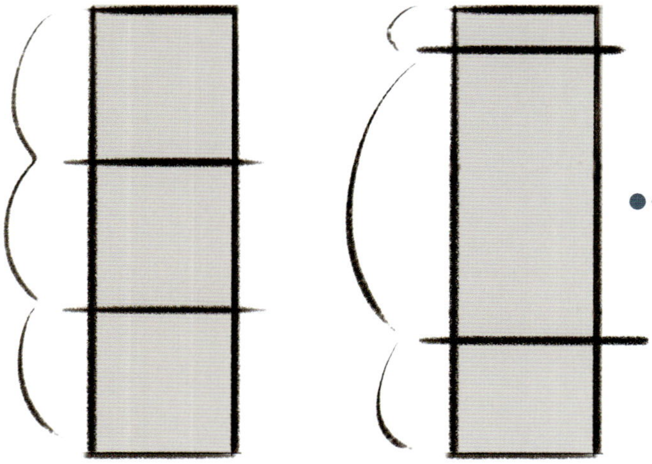

Contrasting forms

One of the most important concepts in design is contrast. It's what makes things visually interesting. Compare these two "ladders" - which is more interesting to look at?

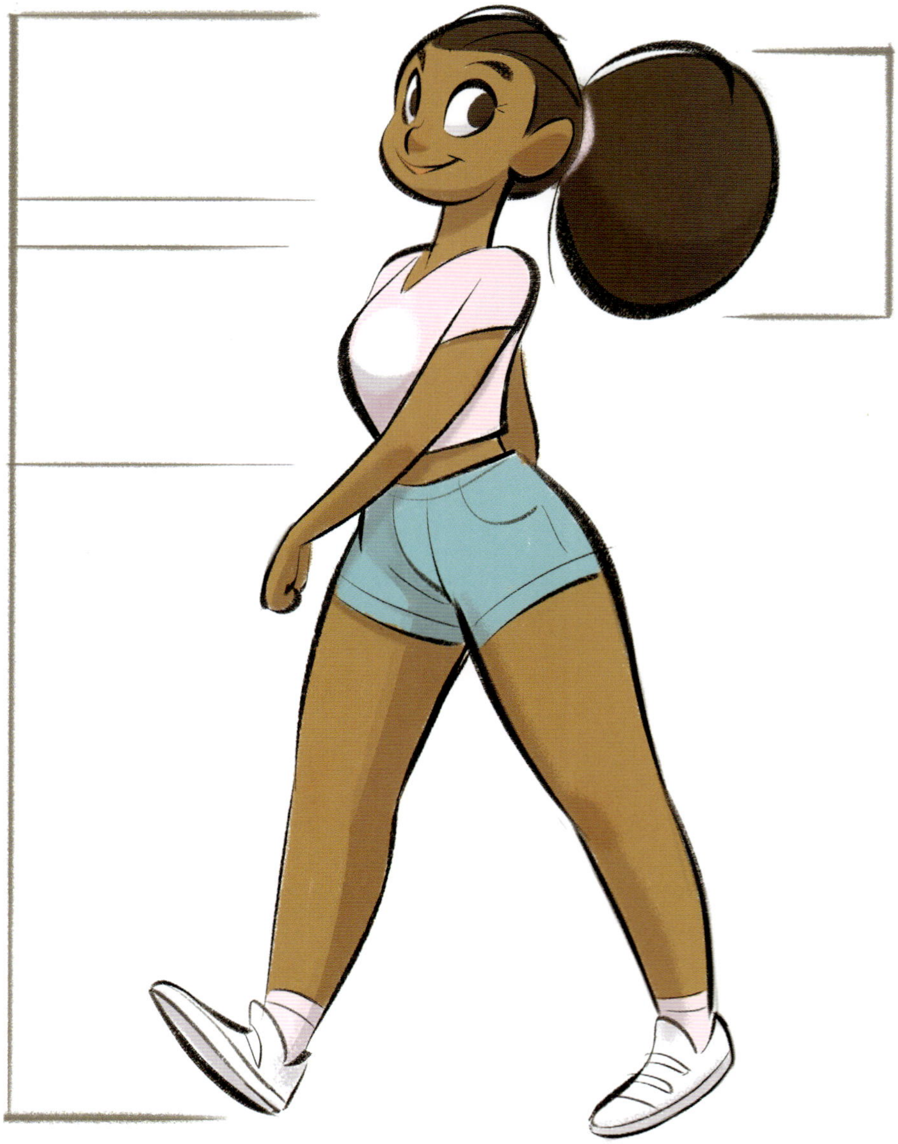

The natural contrast between this character's head size and legs has been pushed. Note how the body is also a different length.

In this more complex design, contrast has been brought into as many elements as possible.

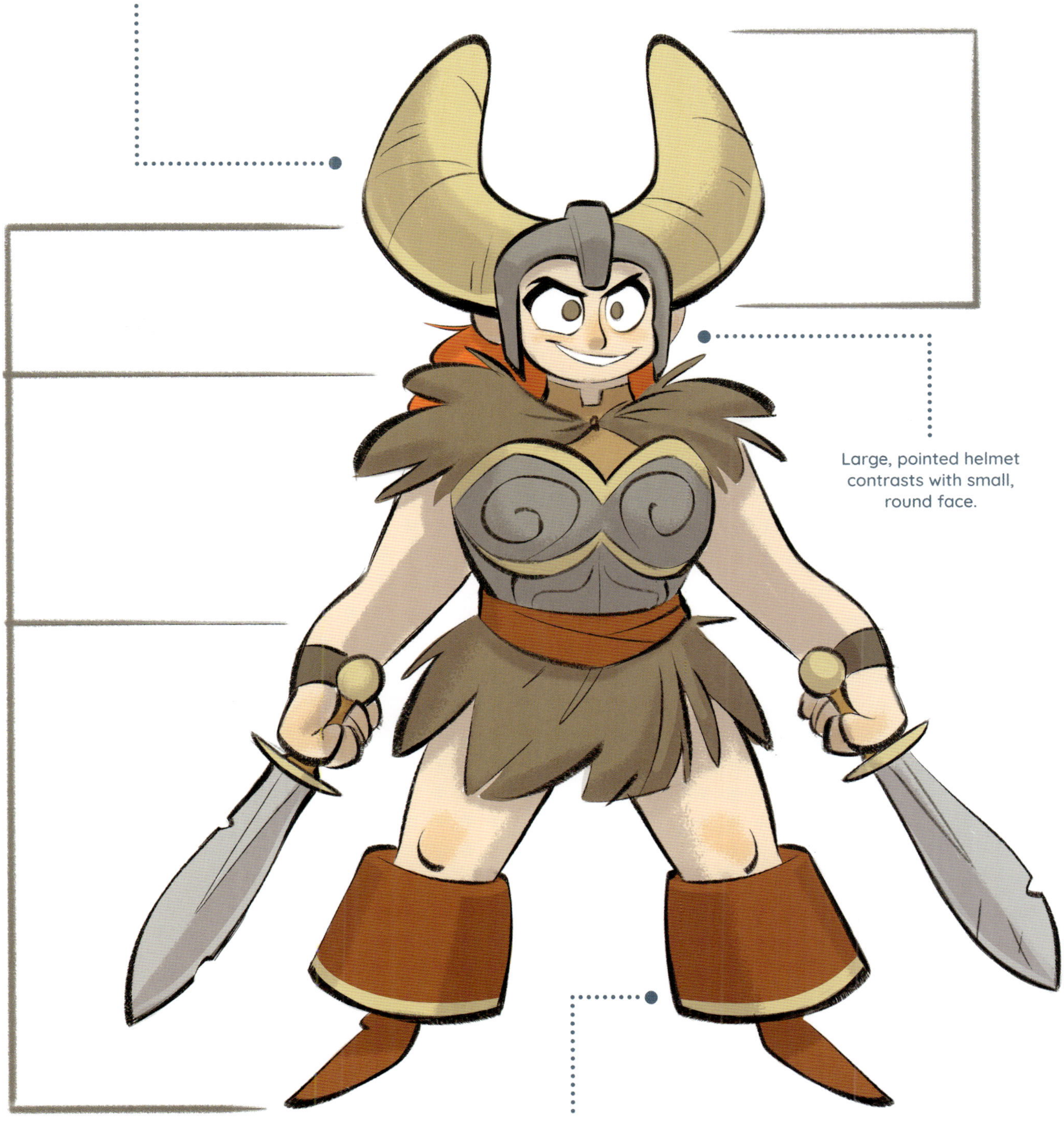

Large, pointed helmet contrasts with small, round face.

Rounded, heavy boots contrast with small, angular feet.

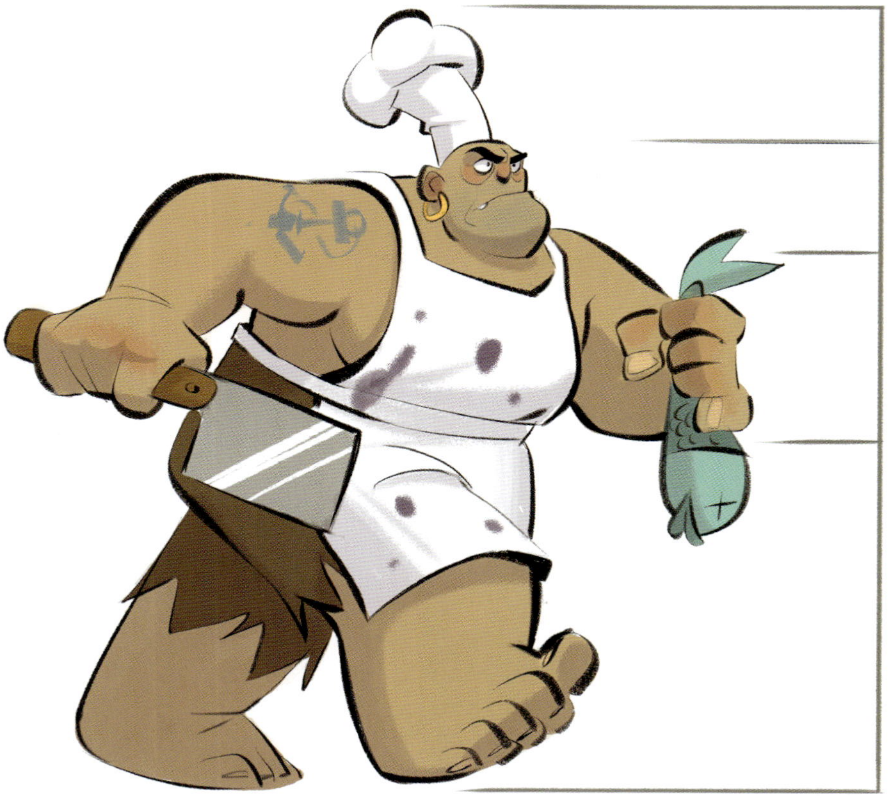

A lot of the fun in this design comes from the contrast of the head with the body – the body is huge and dominating with a relatively tiny head perched on top.

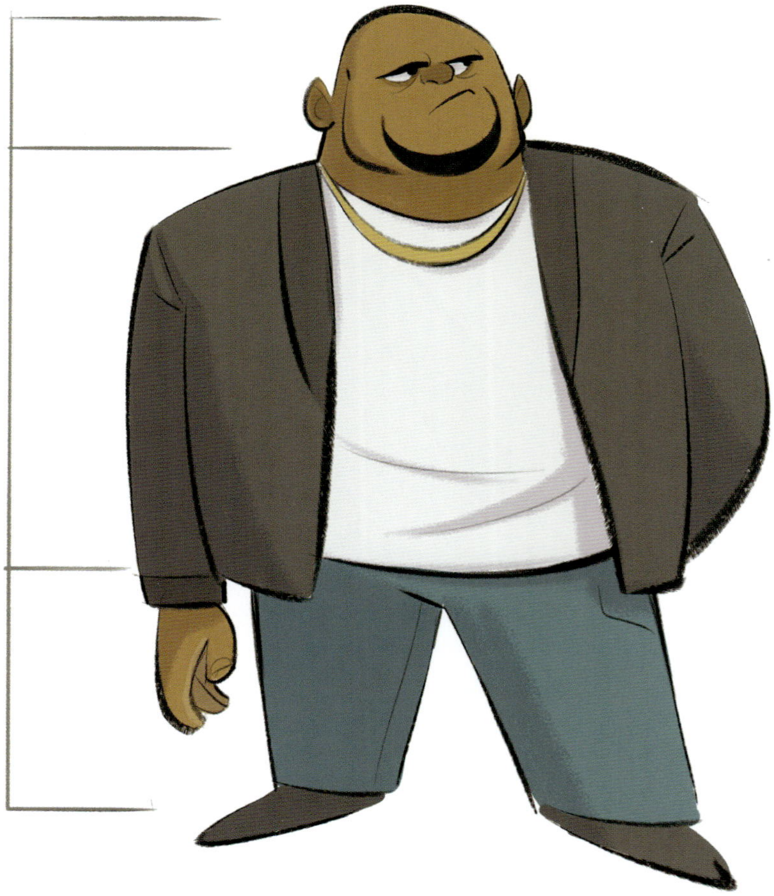

A person's legs are not generally shorter than the main portion of their body, though there are exceptions. Experiment with this and exaggerate things beyond realistic boundaries.

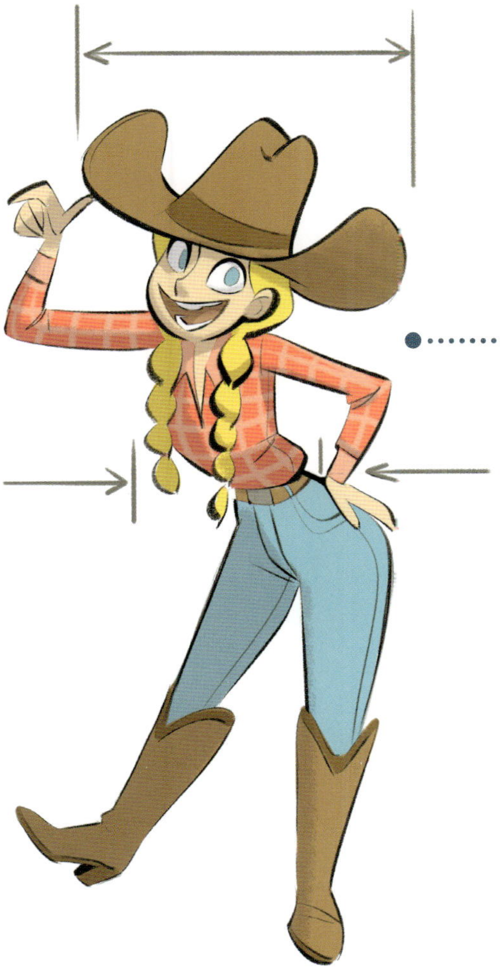

Remember that contrast is not just vertical, but can be horizontal. This character's wide, brimmed hat contrasts well with her thinner body shape.

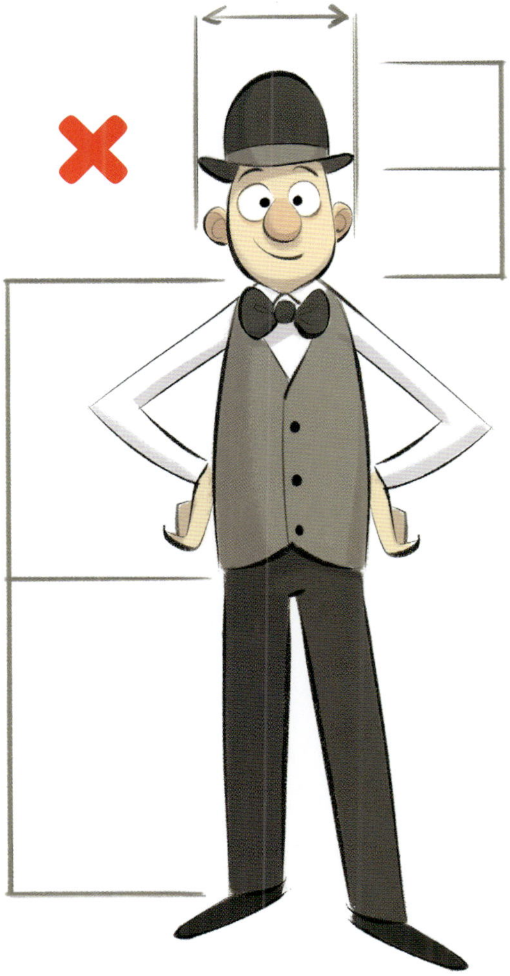

This character has a natural contrast between head and body, but lacks contrast overall. Most of the size relationships are balanced, with little exaggeration. It's not very exciting to look at, but a balanced and very bland character personality might suit these design choices!

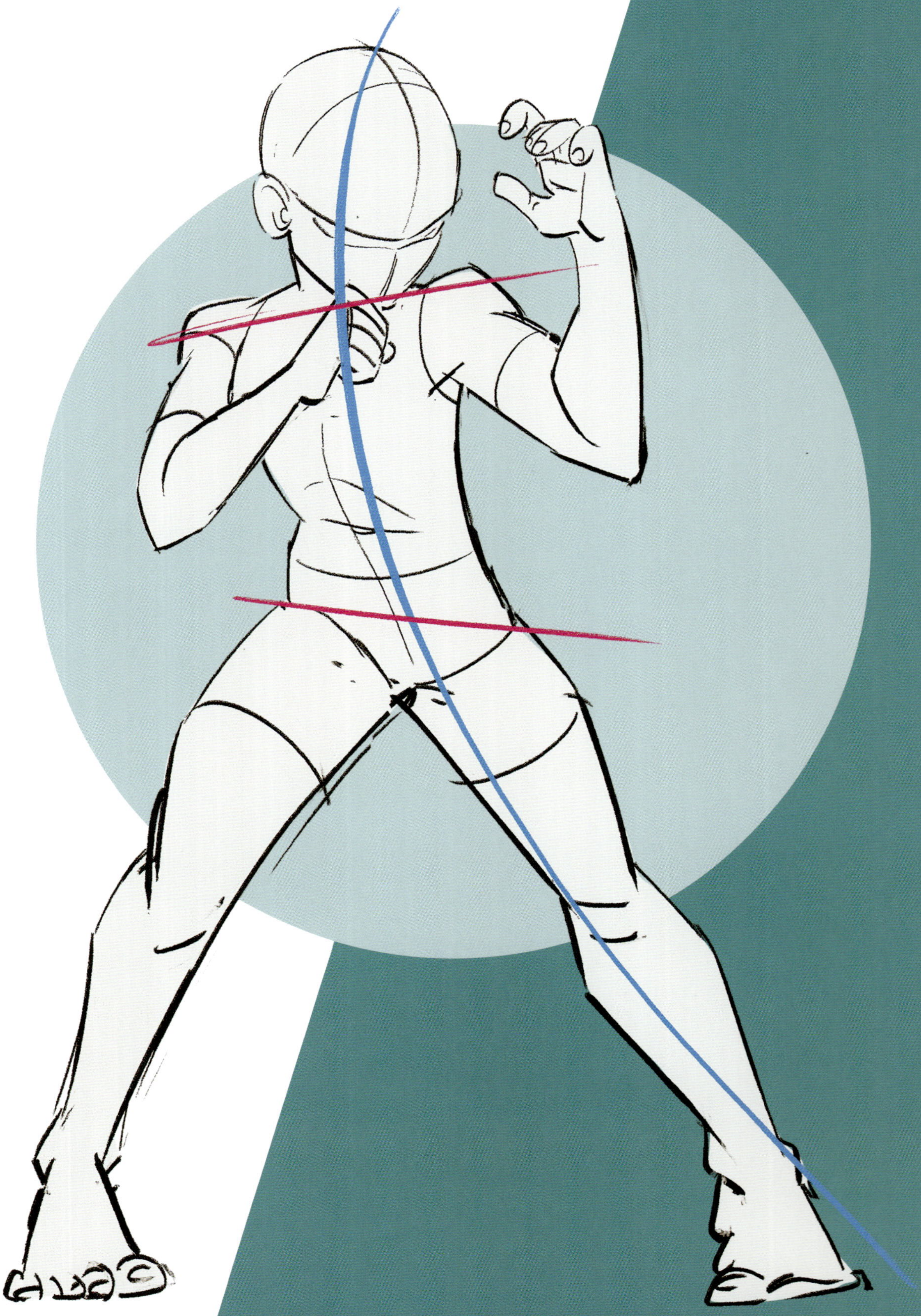

Image by Ida Hem

POSE, MOVEMENT & GESTURE

LINES OF ACTION & MOVEMENT
PAGE 108

HOW TO CONSTRUCT UPWARD FROM GESTURE
PAGE 114

EXAGGERATION OF GESTURE
PAGE 120

POSES LIBRARY
PAGE 128

LINES OF ACTION & MOVEMENT

Ida Hem

When you work as a character designer, a big part of your job is to bring someone else's vision to life. You will often be given a few keywords that describe the character, and then it's your job to visually explain that character in a universal language. If you're lucky, you will be given more descriptive keywords than "happy, fun, and feisty," but more often than not, your starting point will be that vague.

Designing a good character is much more than simply choosing shapes, outfits, and hairstyles. You need to consider how to present that character to the world. How do they plant their feet on the ground? How do they come across? With confidence or shyness? With excitement or sadness? Choosing a pose for your character is an important step in the process. **Pose**, **movement**, and **gesture** are key tools to utilize in order to tell a good story and convey strong personalities.

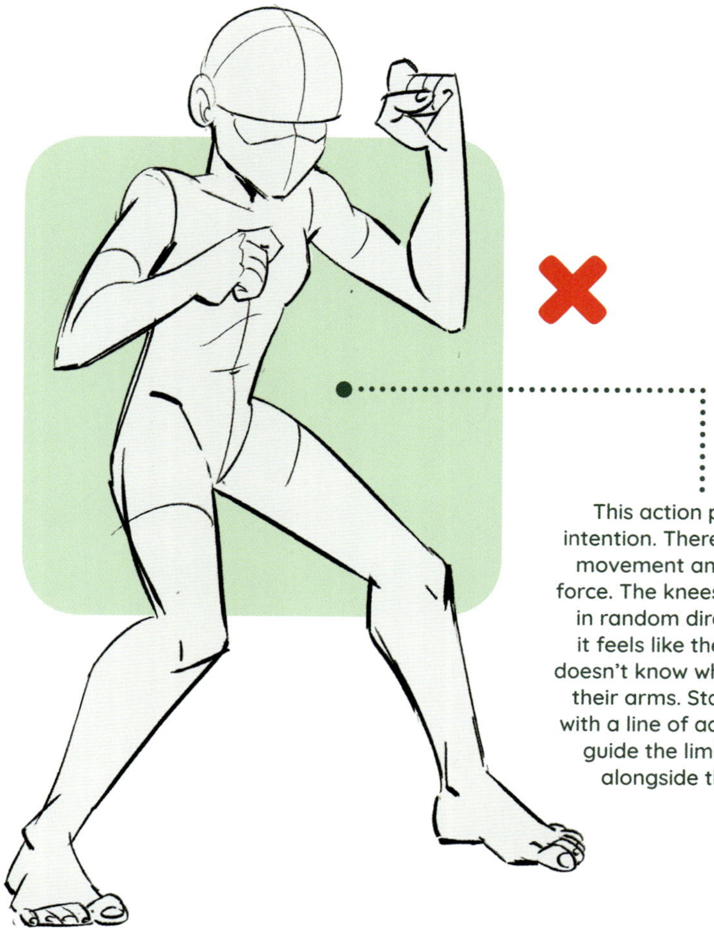

This action pose lacks intention. There is very little movement and not much force. The knees are pointing in random directions and it feels like the character doesn't know what to do with their arms. Starting again with a line of action will help guide the limbs to work alongside the torso.

Line of action is an essential concept used by most artists until it becomes second nature. It's an imaginary line that helps you understand and exaggerate your character's movement. The line of action runs down the character's spine, expressing how much force is in the pose and guiding the direction of the arms and legs. You will see several examples of lines of action in this chapter. Understanding how the concept works and how to utilize it will help you greatly improve your character designs. But think of it as guidance – it's not meant to restrict you. When the line of action is used correctly, it will help you optimize your character's pose, effectively telling a stronger story.

Gesture lines are a form of sketching used early in the process of finding your character's pose. A gesture is essentially a loose sketch based around the line of action. Gestures should be drawn quickly, so you can create lots of them without wasting too much time on the poses that don't work. Drawing lots of poses allows you to exhaust all of your ideas and then lets you pick the best one. Consider this the brainstorming section of the process.

Weight and **balance** are also important to keep in mind. It is common to see "floating" characters if the artist hasn't considered this aspect of the process. A character feels floaty when the weight and balance are not quite right, making the character look less believable. It can either feel like they are about to fall over, or that their feet are not standing on anything. Your goal is to make the audience feel like your character is alive, which is hard to accomplish if the weight is not distributed correctly. You obtain weight balance when the "core," located in the center of the character, aligns with where the character is supporting their weight. Draw a straight line from the core to where your character meets the ground. If they are standing on one foot, that foot should be located directly underneath the core.

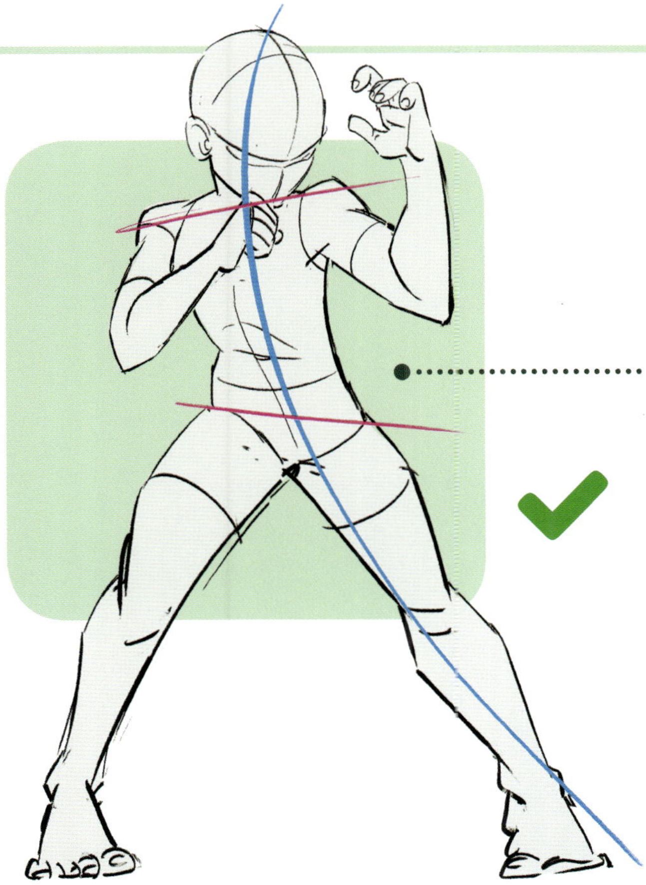

Here is the same pose as the one on the left, but with more intention. The blue line of action is curved back to illustrate a defensive pose. It is aligned with the spine and guides the direction of the character's left leg. The pink lines position the shoulders and hips. Ideally, these should never be completely horizontal, and should point in opposite directions to help with weight balance. There are always exceptions to the rule, but generally this is a good tip to follow.

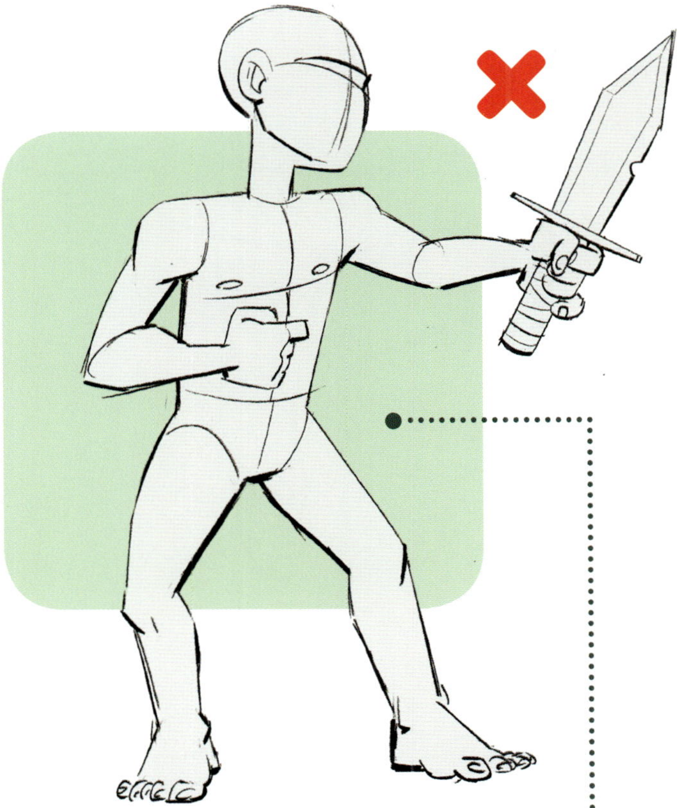

The character's right arm rests in an awkward position within the silhouette. Their hips and shoulders feel stiff because they are parallel to each other. You can improve this by tilting the shoulders and hips opposite each other and implementing a stronger line of action.

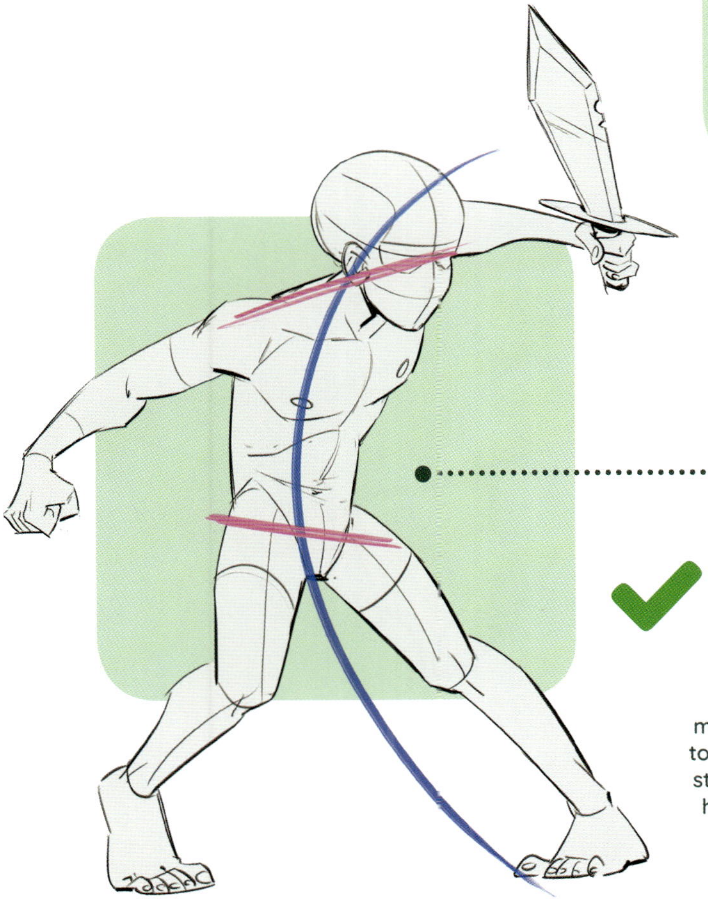

Notice how there is much more energy in this pose. The torso is rarely ever completely straight and the line of action helps you understand which way the spine is curving.

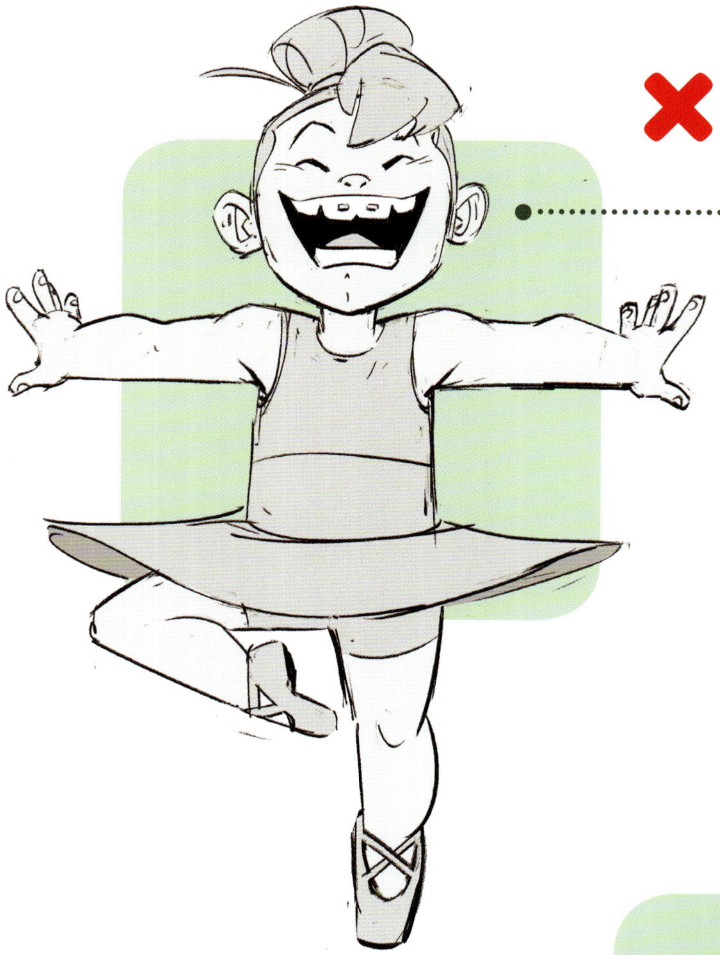

Though this ballerina girl is cute, her pose is rather static. The weight balance feels off and there is no force or direction. The arms are horizontal and aligned with each other, which is never a good choice. Variation is key!

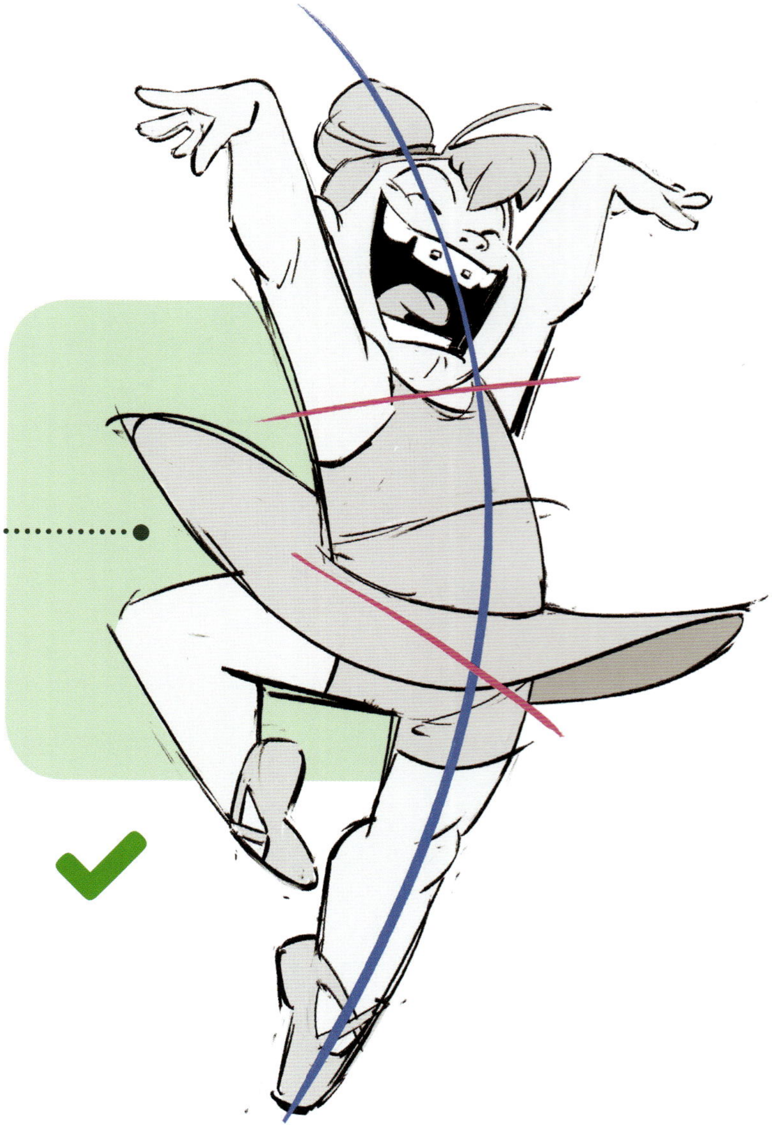

Here is the same character, but with a much stronger line of action. Notice how the arms are no longer horizontal, but instead pulled up to complement the force of the action. A good tip is to make sure your character is in a three-quarter position, rather than front-facing or in profile. This will give them more volume, consequently making them more believable.

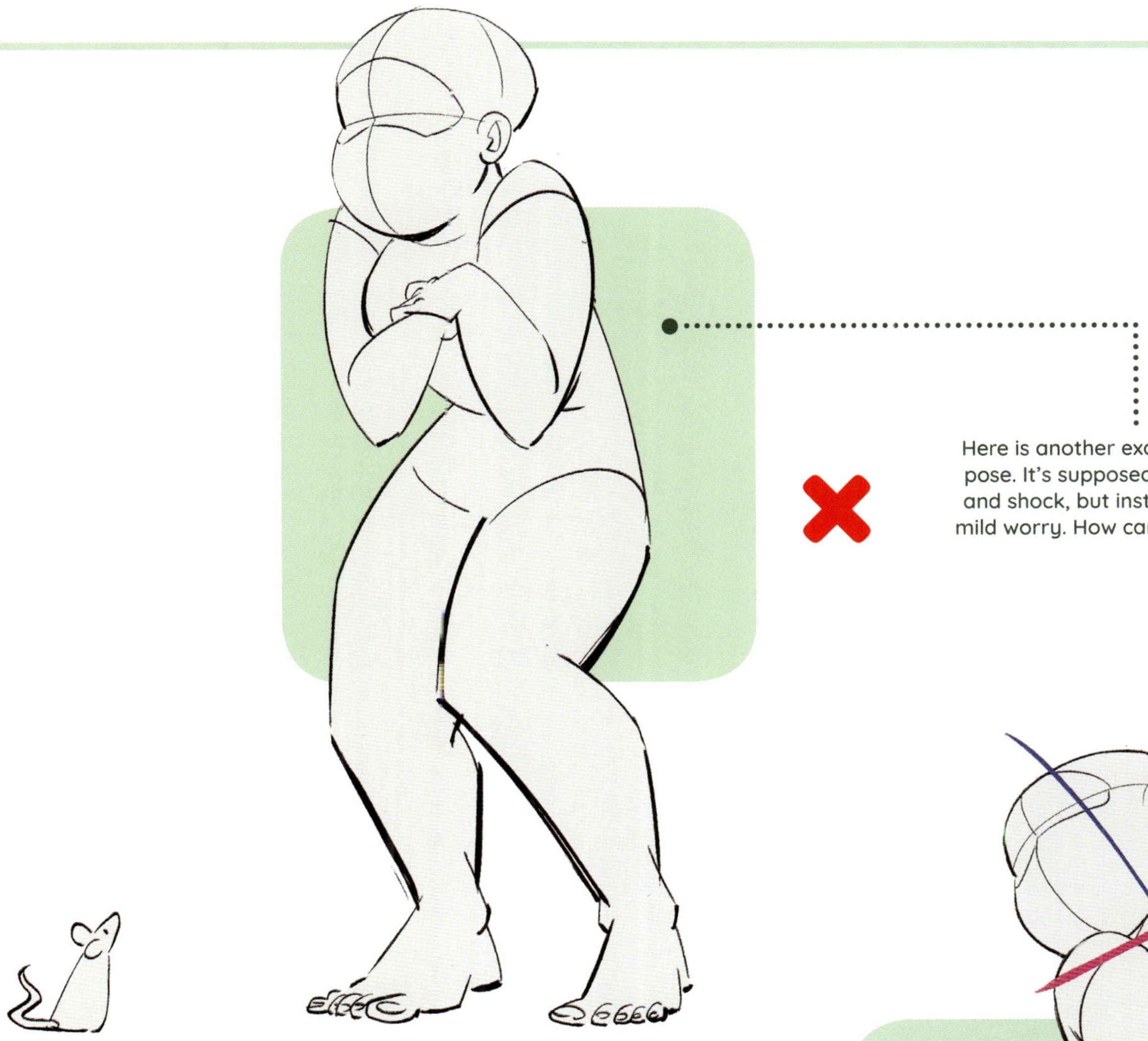

Here is another example of a static pose. It's supposed to express fear and shock, but instead expresses a mild worry. How can it be improved?

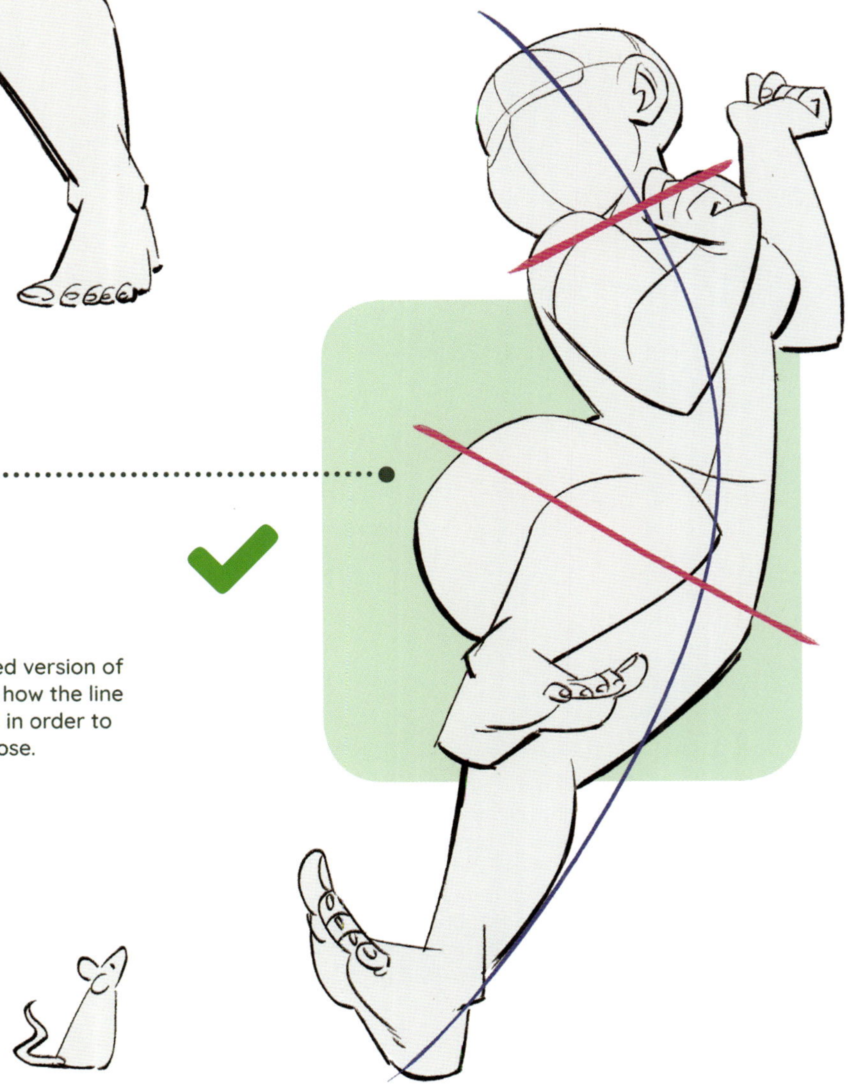

This is a more exaggerated version of the previous pose. Notice how the line of action is more curved in order to emphasize the pose.

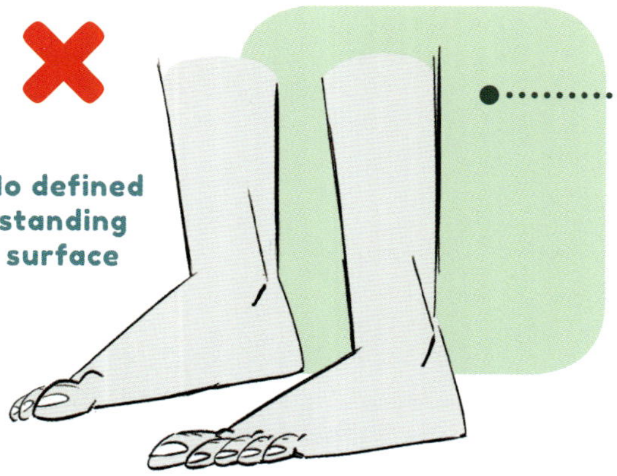

A common mistake made by many beginners is not defining the surface on which their character stands. This can make it look like the character is floating and that there's no weight balance.

Draw a grid on the ground to define the surface perspective. This will make it much easier to see where your character's feet are supposed to go. You should always do this, unless the floor is completely horizontal to the "camera" - but in most cases there will be a perspective.

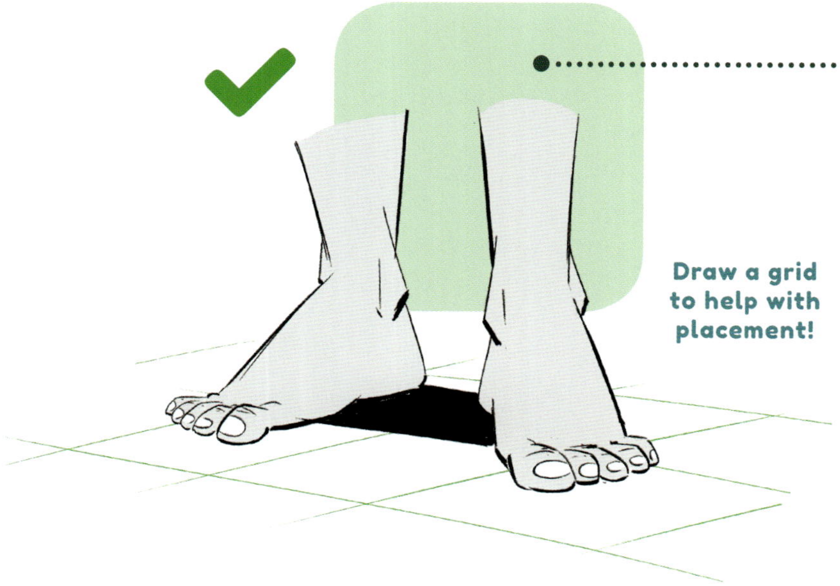

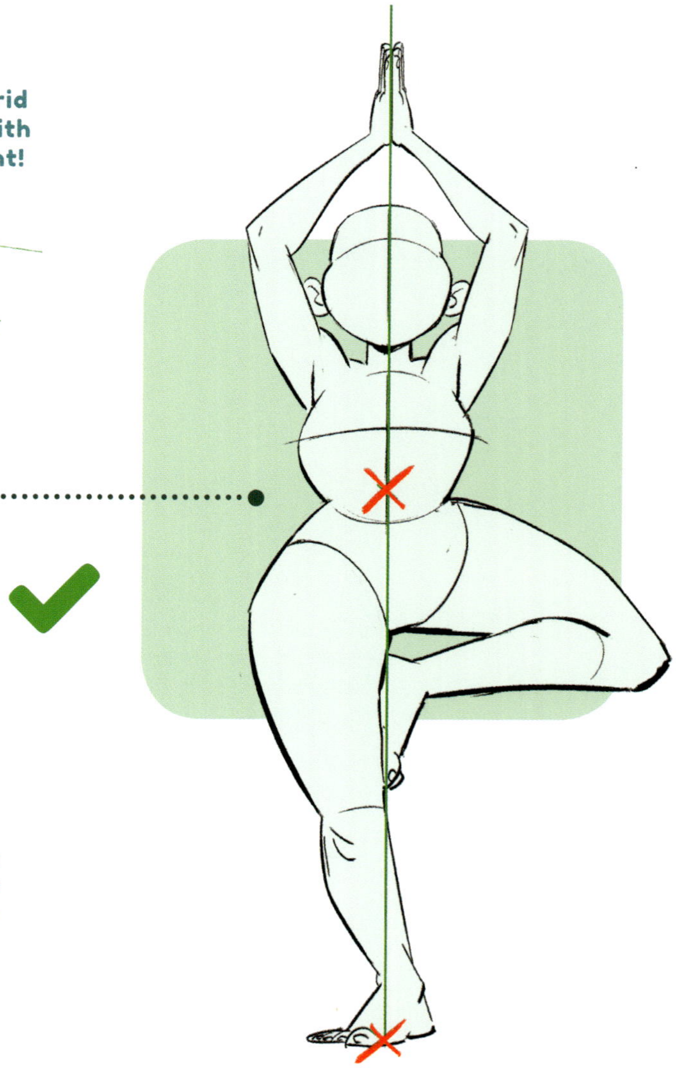

Weight balance is important to every pose. A character's "core" is located in the very center, where the X is in this illustration. This is the core because there is an equal amount of mass/weight around this point. Draw a straight line down to the ground to locate the "point of balance" where the character will support their weight.

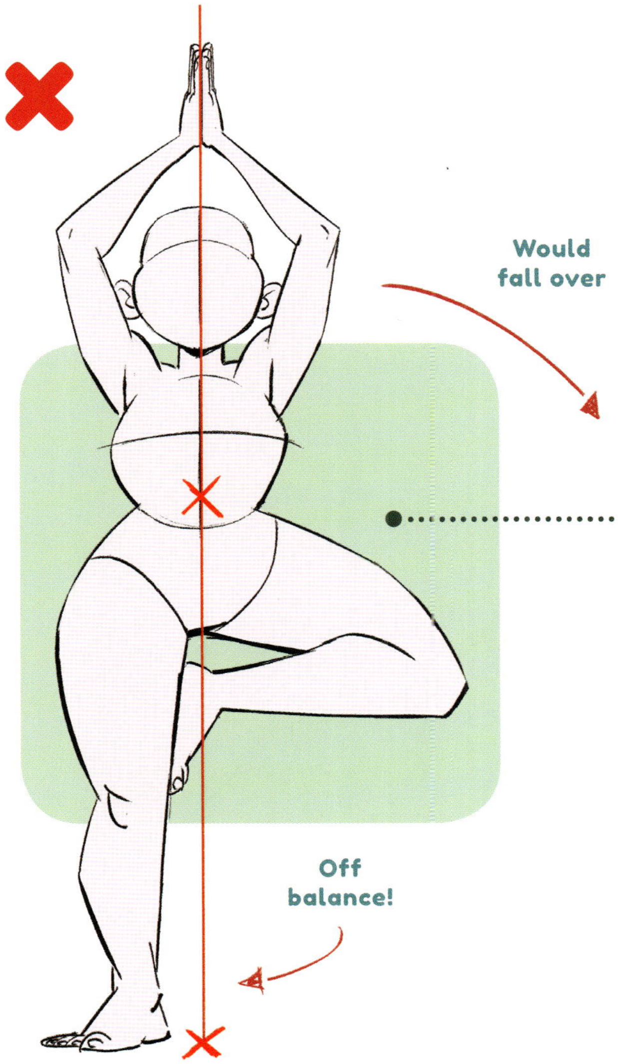

If the balance is off, it means that there is nothing, or not enough, at the point of balance that will support the character's weight. In this case, the leg is too far off, which would realistically result in the character falling over.

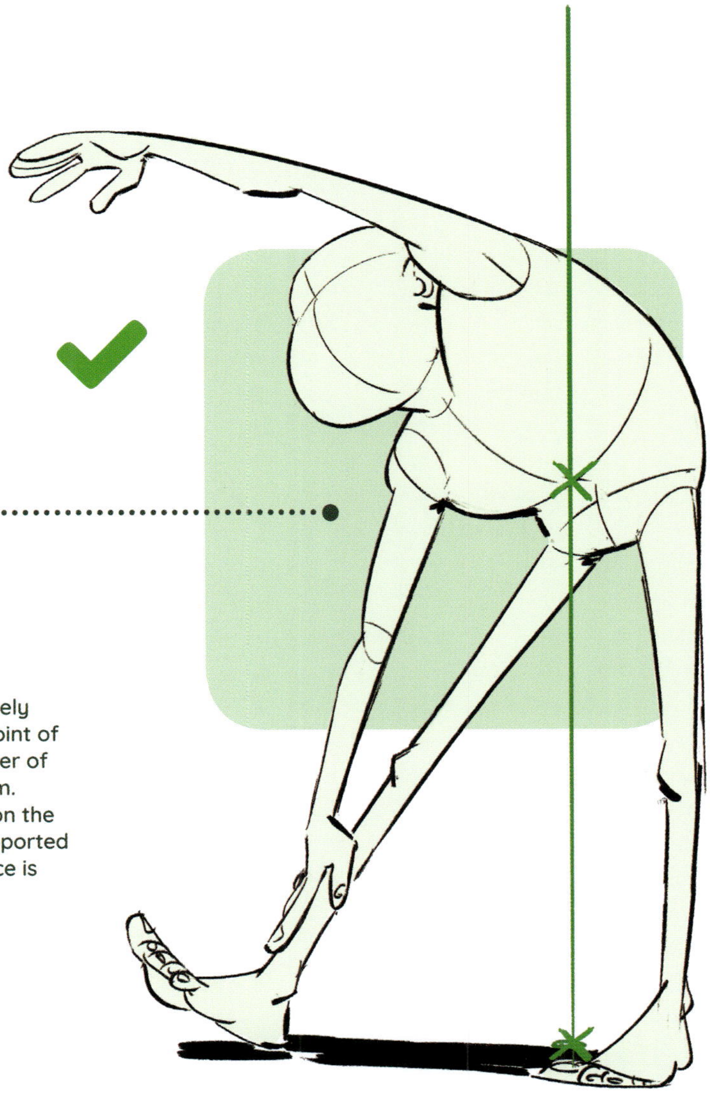

Unless your character is standing completely vertical with 50/50 weight distribution, the point of balance will never be completely in the center of both feet. It will always favor one of them. In this case, most of the weight is balanced on the character's left foot, but some of it is also supported by the right side. Hence the point of balance is closer to the character's left.

HOW TO CONSTRUCT UPWARD FROM GESTURE

Ida Hem

Now that you understand how to approach a gesture drawing, you can move on to construction, solidifying your shapes and lines. You can take a character from a gesture to a finalized design through a step-by-step process. Constructing a character upward from gesture will help you understand the thought process behind the final design, and will help you optimize its potential every step of the way.

The first step of the process is to **establish the line of action**, and then to rough out your idea through contrasting and exaggerating shapes, using your understanding of human anatomy and proportion. Focus on the line of action, making sure it has the force and intention you want your final design to have. A line of action and a proper gesture drawing are the pillars of a good design. If these elements are weak, the final design will be weak as well. As mentioned earlier, gestures should be drawn quickly, allowing you to draw lots of them without wasting time on poses that don't work. This will allow you to exhaust your ideas and options, eliminating the ones that you thought had potential but didn't work on paper. There are no bad sketches in this step.

The second step is to block out the **six key body parts** on top of the gesture, starting to exaggerate to create a stylized shape language. Every artist will approach this differently. It's up to you to find what works best for you - these are merely suggestions to point you in the right direction and give you tools to explore with. The key body parts are the chest, torso, legs, arms, shoulders, and head, because they can all move independently of each other. If you think of them as separate shapes, it will be easier to exaggerate them outside the realms of a realistically built human. For example, you could choose to make the hips twice the size of the chest, creating an exaggerated contrast between the two shapes.

Gesture drawing

Notice how the line of action is curved to push the chest and the hips in opposite directions, making for a curvier final design.

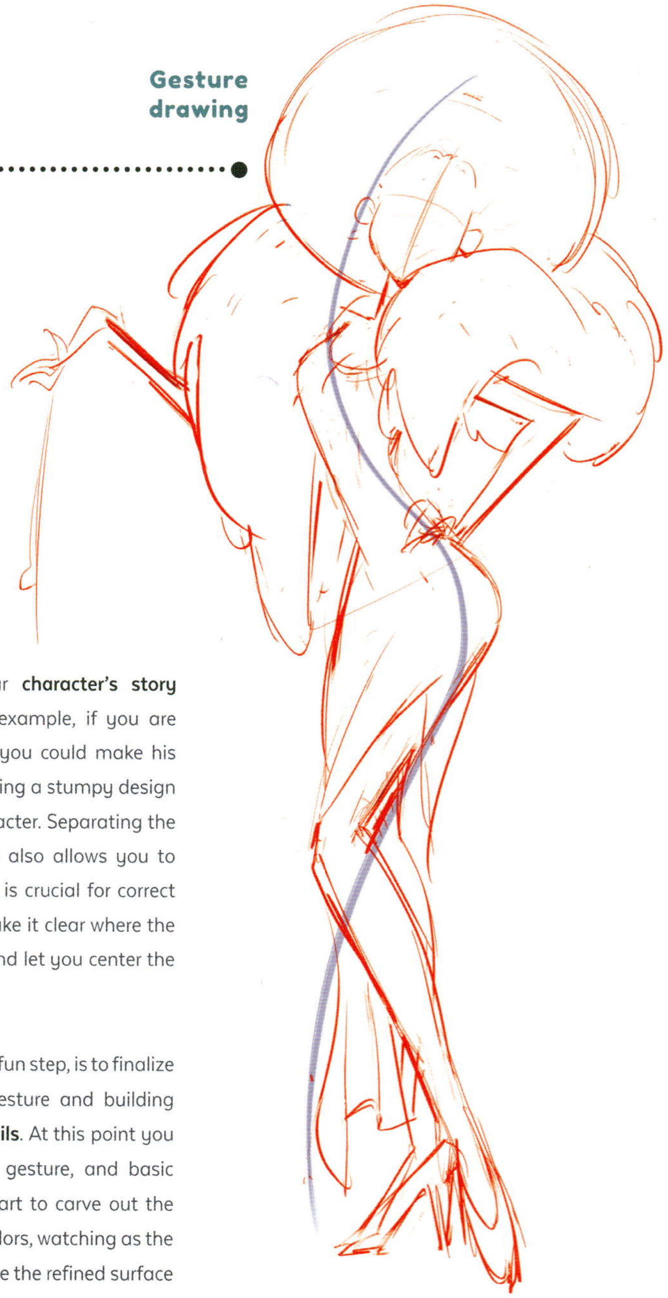

Choose the shapes with your **character's story** and **personality** in mind. For example, if you are designing a grumpy old man, you could make his legs shorter than his torso, creating a stumpy design that would play well to his character. Separating the character into different shapes also allows you to create construction lines, which is crucial for correct volume and anatomy. It will make it clear where the legs connect to the hip bones and let you center the neck between the shoulders.

The third step of the process, the fun step, is to finalize the character on top of the gesture and building blocks, refining the **surface details**. At this point you should have chosen the pose, gesture, and basic shapes. Now you can finally start to carve out the face and clothes, and pick the colors, watching as the character comes to life. Make sure the refined surface details align with the rest of the design. For example, if you are designing a kind-hearted character, round shapes will work in their favor. Keeping the edges soft will make them look friendlier. Always ensure the founding shapes work well.

The hips have been sized up and pushed out to exaggerate the curve, creating a strong contrast between the hips and the chest.

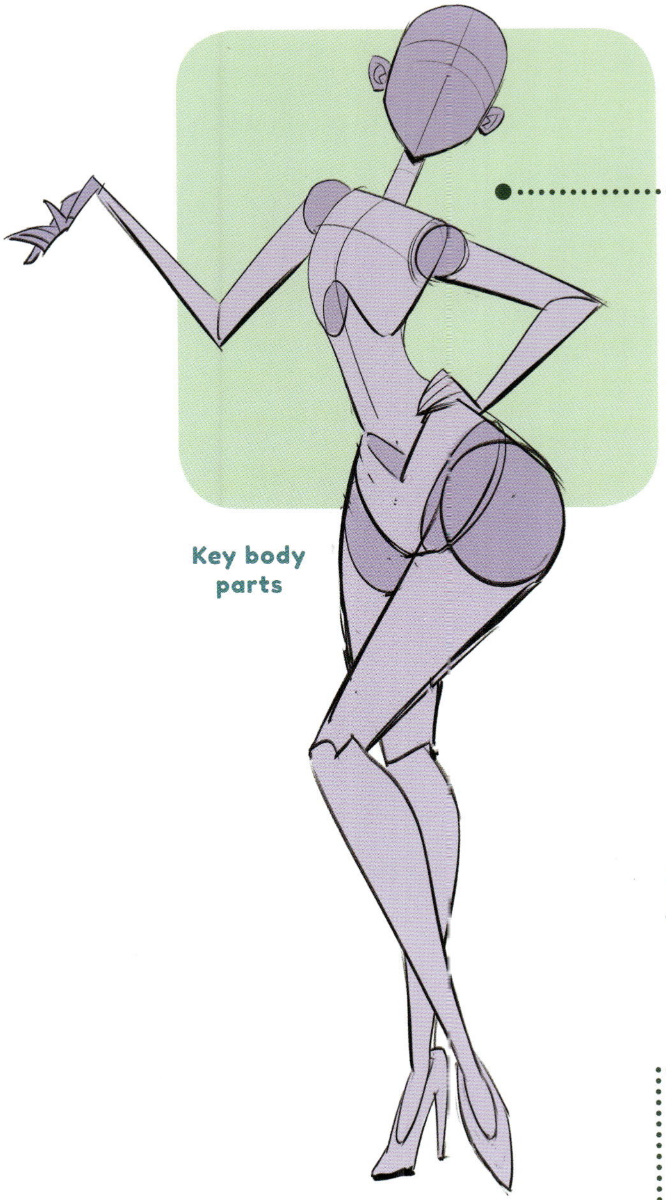

Key body parts

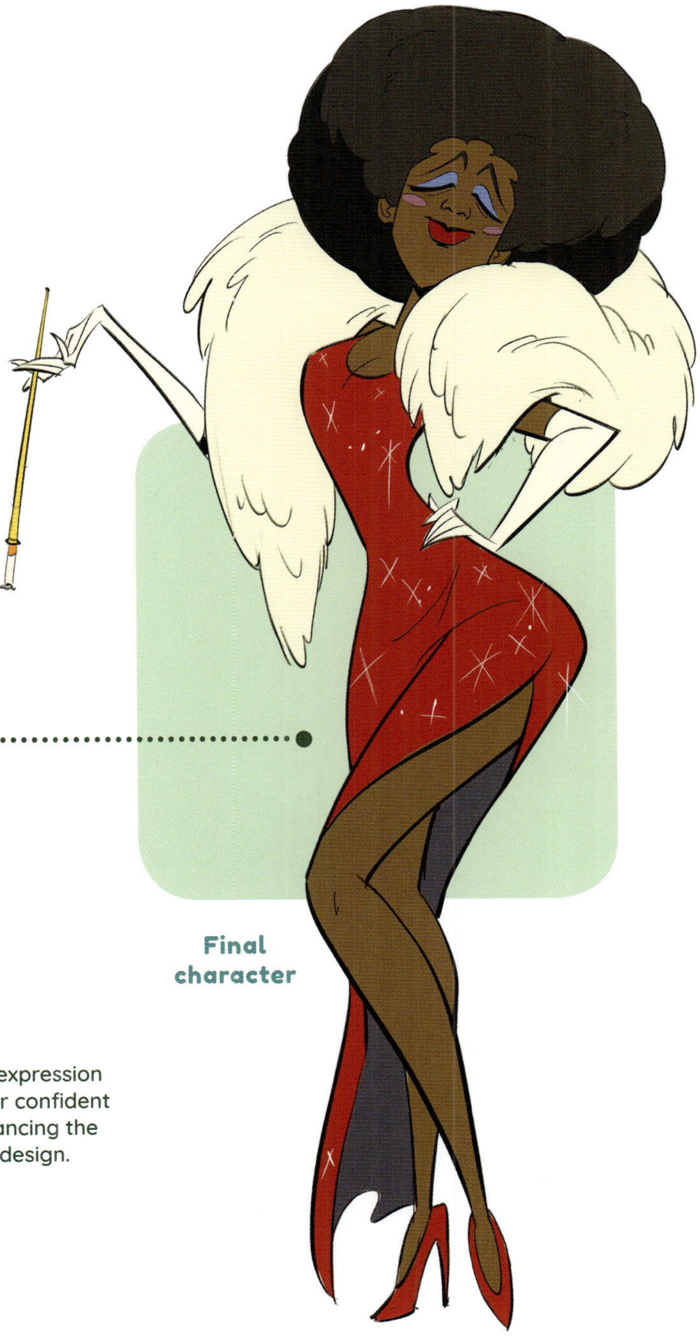

Final character

The facial expression matches her confident pose, enhancing the overall design.

Gesture drawing

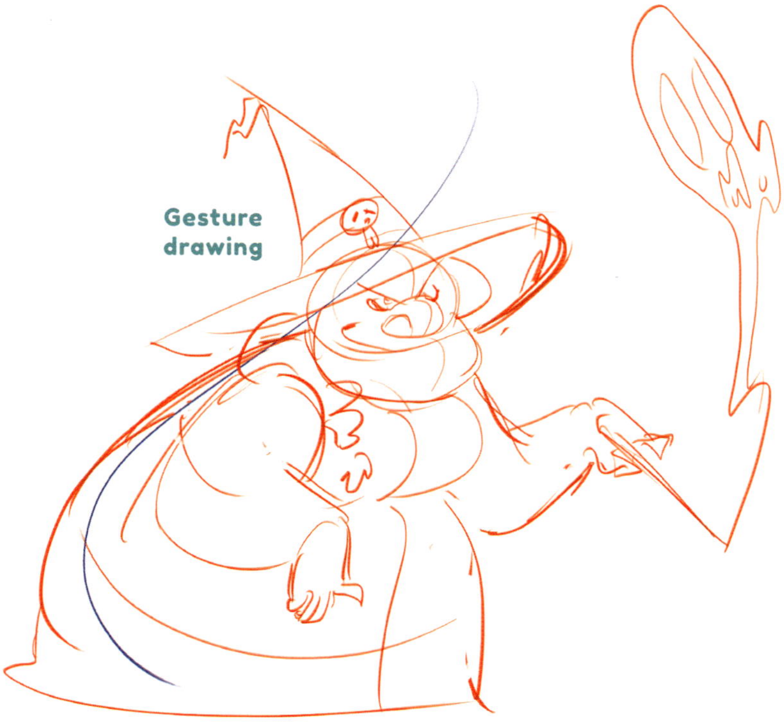

The line of action is curved to make the character lean forward, capturing the creepy nature of a witch.

Key body parts

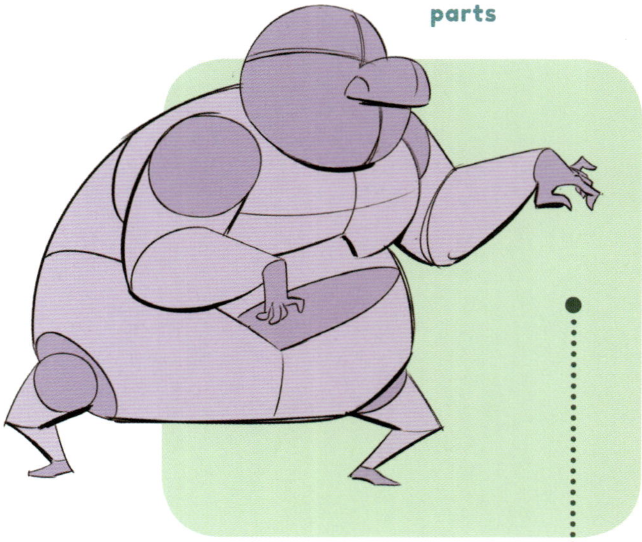

The building blocks solidify the character's anatomy, making it easier to understand. The nose has been enlarged, whereas the hands have been sized down.

Final character

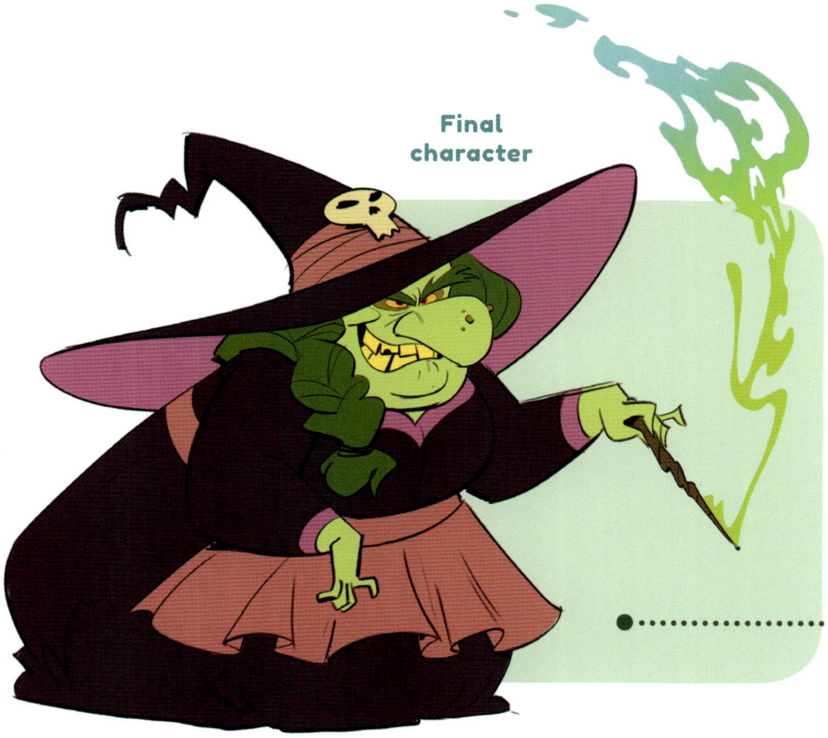

Bushy eyebrows, crooked yellow teeth, and a large droopy nose work with the character's story. The iconic witch's hat shape has been exaggerated too.

The line of action is aligned with the spine. Always look for reference pictures when designing a pose you are not familiar with.

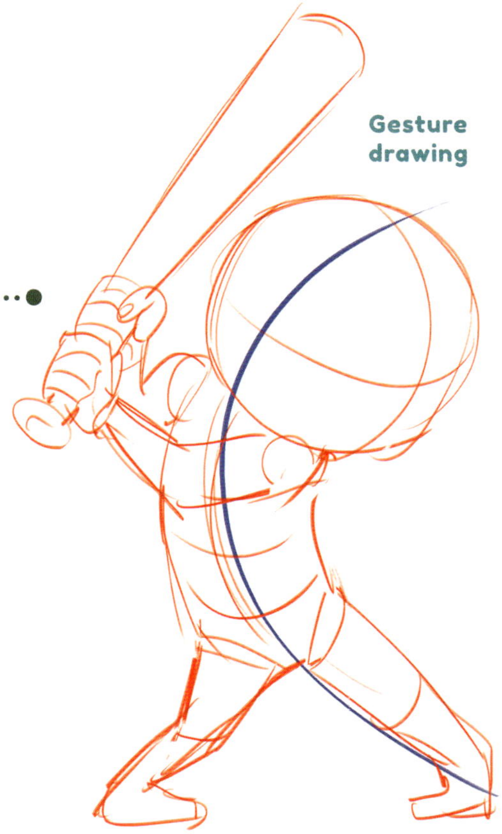

Gesture drawing

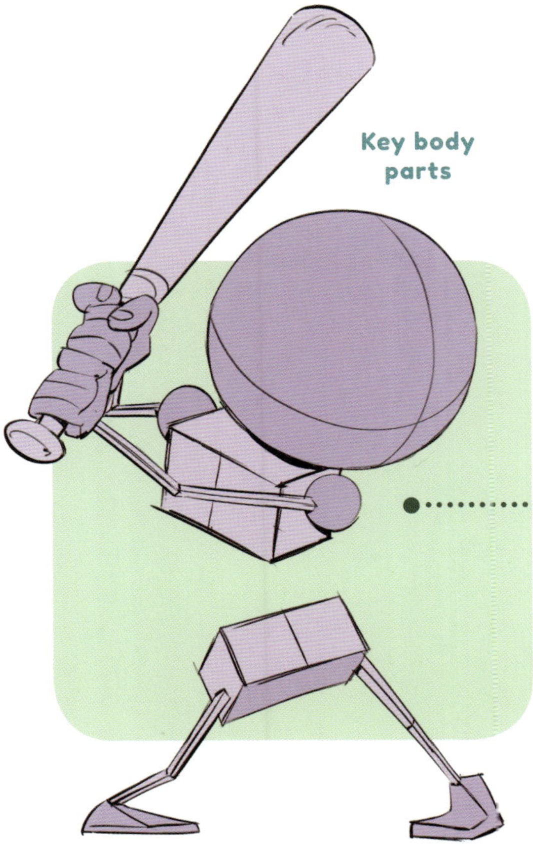

Key body parts

If square shapes help you better understand how the body twists and turns, then use those. Make the process work for you.

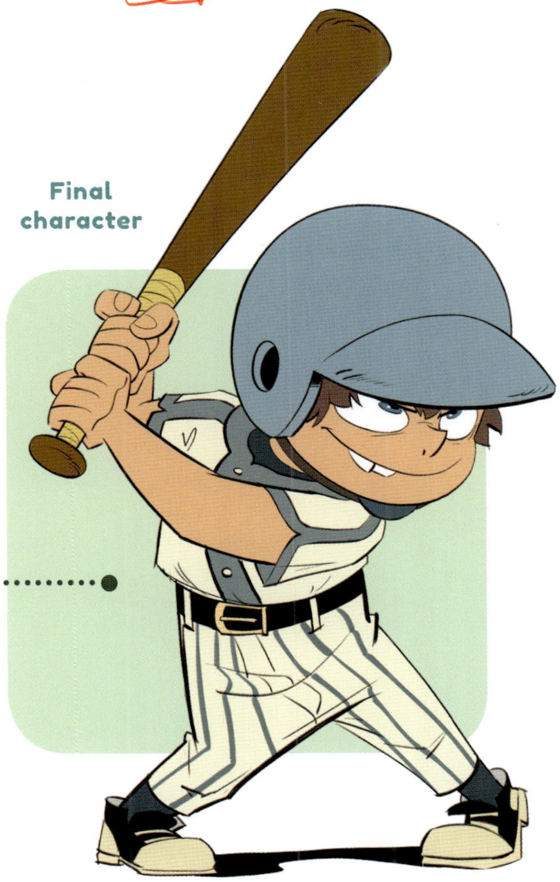

Final character

This character wears a baseball uniform. A t-shirt and jeans would do nothing for the design.

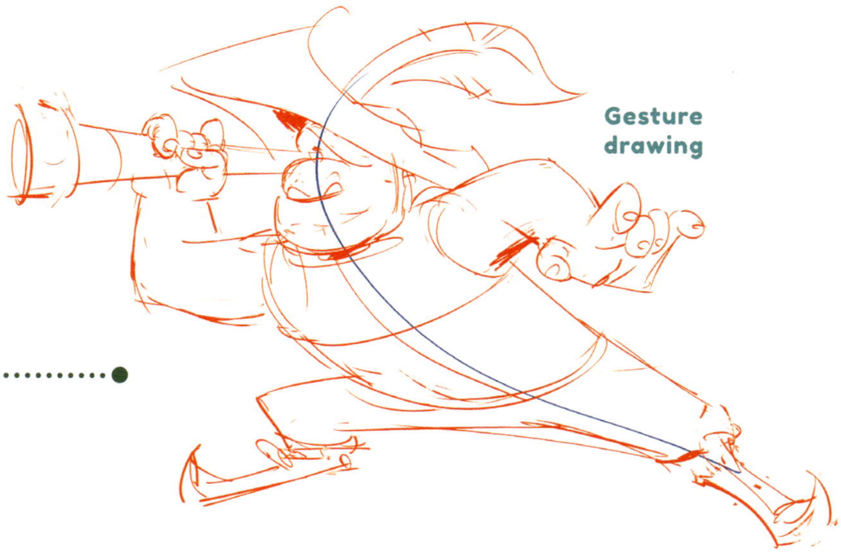

Gesture drawing

This gesture shows the character trying to look at something in the distance, leaning forward to see better. The line of action is curved forward to emphasize this.

Key body parts

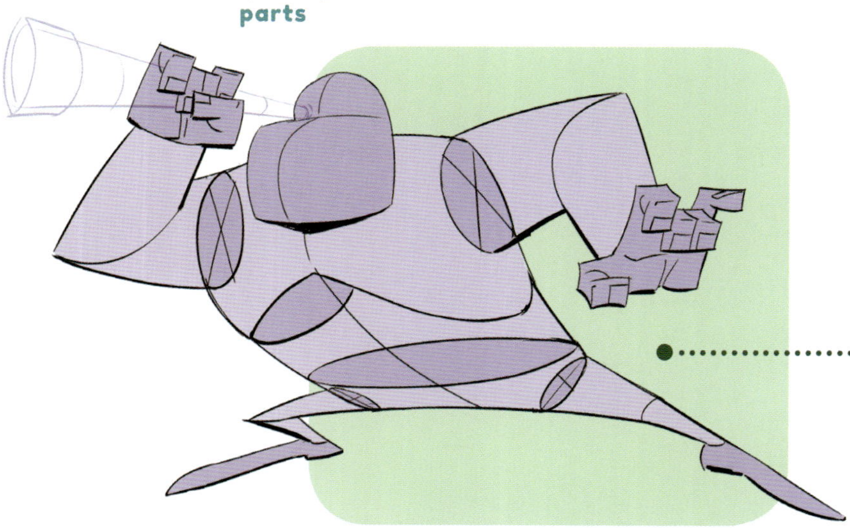

The upper body and hands have been sized up. The telescope has been pushed further up to point in the same direction as the chest.

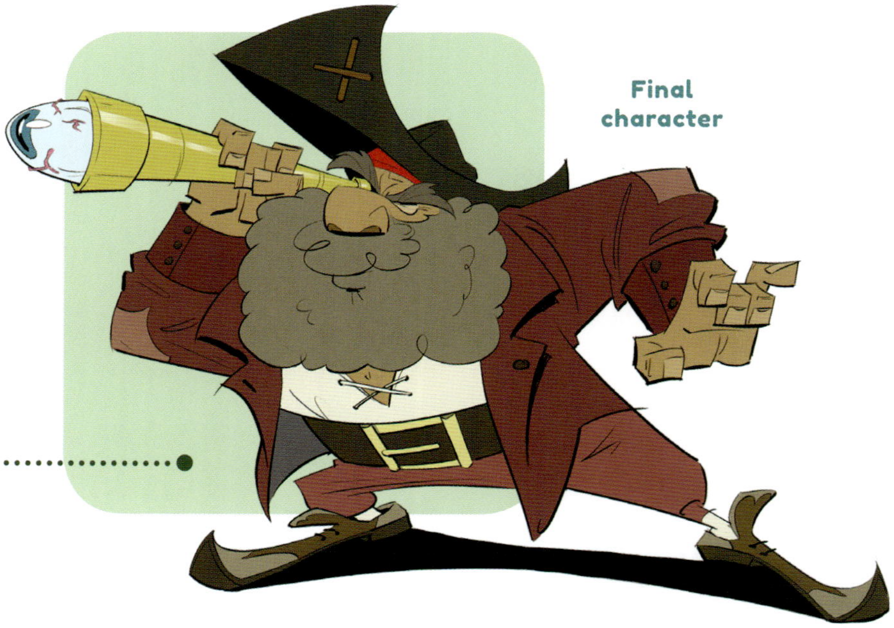

Final character

Notice how many square shapes are used in the final design. Repeating shapes is a good way to unify a design.

CLEAR SILHOUETTE

Being able to instantly read a character's pose is important for clarity. If the audience has to take a second look to understand it, their viewer experience is disrupted. Visualizing the inner lines is an indicator of a good silhouette. Understanding the pose and direction is crucial, so that the character's personality shines through their silhouette.

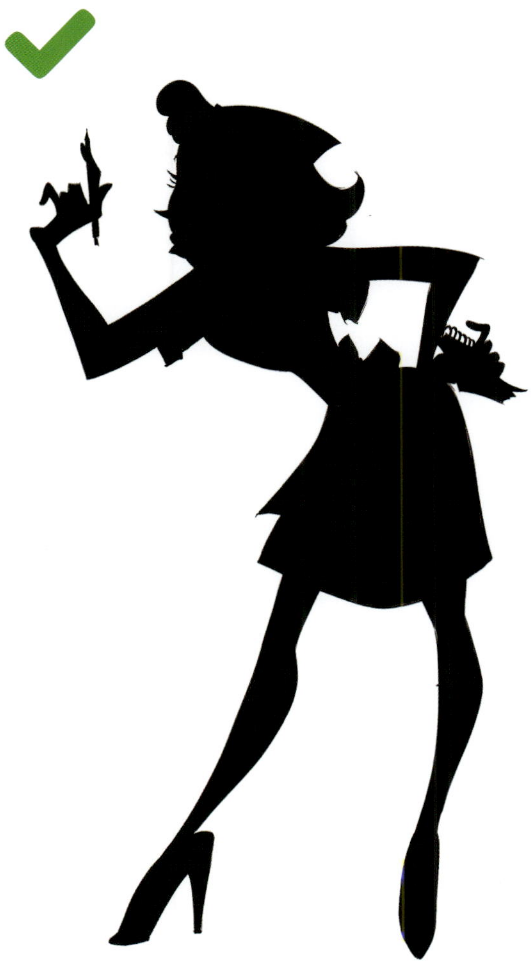

Clear direction

Clear personality

Clear limbs & pose

UNCLEAR SILHOUETTE

This silhouette is unclear – you can't tell what's happening. Is the character facing forward or backward? Where are the limbs? Are they holding something? What are they doing?

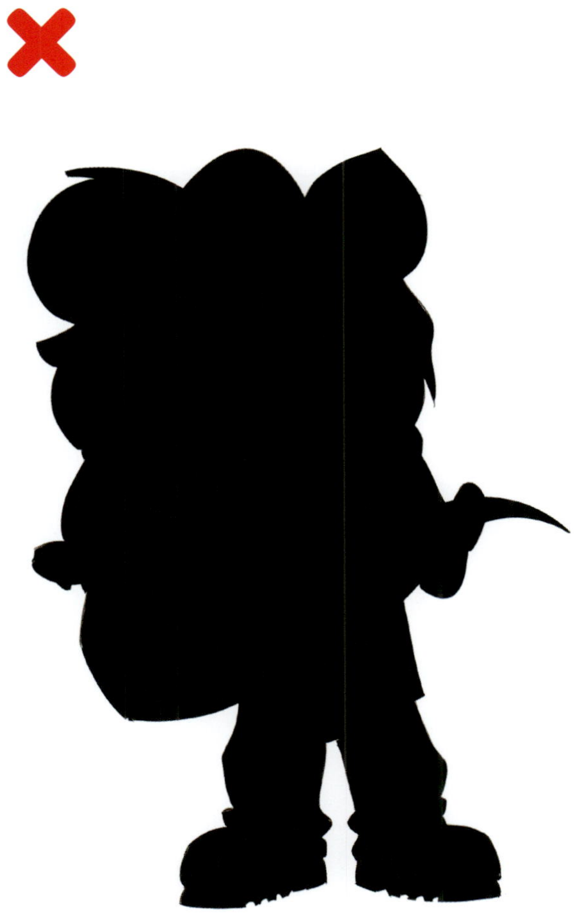

Action?

Limbs?

What is happening?

EXAGGERATION OF GESTURE

Ida Hem

As a visual artist, it is crucial to know how to present your work to portray the correct action, emotion, and mood. Whether you are a character designer, animator, comic-book artist, or storyboard artist, all can benefit from learning how to exaggerate gesture to tell a clear story with a strong personality. **Posing**, **body language**, **movement**, **line of action**, **gestures** – these are all tools you can use to tell a story. While they might feel as if they are second nature, seeing them in theory versus drawing them on paper are two very different things. Only with time and practice can you develop such a skill as second nature.

Developing a good character is not just about design choices and shape language, but also how the character **acts** and **showcases themselves**. Keep in mind what the first impression of the character will be to someone who has never seen them before. The character's personality must shine through in their gesture, and an efficient way to accomplish that is through exaggeration. More often than not, the first gesture sketch will be too subtle. If a design is too subtle, it leaves it too open for interpretation. Your goal is for everyone to see the same thing, without interpreting it in a way that wasn't intended. For example, you would not want a sad character to be interpreted as content, or a confused character to be interpreted as arrogant. Exaggerating the gesture will allow you to **eliminate subtlety**. The design will no longer be interpreted, but instead observed and accepted for what it is. Of course, art is subjective and there are no rules, merely suggestions. If your goal is to achieve subtlety with the intention of your character being open to interpretation, that is still valid, but the key here is *intention*.

This section will explore how to exaggerate gesture to showcase a character's personality in an obvious manner, leaving no room for them to be misinterpreted. This can be accomplished through their line of action, story, focus, silhouette, and overall energy. These are all pillars of great character design.

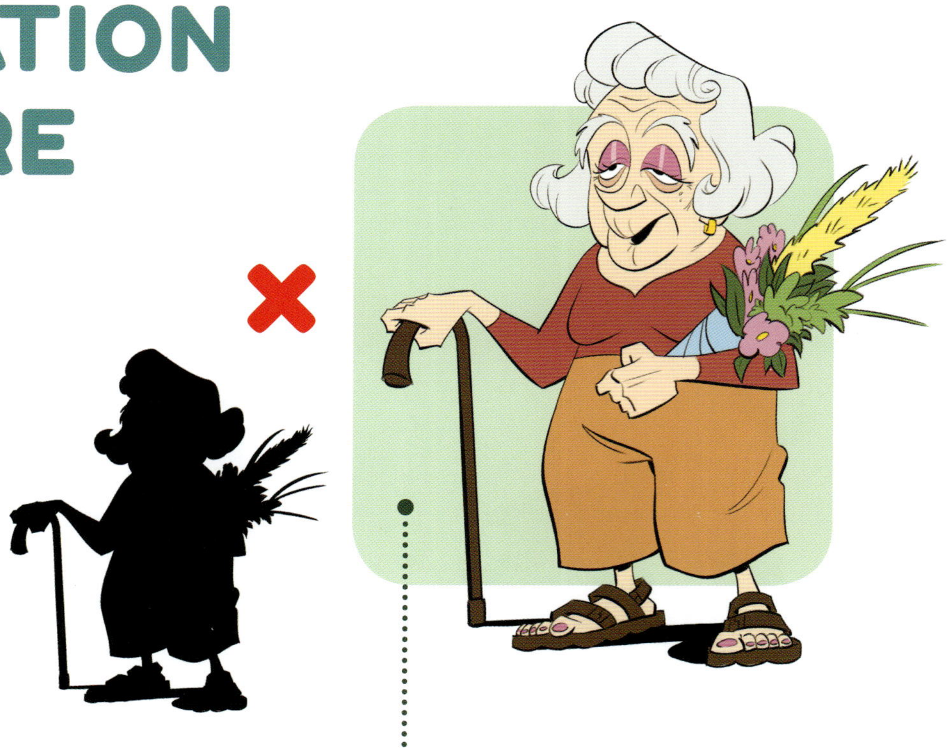

This first gesture is weak because the silhouette is hard to read, and the character isn't supporting herself on the cane. Why is it there if it's not being used? Besides her clothing and appearance, she is not portrayed as an older woman.

You can exaggerate the character successfully by bending her back, making her lean onto the cane to show how old age is taking its toll on her body. This is an example of exaggerating the story aspect of the design.

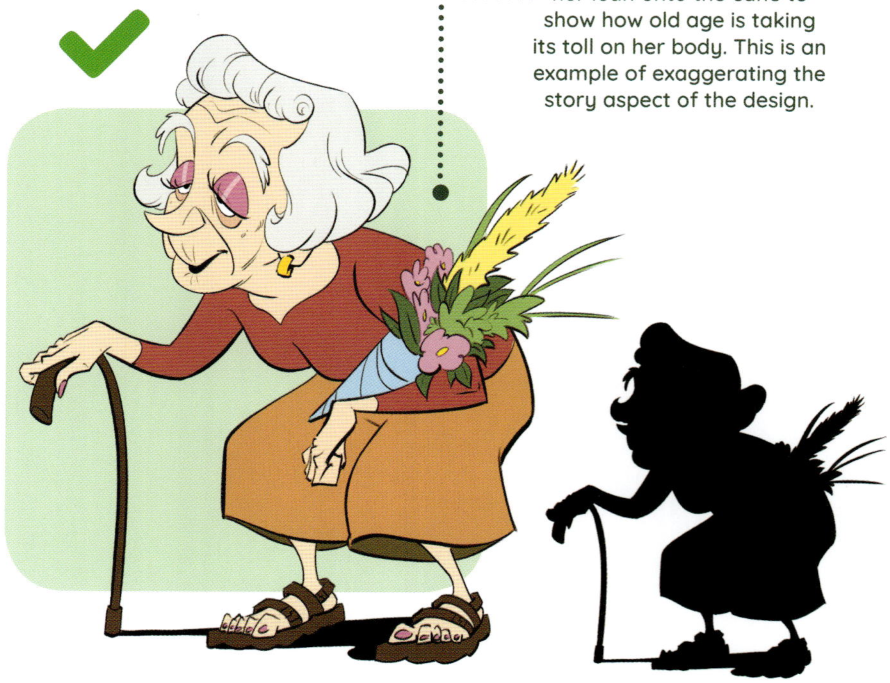

There is no line of action, resulting in a confusing silhouette, distracting tangents (see page 82), and a static pose with very little personality. This can be fixed by focusing on the character's intended personality.

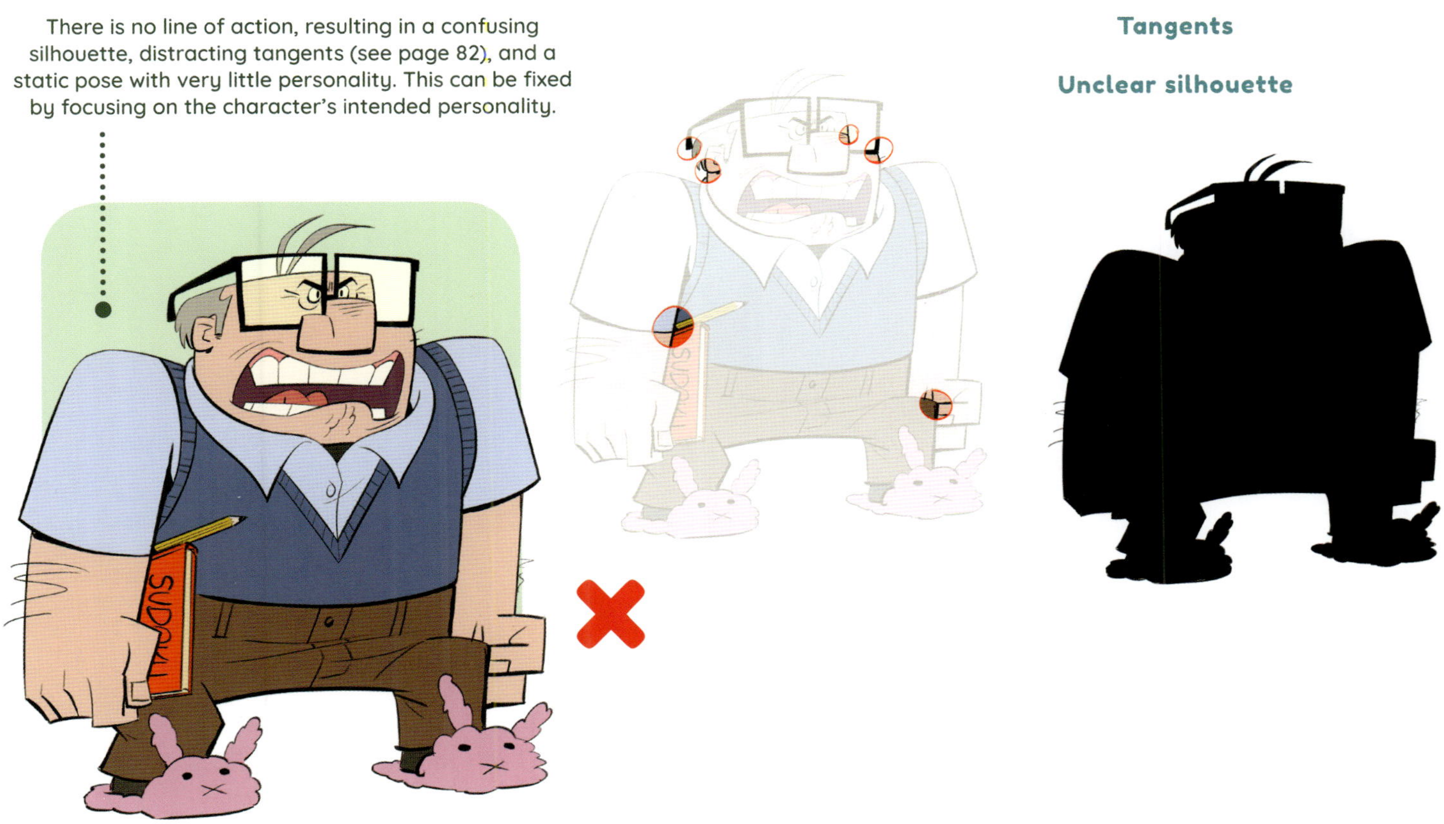

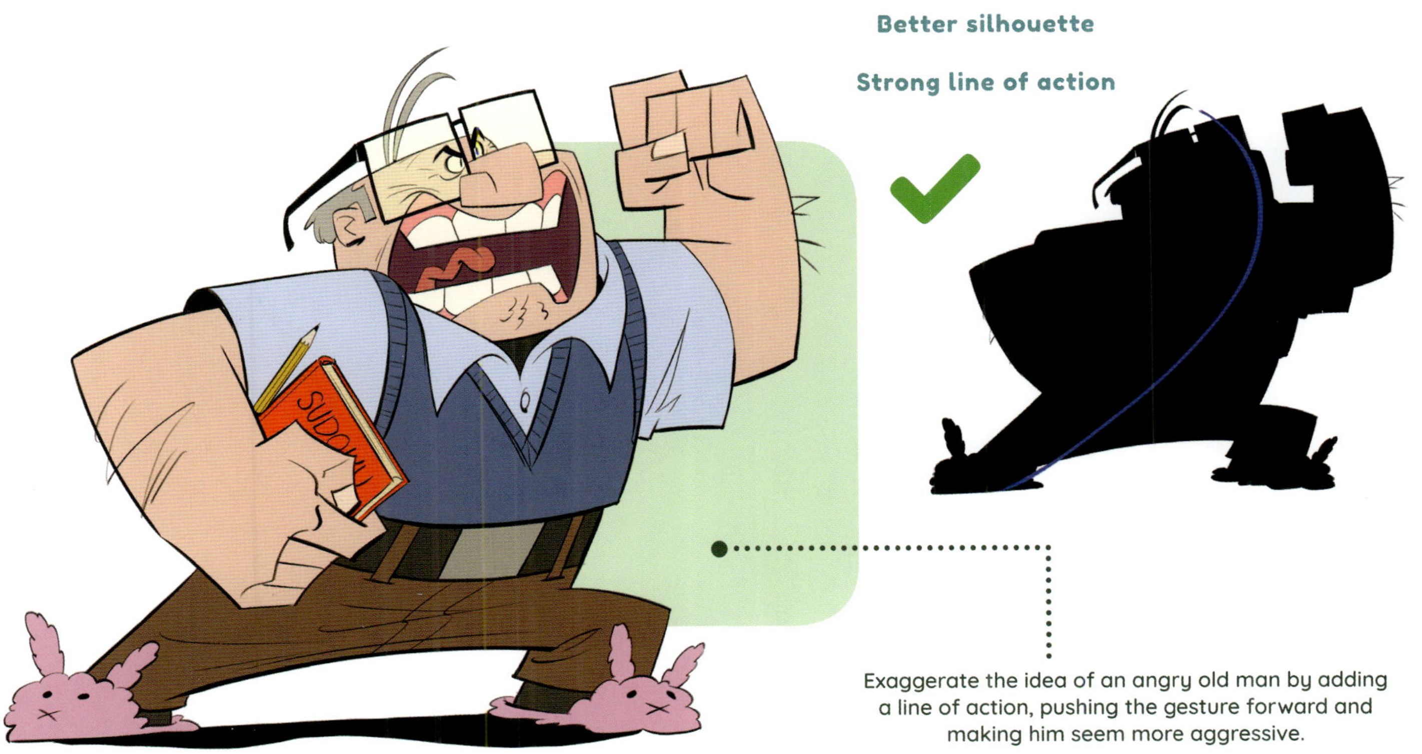

Exaggerate the idea of an angry old man by adding a line of action, pushing the gesture forward and making him seem more aggressive.

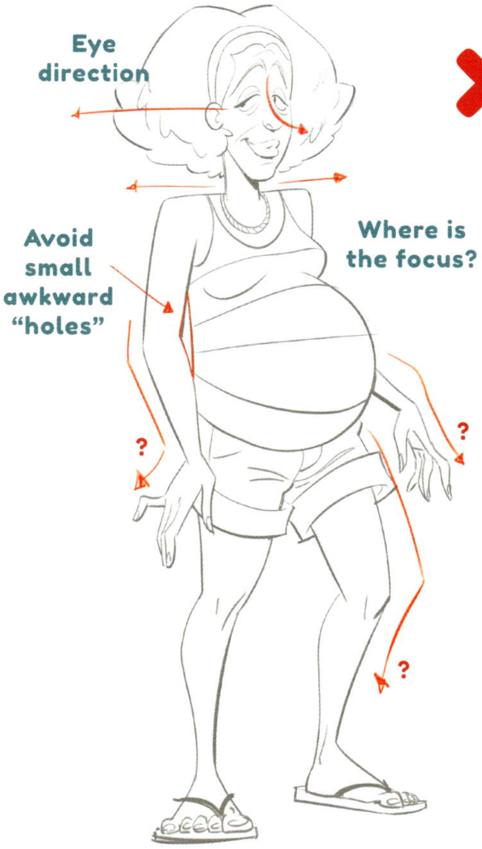

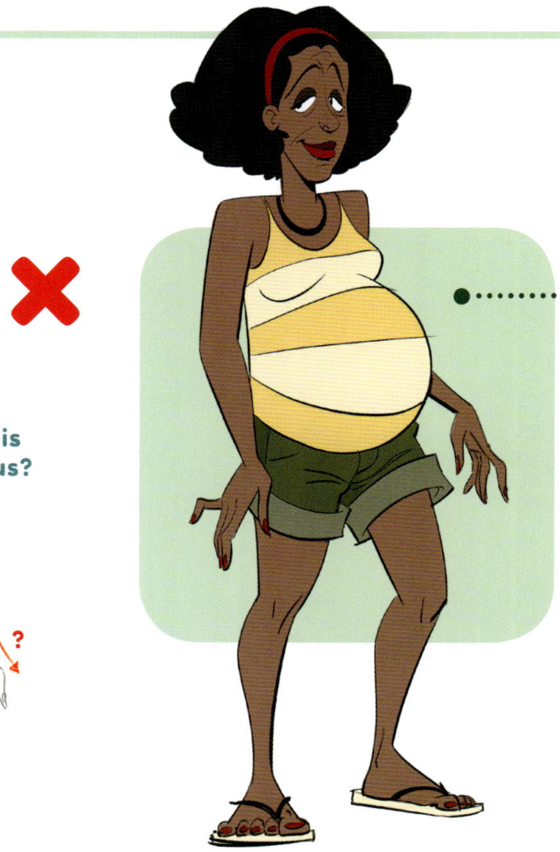

There are a number of problems with this first pose. It lacks direction and focus, and while pregnancy may be a key part of the character's story, the pose places no emphasis on the fact that she is pregnant.

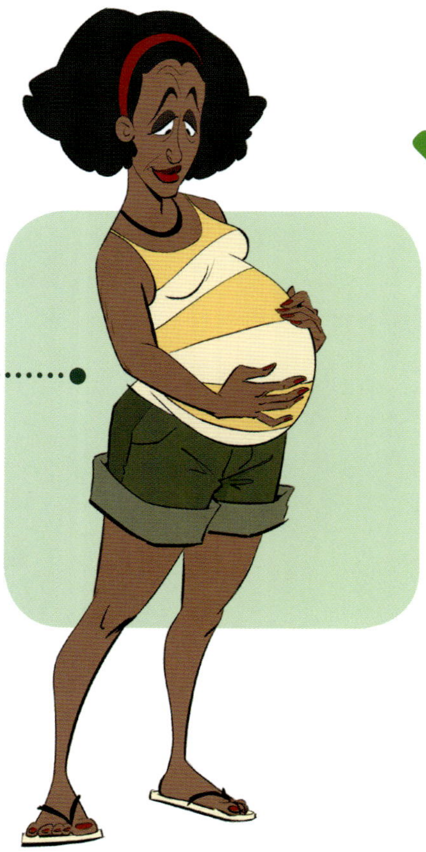

The character's balance has now shifted to compensate for the extra weight, resulting in her hips being pushed forward. Guide the audience's focus and emphasize the character's emotions by using the direction of the limbs and eyes.

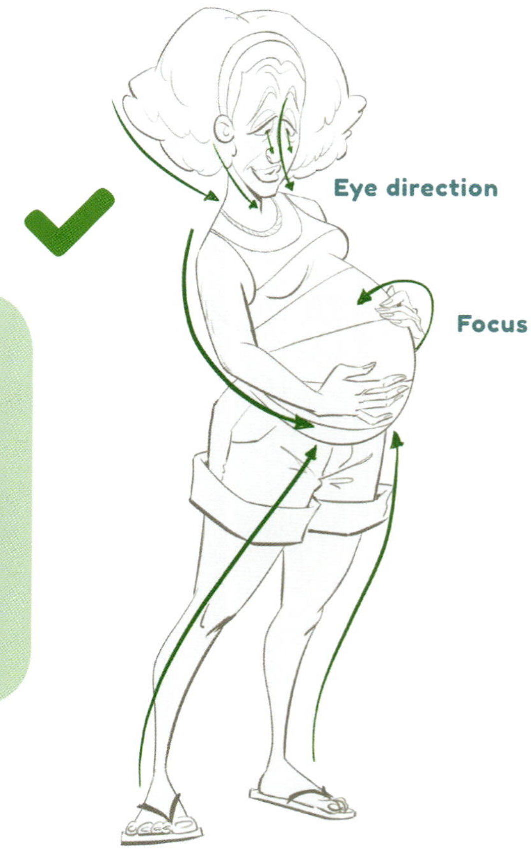

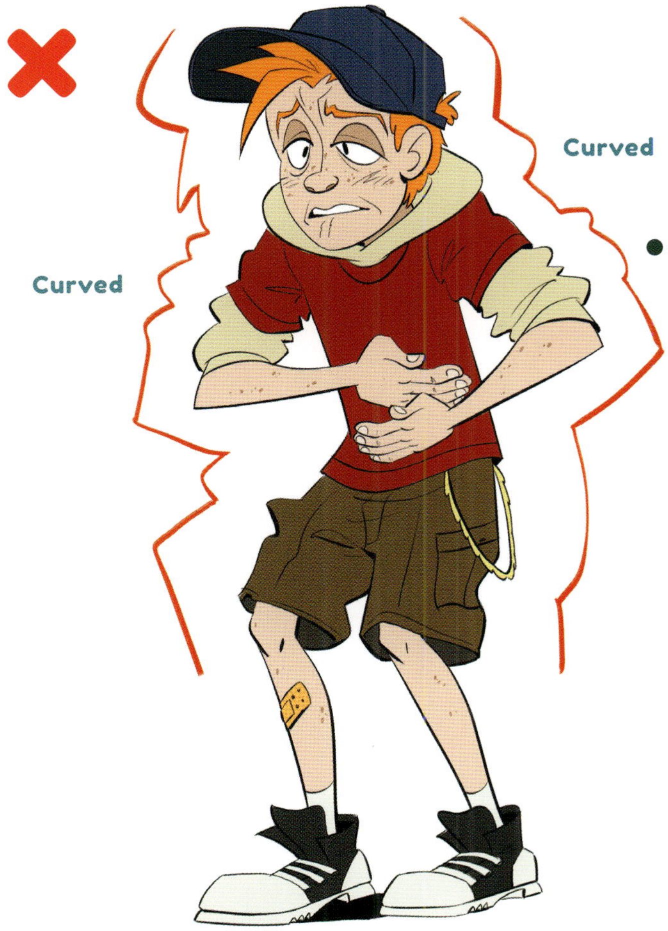

The upper body of a character is rarely ever completely straight. The spine will favor a curve, depending on the pose. However, this gesture lacks the strengthening contrast of curved versus straight that would make the pose more dramatic. This character needs a line of action that works with the intended story.

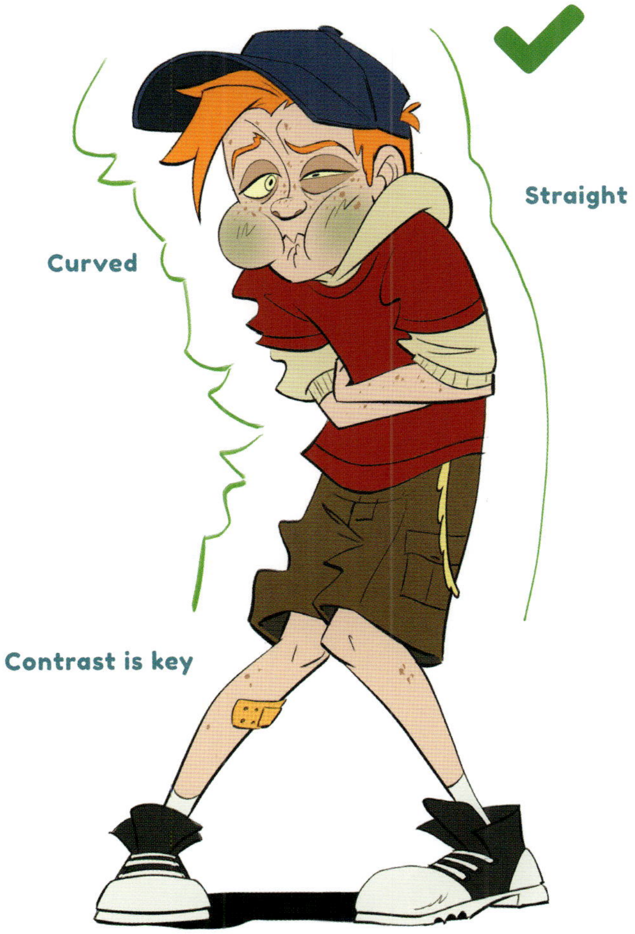

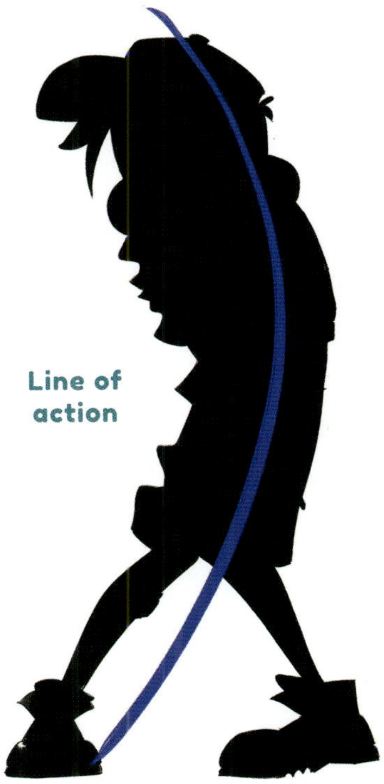

The character is feeling sick, which can be emphasized by bending his body forwards. Pointing the knees inward helps retain the focus, rather than sending it outward from the gesture.

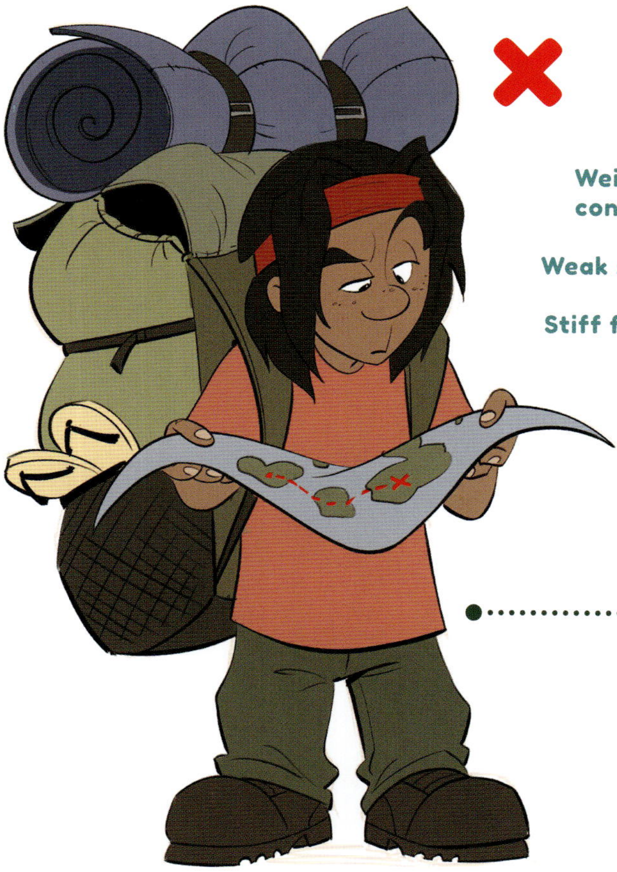

This pose has a weight and silhouette problem. The character's backpack is almost bigger than he is, yet the weight seems to not affect him. Believability is important, so his balance needs to be shifted.

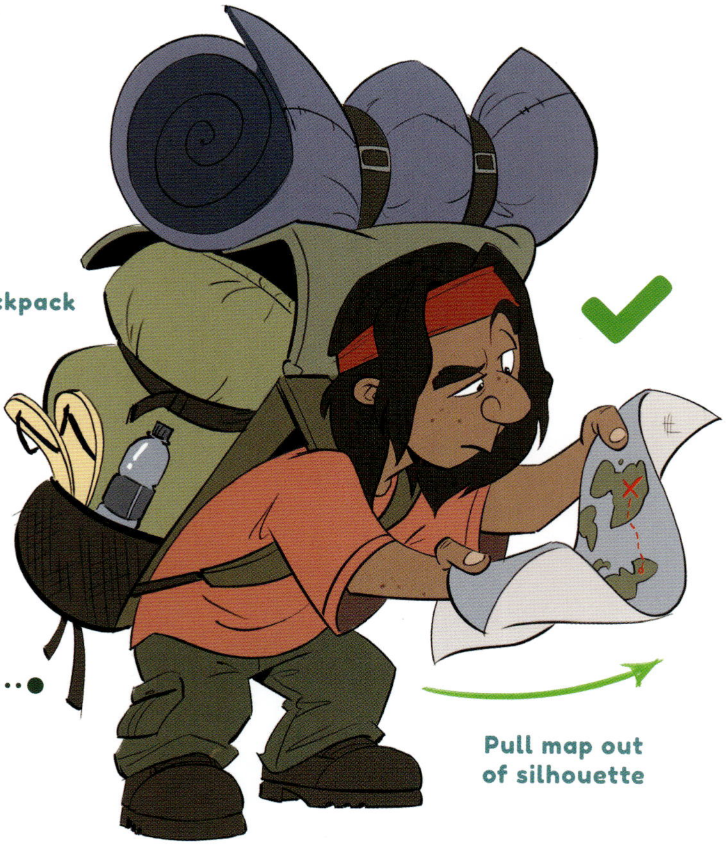

Leaning the character forward allows the backpack to rest on his back, instead of pulling him backward. Three-quarter views always contain more information than a frontal view, so the character has been turned sideways, allowing the map to break out of his silhouette.

Too subtle

Inexpressive silhouette

If this character was turned into a silhouette, it would look as if he was simply sitting instead of having fallen asleep.

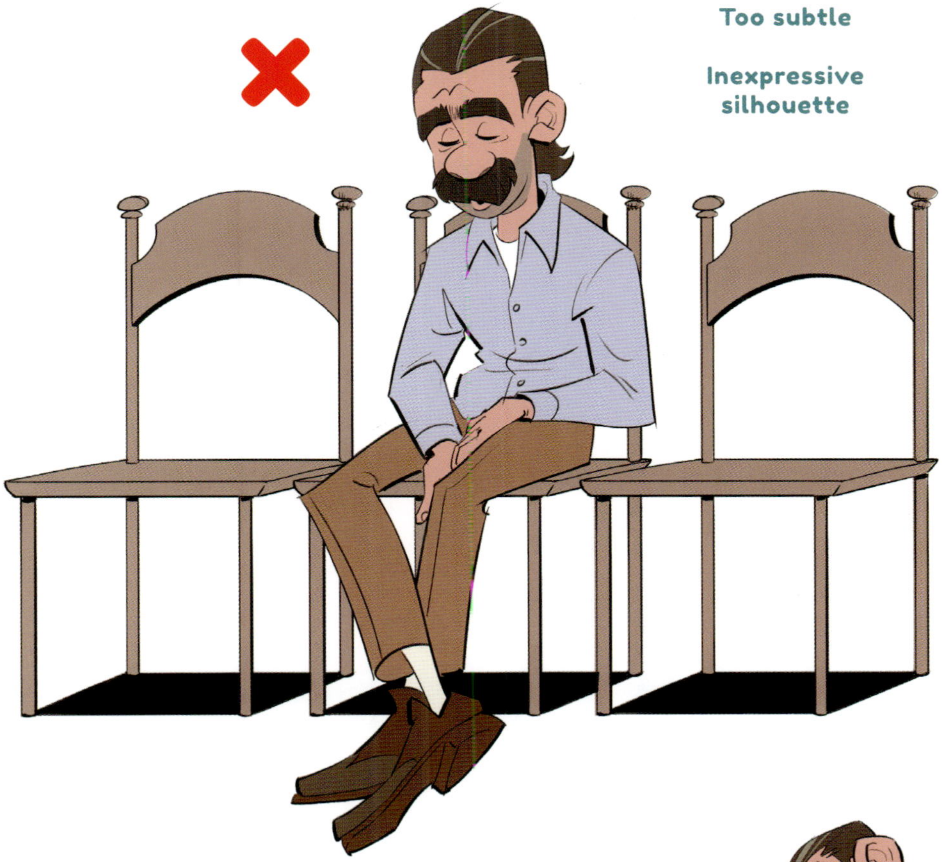

Relax the muscles

Focus on weight

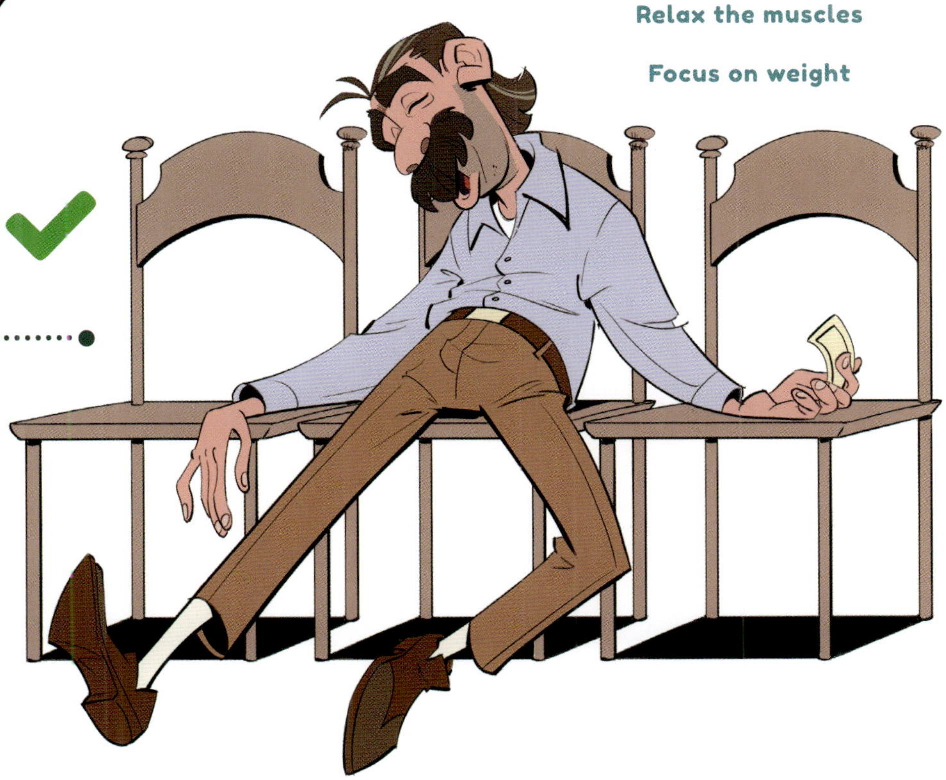

Play into the scenario by exaggerating the features that will clearly tell the audience that the character is sleeping. Relax his muscles and push his weight down into the chairs.

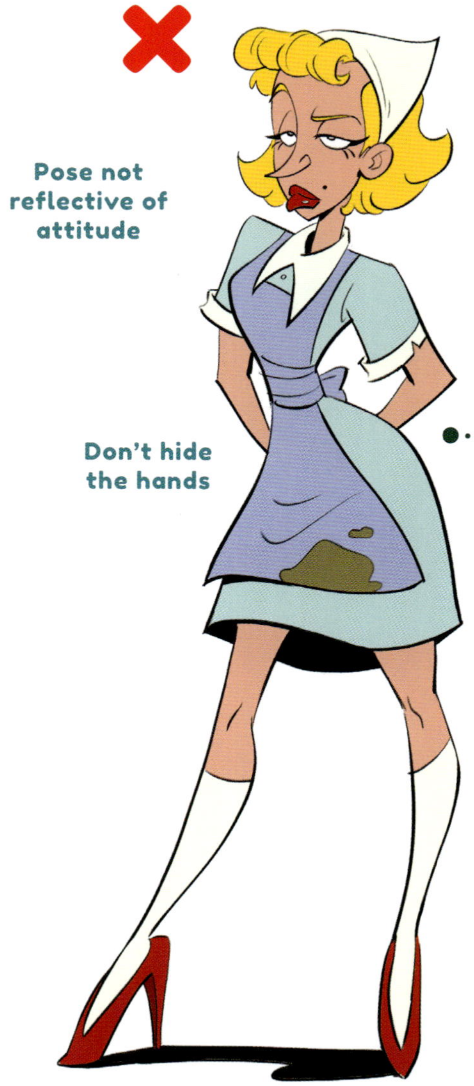

Hands are hard to draw, which is why many beginner artists avoid them like the plague! Instead of avoiding challenges, focus on tackling the parts of a design you know could use some work. Plus, hands can be a great gesture enhancer!

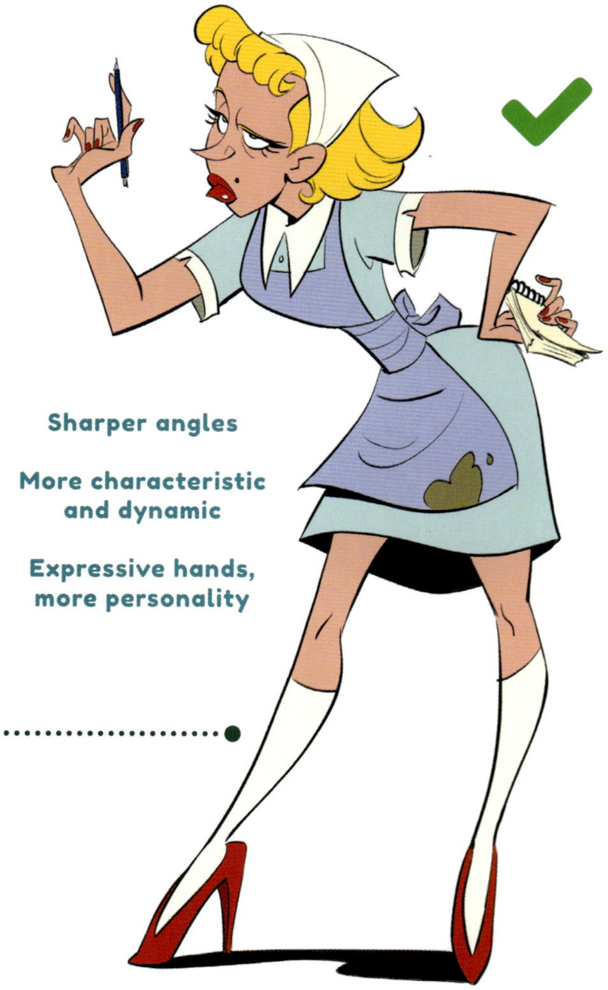

Pay attention to how much the personality and expression are exaggerated by putting the hands on display. They work in harmony with the rest of the body.

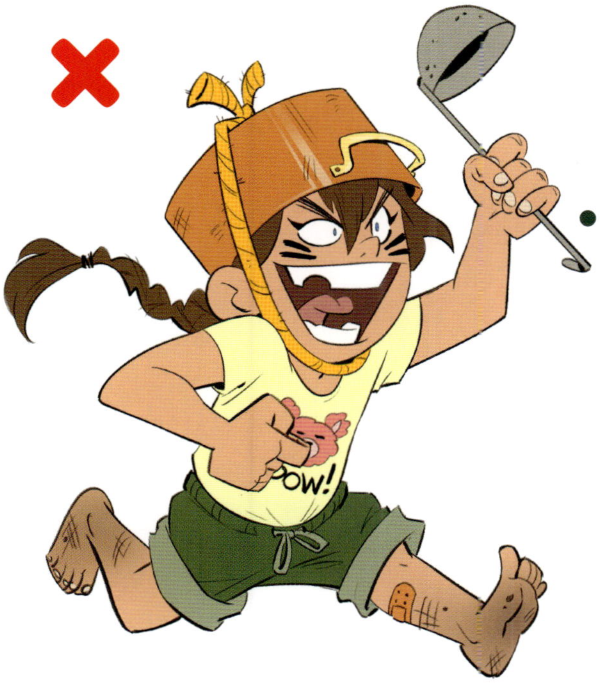

This pose can be exaggerated by integrating a line of action. The character should be leading with her chest, so the line of action needs to curve the spine forward.

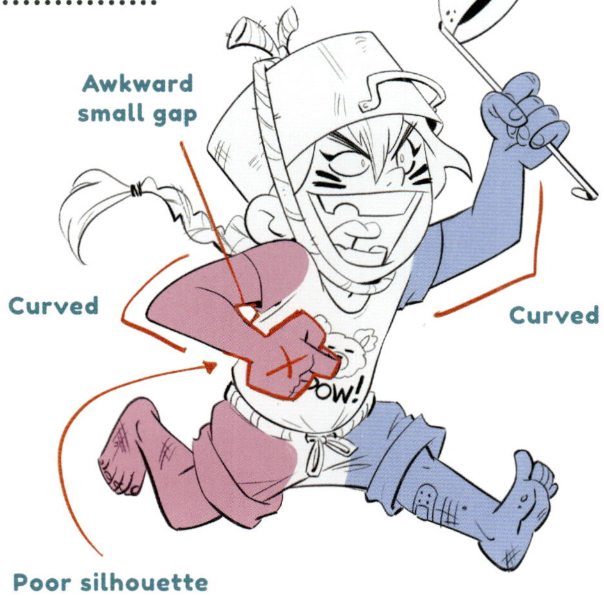

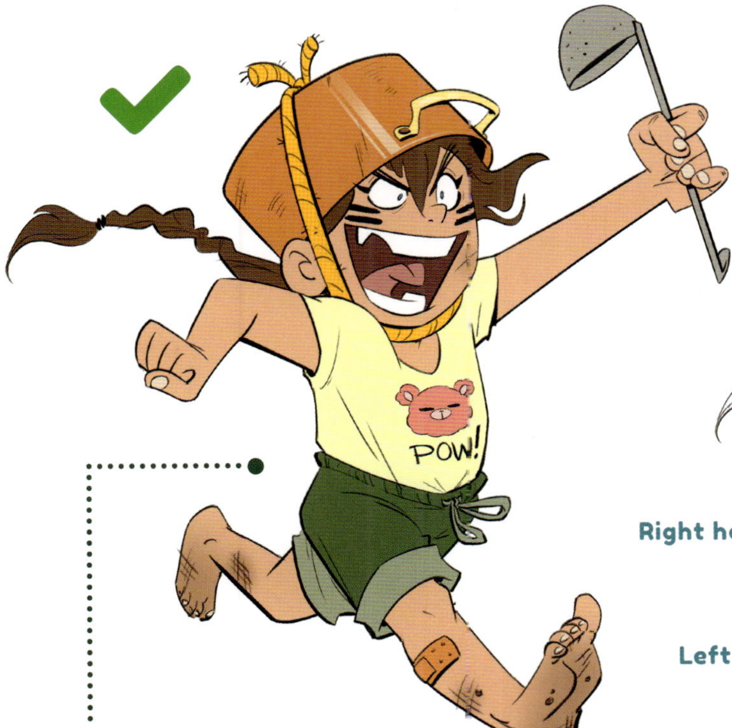

A strong line of action has been added, and the silhouette has been improved by pulling the character's right hand out from the torso. All of this allows the pose to be exaggerated through force and energy.

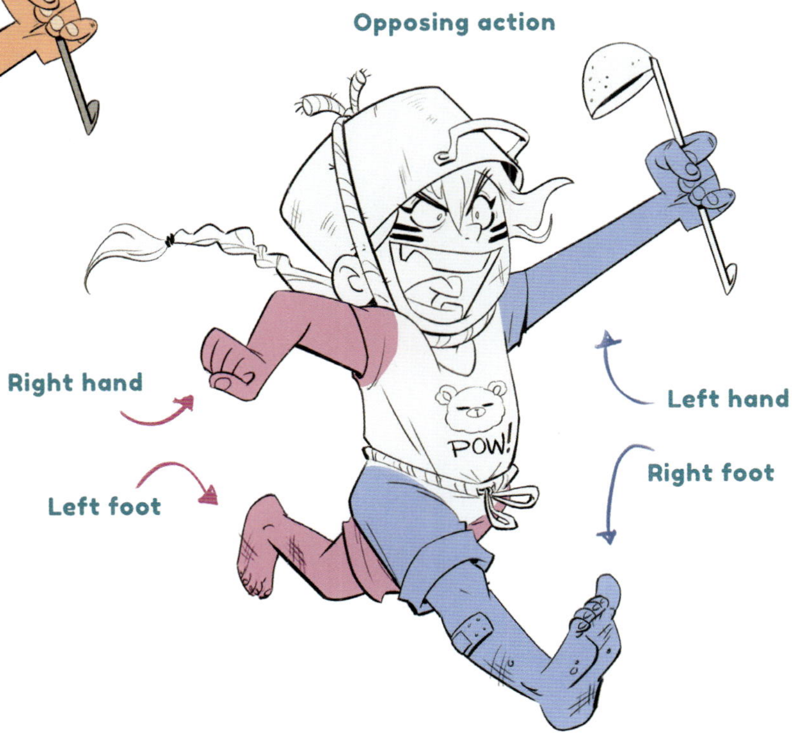

POSES LIBRARY

Kenneth Anderson

Life drawing and observational drawing will improve your knowledge of how people move and hold themselves, while gathering reference from photos, books, TV shows, and films can help build a mental library of pose ideas.

Make sure the key idea behind a pose is clear and simple - the gesture and line of action of a tired character, for example, will vary from those of an energetic character. If the key ideas become confused on the page, the pose will be too.

CROUCHING, CURIOUS

A curious character will likely lean in and reach out to the subject of their attention. A crouched position suggests even more interest.

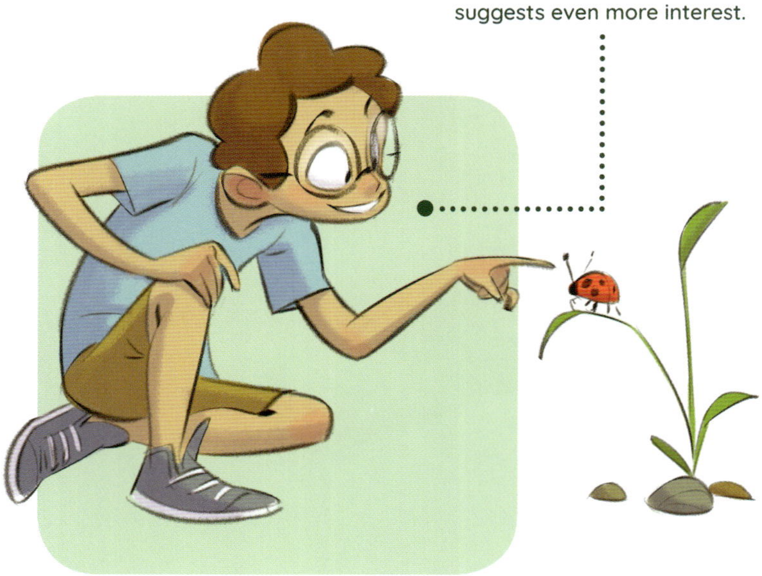

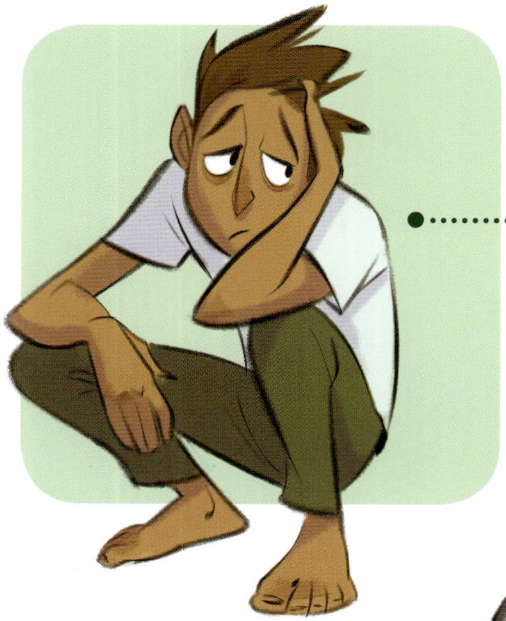

CROUCHING, SAD & TIRED

Some emotions fit well together and are easily synthesized into a singular pose. Sadness and tiredness work well in tandem.

CROUCHING, STEALTHY

A stealthy crouch should feel engaged, full of ready-to-act energy.

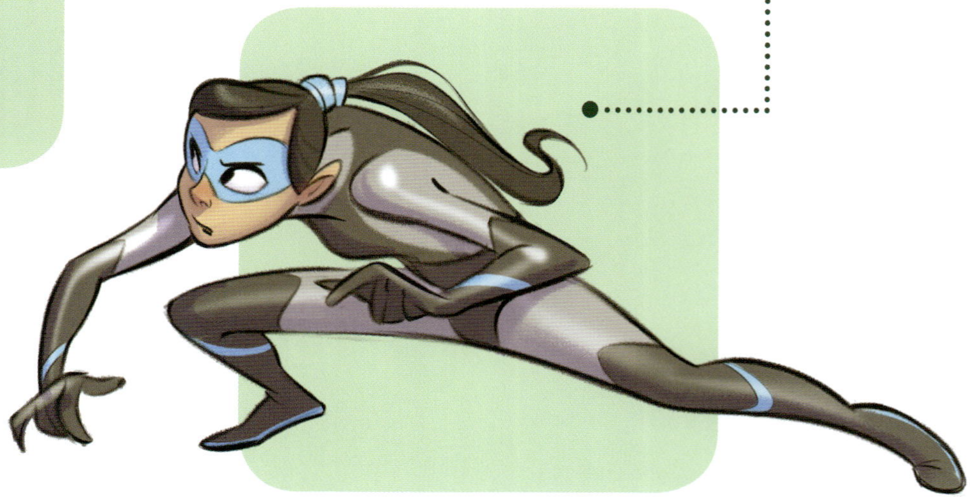

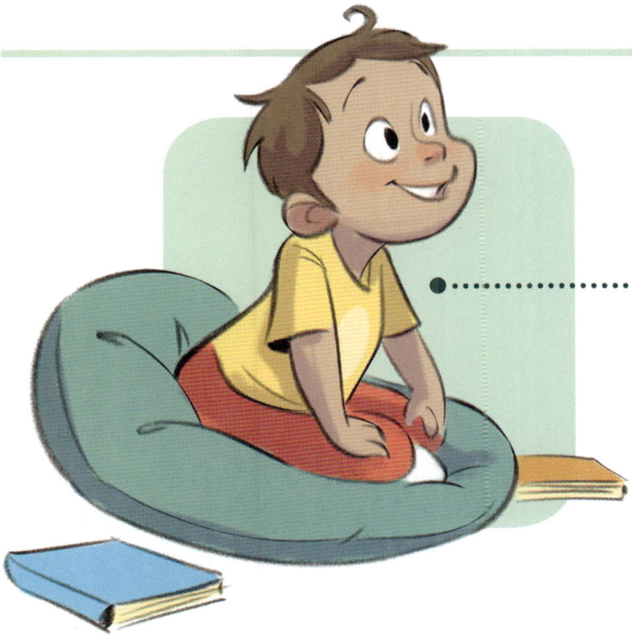

SEATED, EAGER

An eager character will likely lean toward the thing that's caught their attention or that they want, even if seated.

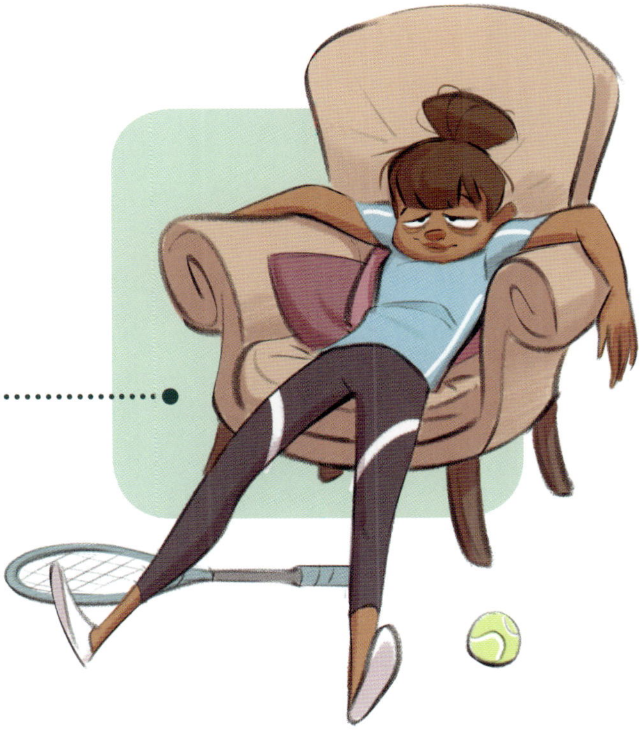

SEATED, EXHAUSTED

A chair is the perfect object to collapse into when tired – how the body molds and contours to the chair helps sell the idea of exhaustion.

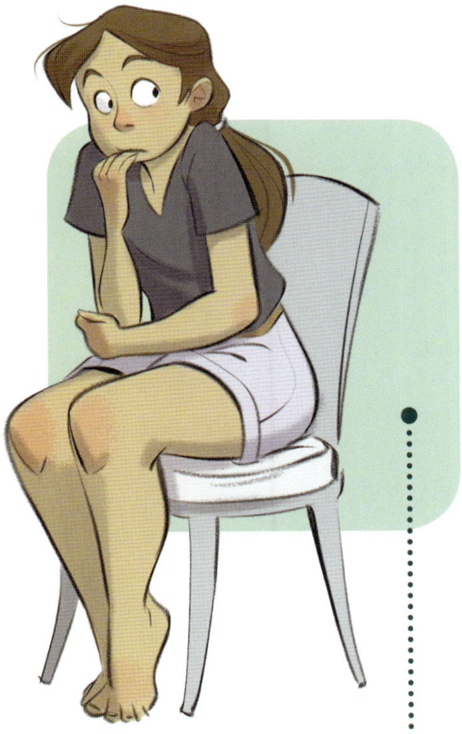

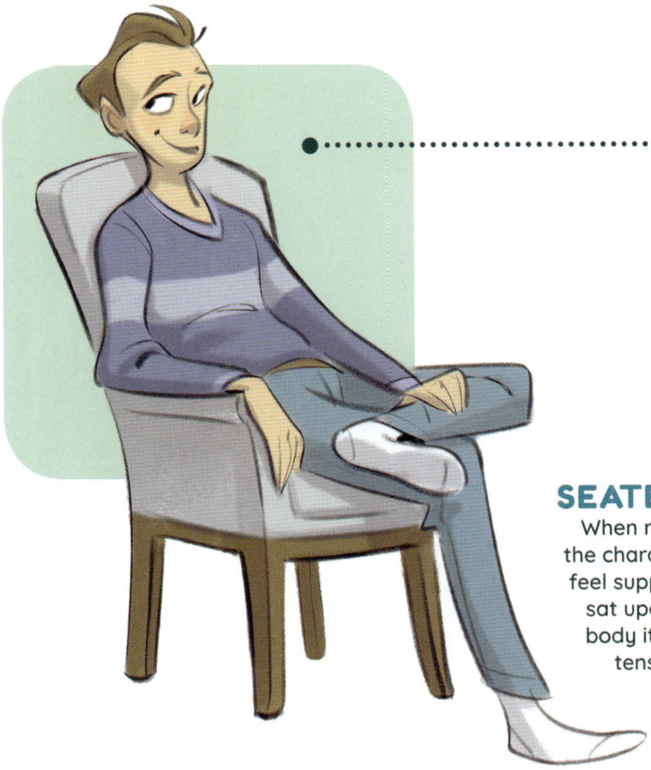

SEATED, NERVOUS

A nervous character can't relax, not even when sitting. Attentive upright body language can help sell this idea.

SEATED, RELAXED

When relaxed and seated, the character's weight should feel supported by the object sat upon, rather than the body itself, with no visual tension in the body.

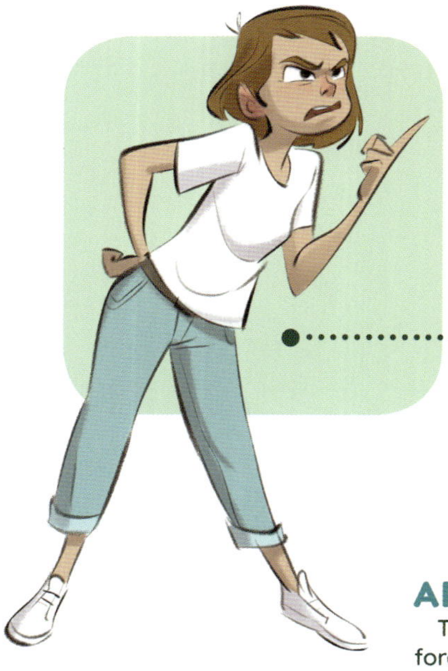

STANDING, ARGUMENTATIVE

This type of pose exudes forceful energy to match the mood that has created it.

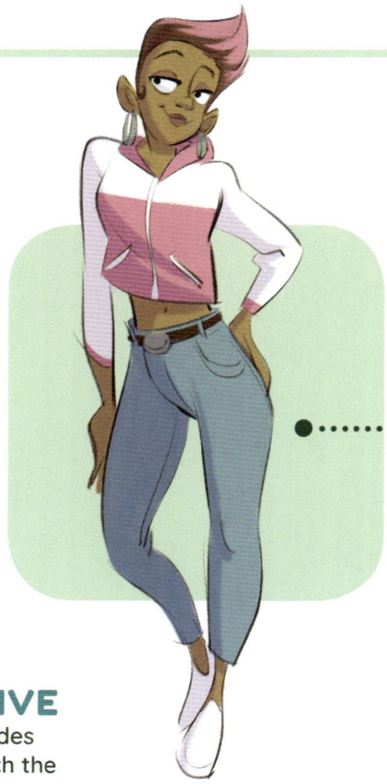

STANDING, CASUAL LEAN

Here the weight of the body is supported by an unseen wall, the energy of the pose relaxed – take away the wall and they will likely fall over!

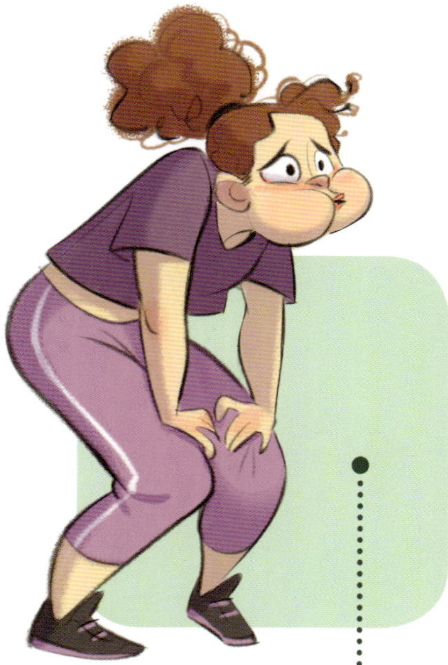

STANDING, EXHAUSTED

It can be hard to stand upright when exhausted. This character is bearing their weight on their legs while trying to catch their breath.

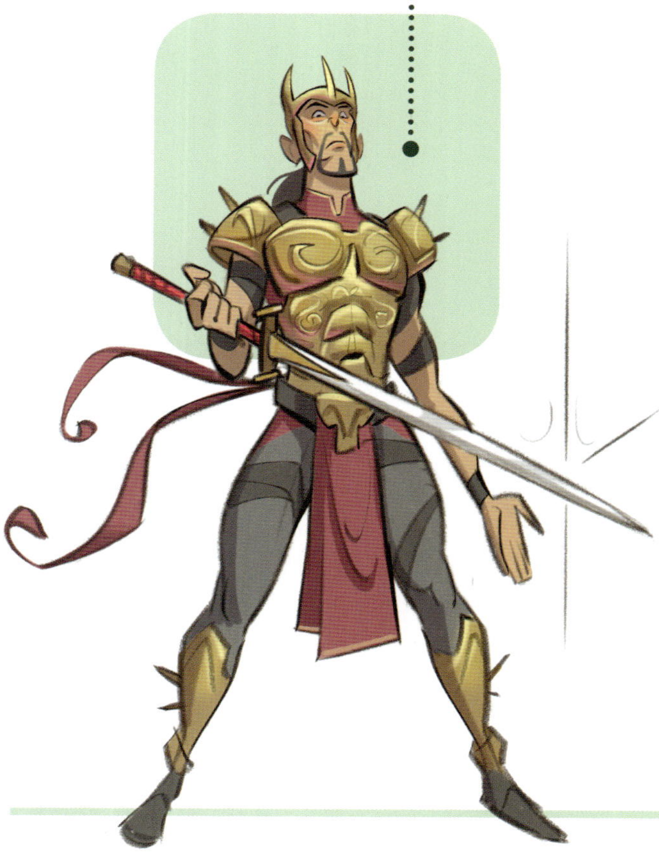

STANDING, HEROIC WITH WEAPON

A wide stance with upright shoulders conveys confidence, readiness, and an air of power – perfect for a heroic vibe.

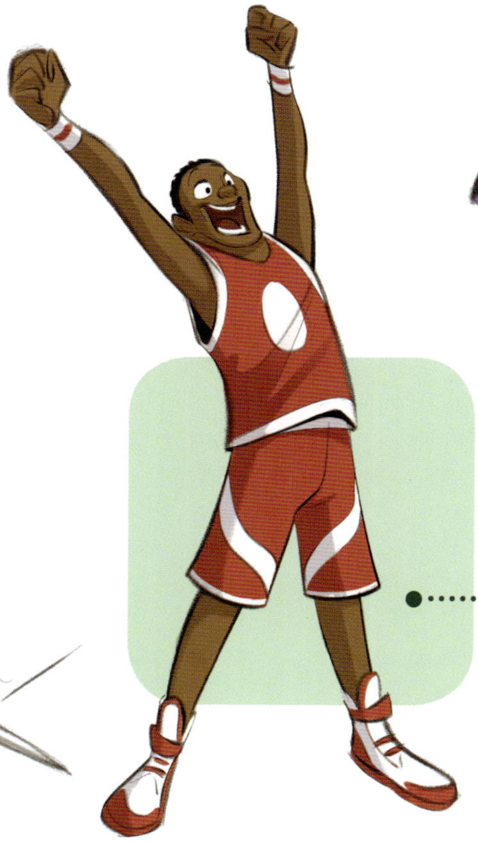

STANDING, TRIUMPHANT

An extreme form of triumph, where the character throws their limbs out with celebratory energy.

Randy Bishop

Each pose you put the character in should match their personality, style, temperament, and physical ability. Exploring different poses is a good way to get a feel for your character, to "break in" the design and work out any kinks. When putting a character through multiple poses, you will be able to watch them evolve and settle into a pose that's comfortable. The design is always better after doing this, so it's wise to hold off making technical pieces such as turnarounds until after you have tested the design in this way.

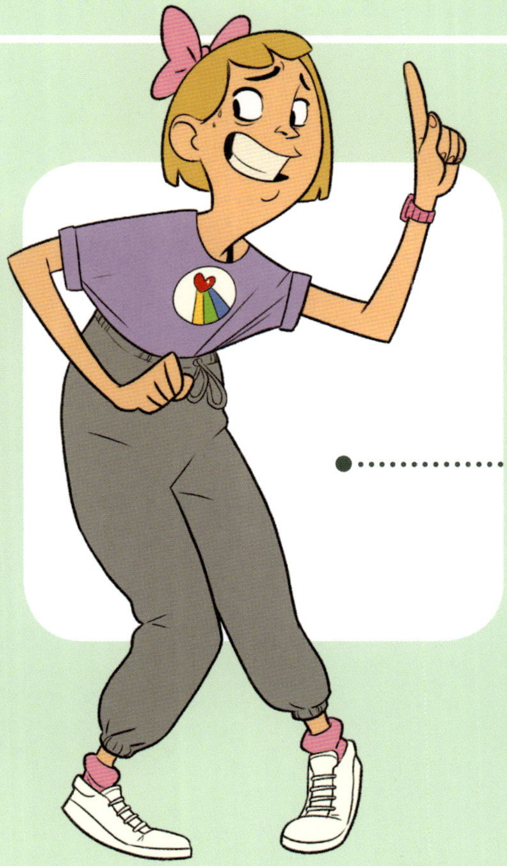

DANCING, EMBARRASSED

Social situations are awkward for many people. Any amount of attention, good or bad, is enough to make this character sweat, with an awkward stance and worried expression conveying discomfort.

DANCING, COMICAL

The lanky limbs, receding hairline, and exuberant facial expression make this dancing dad look doubly goofy!

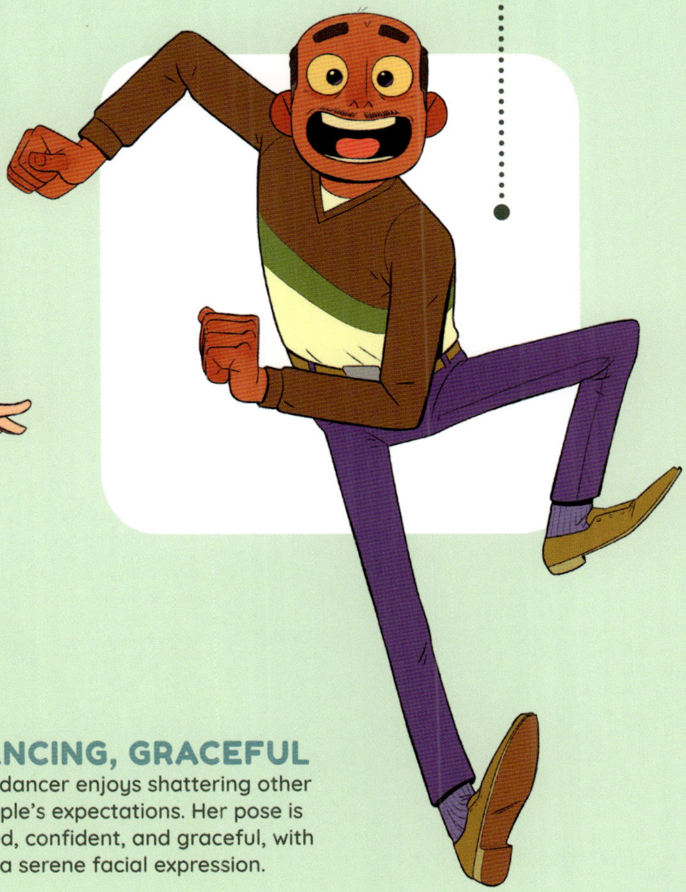

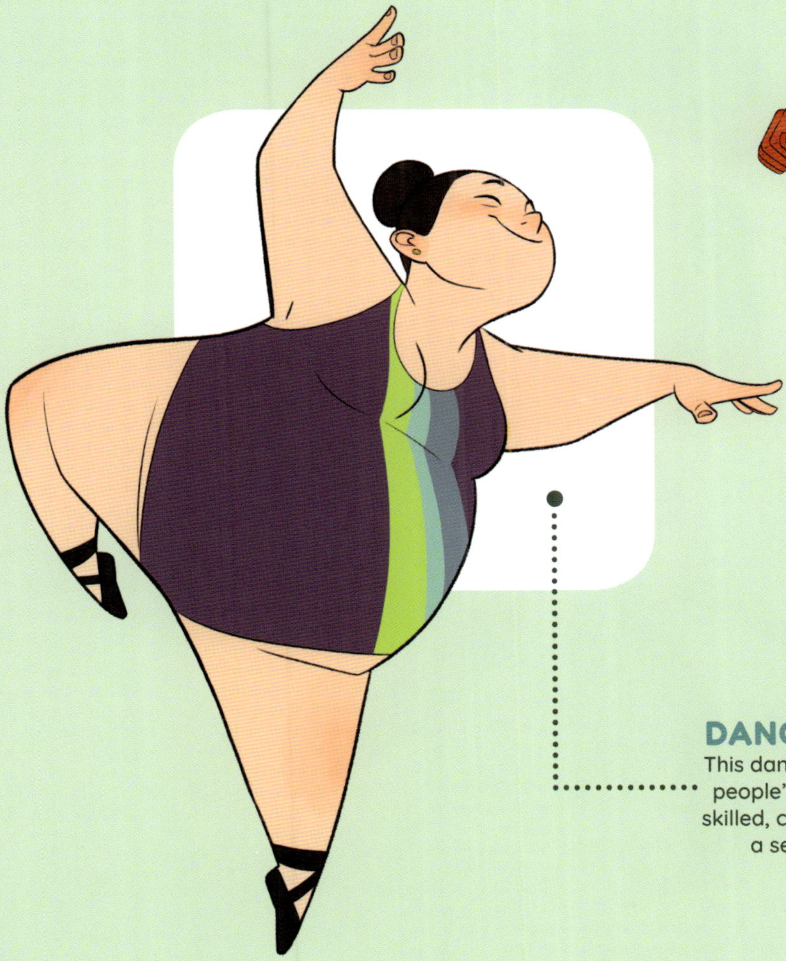

DANCING, GRACEFUL

This dancer enjoys shattering other people's expectations. Her pose is skilled, confident, and graceful, with a serene facial expression.

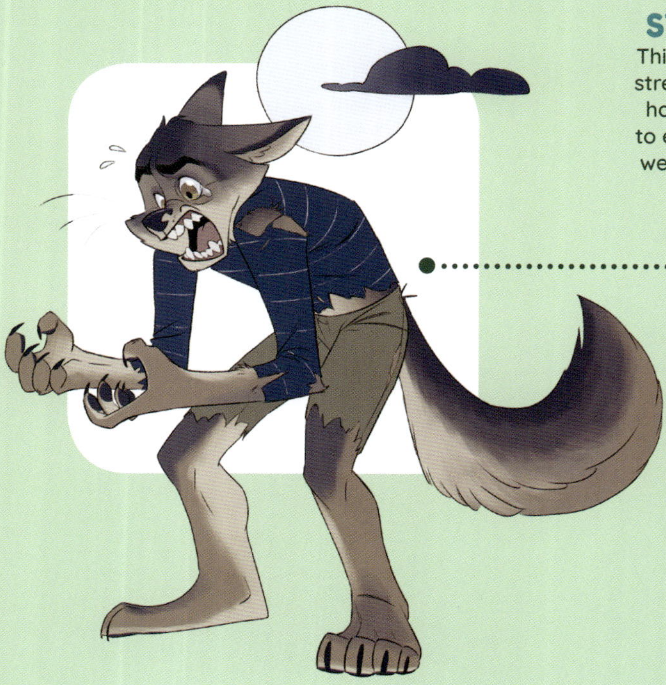

STRESSED OUT

This pose is one of extreme stress and anguish. Imagine how terrifying it would be to experience turning into a werewolf for the first time!

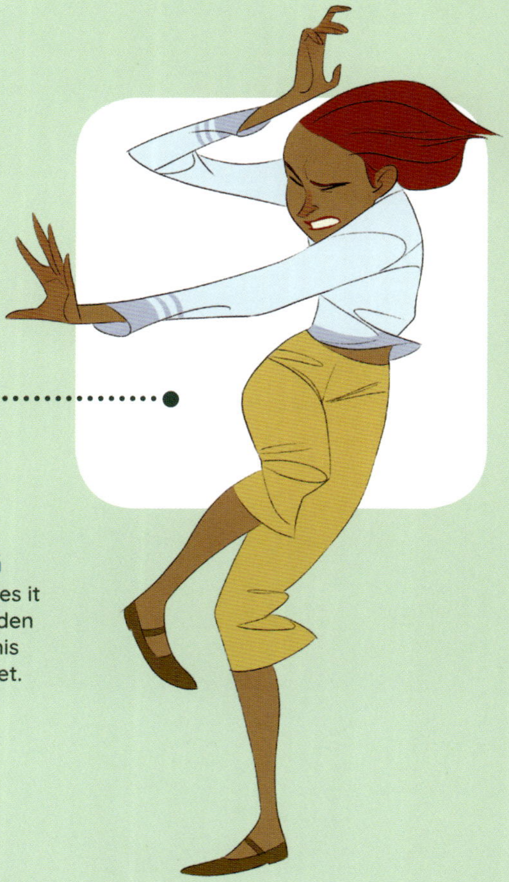

COWERING

This fearful pose makes it look as though a sudden wind could sweep this character off her feet.

WAVING A GREETING

This upbeat character loves waving a cheery hello to his neighbors.

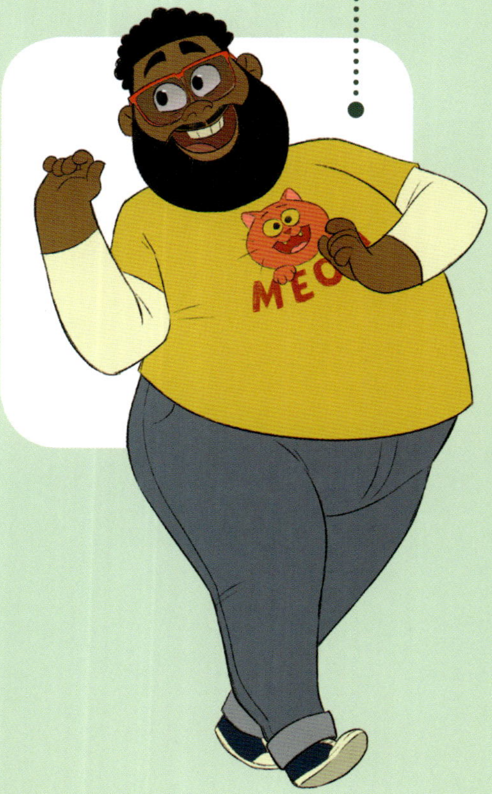

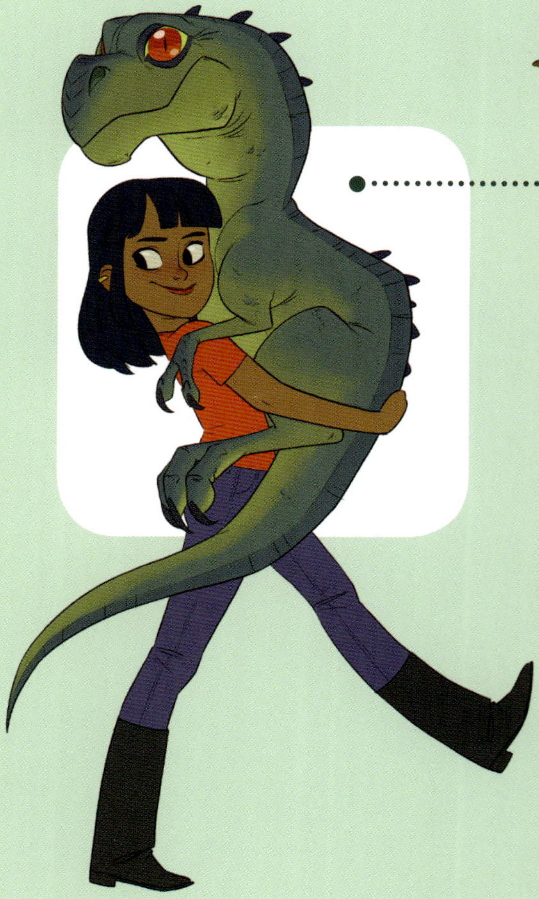

RUSHING, CARRYING SOMETHING

Marching straight through town carrying a dinosaur just screams confidence.

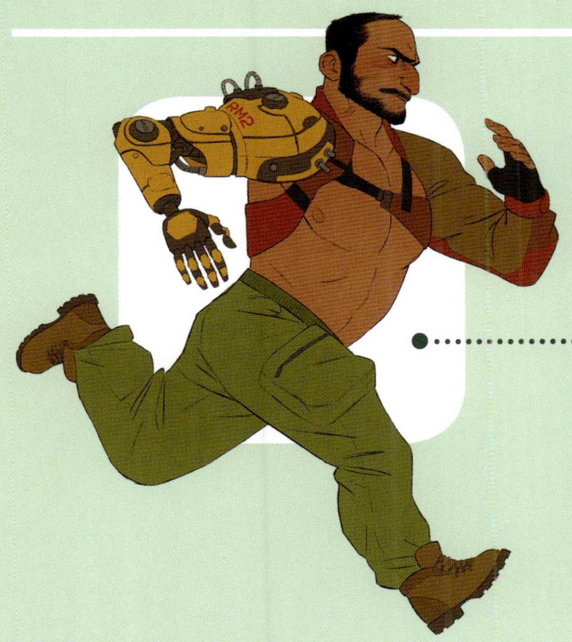

RUNNING, DETERMINED

With his gaze fixed straight ahead and arms and legs pumping, it's clear this character is running with purpose.

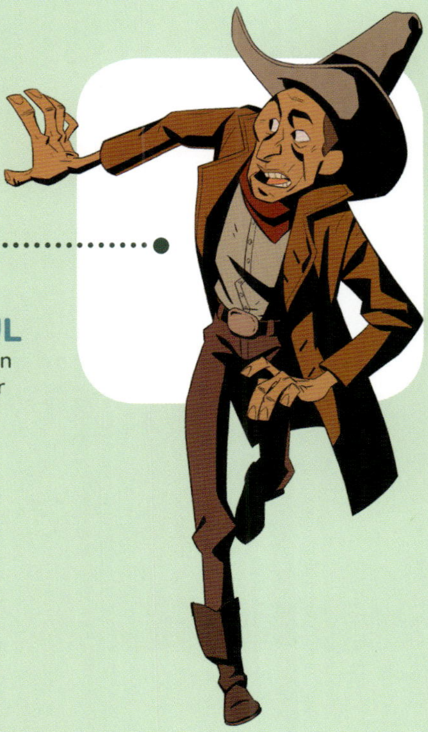

RUNNING, FEARFUL

Looking behind you as you run might be dangerous, but fear makes people irrational.

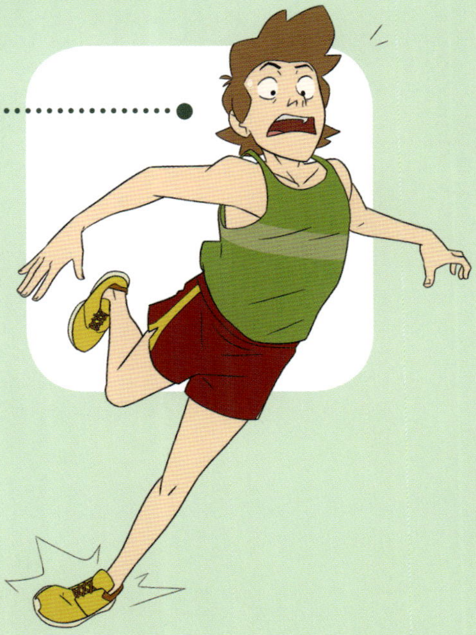

TRIPPING

Show the transition between relaxation and panic in a character's body language as they fall. Surprise registers first on his face, the chest and shoulders lead the fall, and his left hand begins to tense up.

DODGING AN OBSTACLE

Dodging an obstacle usually involves intentionally throwing yourself off-balance for a moment, making the pose doubly tense. On the one hand, there's an object that could injure, and on the other, there's the danger of falling over.

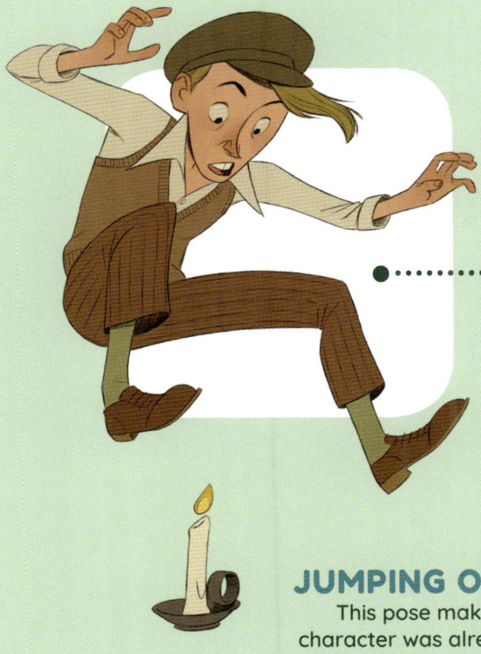

JUMPING OVER AN OBJECT

This pose makes it look as though the character was already moving at a fast pace before he came across the candlestick. If he were simply jumping over it from a stationary position, his motion would be more vertical, and the distance between himself and the candlestick would be greater.

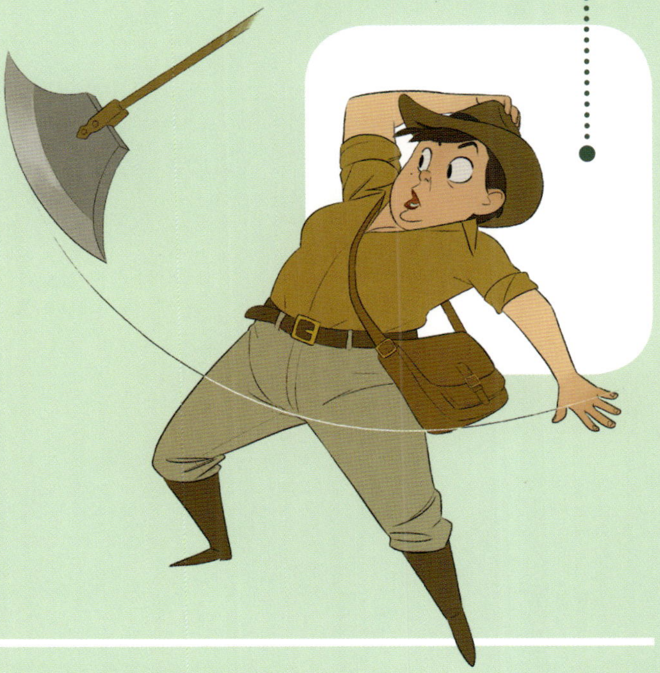

Luis Gadea

Start by choosing a single verb or word that you want to illustrate. Next, draw your character in a selection of rough poses to explore the verb. Think about the silhouette of each pose and check whether the silhouette fully communicates the idea. If it doesn't, go back to your roughs and sketch as many poses as needed to find one that successfully communicates the chosen verb. If you are having trouble, look for references or try posing in front of a camera yourself and analyze what you see.

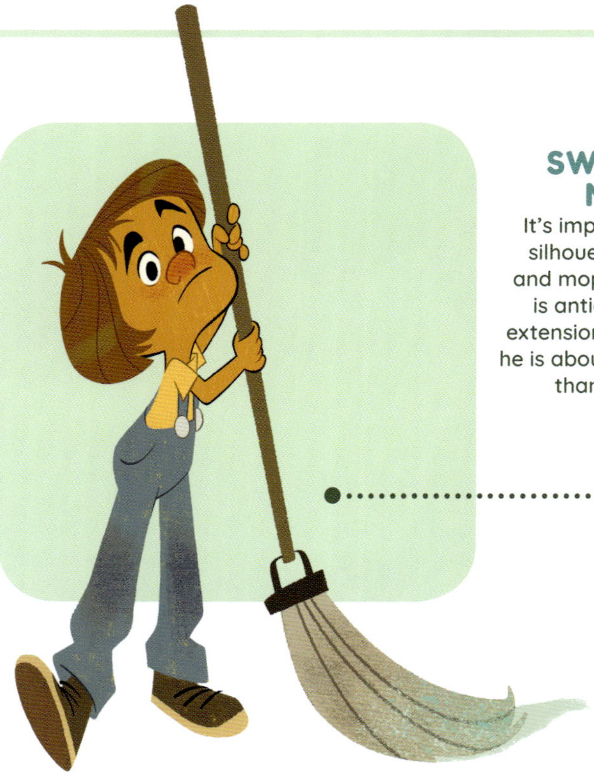

SWEEPING OR MOPPING

It's important to see a clear silhouette of the character and mop in action. Movement is anticipated through the extension of the boy's leg, as if he is about to take a step rather than simply standing.

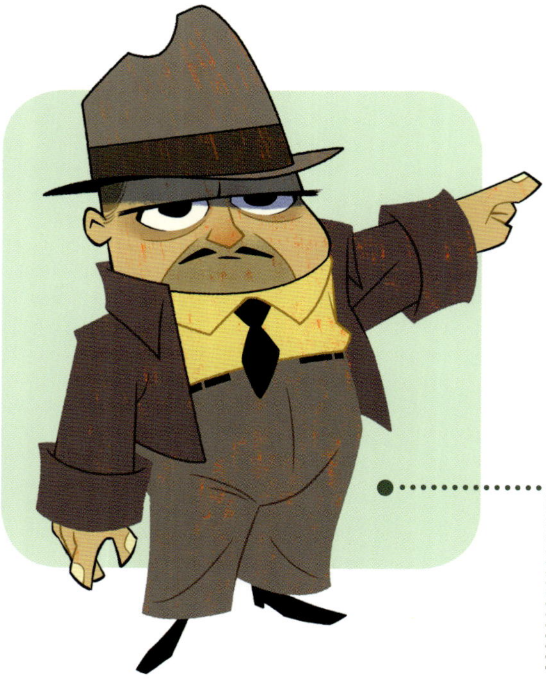

POINTING AT AN OBJECT

The character has a clear inverted "L" shape, drawing attention to the pointing action.

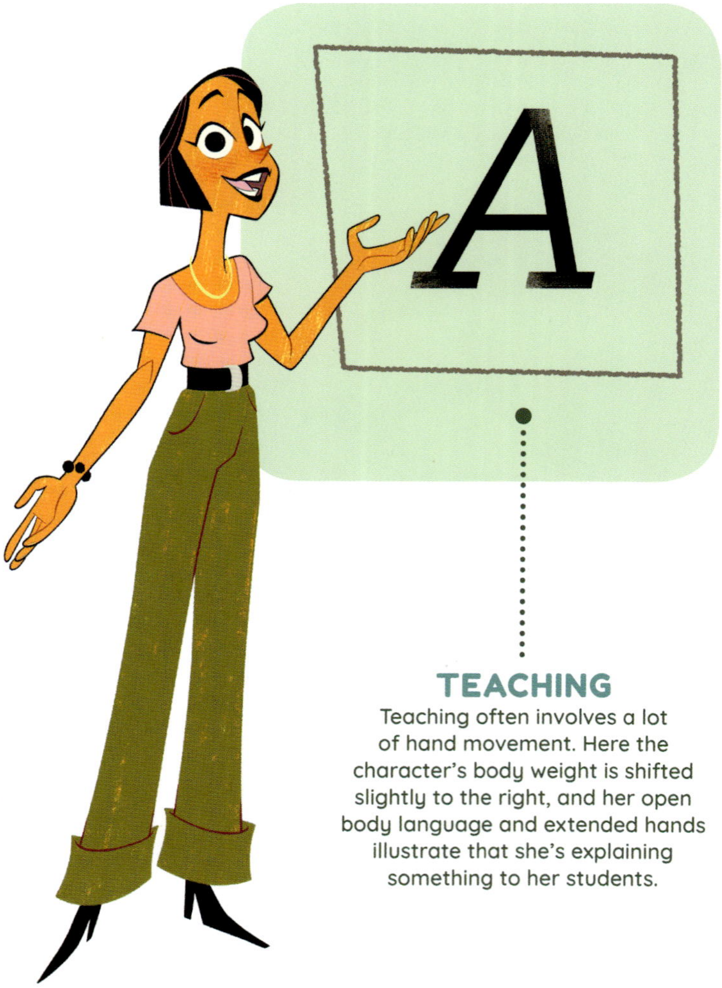

TEACHING

Teaching often involves a lot of hand movement. Here the character's body weight is shifted slightly to the right, and her open body language and extended hands illustrate that she's explaining something to her students.

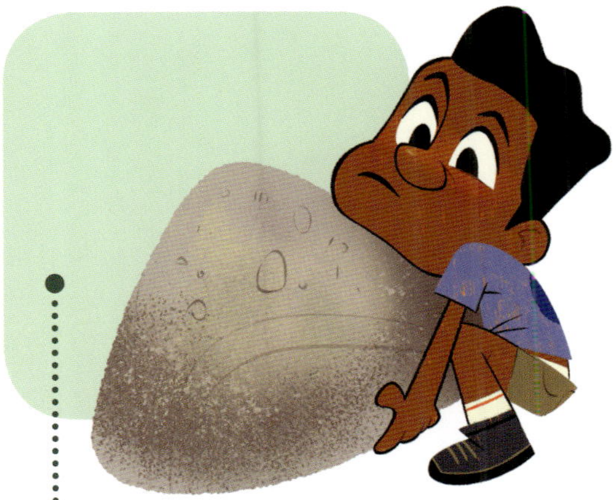

LIFTING A HEAVY OBJECT

A "C"-shaped back illustrates the action of lifting. The character's feet are planted firmly on the ground, with the large rock he's trying to lift obscuring his other foot and hand.

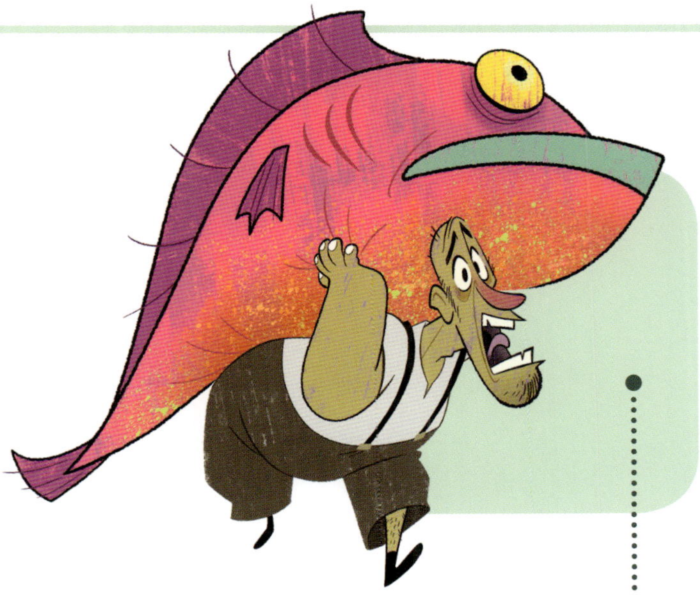

CARRYING A HEAVY OBJECT

Carrying a heavy object on your back will create an inverted "C" shape, the opposite to the pose on the left. If exaggerating the size and heaviness of an object, try showing the character's exhausted pose and expression.

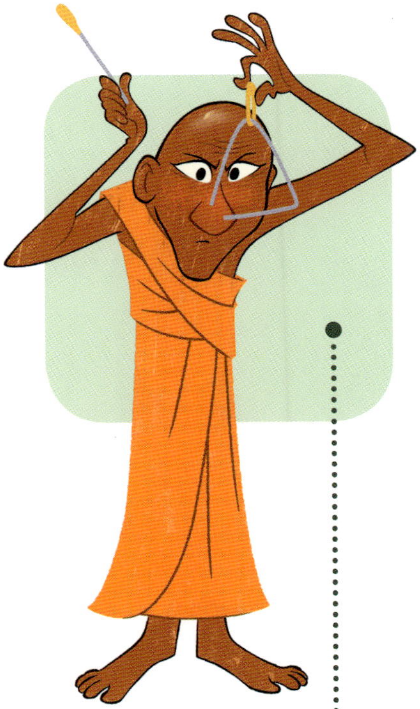

PLAYING MUSIC, FOCUSED

The character's focused eyes, poised arms, and simple body shape draw attention to the instrument and illustrate his concentration and determination.

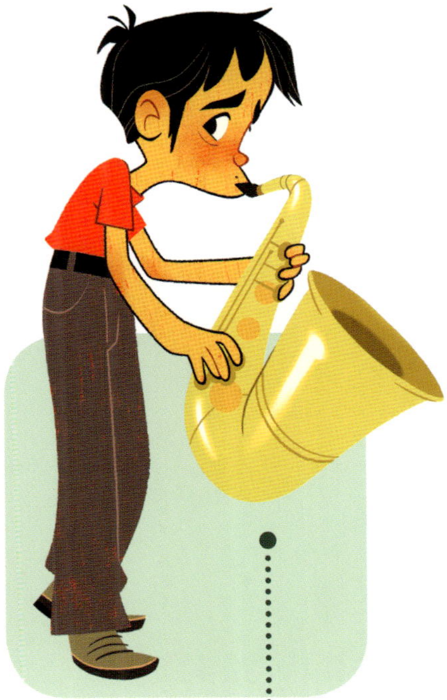

PLAYING MUSIC, NERVOUS

This character's hunched, "C"-shaped back and half-hidden face reveal how insecure and anxious he is. His shy expression, a slight blush on his cheeks, and his feet not completely on the ground convey his lack of confidence.

PLAYING MUSIC, TRIUMPHANT

The opposite of the nervous boy, this girl's confidence and enthusiasm for her clarinet-playing are shown through her upward-facing head and extended leg as she dances from foot to foot.

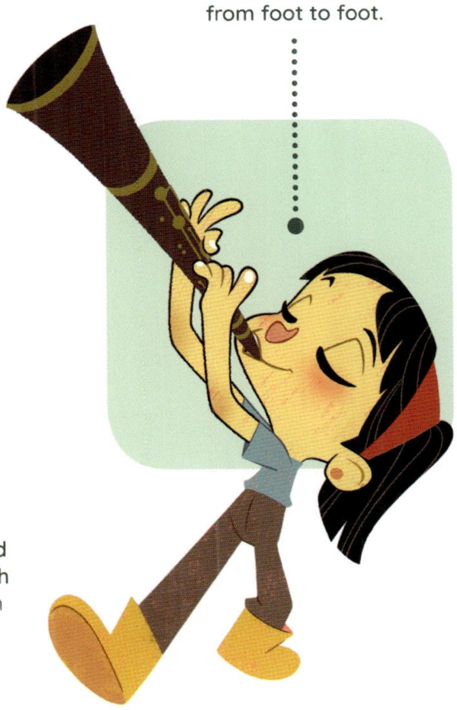

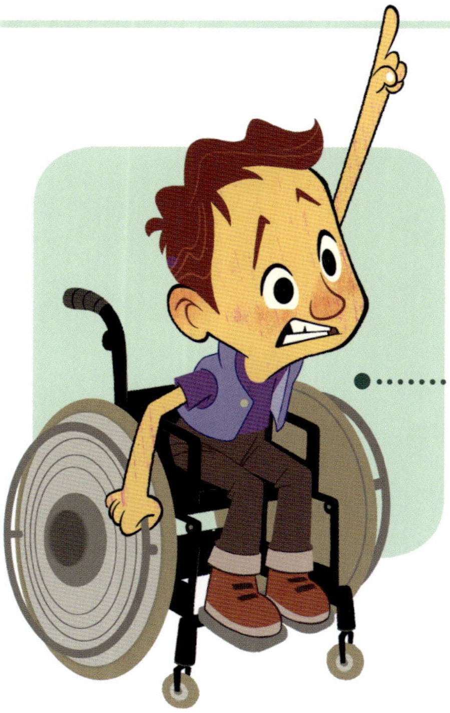

IMPATIENT, FINGER RAISED

Arm straight up in the air and finger pointed in urgency, this character is calling for attention. His head tilted slightly to one side shows his worry and that he really can't wait.

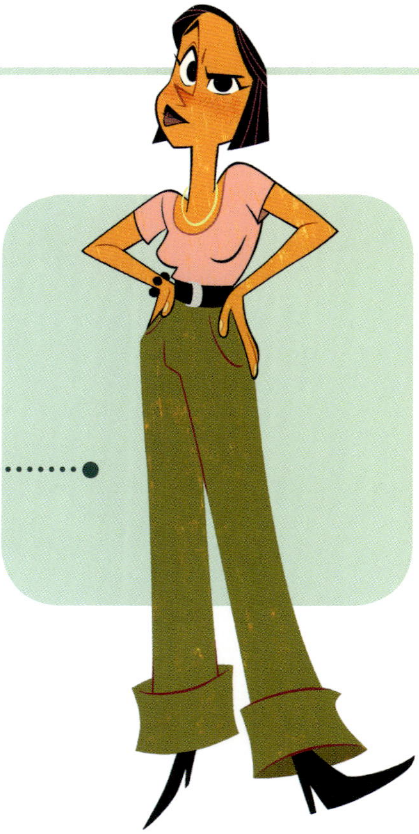

IMPATIENT, HANDS ON HIPS

Here is the school teacher again, but this time she's feeling impatient with her students. There is slight movement to the leg as she taps her foot in irritation.

ARGUING

Both characters lean in close, each blaming the other for the broken phone. The hand gestures illustrate their anger: the clenched fist, the aggressive finger jabbing the chest, and the finger pointing down at the phone.

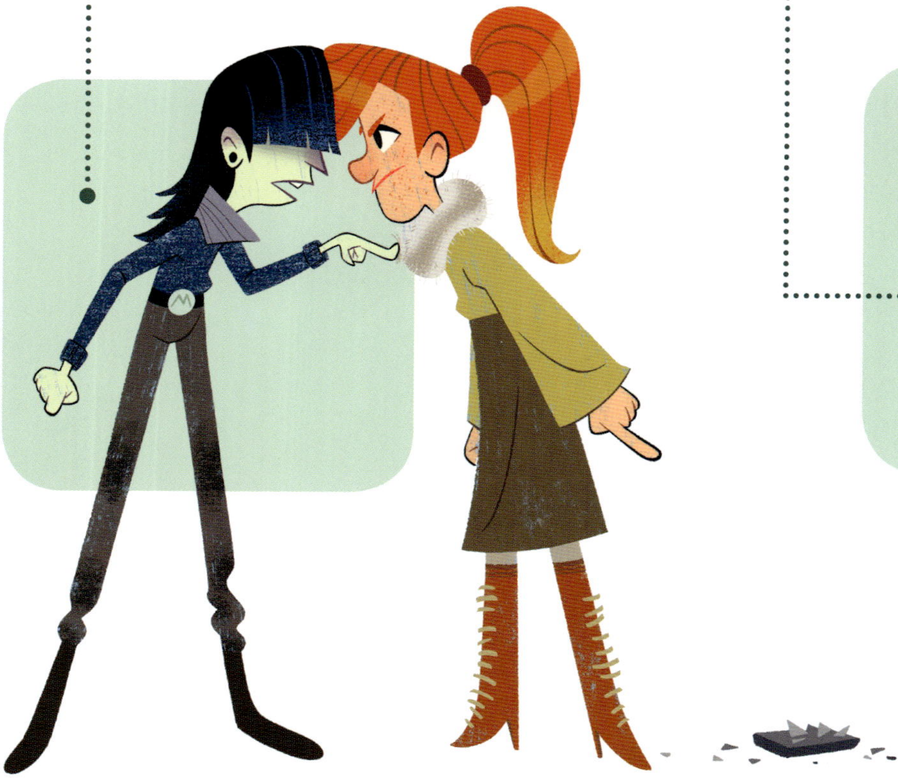

CHATTING & LAUGHING

They are back to being best friends. Relaxed hand gestures and open, upturned mouths illustrate their friendly conversation and laughter.

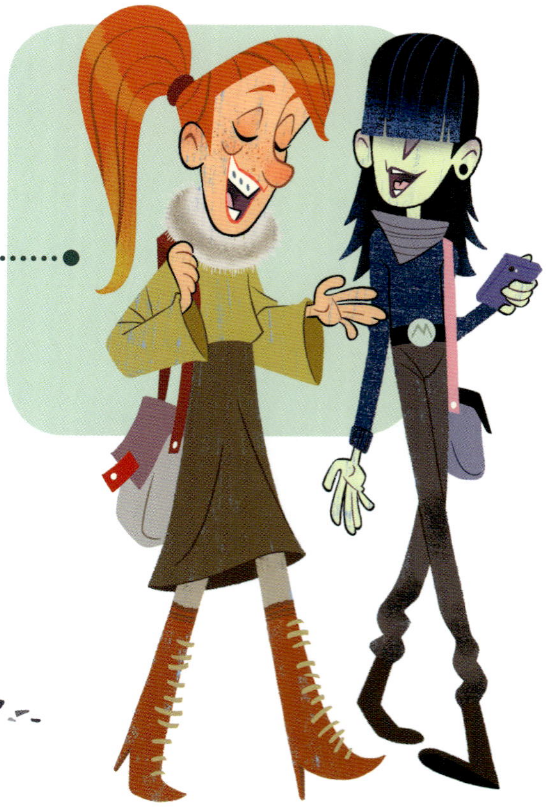

Meybis Ruiz Cruz

You need to practice sketching poses with intention: what the characters are doing, and how they are feeling. Try to explore different ways of portraying the same action or emotion, considering the character and context. For example, a baby eats differently than an adult, and it's not the same action to catch a ball as it is a bridal bouquet or a falling glass. Even a standing pose will change from one person to the next, depending on many different variables.

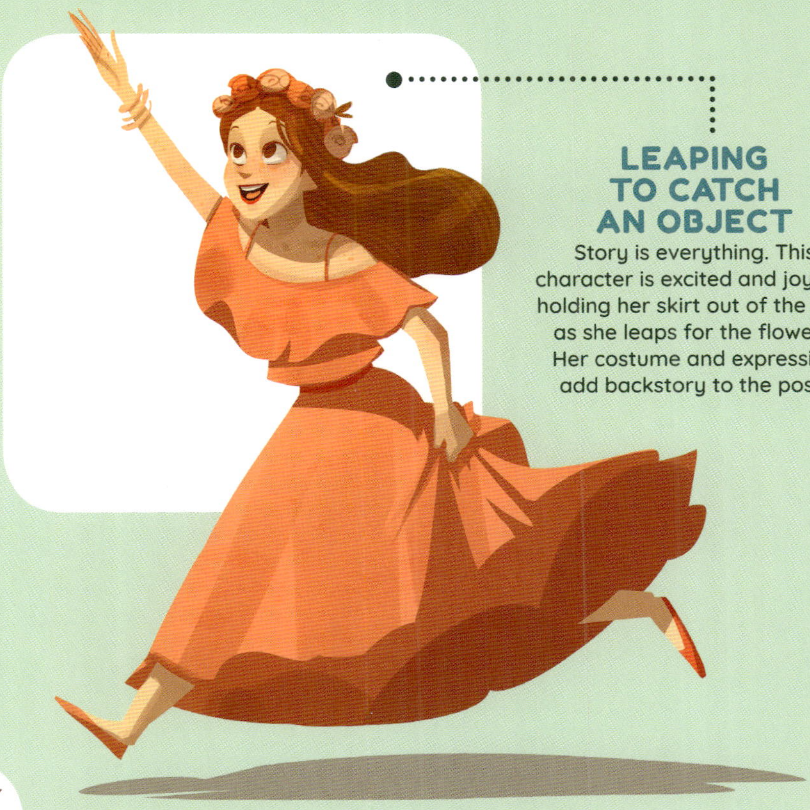

LEAPING TO CATCH AN OBJECT
Story is everything. This character is excited and joyous, holding her skirt out of the way as she leaps for the flowers. Her costume and expression add backstory to the pose.

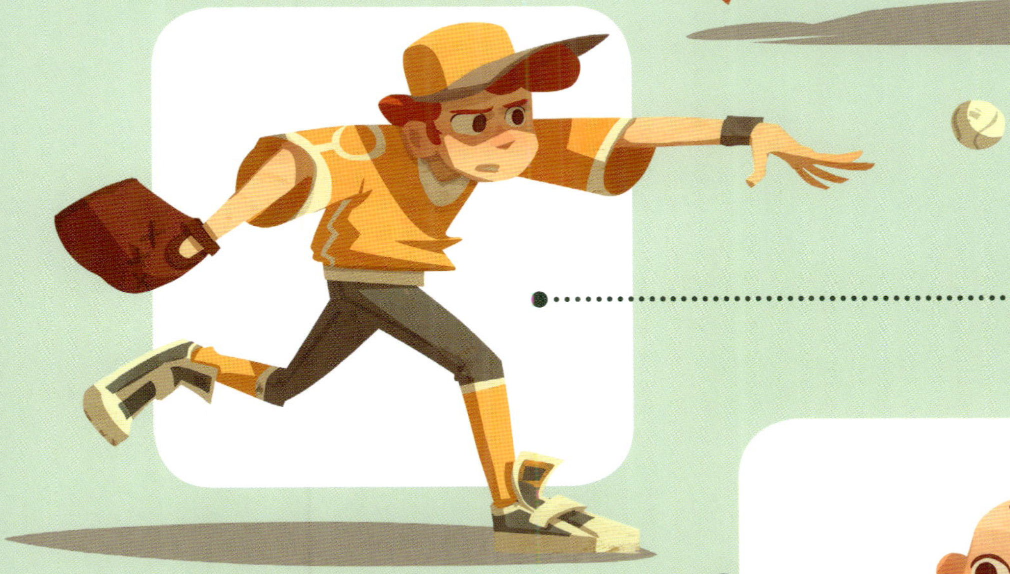

THROWING AN OBJECT, DETERMINED
Silhouette translates into clarity. There is no mistaking the clear positive and negative shapes of this dynamic throwing pose, especially with the additions of the glove and ball.

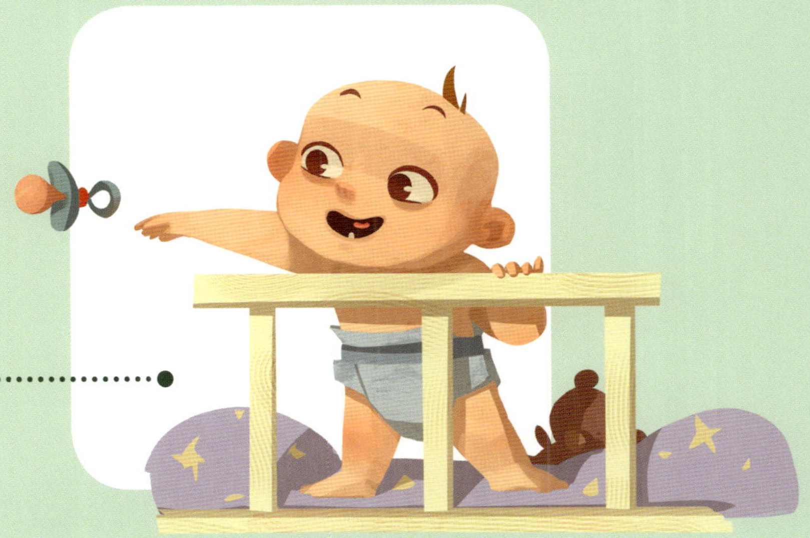

THROWING AN OBJECT, LAUGHING
The emotional state of the character is decisive when creating a pose. This action is the same as above, but the emotion and expression are different, changing the tone to one of fun and mischief.

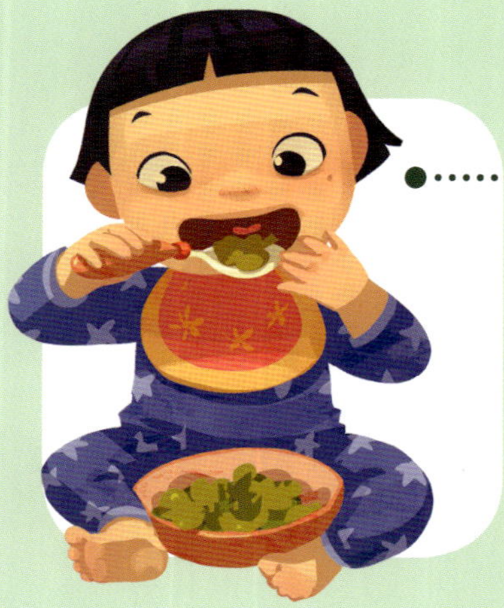

EATING, TWO HANDS

A character's age will greatly influence how they execute any given action, like this toddler using both hands to maneuver a spoon. The motor skills of a toddler, adult, and an elderly person are completely different.

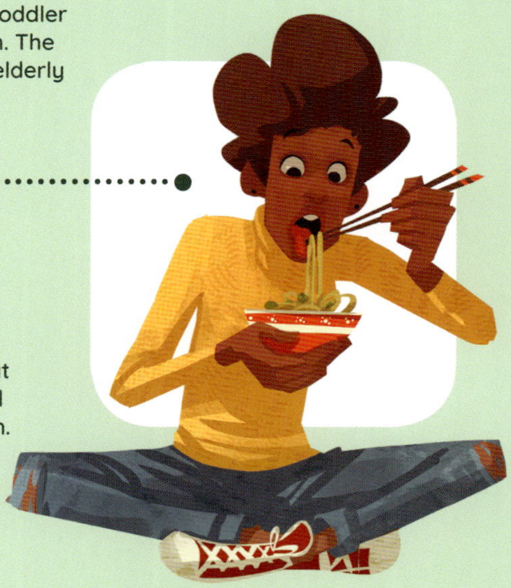

EATING, ONE HAND

Use references. Be your own model. If you need a specific pose and can't find a useful picture online, take a photo of yourself in that pose and then exaggerate it. It's very helpful for tricky poses like this cross-legged position.

TYING SHOELACES

Small details add character and backstory. The band-aid tells you this kid is determined; after a fall he probably stands up, shakes off the dust, and carries on. His enthusiasm for tying his laces adds to his confidence.

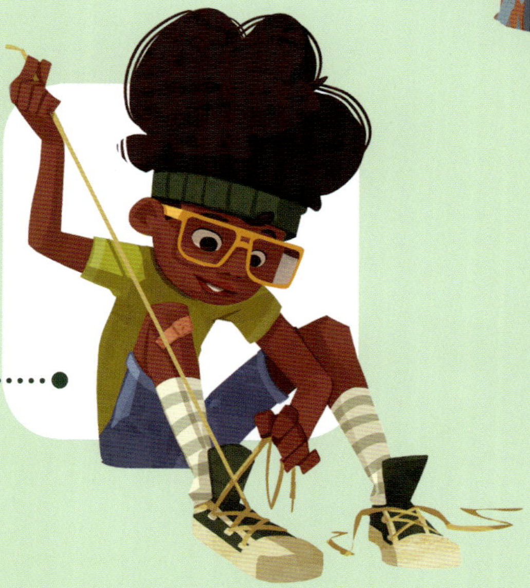

RUSHING TO GET READY

When the idea for a pose is fairly abstract, it can help to use props and universal situations, like a loose tie or an unfinished breakfast while dashing out the door, to improve readability. Familiar, everyday details help the audience relate to this character's life and story.

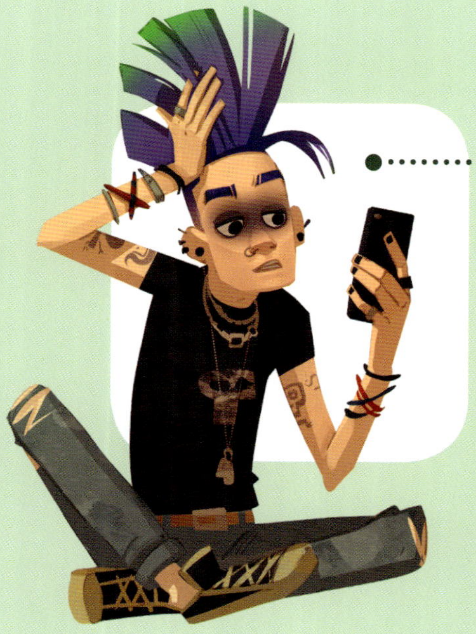

STYLING HAIR OR MAKEUP

Subvert stereotypes. When you hear "styling hair," you probably think of a girl, but vanity is universal and this punk kid cares for his appearance as much as anyone else does! The props, accessories, and costuming are essential to the story of this pose and character.

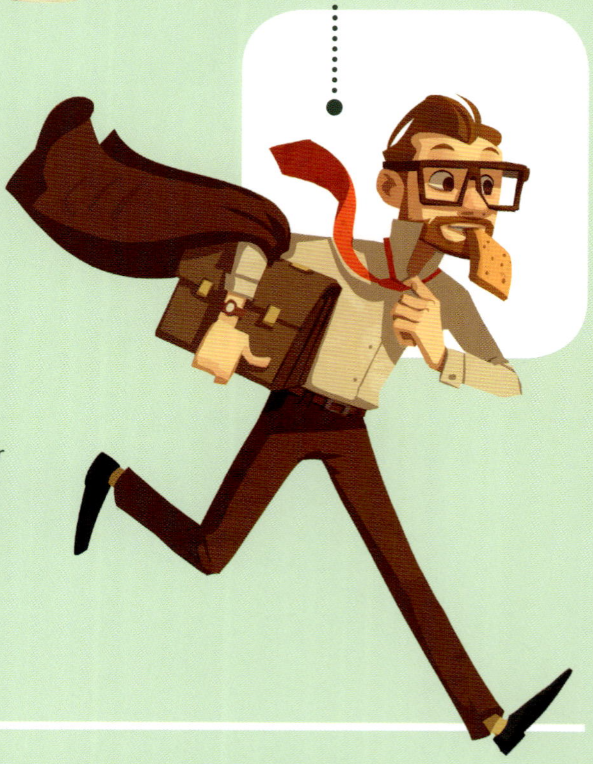

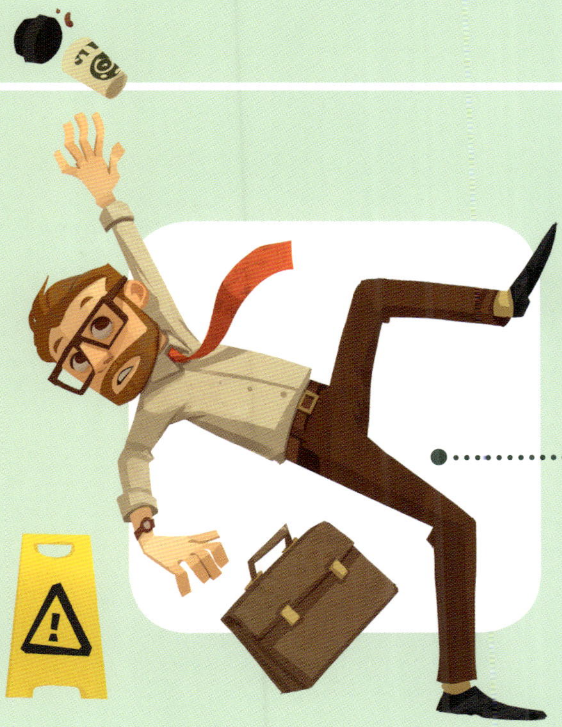

SLIPPING ON A SURFACE

Sometimes you can use the same character if it connects thematically. In this case, it makes sense that someone late and in a hurry would slip on a wet floor.

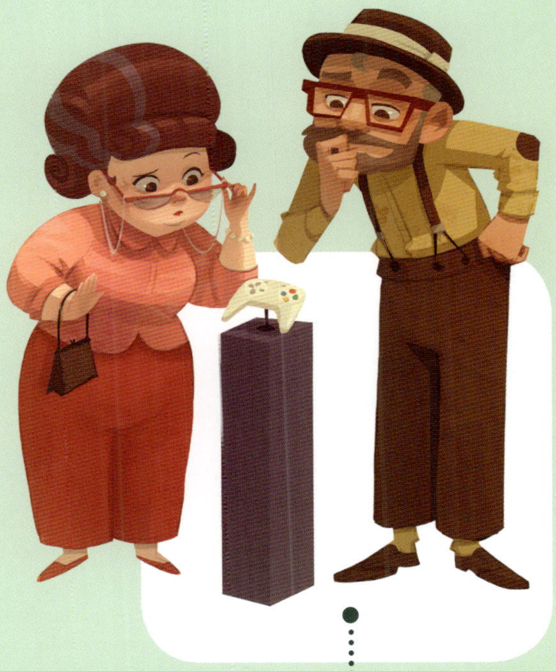

CONFUSED BY AN OBJECT

Anachronisms are handy when portraying confusion. The opposite of this idea could also work, such as two kids confused by a cassette tape or old telephone. Scratching chins and peering over glasses helps convey puzzlement.

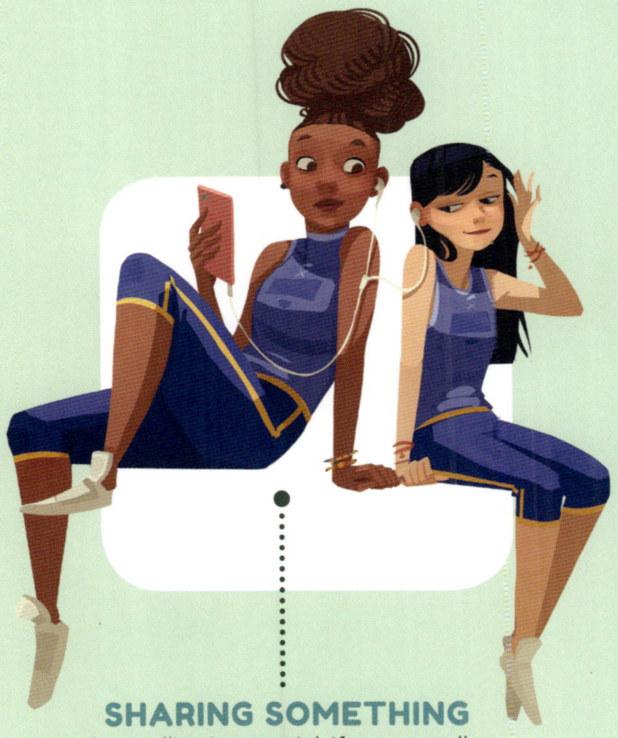

SHOWING AN OBJECT TO OTHERS

Sometimes it helps to think of the emotional response you want to evoke in the audience. How do you want people to feel when they see the illustration? Directing characters' gazes toward the important object helps tell the story.

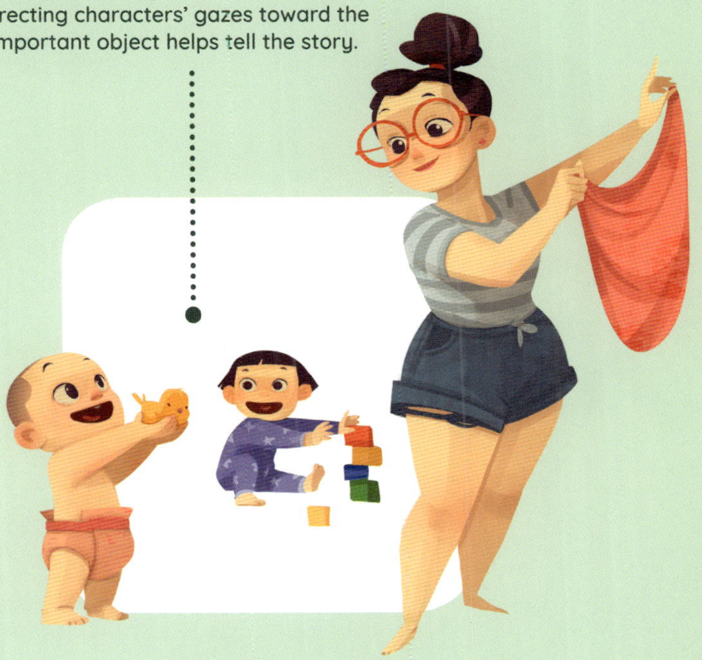

SHARING SOMETHING

Storytelling is essential. If you can tell a small story in a simple drawing, people will engage. What has just happened, or what is about to happen? Earphones act as a prop to connect these characters, both visually and narratively.

Noor Sofi

No two people are alike, so how one person performs a certain action could be entirely different to how another person performs it. Step into your character's shoes and imagine what unique qualities they have that make them stand out from the crowd.

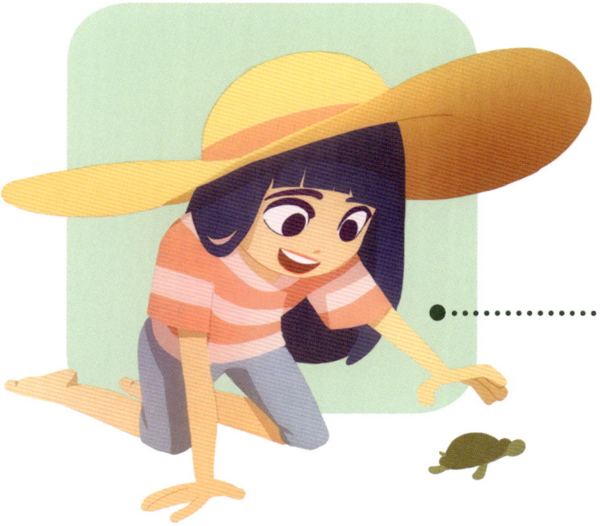

PICKING UP AN OBJECT

Contrasting big and small creates visual interest. This small girl wears a big hat, making her design more interesting, and she in turn is much bigger than the little turtle she's interacting with.

REACHING UP FOR AN OBJECT

As discussed on page 108, a strong line of action will make your poses feel less stiff and more fluid. This character has a strong diagonal line of action, suggesting activeness and energy. Her whole figure stretches upward as she reaches for the book.

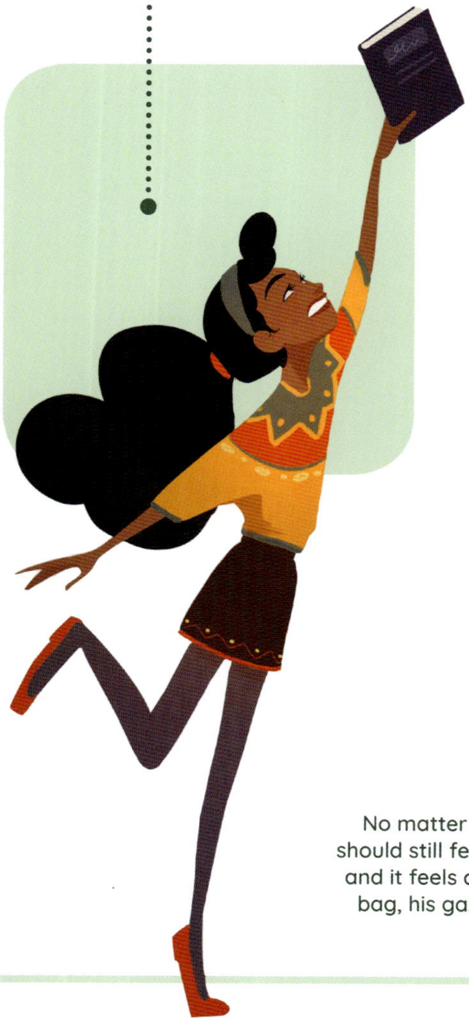

SEARCHING POCKETS

When choosing a pose, make your character's actions easy for the audience to understand. This man searches for something in his pocket, his pose ensuring his pocket is in full view.

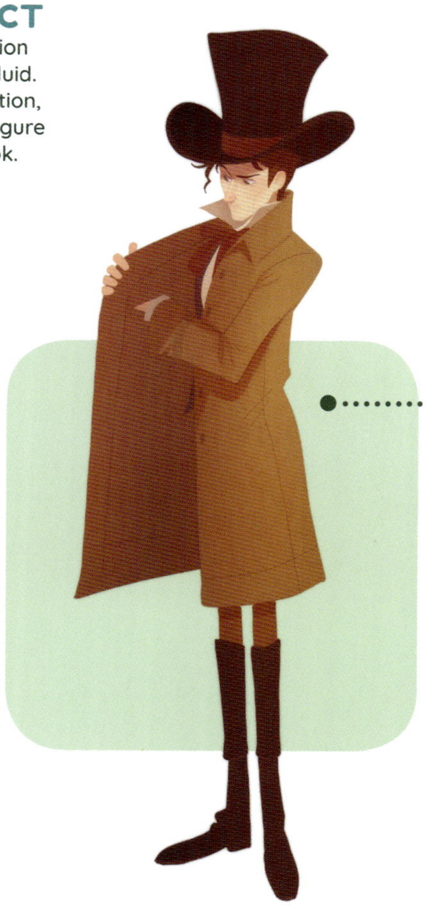

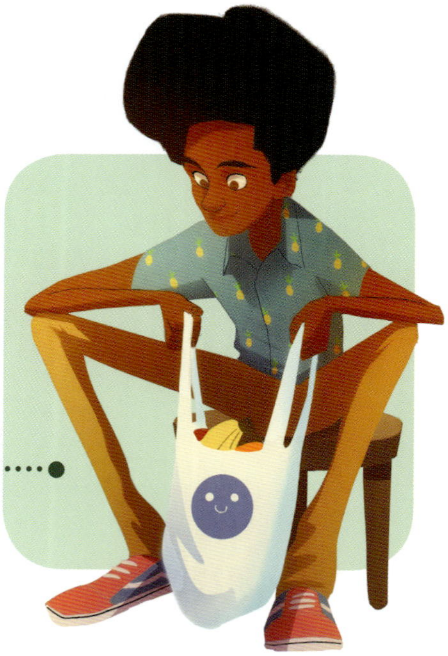

LOOKING IN A BAG

No matter how exaggerated your character is, their pose should still feel natural. Reference was used to draw this pose, and it feels comfortable to the eye. As the character lifts the bag, his gaze directs the viewer to search its contents too.

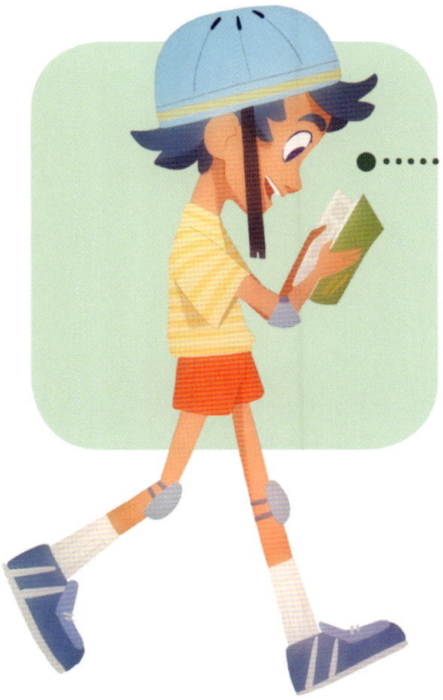

READING WHILE WALKING

A strong silhouette makes for a quicker, easier, and stronger visual read. If you only saw this character's silhouette, you would still be able to see that he's walking while reading a book.

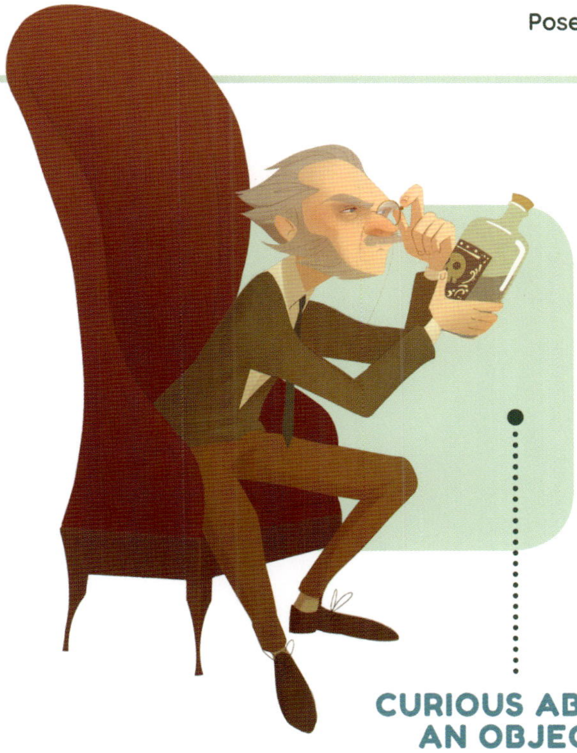

CURIOUS ABOUT AN OBJECT

A character's power center is the part of their body that leads a pose. This old man looks curiously at the contents of a bottle. The action suggests his mind is working very hard, and so his whole body is led by his head, which drives his actions.

SECRETIVE, HIDING AN OBJECT

Ask yourself, what is your character's motivation? You can immediately recognize this young boy's intentions as he sneaks off with an armful of cookies. He wants the cookies for himself, his backward glance hinting that they weren't his to take.

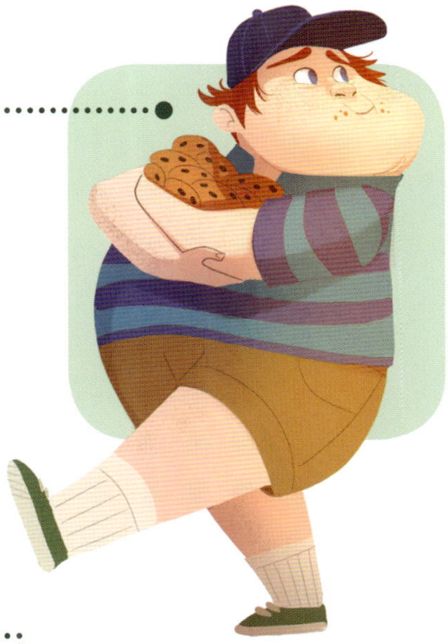

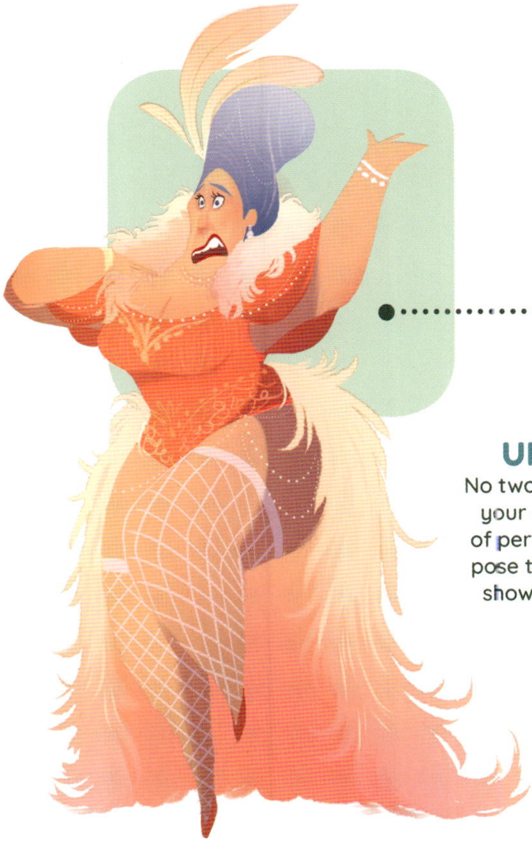

STARTLED BY AN UNPLEASANT SURPRISE

No two people are alike, and the same goes for your characters! Everyone has a unique way of performing actions, so use your character's pose to display their personality. This showgirl shows her displeasure in a much louder way than a quiet librarian might.

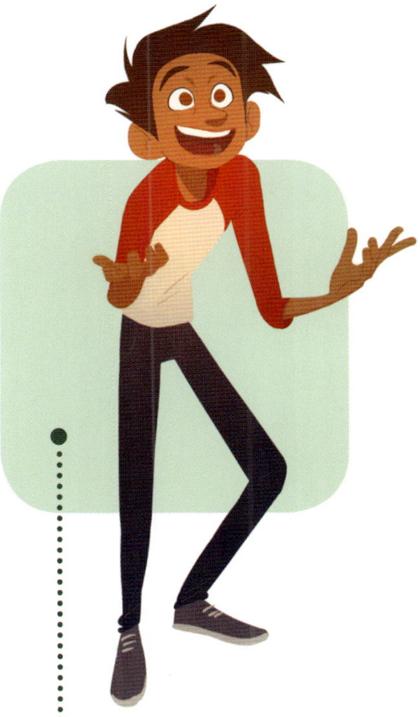

STARTLED BY A PLEASANT SURPRISE

This character's raised eyebrows, wide eyes, open smile, and spread hands help convey his joy and amazement.

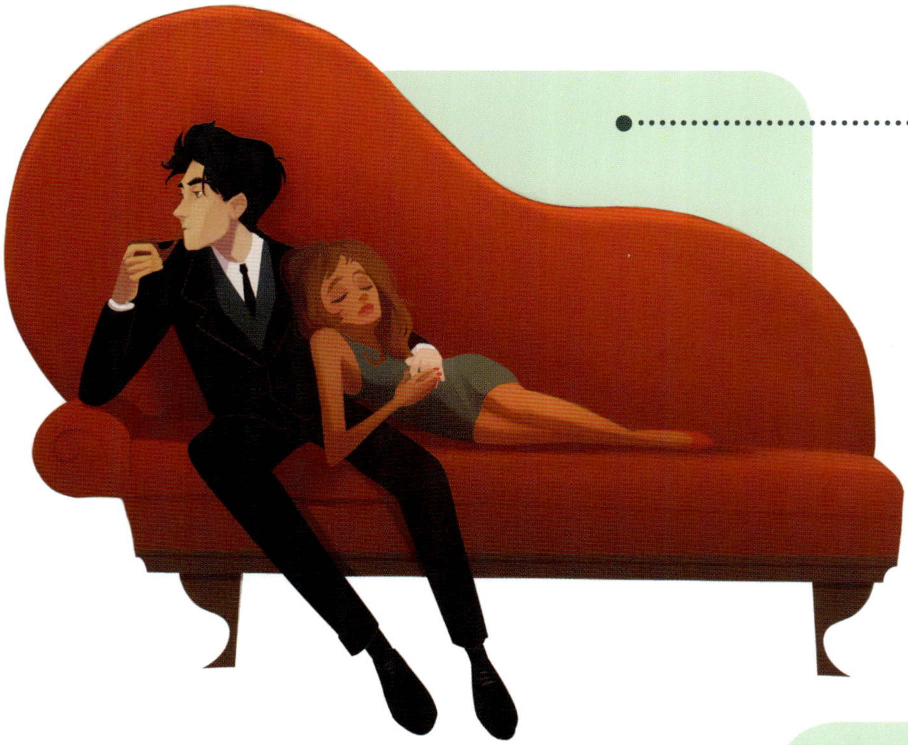

ONE CHARACTER LEANING ON ANOTHER

Looking at human figures like puzzle pieces can make a pose look stiff. These characters are a couple, depicted in the way her figure flows into his. Their limbs, expressions, and lines of action feel relaxed and content.

DRAGGING

Weight will impact how your character moves, whether it's their own weight or the weight of something affecting them. Here, the woman must use her foot as support and lean forward in order to drag the man's weight.

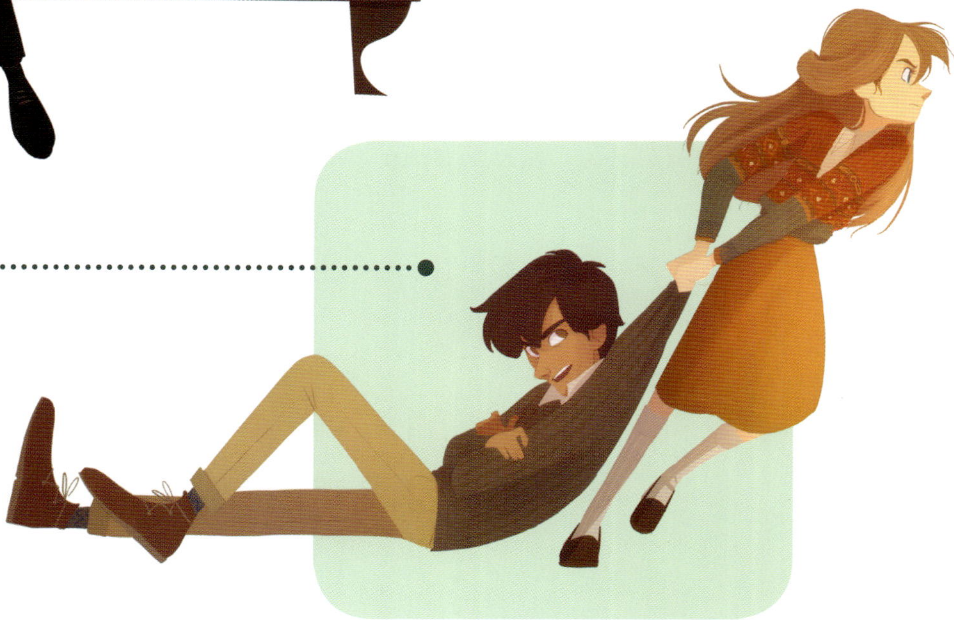

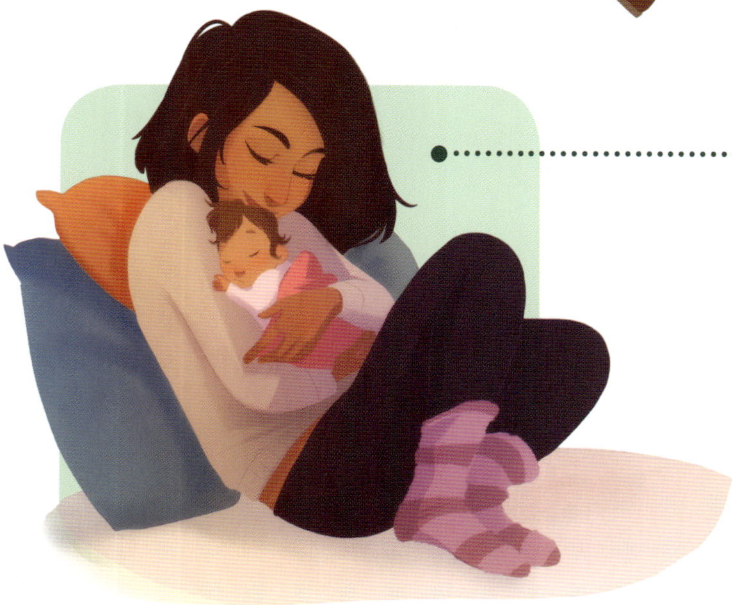

HOLDING CHILD IN ARMS

This mother and baby pose was drawn with organic, curvy lines to convey feelings of warmth and love. The mother's whole body is curled around the sleeping child. The relaxed expressions and warm colors add to the feeling of cozy closeness.

Sweeney Boo

Keep good proportions in mind. Make use of references, but always as inspiration rather than for tracing. Ensure your characters have a sense of gravity and weight – you want them to look like they are interacting with the space around them. Even if they are set against a white background, try to ground them somehow, to avoid drawing weightless characters that look like they are floating.

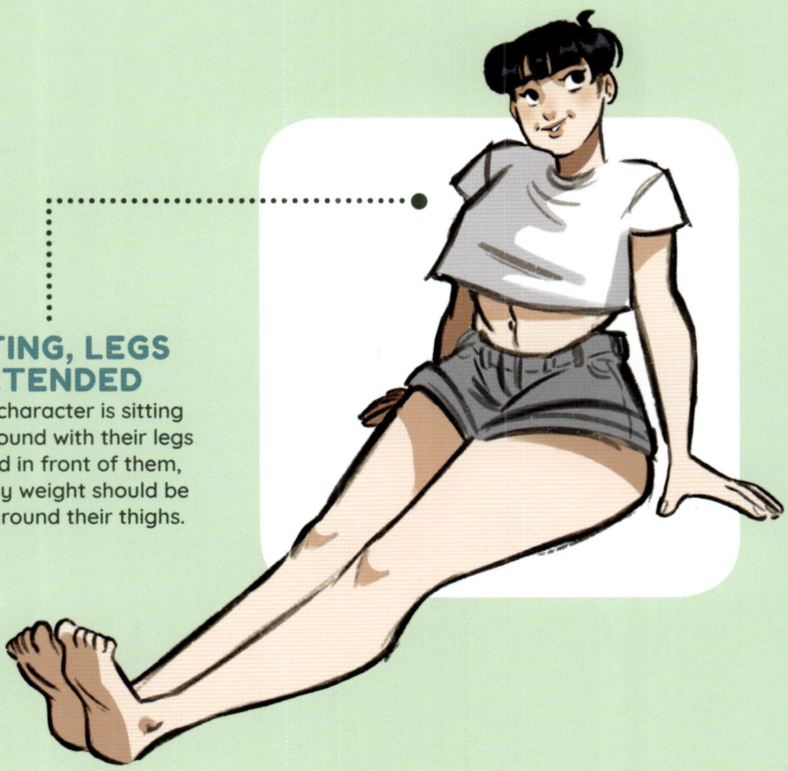

SITTING, LEGS EXTENDED

When a character is sitting on the ground with their legs extended in front of them, their body weight should be thicker around their thighs.

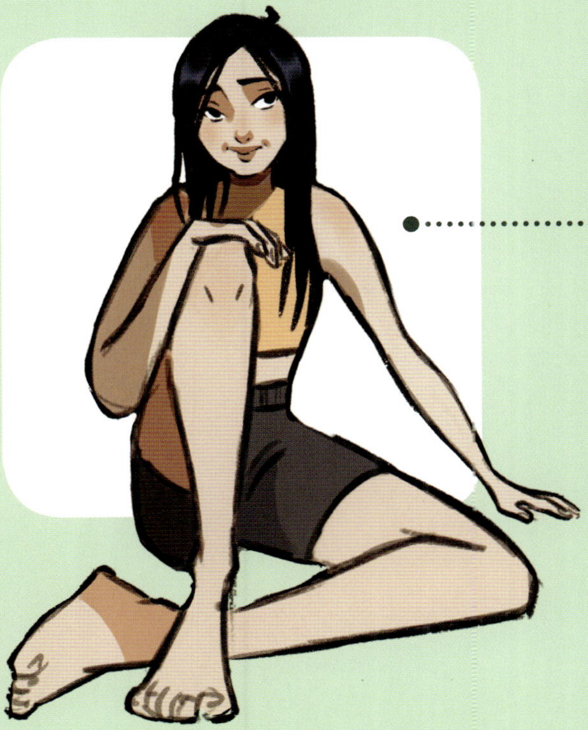

SITTING, ONE KNEE RAISED

The arm extended to the side supports the character's weight and helps to convey their relaxed mood.

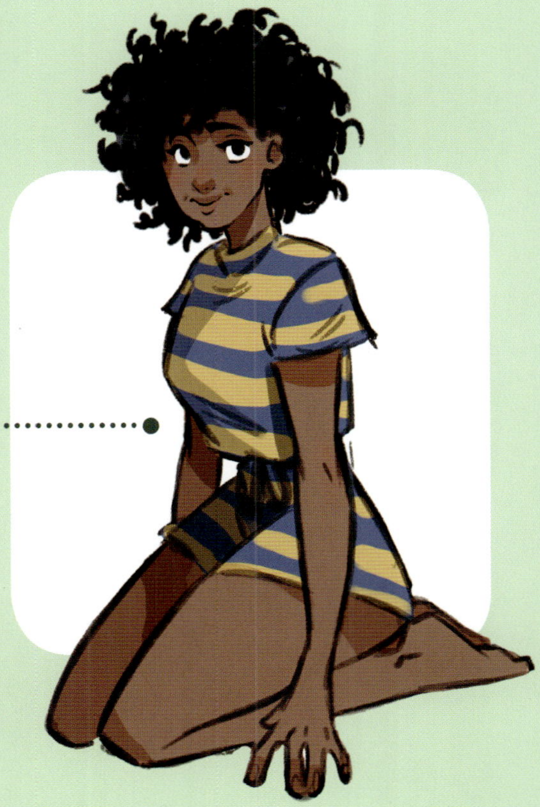

KNEELING, RELAXED

You can convey a lot of personality through the smallest changes in pose and posture. Shoulders up and hands on the ground, the character looks shy and reserved.

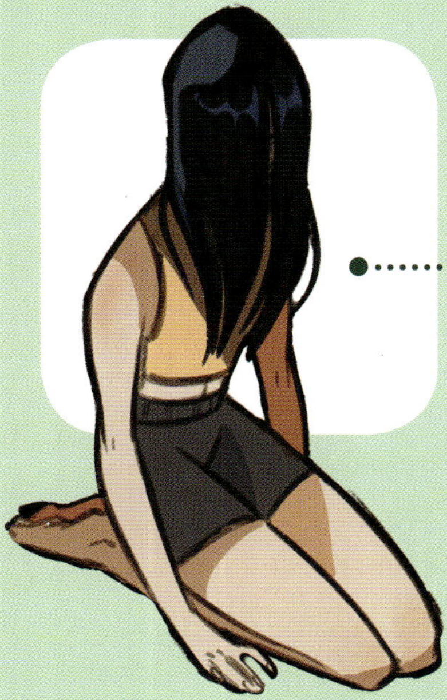

KNEELING, SAD

This character hides behind a wall of hair, her sadness amplified by her drooping shoulders and forward-tilted head.

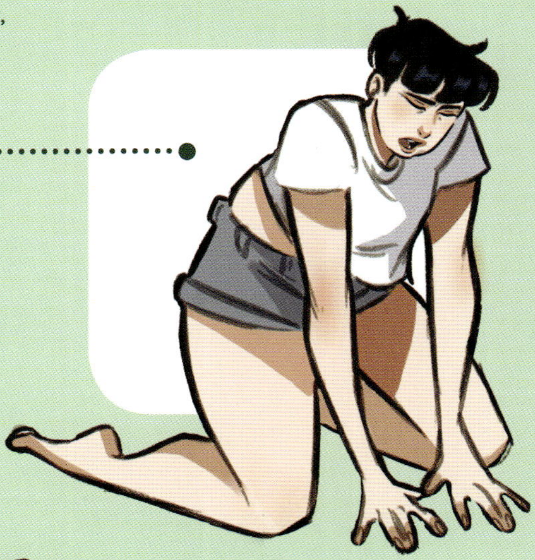

KNEELING, EXHAUSTED

The character leans into the floor, their arched back and open mouth conveying exhaustion and pain.

CELEBRATING, ONE ARM RAISED

A character should wave with their whole body, not just their arm. Her legs, head, and arms are all part of the motion.

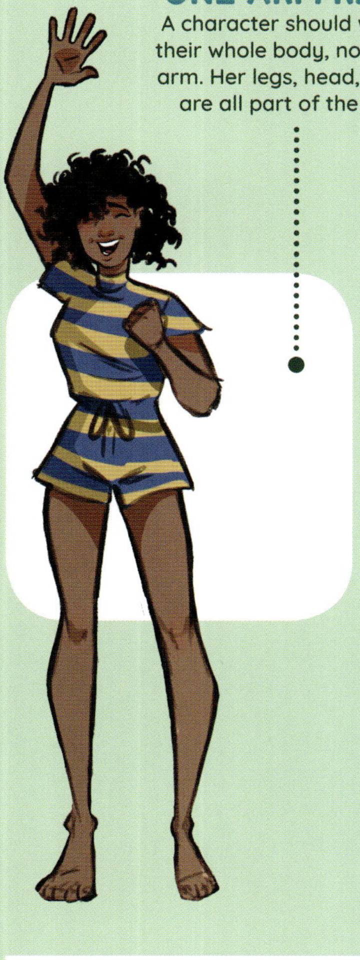

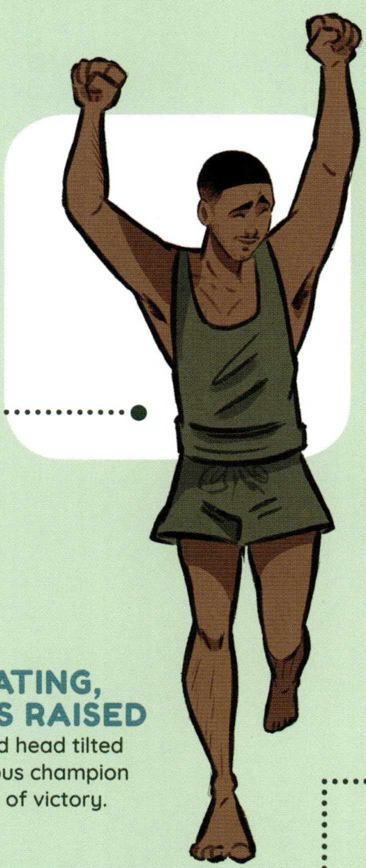

CELEBRATING, BOTH ARMS RAISED

Two arms up and head tilted down, this gracious champion displays a sign of victory.

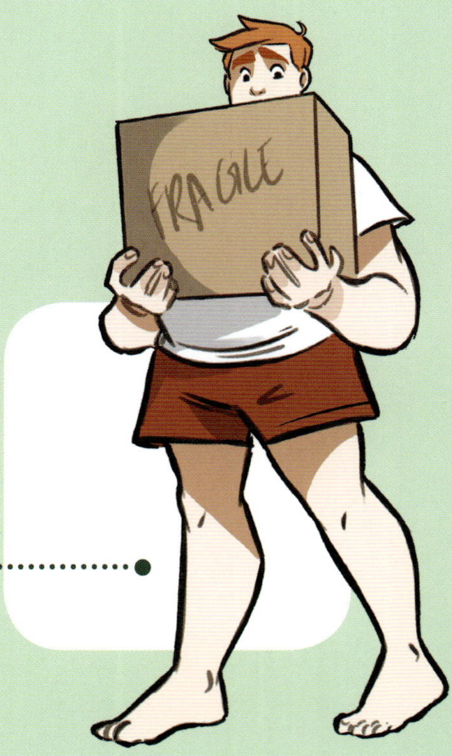

CARRYING AN OBJECT CAREFULLY

This character takes one careful step at a time. His body must show his cautious movement, and his arms the weight of the object he carries.

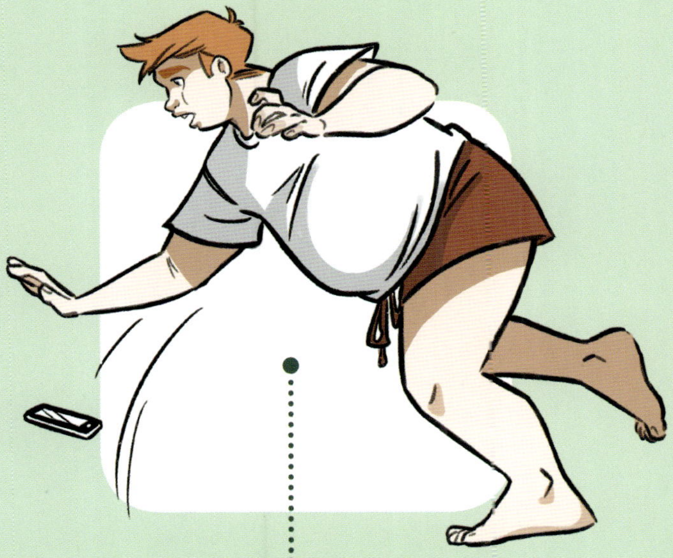

DROPPING AN OBJECT

When dropping an object, a character will mcst likely throw themselves forward as they attempt to catch it. Don't hesitate to exaggerate their movement to ensure the action is powerful.

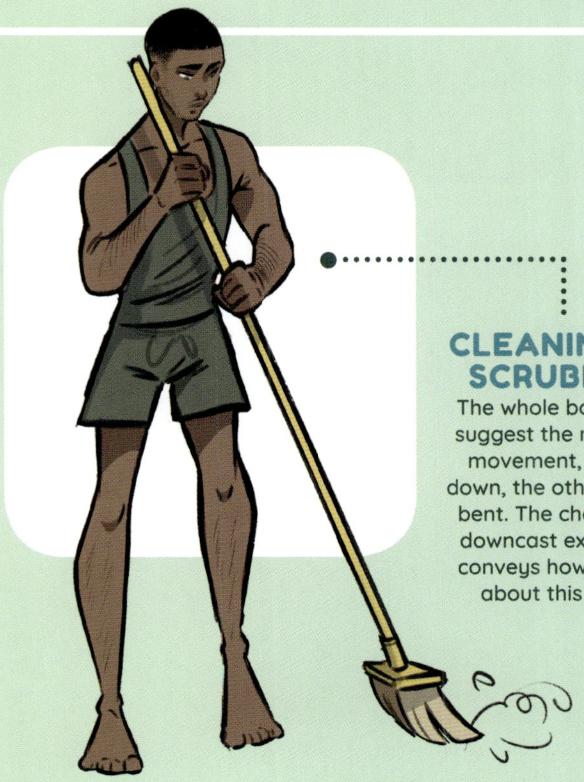

CLEANING OR SCRUBBING

The whole body must suggest the repetitive movement, one leg down, the other slightly bent. The character's downcast expression conveys how he feels about this chore.

KICKING AN OBJECT

When a character is running or kicking, the movement of each arm will always be opposite to the corresponding leg. If the right leg is forward, then the left arm should also be forward, with the right arm and left leg behind.

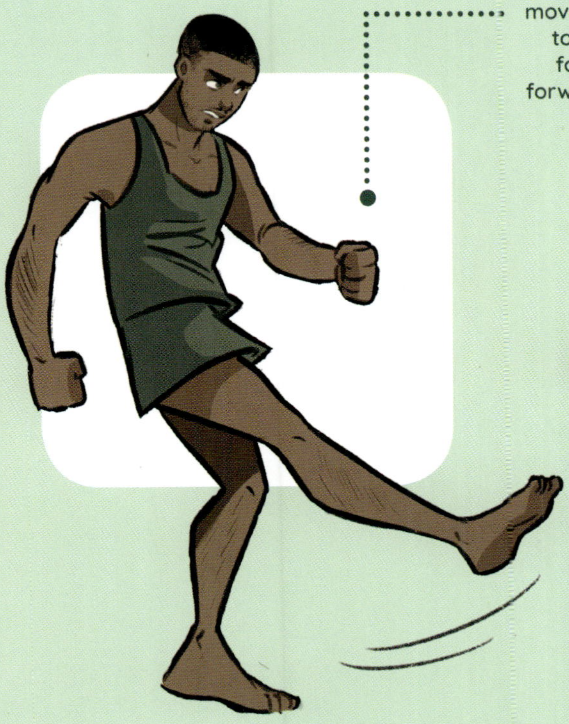

TACKLING AN OPPONENT

When a character kicks, don't forget to put all their weight on the leg that is still on the ground. Meanwhile, the other character's weight is thrown off-balance as he falls!

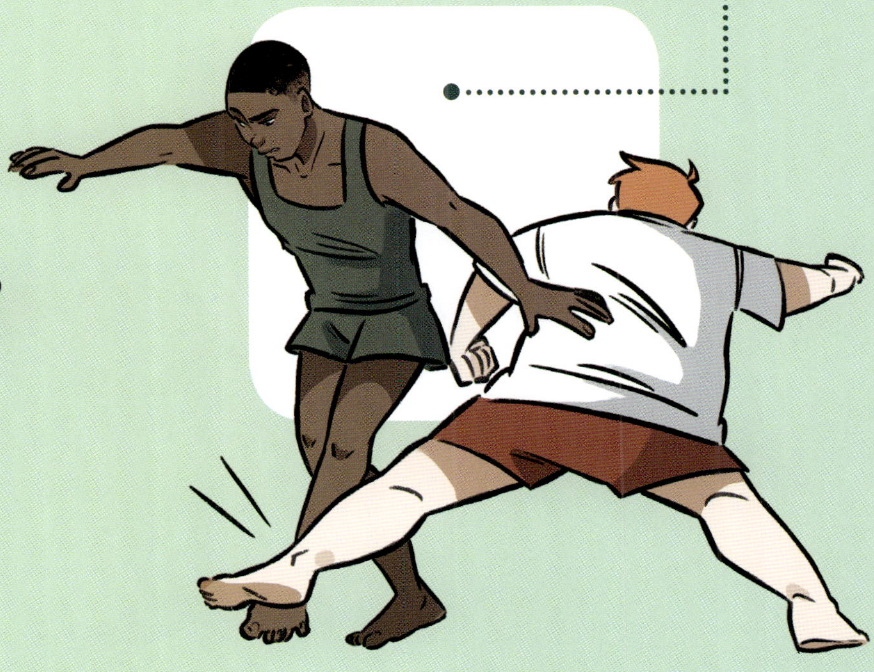

Corah Louise

Every character has a unique way in which they hold themselves and move their body. If you were to sketch multiple characters sat on a bench, they should all be sitting differently; whether relaxed, tense, or a child sitting upside-down, each should be characterful and unique. Once you have decided the story, make sure your character's pose is readable. If you were to remove the details so you were only left with a silhouette, could you still read their pose and emotion?

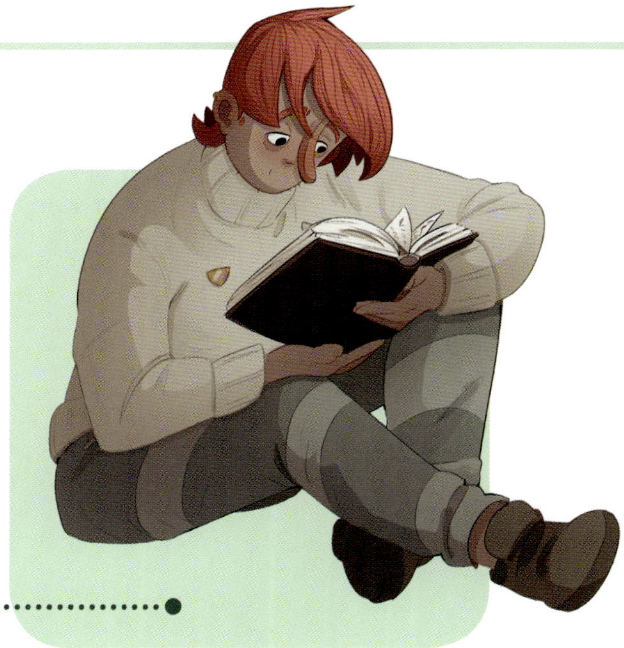

SITTING, READING

This relaxed pose shows an easiness in the body as the character leans in toward the object of their attention – the book.

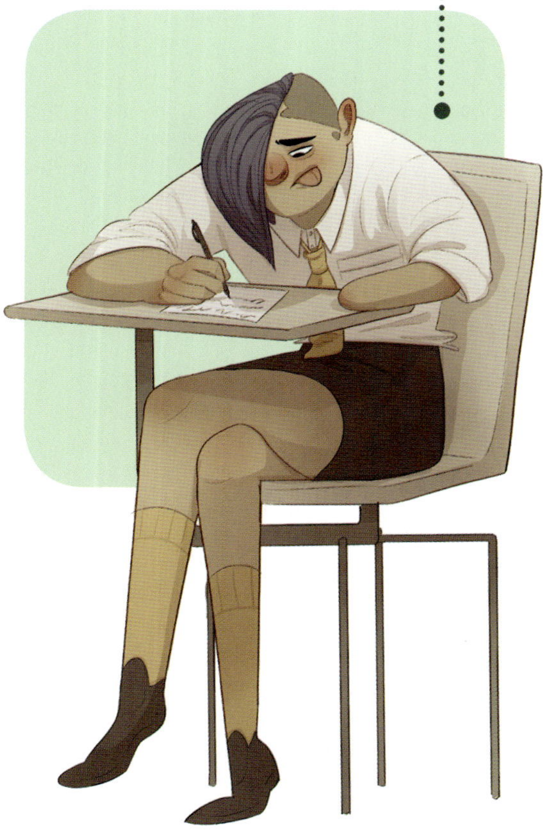

SITTING IN AN EXAM, FOCUSED

The character's body leans in as they focus on the exam paper, but unlike the previous pose, their shoulders are lifted in tension and the angle of their body suggests stress rather than pleasure.

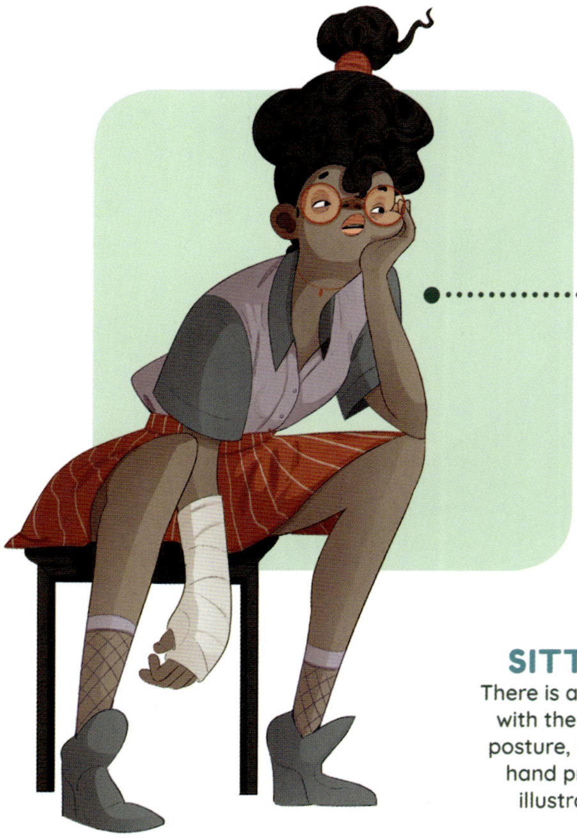

SITTING, BORED

There is a heaviness in this pose, with the character's slouched posture, low-hanging arm, and hand propping up her head illustrating her boredom.

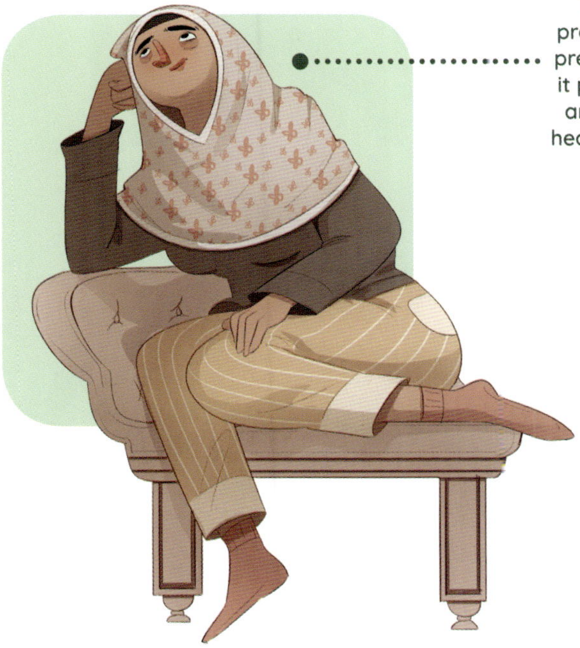

DAYDREAMING

This character's hand props up her head like the previous pose, except here it portrays thoughtfulness and comfort rather than heaviness, as the head isn't being pulled down.

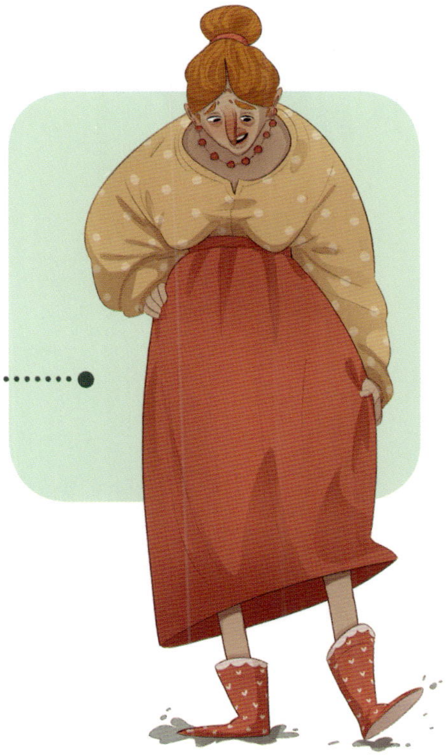

STANDING, LOOKING AT FEET

This character lifts her skirt slightly to show off her colorful new shoes, everything in the design pointing down to them.

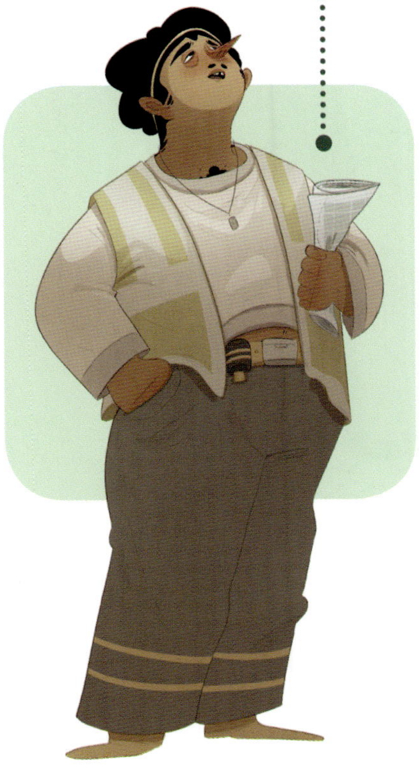

STANDING, LOOKING AT SOMETHING ABOVE

This character talks to someone above him about a work-related matter. With a hand in his pocket, feet spread wide, shoulders low, and his other hand clutching work papers, his pose is comfortable but focused.

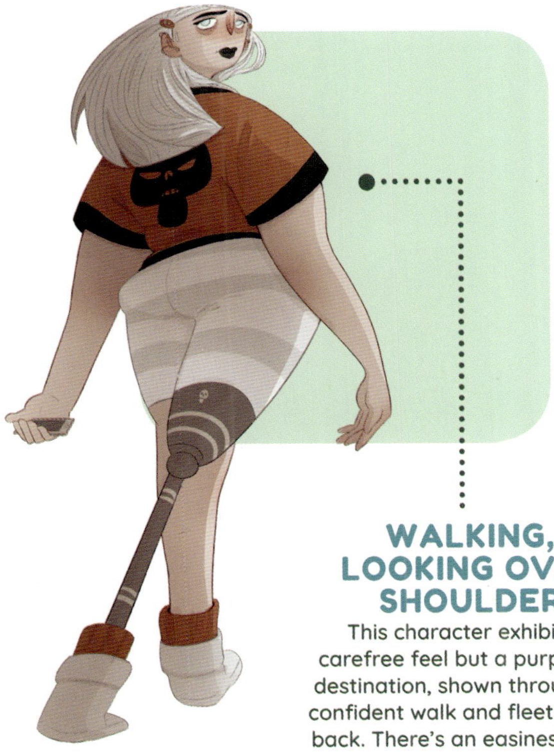

WALKING, LOOKING OVER SHOULDER

This character exhibits a carefree feel but a purposeful destination, shown through her confident walk and fleeting look back. There's an easiness in the swing of the body, but her legs are placed with force.

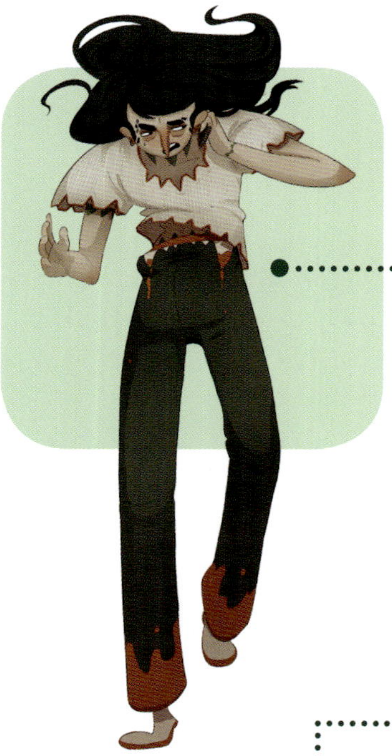

WALKING WHILE TALKING

This character is having a heated phone conversation. He throws his arms about wildly, his body is hunched over in a tense posture, and the movement of his clothes and hair shows his rushed walk.

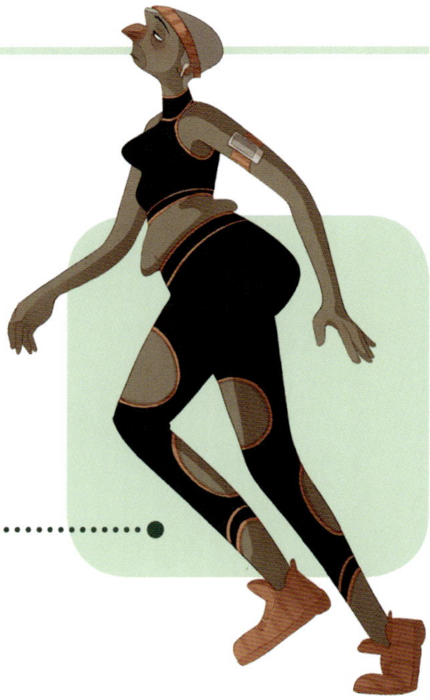

JOGGING, RELAXED

This character goes for a relaxed jog. Her face is neutral, her shoulders low, and there's an ease to the swing of her body with her limbs not extending too far in either direction.

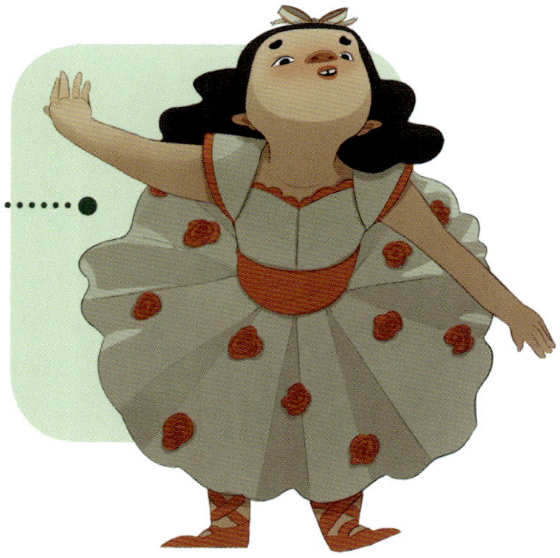

TAKING A BOW

When children take a bow, they often embellish it with a little drama. This character's head is pushed high, her arms are unbalanced, and her raised foot adds an extra flair, portraying her playfulness and innocence.

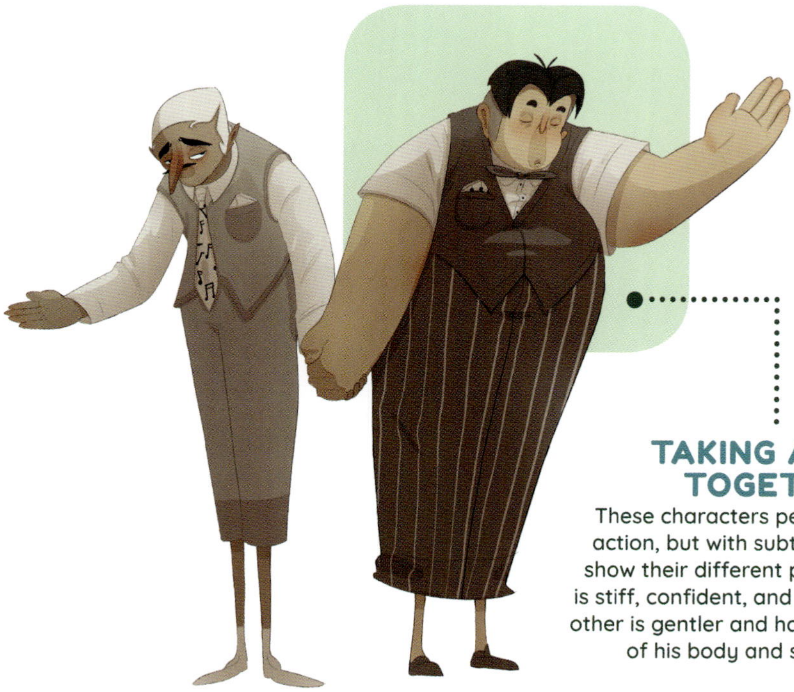

TAKING A BOW TOGETHER

These characters perform the same action, but with subtle differences to show their different personalities. One is stiff, confident, and focused, while the other is gentler and has more awareness of his body and surroundings.

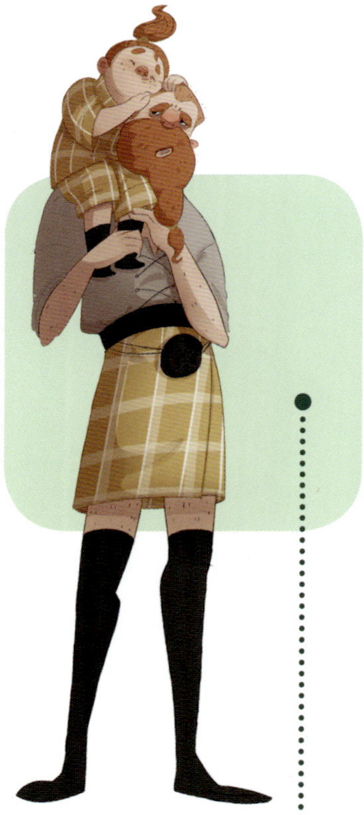

ONE CHARACTER ON ANOTHER'S SHOULDERS

The father is strong and stable, with a wide stance and good hold. The child's trust is shown as she leans her head and body in toward him, revealing their close relationship.

Olga Andriyenko

Human bodies can be complicated to capture in different poses, so simplify your character's body into basic shapes before you go into detail. Think about the movement and direction of the body; when a person is engaged or interested they lean forward, but when scared or avoidant they lean back. It can be helpful to act out the action in front of the mirror, or ask a friend or family member to perform it for you. This will help you understand how the body behaves.

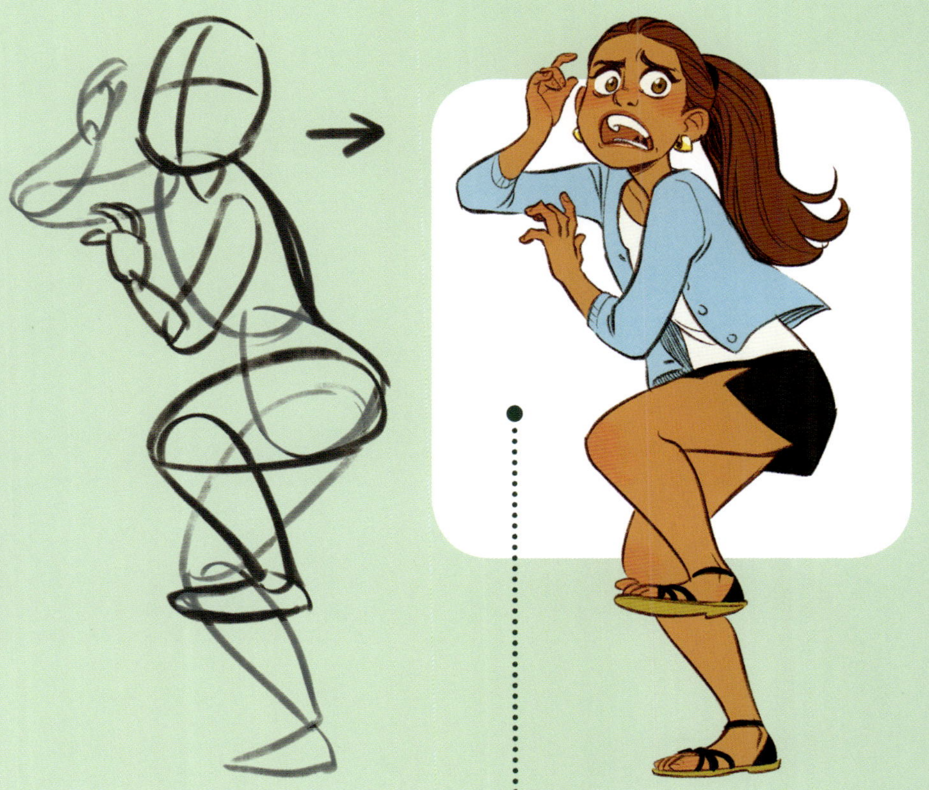

SHOUTING, PANICKED

A panicked character might try to lean away from the source of their fear, but will still look back at it in order to protect themselves. Add some motion to their hair and clothes to illustrate their sudden movement.

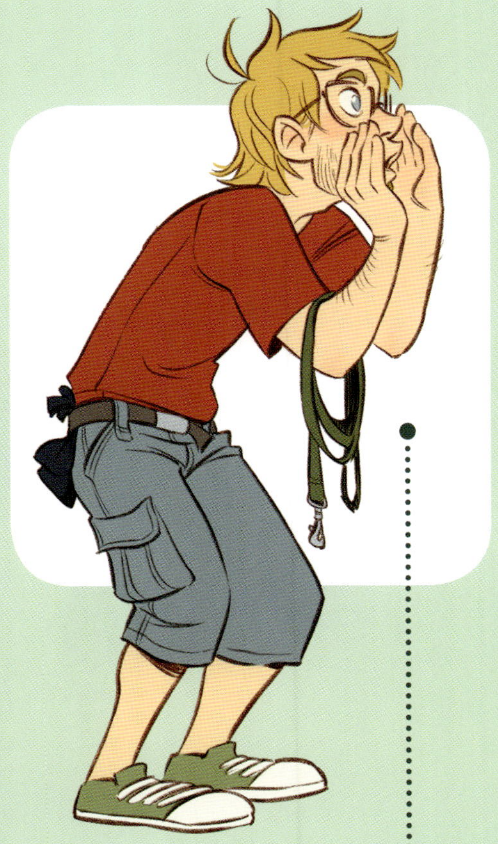

SHOUTING, HANDS AROUND MOUTH

Lean the character forward slightly, as if they're trying to make their shouts carry further.

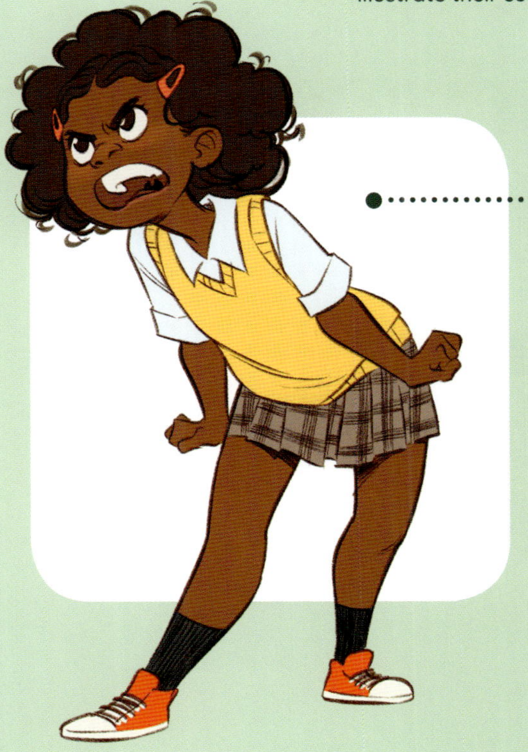

SHOUTING, ANGRY

When angry, a character's body will be full of tension. This can be shown through clenched fists and a wide-legged stance.

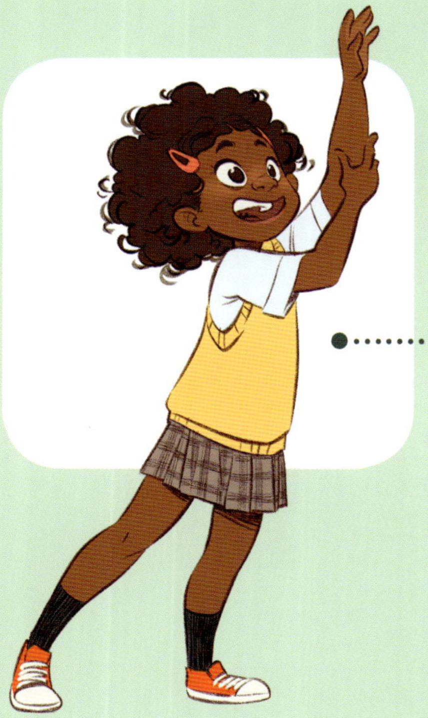

HAND RAISED, TRYING TO GET ATTENTION

Imagine a line of action going through the character's body, pointing to the raised hand. This will help bring more action into the static pose.

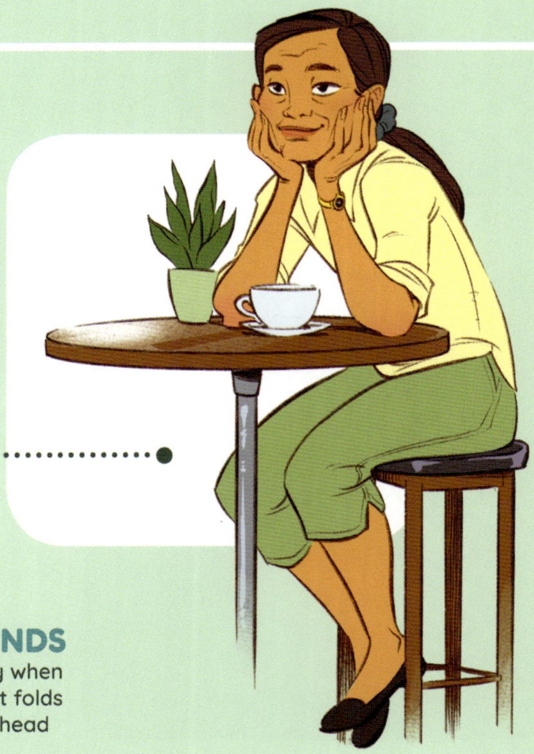

RESTING HEAD IN HANDS

Think about the weight of the body when it's resting on something. Add slight folds to the character's skin where the head touches the hands.

FALLING ASLEEP

When trying not to fall asleep, a character struggles against gravity; not only the eyelids, but the whole body is being pulled down. Use downward-pointing lines in your pose to emphasize this.

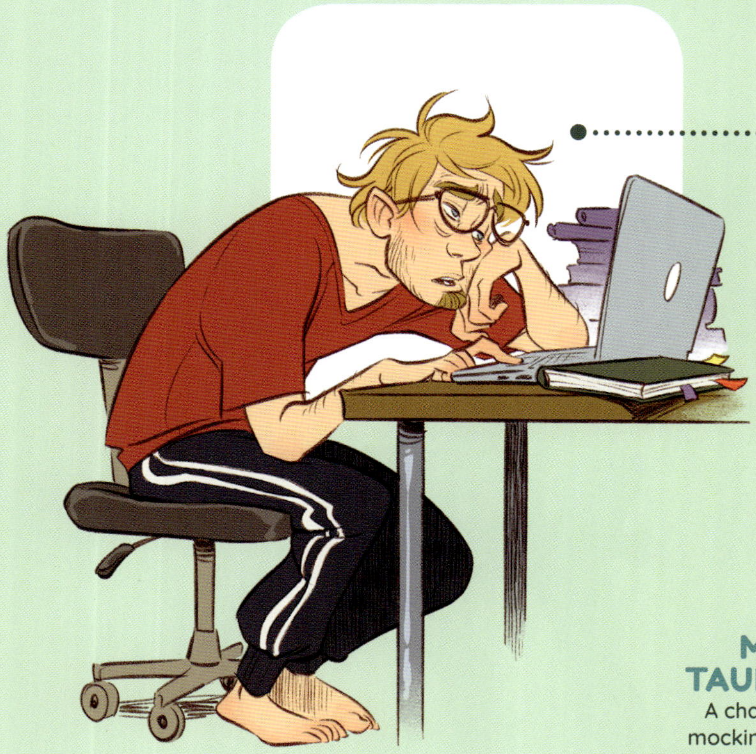

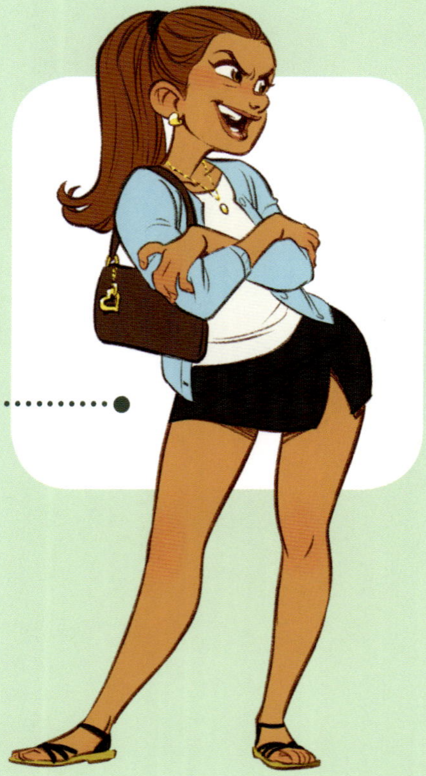

MOCKING, TAUNTING POSE

A character taunting or mocking another is usually overly confident. You can show this by raising their chin and giving them a proud smile.

SITTING, DAZED

A dazed character will not sit upright but should be drawn slightly hunched, perhaps supporting the weight of their body with an arm. A hand holding their head will emphasize their dazed state.

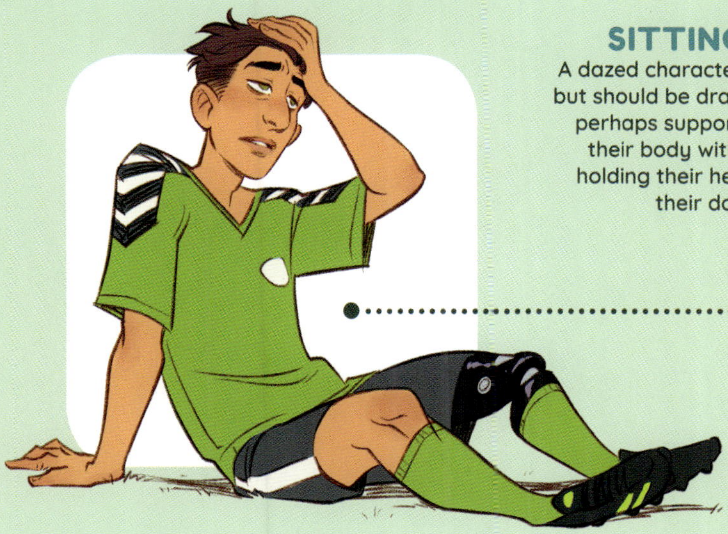

SITTING, LEGS CROSSED

In a cross-legged position, the knees point slightly forward, so don't forget to indicate their shape in your drawing.

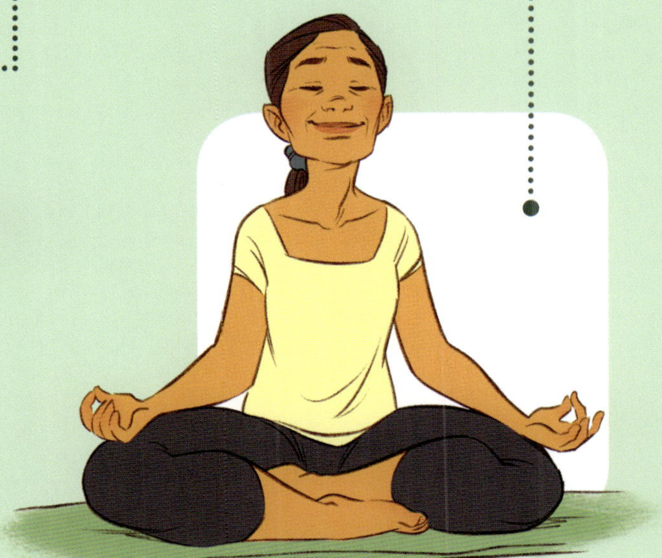

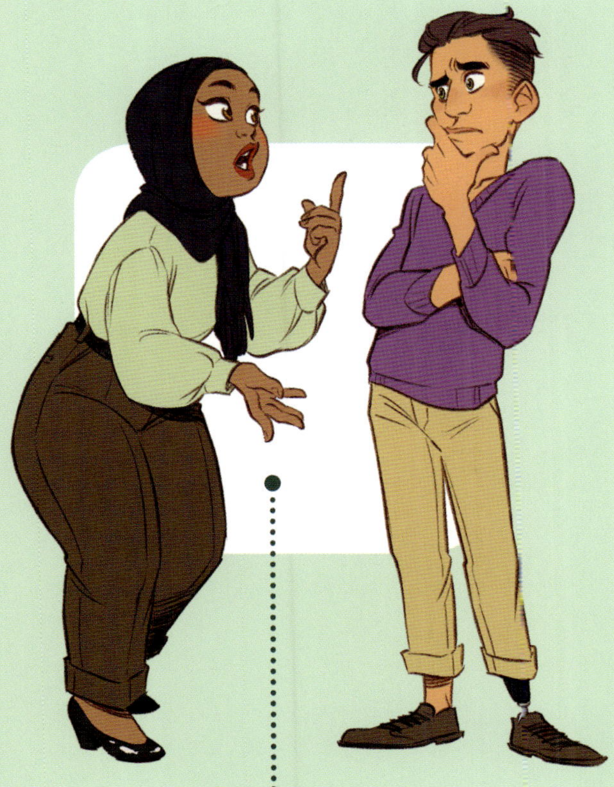

EXPLAINING SOMETHING

When explaining something or trying to convince, a character might lean forward and use their arms to gesticulate and make their point clearer.

RELUCTANTLY LISTENING

A reluctant character might lean slightly away from their conversation partner and even indicate their skepticism with a closed stance (crossing their arms, for example).

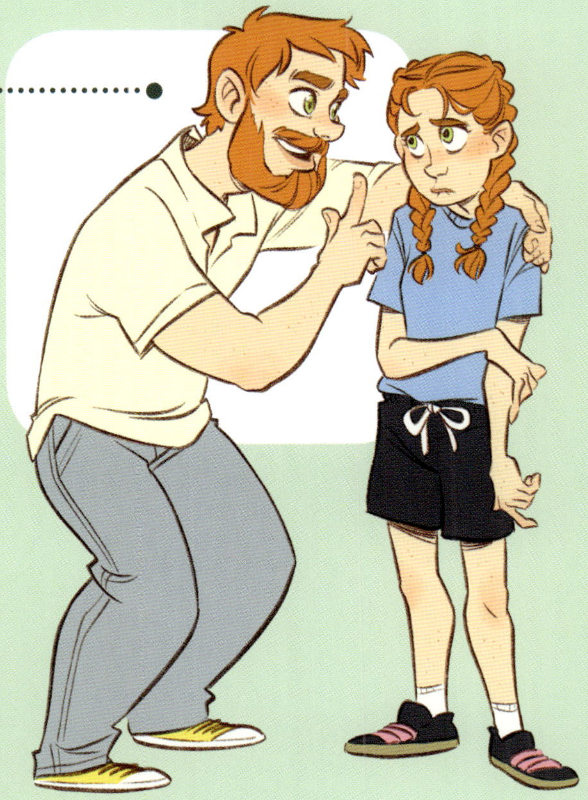

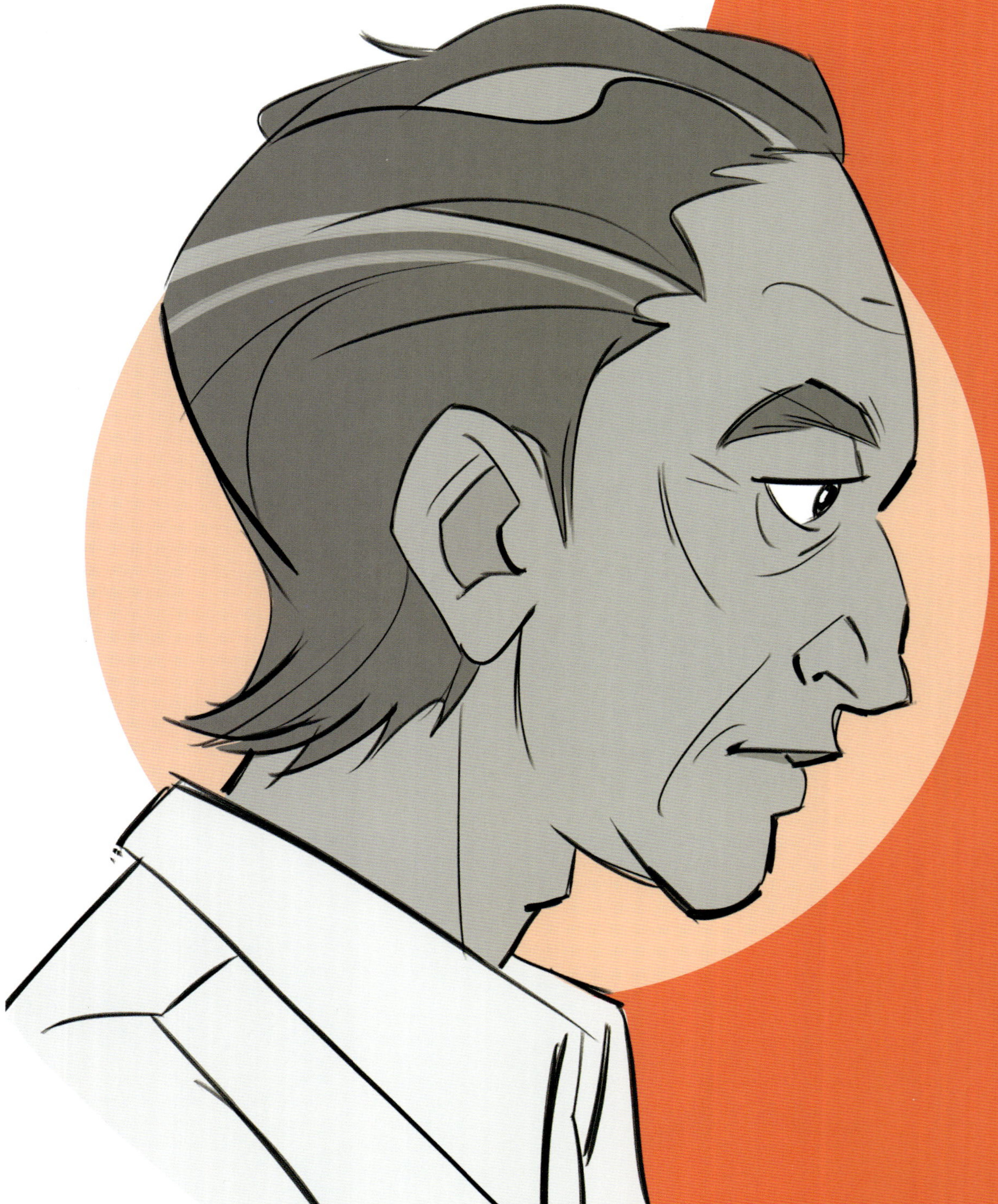

Image by Ida Hem

THE FACE

CONSTRUCTING THE FACE & HEAD
PAGE 154

EXAGGERATING SHAPES
PAGE 162

EXPRESSIONS
PAGE 166

EXAGGERATING EXPRESSIONS
PAGE 170

EXPRESSIONS LIBRARY
PAGE 174

CONSTRUCTING THE FACE & HEAD

Ida Hem

To make a drawing feel believable, it is crucial to understand three-dimensional space, even though we are drawing on a two-dimensional plane. What would a face look like in real life? We can achieve a believable result by using construction lines, and making sure the inner details of the face, such as the eyes, nose, mouth, and hairline, match with them.

Each artist approaches this stage of the process differently, because we are individuals who find our own way to thrive in our craft. An experienced artist may work freehand. If you see a skilled artist drawing without construction lines, it means that they are visualizing the lines in their head. Construction lines will always be a part of the process, consciously or subconsciously. If you consider yourself a novice artist and want to improve your work, you should physically draw the lines. You may be surprised at the amount of information you learn.

Using building blocks and construction lines together is the best method for learning three-dimensional space. Building blocks are essentially shapes that describe the mass of your subject without any detail or character. Adding construction lines over these building blocks, to see how they curve through space, is a great exercise to improve your design skills and understanding of the subject.

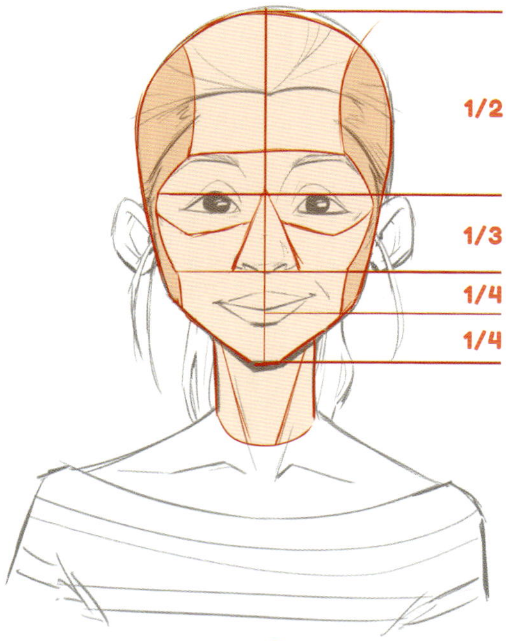

When drawing a front view, focus on the eyes, nose, and mouth placement. If they are not aligned with the centerline, the face will not look quite right.

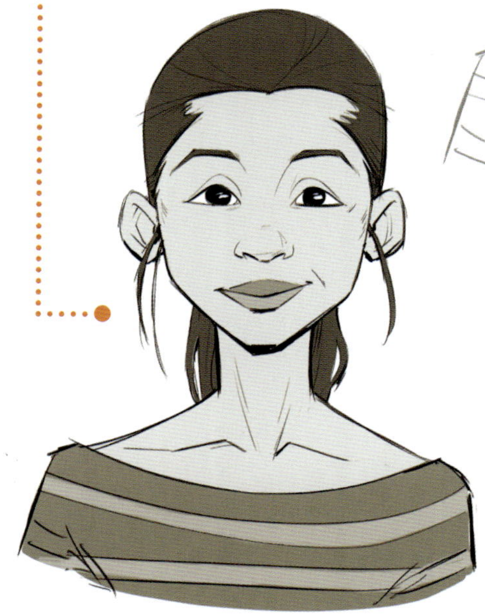

This front view of a female character has soft edges and round shapes, which make her seem sweet and gentle.

Constructing the head

Basic facial construction begins with the skull. Think about the big shapes before you approach details. The base of the head is a circle, with lines coming down on each side to form the jaw, tapering into the chin. You can then draw three straight lines through the face to establish where the eyes and nose are. They are usually placed within the bottom half of the face, as you can see above. A straight line down the vertical center of the face indicates where the nose will be. You can then use this line to place the eyes on either side, and the mouth halfway between the nose and chin.

These construction lines do not change depending on the sex of your human subject. The building-block shapes, however, will definitely change depending on the characteristics you wish to highlight. A traditionally masculine male character tends to have rougher edges and sharper shapes, like squares. A traditionally feminine woman tends to have rounder, softer shapes, like ovals. It is your job as a character designer to learn these shape languages in order to describe your subject correctly. However, a character does not have to be tied to traditional shapes based on their sex. A female character can be drawn with square shapes that make her look stronger and sturdier, and still be feminine. The same concept can be applied to a male character.

A male character tends to have a more angular face and thicker neck than a female character. Other than that, their construction is almost the same.

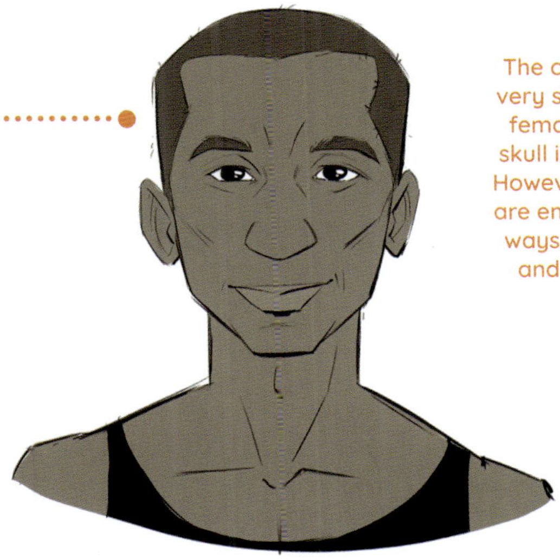

The construction lines are very similar to those of the female face because the skull is built the same way. However, different features are emphasized in different ways, such as a wider jaw and more angular chin.

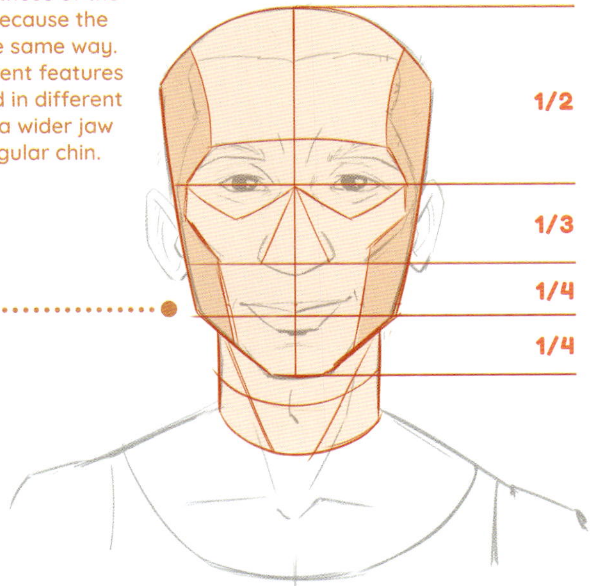

In profile, focus on the shape of the nose, brow ridge, lips, and chin. From this angle, you can see how the eyes are set back in the head, as they are placed deep into the skull.

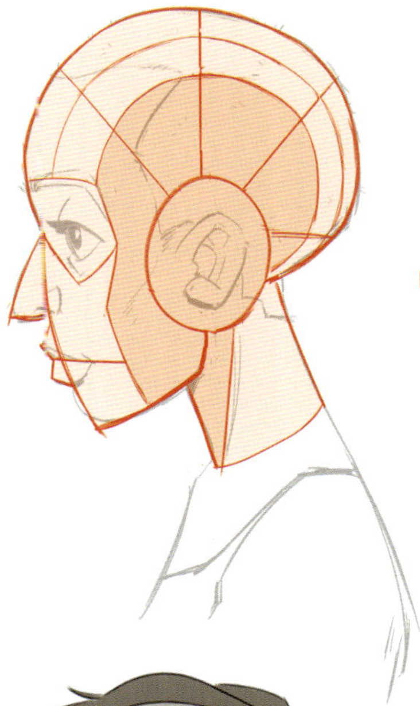

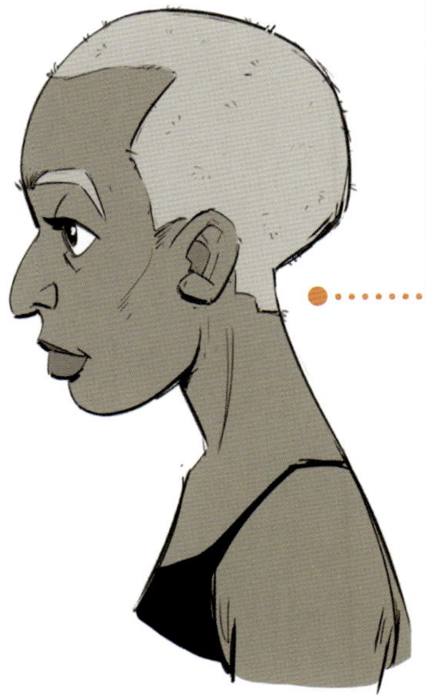

Always start with a circle for the top of the head to determine three-dimensional space. Draw a curved line down to determine the front of the face.

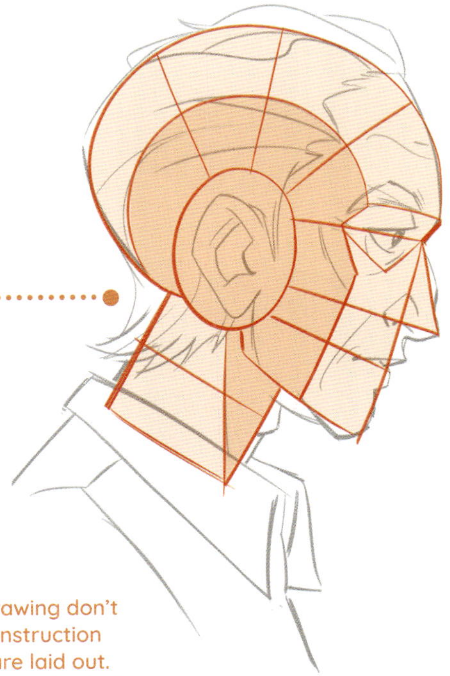

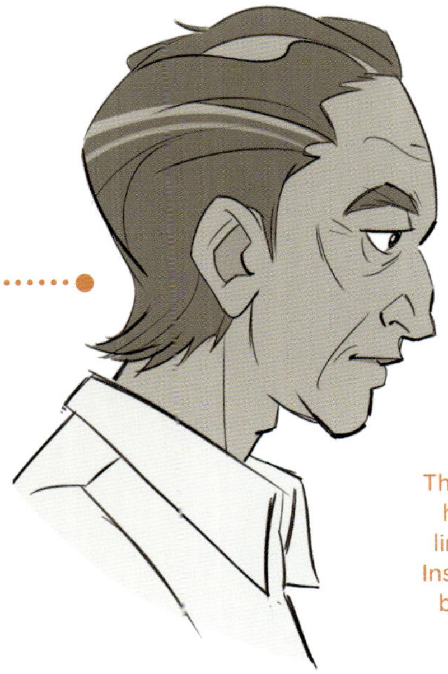

The male profile view tends to have a strongly defined brow bone. The nose is more angular and the lips are thinner. These are just some common traits and not rules to be strictly followed.

The outlines of your drawing don't have to follow the construction lines exactly as they are laid out. Instead, look at them as a physical base where you can add clay to mold the details on top.

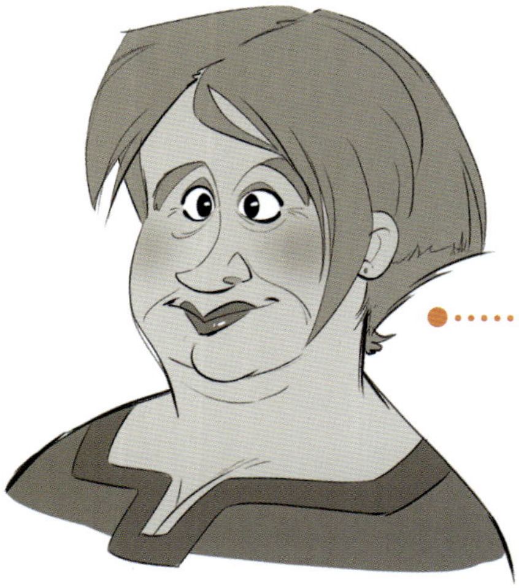

A three-quarter view of the face is considered the most important view and is usually the first one drawn, as it holds the most three-dimensional information.

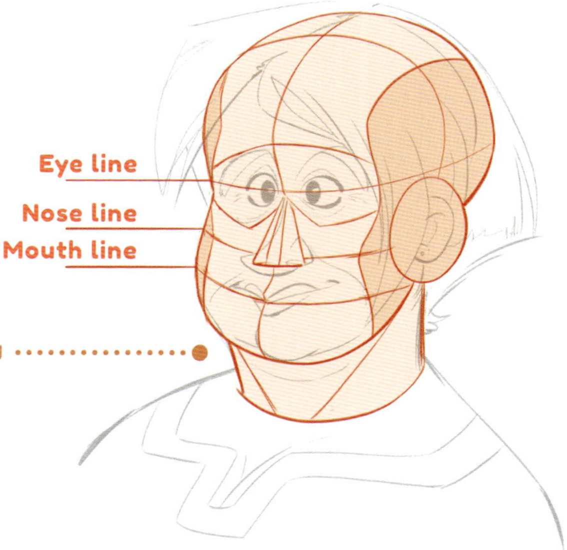

Consider the three-dimensional space and shapes. When drawing horizontal lines across the head shape for the eyes, nose, and mouth, curve the lines as you would around a ball.

As you can see here, a male character can have soft edges and rounded shapes, and still come across as masculine. The goal is to know the rules so that you can break them.

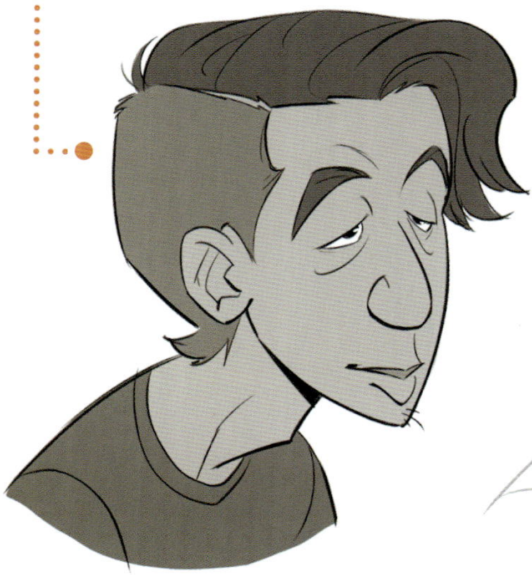

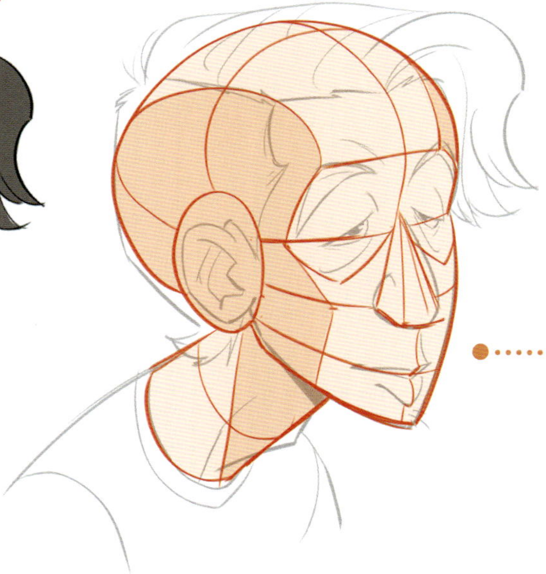

Notice how the construction lines for the nose are triangular, but the final shape of the nose is round. The construction lines do not determine the outcome – they only help toward it.

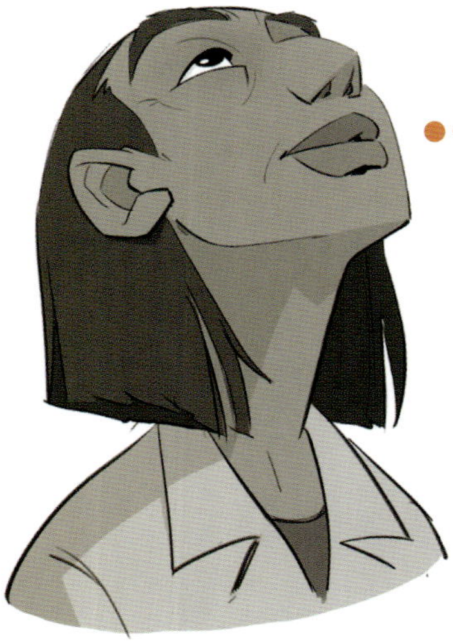

When the head tilts backward, think about what parts are affected by perspective. Usually, the hairline will disappear, while the space under the chin and nose becomes more prominent to the viewer.

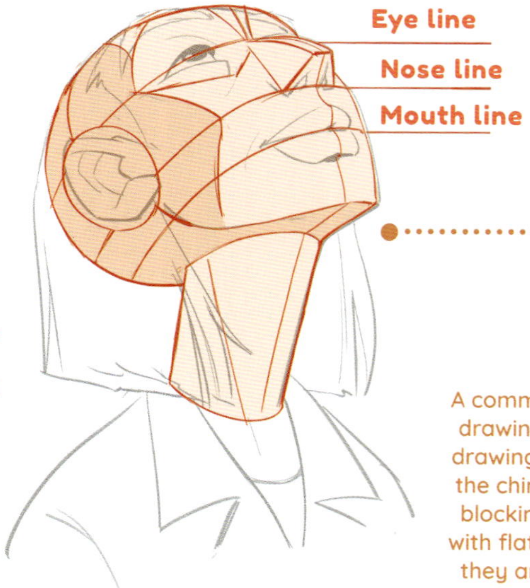

A common mistake when drawing this pose is not drawing the space under the chin or the nose. Try blocking in those areas with flat planes to ensure they are not forgotten.

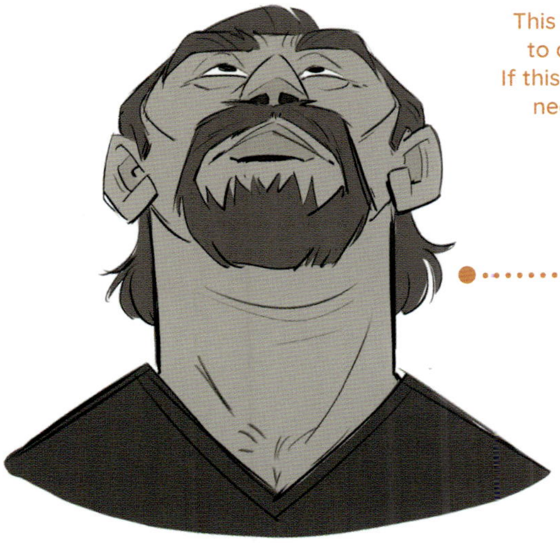

This frontal upshot is a challenging view to draw, as we don't see it that often. If this were a project, the animators would need this view to animate on-model, so make sure you practice it!

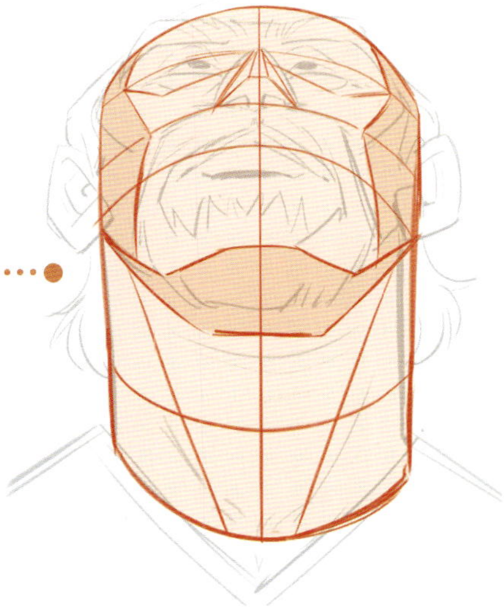

When a head is tilted backward, the horizontal construction lines come closer together, resulting in the facial features also coming closer together. If the angle is extreme, the mouth might even overlap the nose.

When the head is tilted forward, the top of the head becomes the most prominent part of the pose, resulting in the nose overlapping the mouth, and the chin appearing smaller.

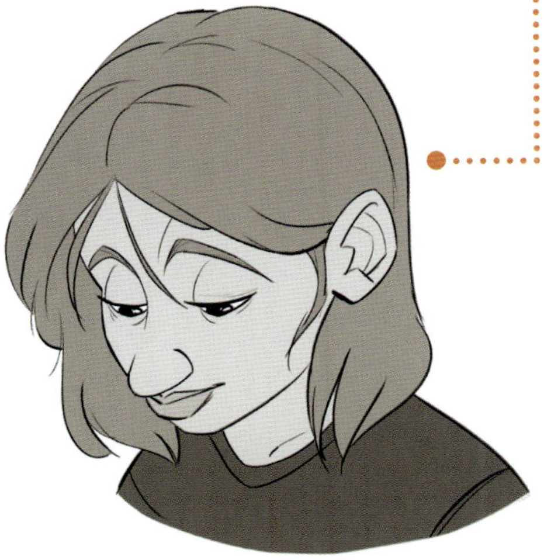

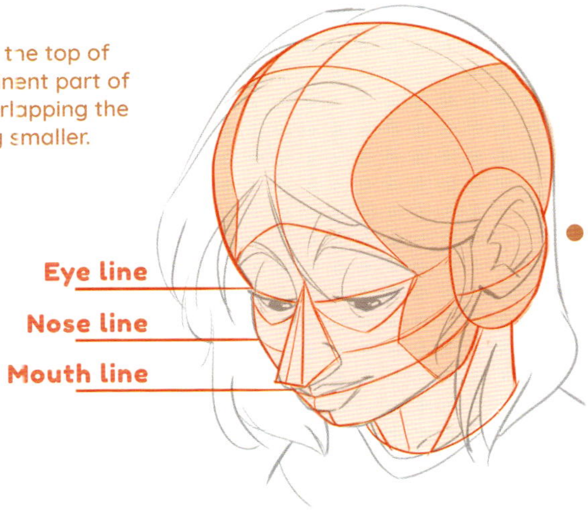

The curve of the horizontal lines is pointed downward because the eyes, nose, and mouth are located at the bottom half of the head.

When drawing a frontal downward shot, lower the eyebrows so they overlap the eyelids. Depending on how drastic the angle is, the nose may even overlap the mouth.

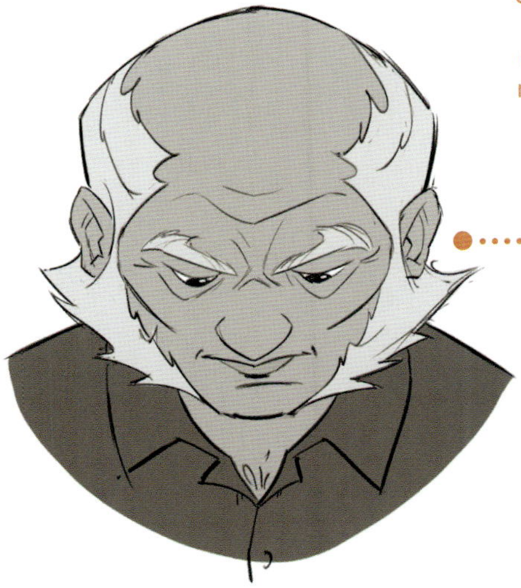

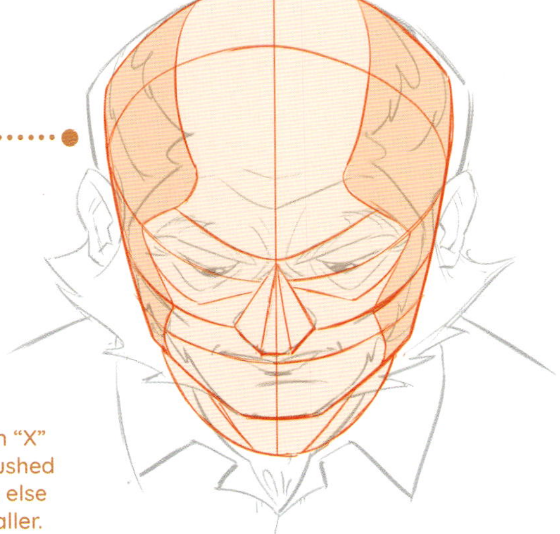

The construction lines intersect in an "X" at the top of the head. This part is pushed forward at this angle, so everything else is pushed backward, appearing smaller.

VISUAL WEIGHT MARBLE THEORY

When designing a face, key elements you should consider include positions of features, types of shapes, and the use of contrasting shapes. When we know how to construct a realistic face, it is then easier to exaggerate the shapes to make fun, cartoony characters. The nose will always be on the center line, but it could be closer to the eyes rather than the mouth. Changing its placement and shape can change your subject's characterization. The nose could be a square shape and take up most of the face, to express a solid, rigid personality. If you make the eyes small next to a big nose, you create contrast. Contrast is key and makes for more interesting visuals. One way to explore contrast is by using the **marble theory** of visual weight as a guide.

In marble theory, the dots represent the eyes and the line represents the placement of the nose. The flatter the nose line is, the younger the subject will look. The more pointed downward it is, the older they will look. The goal is to sketch out the marbles (eyes) and line curves first to help you exaggerate and explore.

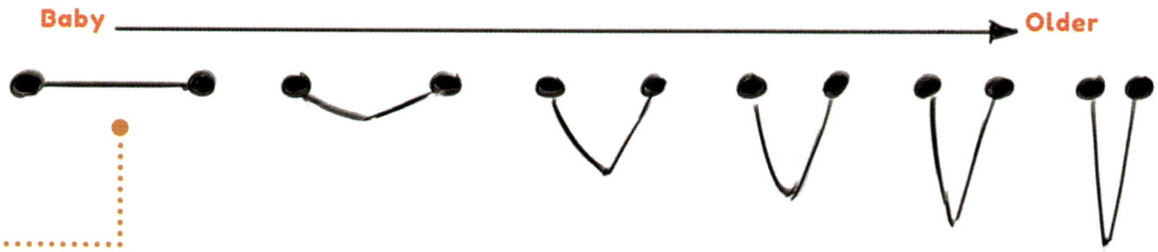

Notice how the line curve is shallow, so the character looks quite young. Her eyes are far apart, which can make a character look less focused and intelligent, like Sid the sloth from Blue Sky's *Ice Age*. This isn't always the case, but is a good trick to keep in mind.

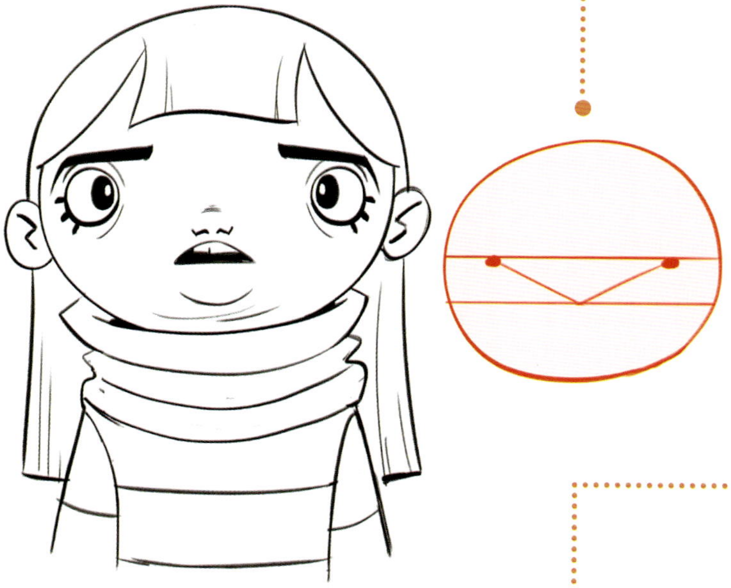

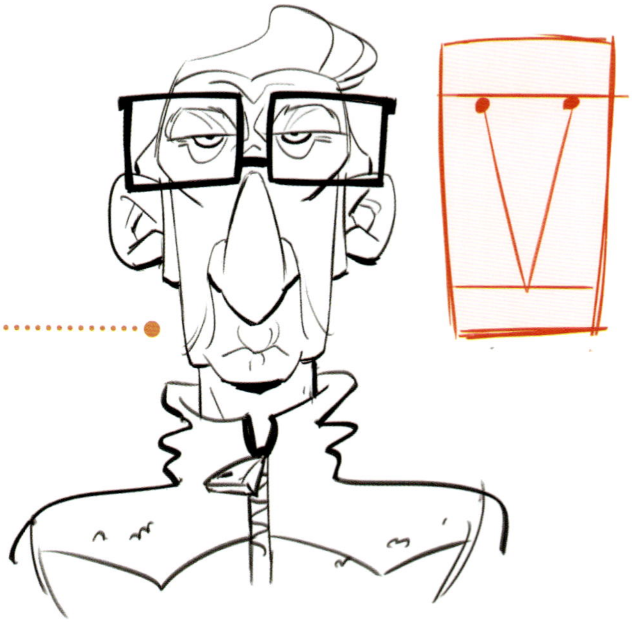

Here is an example of the opposite effect, where the line curve is steep. When a face is long like this one, the result comes across as older. Details such as wrinkles and a large nose add to that idea.

On this character, the eyes are close together, but the line curve is also shallow, making the subject look younger. Look at how small the face is compared to the rest of the head. Contrasting something small with something big is always visually appealing.

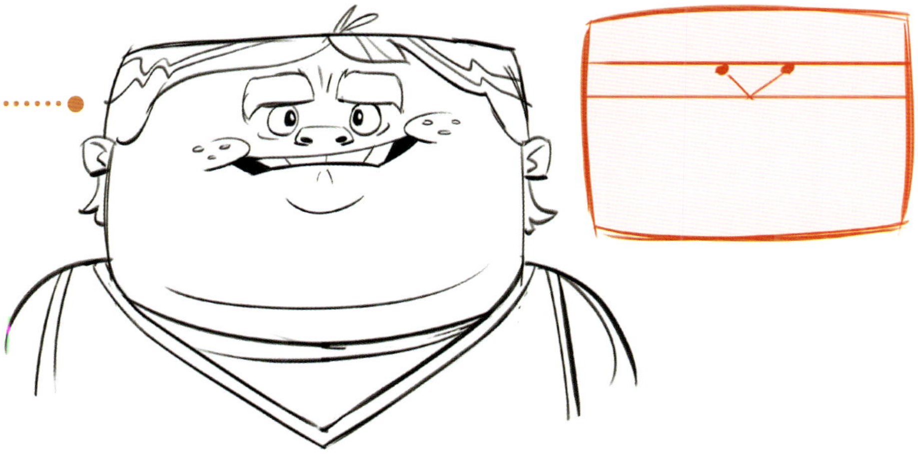

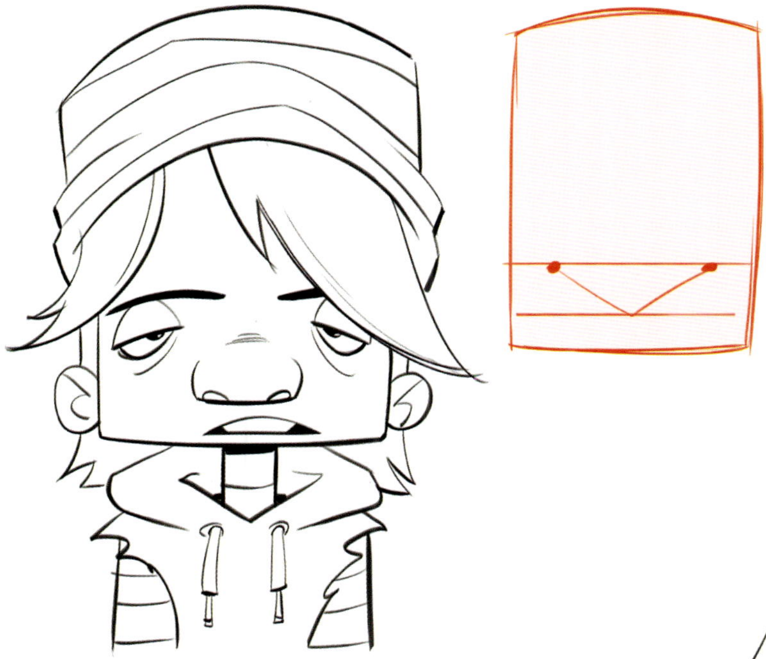

Sliding the lines and marbles around the head shape alters their effect. It is an easy, time-efficient way to push the design without wasting effort on details. This design looks like a teenager, which is helped by use of a mid-way line curve for the nose.

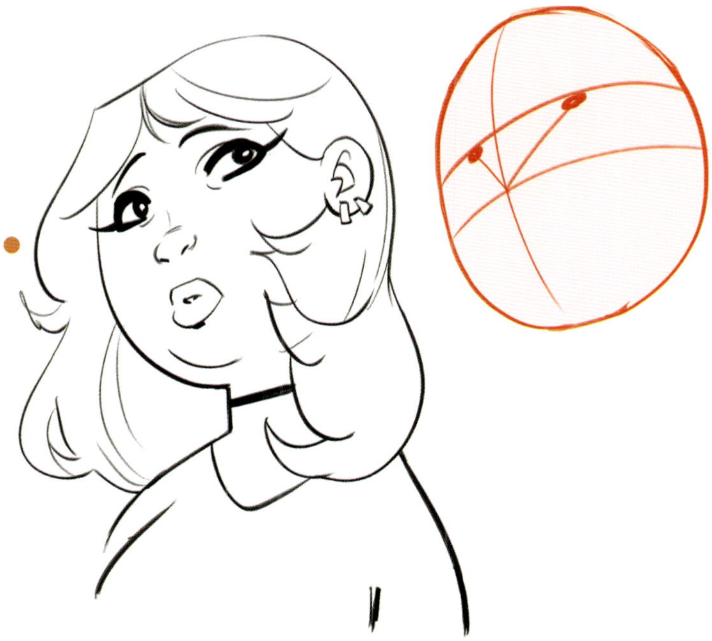

This is an average-looking face with somewhat realistic proportions. She is an adult, but on the younger side. The eyes and line curve are proportional to the head, without extreme exaggerations. Not all designs have to be excessively exaggerated – it depends on the style you are aiming for.

You can apply this visual weight method no matter what angle you are drawing. Here is an example of a long, oblong head with a small face, creating a character with intense, angular features.

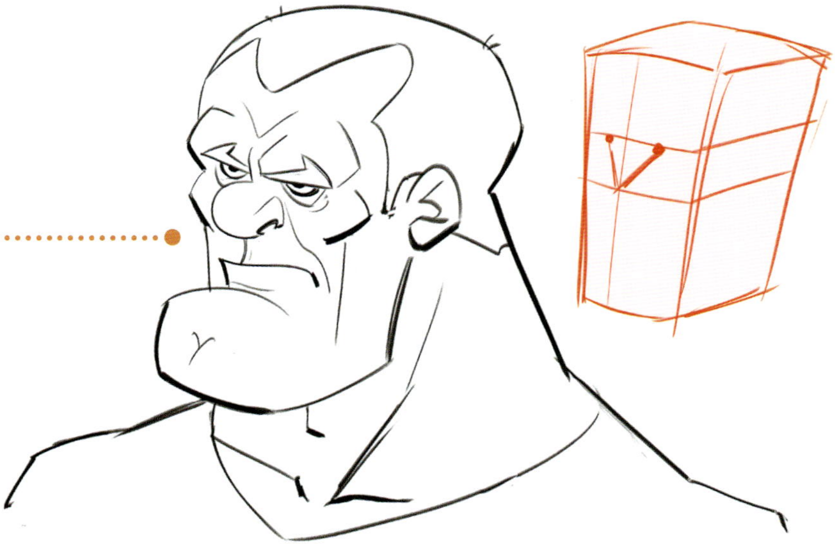

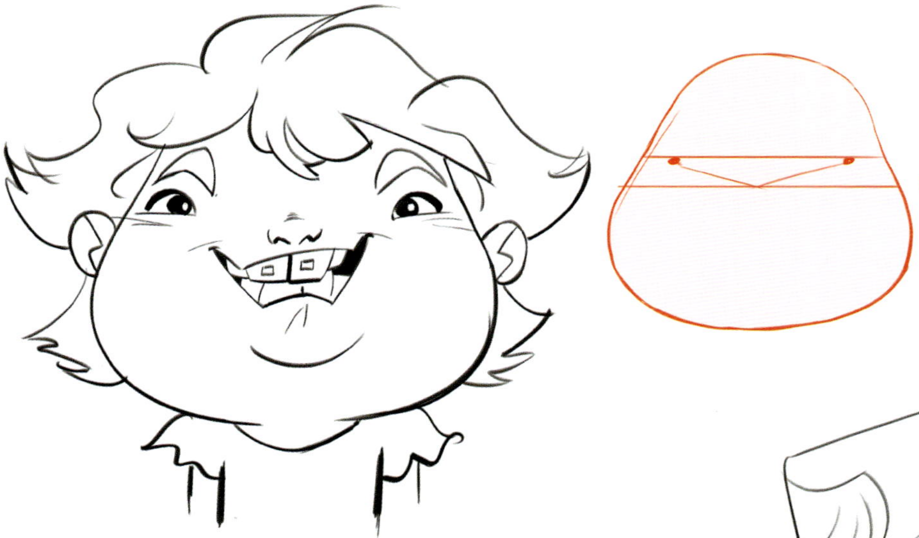

This is another take on the first example of a young character with far-apart eyes. It doesn't matter what head shape you choose, but rather the placement of the eyes and the nose in relation to each other.

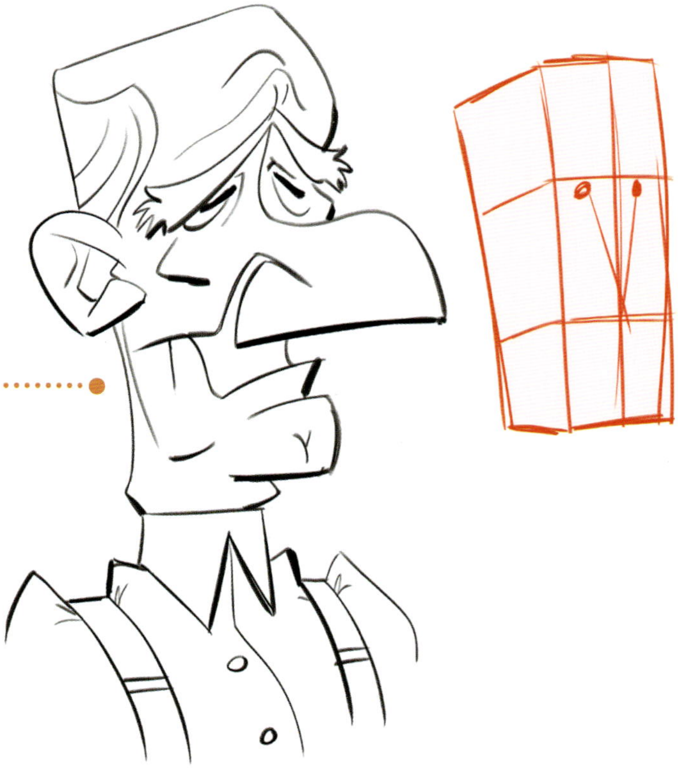

Here is an example of an older character from a three-quarter view. Notice how the space between the eyes and the bottom of the nose takes up half the face.

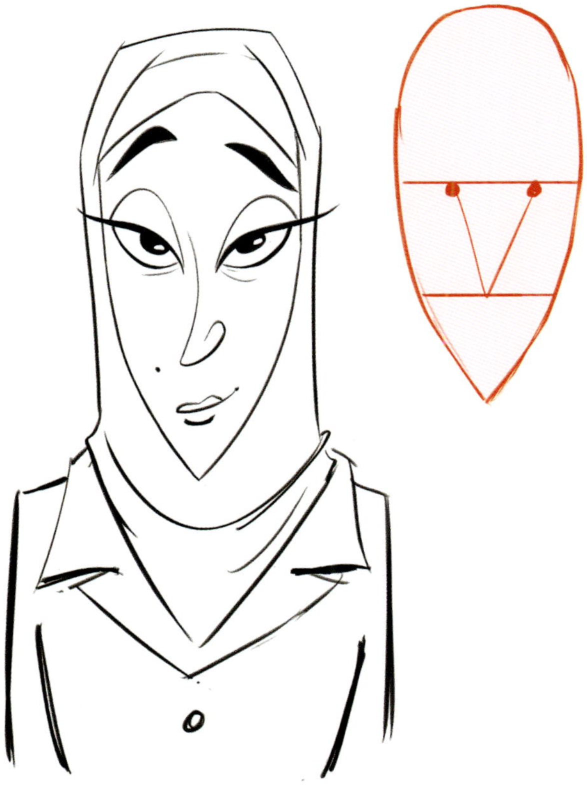

This is an oval face with a pointed chin. Notice how the length of the character's nose makes her look a little older, like a person in their early thirties.

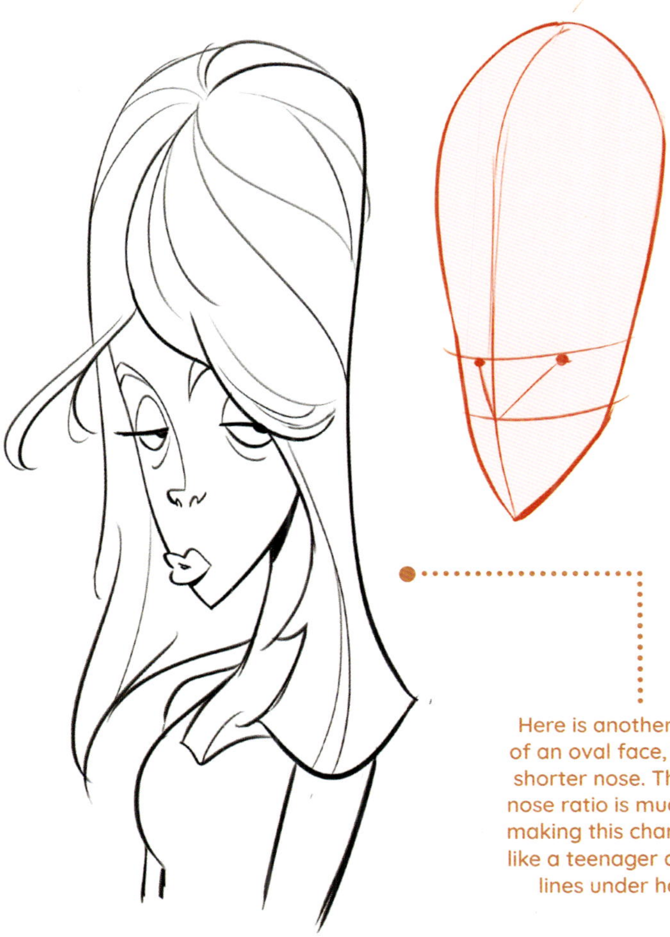

Here is another example of an oval face, but with a shorter nose. The eye-to-nose ratio is much smaller, making this character look like a teenager despite the lines under her eyes.

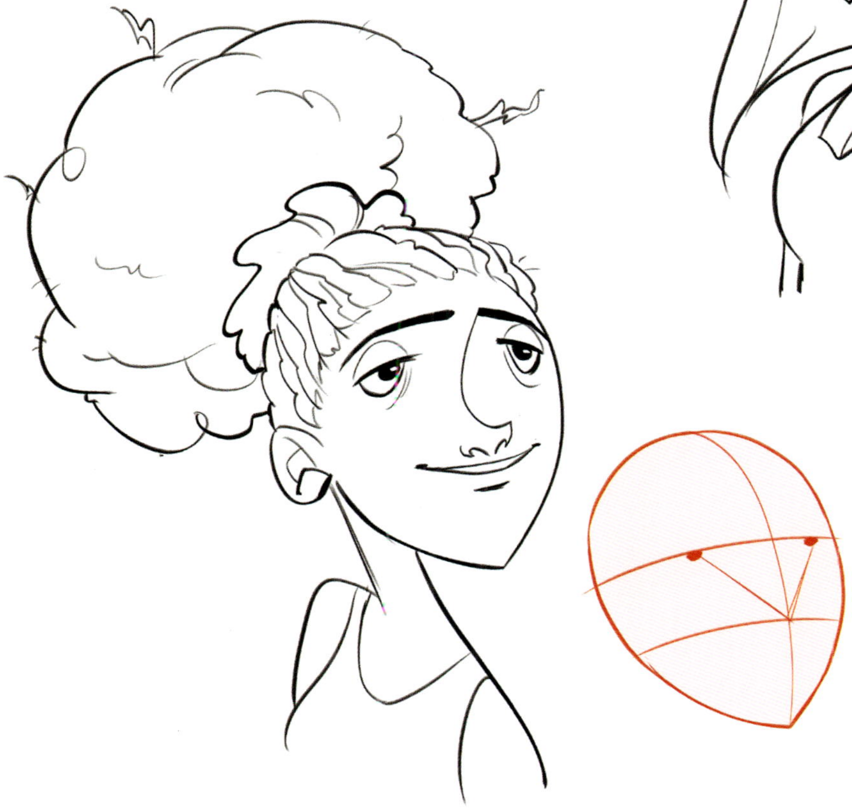

This is another example with quite an even ratio between the eyes and nose, again resulting in a young adult. The eyes are far apart, but they don't appear to be because the nose is also placed farther away.

EXAGGERATING SHAPES

Ida Hem

As character designers, we don't speak English – we speak in shapes! Shape language is universal and doesn't need any words, meaning that no matter what country the viewer is from, they will understand. As you are probably aware of by now, you can apply certain shapes to a character in order to achieve a certain result. For example, square shapes can result in someone who looks stubborn, rugged, and rigid like a rock. Round shapes can convey someone soft, kind, and gentle. Triangles can suggest someone dangerous, fast, and angular. The same applies for the head and face, as it does for the entire figure.

Character designers can take these traits and exaggerate them in order to highlight an idea. When you exaggerate a shape, it means that your character becomes more "cartoony." For example, Stewie from *Family Guy* has a head shaped like an American football. That shape is extremely exaggerated, but results in something unique and characteristic. Disney's Mickey Mouse is essentially just iconic round shapes. When your character has strong, distinct shapes, the result will be something recognizable that sticks in the head of your audience.

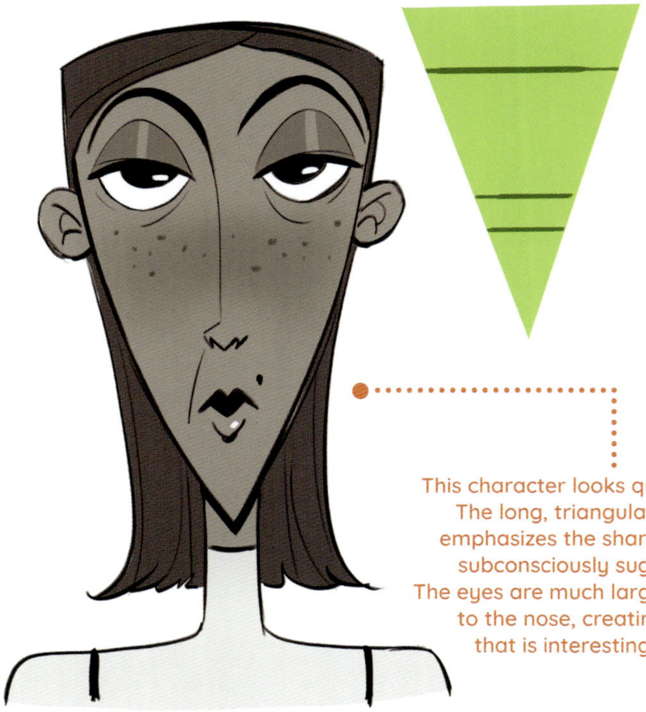

This character looks quite intimidating. The long, triangular head shape emphasizes the sharp edges, which subconsciously suggest danger. The eyes are much larger in comparison to the nose, creating a contrast that is interesting to look at.

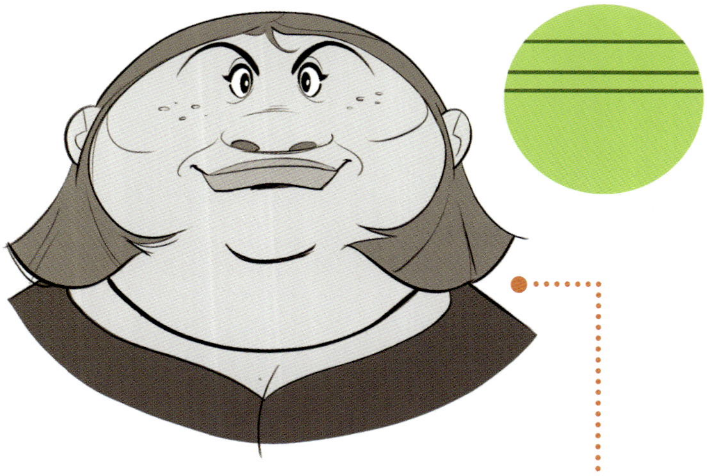

This head shape is completely round and has no sharp edges, making the character look less intimidating than her triangular counterpart. She looks like the chatty, sweet lady at a front desk, greeting you with a smile.

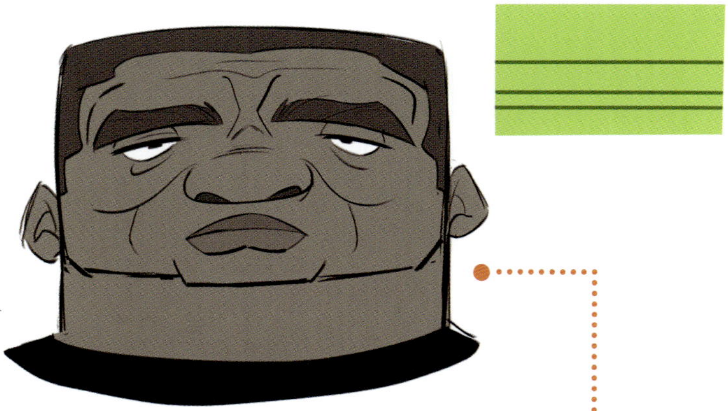

This character looks rock-steady, like an earthquake couldn't move him. This is because the basic shape is a horizontal, elongated square. This shape feels like you couldn't push it over unless you lifted it up, making the character look strong and stable.

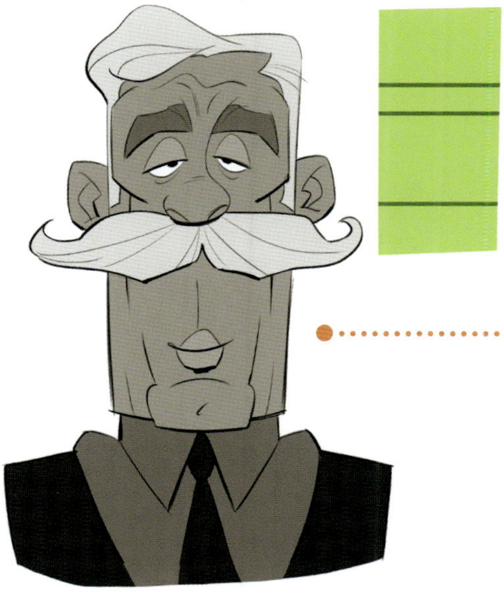

Here we have a vertical rectangle as a basic head shape. It is technically a square, which in this case makes the character look stubborn. Since the shape is vertical and tall, it gives the effect of someone snooty or regal. The mouth is further down on the face, which adds to the smug attitude.

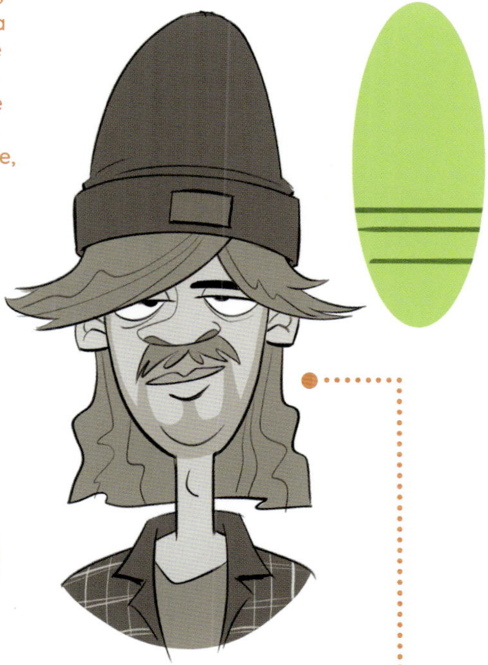

This is the least intimidating character you will ever see – he looks like a laid-back guy who would say “yes” to anything! His basic head shape is a long oval, with the face concentrated in the bottom half. The round edges make him look soft and sweet. Even his hair looks soft.

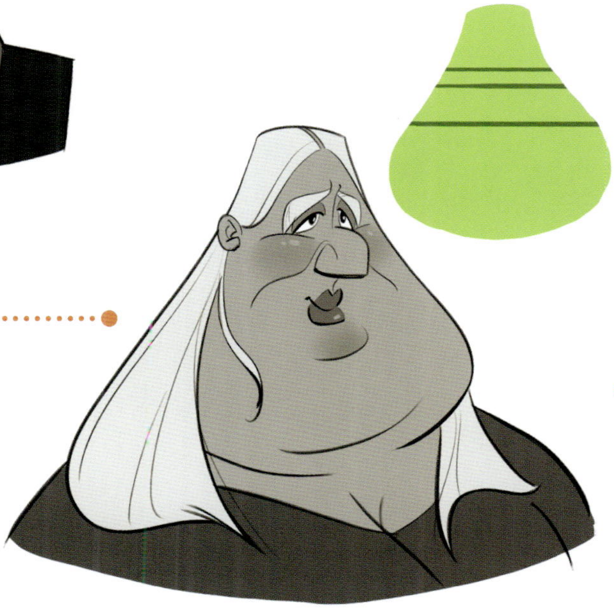

“Soft and sweet” can come in more shapes than just circles or ovals. The key is to have soft edges or no straight lines at all. This character has a pear-shaped head and still comes across like a kind, gentle soul. The bigger mass at the bottom of the pear shape exaggerates the feature of being heavier-set.

Here we have a fun, wonky shape to work with. The head is shaped like a mushroom, which is an unusual shape, and that comes across in the character. He looks friendly, because there are no sharp angles, and he also looks like a fun personality because the shape is fun!

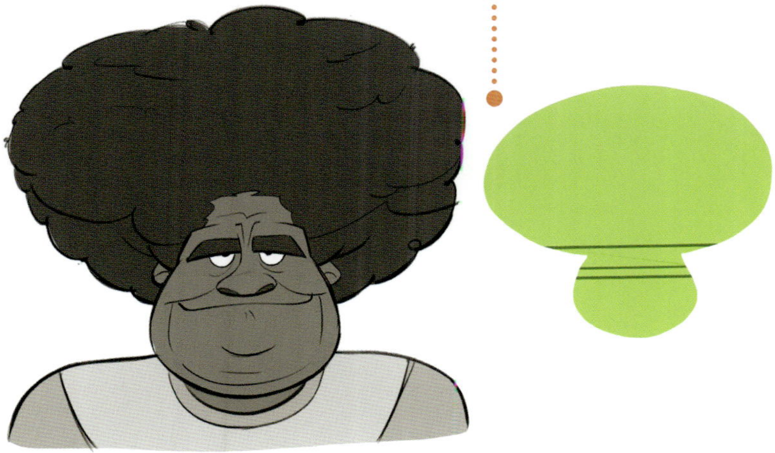

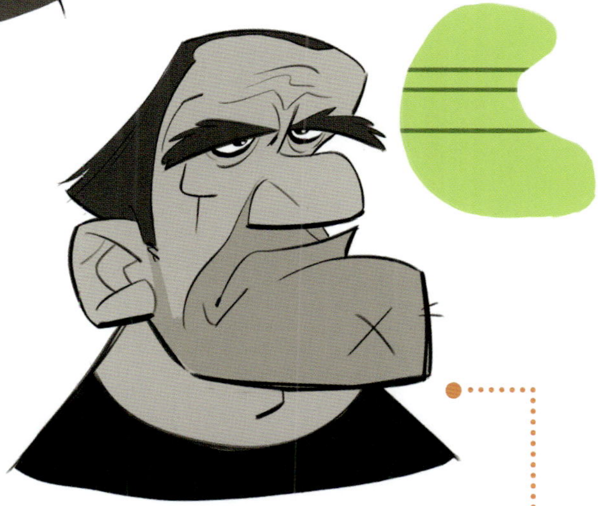

This basic shape is a bean, which is another unusual shape that can yield good results. This is why you should always think outside the box and try as many shapes as possible. The bean shape exaggerates the awkwardness of the character, and his heavy underbite, which makes him look stubborn.

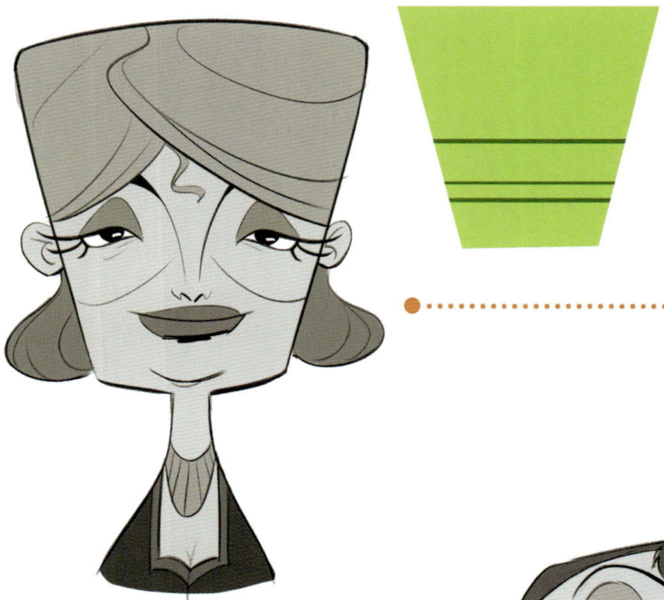

This character's head is a square with a wider top, also known as a trapezoid. The square gives us a strong feature, while the wide top makes her look brainy. This combination of features can make your character look like a leader – she looks like someone who could be a town mayor.

Having a wide shape of any kind will make your character appear solid, as it feels like that shape is harder to knock over. This horizontal oval head shape makes the character look kind, but also strong and solid. She has large, full cheeks, which also make her look soft.

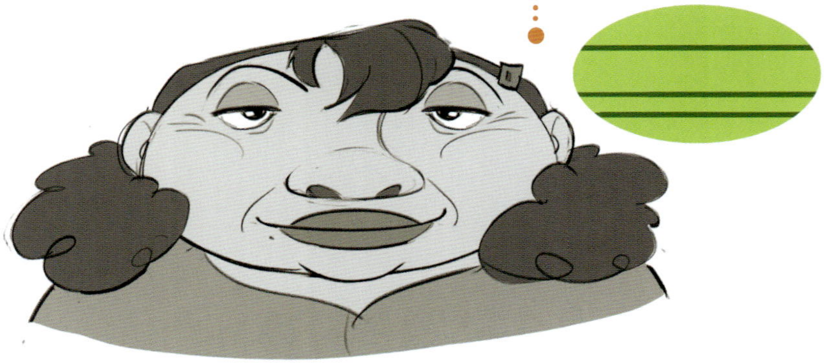

Here we have another example of a trapezoid, but with the wide part at the bottom. This gives the effect of a strong character with a solid base. Notice how the square shape has been repeated in the eyebrows, ears, and chin. Repeating shapes within the design is a great way to unify your subject.

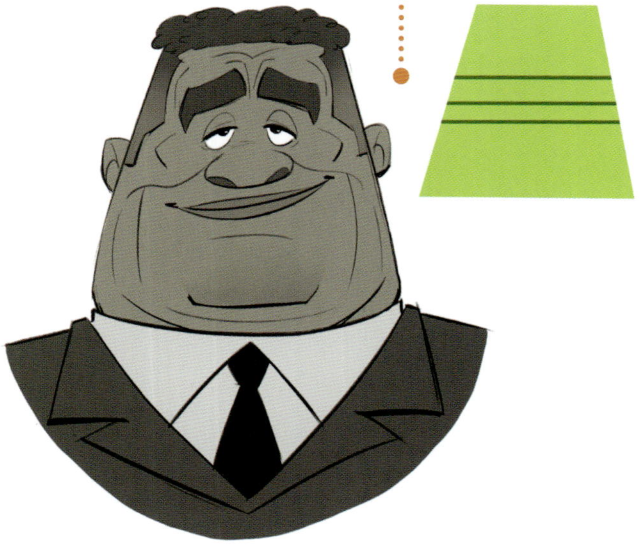

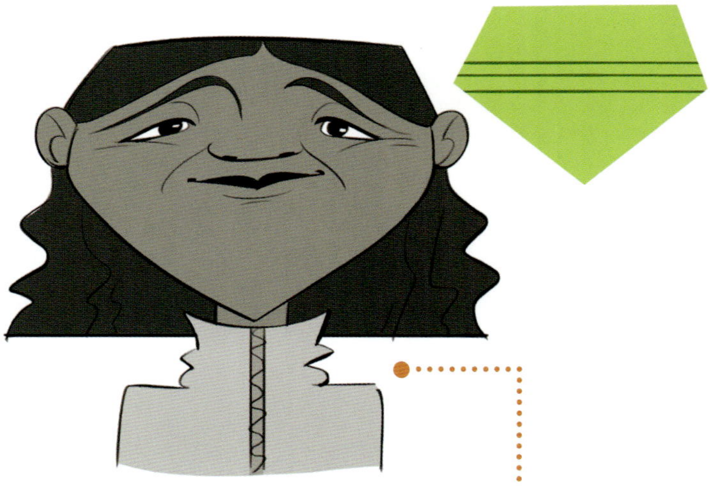

This character has a pentagon-shaped head. The facial features are close together, giving her a bigger chin. This makes her look tough, like she's a boxer who can give a good punch. The top of her head is square, which also helps exaggerate her strong features, and the pointed chin makes her look agile.

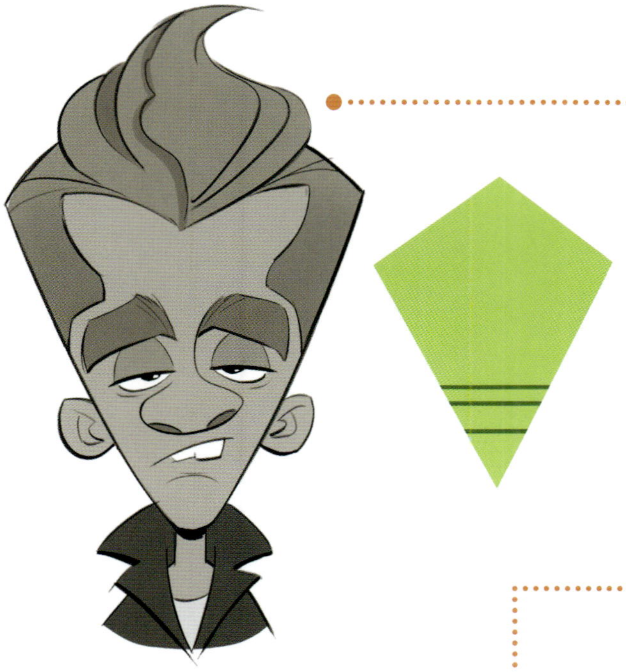

Here we have a very brainy, smart character. Whenever the top of the head for a character is enlarged, it can make them look intellectual and quick-witted. His head is shaped like a kite – a very dynamic shape due to its sharp angles.

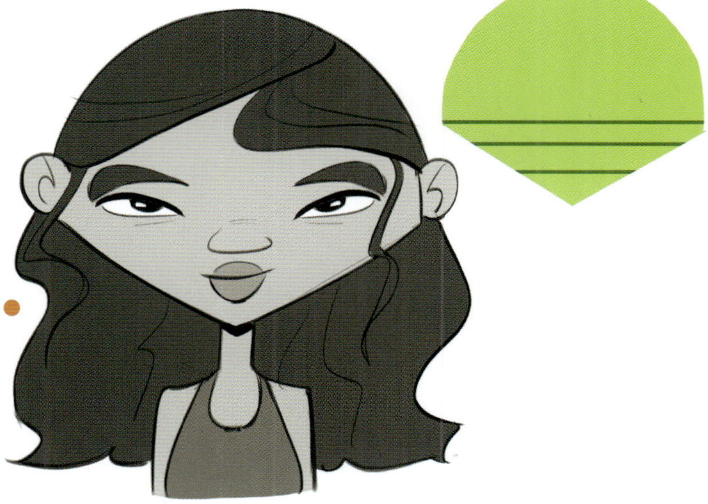

This is a sweet-looking character with a bit of an edge. She has a sharp chin, but overall soft features. Combining shapes like this can make a face look more complex. Her big eyes make her look friendly, and her nose is vertically very close to her eyes, making her look young.

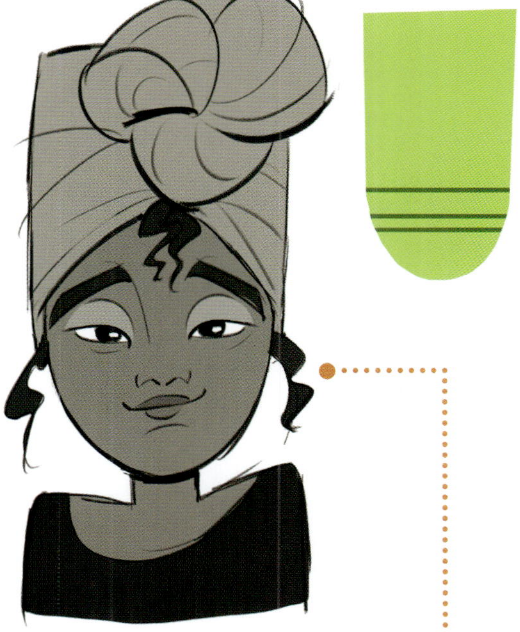

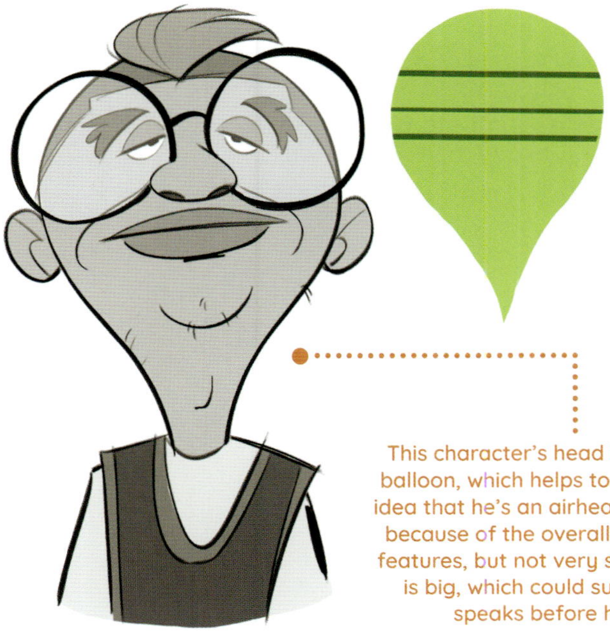

This character's head is shaped like a balloon, which helps to exaggerate the idea that he's an airhead. He looks kind, because of the overall round and soft features, but not very sharp. His mouth is big, which could suggest that he speaks before he thinks.

This is a complex shape as it is a rectangle and a circle combined. The character's face looks very amiable and approachable, and her big, square head makes her look smart and solid. These features make her look like a teacher – someone who can guide and teach with patience.

EXPRESSIONS
Ida Hem

Humans can express a wide variety of emotions, such as happiness, sadness, disgust, surprise, anger, and fear. Some are complex and others are straightforward. It's important to be able to communicate what a character is thinking and feeling because that is how the viewer connects with them. Expressions can be harder to read in cartoon characters than they are in real-life humans, because cartoons are simplified and less nuanced.

In this section of the chapter, we will focus on some basic expressions that will help you understand how the primary and secondary features of the face work. The primary features are marked with red on the faces shown here. These are the eyes, including the surrounding skin/muscles and brows, and the mouth, including the lips and the skin/muscles around them. These are primary features because they are the most expressive parts of the face. The secondary features, marked in blue, include the cheeks, nose, and forehead. These features have far fewer muscles, so are less expressive, but they interact with the primary features and can be used in more unusual expressions. Secondary does not mean "less important" – it just means they are used less often. For example, if a character is sucking in their cheeks, the "secondary" feature of the cheeks plays a much bigger role in that expression.

To create believable expressions, we need to study these facial muscles and interactions. For example, if a character's mouth is smiling, the eyes should be smiling as well. The corners of the mouth push the cheeks up, which push the bottom eyelids up, in a sort of domino effect. When we squint, our mouth usually moves up closer to our nose, because our muscles automatically pull them upward. The best way to study expressions is simply by using your own face. Take photos of yourself acting out an emotion and feel how your muscles move. Many character designers and animators keep a mirror on their desk for quick and easy reference.

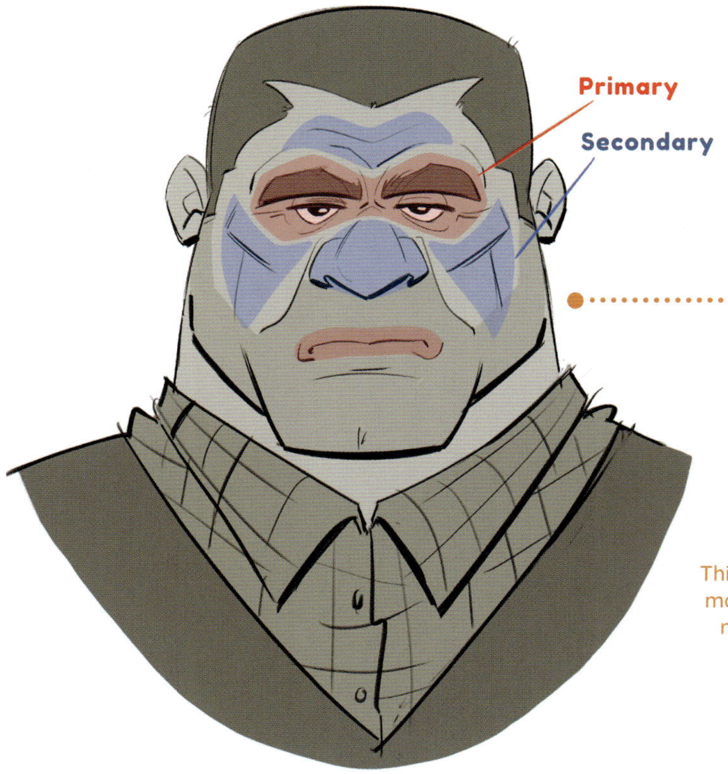

This is an example of a male character with a neutral expression.

This is an example of a female character with a neutral expression.

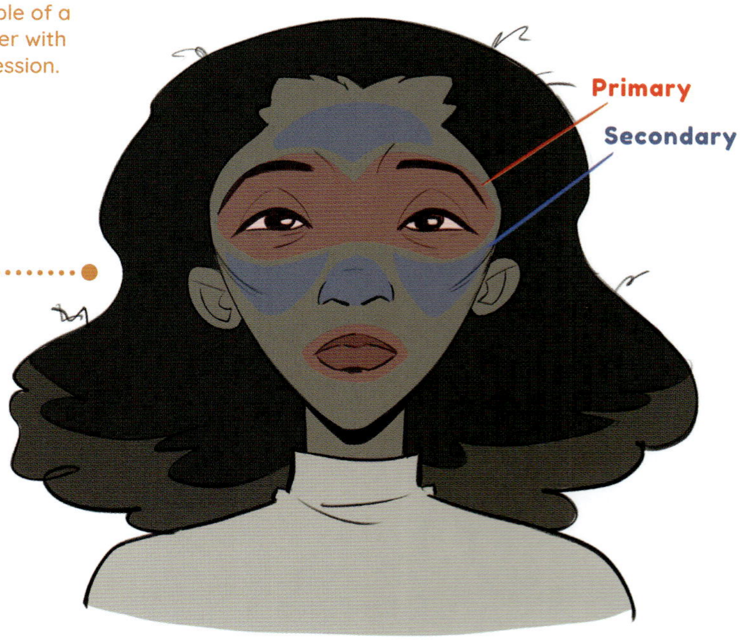

When a character is happy, the eyebrows and bottom eyelids are pushed upward. The corners of the mouth push the cheeks up.

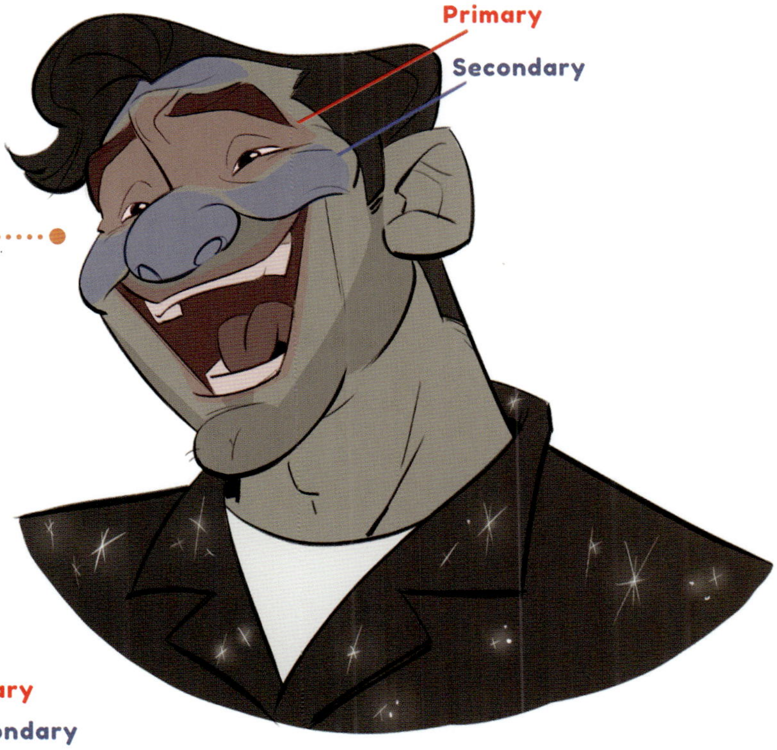

A sad character demonstrates the opposite effect to a happy character. The muscles tend to relax much more, while the inner corners of the eyebrows go up.

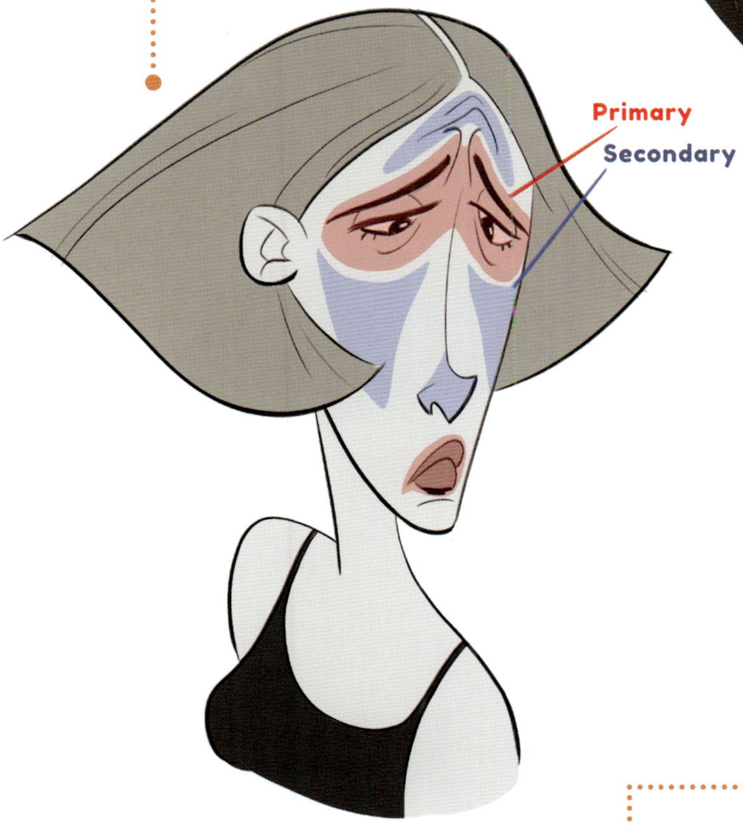

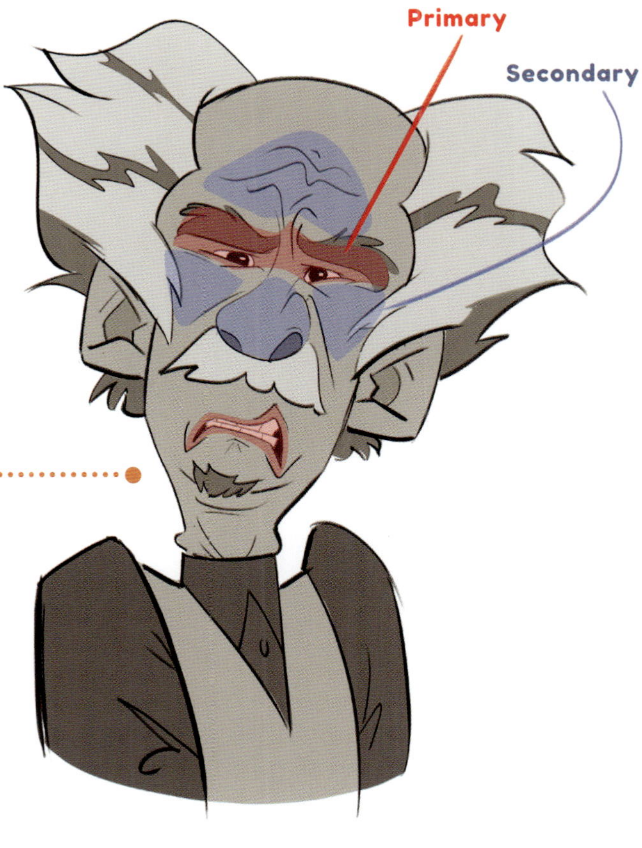

When a character expresses disgust, they tend to squint and the upper lip pulls up. Notice how the nose also pushes up, acting according to the eyes.

Sadness and fear have some similarities. The difference is, when you are afraid, your muscles tense up – and notice how the eyes are wide open.

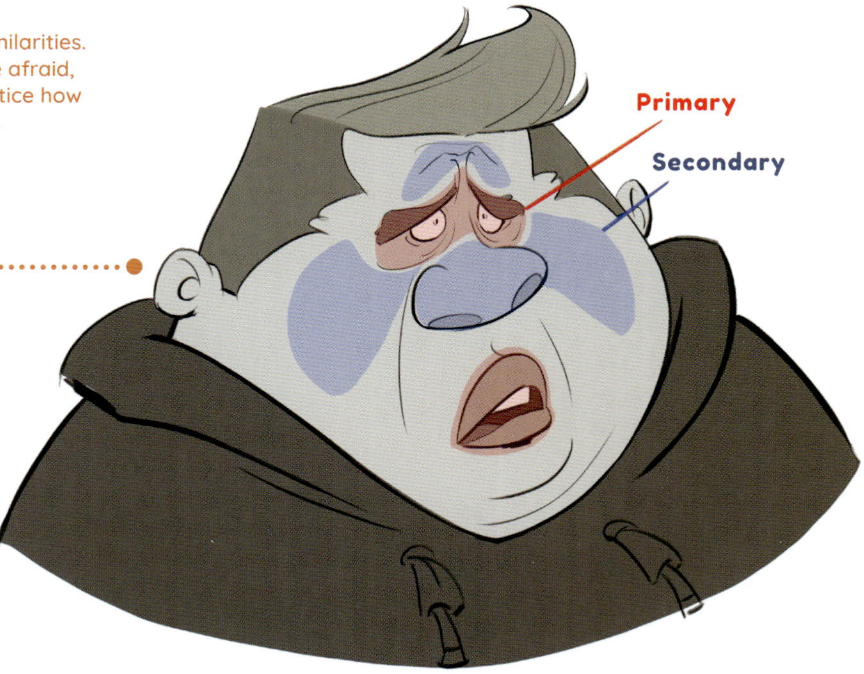

A surprised expression can be accomplished by having all the muscles pull away from each other. The eyebrows will pull up, while the mouth will go down. The eyes are wide.

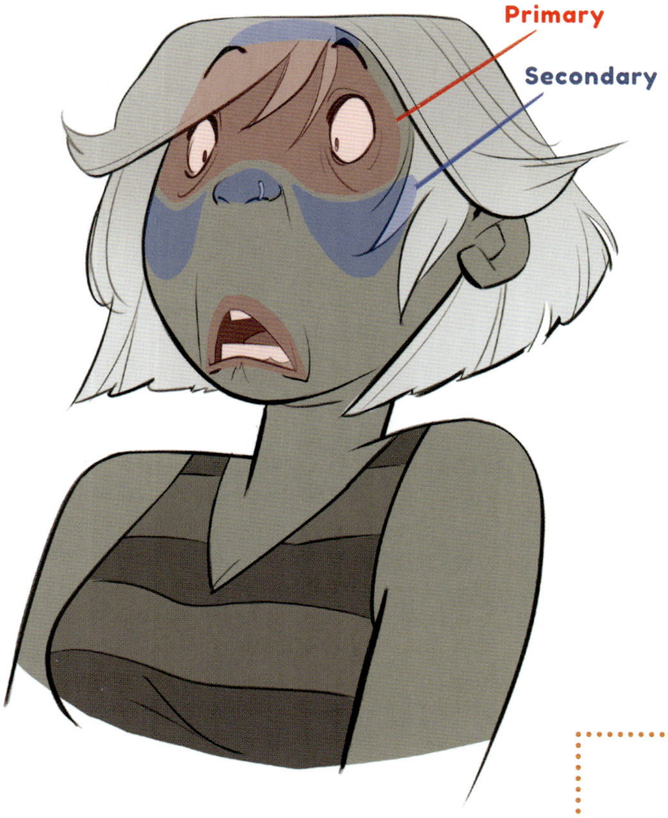

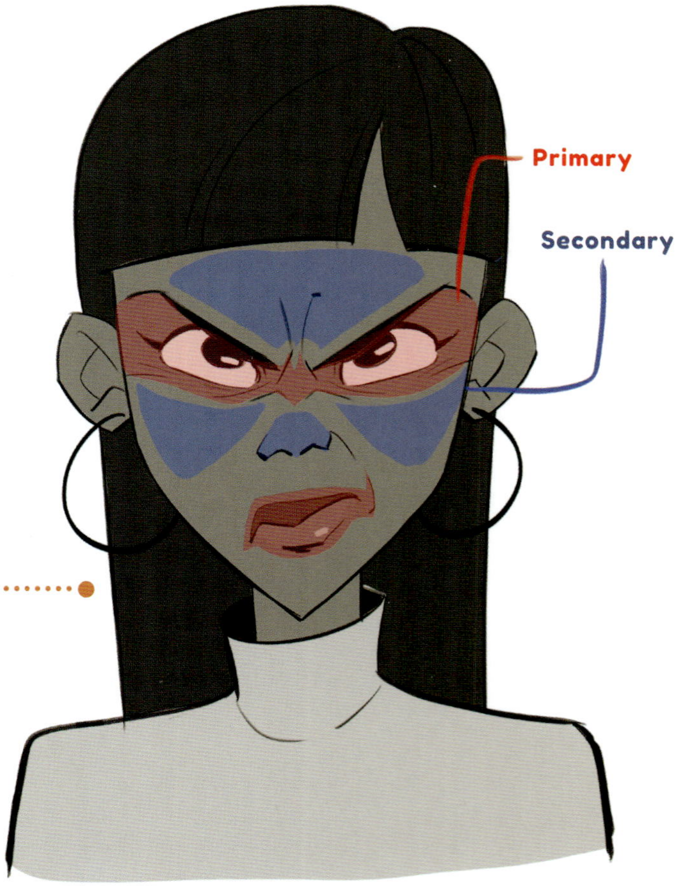

When a character is angry, the focus is on the area between the eyebrows and the eyes. Every muscle pulls toward that area.

This is a compilation of all expressions with their typical traits listed for reference. Take these traits and play around with them to see what results you can get!

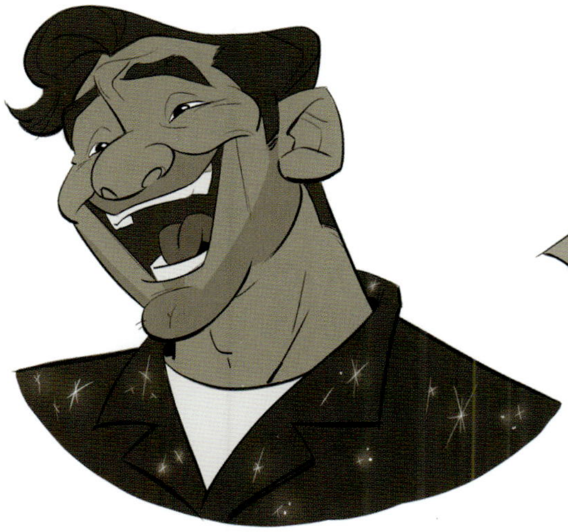

HAPPY

- Wrinkles around eyes
- Corners of mouth go up
- Cheeks go up

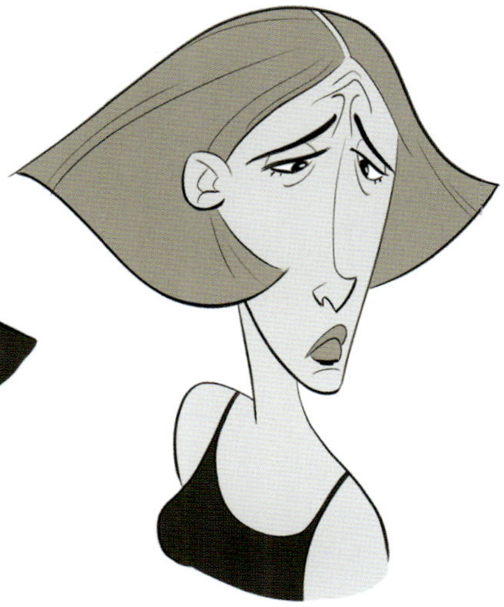

SAD

- Corners of mouth go down
- Cheeks relax
- Inner corners of eyebrows go up
- Forehead wrinkles

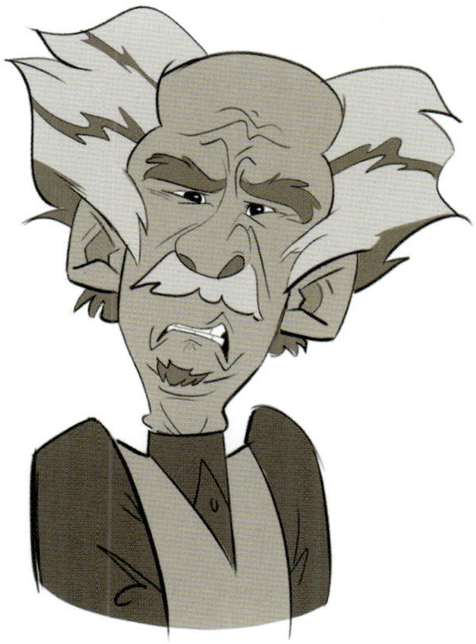

DISGUSTED

- All muscles pull toward center of face
- Cheeks go up
- Wrinkles form around eyes & forehead

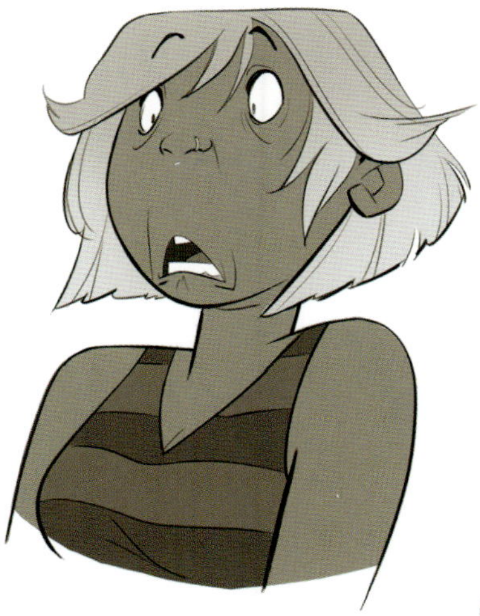

SURPRISED

- Corners of mouth push down
- Eyes widen
- Eyebrows go up
- Face muscles pull outward
- Pupils shrink

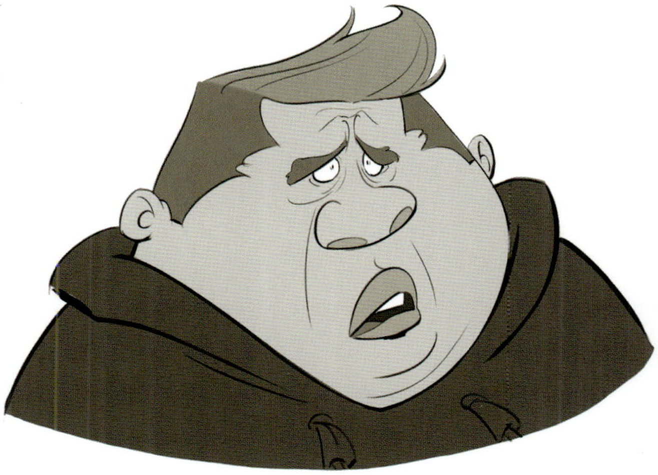

AFRAID

- Muscle focuses in forehead
- Mouth relaxes
- Inner corners of eyebrows go up

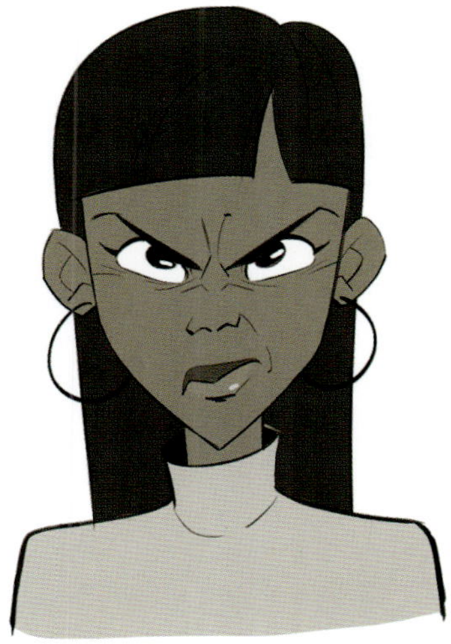

ANGRY

- Face muscles tighten between eyes
- Corners of mouth go down
- Inner corners of eyebrows go down

EXAGGERATING EXPRESSIONS

Ida Hem

Now that we understand the importance of a strong, believable expression and how to work toward it through the primary and secondary features, we can discuss how to exaggerate emotions. As mentioned earlier, the emotions of cartoon characters can be harder to read than those of real-life humans. That is why we need to exaggerate drawn expressions so that the audience can interpret the character quickly and easily. When exaggerating an expression, you need to narrow it down to the primary features (eyes, eyebrows, mouth), take those shapes, and see how far you can push them without breaking the character design.

We are so familiar with the human face because we see it every day, and if something in a design is just a little bit "off," the viewer will immediately be drawn to it. If they need more than a second to understand what's happening, it means the design is not working. When the expression and the design work together effectively, the character becomes dynamic, interesting, and believable.

APPEAL IS THE GOAL

Creating something believable is arguably the most difficult part of character design, because for that we need appeal. Appeal is hard to teach. It is something you have to find through practice. Appeal comes when everything works in harmony together, and when you can read an expression without second-guessing. It comes when the character sits perfectly in a three-dimensional space, and you feel like you could reach your hand into the screen and grab them. Appeal comes when you believe the character is real.

To the left, we have a happy character. Below, we have the same emotion, but exaggerated. The brows, cheeks, bottom eyelids, and corners of the mouth are all pushed up, but emphasized even further to highlight the emotion.

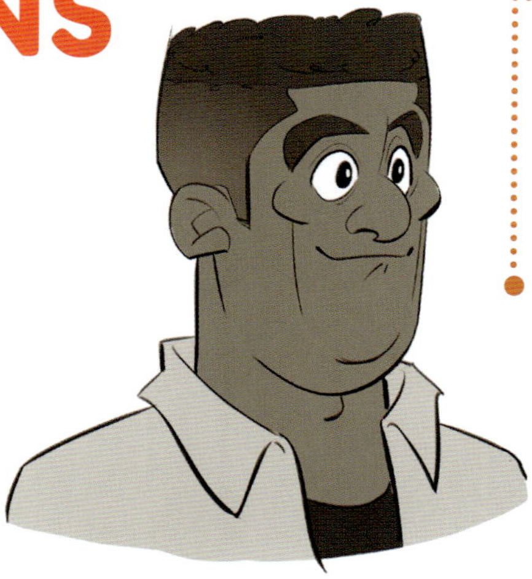

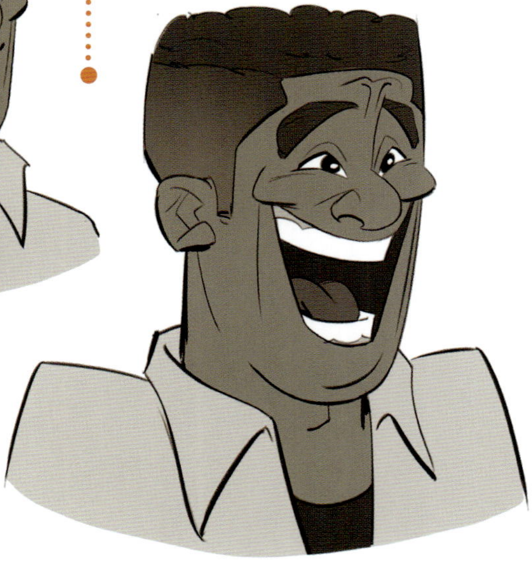

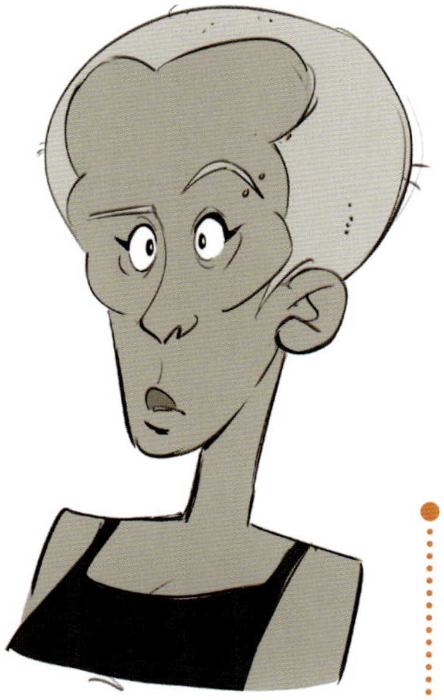

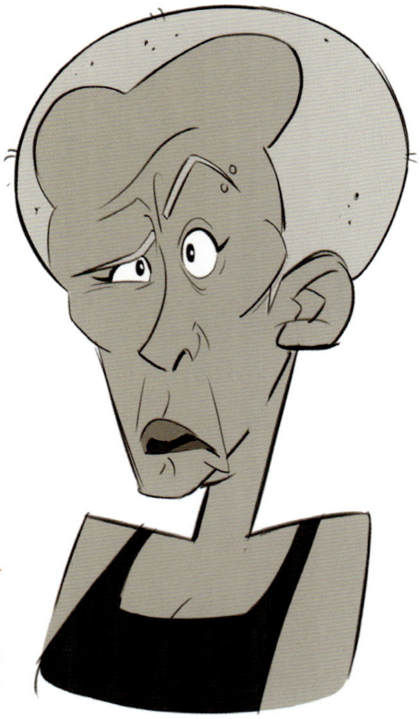

We can push this puzzled expression by further exaggerating the eyebrows. One brow is pushed down, and the other is pushed up to form a shape unique to this emotion. The mouth is pushed down to highlight the eyebrows through opposing action (when two things move in opposite directions).

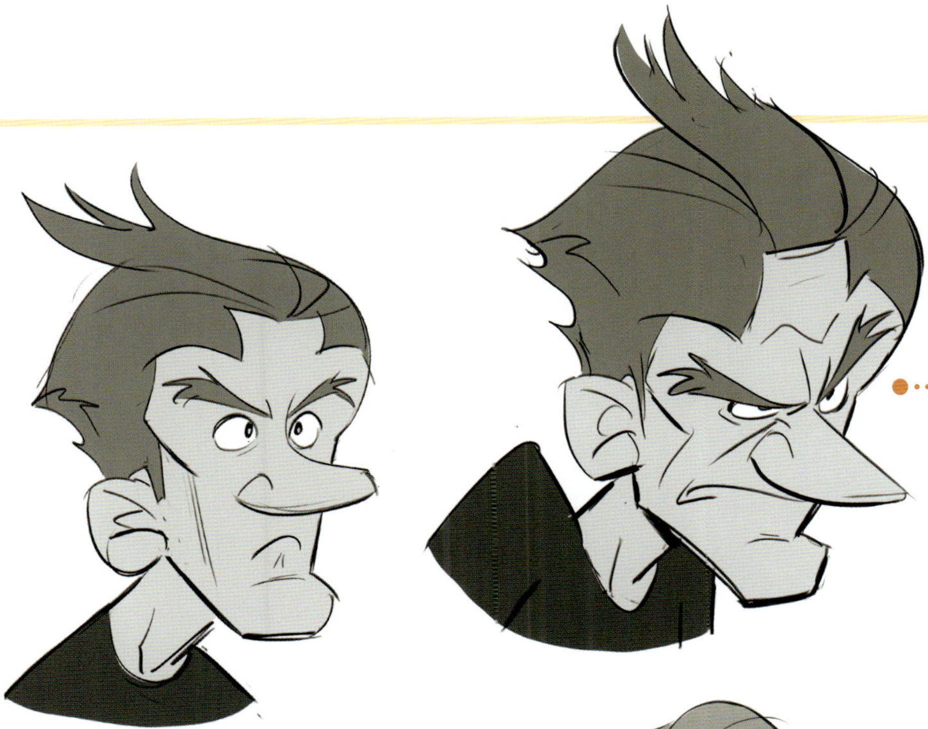

Both versions of the character are expressing anger, but the one on the right feels more convincing. The inner corners of the eyebrows push down over the eyes, and the mouth also plays a big role, pulling down at the corners. The head is tilted forward to emphasize the angry brows even more.

This character is very nervous, like she did something she wasn't supposed to do. The mouth shape has been extremely exaggerated into a wide, guilty smile. The guilty element of the expression can be found in her eyes, as they express panic through the small pupils, wide eyes, and tense eyebrows.

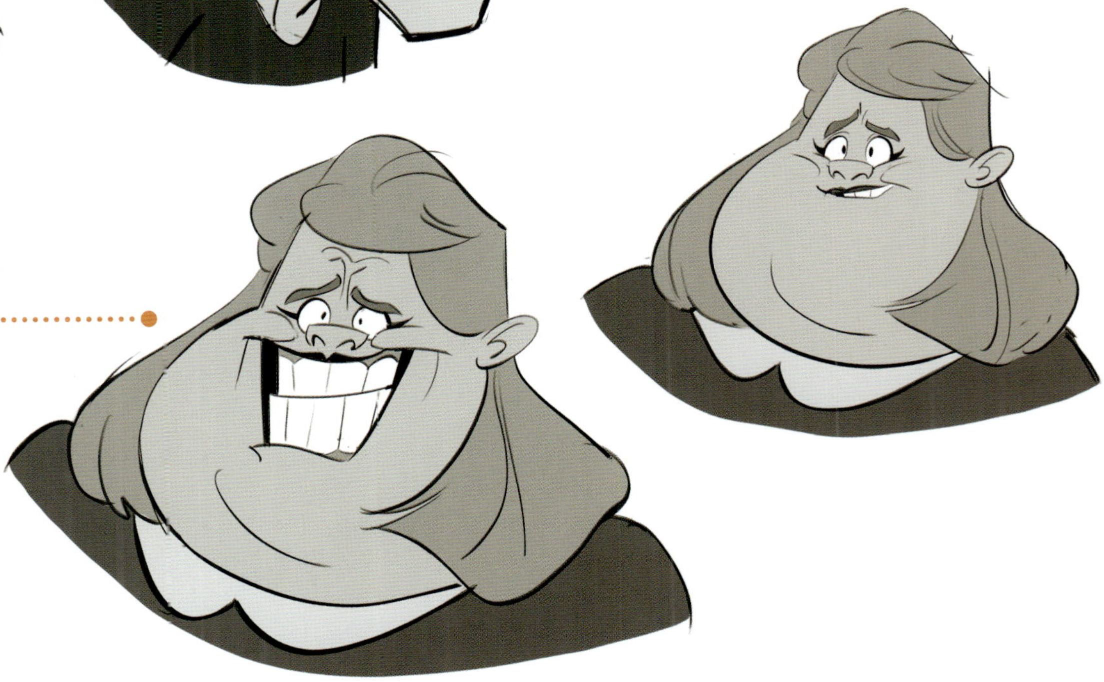

When a character is sad, all their muscles tend to relax, except for the corners of their mouth and the inner corners of the eyebrows. Notice how the left version is standing up straight, in comparison to the right, where he is slumped over. We can exaggerate this emotion by letting the character give in to gravity.

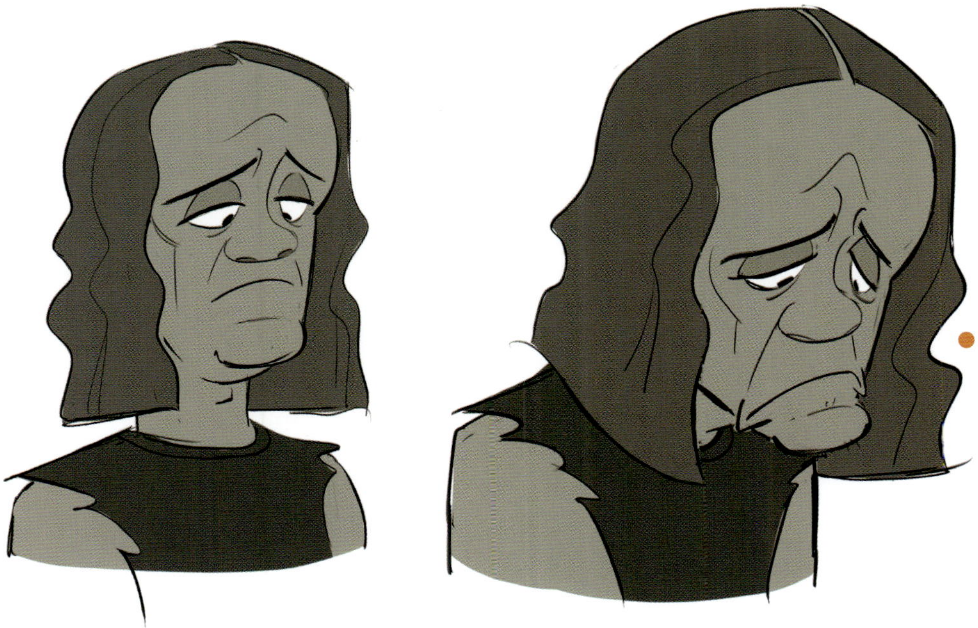

Shock and surprise are rather extreme emotions in themselves, and should always be exaggerated. If they are not, the character can come across as just mildly interested, like the version on the left. Exaggerate the emotion by widening the eyes and shrinking the pupils. The eyebrows push up and the mouth pulls down, elongating the face, which you can convey by stretching out the face shape.

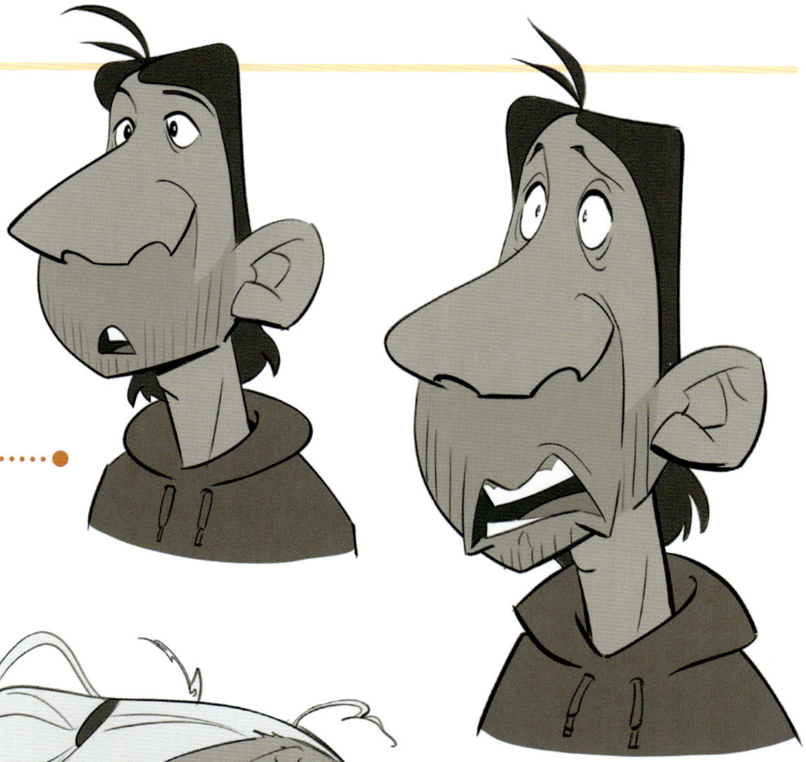

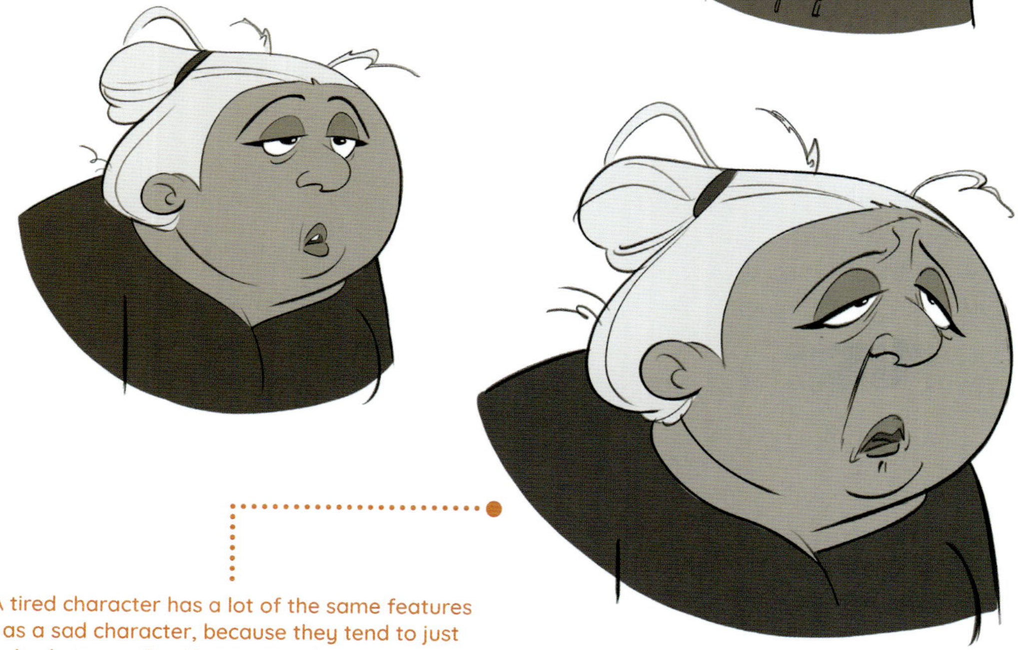

A tired character has a lot of the same features as a sad character, because they tend to just give in to gravity. However, in this expression, the primary focus is not on the eyebrows, but the heavy eyelids. When someone is tired, they struggle to keep their eyes open. We can exaggerate this feature by drooping the outer corners of the eyes down and making the eyelids a bigger shape than the eyeballs.

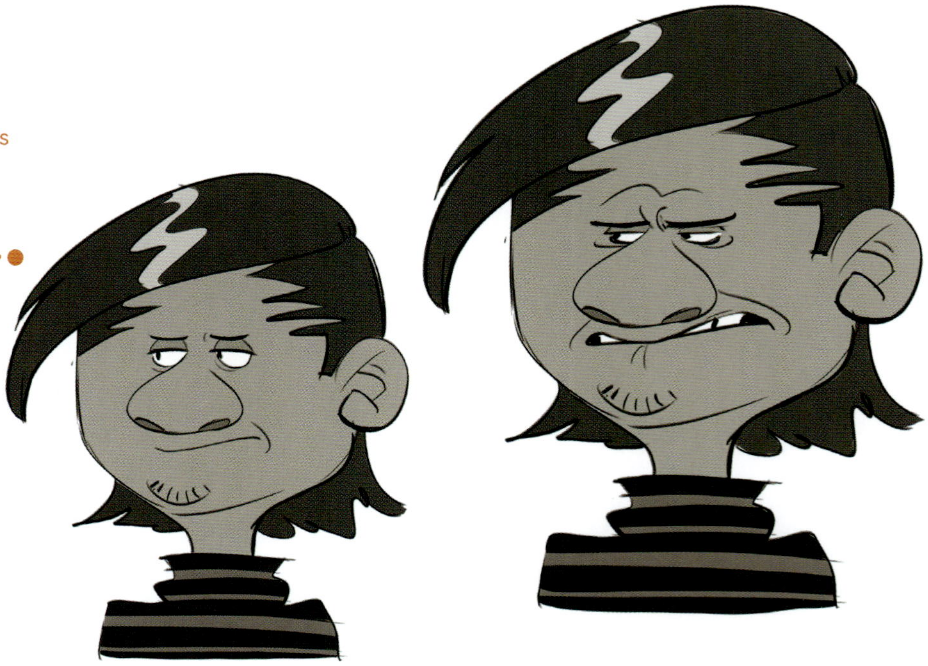

Here is an example of a character side-eyeing someone in annoyance. The left version looks mildly bothered, and could be interpreted in many different ways, while the right version looks completely fed up. When someone is staring in disgust, they usually tend to squint, so we can push that feature as far as possible to leave no room for misinterpretation. The upper lip also tends to pull up in this particular expression.

HAIRSTYLES

When designing an original character, you need to keep their personality in mind. Your character is the one who chooses their hairstyle, not you. Think about the kind of lifestyle your character lives. Are they messy? Neat? Active? All of these are important determining factors that should go into the design process. If your character is athletic and active, with long hair, then they will probably have their hair pulled up and out of their face. If your character is messy, consider a loose, unbrushed hairstyle. These are all traits that reflect your character's personality and story. Don't stop at your first sketch – explore many different options and silhouettes.

The first hairstyle looks neat, as the hair is straight and smooth. The second hairstyle comes across as fun, loose, and free. The third hairstyle would be practical for a hard worker, as the hair is pulled back and out of the way.

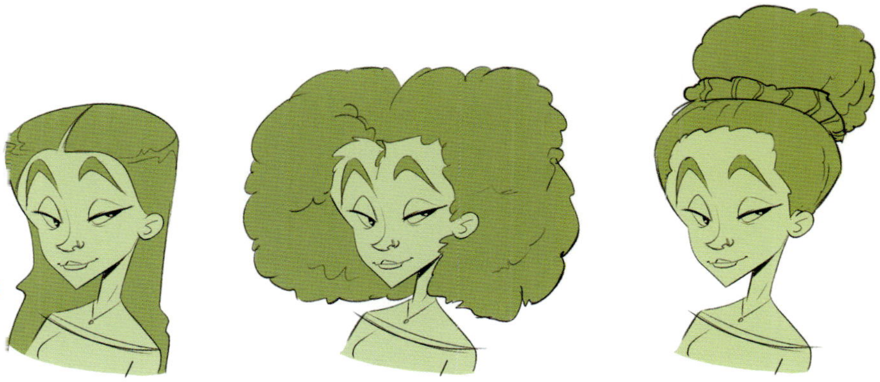

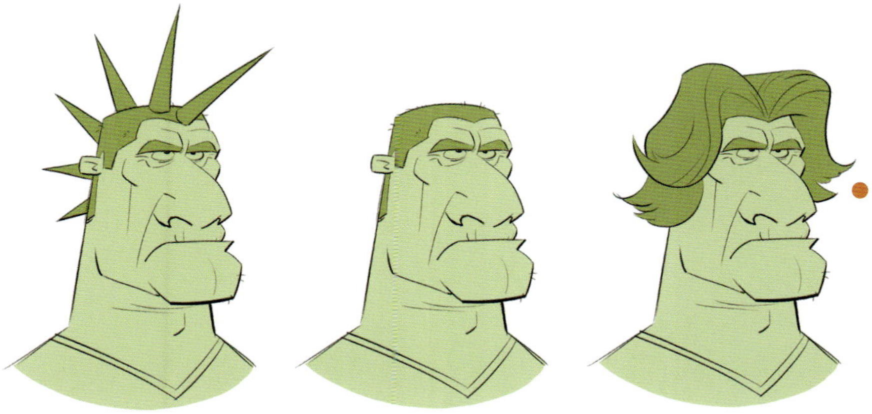

The first hairstyle obviously looks quite rebellious. The second hairstyle looks like a strict, no-nonsense type – maybe military. The third hairstyle option is more loose and flamboyant.

The first hairstyle makes the character look older and like someone who cares for their hairstyle. The second hairstyle is more strict and neat, due to the hard angles. The third option makes her look like she's busy, with her hair up and out of the way, and like she doesn't worry too much about it.

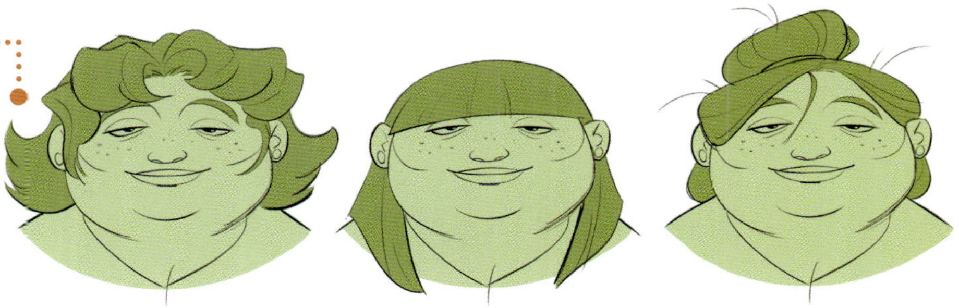

EXPRESSIONS LIBRARY

Kenneth Anderson

Human beings are adept at recognizing and decoding facial expressions, which can make your job as a designer difficult – it can be tricky to get expressions just right! Remember the basic anatomy at play in the face – the jaw bone is the only articulated joint that hinges up and down, with a bit of lateral movement. The rest of the facial expressions come mainly from the muscles surrounding the eyes and mouth. Studying facial anatomy and designing from reference will really help.

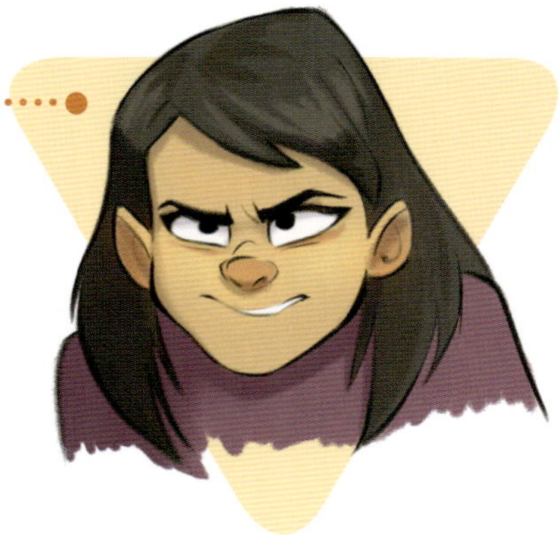

ANGRY, ABOUT TO ARGUE
Creased eyebrows and an almost-snarl, combined with hunched shoulders, suggest a character about to expel some pent-up angry energy.

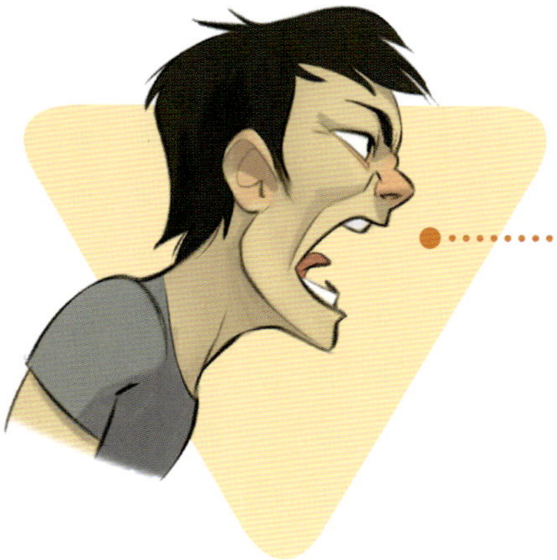

ENRAGED, SHOUTING
A wide-open mouth paired with a creased brow and narrowed eyes can only mean one thing: shouting!

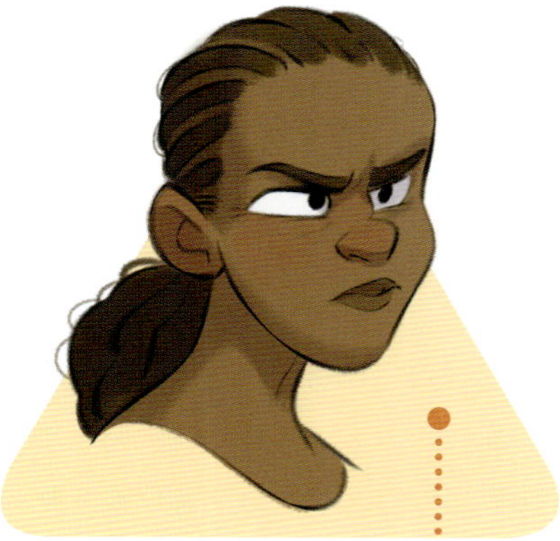

MILDLY ANGRY, FROWNING
The start of a frown combined with a downturned mouth is likely the sign of mild anger brewing.

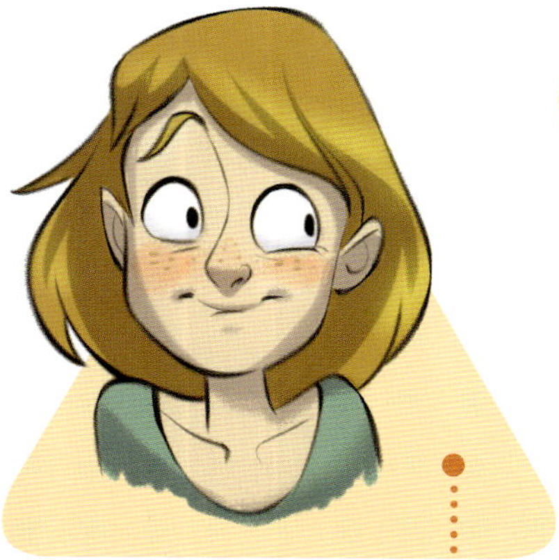

MILDLY EMBARRASSED
Wide eyes, pursed lips, and raised eyebrows are one way to suggest mild embarrassment.

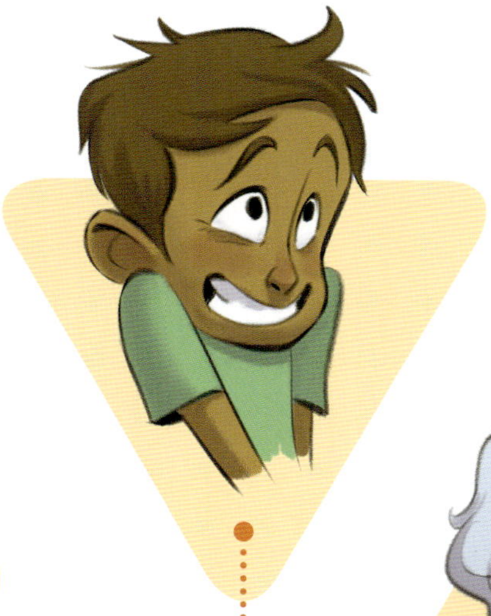

EXTREMELY EMBARRASSED
This smile, combined with the character's apologetic eyes and downward tilt of the head, convey extreme embarrassment.

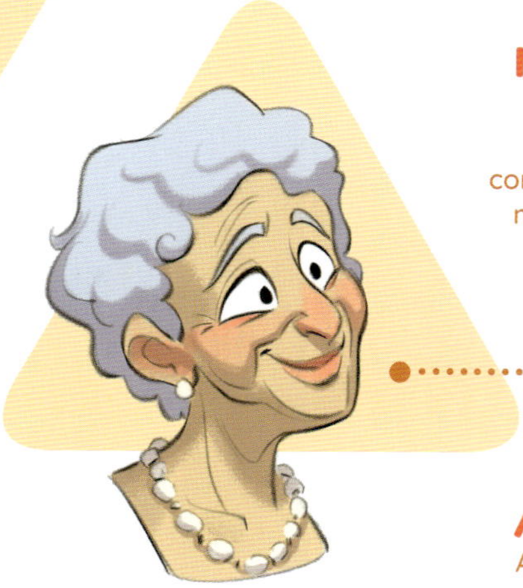

GENTLE, AFFECTIONATE
A subtle smile that pushes up the bottoms of the eyes makes this expression feel genuine and warm, while the open eyebrows enhance the affectionate vibe.

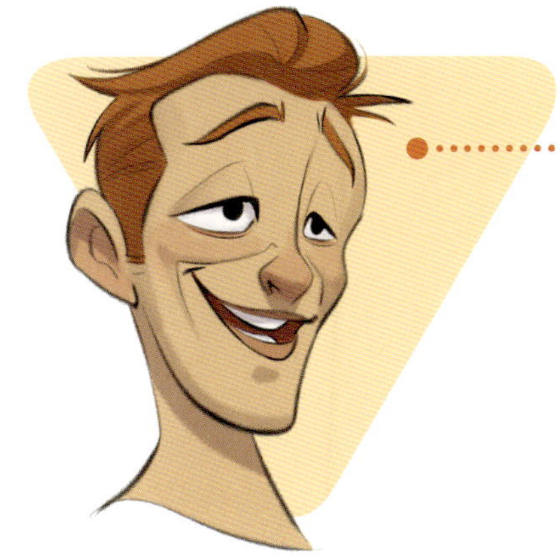

LOVESTRUCK

"Lovestruck" is a tricky expression to design without making a character look a bit dopey! The asymmetrical, unfocused gaze, raised brows, and wide smile make him look affectionate and slightly dazed.

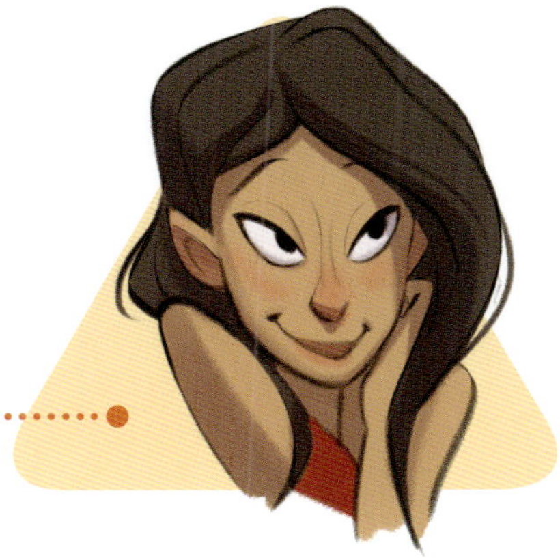

SHY, COY

Head tilted down with eyes looking up suggests a shy character subconsciously trying to hide from the person in front of them.

DEVIOUS SMILE

This version of a devious smile isn't a million miles away from a sneer. Eyebrows might be creased, revealing true intent.

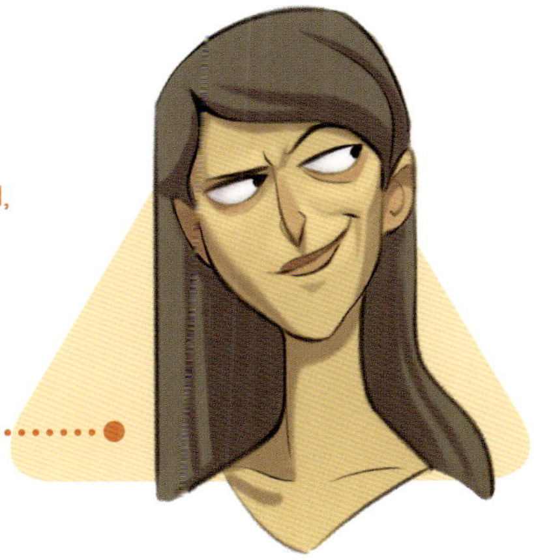

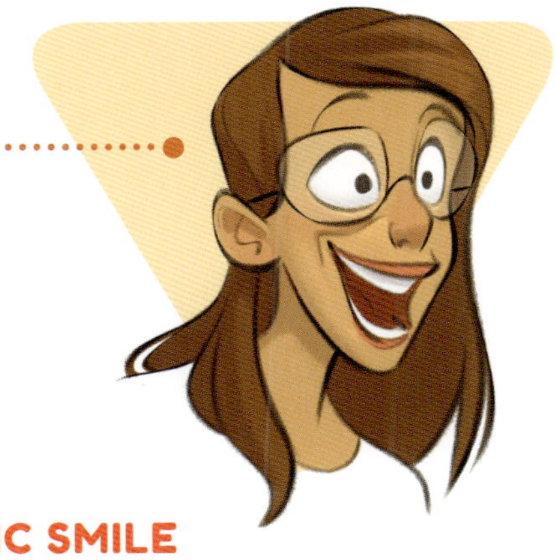

ENTHUSIASTIC SMILE

An enthusiastic smile is big and full of energy, with the high eyebrows and wide-open mouth reflecting that.

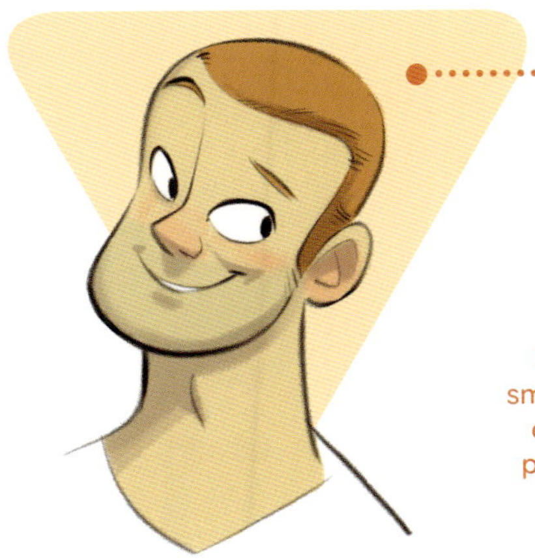

RELAXED SMILE

Most of the work in a relaxed smile will be in the mouth, but the eyes and eyebrows come into play too, no matter how subtly.

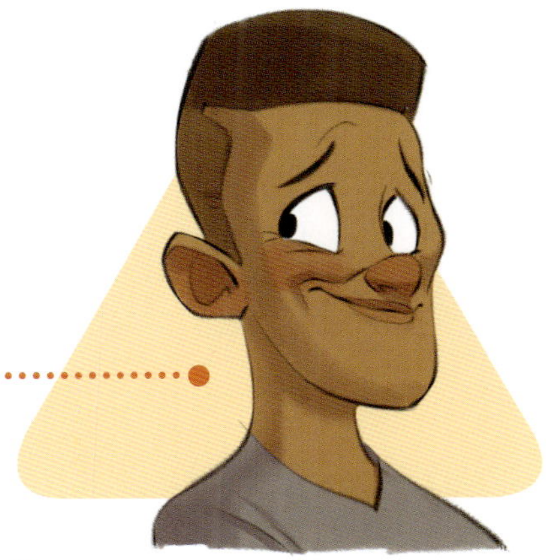

RELUCTANT SMILE

The mouth might be making an almost smile shape, but the reluctance comes through in the eyebrows and eyes.

Randy Bishop

Expression sheets – sheets showing different facial expressions for a character – serve two primary purposes. The first is to explore how far you can stretch or squash a character's facial features before the design breaks. If you stretch a design beyond its inherent limits, it will look wrong to your audience – the closer a style is to representing reality, the less room there is to exaggerate expressions. The second purpose is to show the production team exactly how your character emotes, so they can move forward without needing to guess how your character's face moves.

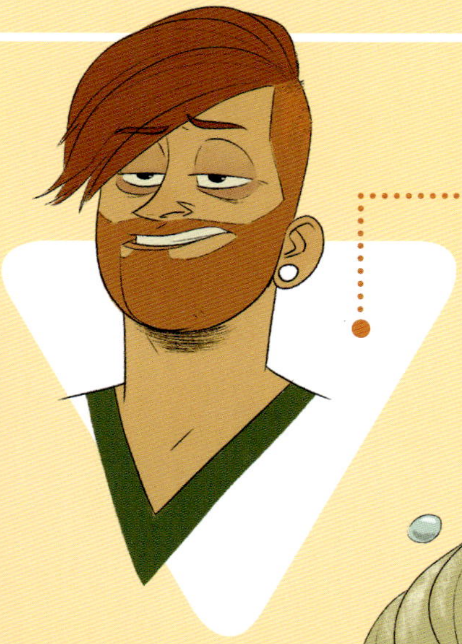

SKEPTICAL

Skepticism is a strange cross between boredom and surprise. It's impressive that people can capture the juxtaposition inherent in sarcasm on their faces, and even more impressive if you can recreate it on a character.

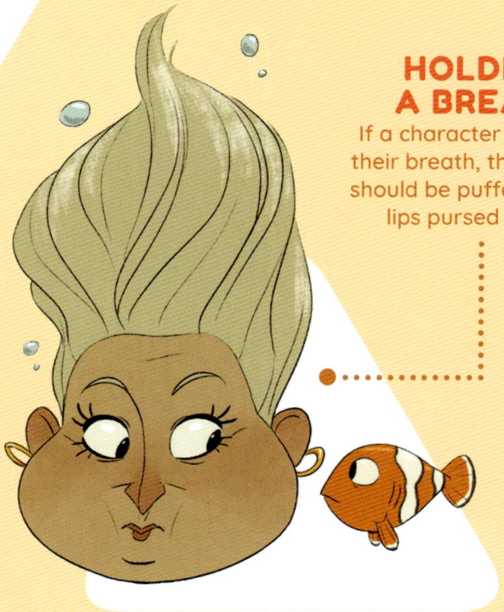

HOLDING A BREATH

If a character is holding their breath, their cheeks should be puffed out and lips pursed tightly.

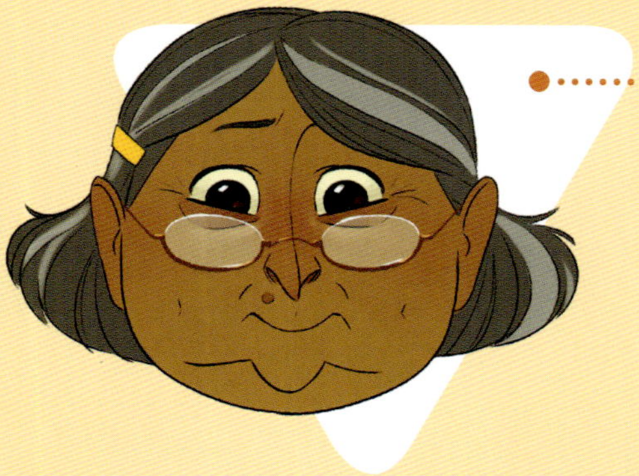

TRYING NOT TO LAUGH

People tend to bite the inside of their lips together when they are trying not to laugh. This results in a small smile that is a little lower than normal.

GUILTY

Guilt can express itself as a combination of sadness and disgust. The character's eyes are sad, but their mouth betrays disgust at their actions.

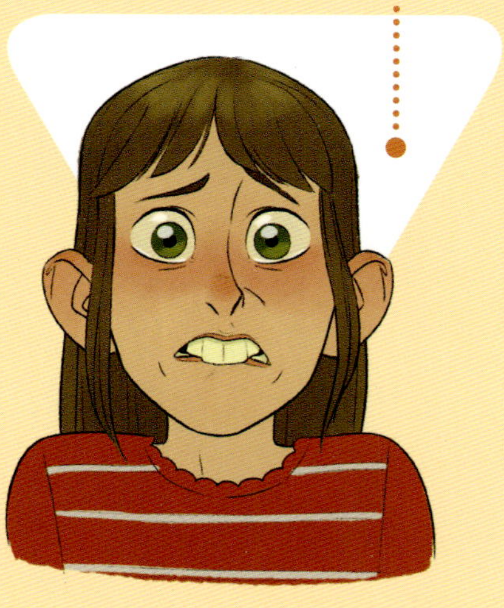

STICKING TONGUE OUT

The character's whole head is thrust forward to emphasize the tongue. His nose wrinkles up and brows draw down to exaggerate his disdain.

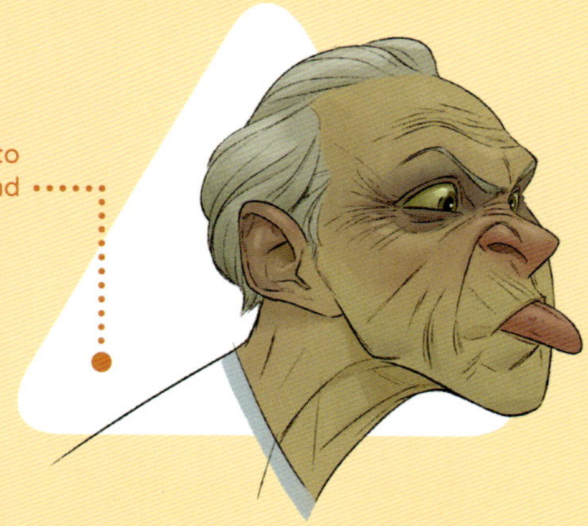

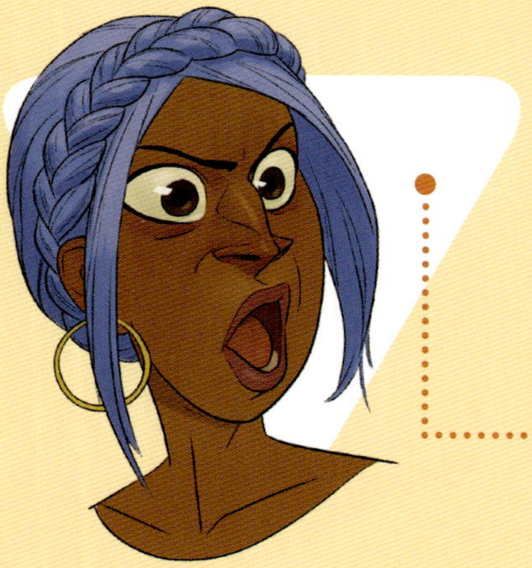

OUTRAGED GASP

For an outraged gasp or exclamation, most of the face will pull upward toward the spot between the eyes, while the corners of the mouth will pull downward.

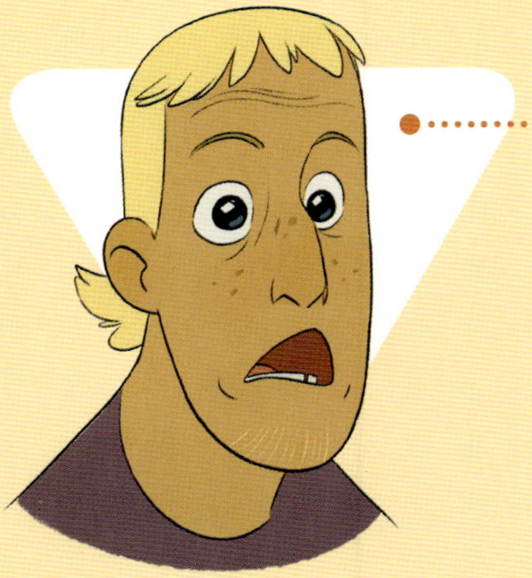

AMAZED, OPEN-MOUTHED

Think of amazement as the face being stretched up and down simultaneously. The eyebrows come up, the eyes open wide, and the mouth drops down.

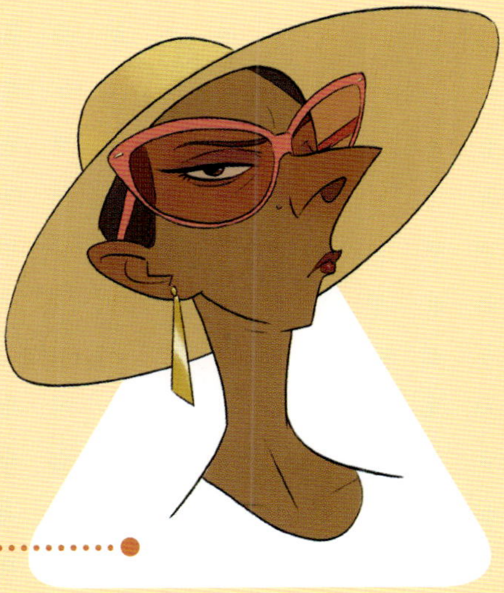

ALOOF

Making a character feel aloof can be achieved in a number of ways. In this case, the character's head is tilted slightly back to make it seem like she's looking down at everyone.

CHEWING, EATING

People often chew their food on one side of their mouth, meaning one cheek will be bulging and the other won't.

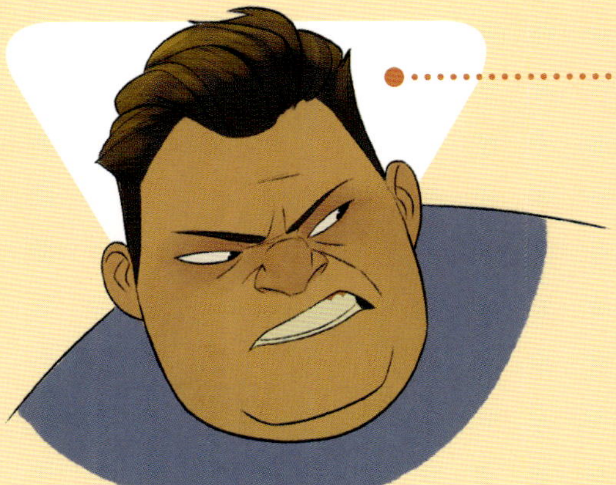

SCORNFUL

Scorn is a dismissive twist on anger. Lifting one side of the upper lip and making the character look at the object of scorn out of the corner of their eye works well.

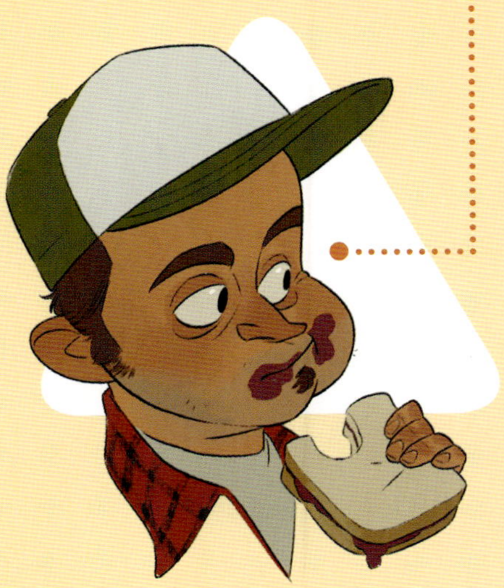

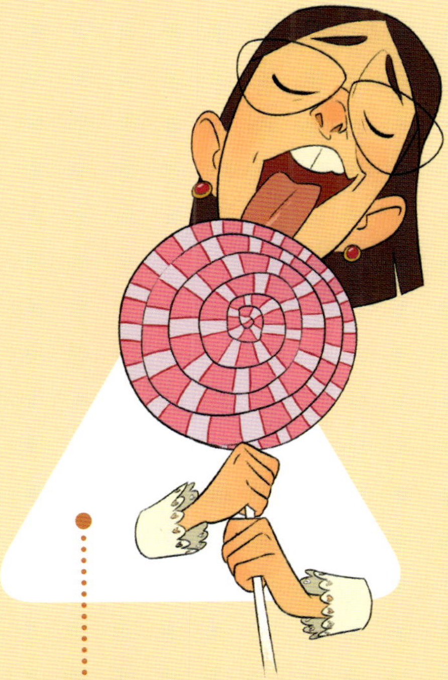

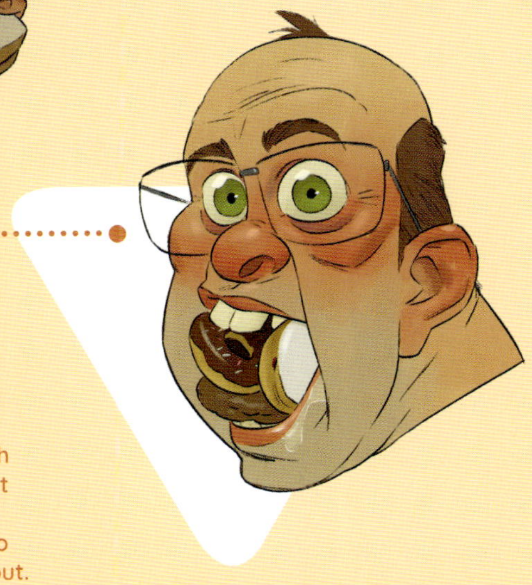

MOUTH FULL OF FOOD

If someone has so much food in their mouth that they can't completely shut it, it's impossible to stop drool from spilling out.

LICKING A LOLLIPOP

When a character licks something, it reads better to have their whole head moving, dragging the tongue along behind it.

Luis Gadea

Consider the story behind the character. Who are they? How do they react to certain situations? What is their role within the story? Ask these questions and write down the answers to build a character profile. Then grab a mirror, put yourself in the character's role, and have fun acting out the faces you need to create.

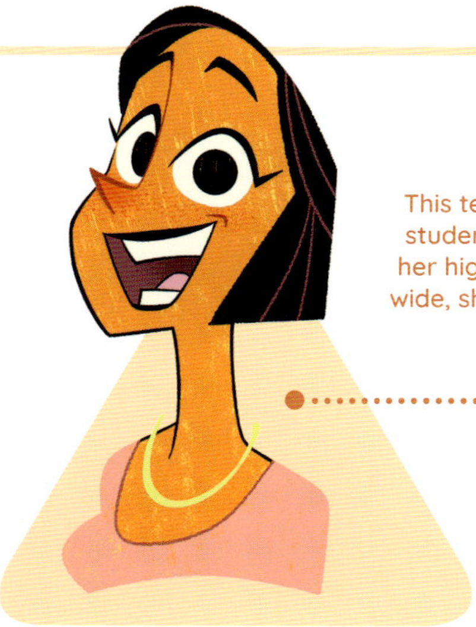

OPTIMISTIC

This teacher is optimistic about her students' progress. Free of doubts, her high eyebrows, large pupils, and wide, shiny smile show her happiness.

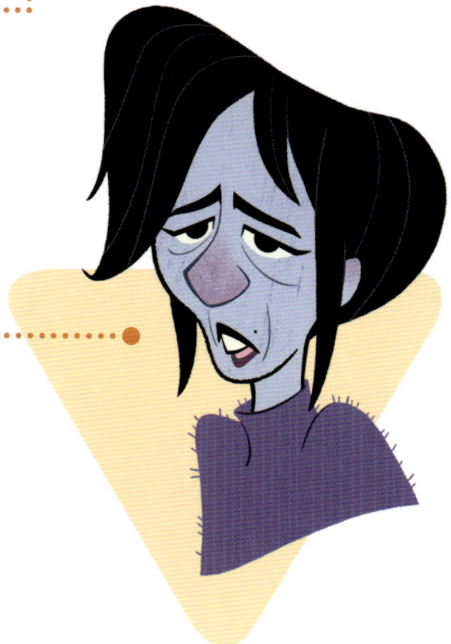

PESSIMISTIC

This character's eyebrows and eyes are tilted downward, pulled down by her pessimistic attitude. Her shoulders shrug upward to create the impression that she no longer cares.

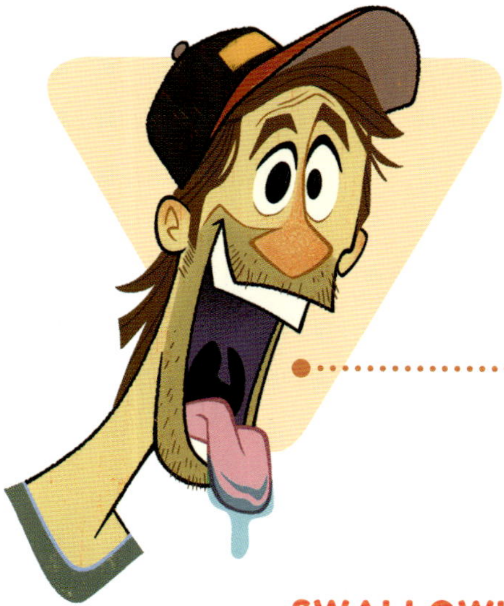

HUNGRY

You can exaggerate a salivating expression to make it more cartoon-like. This character's asymmetrical pupils, wide-open mouth, and hanging tongue illustrate the intensity of his desire for food.

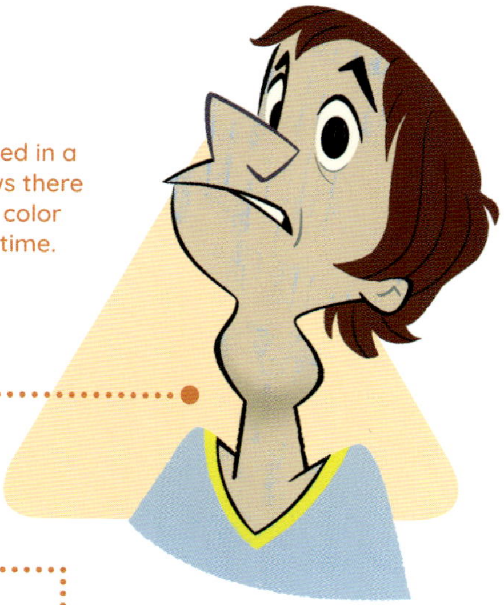

SWALLOWING

This character's nervous gulp is emphasized in a cartoon-like way. His elongated neck shows there is something stuck in his throat, the cool color scheme suggesting he's having a tough time.

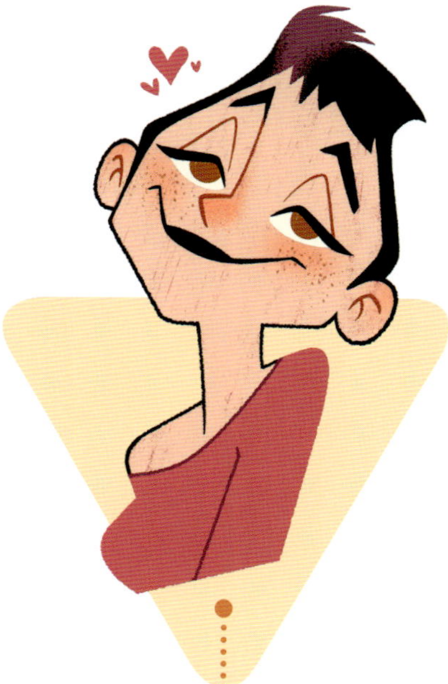

SIGHING

This character raises a shoulder while tilting her head to the side as she sighs. Her smile is big, her eyes melting with love.

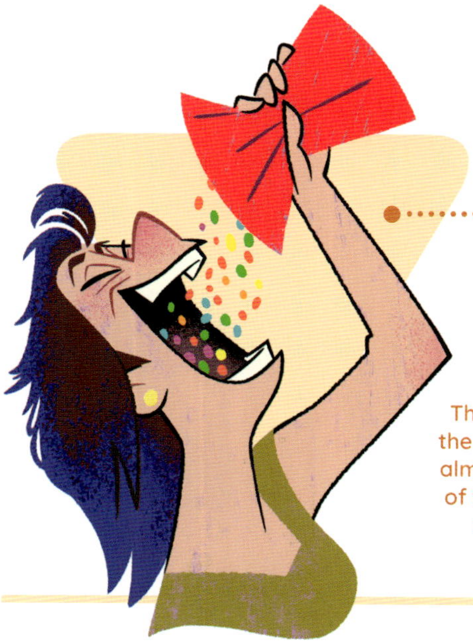

GULPING FOOD

The entire body tilts back to allow the mouth to open as wide as it can, almost shrinking the upper features of the character's face. Remember to exaggerate when you can.

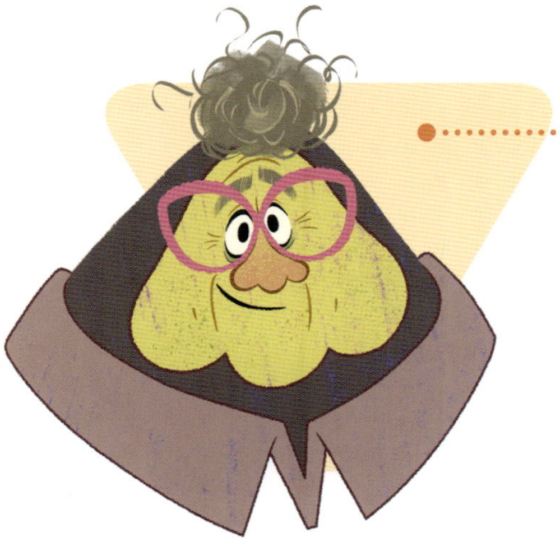

KIND

This old lady's design and expression are full of curves, conveying her kind, gentle nature.

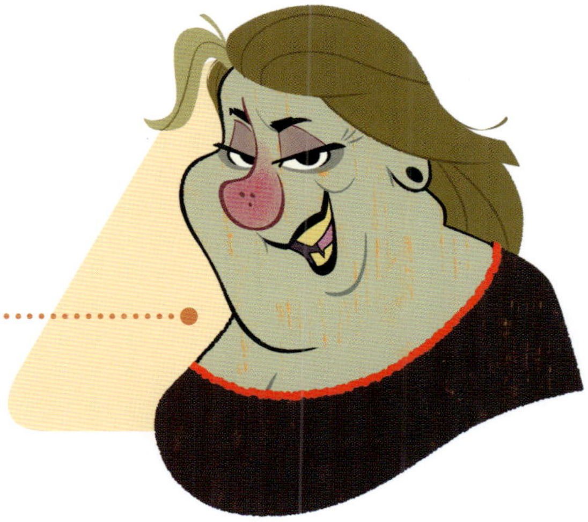

MEAN-SPIRITED

This character enjoys being mean, her smirk communicating that she knows she's being deliberately unkind. Her eyes are almost hidden by her eyelids to create a "V" shape.

UPTIGHT

This character's eyebrows form a straight line to exaggerate his tense stare. The lines on his forehead and face hint at his unease.

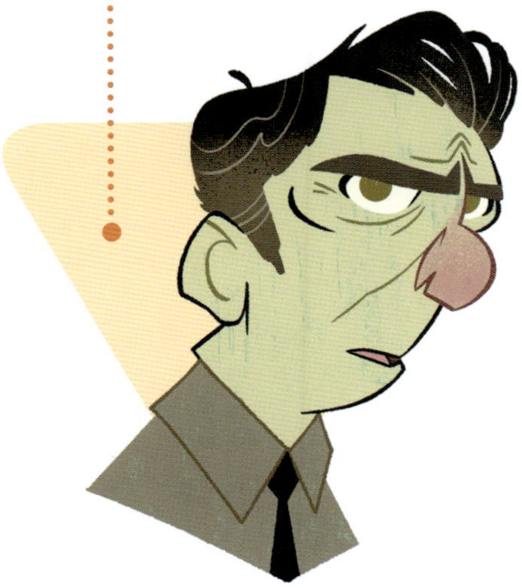

IRRITATED

This character's crooked mouth, bared teeth, and eyes disappearing into his eyebrows show his intense irritation.

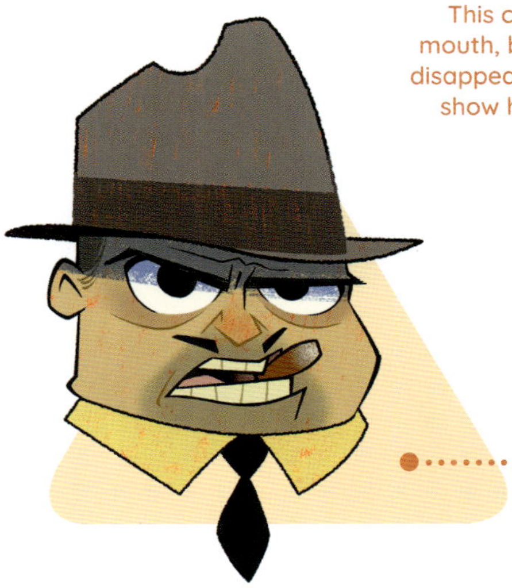

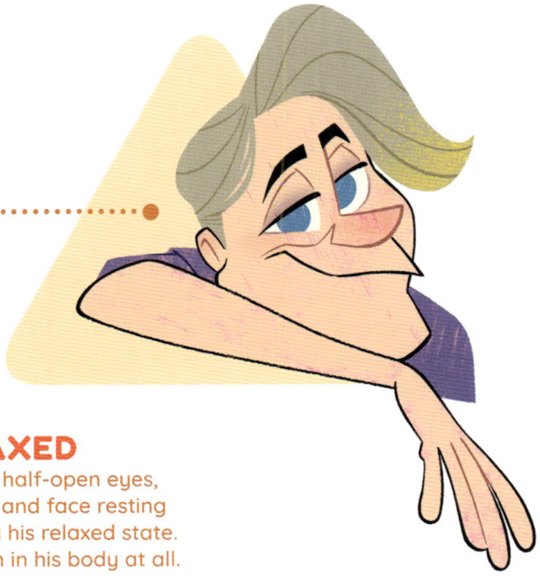

RELAXED

This character's half-open eyes, calm expression, and face resting on his arm convey his relaxed state. There is no tension in his body at all.

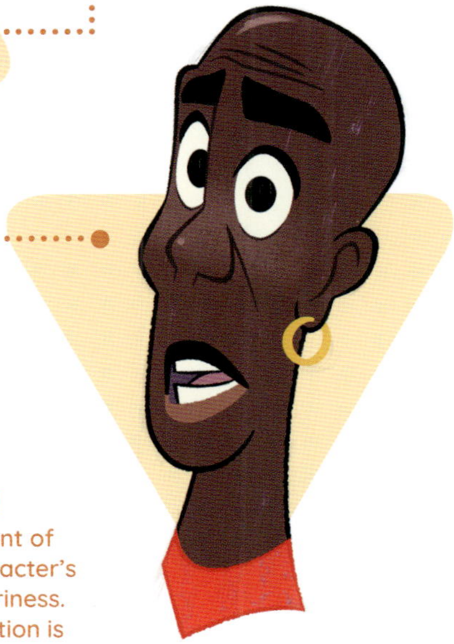

SKITTISH

The increased amount of white around this character's pupils hints at his wariness. The overall line of action is tilted backward to illustrate his insecurity and edginess.

Meybis Ruiz Cruz

Take some time to learn about the different facial muscles and how they push the cheeks, eyebrows, mouth, and nose to show different emotions. Observe real people and study actors, both expressive and nuanced, and notice the small details in their performance, like a subtle twitch of the lip or a tic in the eyebrow. Remember that faces, like bodies, have a line of action that can be stretched and compressed depending on the expression.

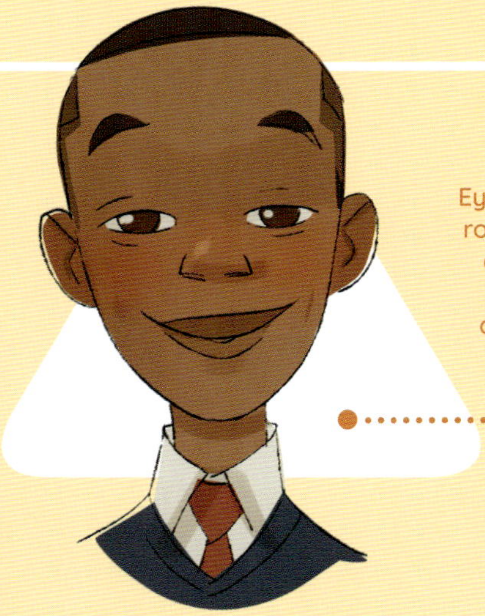

ROMANTIC

Eyelids down and eyebrows up can convey a romantic or sleepy mood, so adding a smile and slight blush help make this romantic expression clearer. A more cartoon-like approach would be to draw "heart eyes."

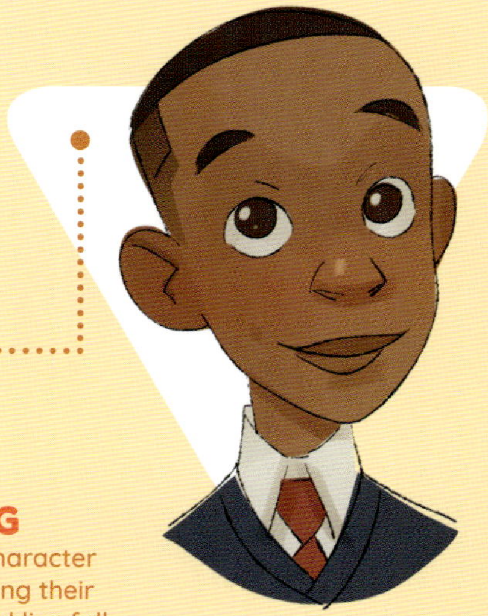

HOPEFUL

Some emotions are more subtle and depend on context. Is this character hopeful about his crush liking him back, or about the teacher canceling that last-minute pop quiz?

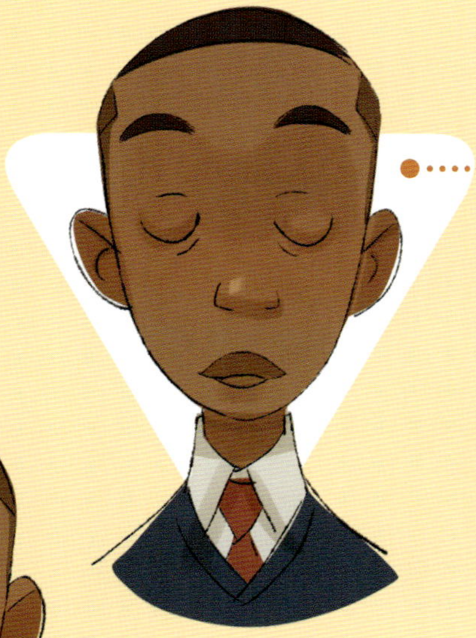

MEDITATING

When meditating, your character should be relaxed, including their facial muscles. The jaw and lips fall slightly, and the eyes are closed. The eyebrows are lifted to show intention, so he doesn't look asleep.

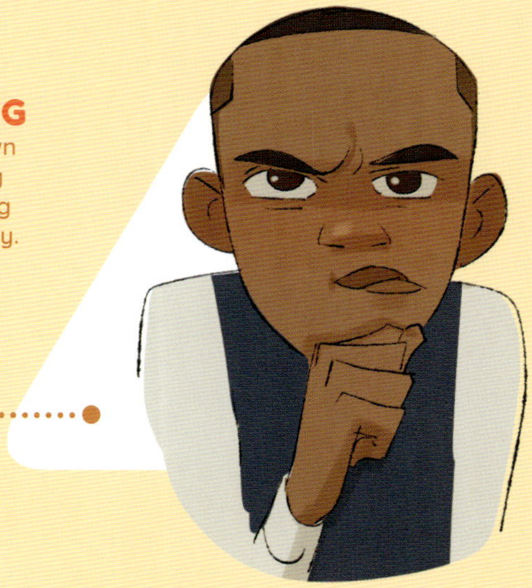

CONCENTRATING

Some people tend to frown when focusing – knotting their brows and tightening their lips to the side slightly.

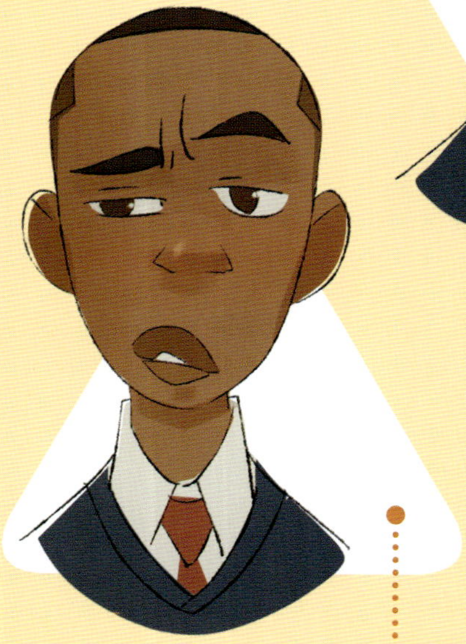

MUDDLED

When perplexed or confused, a character will raise an eyebrow and drop their jaw, causing the mouth to open slightly. The face will appear a little stretched as a result.

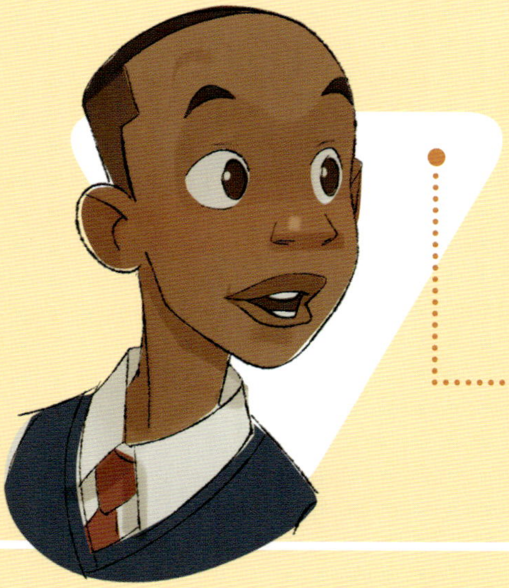

DISTRACTED

A butterfly flying by in class is a beautiful distraction; the same butterfly resting on your nose when you are meditating is an annoyance. In this case, the character's wide eyes and open, slightly smiling mouth suggest a pleasant distraction.

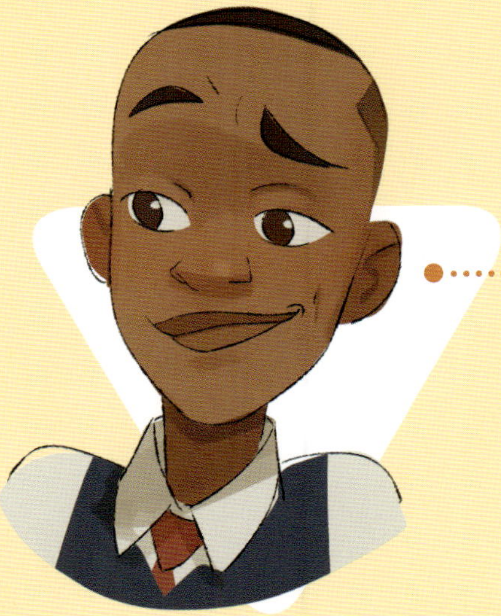

PROUD

Being proud of a petty achievement might come across as cocky, while a parent's pride could be more emotional. This character's asymmetrical smile and raised eyebrow convey the former!

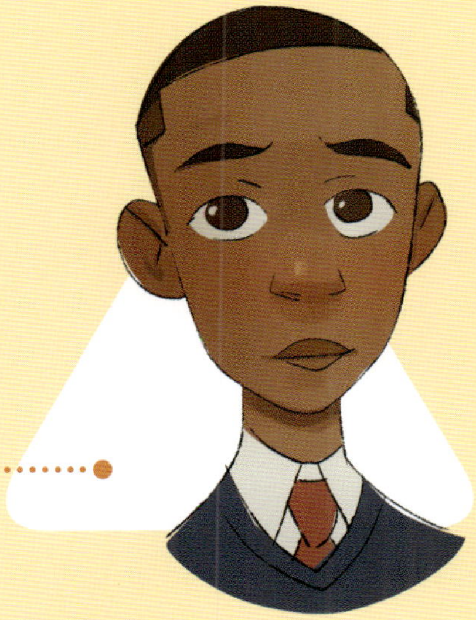

MODEST

This expression is almost neutral, suggesting the character is quite reserved. However, his subtly worried brows and pursed lips add an element of shyness.

CAUTIOUS

A character could be cautious about an unknown and likely dangerous object, or about someone's intentions, or maybe about how they will explain a broken window to their parents.

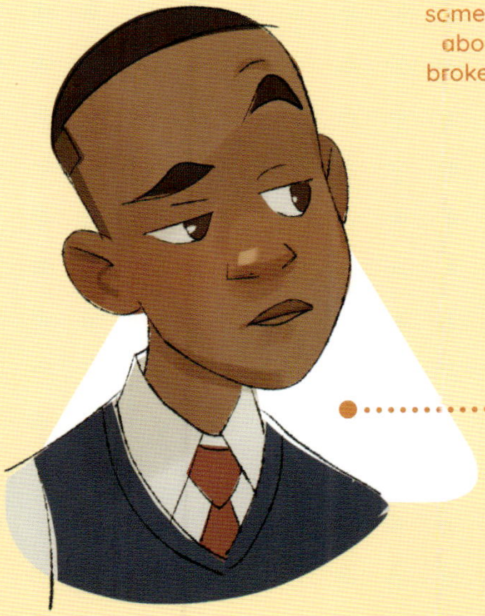

INTIMIDATING

A forward lean with the eyebrows down, mouth tight, nostrils flared, and wrinkles indicating tension in the facial muscles conveys an angry and intimidating character.

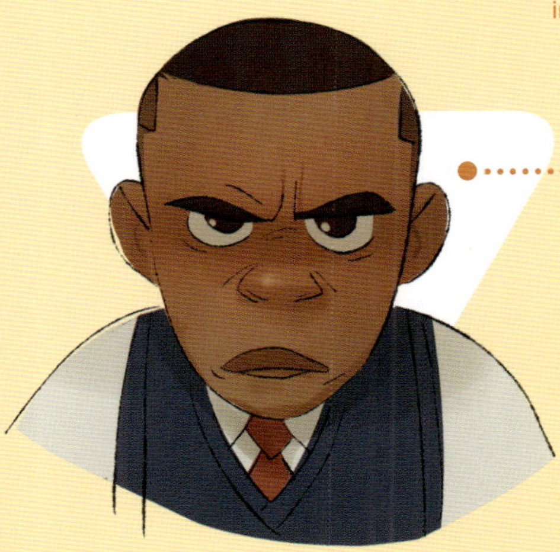

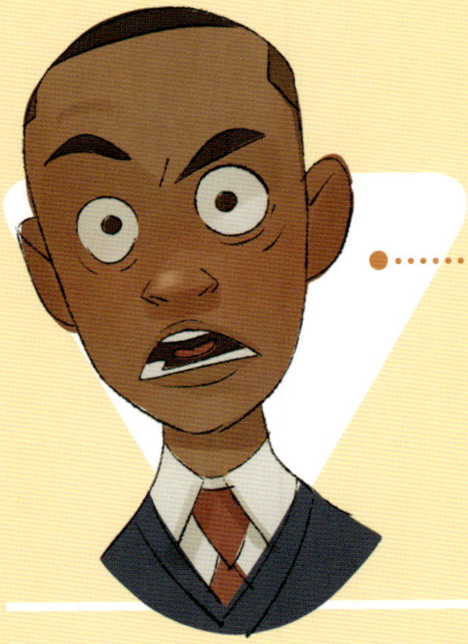

WILD-EYED

Pupil size can help depict different emotions. Big pupils can make a character look cute and innocent, while contracted pupils represent an unbalanced and irrational state.

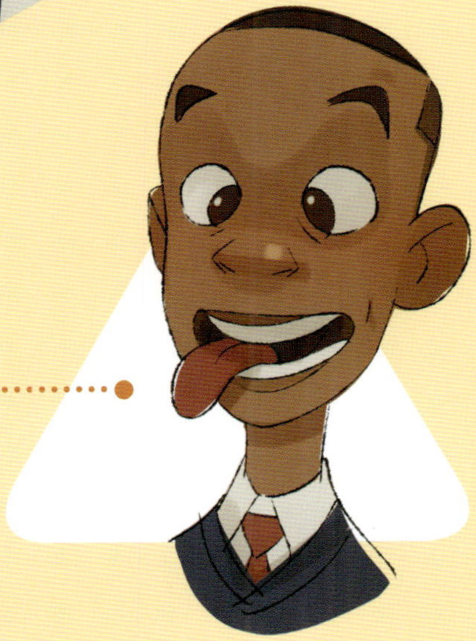

SILLY

Crossed eyes, a big grin, and a poked-out tongue create an unmistakably playful expression. Grab a mirror and start making silly faces like no one is watching, then pick one and draw it.

Noor Sofi

When designing expressions, make them specific to your character. Everyone performs expressions in their own unique way, so before creating a successful expression sheet you must first understand who your character is. Are they an arrogant knight? A sleazy thief? There are general rules that can guide you in drawing accurate expressions. Any time your character questions something, raise one of their eyebrows. If they are scared, make them seize up, frozen in fear. When they are happy, draw them with soft eyes and a relaxed smile. Understanding a little acting and human psychology can help when designing expressions.

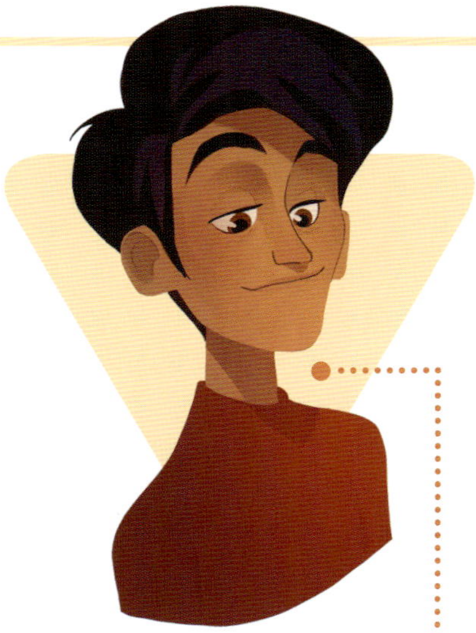

IMPRESSED

To be impressed is a combination of confidence, cockiness, incredulity, and admiration. Show this by tilting the character's head upward, with raised eyebrows and an amused smile.

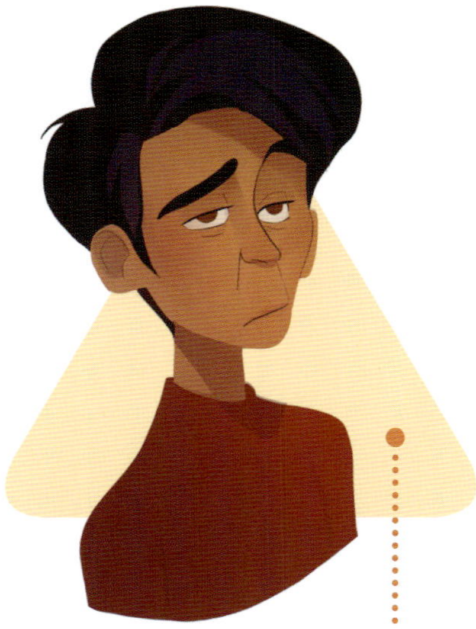

UNIMPRESSED

To be unimpressed implies a character feels they are in a place to pass judgment. Show this by pairing one raised eyebrow with a deep-set frown as they look upon who or what they are unimpressed by.

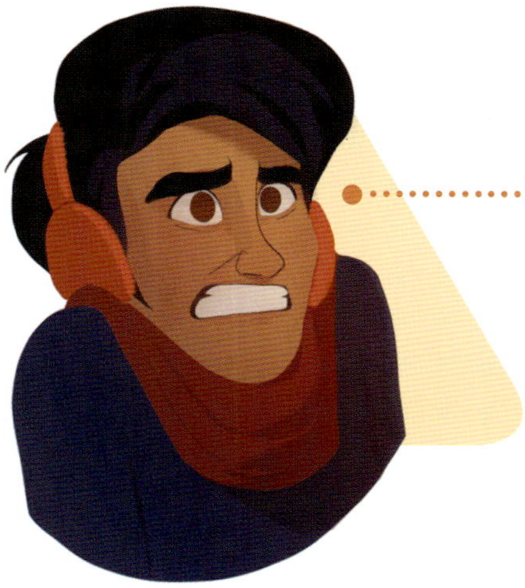

COLD

Like water, people start to seize up when cold. The character's whole body and face should tense up. The shoulders draw closer to the body in search of warmth, while the teeth are bared as they chatter.

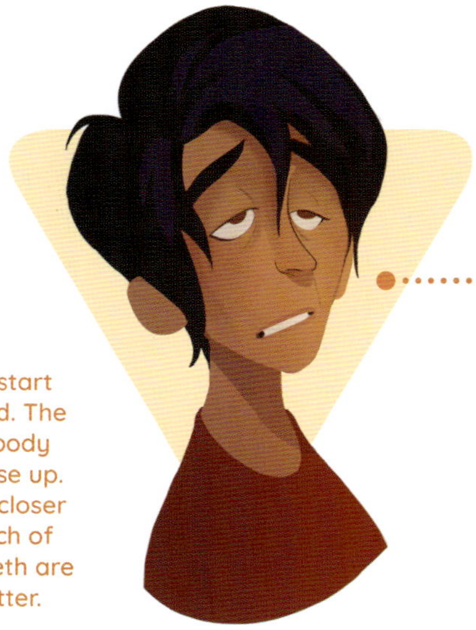

HOT

Like wax melting off a candle, everything in a character's expression should convey that hot, melting feeling – think sagging eyes, drooping shoulders, and hair sticking to their forehead.

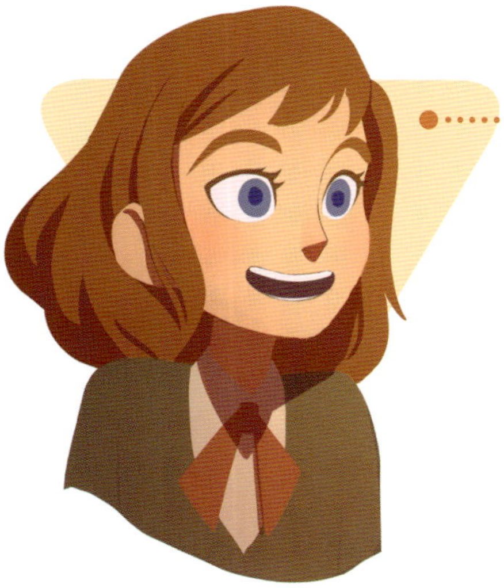

ELATED

When you are happy, it feels like everything in your body lifts up, including your facial features. A happy expression will include a big smile, with bright eyes and raised eyebrows.

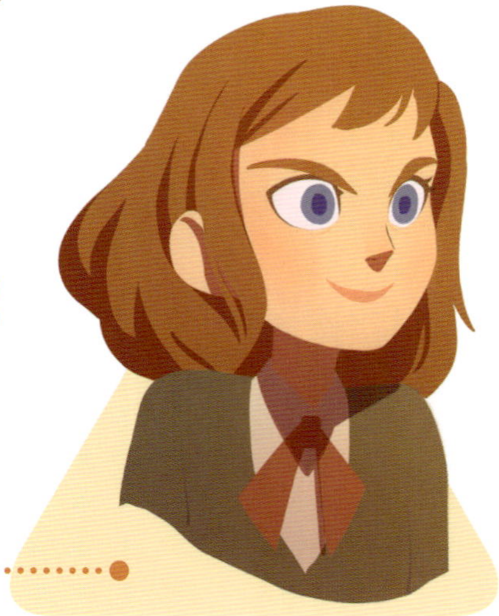

CONFIDENT

Confidence comes from a sense of self-assurance and determination. This character locks their eyes on their target, with eyebrows furrowed in resoluteness, while sporting a smile.

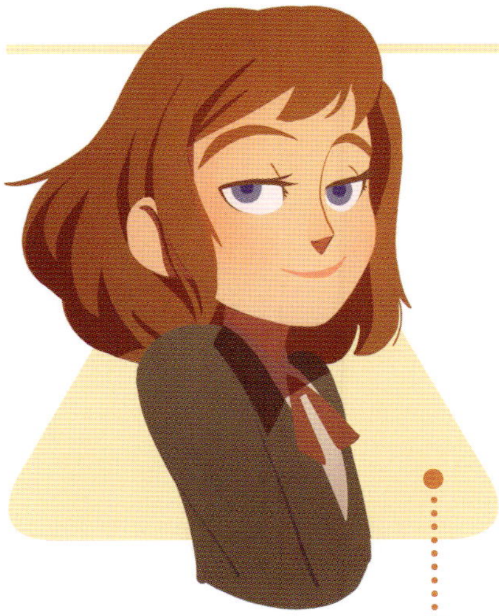

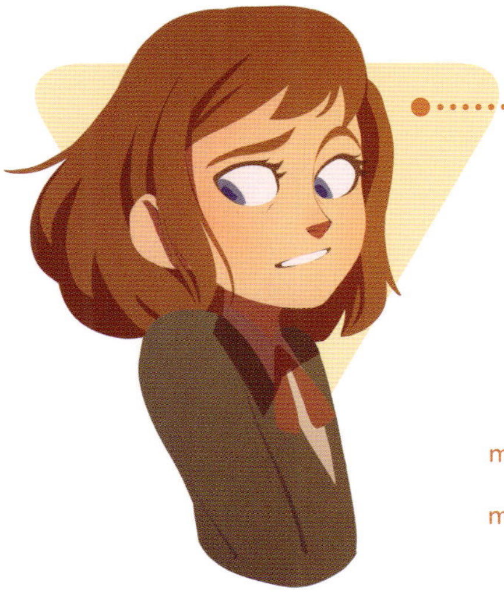

AWKWARD

When a person feels awkward, they will often look anywhere but at the thing that is causing them discomfort. Give the character a sideways glance, clench their teeth, and raise an inquisitive eyebrow as they try to figure out why they feel so awkward.

GOOFY

To draw a goofy expression, make some of the facial features a little wonky. This character's mouth is slightly skewed, with her eyebrows a little off-kilter too.

SASSY

Sass is another form of confidence, but with a touch of humor and arrogance, and sometimes a little flirtation. Raise the character's eyebrows to give them half-lidded eyes, and add a smile.

MISCHIEVOUS

To capture a mischievous expression, draw the character slyly looking off to the side, as if they are checking to see if someone is watching, and sneakily smiling to themselves. Lift one of their eyebrows, as if they are questioning how things might turn out.

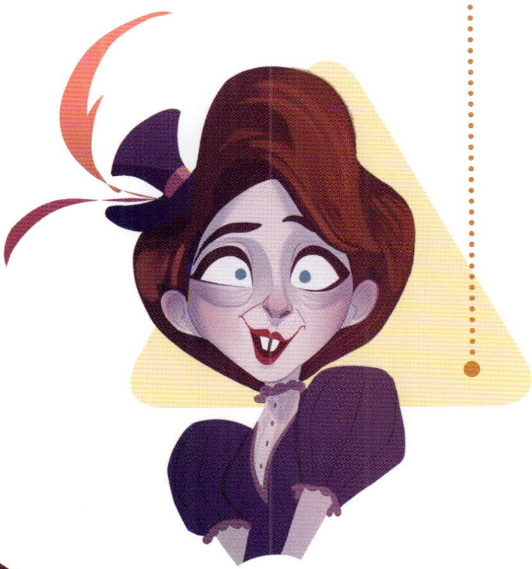

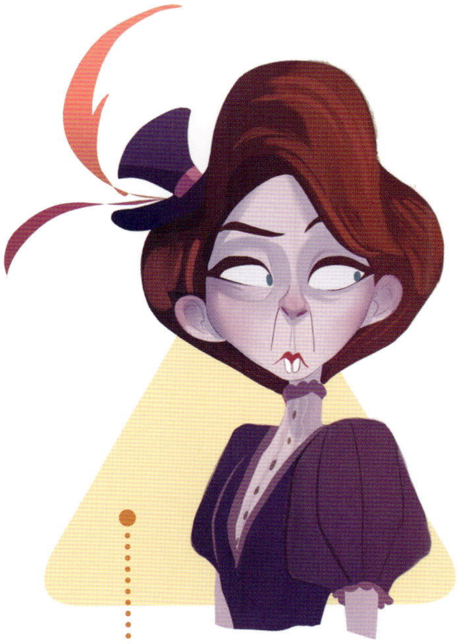

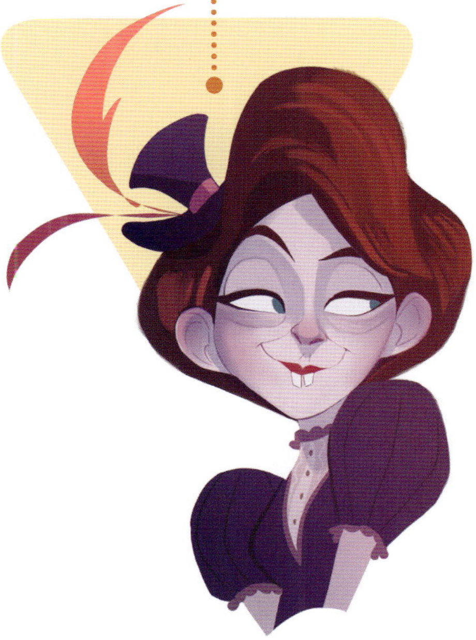

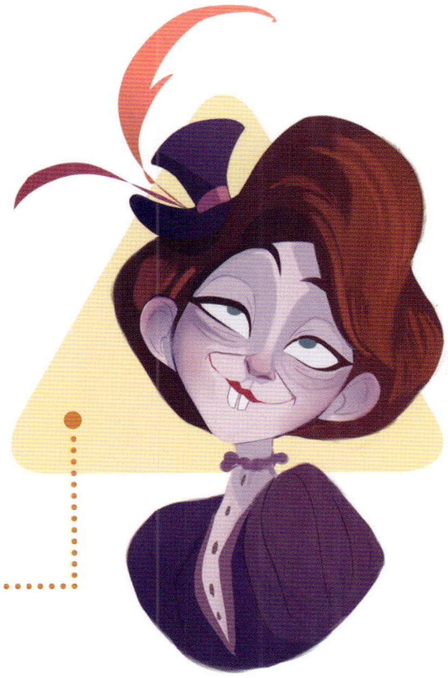

SUSPICIOUS

When suspicious, you are on alert. Like a guard dog, this character stands tall and perfectly still, quietly listening to see if their suspicions are true. They glance to the side with an inquisitive brow.

DAYDREAMING

Capture a daydreaming expression by drawing the character looking up, as if staring off into the clouds. Droop their shoulders to make it seem as if they are sighing as they leave reality and give into the dream.

Sweeney Boo

Creativity and consistency are important when designing a character's expressions. Don't be scared to exaggerate some of their features to drive home their emotions and actions more intensely. The eyes should be the center of each emotion you draw; focus on making them the most important part of the design.

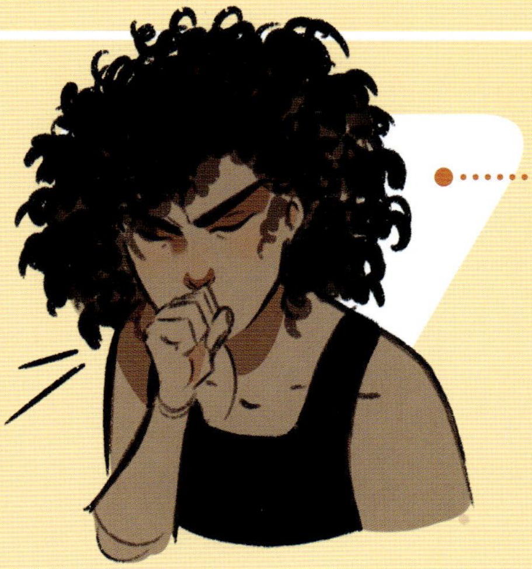

COUGHING
When coughing, a character will most likely lean forward a little. Their mouth may be hidden behind a clenched fist or open hand used to catch the cough.

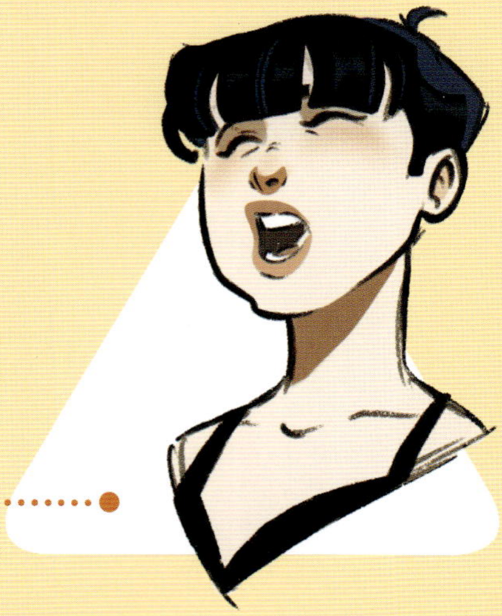

PRE-SNEEZE
To capture a character just before they sneeze, draw them looking up with their head titled slightly back.

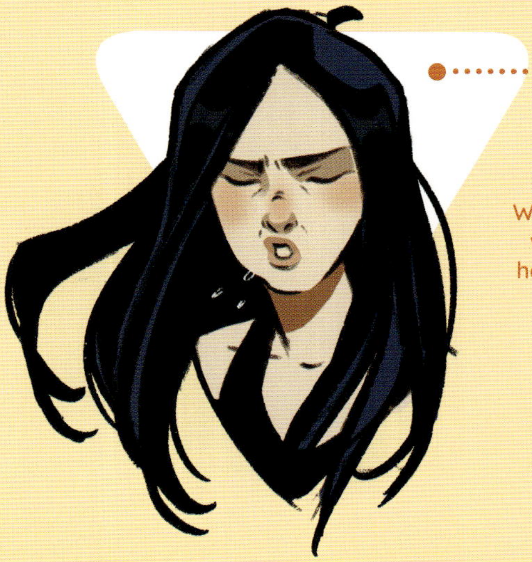

SNEEZING
When sneezing, a character will suddenly thrust their head forward, eyes closed.

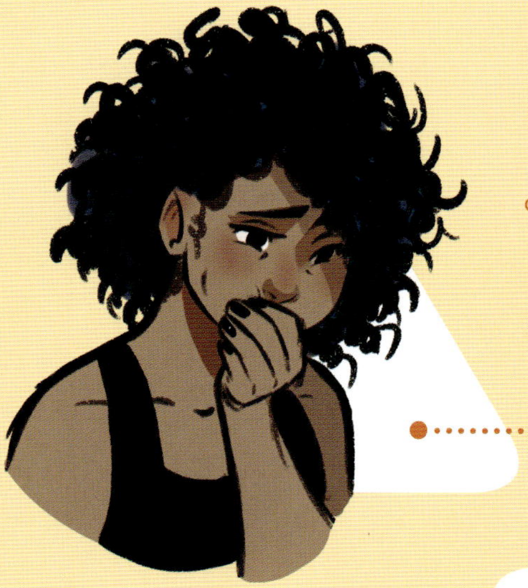

RETCHING
Show your character is about to vomit by placing a hand over their mouth, puffing out their cheeks, and raising the eyebrows to show their concern. This character is unwell, her shoulders down and head tilted to the side in exhaustion.

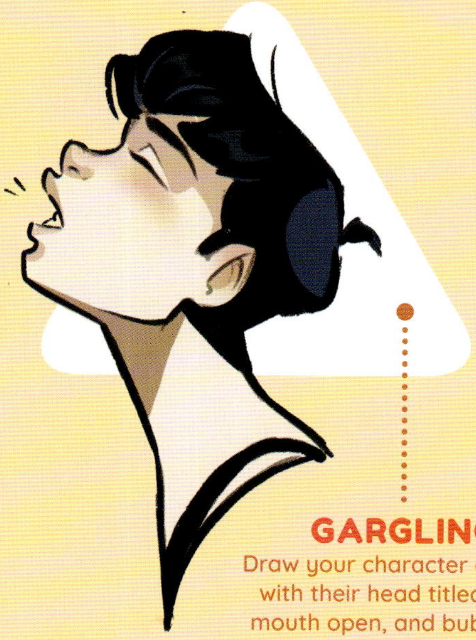

GARGLING
Draw your character gargling with their head titled back, mouth open, and bubbles or liquid in their mouth.

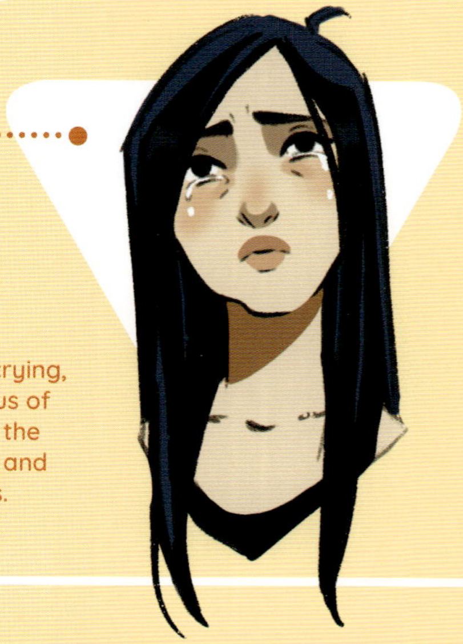

WEEPY
When capturing a character crying, their eyes should be the focus of the expression. In this case, the character's eyes are tearful and puffy with worried brows.

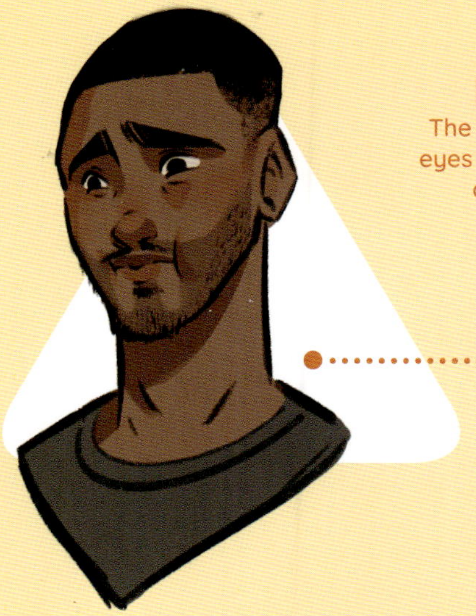

NAUSEOUS

The character's distressed eyes and puffed-out cheeks convey his nausea.

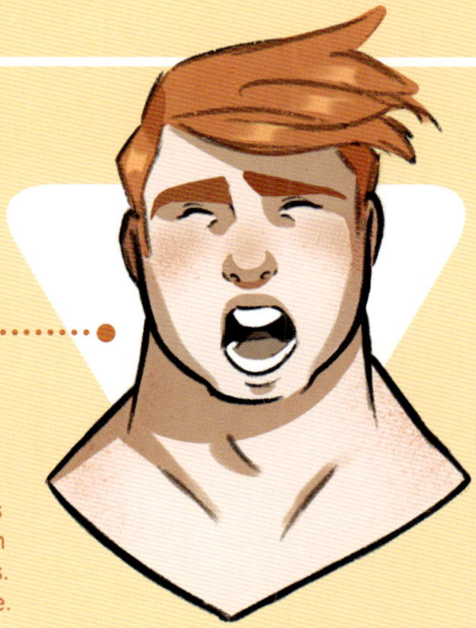

YAWNING

Illustrate a character's yawn with a wide-open mouth and closed eyes. Feel free to exaggerate.

SNORING

This character's open-mouthed snore, drool spilling from the corner of his mouth, and relaxed expression show he's in a deep sleep.

SLEEPING

To show a character is fast asleep, close their eyes and give them a restful expression as their facial muscles relax.

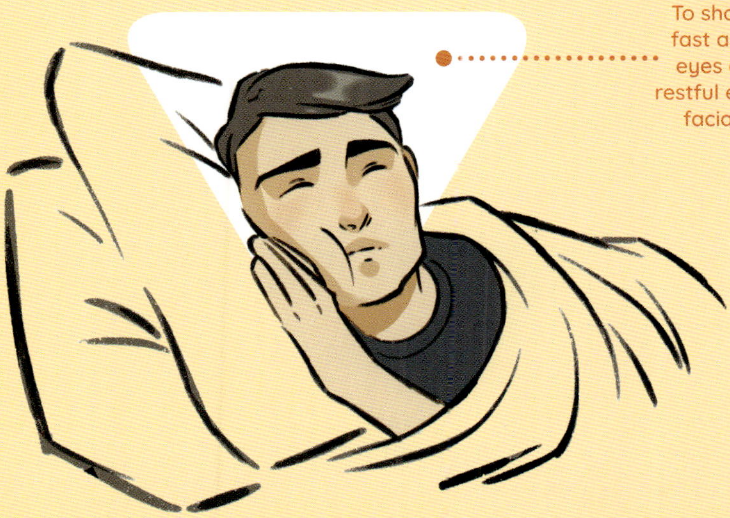

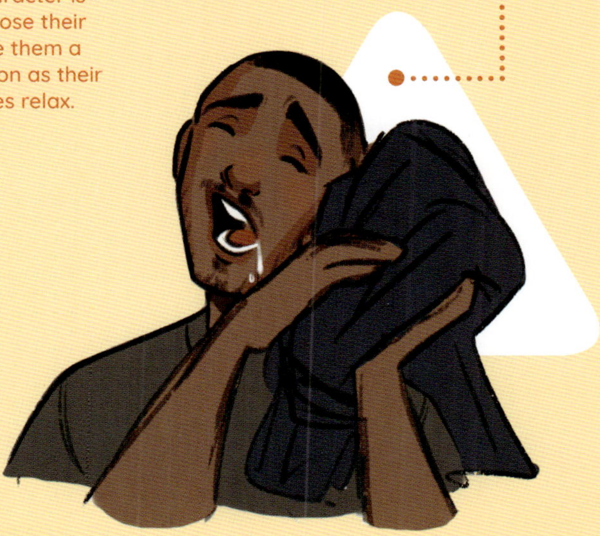

SHARP PAIN

An intense grimace can convey pain. The more exaggerated the grimace, the sharper the pain!

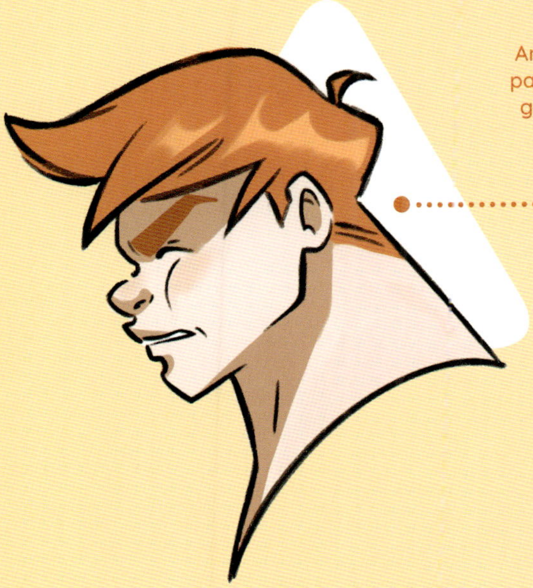

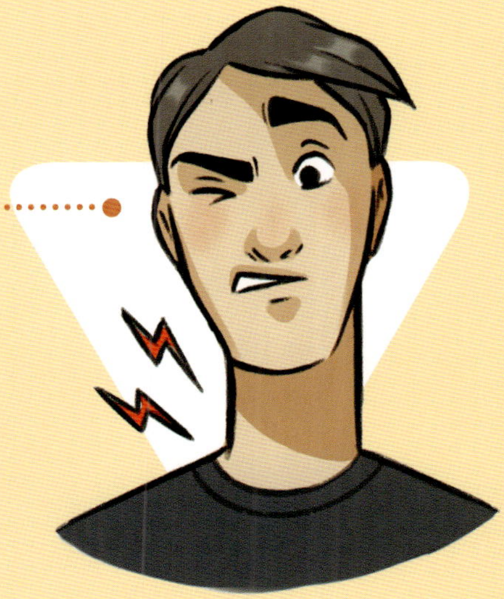

ACHES & PAINS

Adding small shapes and lines can help illustrate the source of a character's aches and pains.

Corah Louise

The purpose of an expression should always be clear, even if it is only subtle, to ensure that everything on the face works toward showing the chosen emotion. If the eyebrows, for example, are not doing their job, then the whole expression could fail. Study your own reflection while making different expressions - watch how your eyebrows raise or furrow, or how your nose scrunches or your nostrils flare. You might observe different ways the face moves that perhaps you hadn't noticed before.

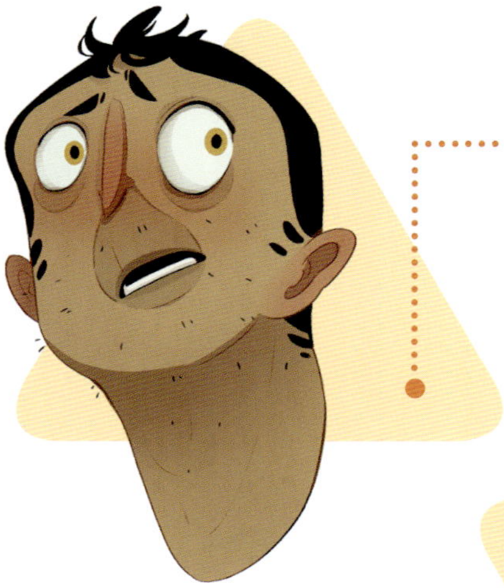

TERRIFIED

Though this character's face turns away from the feared object, his eyes can't help but look back. Notice how his eyebrows are furrowed with worry, his eyes bulging and mouth tense.

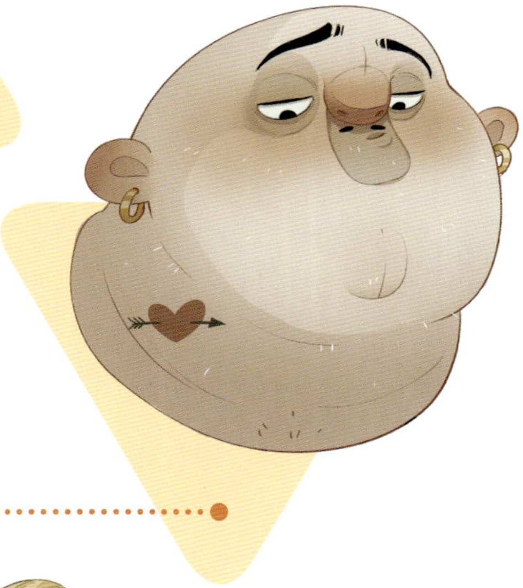

THOUGHTFUL

This character's head is angled slightly in thought, a small smile plays on his lips, and his eyelids are heavy in contemplation. His eyebrows are raised, questioning what's running through his mind.

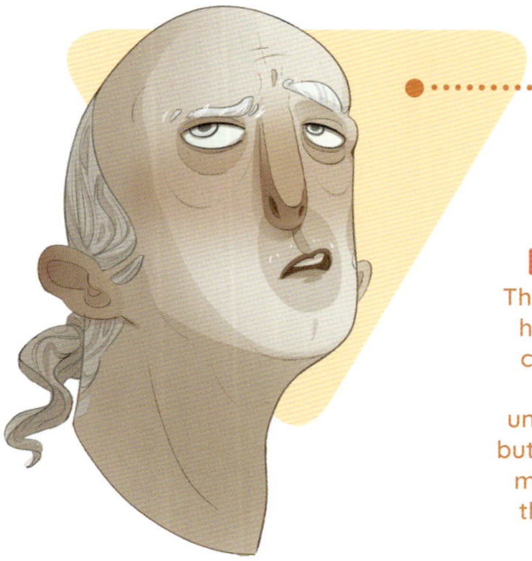

MILDLY DISGUSTED

The character turns his head away from the cause of his disgust. His eyebrows are unbalanced (furrowed but questioning) and his mouth is pulled up to the side in revulsion.

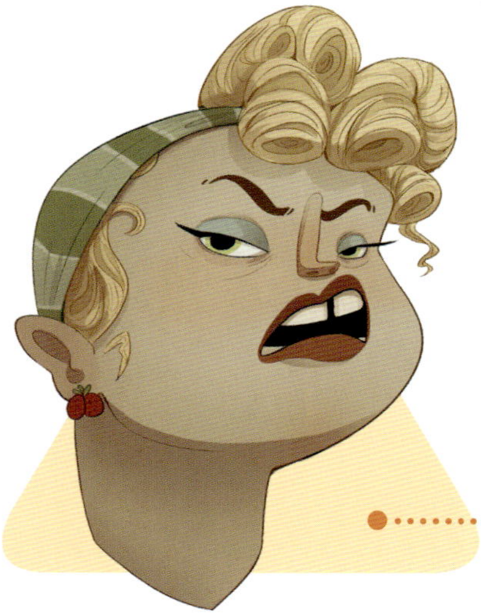

STRONGLY DISGUSTED

This is an exaggerated version of the mildly disgusted expression. The mouth is pulled harshly up and to the side in horror, making the nose turn up and eyebrows furrow dramatically.

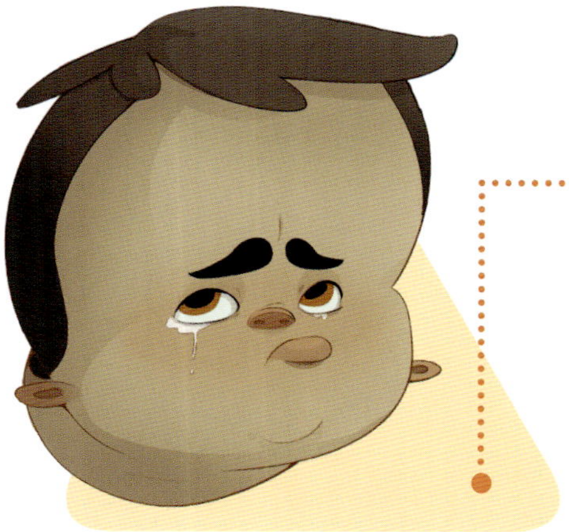

SULKY

This character's head is weighed down while his tearful eyes look up, making him appear young, innocent, and moody. His eyebrows are pulled in tightly and his bottom lip juts out as he sulks.

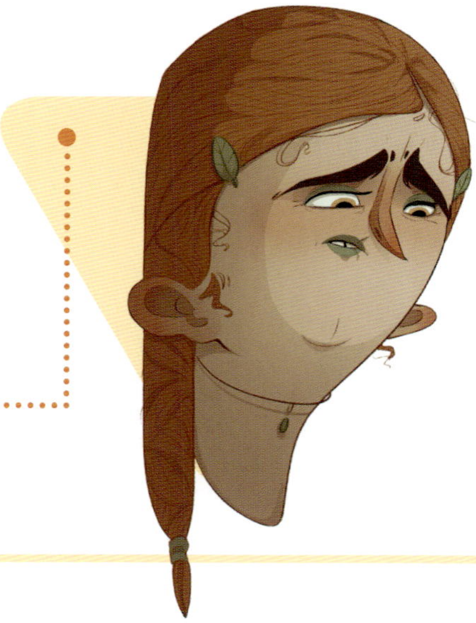

ANXIOUS

The character's head is angled down and her eyes are thin and anxious. Her lip is pulled up high into her teeth and her eyebrows are furrowed tight with worry.

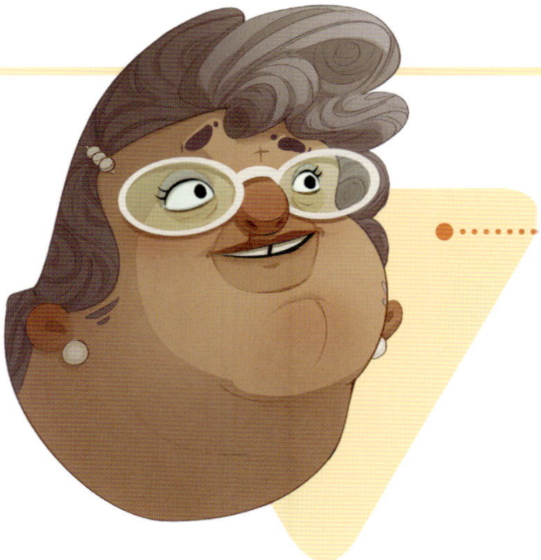

CHEERFUL

Here is an easygoing, cheerful expression. The character's simple smile pulls the lower eyelids up slightly. The joy in the high eyebrows lifts the top eyelids, opening the eyes wider.

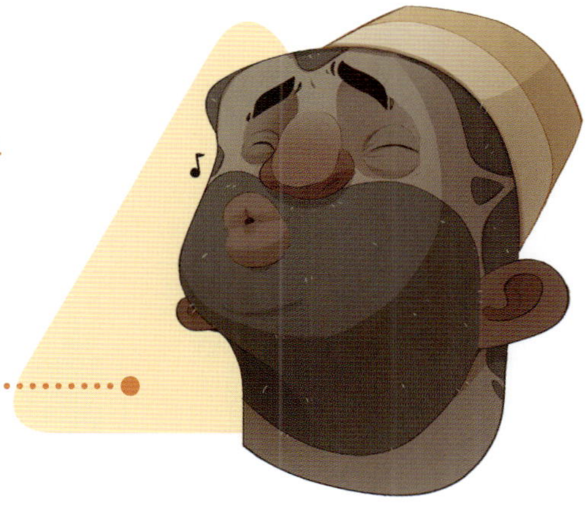

WHISTLING

This character's carefree and joyful emotion is shown as he throws his head back, closing his eyes as he pulls his lips up high to whistle. His unbalanced, high eyebrows suggest a playfulness to his character.

SINGING

This character's head is thrown back as she belts out a tune. Her closed eyes and furrowed eyebrows convey her focus, while her wide-open mouth and movement of the tongue show she is singing.

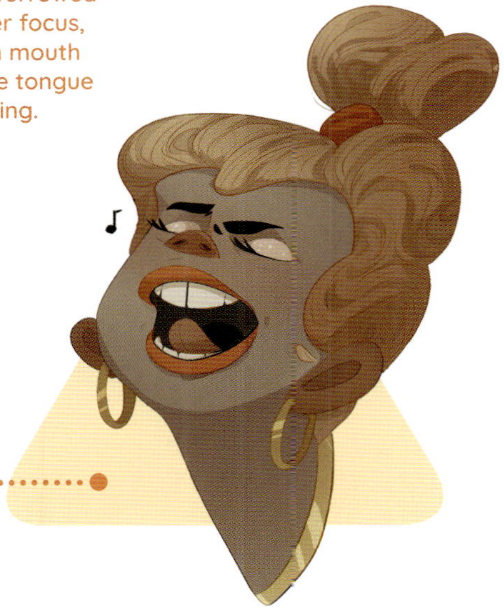

PLEASANTLY SURPRISED

Raised eyebrows and wide eyes reveal this character's shock. She wears a small smile, her mouth dropping open slightly to suggest a pleasant surprise.

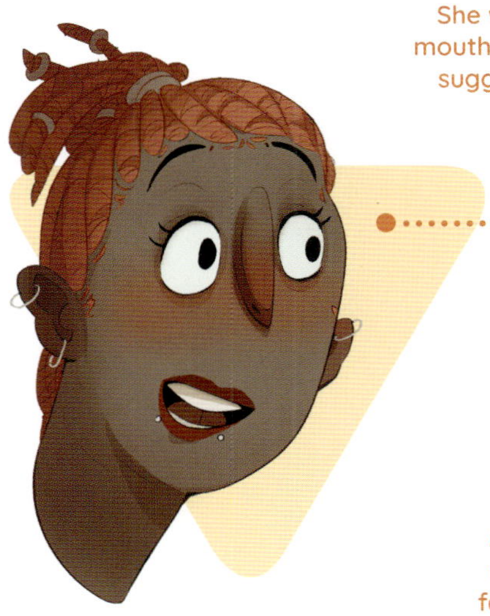

OVERJOYED

A jubilant smile takes up much of this character's face, showing all her teeth in a wide grin and causing her eyes to squint slightly. The eyebrows are lifted high with joy.

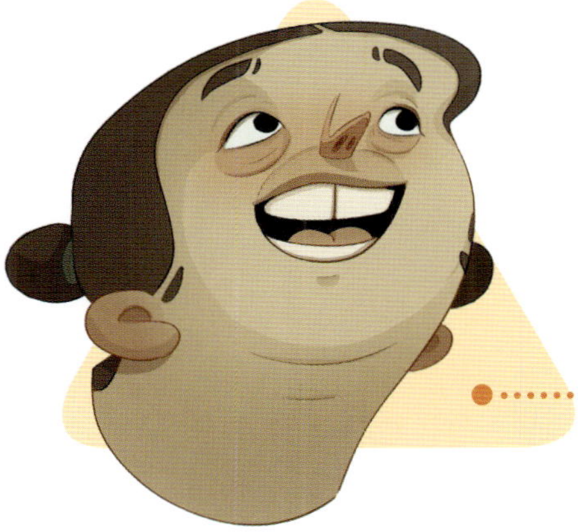

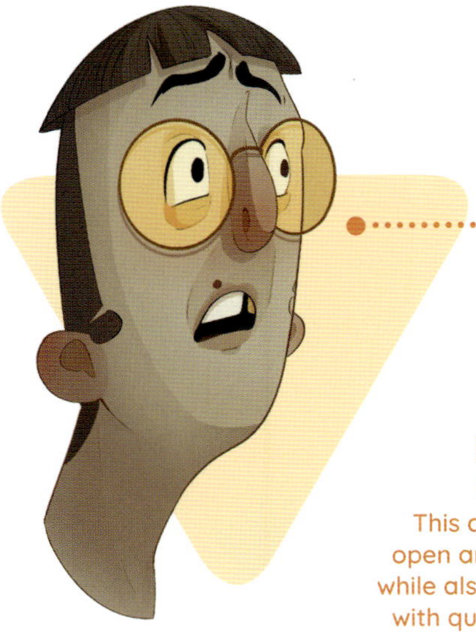

FEARFULLY SURPRISED

This character's eyes are wide open and eyebrows high in shock, while also unbalanced and furrowed with questioning. His mouth drops low at the corners in worry.

Olga Andriyenko

Looking in the mirror or using your selfie camera are valuable techniques for studying expressions. Try out different levels of an emotion and watch how your face moves, studying which parts of it tense or relax. Pay attention to how wide your eyes and mouth open, as well as the shape of your eyebrows. Do distinctive creases and wrinkles form in certain areas of the face? This usually happens when an emotion is very intense.

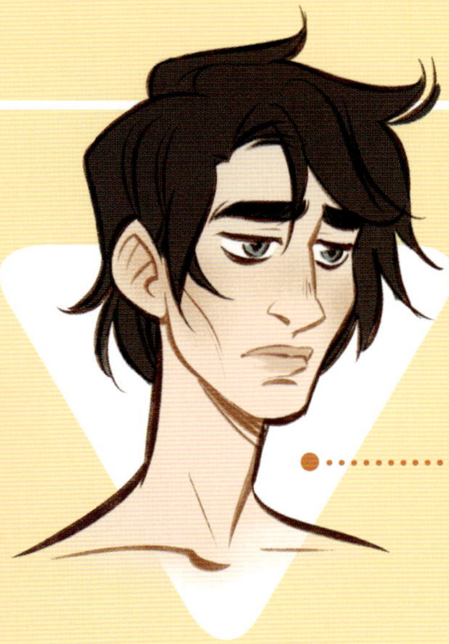

MELANCHOLY
Melancholic expressions are very low-energy and have little going on in the face. Lower the character's upper eyelids slightly and let their eyes look downward.

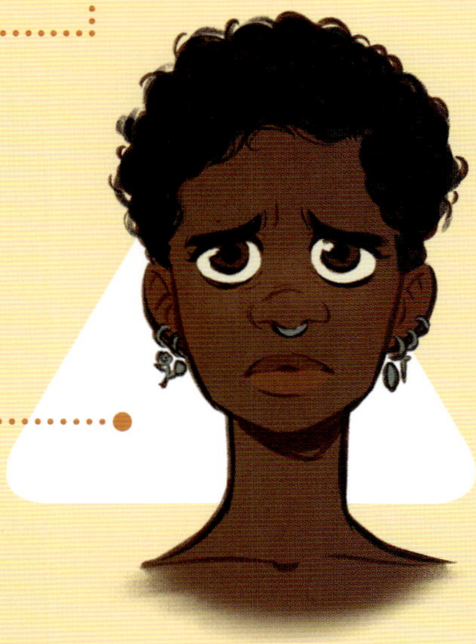

SAD
Sadness can be depicted by a sense of heaviness: This character's eyebrows are low, pushing down on her eyes, and the corners of her mouth are pulled down slightly.

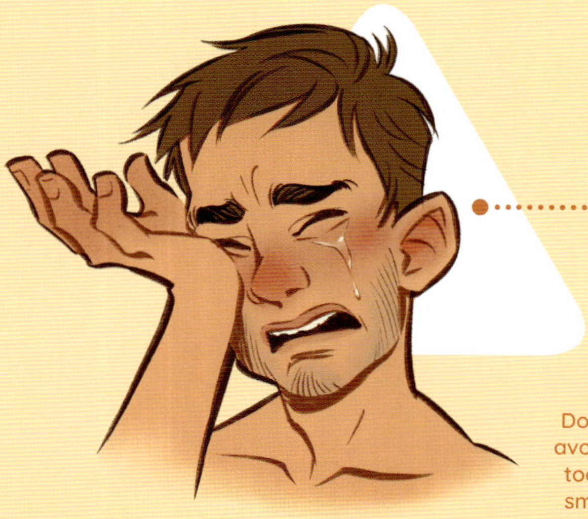

UPSET, CRYING
Use a character's hands to emphasize intense emotional expressions. There is stronger blood circulation in the face when crying, so the cheeks and nose will redden.

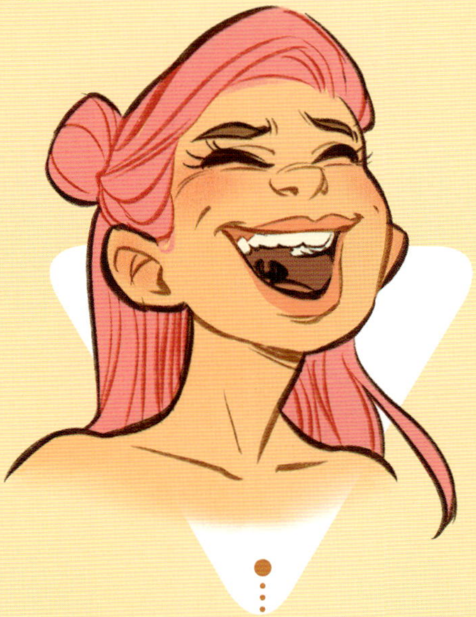

SLIGHTLY LAUGHING
Don't be afraid to show some teeth, but avoid drawing lines between every single tooth – this can look creepy. To make a smile or laugh seem honest, ensure the character's eyes are smiling too, by giving them a slightly upward-curved lower lid.

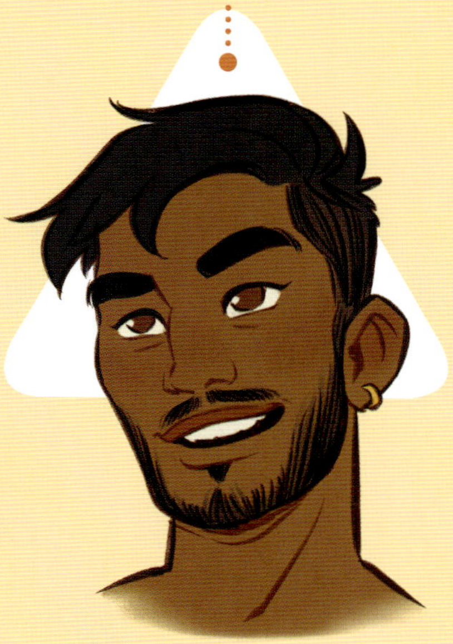

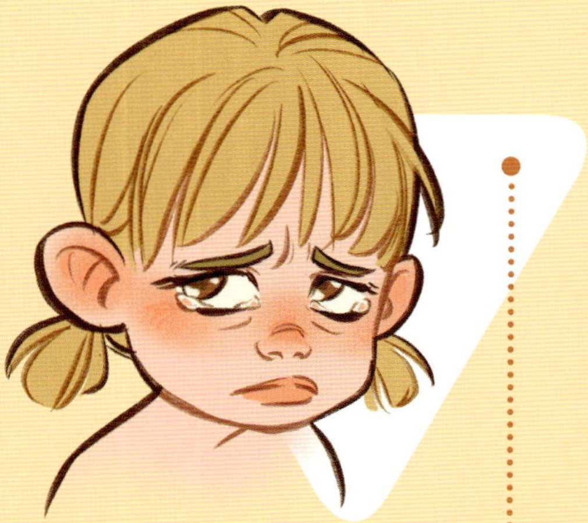

FROWNING, TEARFUL
When tears start to form, they usually collect in the corners of the eye along the lower lid before they spill out.

UPROARIOUS LAUGHING
For a big laugh, tilt the head upward and back slightly, and emphasize the energetic emotion with some lines around the eyes and mouth.

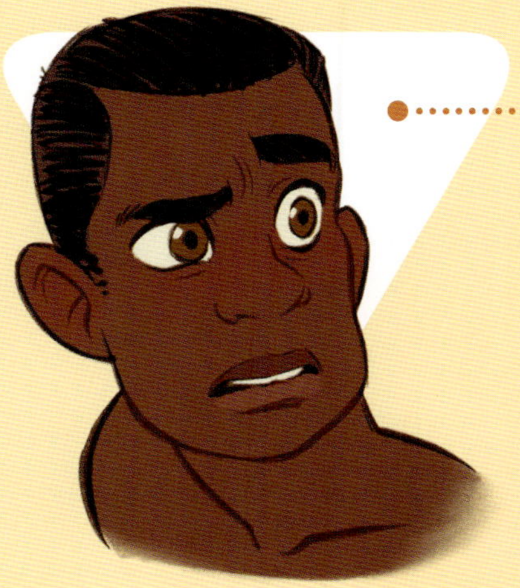

CONFUSED & WORRIED

Confusion can be depicted with asymmetric eyebrows: one lowered and one raised. A slight biting of the lip can show worry and nervousness.

CONFUSED BUT AMUSED

Combine asymmetric eyebrows with a slight laugh to show when a character is confused, but amused too. The corners of the mouth can be asymmetric as well, as if the character is not sure whether to laugh or not.

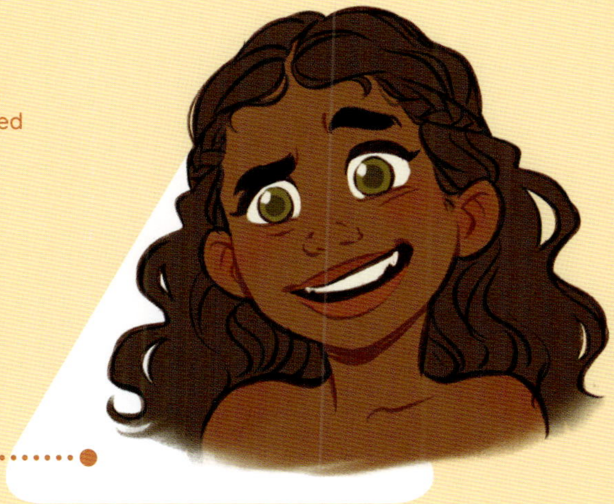

SLIGHTLY TIRED, DISTRACTED

The most obvious sign of tiredness is dark eye circles due to stress or lack of sleep. The character's head might be drooping, needing to be supported by a hand. The eyes pointing sideways indicate distraction.

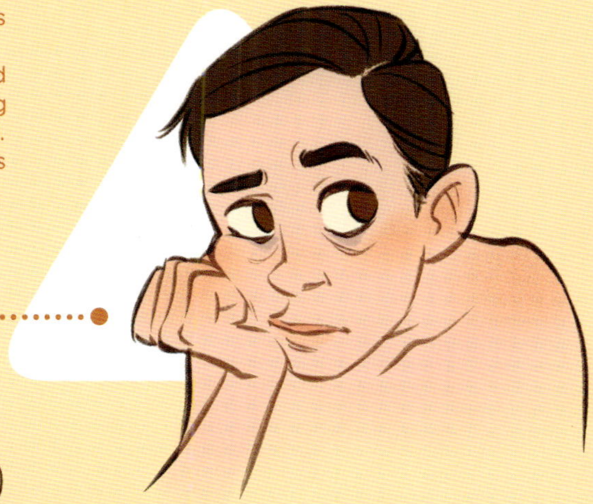

EXHAUSTED

Illustrate intense exhaustion with a big sigh or a yawn.

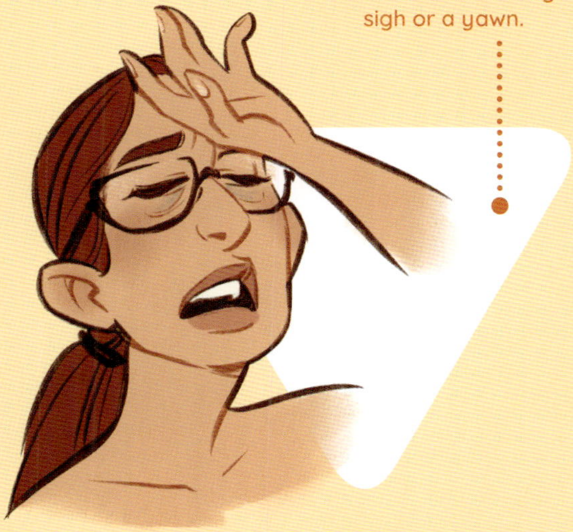

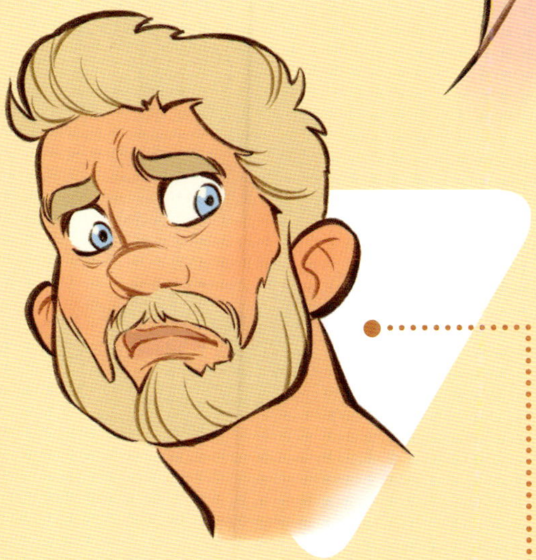

SLIGHTLY WORRIED & AFRAID

When someone is scared or worried, their eyebrows pull together and slightly upward, with wrinkles forming between them. This character's eyes are open wide, with the irises and pupils reduced in size.

MODERATELY FRIGHTENED

A frightened character will try to pull themselves away from the danger – show this by tilting their head back. Clenched teeth can help illustrate how tense they are.

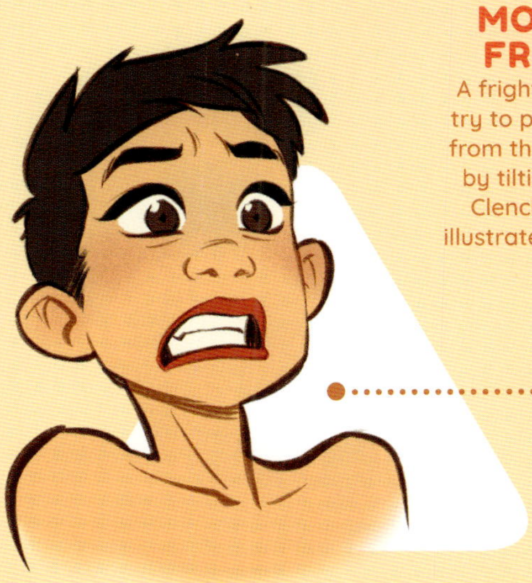

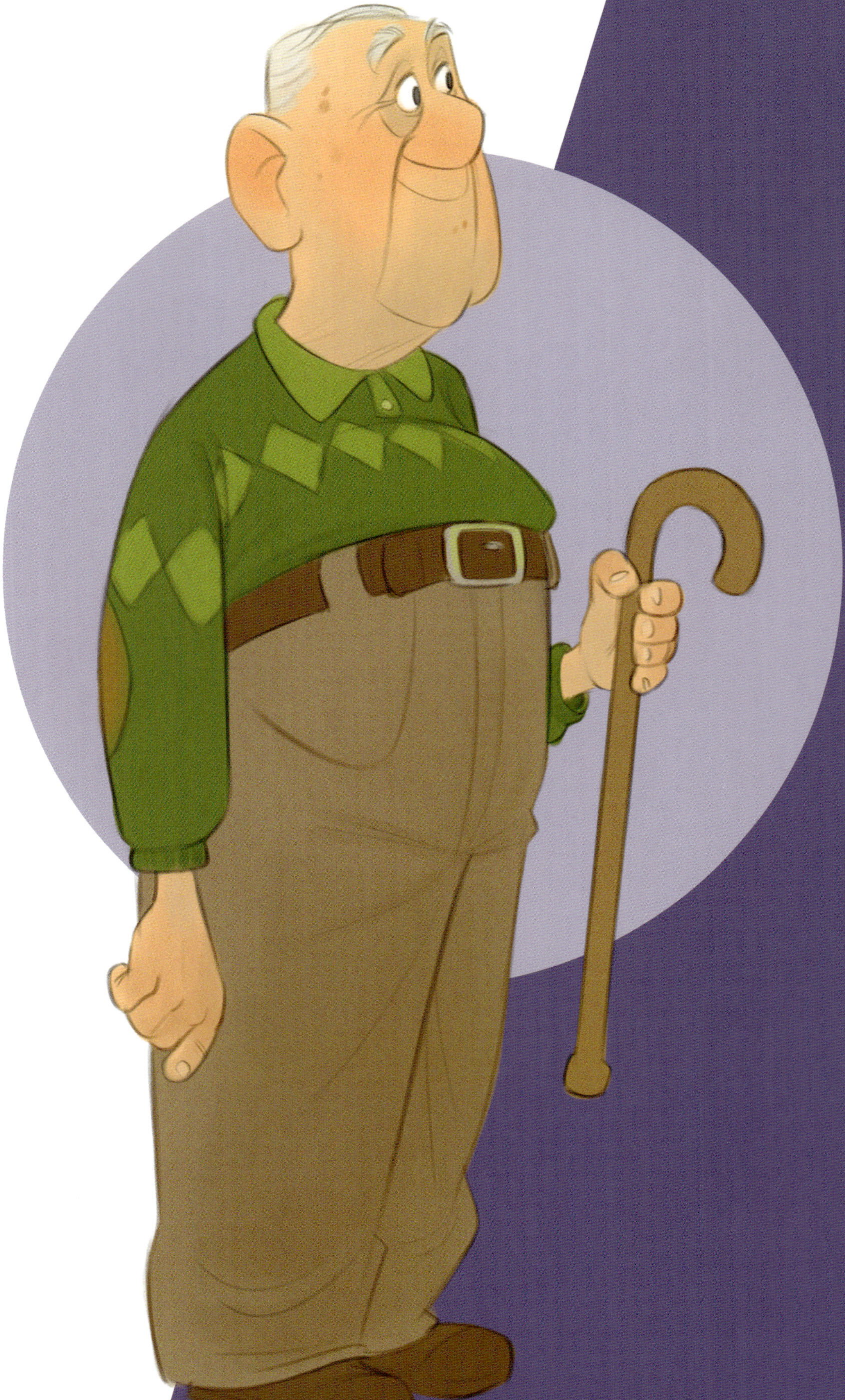

Image by Tom van Rheenen

AGE

COMMUNICATING AGE
PAGE 192

BABY CHARACTERS
PAGE 197

CHILD CHARACTERS
PAGE 198

TEEN CHARACTERS
PAGE 200

ADULT CHARACTERS
PAGE 202

ELDERLY CHARACTERS
PAGE 204

CASE STUDY: THE LIBRARIAN
PAGE 206

COMMUNICATING AGE

Tom van Rheenen

Age is an important part of character design. There might be times where you need to show your character at different points in their life, through flashbacks or to show the passage of time. But even if you only show the character in a specific moment in their life, it is important to understand the workings of age on the human body. You might be tasked with designing a character at a specific age, or to show the difference in age between two characters. A character's age will always tell the audience something about them, so be sure to use it to your advantage as a designer.

This chapter will cover the basics of how the human body changes over the course of a lifetime, and demonstrate general principles you can follow to communicate the age of a character, allowing you to capture every stage of their life.

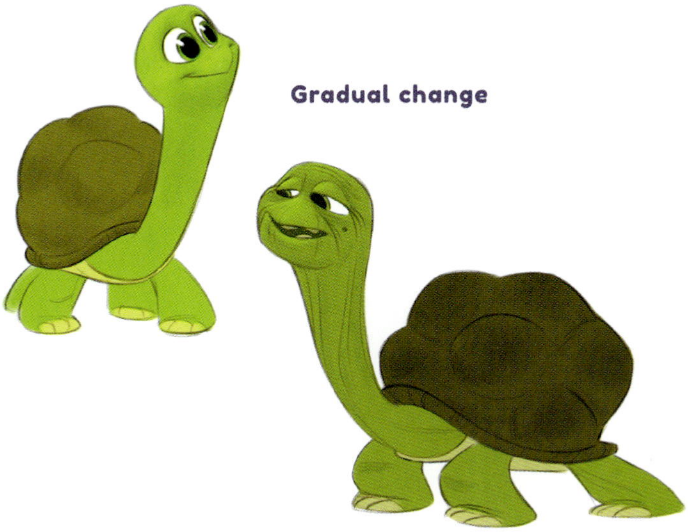

Gradual change

HOW CHARACTERS CAN CHANGE

Stories are almost always about transformation. Readers are often bored by stories in which a character does not change in some way. They want to see a character develop, advance, or regress - perhaps tragedy being the exception, where the lack of change is their fatality. But how can you convey such change in your character designs?

Change can be gradual or abrupt. The former happens step by step - perhaps as a character becomes progressively more tired from their office job, wrinkles start to set in, eyes start to gray, and their posture and walk become increasingly slouched. There is great tragedy in slow demise. Conversely, a character might change abruptly. A certain life event could transform a shy wallflower into the life and soul of the party. Such abrupt change can be considered a metamorphosis - a caterpillar turning into a butterfly being the most iconic.

There are three types of character change or evolution: **physical**, **social**, and **psychological**. One, two, or all three of these can play a part in the transformation a character goes through. Perhaps the shy wallflower now dazzles in bold, colorful clothing, but on the inside she is still the same timid girl, not at all comfortable with her new wardrobe. Her transformation is physical, but not psychological. Or perhaps the shy wallflower might realize she is not comfortable in her new role and returns to her modest wardrobe, but with newly gained confidence and acceptance of who she is. This is a psychological change.

Abrupt change

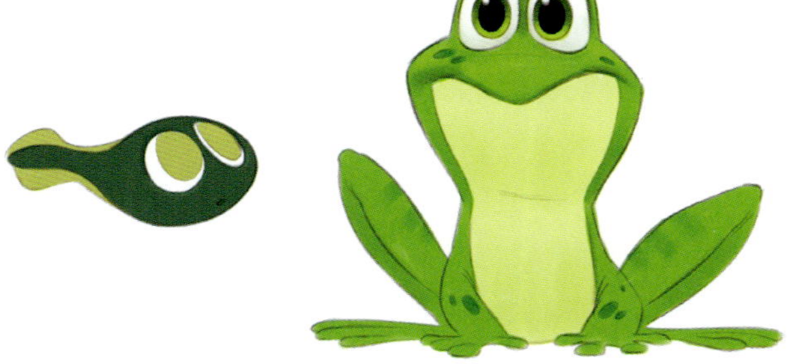

USE YOUR TOOLBOX

As the human body comes in a wide variety of shapes and sizes, it is impossible to cover everything here. This chapter will cover general principles and broad observations that distinguish different age groups. Think of these as guidelines rather than strict rules to abide by when designing characters. Sometimes your character might call for different design choices that go against these general principles - often this is what will make your design more unique! Revisit these principles when a part of your design is not working. Use them as a toolbox for when something needs fixing, not as a blueprint that must be followed at all times.

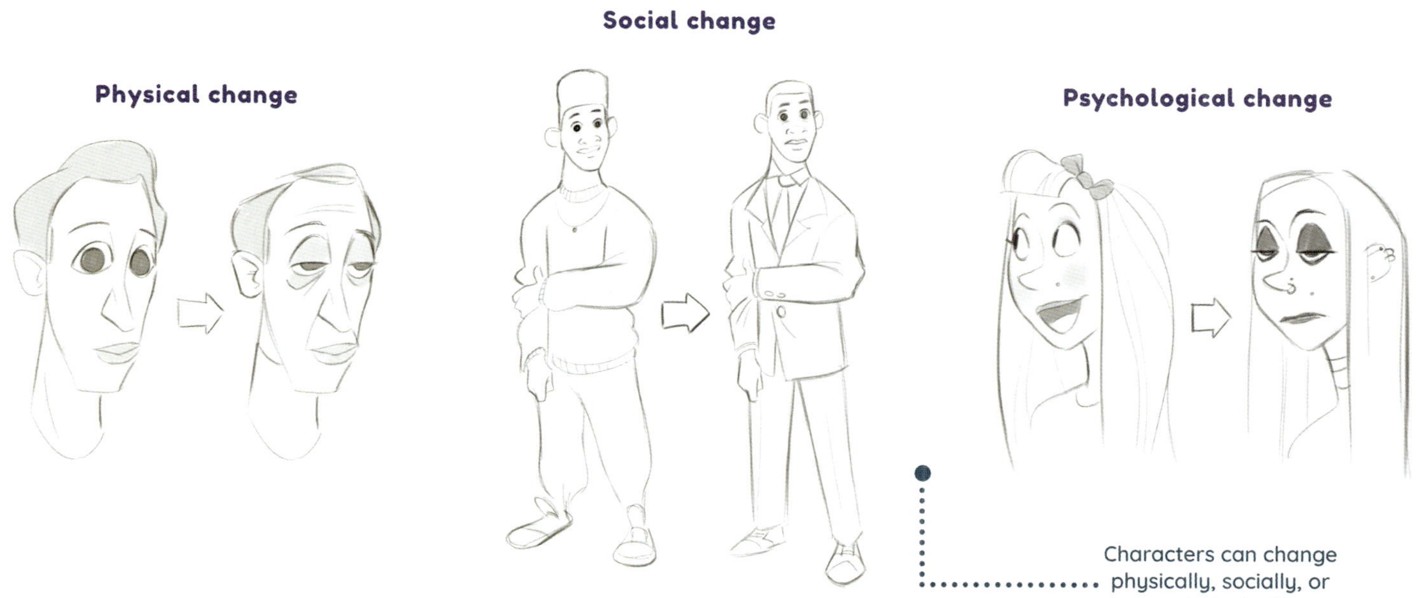

Characters can change physically, socially, or psychologically.

SHAPE & POSTURE

The human body changes drastically throughout its lifespan. Babies, adults, the elderly – they all have the same body parts, but differ greatly in how they look. So how does the body age? The cranium stays relatively the same shape and size throughout the human life. The jaw, however, changes over time. Babies tend to have a much smaller jaw and therefore a rounder head, whereas in adults, the jaw becomes more prominent, elongating the head.

When designing characters, shape language can be used to distinguish different age groups. In babies and toddlers, shapes tend to be round and soft. As characters transition toward adulthood, shape language might become squarer with stronger angles. For elderly characters, shapes grow more crooked with even sharper angles. These are guidelines, however – not rules. If designing a sweet old lady character, you may wish to opt for softer, rounded shapes.

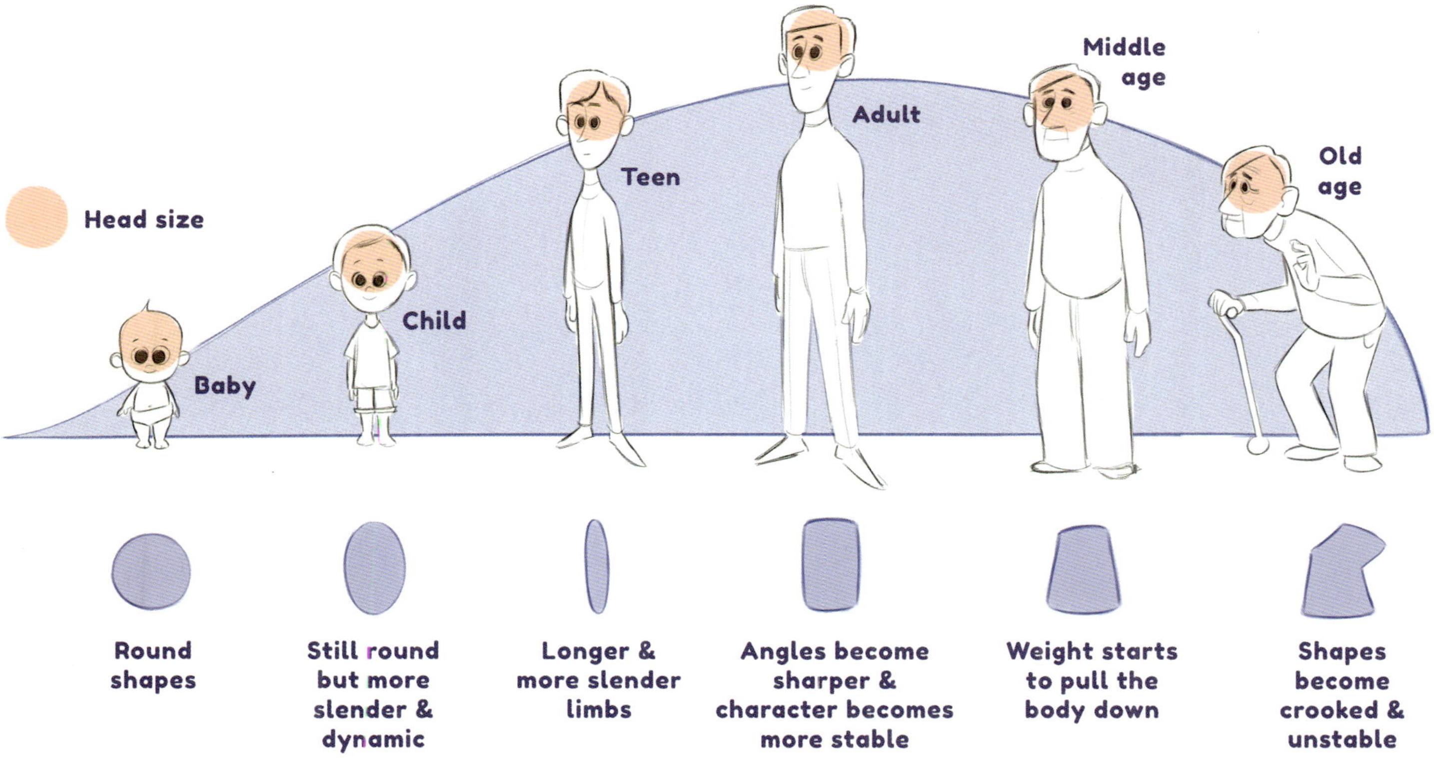

Another aspect of the human body that can reflect change over time is posture. Posture can of course change temporarily – a certain mood or mindset might cause a character to slouch or hunch their shoulders – but changes to posture can also be of a more structural nature. As the body ages, muscles get weaker, including the muscles that keep your posture upright. For this reason a person might develop a hunch as they grow older, hence the crooked shape language you might use when designing an elderly character.

Posture changes over a character's lifetime, which can help signify their age. In these examples, the S-shaped gesture of the spine becomes more angled over time.

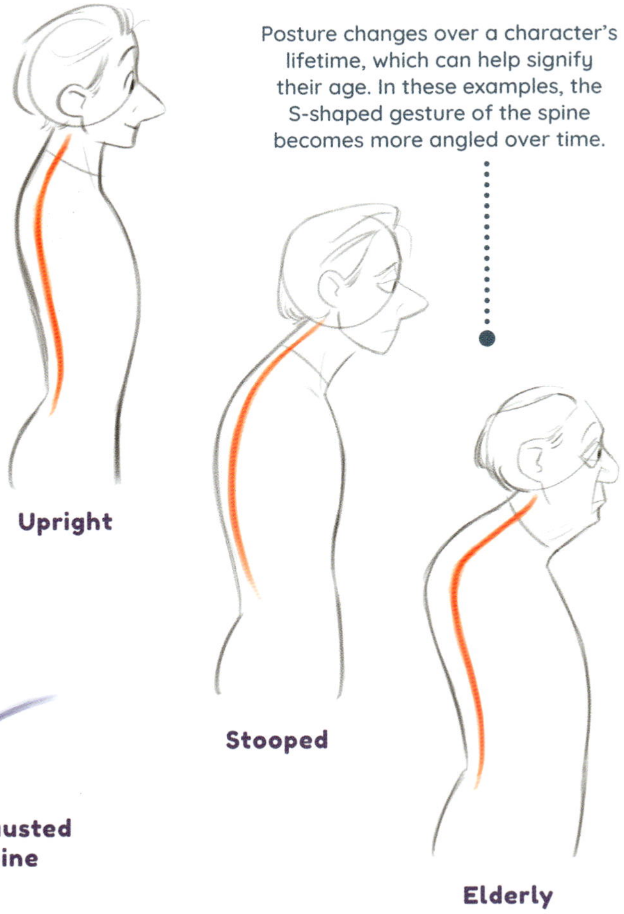

An energetic, youthful posture will have the chest pointing outward, whereas a more exhausted, aged posture might have the chest slouching inward.

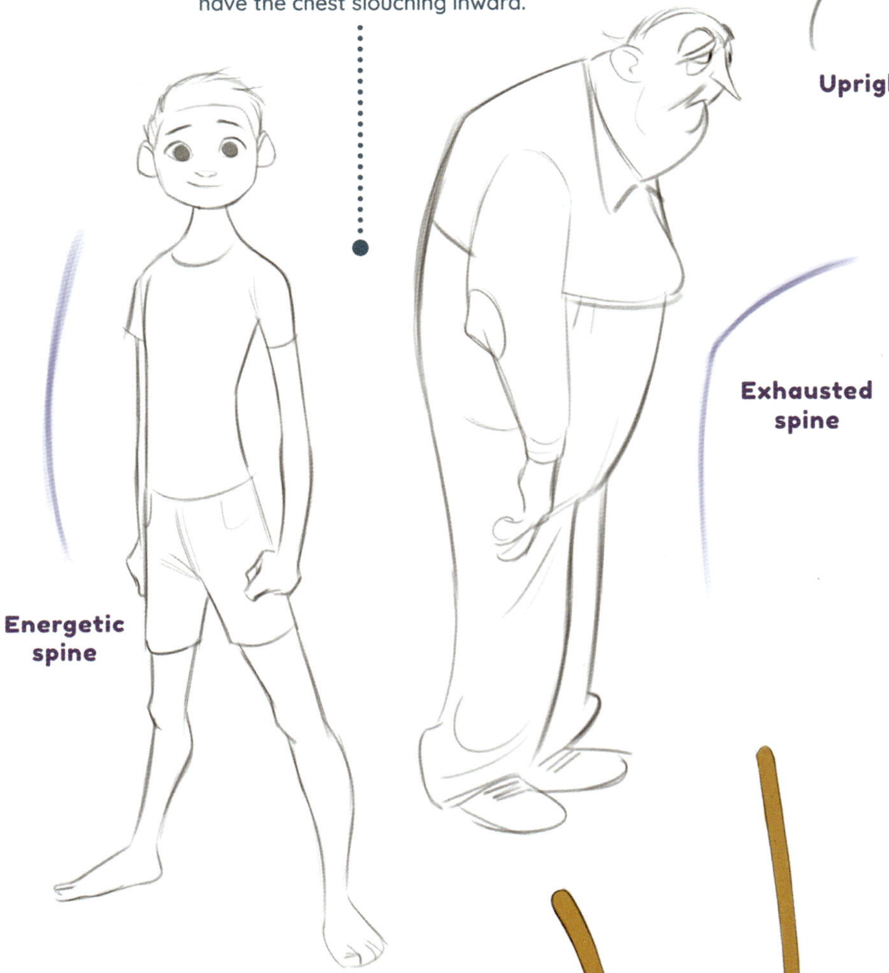

When posture and shape language are applied, even a broom can communicate age.

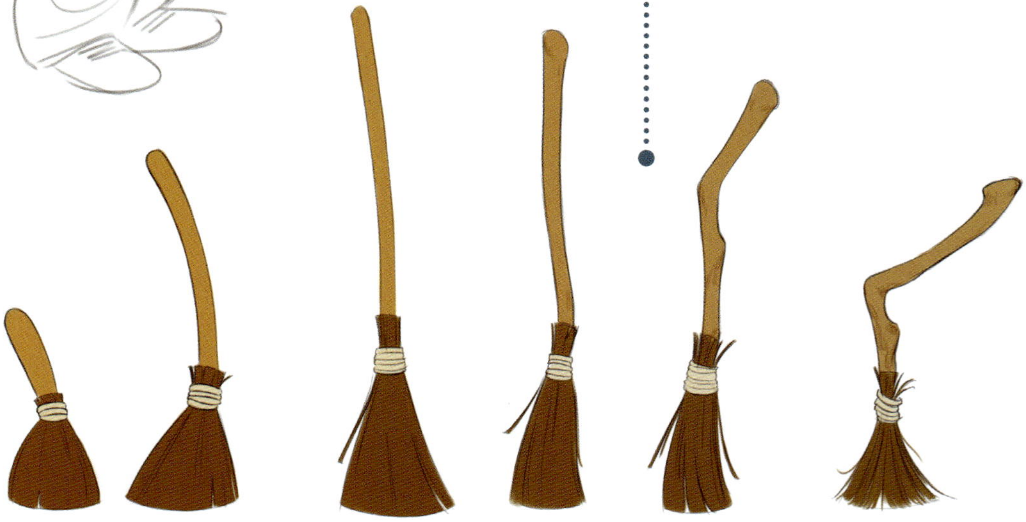

The life of a broom

WEIGHT

A layer of fat sits on top of the bones and muscles that make up the body. As fat is not always distributed evenly, it results in a variety of different body shapes. A person can be underweight or overweight at any age, but this manifests very differently at different ages.

Young people tend to be more active and their metabolisms are faster because their bodies are still growing. For this reason, teens are often slimmer than those who are more mature in years, and their weight is distributed more evenly across the body. As the body gets older, however, weight can start to build in specific areas, creating a greater variety in body shapes. The difference in weight distribution between genders also becomes more apparent in adulthood. As mentioned on page 96, for men, weight predominantly sits on the belly, whereas for women it tends to center around the hips.

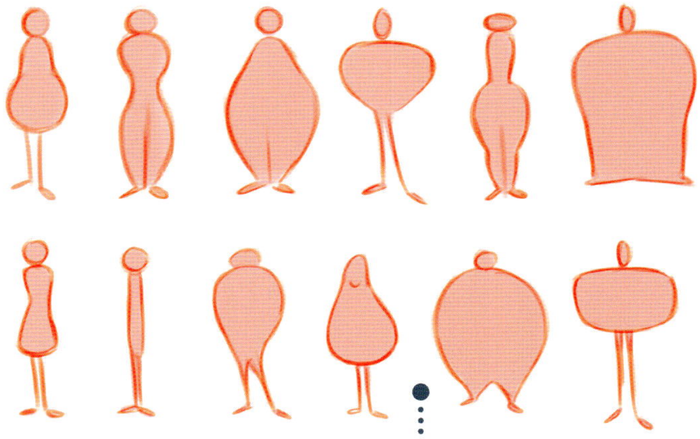

Weight gain can result in a variety of body shapes.

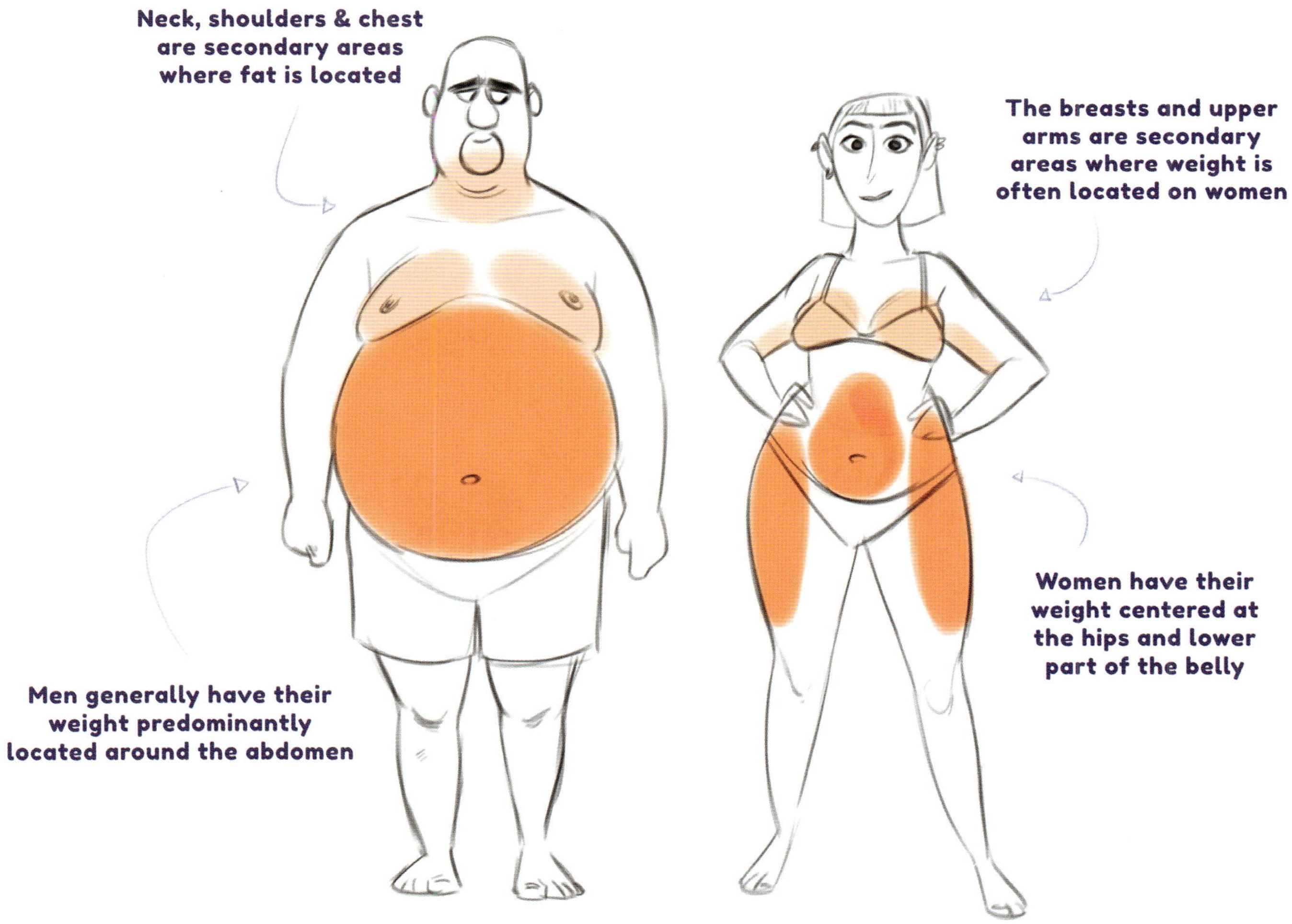

WRINKLES

The elasticity of the skin is another thing that changes with age, altering the type of wrinkles that form. A baby's skin is thick and elastic, and therefore most wrinkles are folds: a squash between two volumes. These are noticeable in the cheeks but are most prominent around the neck, ankles, and wrists. The skin loses this flexibility as it ages, and different kinds of wrinkles start to form, noticeably in the face. When people talk and express themselves, the skin in their face moves, being squashed, stretched, and folded as different emotions are expressed. But when the skin loses its flexibility, all the stretching and folding starts to leave a more permanent imprint. This is most noticeable around the eyes, forehead, and mouth. These wrinkles echo the emotions a person has most expressed throughout their lifetime, so when designing an older character, the choice and placement of wrinkles can tell the audience a lot about a character's history.

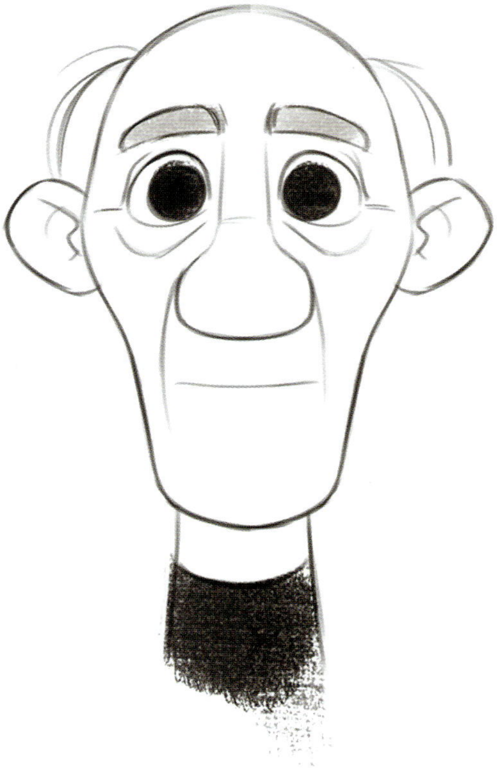

Neutral

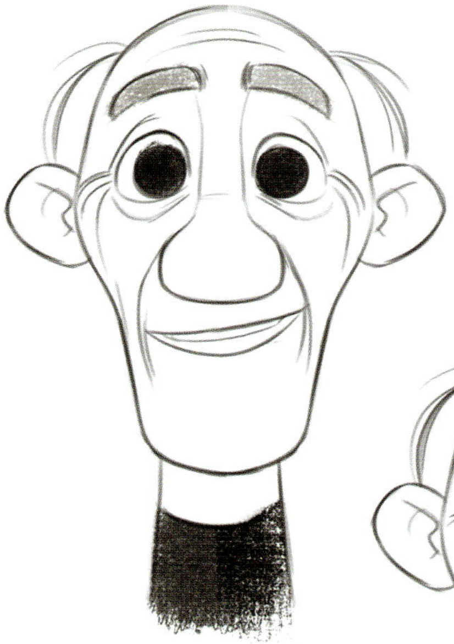

Happiness

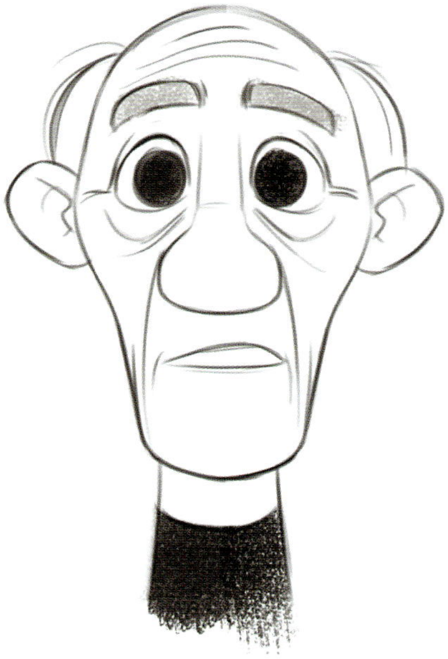

Surprise

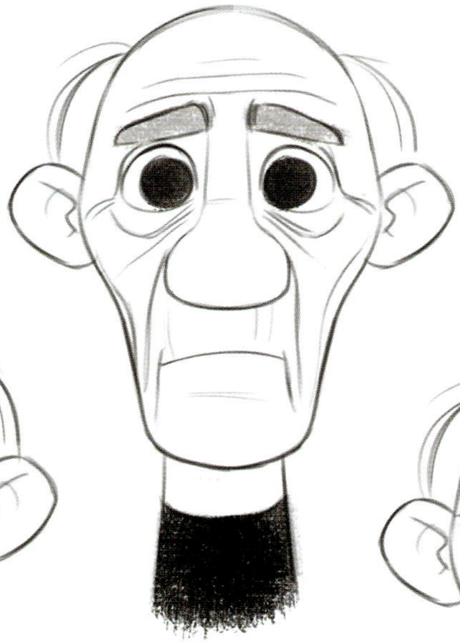

Sorrow

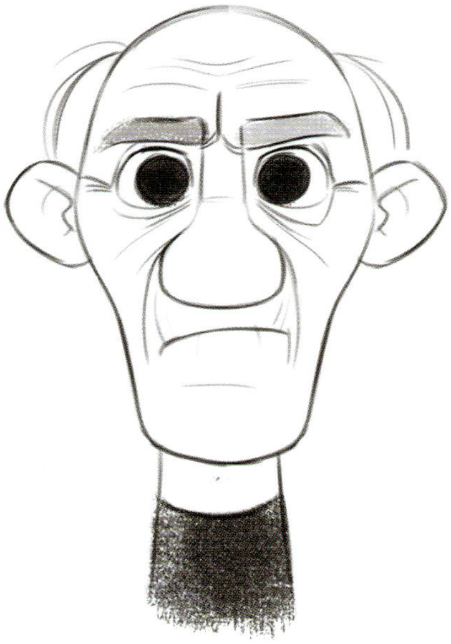

Anger

BABY CHARACTERS

Tom van Rheenen

SPACING THE CUTENESS

Let's start at the very beginning of childhood. Baby animals, whether they are puppies, kittens, or human babies, are all adorable – but what makes them adorable? What sets babies apart visually? Most noticeably, a baby's proportions are very different to those of an adult. If you have seen medieval paintings of babies that look just like miniature adults, you will know that wrong proportions can give very unsatisfactory results.

First of all, consider head-to-body ratio: babies have a very large head in relation to the rest of their body. Their facial features tend to be spaced differently too, mainly positioned in the lower half of the face. Babies also have a lot of fat: baby fat. Their forms are therefore very round and soft – you will not find many sharp angles in babies, as you saw on page 39. Drawing soft, rounded shapes for infant characters will help make your designs appear more sweet and baby-like.

Proportions are what help make babies cute. They have relatively large foreheads and small jaws with soft, round cheeks.

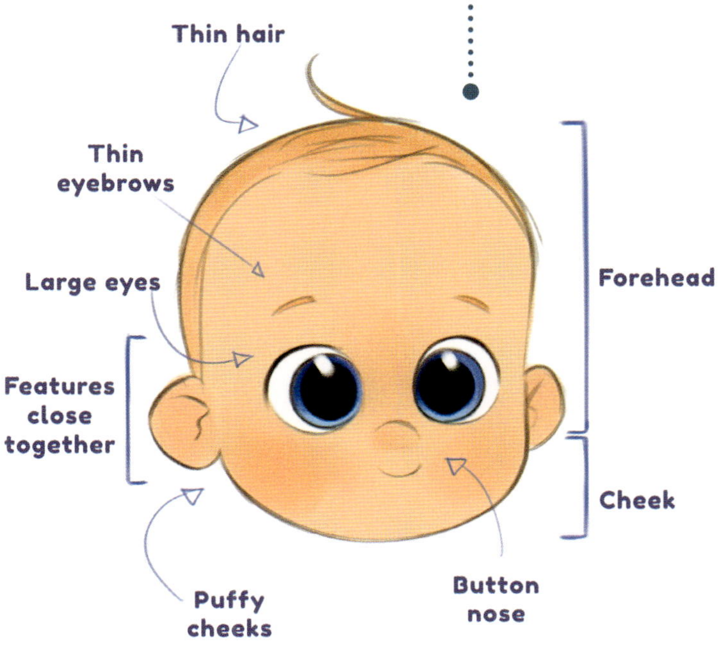

BABY STEPS

Another feature that sets babies apart is their development and expression of motor skills. They are still learning how to find their balance, move around, and hold things, which creates a very distinct style of movement. There will be a lot of squatting, and lots of legs and arms reaching out to find balance. Babies also tend to push out their chest and backside, giving them a unique, baby-like waddle that can make them look very unsteady.

Babies are still learning to find their balance, giving them a distinct style of movement.

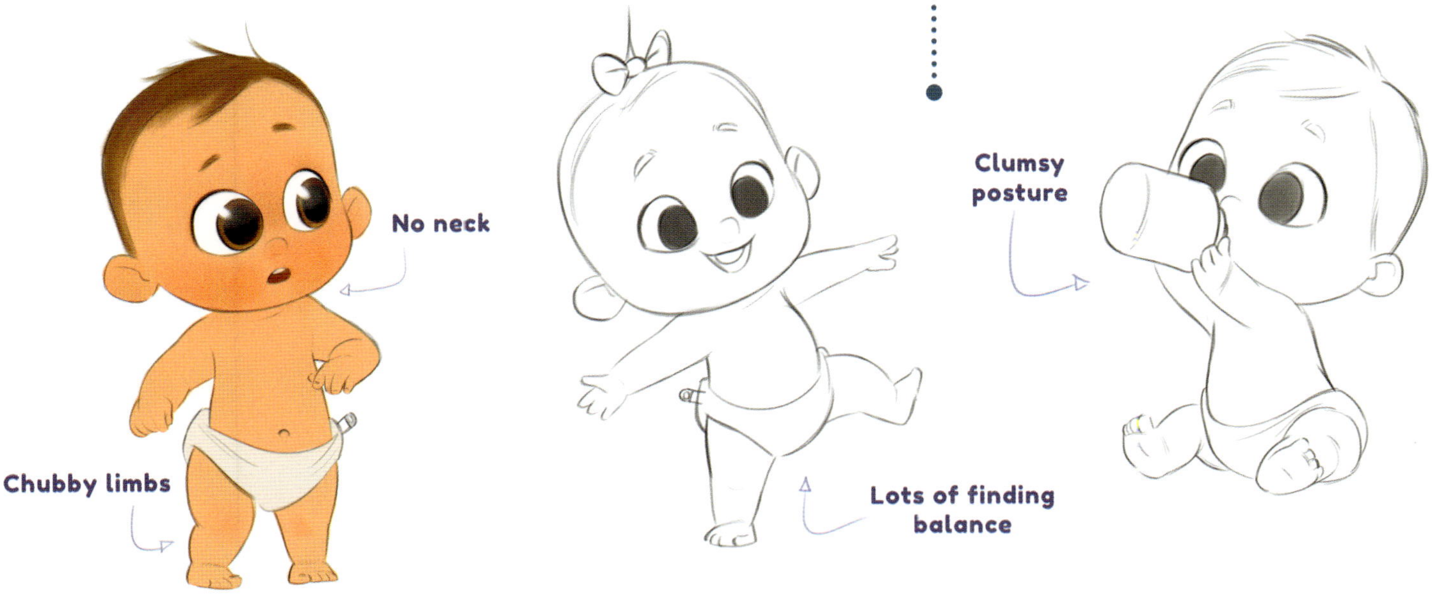

CHILD CHARACTERS

Tom van Rheenen

The body changes rapidly during the transition from baby to child. A child at three years old will look very different to a child at six. It can therefore prove tricky to capture the true age of a character in your design. However, there are some general changes you can keep in mind to guide you. First of all, children start to lose a lot of their baby fat as they grow. The neck becomes more apparent (though still relatively small), limbs become more slender, and features begin to form in the face - most noticeably, a child will start to lose their chubby baby cheeks.

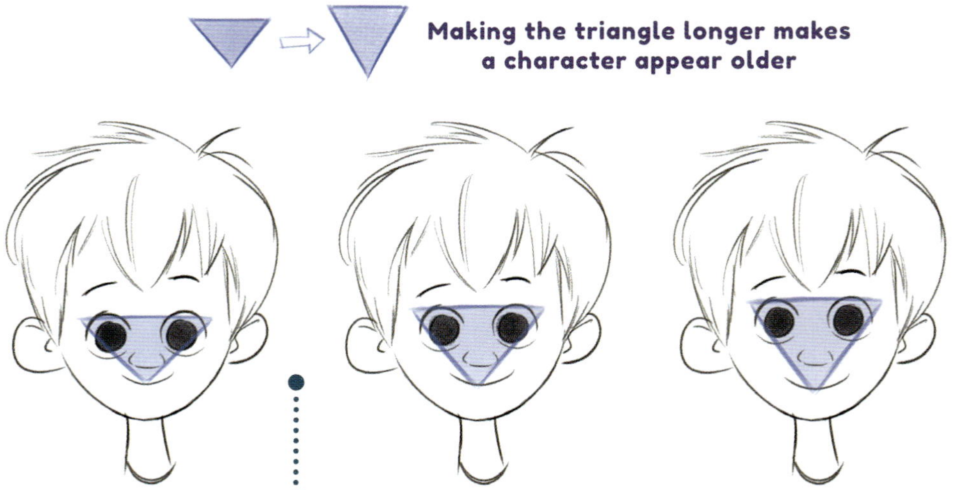

Use the face triangle tool to position the features of your character, allowing you to more easily depict their age.

FACE TRIANGLES

A good way to control the age of the character you are designing is to pay attention to how their facial features are spaced. Imagine a triangle that contains the eyes, nose, and mouth, and observe its location on the face, as you did with the marble theory on page 158. As you grow older, that triangle tends to elongate, with features appearing more spaced out within the face. The space above the triangle decreases, demonstrating how the forehead starts to appear smaller as you age.

A PLAYFUL LIFE

Of course, designing child characters is about more than just proportions. Remember, you are designing a character. Spend some time thinking about what defines children. Imagine what the character might get up to all day and how you will depict that visually. Are they climbing trees? Then their clothes are probably covered in dirt; there might be scratches on their knees, and maybe a twig stuck in their hair. What about a more reserved or creative child? Perhaps they like playing with crayons and paint, making a mess, or they might have found solace in a soft toy or imaginary friend. These details will add another layer of life to your character.

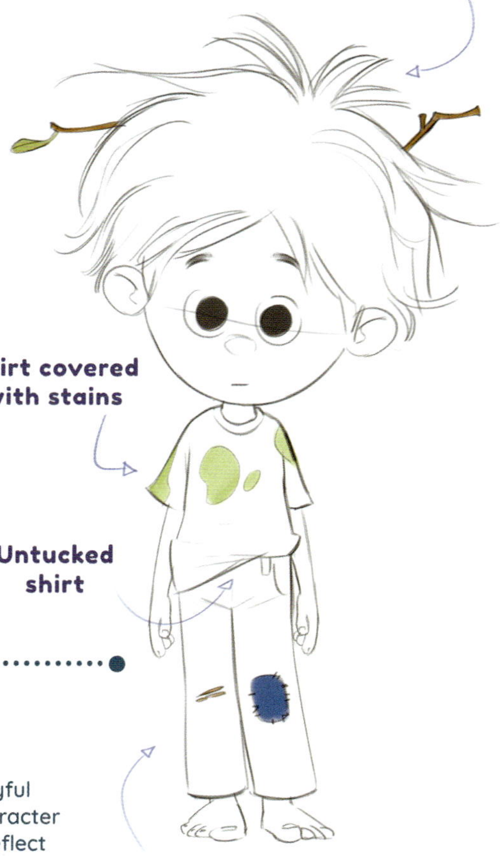

Children have a wild and playful lifestyle. Think about how a character spends their time and try to reflect that in their appearance.

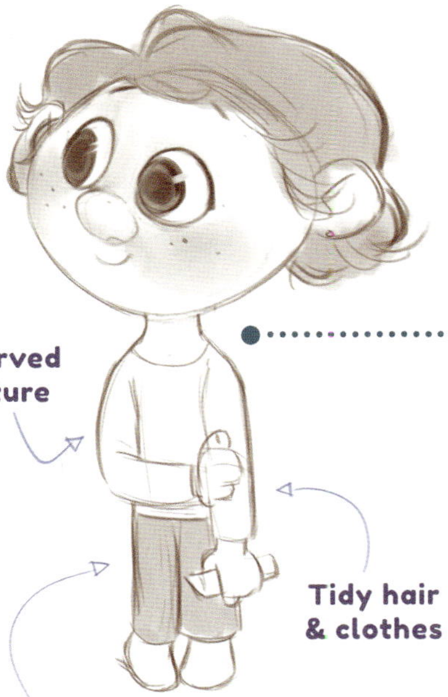

Reserved posture

Tidy hair & clothes

Don't be afraid to experiment with proportions, such as a big nose

Compared to the child on the previous page, this character's pose and appearance make her come across as quiet, neat, and a little shy.

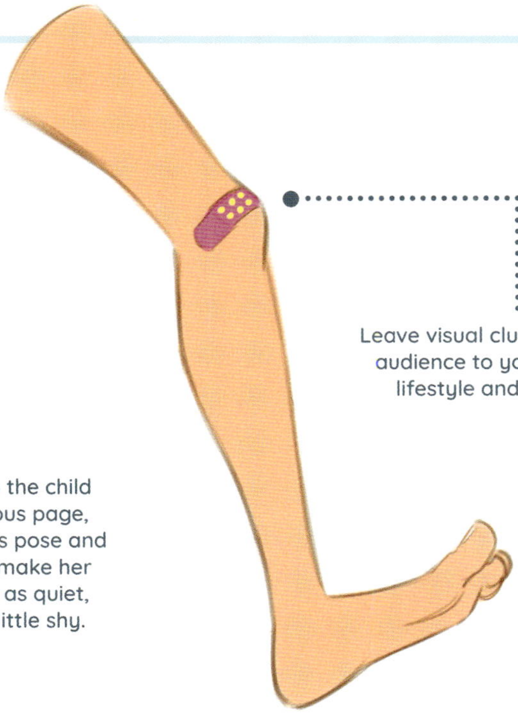

Leave visual clues that alert the audience to your character's lifestyle and personality.

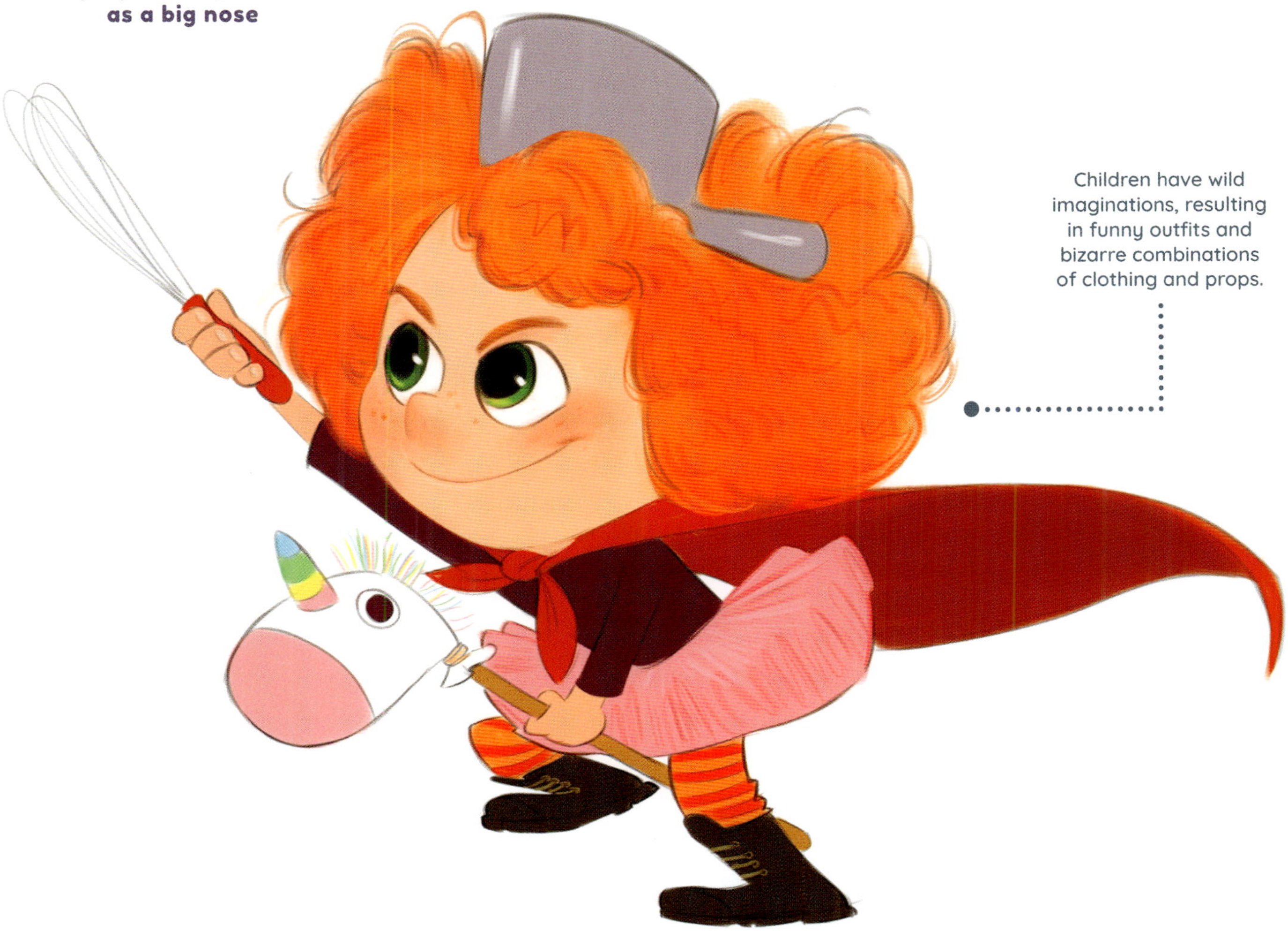

Children have wild imaginations, resulting in funny outfits and bizarre combinations of clothing and props.

TEEN CHARACTERS

Tom van Rheenen

Teenage bodies are undergoing a lot of change, growing suddenly and experiencing an influx of hormones. There are a lot of new things for teen characters to get used to.

NEW HEIGHTS

Teens can experience rapid growth, sometimes growing so fast that their muscles and motor skills have to play catch-up. Because of this, teen bodies can behave a bit clumsily, their muscles not having grown into their new longer limbs yet. Changes can also be observed in a teen's face. The jaw starts to become more apparent, the nose becomes more pronounced and defined, and the neck grows longer and more visible. While a child's features are still very soft, in teenage characters you can begin to introduce some harder angles, straighter lines, and more defined shapes.

EMOTIONAL ROLLERCOASTER

Another change teens have to endure is the emotional rollercoaster caused by an increase of hormones. This is a period in which they might start to rebel against their parents and feel the need to find their own identity. Of course, they have no clue what to do with this newly fought freedom, which can result in pink hair, pierced ears and noses, and lots of dark makeup. The teenage years are a period in which teens try to express themselves in the most outspoken of ways. Searching for a new identity, teens tend to cling together, forming groups based on their interests or choice of appearance. When designing teen characters, do not miss the opportunity to explore different costumes, accessories, and ways to convey their interests.

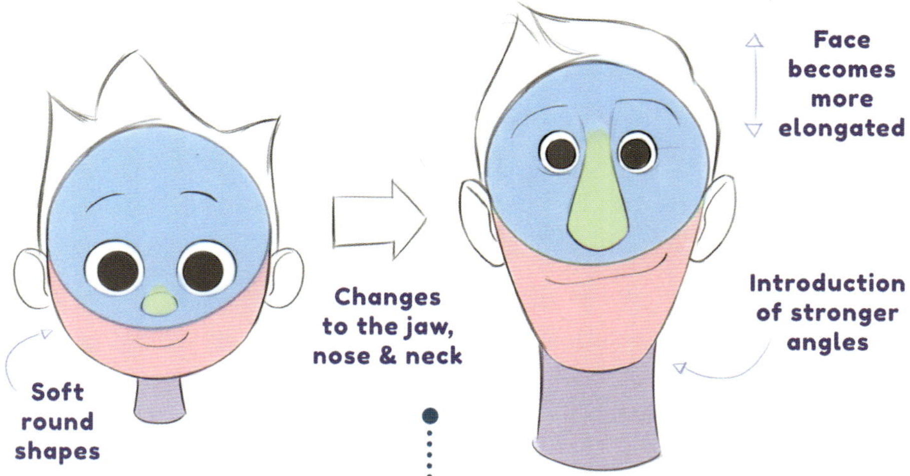

The face can change a lot when transitioning from child to teenager. Bones become much more apparent, making the jawline and nose more prominent.

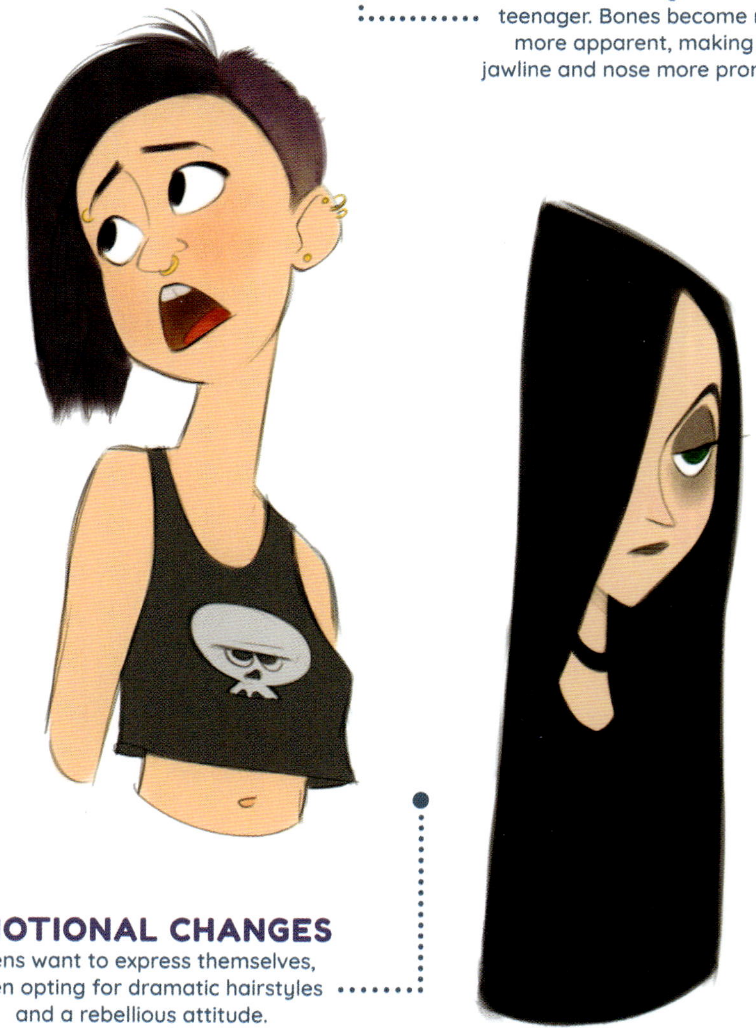

EMOTIONAL CHANGES
Teens want to express themselves, often opting for dramatic hairstyles and a rebellious attitude.

EMBARRASSMENT

One emotion that plays a big role during teenage years is embarrassment. Teens can be incredibly embarrassed by their parents and siblings, and sometimes even ashamed of themselves. Pimples, braces, sweat, hair in new places – all of this can make teens feel incredibly awkward and insecure, which you need to convey with their posture, facial expressions, and overall acting.

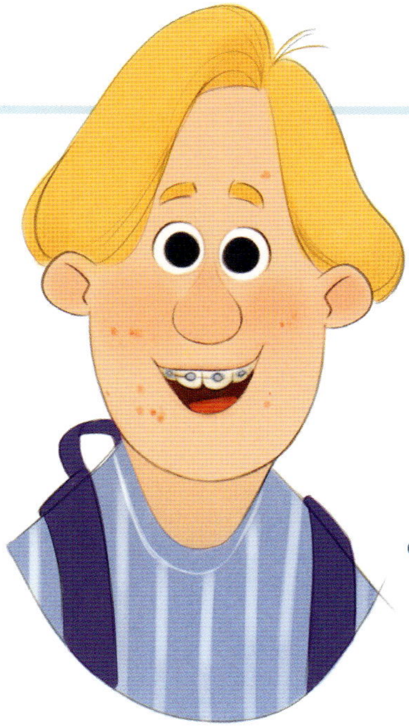

PHYSICAL CHANGES

Teens are often subject to braces and acne. Such details will make your character relatable.

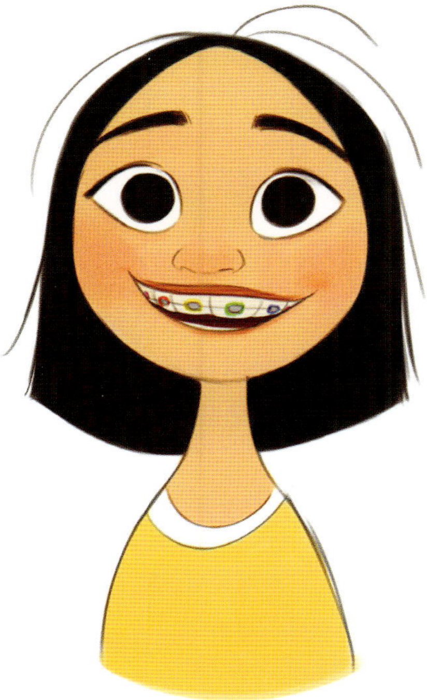

Braces may not be fun to wear, but they can be a fun design detail that adds awkward charm to a character's smile.

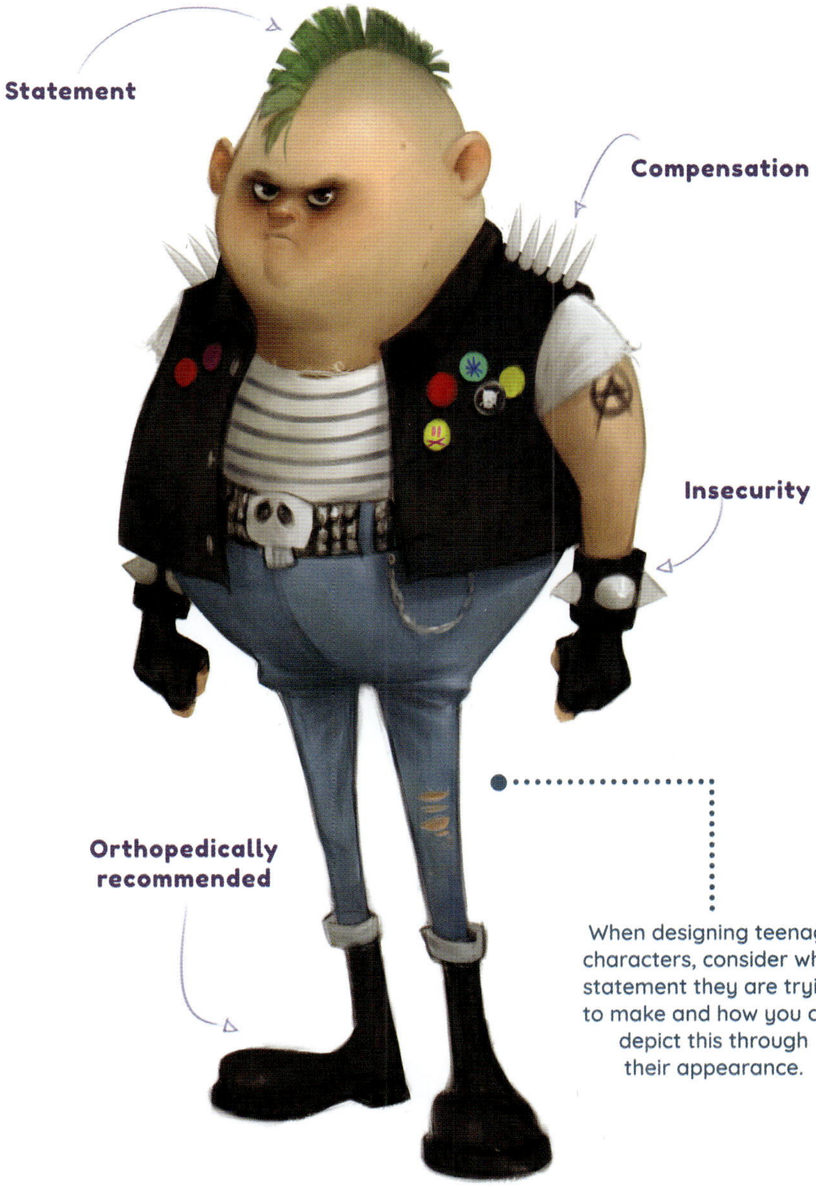

When designing teenage characters, consider what statement they are trying to make and how you can depict this through their appearance.

ADULT CHARACTERS

Tom van Rheenen

RESPONSIBILITIES

Next up is adulthood. There are two major changes that come when growing from teen to adult. Firstly, there is often a transition in lifestyle – moving from a life of play and party into a life of work and responsibilities. No longer supported by their parents, twenty-somethings need to look for an apartment and a job to pay the rent and bills. Many start to focus on starting a family or advancing in their career, both of which can result in joy, but also tiredness. All these responsibilities can be very stressful, affecting a person's mood. Adults tend to be more tired, less playful and frivolous, and less able to experience the same level of enthusiasm and wonder that children feel toward life.

BODY CHANGES

The second major change adults face is weight gain. Once the body is done growing lengthways, it starts looking for different directions to explore. This is due to a slowing-down of the metabolism. However, adults are also more muscular compared to teens. As fat and muscle becomes more emphasized, adults start to show a bigger difference in appearance based on the individual make-up of their bodies. As adults gain weight, the fat will sit on different parts of the body, resulting in a greater variety of body shapes.

Adult features also become more pronounced, with features like a crooked nose or sharp jawline becoming more apparent. Play around with more plane changes in the face and introduce sharper angles.

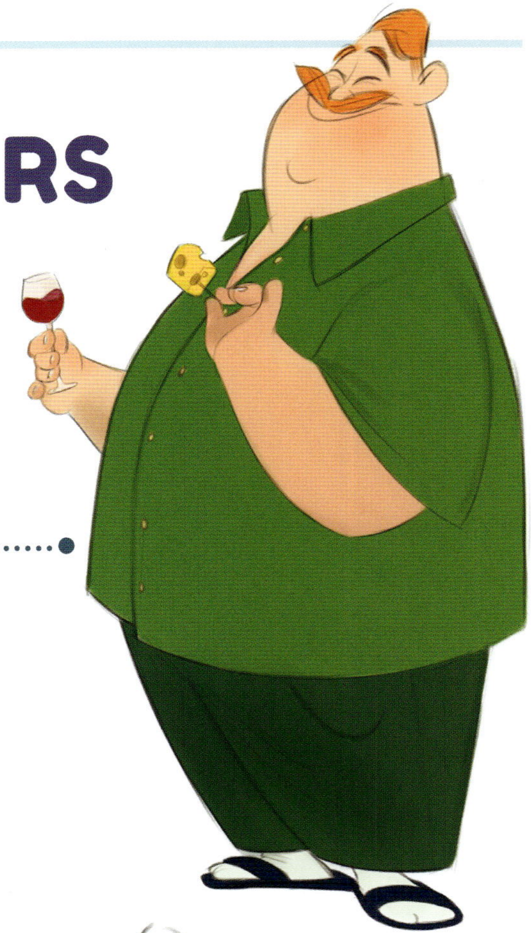

Adults are often portrayed as being less expressive and more boring than children, but they can still be fun characters, with more grown-up tastes and interests to explore.

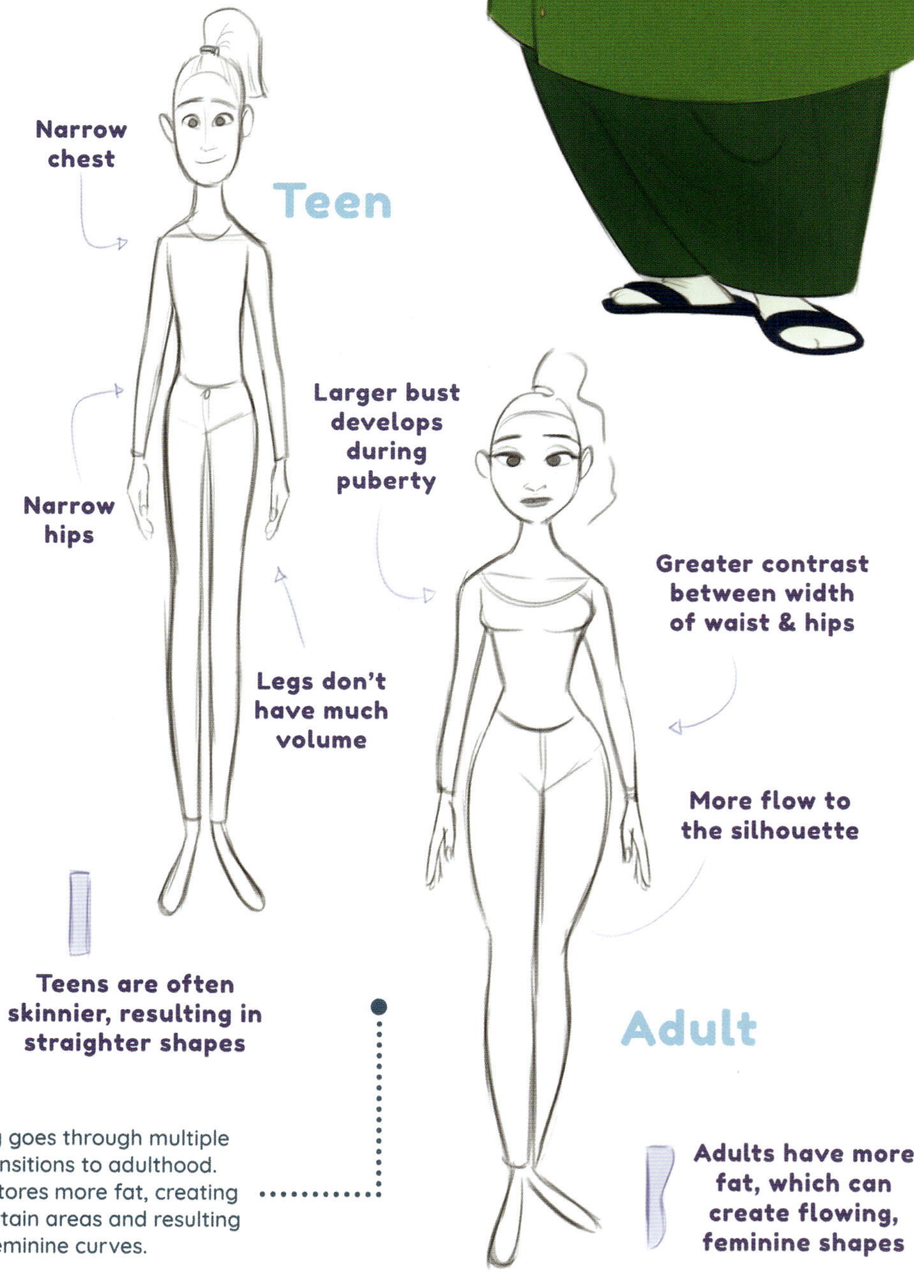

The teenage body goes through multiple changes as it transitions to adulthood. The female body stores more fat, creating more volume in certain areas and resulting in more feminine curves.

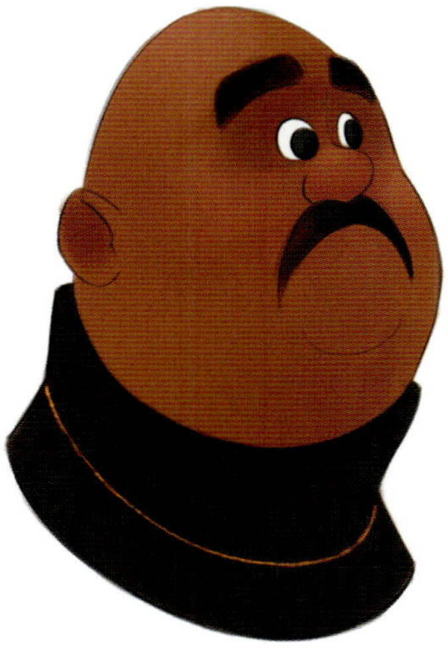

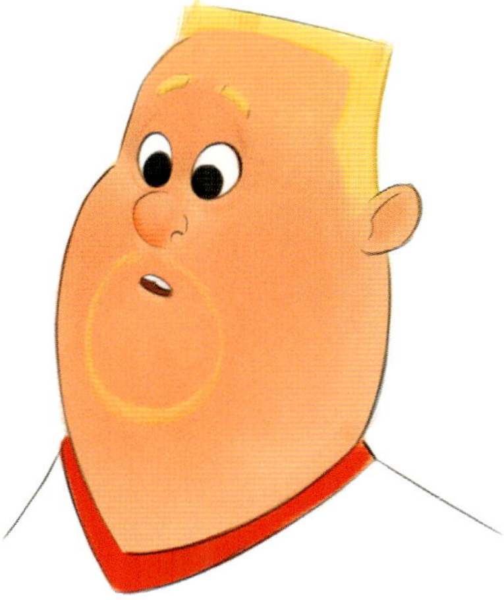

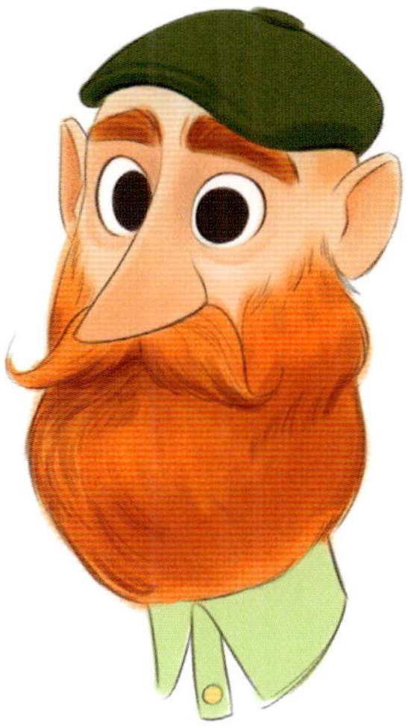

Men start to grow facial hair as they transition into adulthood. Beards are a great feature for giving your character more personality.

You can use clothing and style to convey a lot about a character's hobbies, lifestyle, and personality. How do they spend their free time? How have the routines of adulthood influenced them?

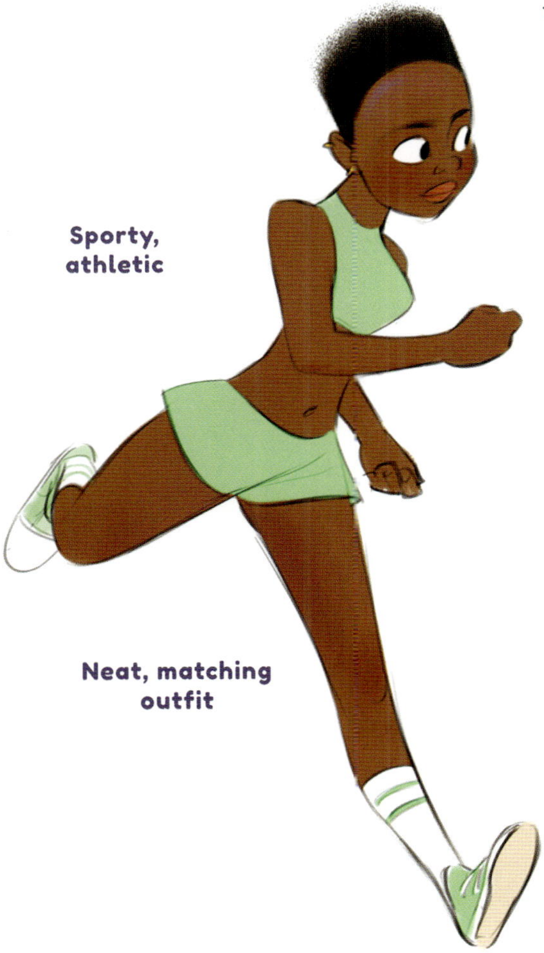

Sporty, athletic

Neat, matching outfit

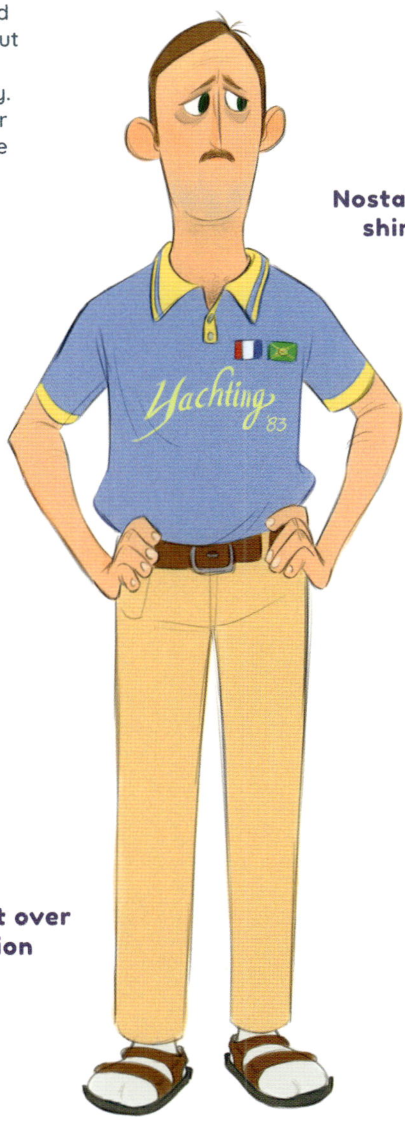

Nostalgic shirt

Comfort over fashion

ELDERLY CHARACTERS

Tom van Rheenen

SIGNS OF THE TIMES

The skin loses elasticity as the body ages, meaning wrinkles set in more permanently and the skin starts to sag. The skin also becomes thinner and starts to hang more loosely. You can see this most around the bones that sit closest to the surface, for example in the fingers, knees, and around the cheekbones and nose. Also, the nose and ears keep growing throughout the body's lifespan, so you can push these features in your character design.

As the body ages, muscles tend to become weaker, which can result in a hunched posture and unsteady, hesitant movement. As the body weakens, some older adults become more dependent on their surroundings, be it friends and relatives, or supportive items, such as walking sticks or false teeth. This dependence can lead to insecurity as seniors recognize their own frailty and ill health, but keep in mind that the aging process affects each person's mind and body differently.

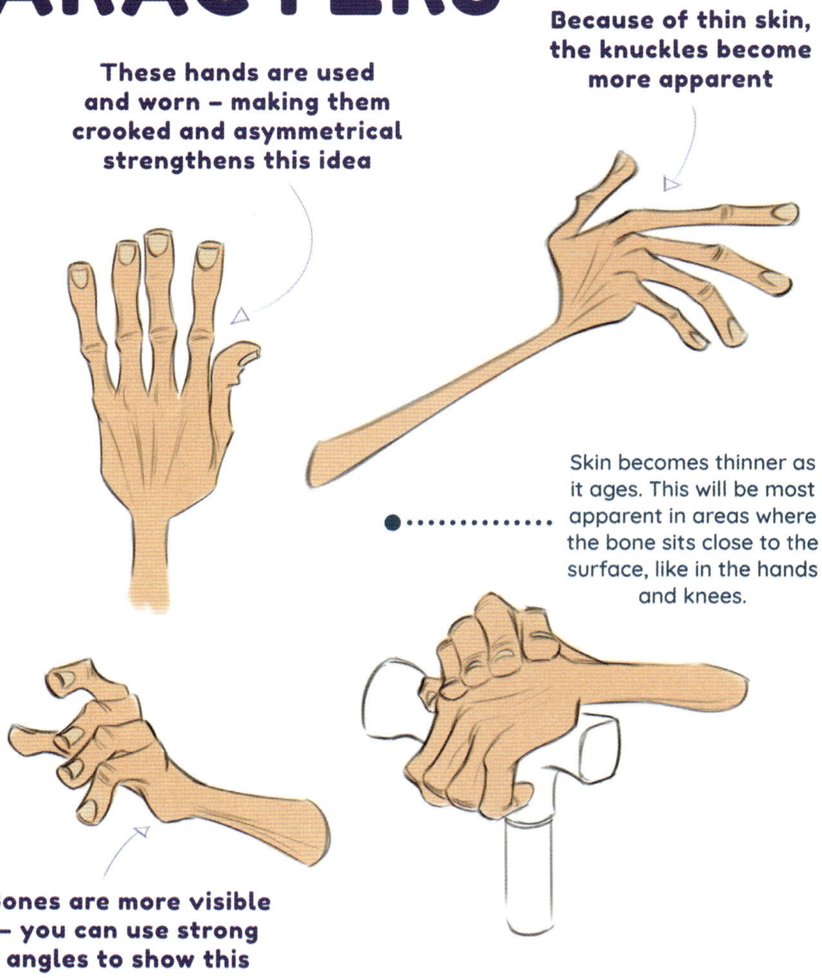

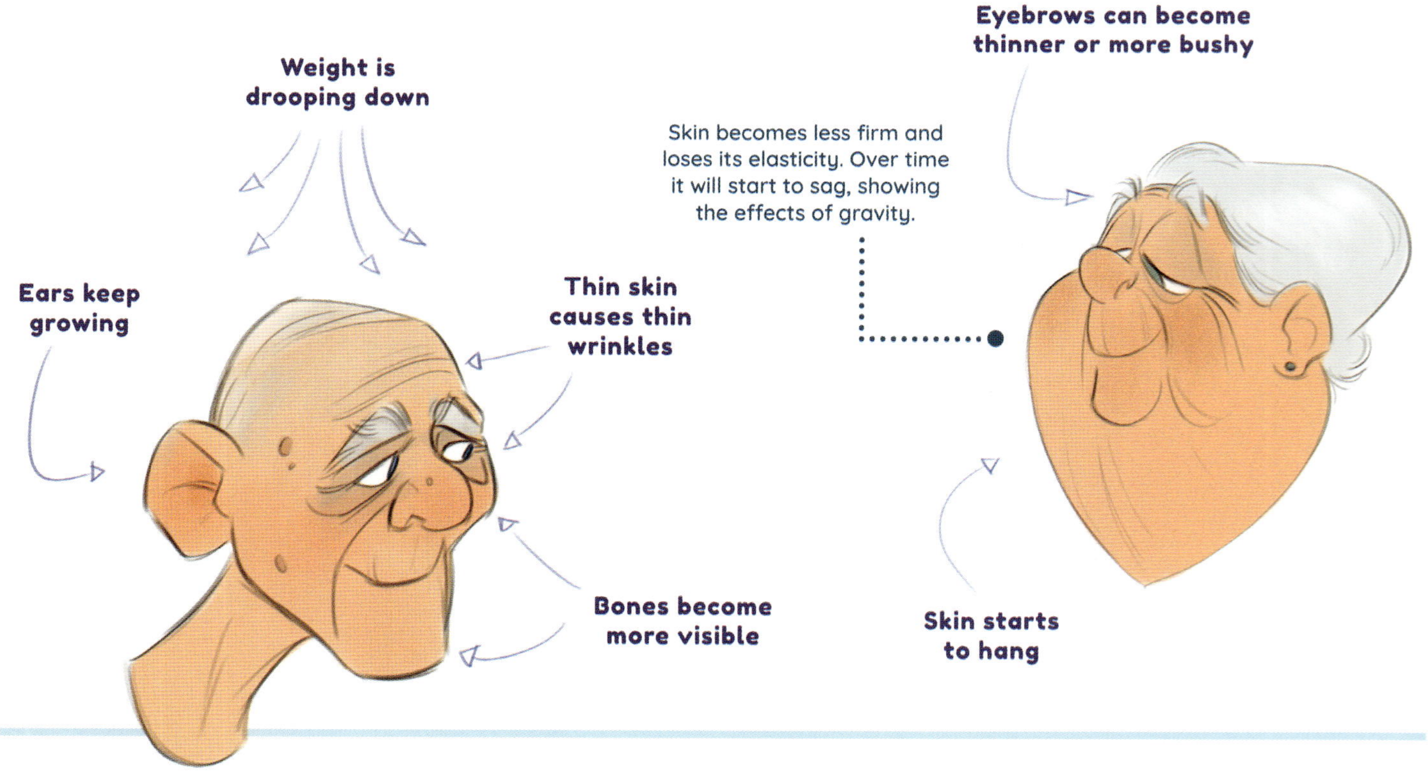

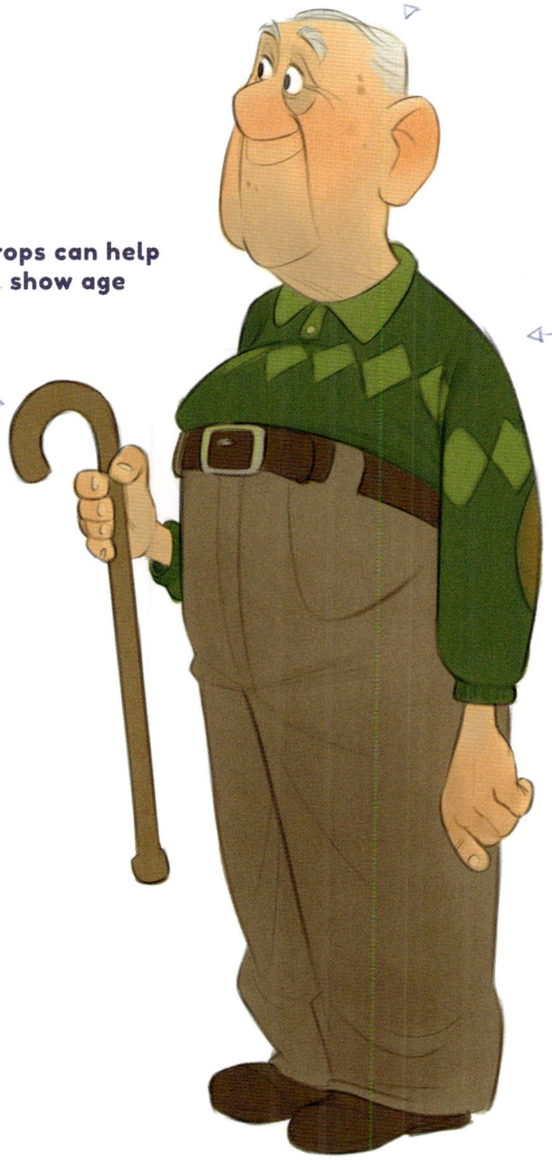

Use posture to depict the age of an elderly character by making the spine more hunched or crooked.

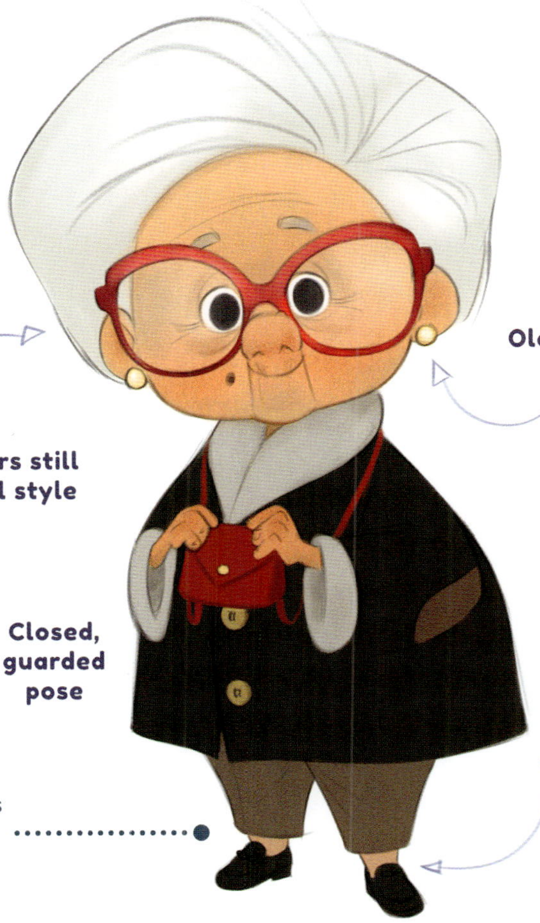

The body shrinks as it grows older, making some people appear more compact.

CASE STUDY: THE LIBRARIAN

Tom van Rheenen

Now you have read about the different ways to communicate the age of a character, let's use this knowledge to design a character at different points over the course of their lifetime.

Meet Ralph, an introverted librarian. Ralph enjoys a quiet life with no crazy heroics, and is all too familiar with the insecurities many experience. He is shy and does not know how to connect very well with the people around him. He has found solace in books and could not have wished for a better environment in which to spend his days than a quiet library.

Ralph has a very solitary nature and prefers to be alone. He loves the night as it is quiet and the perfect time to get lost in his books. He also keeps a very sharp eye on anyone in the library, making sure nobody makes a sound. These qualities might remind you of an owl, another solitary nocturnal creature defined by its sharp eyes and sensitivity to sound. Ralph's design is imbued with owl-like features, including bushy eyebrows, a sharp, beak-like nose, and large eyes. His neck is obscured by a high collar, again a reflection of an owl's hidden neck and posture. Yet while owls tend to have a strong, compact shape, Ralph has long, thin legs to make him look more frail and insecure. His library days provide the starting point for his design, as it is this life stage that allows these owl-like features to show the most.

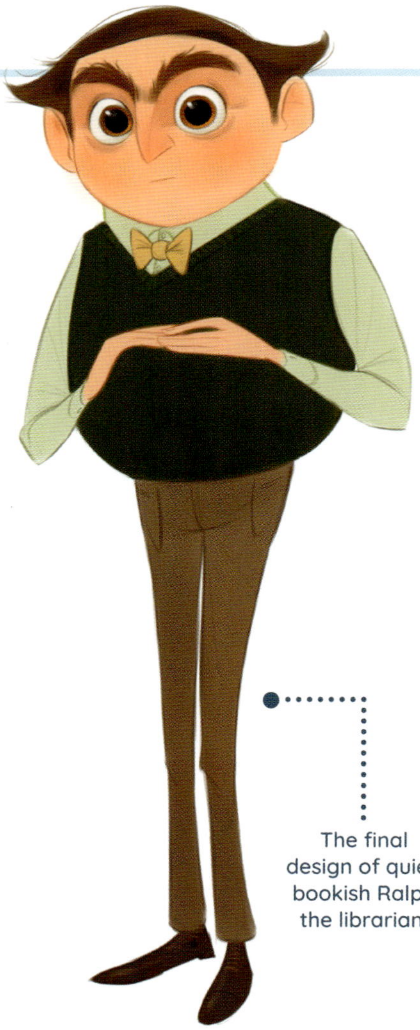

The final design of quiet, bookish Ralph the librarian.

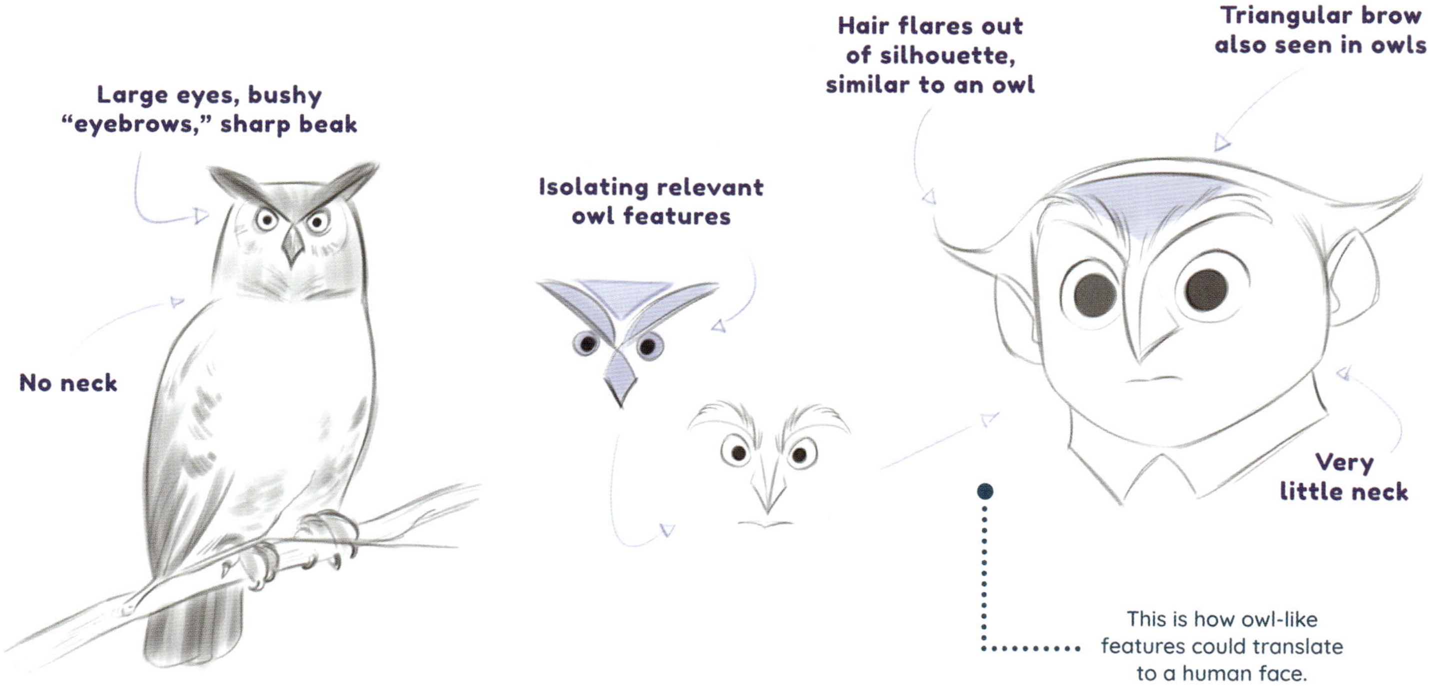

This is how owl-like features could translate to a human face.

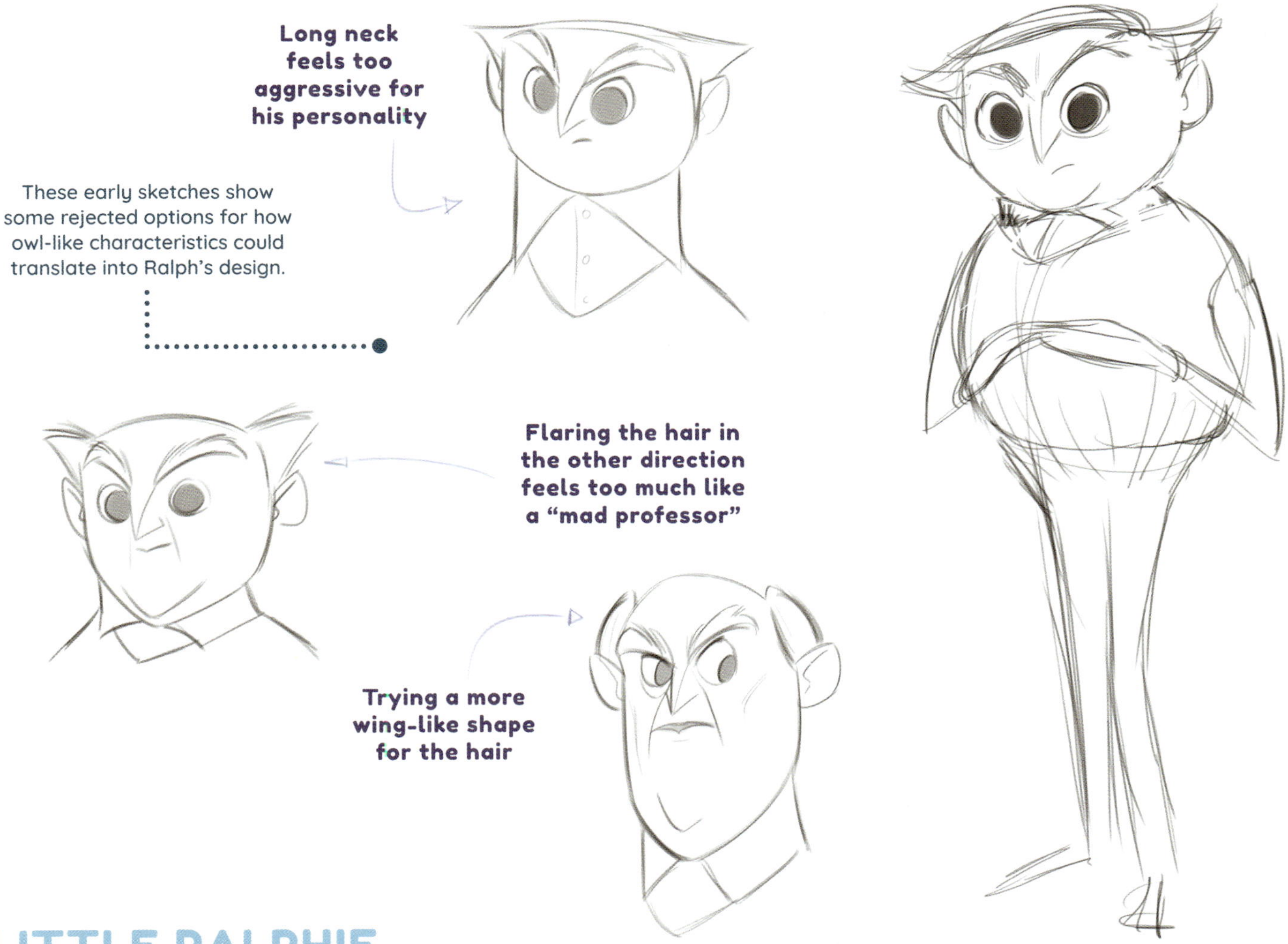

LITTLE RALPHIE

The challenge comes in translating Ralph's owl-like features onto his infant self. His sharp beak-like nose will look odd and out of place when put on a cute, chubby baby. The key is finding a balance and hinting at those features, while keeping the proportions and angles believable for a baby. Here the sharpness and the presence of the nose bridge are reduced, though there is a still a slight angle, so you can tell it is not a typical baby nose.

It can help to give your character a few iconic features that can be repeated throughout the different stages of their life. This could be a ridiculous hairstyle or hair color, a mole or birthmark, or simply something that will let the audience know immediately that this is the same character. Ralph's tufty, owl-like hairstyle is a feature that can be repeated throughout his life. Babies often have a few strands of hair on top of their head, which lends itself perfectly to two strands that fit Ralph's owl-like hairstyle.

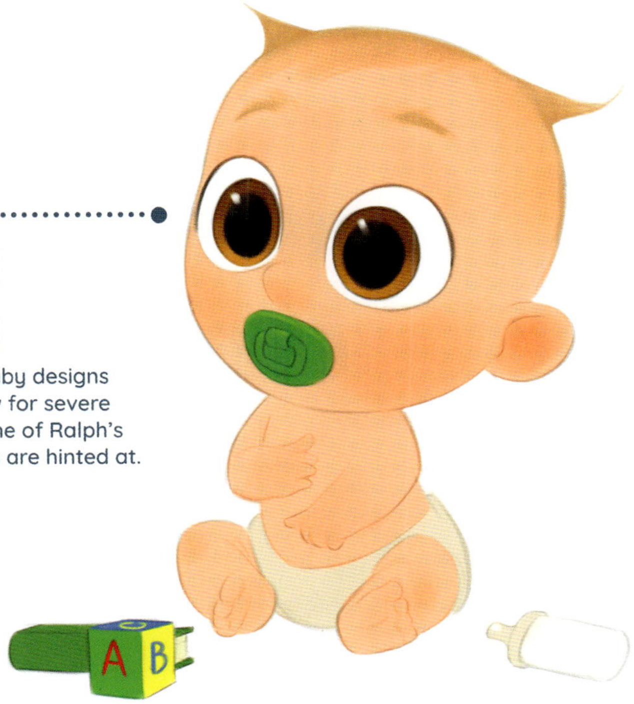

Although baby designs do not allow for severe features, some of Ralph's owlish features are hinted at.

CHILDHOOD YEARS

Children are often intrigued by their surroundings, experiencing wonder at everything they see. They like to question things and keep an open mind to the world around them. As a child, Ralph experiences similar feelings, his wonder and curiosity depicted in his wide-eyed expression. However, he also has a slightly guarded pose, shielding himself with a book, which hints at his shyness and his impending retreat into books.

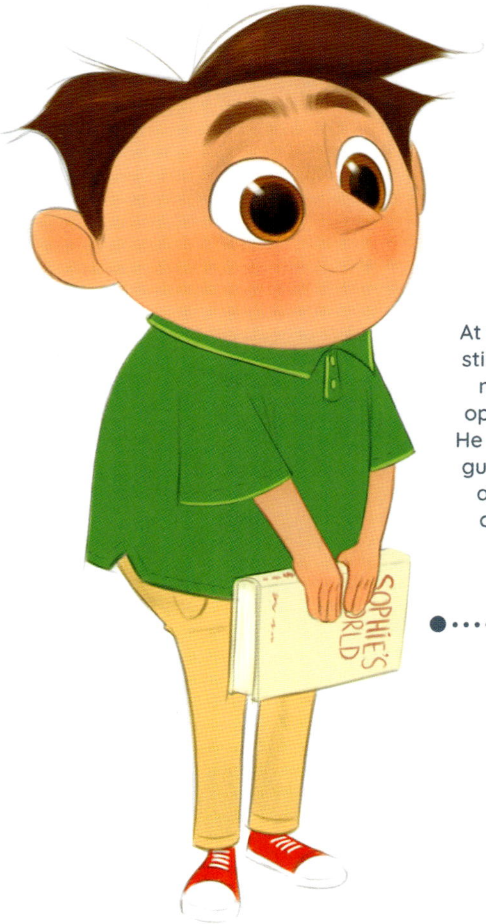

At this age Ralph is still quite innocent, naive, and very open to the world. He is already a little guarded, however, as shown by his closed posture.

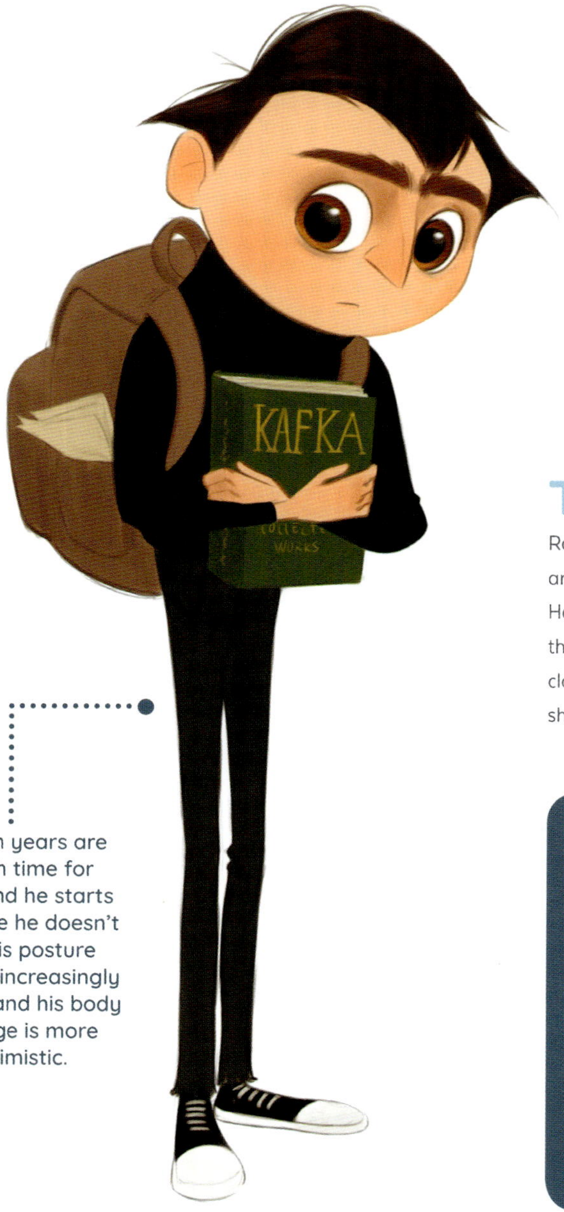

The teen years are a tough time for Ralph, and he starts to feel like he doesn't fit in. His posture becomes increasingly guarded and his body language is more pessimistic.

TEEN RALPH

Ralph's teenage years are climactic in his struggle to connect with others. Teens are often insecure and crave validation, and it is easy to feel like an outcast. Here Ralph wears dark clothing, creating a strong value contrast and showing these years as more dramatic for him. Out of all the stages of his life, his teenage clothing has the most contrast. He has even decided to dye his hair a darker shade. His closed-off, guarded pose reveals his feelings of shyness and insecurity.

COLOR

Another factor that can help strengthen the consistency of a character is the color palette. Even though Ralph's clothes change throughout his life, they remain within the same palette, with an emphasis on green. Even when he wasn't wearing many clothes as a baby, the green is introduced in his pacifier. The green is desaturated as the years pass to emphasize the aging process and colors fading over time.

ADULT RALPH

Over time, Ralph's eyebrows have become thicker and a bit bushier. His features, such as his nose and jawline, have become sharper and more pronounced. His weight has changed too. Growing into his teenage years, he lost his childlike chubbiness, but now in adulthood he has gained weight again, this time more concentrated around his belly. Additionally, his hair has become progressively thinner. As he grows older, these elements will change even more.

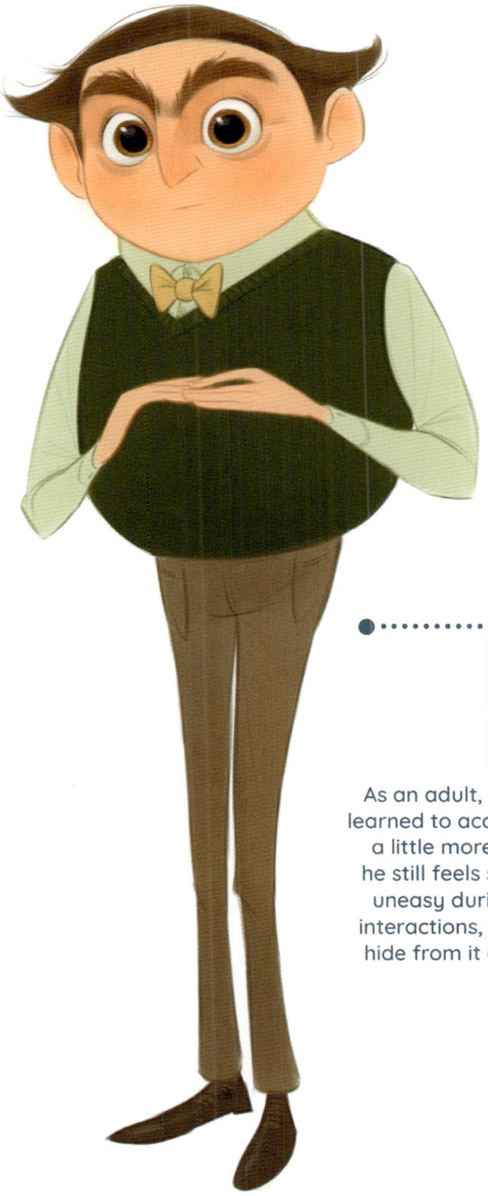

As an adult, Ralph has learned to accept himself a little more. Though he still feels somewhat uneasy during social interactions, he doesn't hide from it any more.

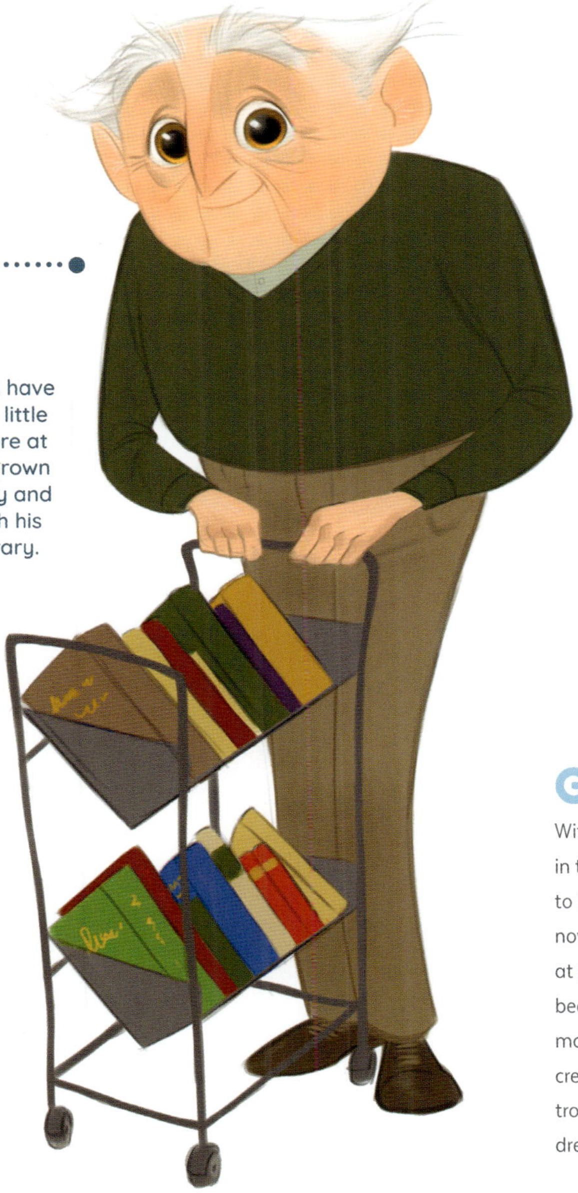

His older years have made Ralph a little softer and more at ease. He has grown psychologically and is content with his life at the library.

GOOD OL' RALPH

With the years, Ralph has come to accept who he is and has embraced his place in the library. He is more soft-tempered, he wants less of people, he is less eager to be accepted, and he is less tortured by the feeling that he is different. Ralph now walks through the library with a calm smile on his face, feeling at home and at peace. He has lost most of the hair on top of his head, but his eyebrows have become bushier. Additionally, his posture has become more hunched, his chest more boxy and weighed down. Even though he is more frail, his wider trousers create the impression that he is more emotionally grounded. For him, wider trousers have become a fashion staple, being comfier to wear and making getting dressed much easier.

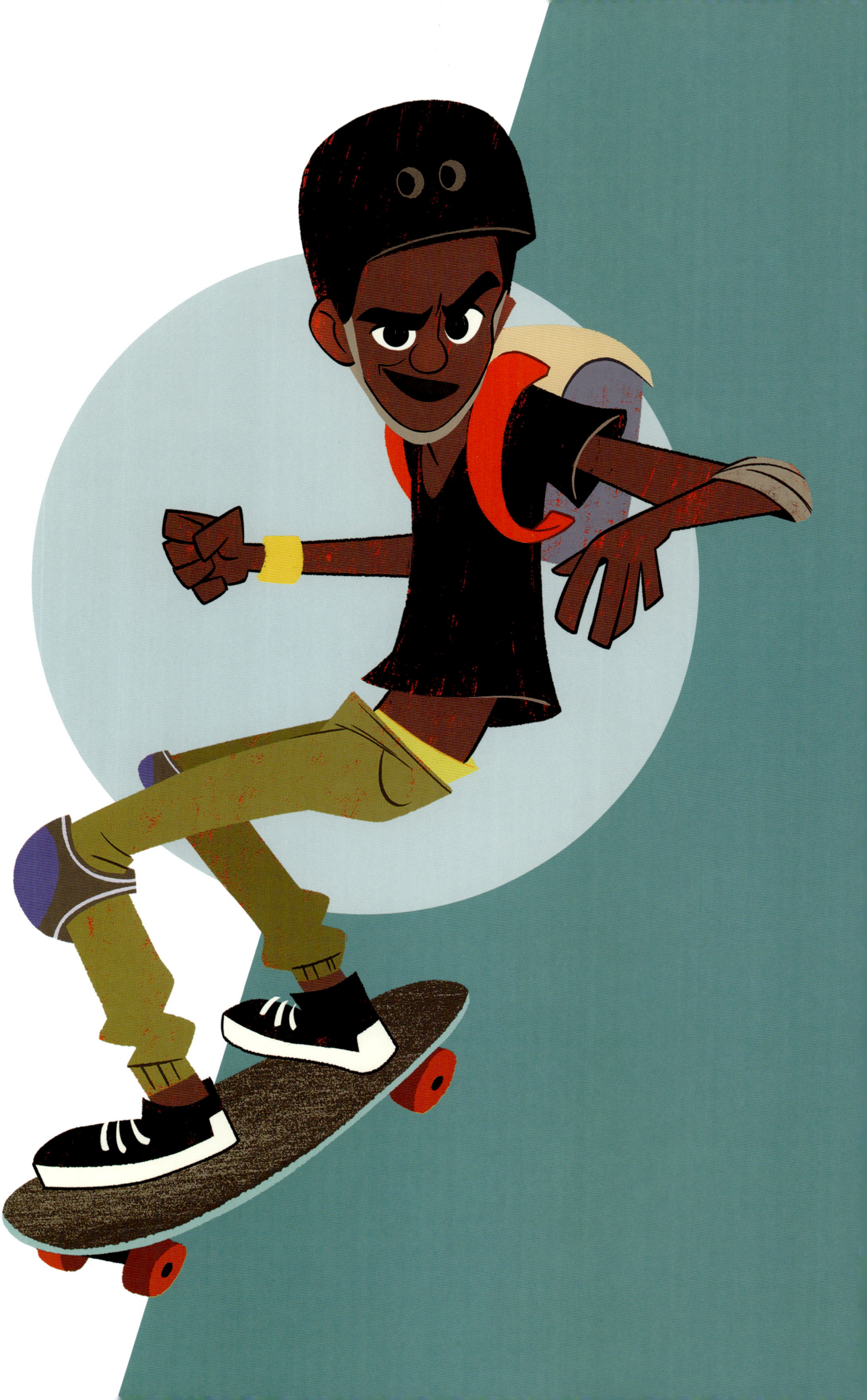

Image by Luis Gadea

ACCESSORIES

OVERVIEW
PAGE 212

COSTUME LIBRARY
PAGE 216

HAIRSTYLES LIBRARY
PAGE 224

PROPS LIBRARY
PAGE 232

OVERVIEW

Guilherme Franco

You might think of accessories such as props, costumes, and hairstyles as toppings on a cake – elements that provide a character with an extra level of detail. However, they can be a lot more than that. When linked to a character's story, accessories, hairstyles (see page 224), facial hair, and clothes add a different **level of depth** that can amplify the viewer's perception of a character.

Deciding what accessories to add to a character and their costume is never an easy task. As you will have gathered already, the first step is **research**. After brainstorming your initial ideas or receiving the brief, research enables you to expand your visual library on the subject matter you are going to draw. You may find you accidentally come across elements you had not initially thought of, which can help you create unique connections and more original designs.

The less you know about a topic, the more time you should spend researching and learning about it. When specifically researching clothes and accessories for a character, have a keen eye for detail and take note of ornaments, patterns, and textures that will help you to accurately represent a prop and prevent it from looking too simple or misplaced. Good observation is key to understanding the subject you need to draw, and is a skill you can only attain through practice. It takes time to be able to accurately recreate the elements you see in your research.

When it comes to adding clothing, hair, and props to your characters, think about their **hierarchy of importance**. It is easy to become overwhelmed by references and to end up choosing too many or too few accessories, which can harm the readability of your character. To avoid this, start by choosing a **main prop** that is the most meaningful or important to your character and their story – the one that defines them the most. Once this is chosen, you can start on the **secondary accessories** – props that are still meaningful but do not carry the same emotional weight as the main one. After these, you can add **tertiary accessories** that are not necessarily meaningful, but are there for **aesthetic reasons** or to **support the silhouette**. Choosing one accessory for each of these hierarchical levels will give you three accessories to start with, and sometimes that is more than enough. Always keep an eye on the overall flow and readability of the design to ensure the props do not break the initial structure of the character. They should maintain the momentum of the character's movement and respond accordingly to their actions.

As an example, imagine a character in a world where vampires are treated like pests and humans need to hire professionals to deal with these infestations. For most exterminators, this is just a routine job, and they are unmoved by the sight of vampires crawling through old barns or hiding in dusty attics. This character, however, is terrified of vampires. After graduating from college, she finds herself having to work for her father's vampire extermination company, Vamps-B-Gone, which leads to extremely humorous events. Her accessories and equipment need to show her fearfulness and how she always over-protects herself for the inevitable encounters with vampires in her line of work.

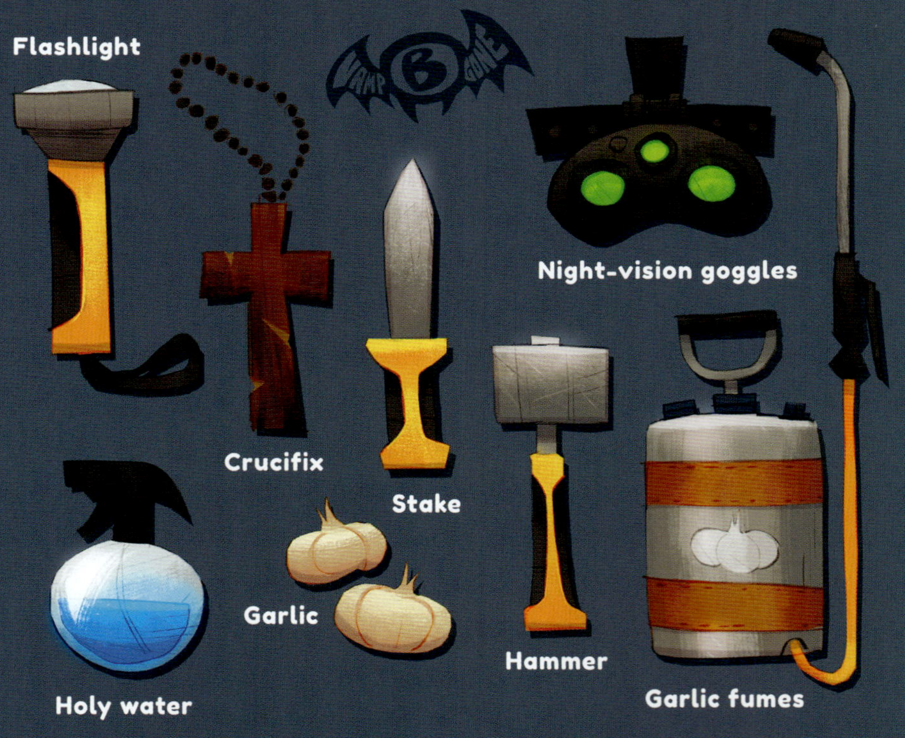

Consider what props will tell a character's story. For this character, who is a vampire exterminator, old vampire-killing devices have been reimagined as modern-day tools. Some items, however, remain the same throughout the ages.

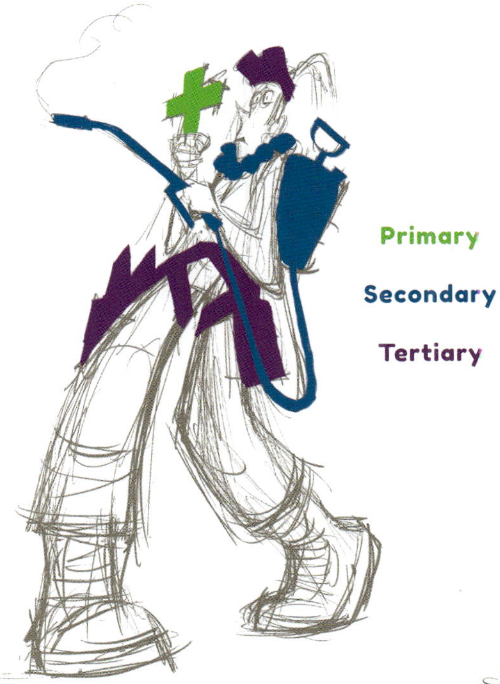

Thinking about the hierarchy of accessories will help you when creating the first roughs of your character. Write down a few keywords to help you sketch the pose and expression.

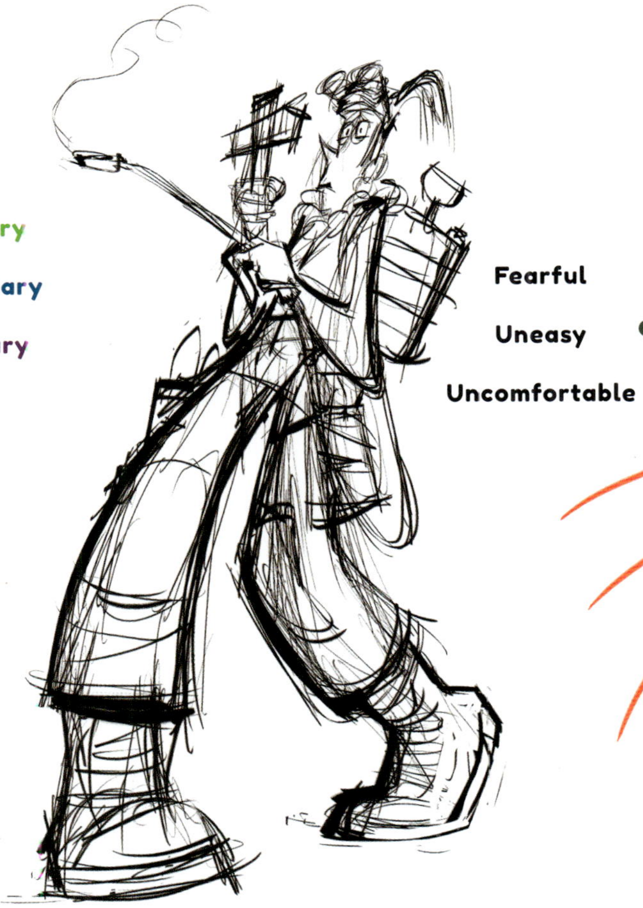

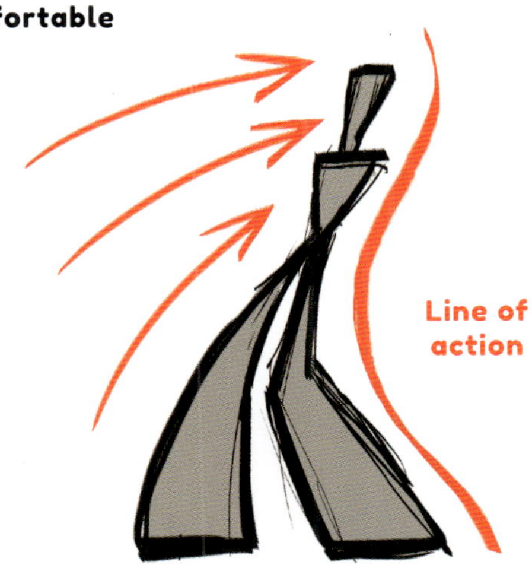

Clean up the lines to check if the silhouette is working. The main accessory (the crucifix) can be seen even at this early stage and is a focal point of the design.

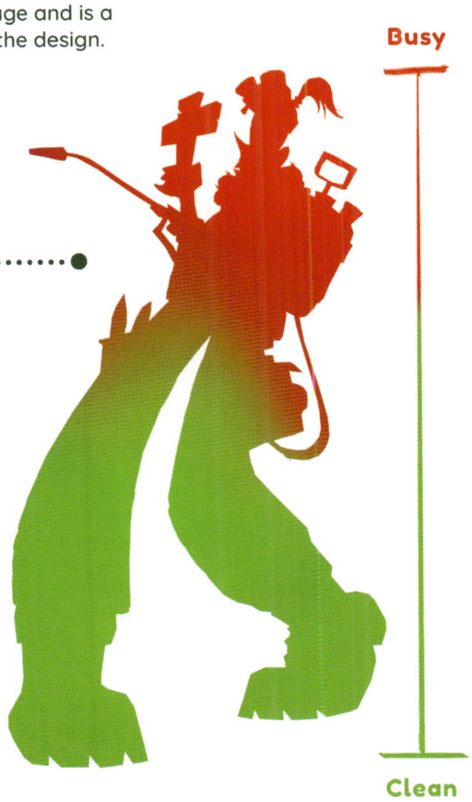

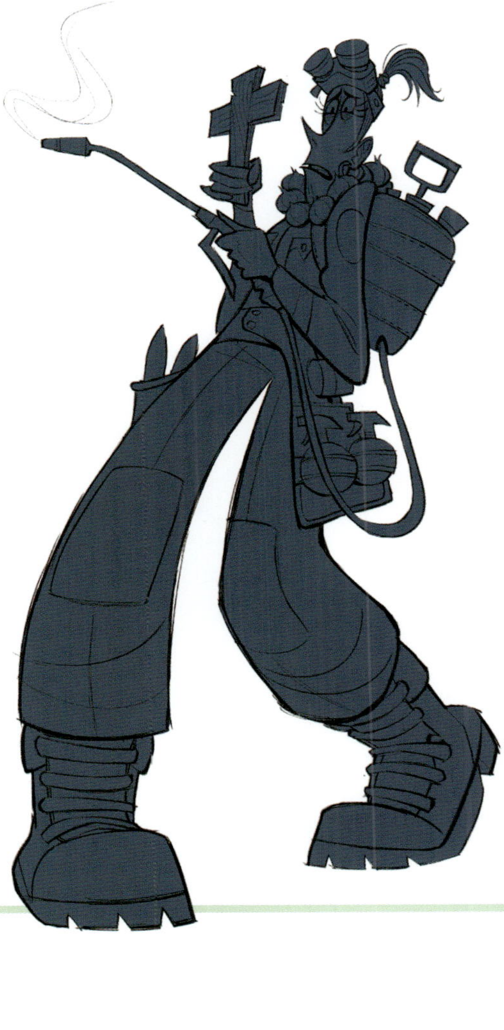

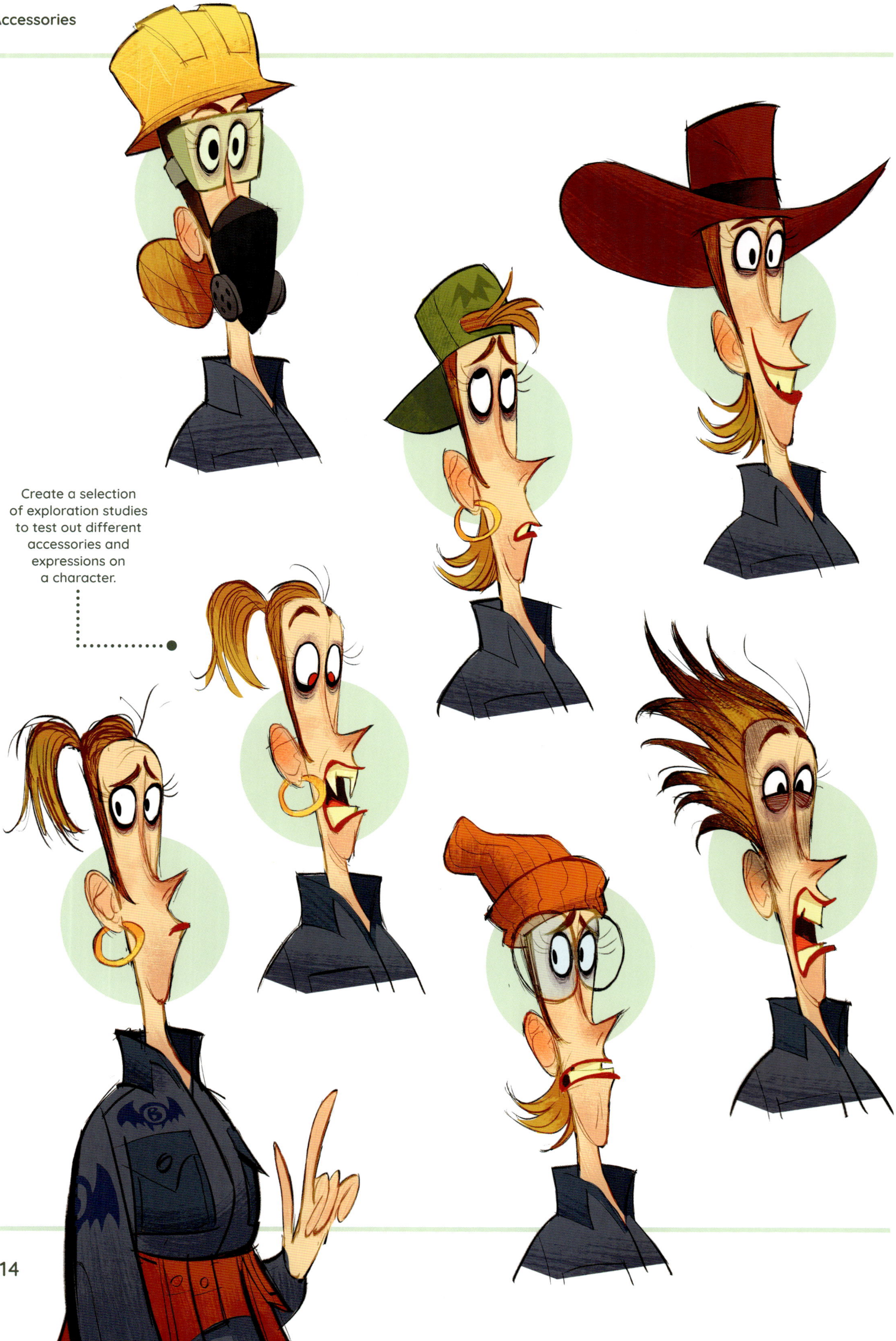

Create a selection of exploration studies to test out different accessories and expressions on a character.

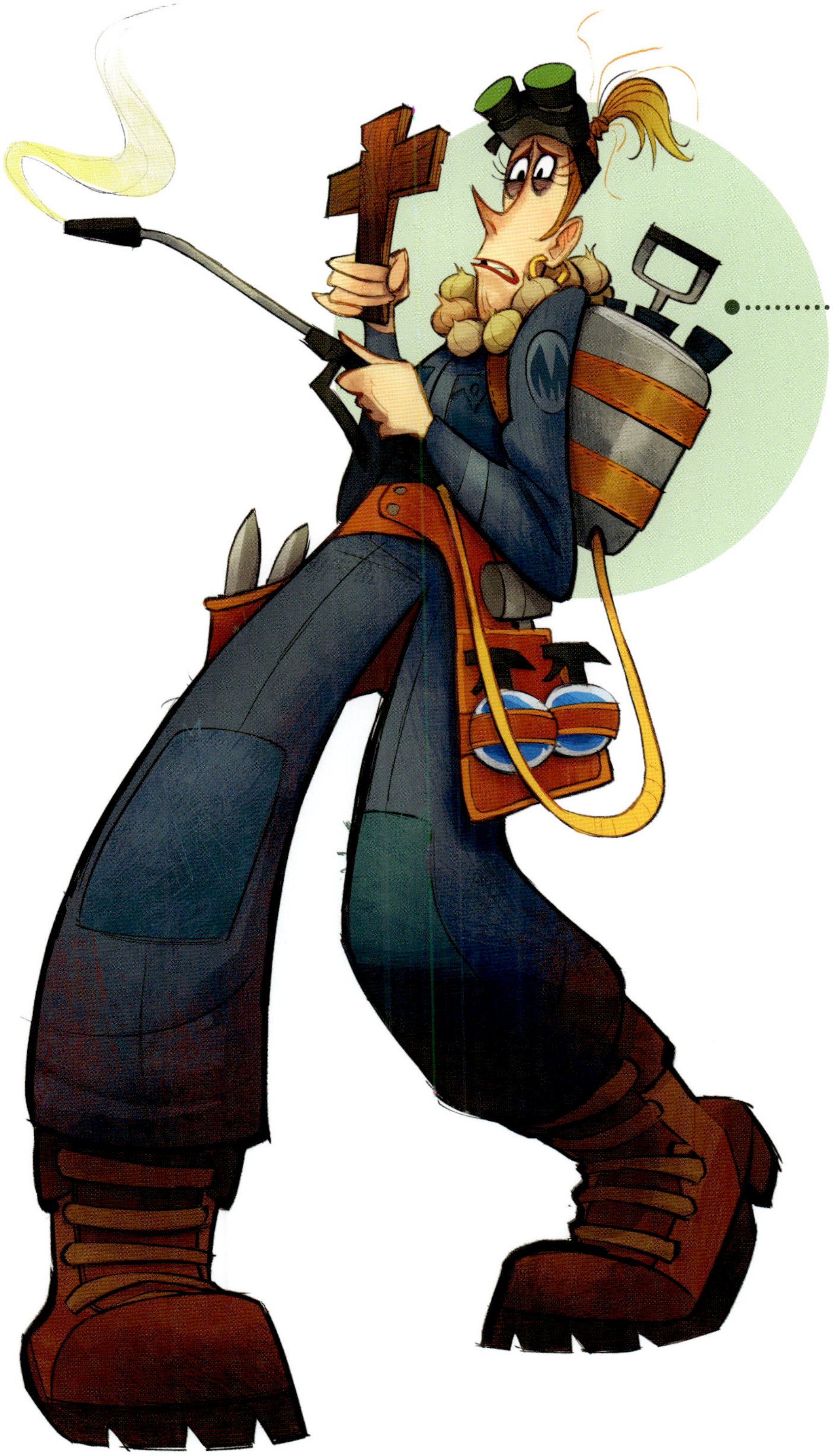

The crucifix is the oldest of the character's accessories, maybe a family heirloom, and contrasts with her more modern tools.

Without her accessories, the character feels generic and completely powerless. The whole idea of the character over-protecting herself is lost.

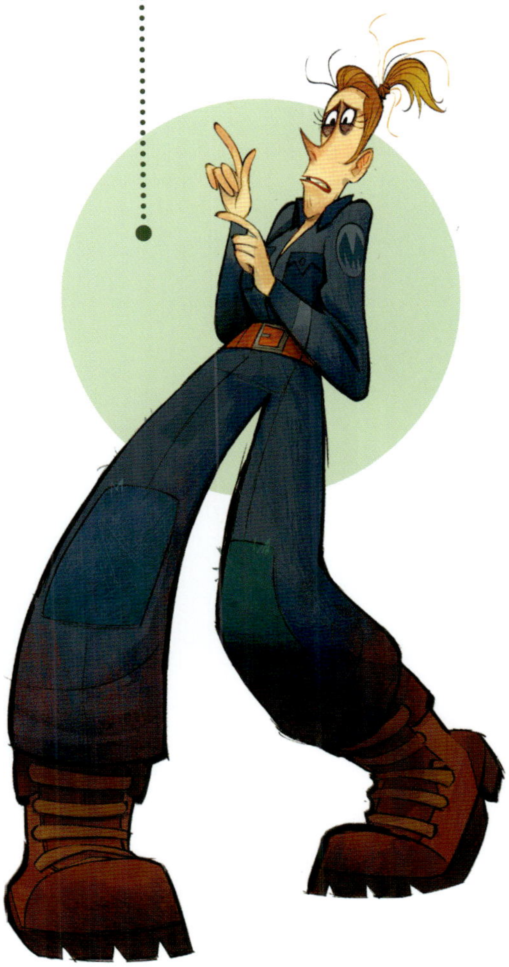

COSTUME LIBRARY

Kenneth Anderson

Character costumes should serve a number of purposes: to tell the audience something about who a character is (status, wealth, occupation), where a character is (time, place, and setting), and add visual interest to a design. The clever use of costume can manipulate a character's silhouette, shape language, and form.

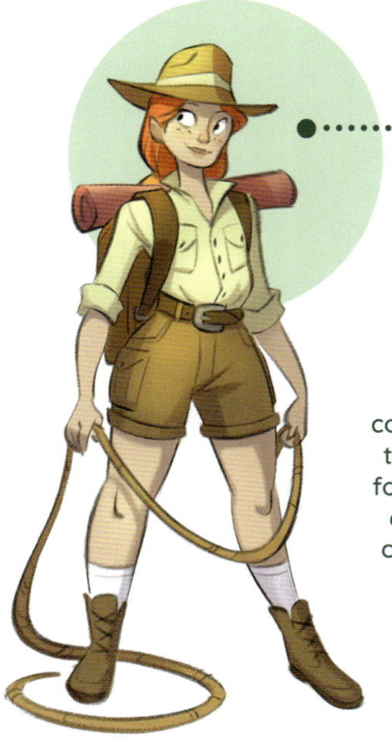

This character's costume immediately tells us she is ready for adventure, taking cues from popular culture and real-life adventure attire.

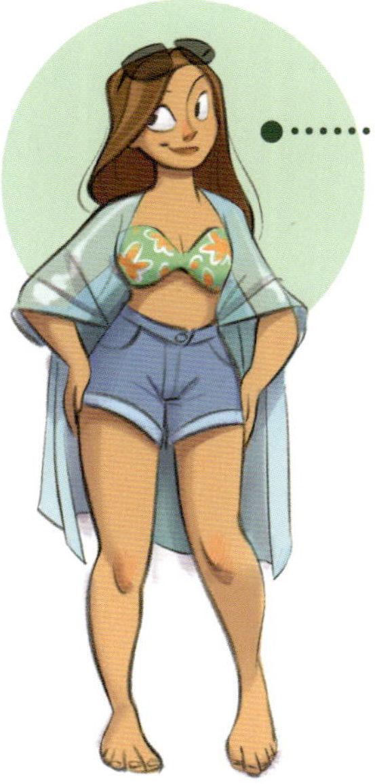

A character's outfit must be practical to their environment and tell the story. In this case it should be obvious the character is going to the beach.

Pyjamas come in many different forms – the type a character wears will say something about who they are.

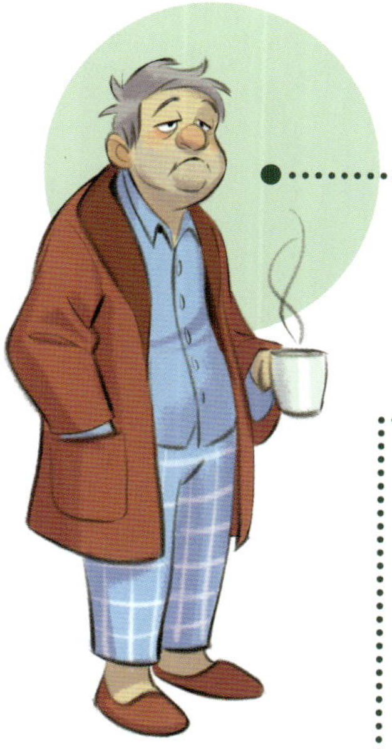

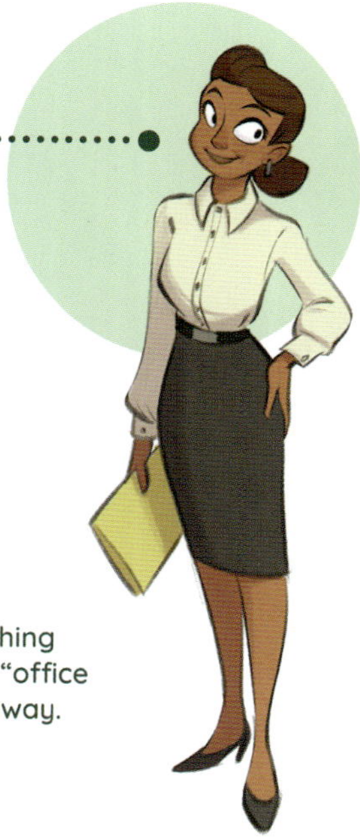

This classic clothing combination says "office wear" straight away.

When popular culture has defined a particular archetype, such as a pirate, it is necessary to work within the "rules" while still being creative and finding ways to show the character's personality.

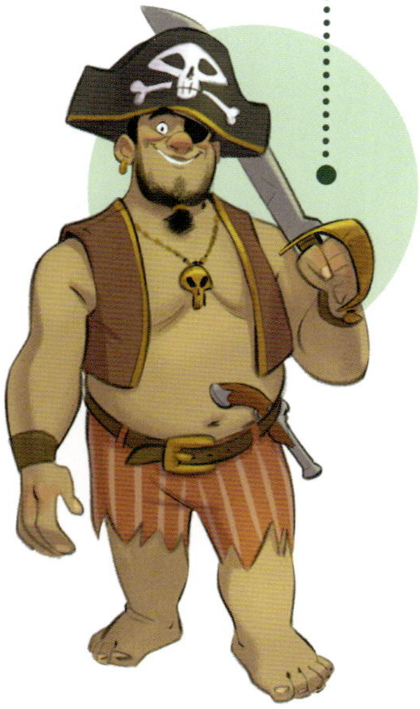

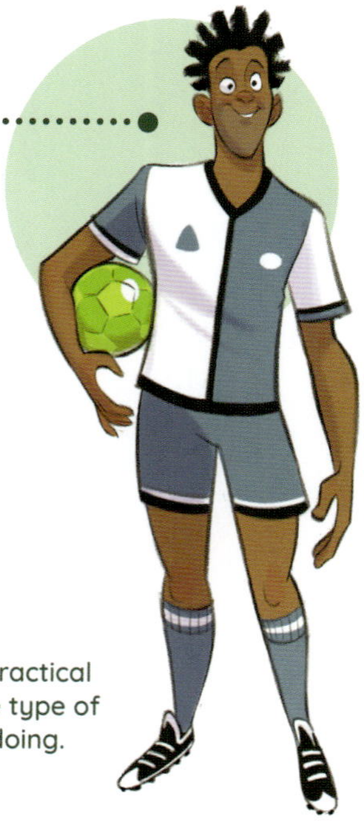

Sports clothing is extremely practical by nature and must reflect the type of actions a character will be doing.

Randy Bishop

Costuming is an important part of the design process that can sometimes be neglected. A thoughtfully designed costume can make or break a design. Think first about your character's role in the story you're telling. The costume's functionality is important, as is the way it affects your character's silhouette. If your character is an assassin who needs to go unnoticed, you might consider practical, dark clothing that won't snag on anything as the character sneaks through the night. A thoughtful approach to costume design can add a level of professionalism to your work that can set it apart.

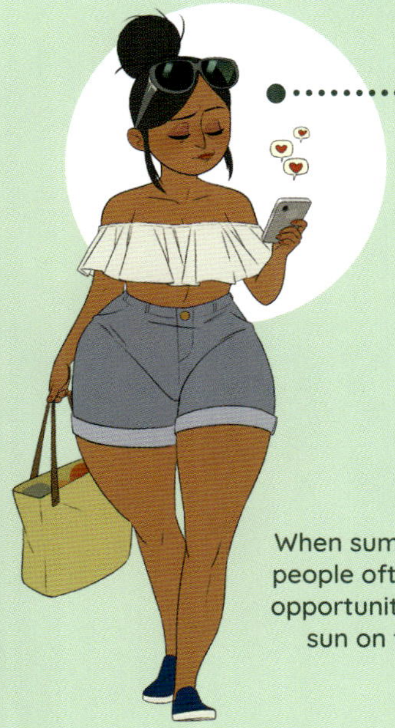

When summer comes, people often relish the opportunity to feel the sun on their skin.

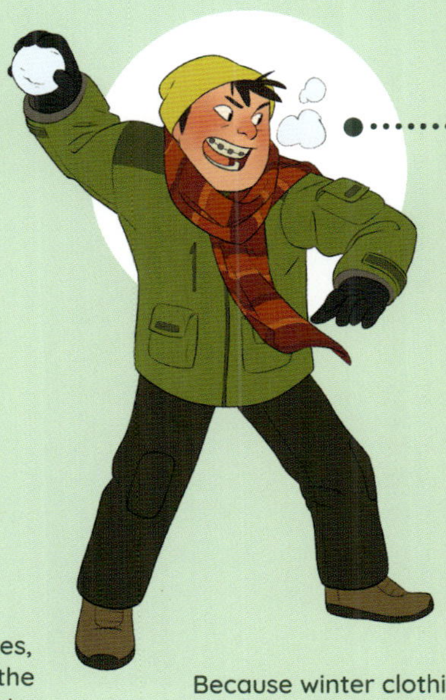

Because winter clothing tends to contain more padding and thicker materials, a character's anatomy can be almost entirely obscured.

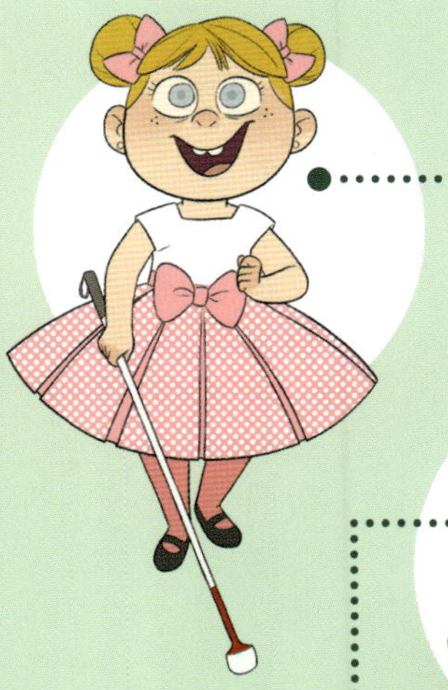

Nothing says "cute" like bows and polka dots on a dress.

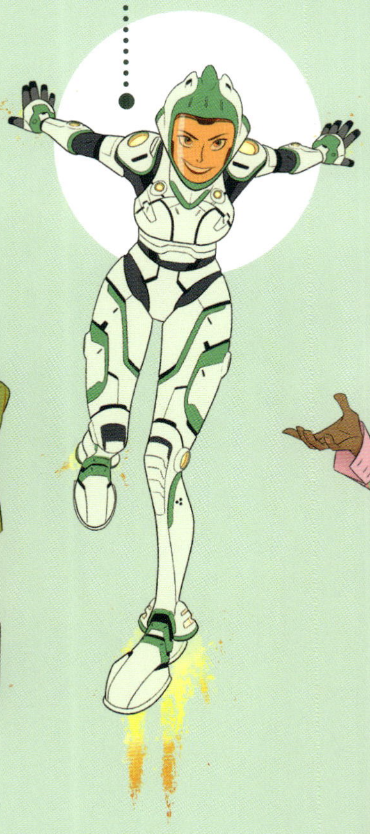

Armor is a good way to make your character appear powerful or threatening.

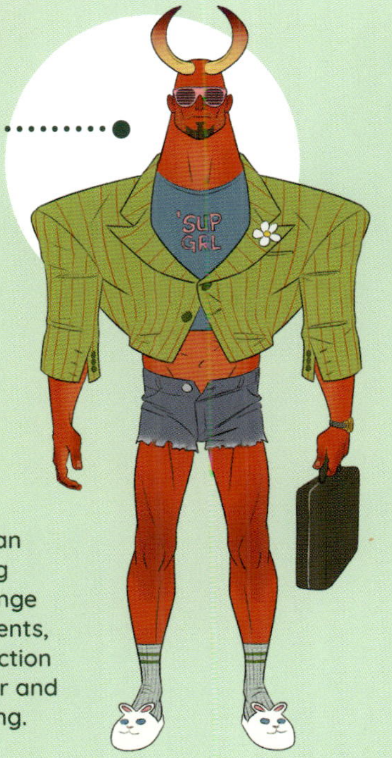

A humorous outfit can be created by using ill-fitting clothes, strange combinations of garments, or an obvious contradiction between your character and what they are wearing.

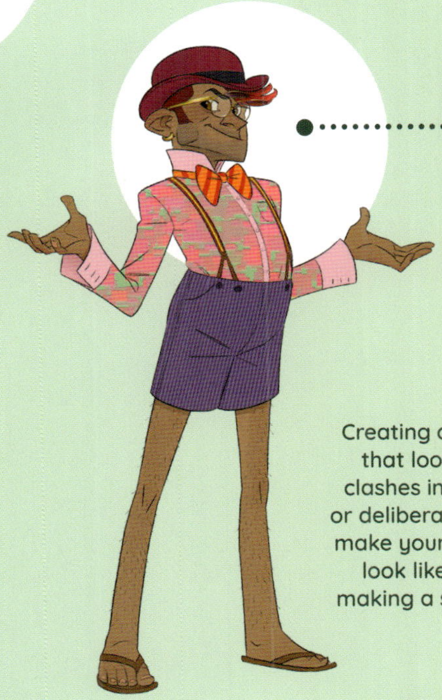

Creating a costume that looks like it clashes in a careful or deliberate way can make your character look like they're making a statement.

Luis Gadea

Costumes, like any other part of a character, can be stylized. Think of the costume like a character in itself, with personality and story. Consider the shape and silhouette you want your character to have. Can you push the shape of the costume? Try to exaggerate it if the style of the character and brief allows. Exaggerating certain aspects will add value and distinctiveness to your character, while also providing a touch of humor.

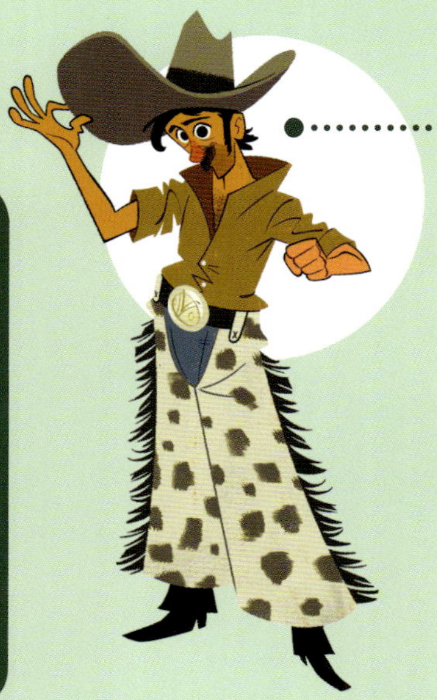

Exaggerating the cowboy's hat and chaps improves the silhouette and makes the character a little funnier. Always make sure that details like the position of the hand on the hat can be read clearly by the viewer.

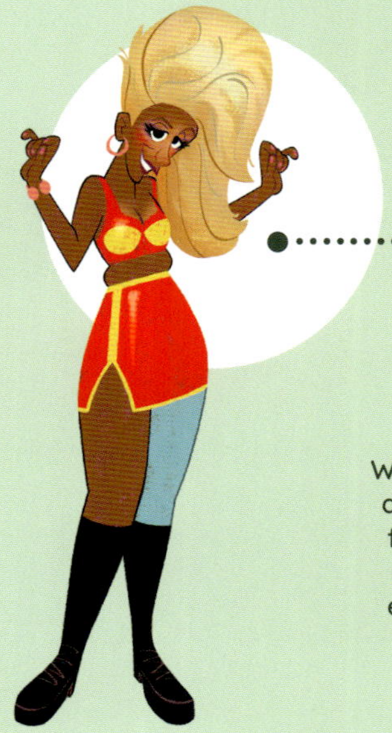

When designing a glamorous drag queen, use references for inspiration, make good use of color, and consider exaggerating the hairstyle for a bold silhouette.

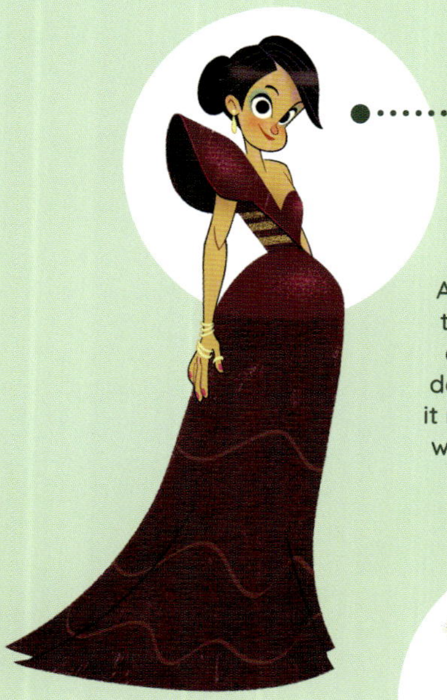

Asymmetry helps to make this design a success. The asymmetrical shape and detailing of the dress make it more interesting, while the woman is kept very simple.

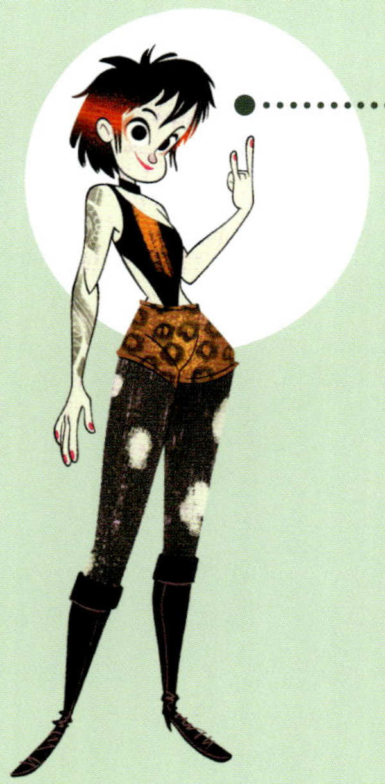

Always consider pose and how the silhouette will read. This punk rocker's outfit contains an interesting combination of textured fabrics, though the colors are limited to a few hues.

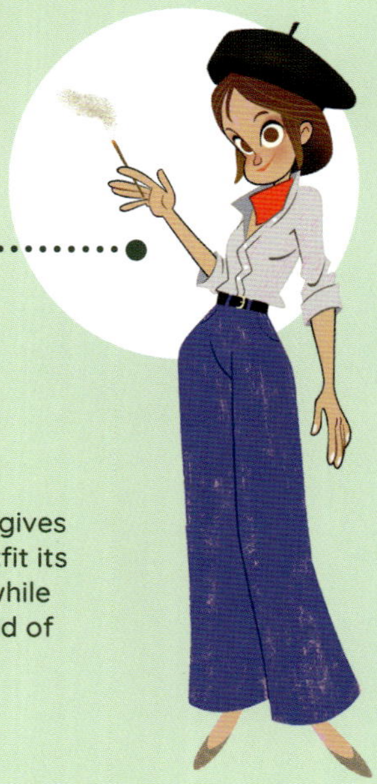

Adding a few props gives this chic Parisian outfit its finishing touches, while keeping a clear read of the silhouette.

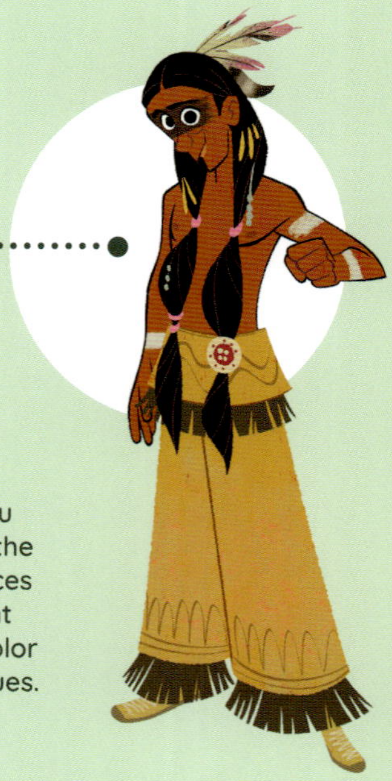

Do not feel like you have to stay within the colors your references dictate. Experiment and explore other color combinations or values.

Meybis Ruiz Cruz

Clothing can say a lot about a person and their context. Is your character rich or poor? Vain or modest? Introverted or extroverted? Do they exist now or a century ago? In medieval France or early 20th-century Shanghai? Even in the same period, outfits change from one place to the next depending on climate and culture. Research is essential when designing costumes – even more so if your subject is from another time and place. If they exist in your time and zone, observe from reality; study people on the streets and take notes.

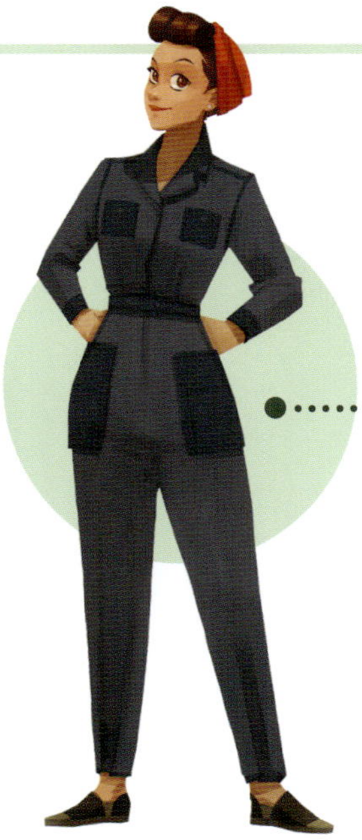

In the 1940s, many women had to start doing all kinds of jobs while men were away fighting in the war. Practicality was essential – think durable fabrics and hair pinned up or covered.

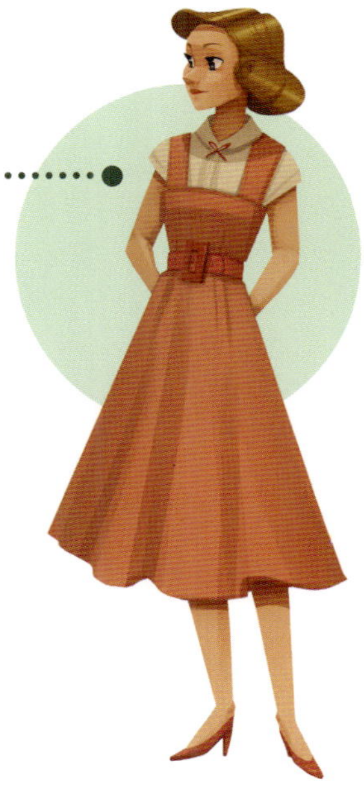

With men returned from the war, many women returned to the home. The 1950s saw a more traditional style of clothing that emphasized a feminine silhouette and used softer pastel colors.

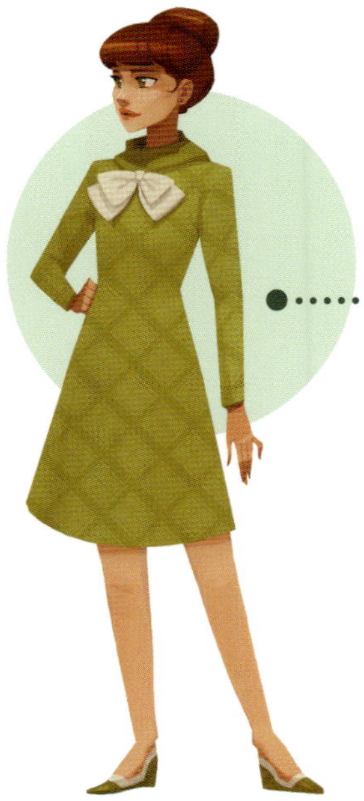

The A-line silhouette is characteristic of the 1960s, with trapeze-shaped dresses and heavy use of plaids, saturated colors, and bolder patterns.

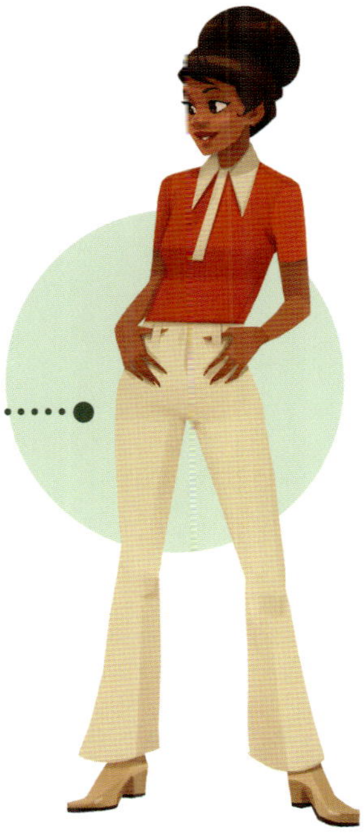

The 1970s were a time of extremely tight clothing, featuring big shirt collars and full, bell-bottom pants.

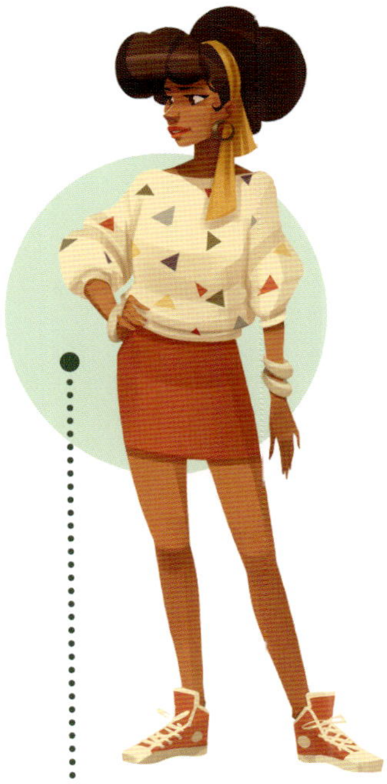

The 1980s brought bolder patterns and brighter colors, influenced by the Memphis design movement. Silhouettes changed to a more relaxed fit and everything became bigger, including the hair.

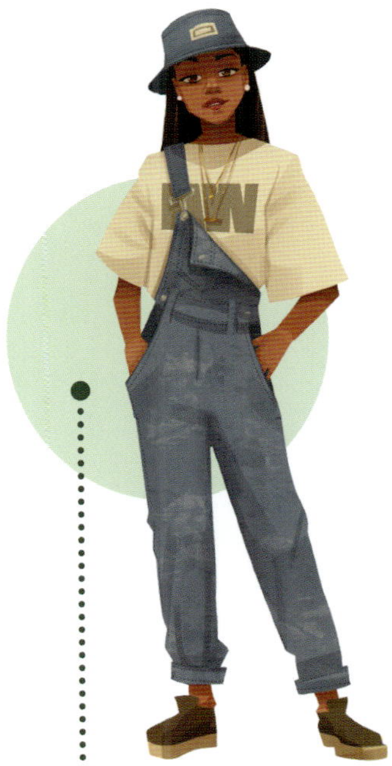

Light-wash denim dungarees, a hat, and a baggy t-shirt was a go-to look in the 1990s, often paired with jewelry and gigantic-soled shoes.

Noor Sofi

Be creative when exploring costumes. Rather than creating a generic princess outfit of a pink dress with puff sleeves, try to explore something different. A princess's outfit could be inspired by an ancient tiger tribe that her kingdom descends from, or perhaps she is a goth princess who only wears black. Let your character's costume say something specific about who they are as an individual.

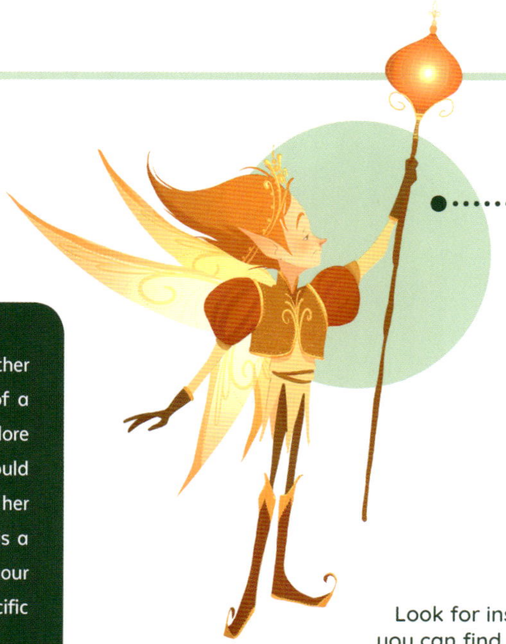

The color of a costume can suggest a lot about a character. This fairy wears a warm color scheme. As fairies are often tied to nature, you can assume he's an autumn fairy.

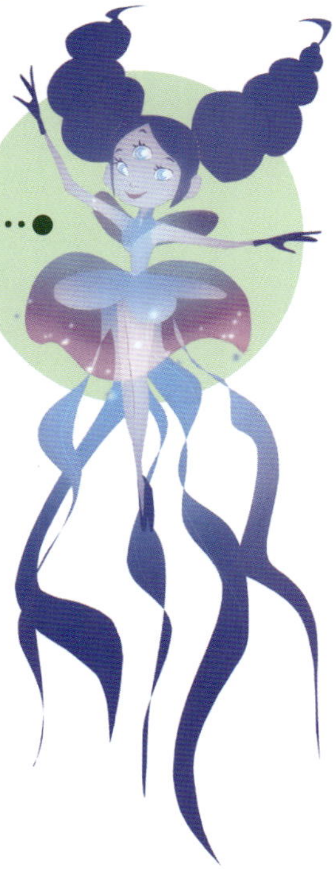

Look for inspiration wherever you can find it. This costume was inspired by a jellyfish, as underwater creatures can often remind people of otherworldly beings such as aliens. The bioluminescence of jellyfish also provides the costume with a sci-fi feel.

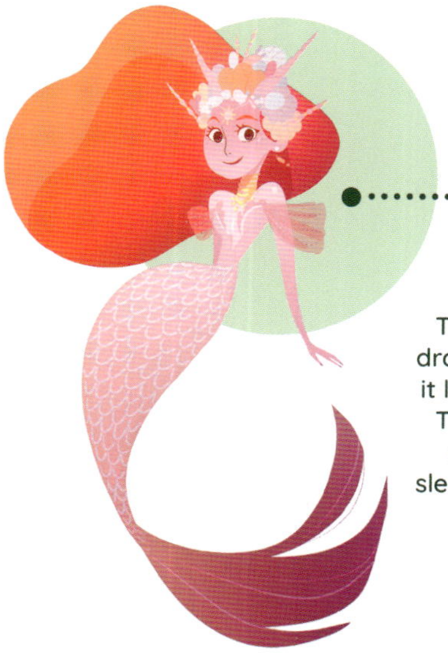

This mermaid costume was drawn with the idea of making it look like a glamorous dress. The repetition of the scales and the off-the-shoulder sleeves help create an elegant ball-gown feel.

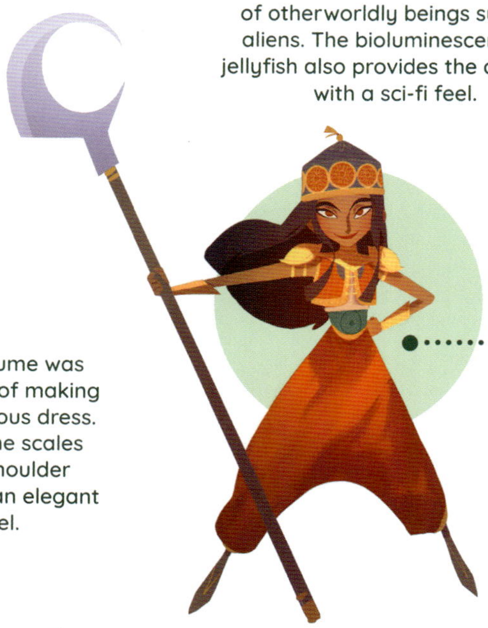

For this Arabian-inspired warrior, research of ancient Persian warriors and other warriors from that region was carried out first.

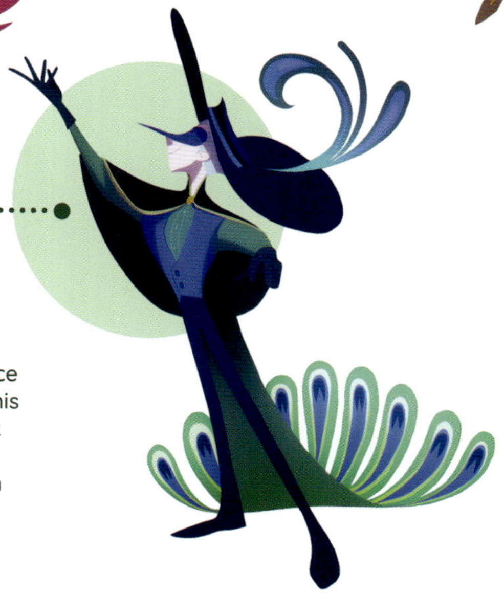

Peacocks are often associated with flamboyance and vanity. Not only does this character wear a peacock costume, but he displays a sense of flamboyance in his pose to showcase his confident personality.

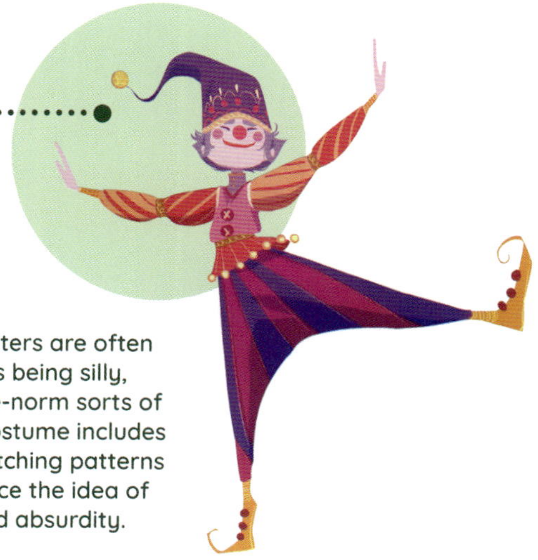

Circus characters are often depicted as being silly, outside-of-the-norm sorts of people. This costume includes varied, mismatching patterns to help enforce the idea of silliness and absurdity.

Sweeney Boo

Fashion is varied enough that there are countless options for creating a powerful character design. In comics, you will often see outfit designs that continue the same costume tropes and stereotypes that audiences are familiar with, but do not forget that you have the tools to go beyond those and design something different.

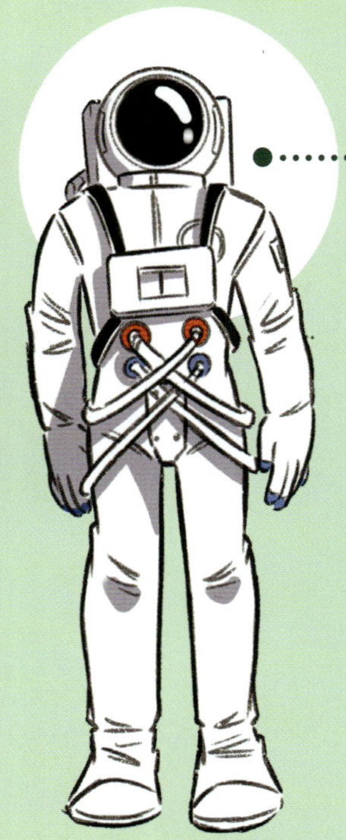

Use real-life space suits as reference when designing astronauts and space characters, simplifying the suit designs as needed.

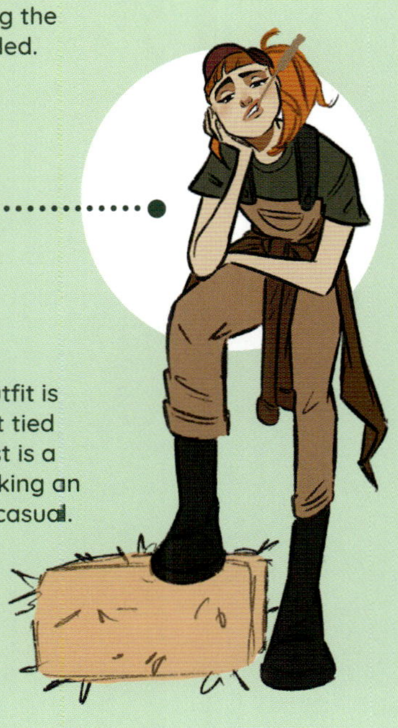

This farmer's outfit is practical; a shirt tied around the waist is a simple way of making an outfit look more casual.

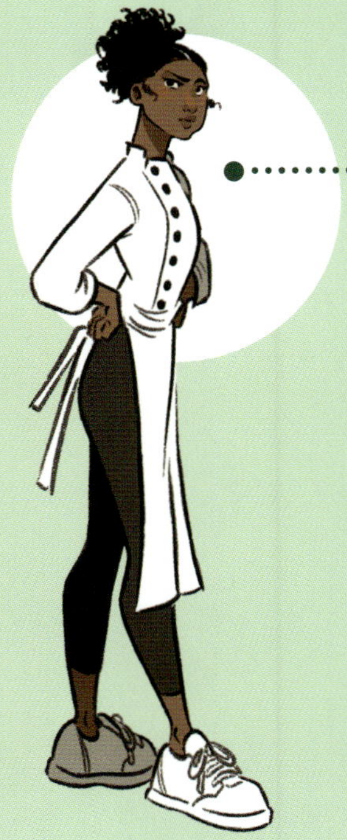

This chef keeps things neat and tidy by wearing a simple, clean-lined outfit with her hair up and out of the way.

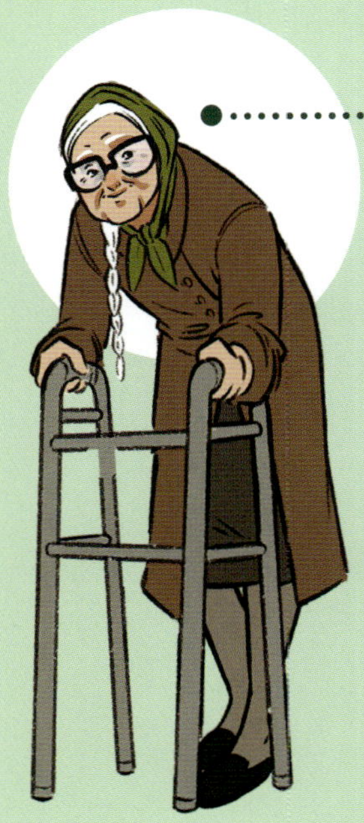

With her long coat and scarf tied neatly at her neck, this grandma is classic yet classy.

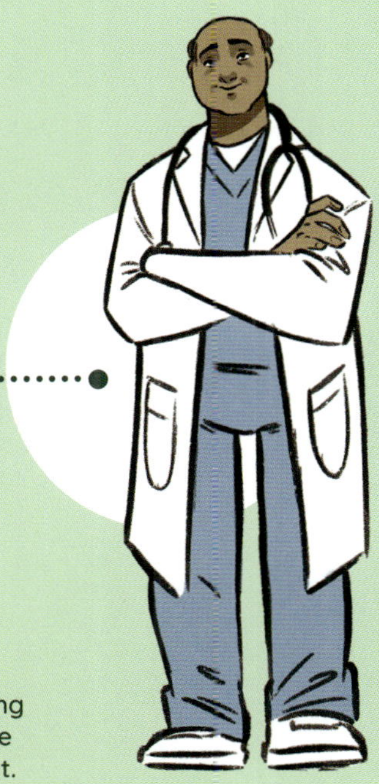

This doctor keeps things simple, wearing plain scrubs and the signature white coat.

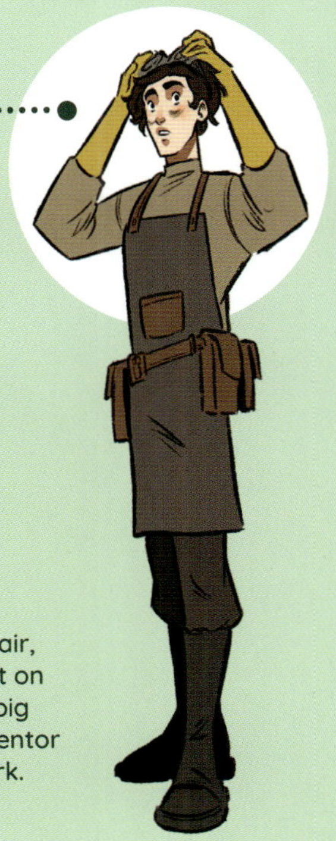

With tousled hair, smudges of dirt on his face, and big goggles, this inventor is hard at work.

Corah Louise

People dress with purpose, even if they do not do it intentionally. The clothes you feel comfortable in will often reflect what you want to portray about yourself, the people you hang around with, the art you appreciate, and the time you live in. The same goes for your characters. When dressing a character, think about why they would be wearing those clothes. What colors would they pick? Do they want their outfit to help them blend into the background, or to make them stand out? Do they dress a certain way to appease others, or do they intentionally do the opposite? Consider their personality and how you can use their outfit to represent their character.

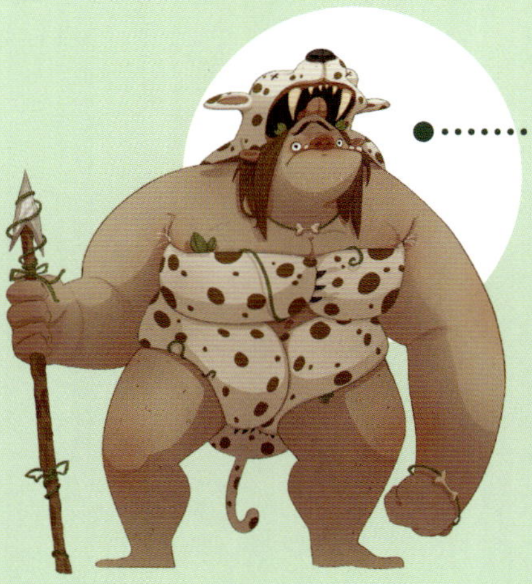

Resources and accessibility are key here. This caveman can only make his clothing from what is to hand, turning raw materials into something purposeful and useful, but we can still add a twist of fun.

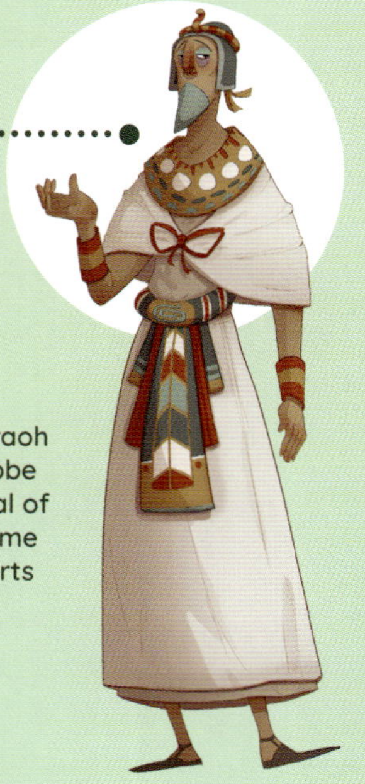

This flamboyant Egyptian pharaoh wears a highly accessorized robe with bright pops of color, typical of the era. Always research the time period first, then select the parts that suit your character.

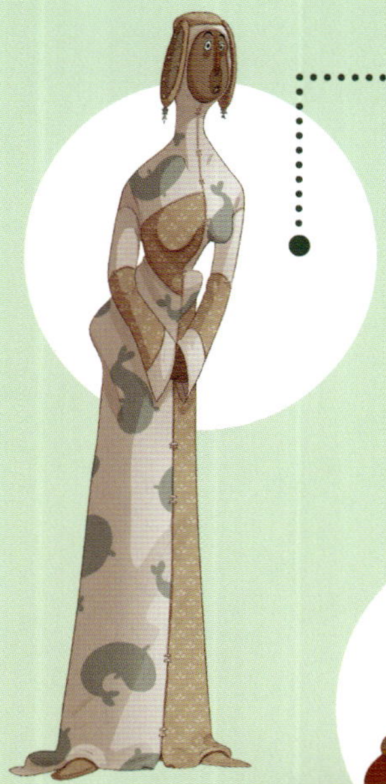

A lost and confused character from the Middle Ages. Everything about her outfit looks uncomfortable. The murky colors suit her forlorn personality, the headpiece drooping down like puppy ears.

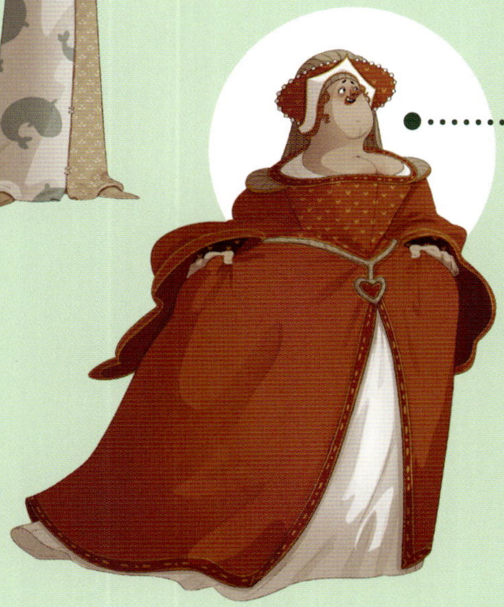

The wide, bouncy, brightly colored dress reflects the bold, fun, and lively personality of this Tudor character. The heart detailing further hints at her friendly manner.

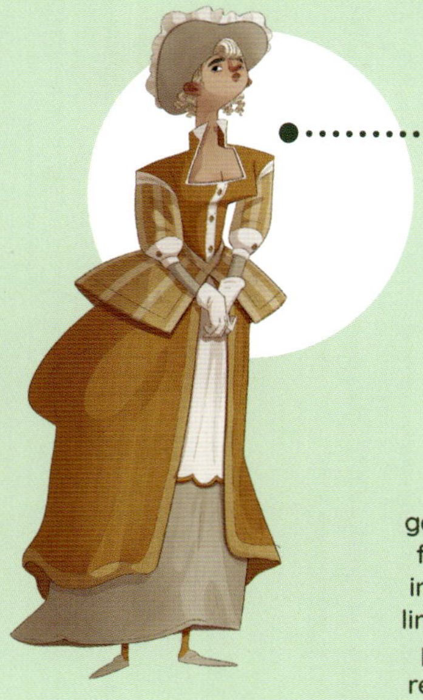

This Victorian character exudes affluence, vanity, and superiority. Her stiff yet feminine clothes with their angled edges contain minimalistic colors, reflecting her haughty persona.

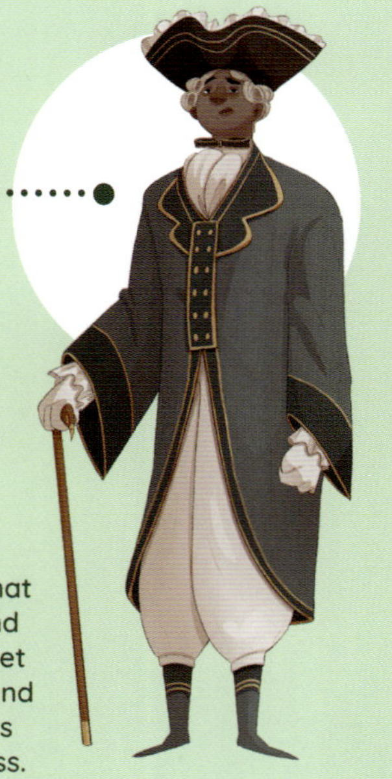

This Victorian gentleman wears a hat for added height and importance. His jacket lined with gold trim and pristine white gloves reveal his higher class.

Olga Andriyenko

When designing costumes for your characters, internet search engines are your best friend, along with books, magazines, and movies. Consider the time and location your character exists in, as well as their personality and living conditions. It is helpful to create Pinterest boards, collate folders with saved images, or collect cutouts from magazines to gather inspiration for your character before you start drawing.

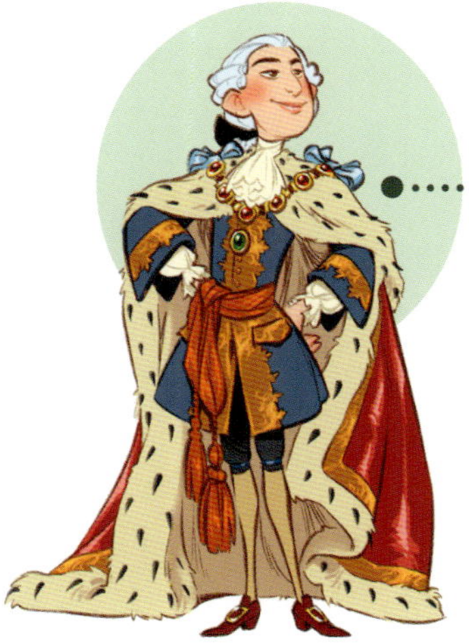

A royal character will likely want to show off their riches. Do not be subtle with ornaments, precious metals and stones, furs, and lace. This prince is inspired by the Rococo era.

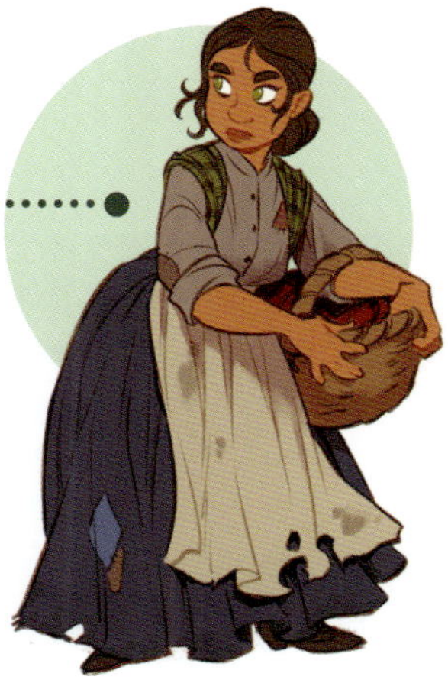

A pauper character will have worries more pressing than the latest fashion. Their clothing will be on the practical side and show signs of age and wear-and-tear, as well as repairs.

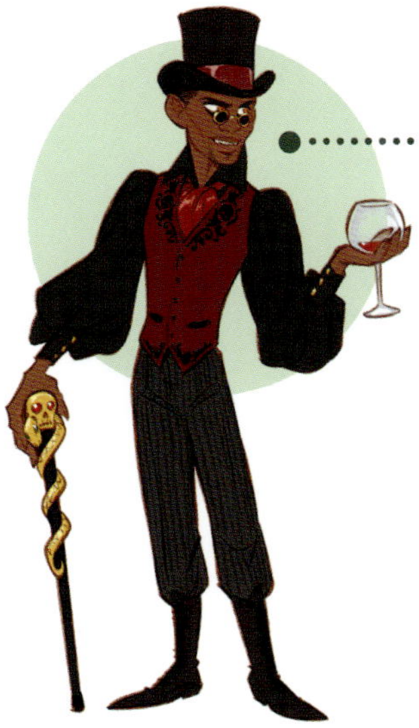

Gothic clothing is often inspired by Victorian fashion. Keep the colors dark and add spooky ornaments and accessories such as skulls, snakes, bats, and spider webs.

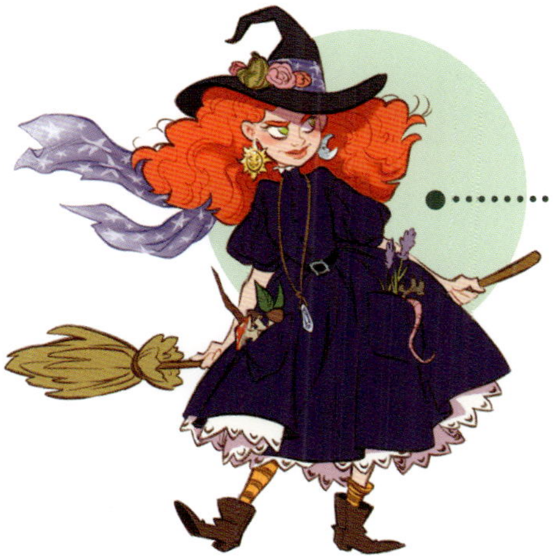

Show the magical interests of witch or wizard characters by decorating their costume with celestial bodies and all kinds of strange talismans they might use for their magic.

Superheroes often wear practical, stretchy, full-body suits to allow them a full range of motion in their superhero battles. Give your hero a theme and reflect this in their name and costume design.

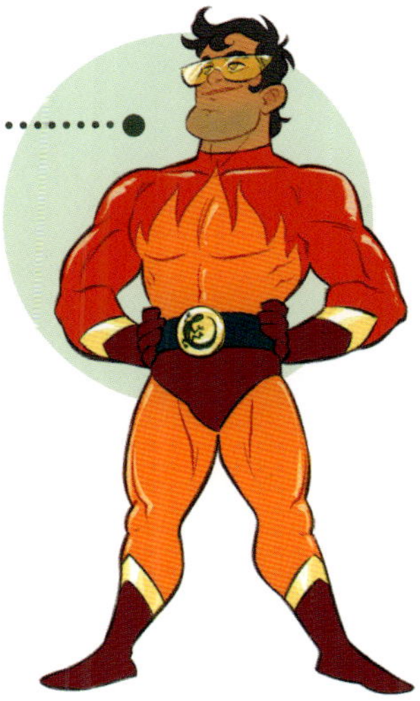

Villains love capes! Their costume designs and colors are often inspired by dangerous animals, like the venomous snakes used in this character's costume.

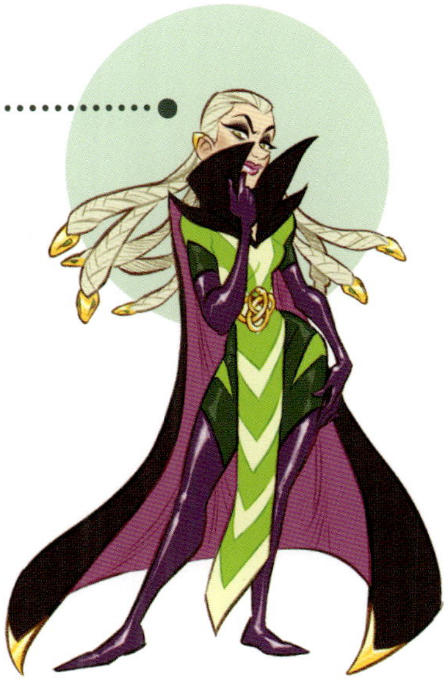

HAIRSTYLES LIBRARY

Kenneth Anderson

Facial hair can tell you a lot about a character. How a character wears their beard or moustache will likely reflect their attitude to their own appearance, or suggest who they are and their place in society, much like their costume and props will. Think about the underlying head shape beneath the facial hair, as ultimately it will affect the shape of the beard or moustache. Also, be mindful of ethnicity and how different characters will have different hair types, as this will also affect their facial hair.

Fancy facial hair comes in many forms. It is important to make clear the time and energy that went into crafting it, while keeping it neat and tidy.

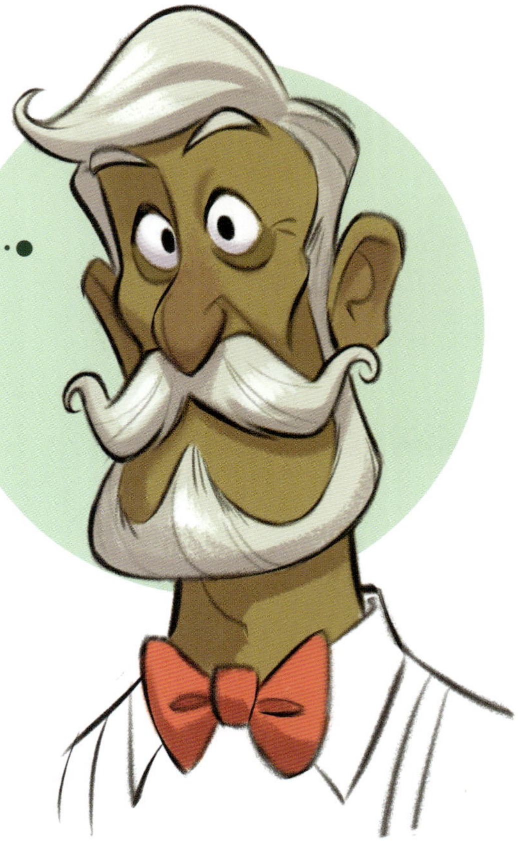

Big, long beards left to their own devices will hang differently depending on the hair type and the shape of the character's head.

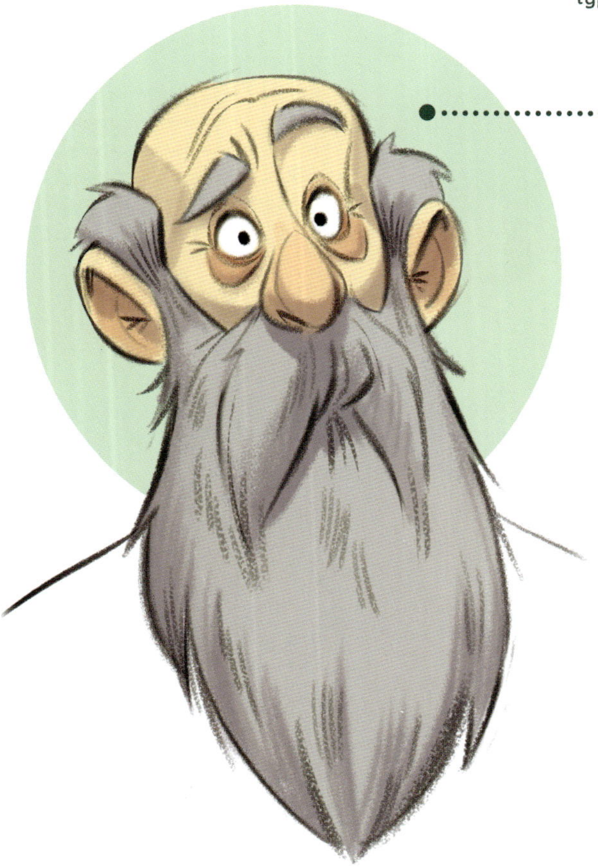

A beard can be used to frame a face and accentuate parts of it. In this case, it follows the planes of the face shape and frames the character's mouth.

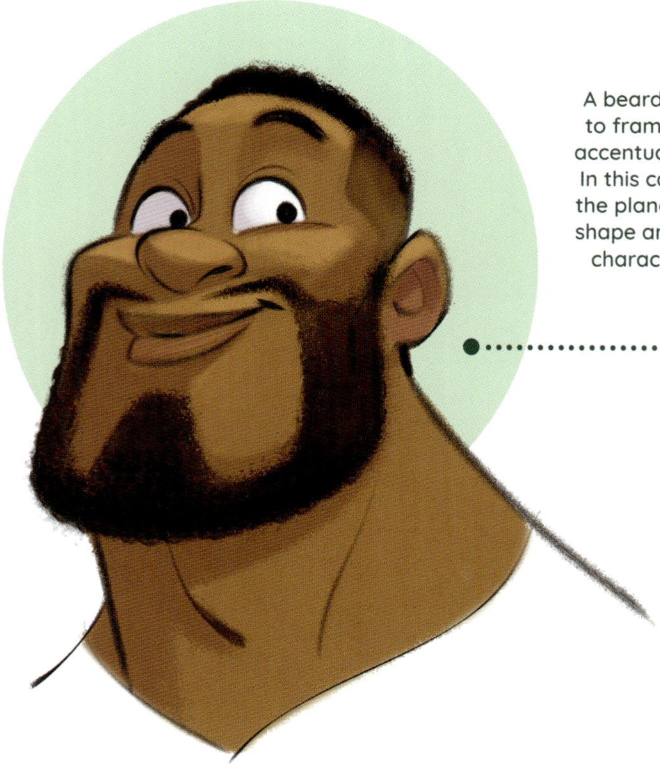

Randy Bishop

The way a character grooms themselves can say a lot about how they see themselves, or at least how they wish others to see them. A well-coiffed head of hair can take time and effort, which tells an audience that the character spends time thinking about their appearance. Hair that is unkempt tells an audience that the character doesn't really care how others see them, doesn't want to appear to care about this, or doesn't have time to think about it.

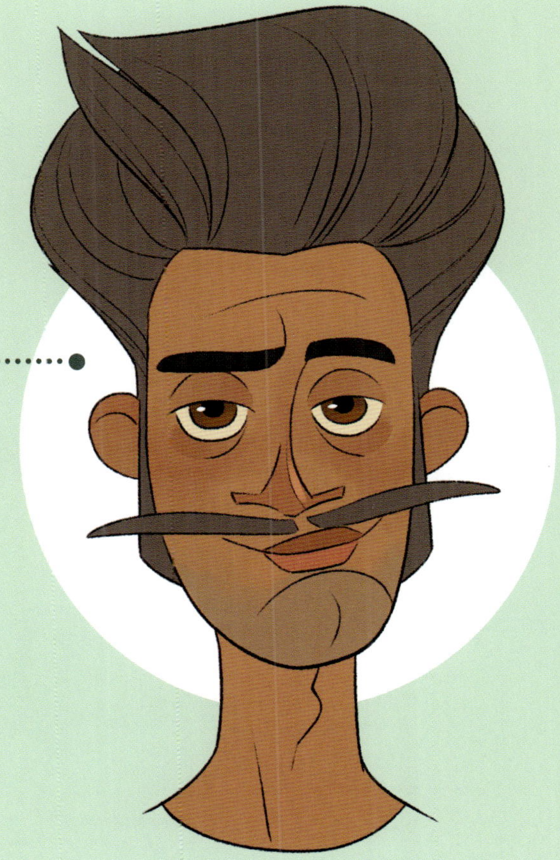

A big, well-styled hairdo can make a character appear self-confident.

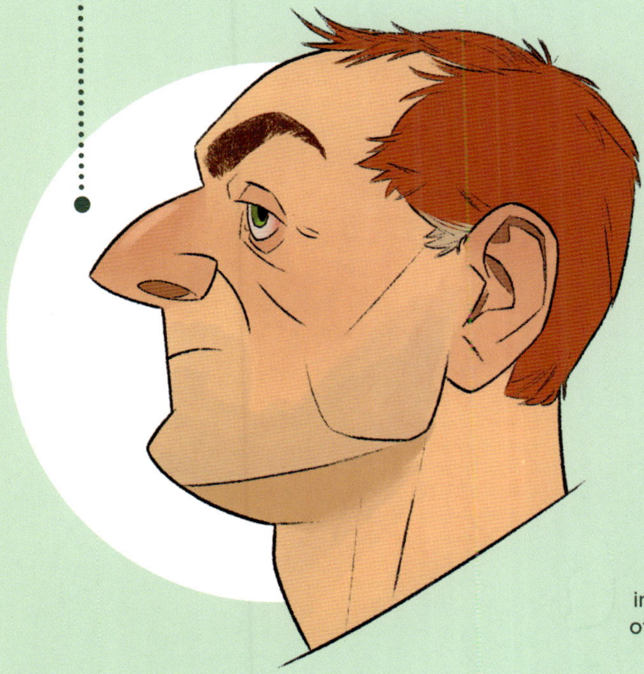

A receding hairline or thinning hair not only ages a character, but makes them look like they have experienced a level of stress over the years.

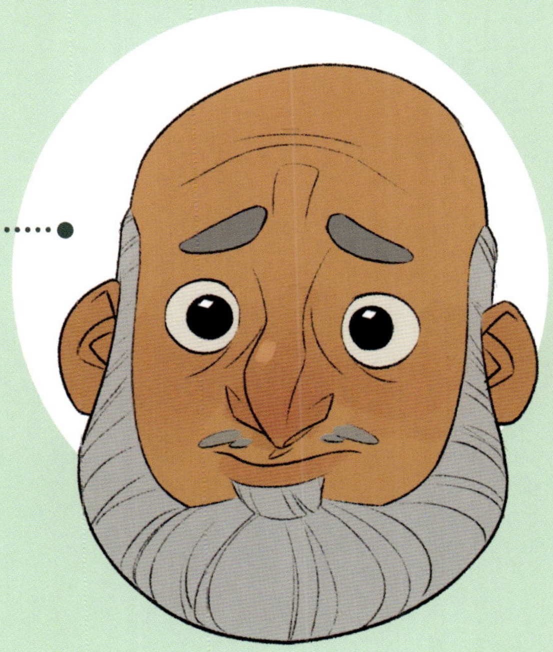

A bald head indicates age and often wisdom, too.

Luis Gadea

Everyone has their own rituals for styling their hair, from the complicated and time-consuming to a speedy one-minute routine. Even if someone does not spend any time on their hair, this still tells something of their personality. When designing a character, think about the silhouette of their hair. Find a balance between it and the character. Avoid drawing so much attention to the hair that it distracts from the character's face, unless this is on purpose and part of the story.

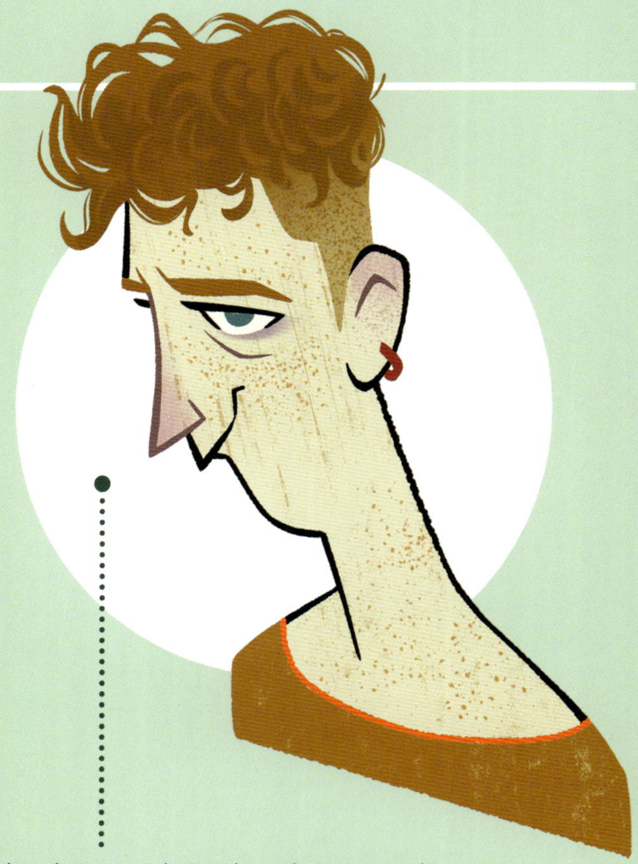

Try to match a character's hairstyle to their personality. With curls on top and fading around the sides, this character is someone who cares about his appearance. Adding a gradient color from the sideburns up creates the effect of fading.

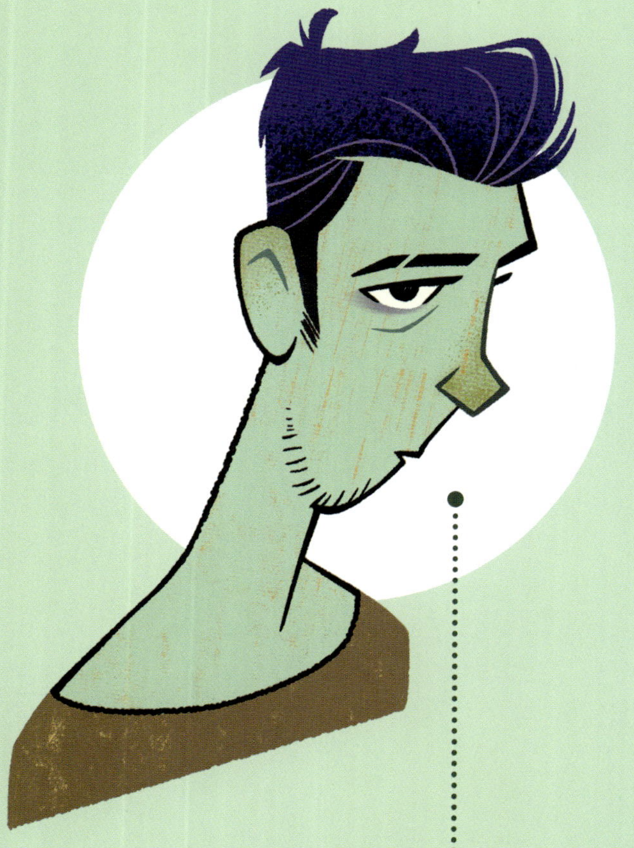

You do not need to draw every single strand of hair, one by one. Think of the hair as one entire shape, then add details here and there. This character's hair has a black base with a few highlight lines to show the direction of the style.

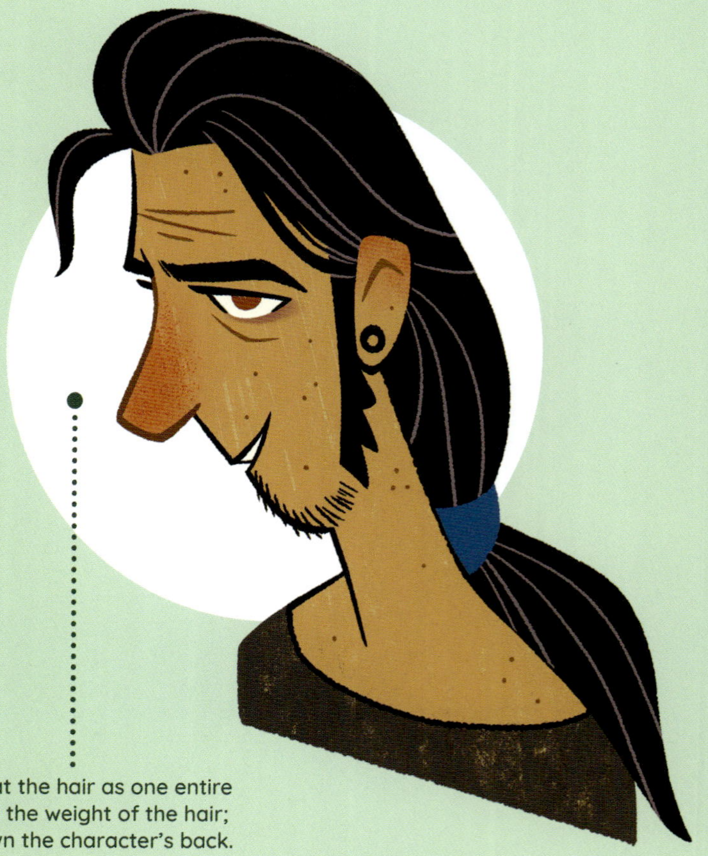

With longer hairstyles, you can also treat the hair as one entire shape. Add a few flowing lines to depict the weight of the hair; in this case, it is very long, so it falls down the character's back.

Meybis Ruiz Cruz

Hair can emphasize personality as well as helping to communicate a character's emotional state, like how some people play with their hair when distracted, or how hair stands on end when someone is scared. Hair can also help describe a time period and place. Most people will recognize the white powdered wig of 18th-century Europe as much as the signature hairstyle of a samurai.

There are myriad different bob hairstyles; this one is the Dutch bob, created by Mary Thurman and later popularized by 1920s flapper Louise Brooks. It is practical and easy to style.

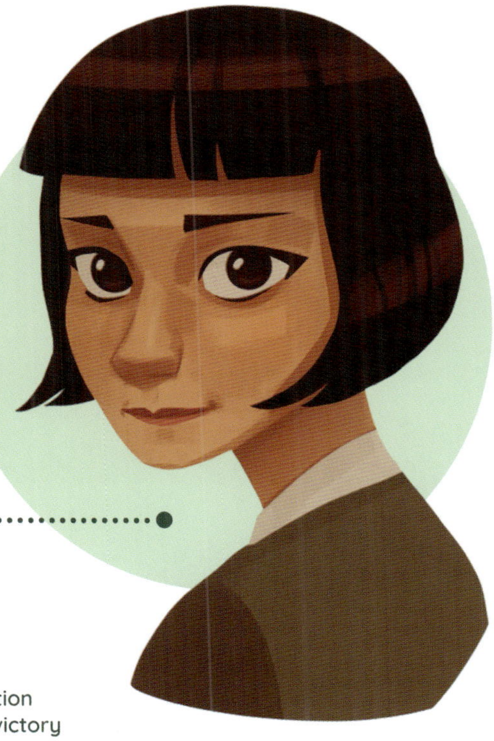

Allegedly named after an aviation maneuver used in World War II, "victory rolls" were popular in the 1940s. The hairstyle is very structured, with the rolls framing the face and giving height to the hair.

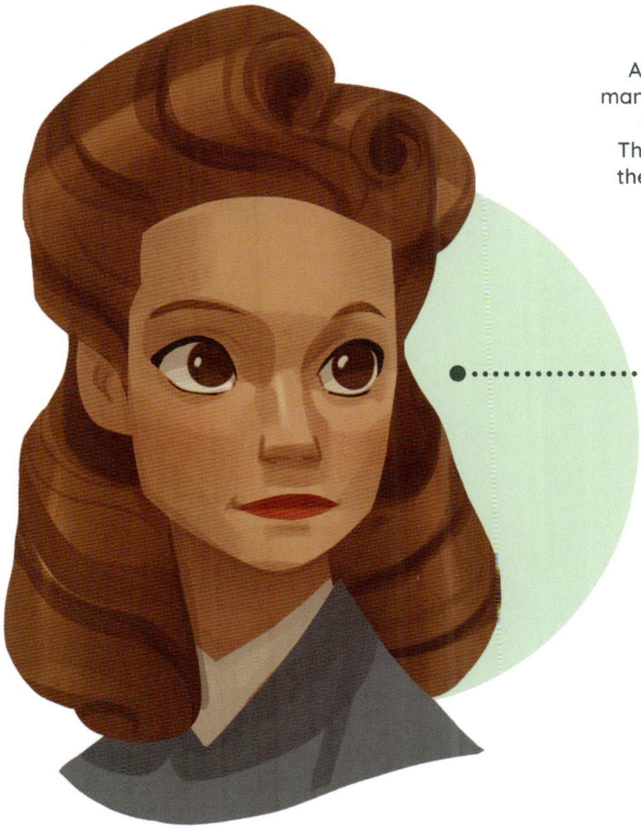

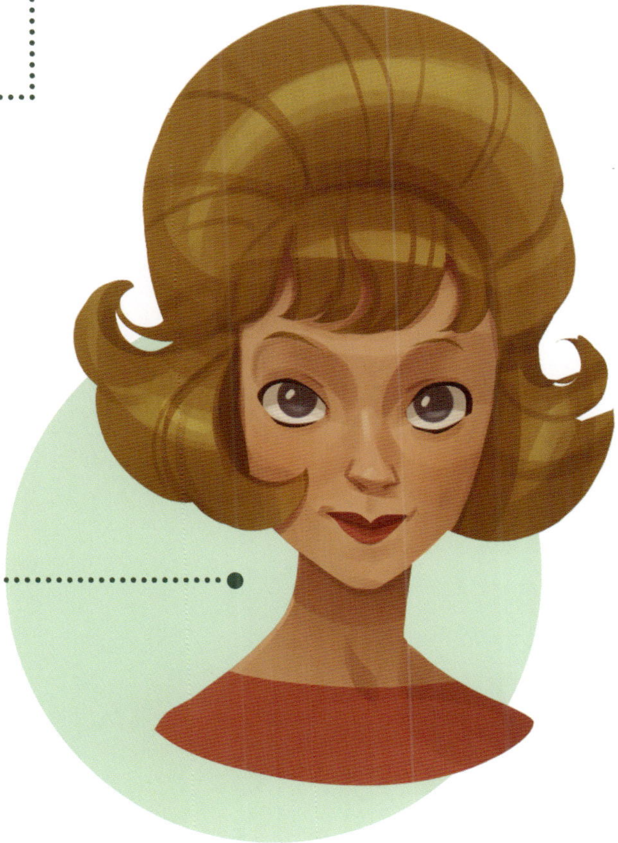

The beehive was created by Margaret Vinci Heldt in the 1960s. It has a round and conical appearance, and is all about volume and height.

Noor Sofi

Hair can be a distinctive feature of any character and can say a lot about them. If a girl's hair hangs in front of her face, you might guess that she is shy or reserved. But however you style your character's hair, you must also consider the reality of how hair works. Different types of hair have different design strategies to follow, as demonstrated here.

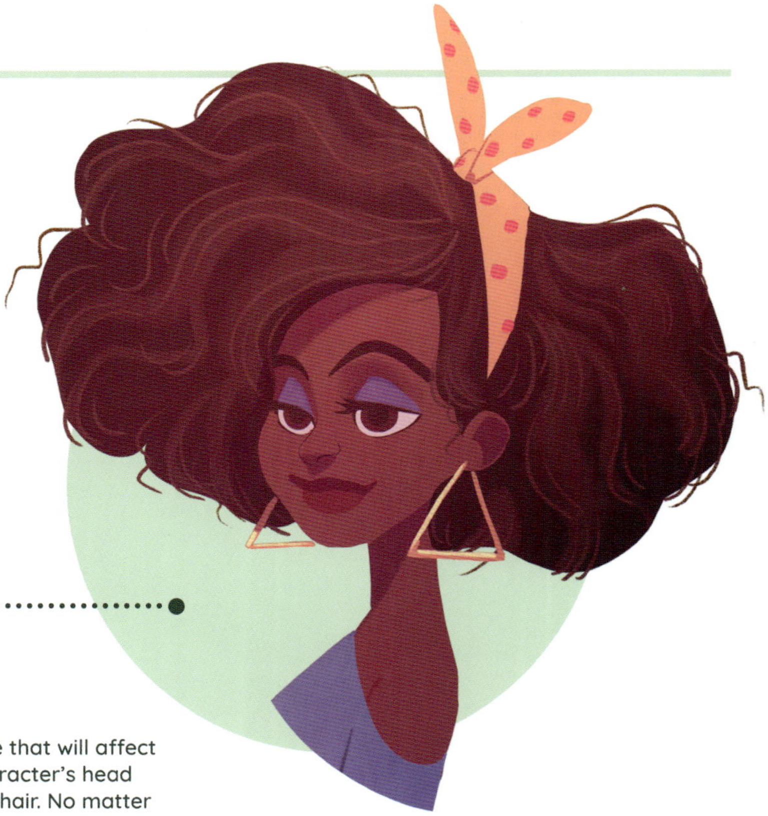

Tight, curly hair will have more of an overall shape that will affect the character's silhouette. For example, this character's head takes on a more boxy shape because of her thick hair. No matter how she moves, the shape of her hair will rarely change.

Straight hair is like a smooth waterfall cascading downward. To give it more visual interest, you can add a few flyaway strands to break up the shape.

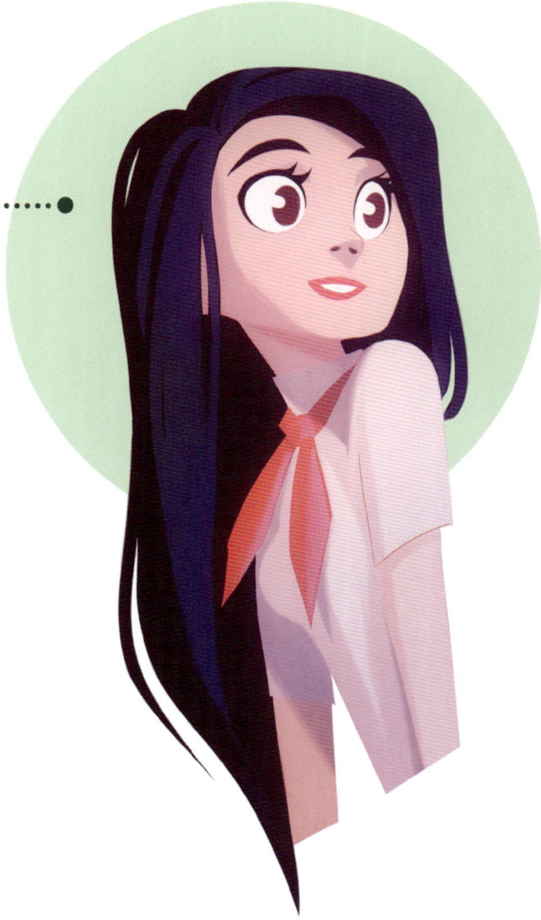

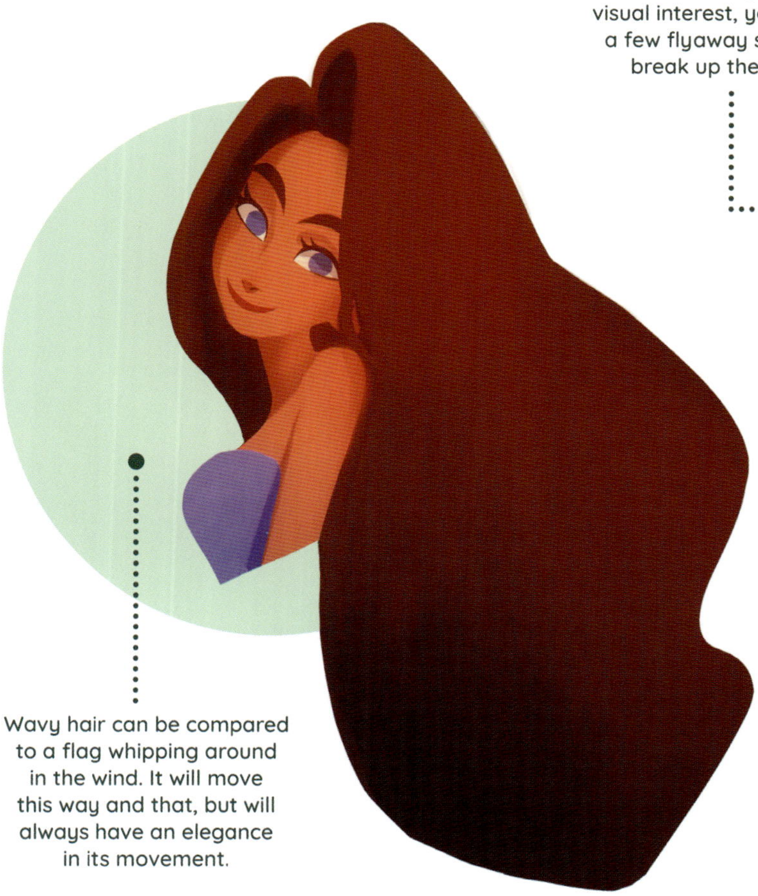

Wavy hair can be compared to a flag whipping around in the wind. It will move this way and that, but will always have an elegance in its movement.

Sweeney Boo

Hairstyles are like outfits. Playing a key part of your character's design, they offer a wide range of possibilities. It might seem easier to go for a simple style or what makes the most sense for a character, but do not hesitate to push your design a little further. Sometimes a simple accessory, piece of clothing, or hairstyle can help give a character a more serious or more casual look.

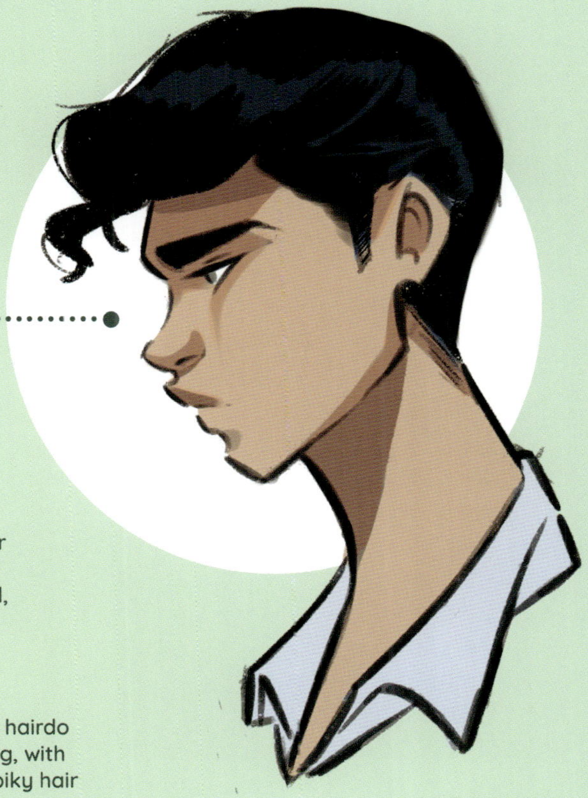

The Elvis-style pompadour hairdo is voluminous and often slicked back with gel, giving it an iconic shine.

A punk or Mohawk-style hairdo is edgy and eye-catching, with shaved sides and long, spiky hair down the center.

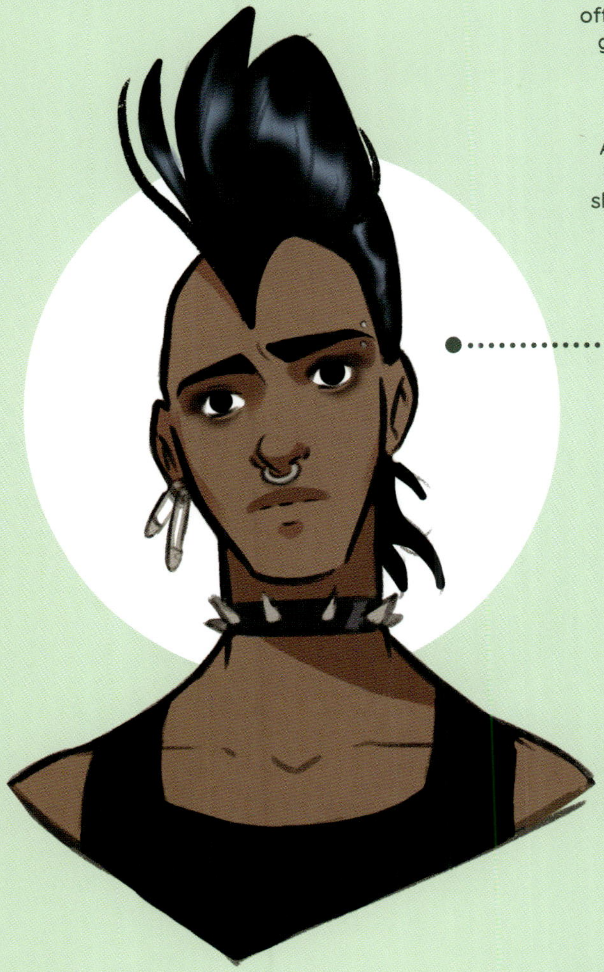

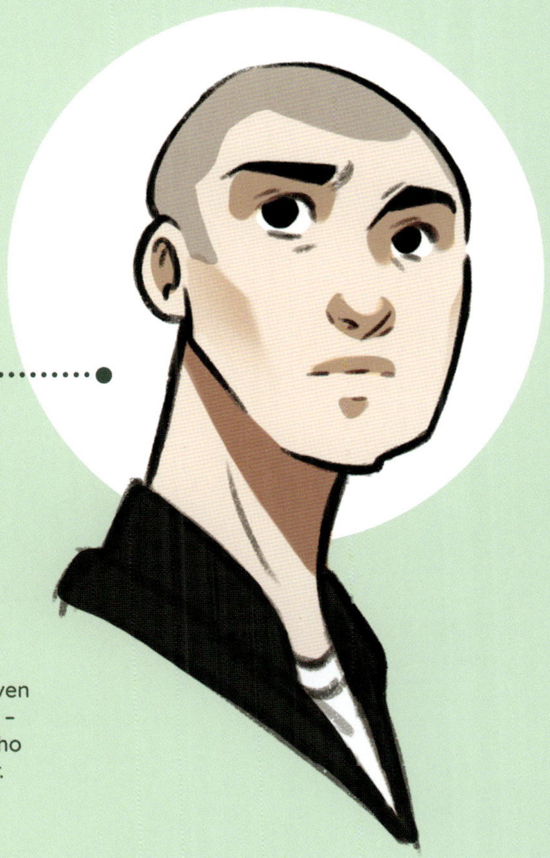

A "buzz cut" or clean-shaven head requires no styling – perfect for characters who do not want the bother.

Corah Louise

Hair acts as an extension of a character's personality, changing their silhouette and providing extra shape and dimension. The way their hair is (or isn't) styled can tell a lot about their story, personality, and fashion sense, and can even suggest different personas. Styling hair hanging over a character's eyes can make them look shy, mysterious, or unapproachable, whereas having it tied too tightly can make them look uptight or strict. Be intentional with your choice of hairstyle and let it tell a story. Try matching hairstyles to different personalities and experiment with how hair can create a more interesting silhouette for your character.

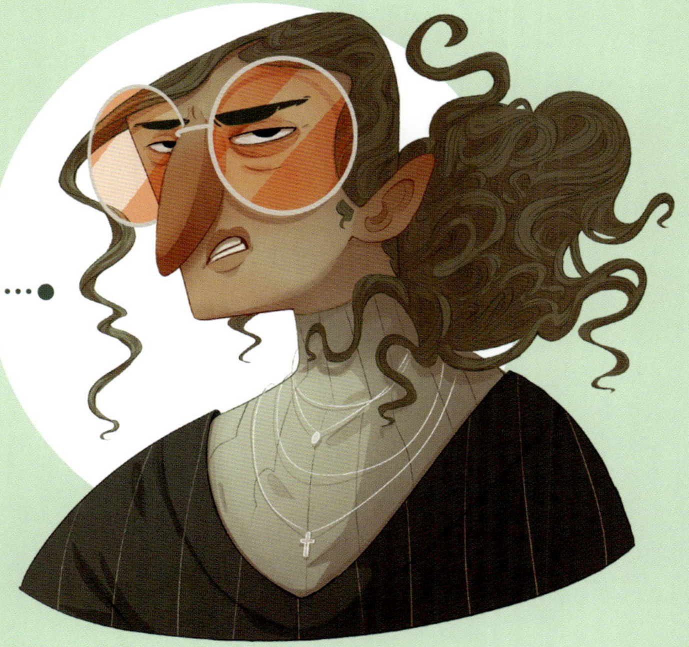

This character has not got the time or attitude to be patient with her unruly hair – it is quickly tied back, out of the way, but it does not stay there for long.

This tidy updo has a clean silhouette. The plaits on this character are clear, readable shapes and do not touch the shoulders, making for an overall tidier design to represent her neat personality.

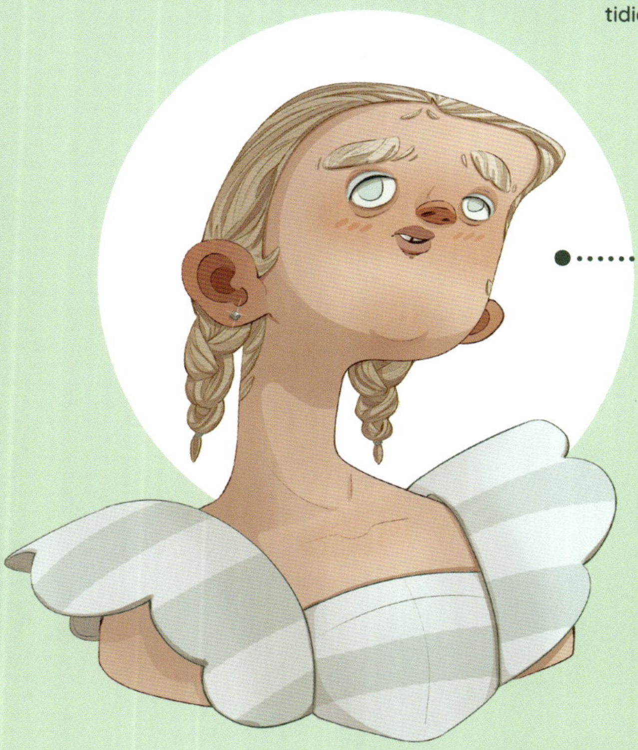

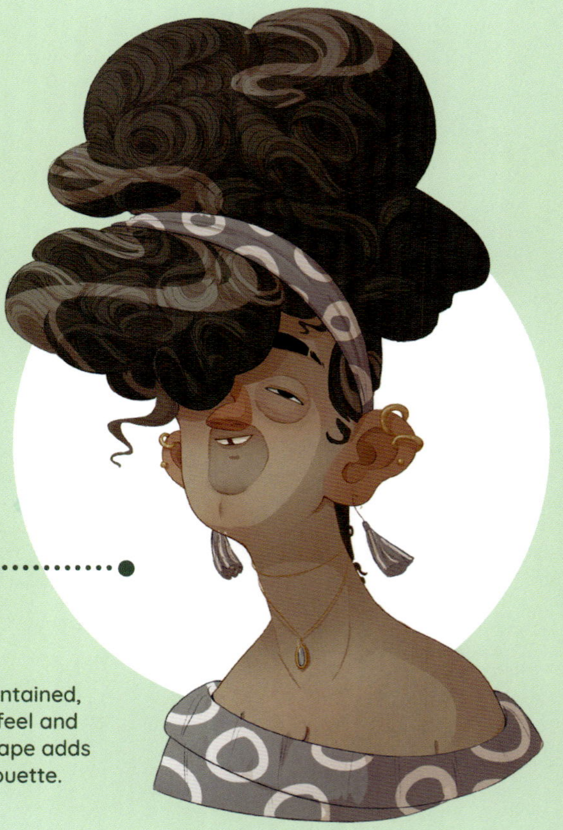

This character's big hair cannot be contained, hanging over one eye for a carefree feel and bold look suggesting creativity. The shape adds an interesting dimension to her silhouette.

Olga Andriyenko

When designing hairstyles for your characters, start by drawing the rough shape of the hair, then add in some individual strands of varying thickness. Avoid drawing too many single strands of hair or the results will end up looking quite heavy and distracting.

Imagine dreadlocks like soft tubes, but give them a slightly irregular shape. You do not have to draw every single one - just enough for the viewer to fill out the rest in their mind. When you are happy with the positioning of the locks, draw in some curved lines to indicate texture and volume.

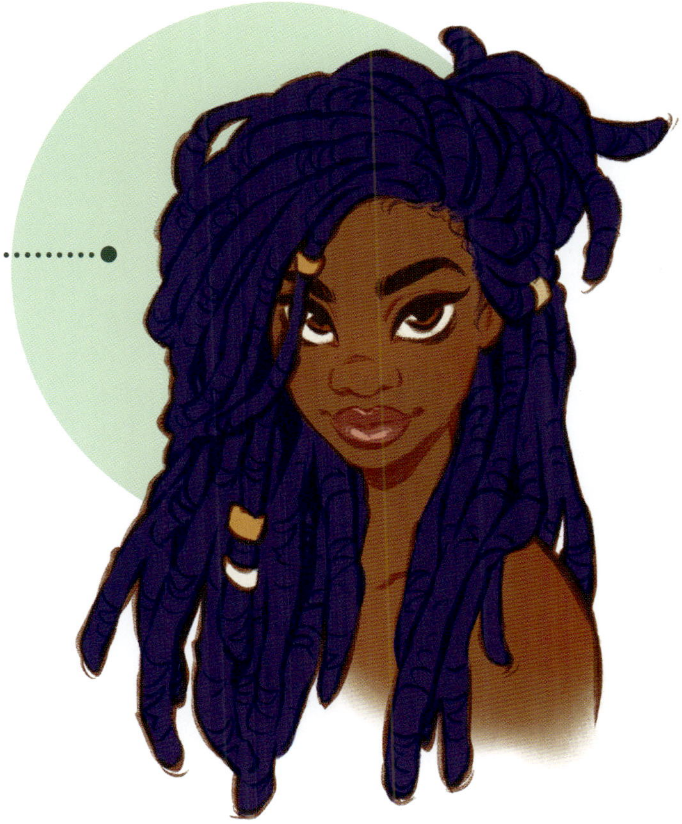

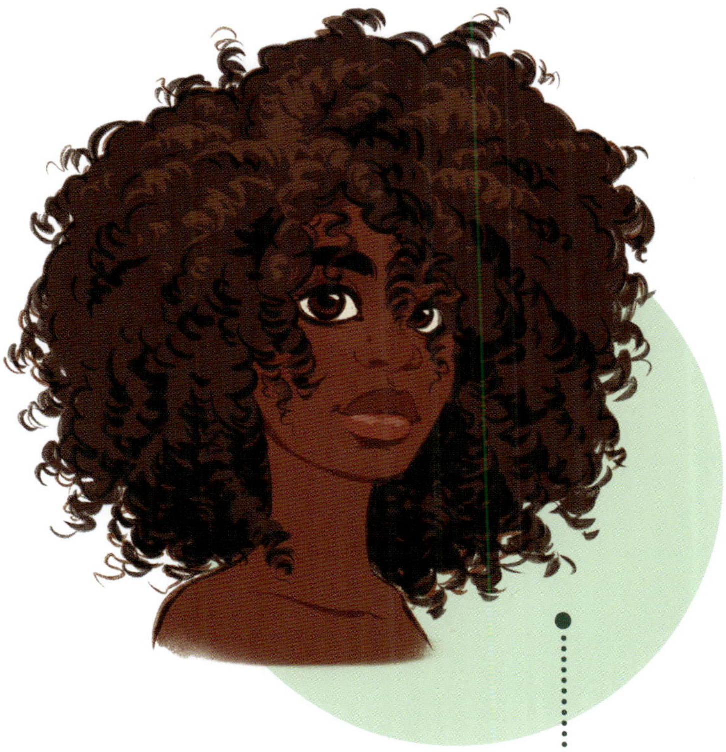

For afro hair, start by drawing a soft cloud shape around the head to work out the hair length and overall form. Add detail by drawing individual locks of hair, varying their thickness and length slightly for a natural-looking result.

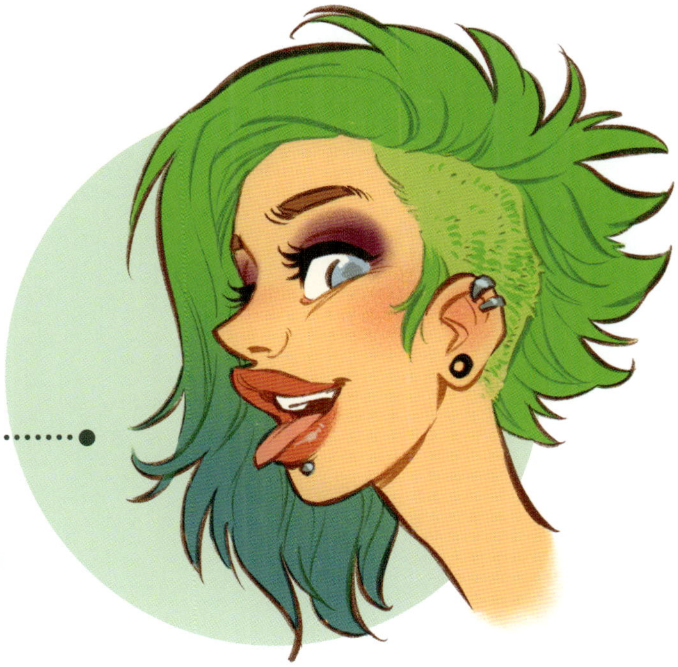

Punk hairstyles often feature bright colors - sometimes several different colors in the same hairstyle. When designing a partially shaved hairstyle, use a more transparent version of the main hair color to illustrate the skin showing through the short hair, then draw some stubble for texture.

PROPS LIBRARY

Kenneth Anderson

A prop should match the design style and proportions of the character. For example, if the prop is super realistic but the character is very stylized, they will look odd when placed together. In some cases, a prop may be especially unique to a character, such as an iconic weapon that becomes part and parcel of who they are.

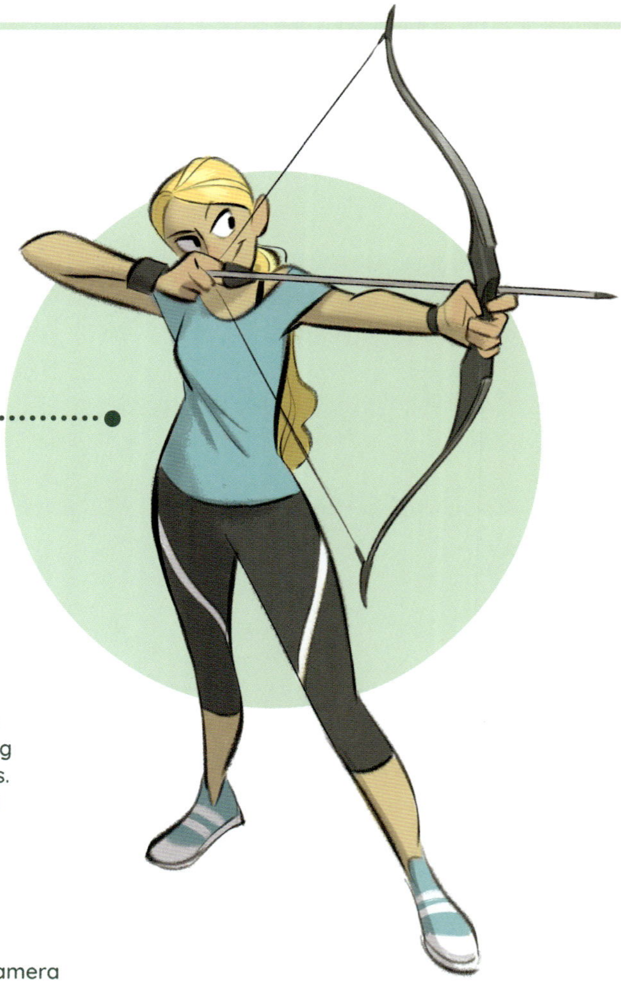

Bows and arrows come in many different forms despite generally adhering to the same iconic shapes. The details are what will differentiate them.

Almost everyone owns a camera of some kind, but the type of camera a character uses can say something about how seriously they take their photography.

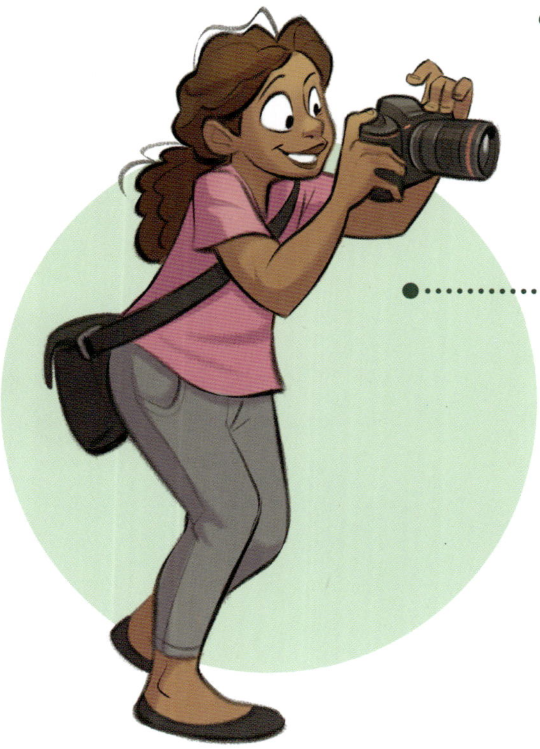

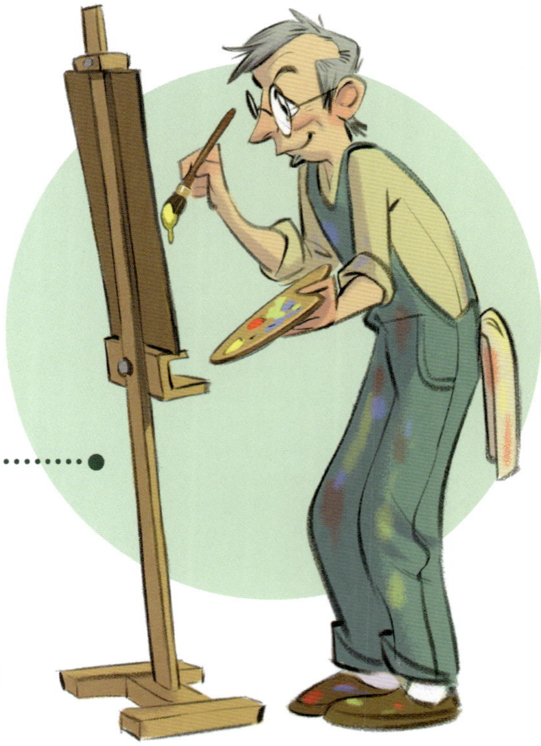

For a creative hobby such as painting, many different tools might be necessary, all at the same time!

Randy Bishop

Props are like the icing on the cake of your design. They can add a touch of flair or provide extra insight into who a character is. You can tell a lot about a person by what they choose to carry around with them. Do they always have the latest phone, or do they wait until their old phone completely dies before replacing it? What sort of books do they read? If they carry a weapon, is it one that favors strength or skill? Perhaps they wear a bracelet their child made for them? These little details can be really satisfying for an audience to pick up on.

A motorcycle, Jet Ski, or similar vehicle almost always indicates a free-spirited character.

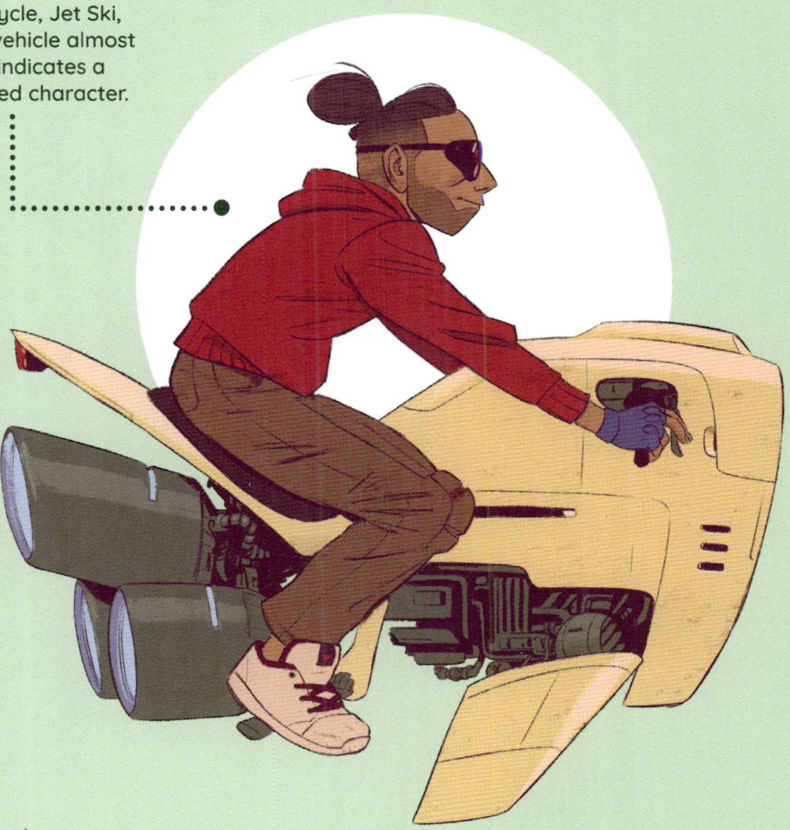

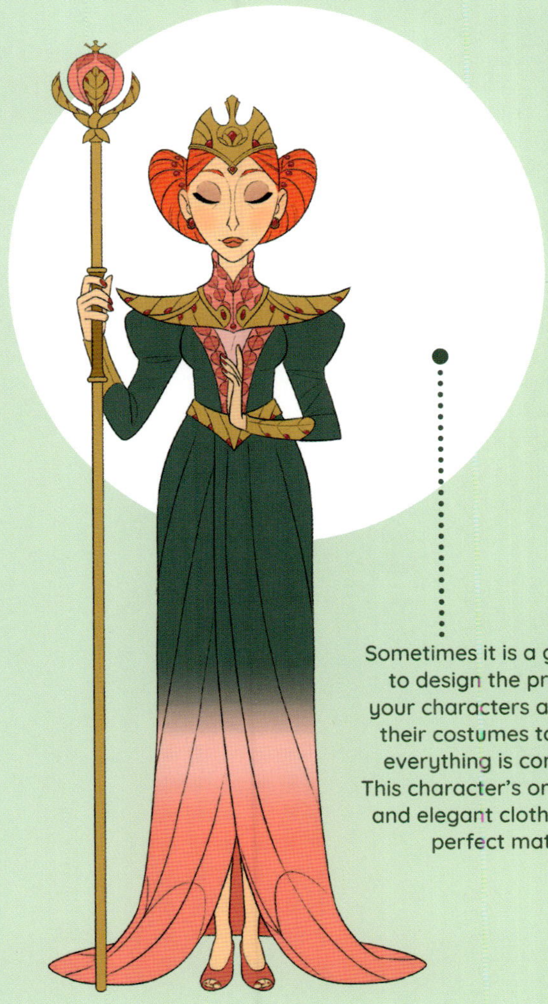

Sometimes it is a good idea to design the props for your characters along with their costumes to ensure everything is consistent. This character's ornate staff and elegant clothing are a perfect match.

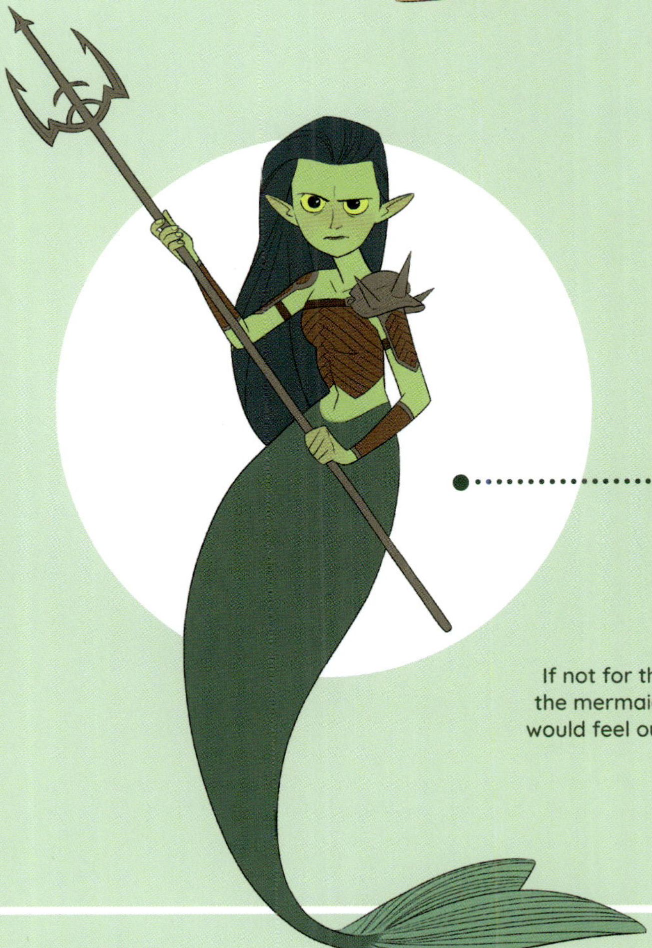

If not for the armor, the mermaid's trident would feel out of place.

Luis Gadea

You can stylize props to make them more visually interesting and to complement the character's personality and style. Start by designing a regular object, then try pushing the asymmetry of it: distort the corner, skew it on one side, or push some elements of its silhouette to make it more striking.

You also need to make your props believable, so they fit seamlessly with your character and are not just floating beside them with no purpose. Make the hands holding the prop look like they are actually touching it. Study yourself using objects and try to recreate what you see.

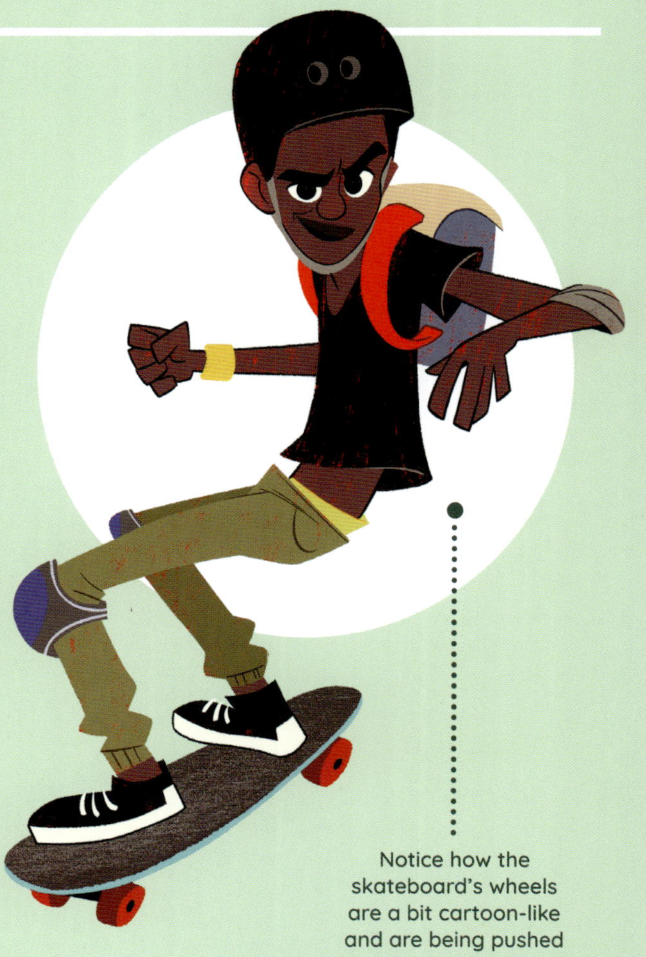

Notice how the skateboard's wheels are a bit cartoon-like and are being pushed down by the character's weight. The helmet plays two roles: it is a helmet, but also follows the same shape as an afro, which could help with visual consistency when the helmet is removed.

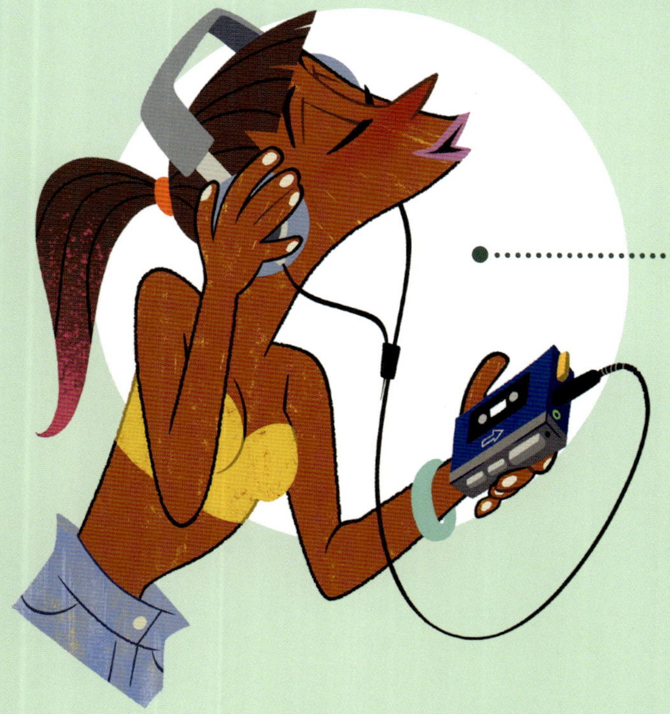

This character's style is from the 1980s and 1990s, so her music player needs to fit the era too. The wire is easy to distinguish and shows the connection between device and headphones.

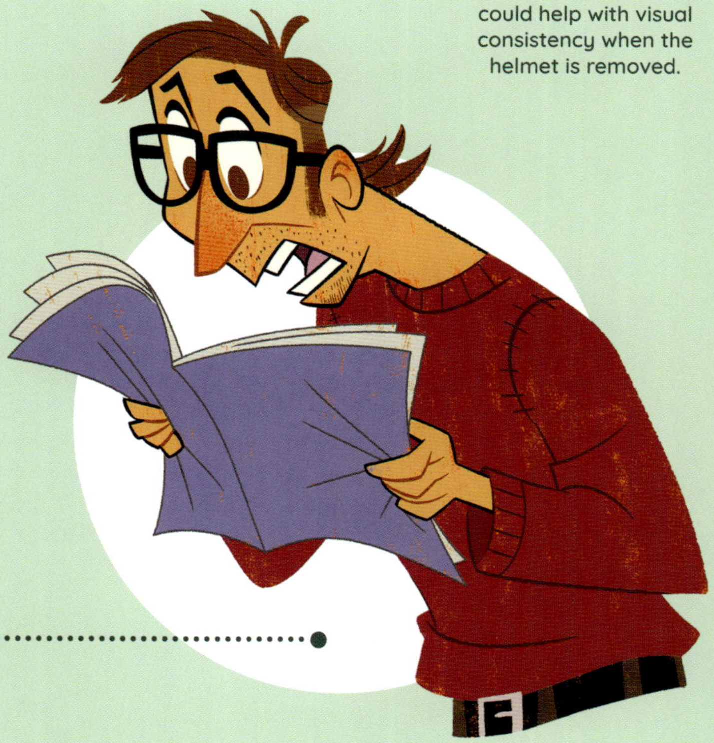

Even with a simple prop like a magazine, you need to think about the bigger story in which it plays a part. As the character reacts to something he has read, the magazine will be affected accordingly. Drawing wrinkles and creases shows where the pages are being crumpled in his grasp.

Meybis Ruiz Cruz

When designing a character handling a prop, it is essential to consider their proportion, weight, size, and how that will impact their interaction. Imagine a toddler carrying a bass guitar, then how differently an adult would handle it.

Be conscious of the visual language of the character and the level of stylization. A prop should match the character's style and yet still be readable. Study the object carefully and determine what characteristics are essential for its recognition; then you will be able to simplify it and adapt it to any style while keeping it readable.

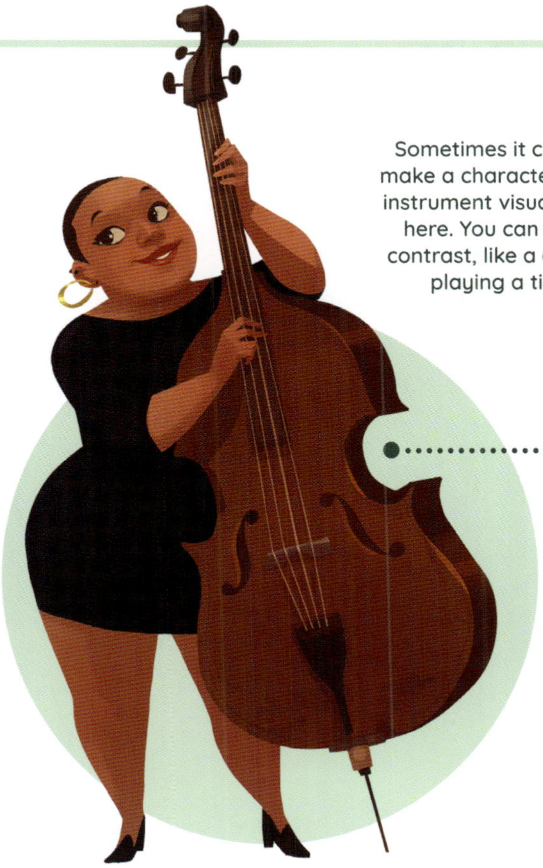

Sometimes it can be fun to make a character match their instrument visually, as shown here. You can also create contrast, like a colossal man playing a tiny violin.

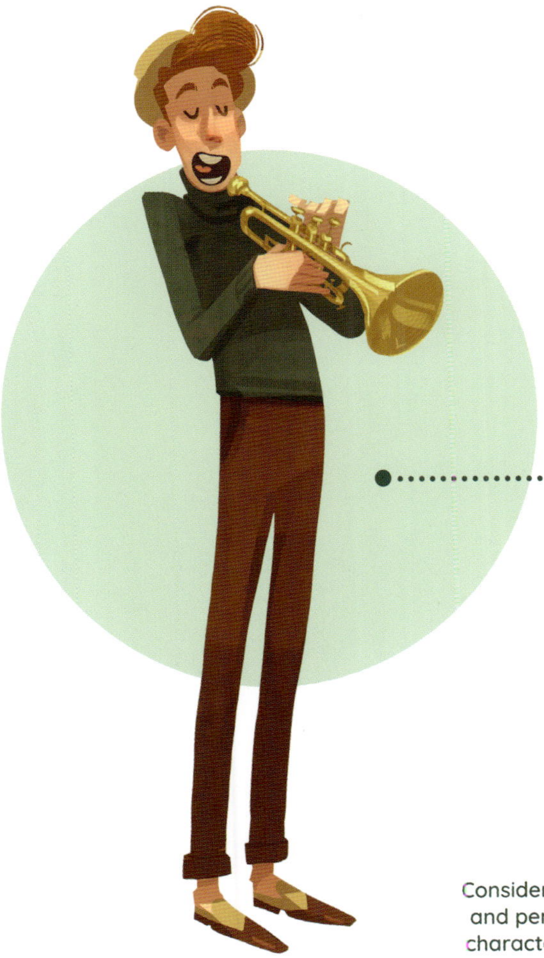

Consider the moment of the interaction you want to portray; is it before the performance, during, or afterward? This will affect how you approach the pose.

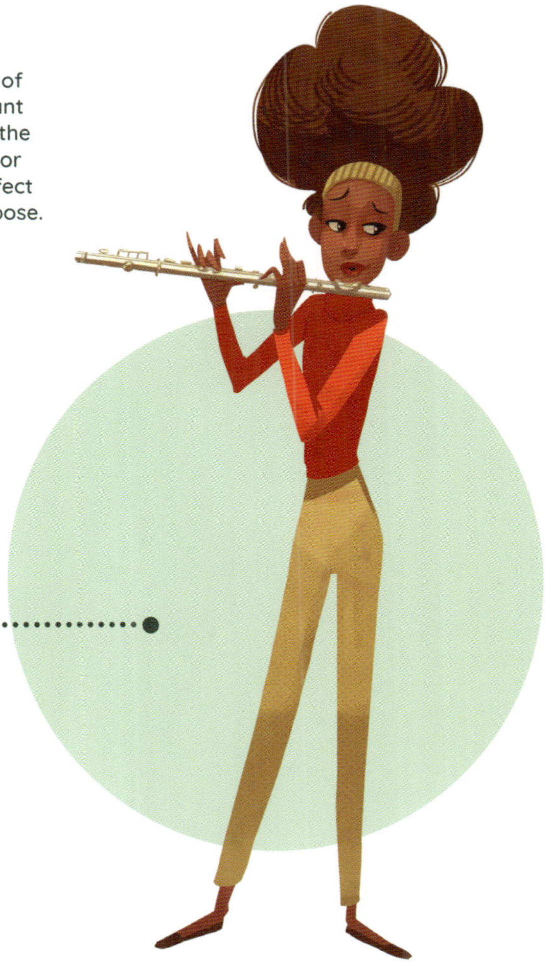

Consider the character's expertise and personality. You can tell this character is playing effortlessly – just enjoying the moment, extremely confident, even a bit cocky.

Noor Sofi

When drawing a character with a prop, you have yet another opportunity to tell a story. How does your character feel about the prop? How do they use it? Does it have any special or specific meaning to them? When designing a prop, try to make it specific to your character. If the two are connected in some way, show this relationship. This could be through certain design choices, like the character and prop looking visually similar, or it could be in how your character reacts to the prop.

A prop can help provide a certain tone or atmosphere to your character. Here a boy picks a bunch of flowers, conveying a sense of beauty and peace.

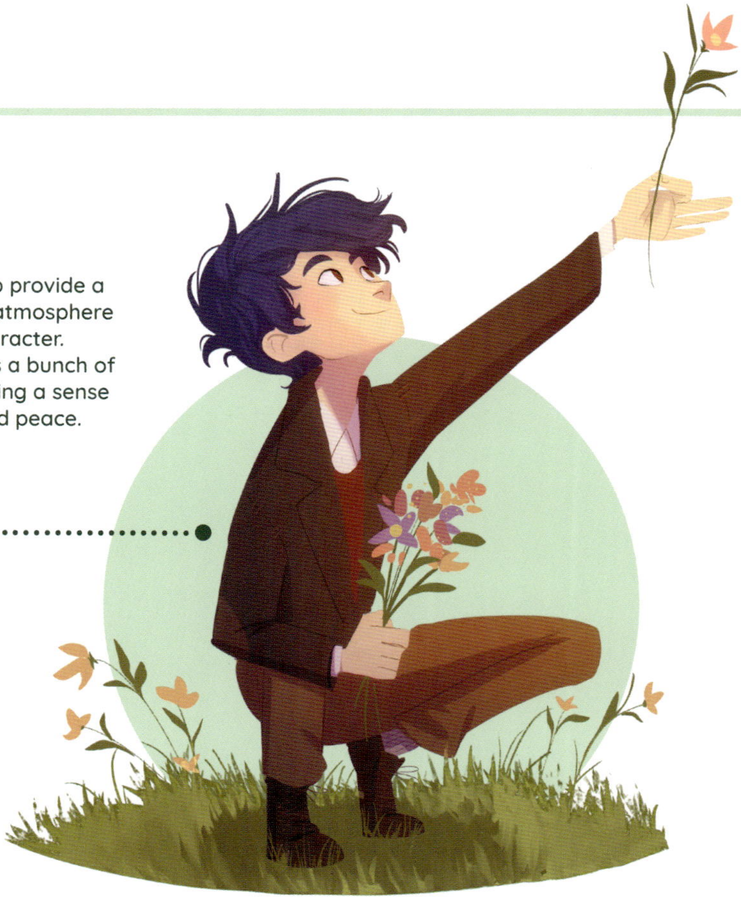

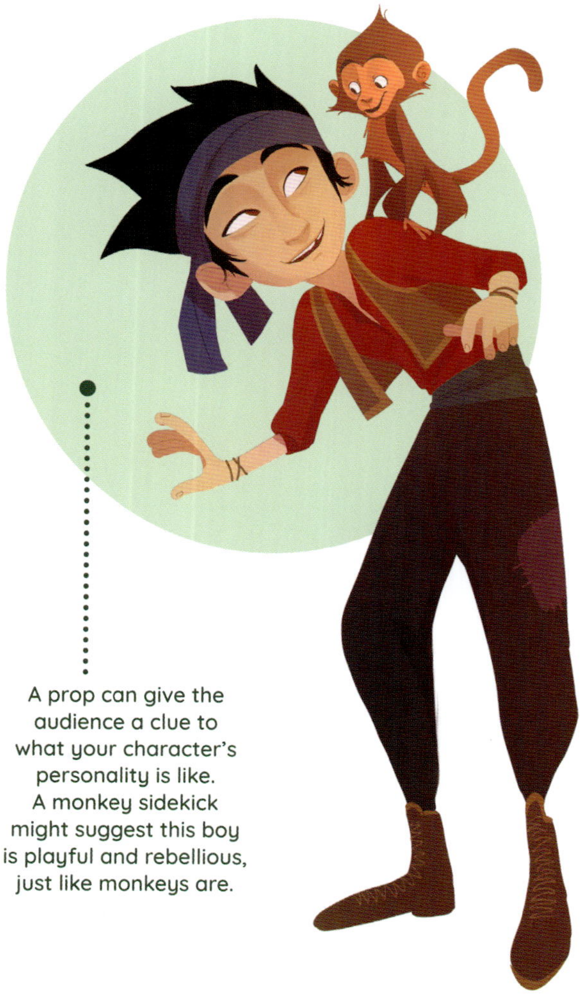

A prop can give the audience a clue to what your character's personality is like. A monkey sidekick might suggest this boy is playful and rebellious, just like monkeys are.

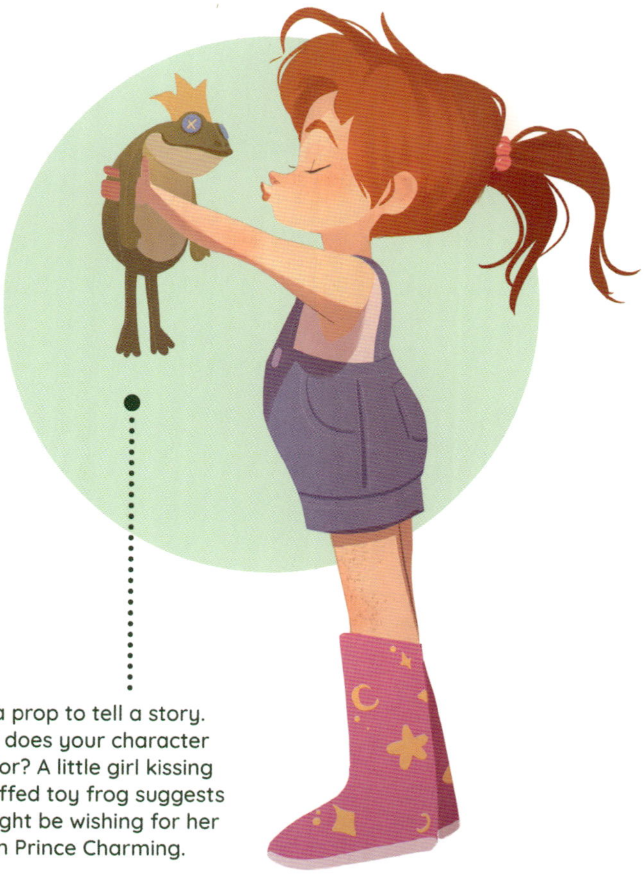

Use a prop to tell a story. What does your character wish for? A little girl kissing her stuffed toy frog suggests she might be wishing for her own Prince Charming.

Sweeney Boo

When designing props, it is important to consider gravity; every object has a weight that needs to be taken into consideration when interacting with or carried by a character. Props can also tell the audience a lot about a character's personality, depending on the way they use or carry it.

Hint at your character's personality through the way they hold their coffee cup. One-handed can look confident and carefree, whereas a two-handed grip can make them appear endearing and shy.

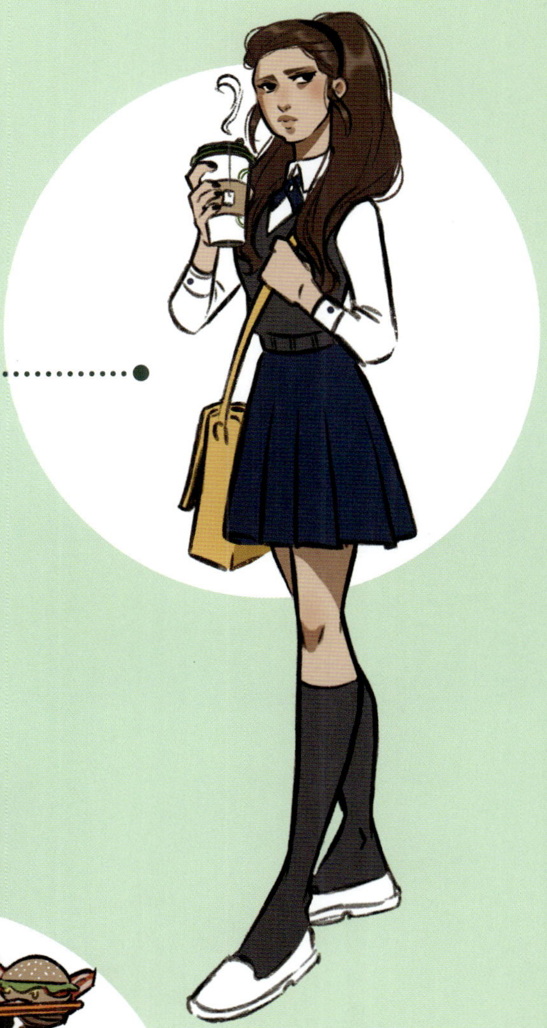

A skater character drinking from a carton of fruit juice can suggest he is holding on to elements of his childhood and is not ready to grow up yet.

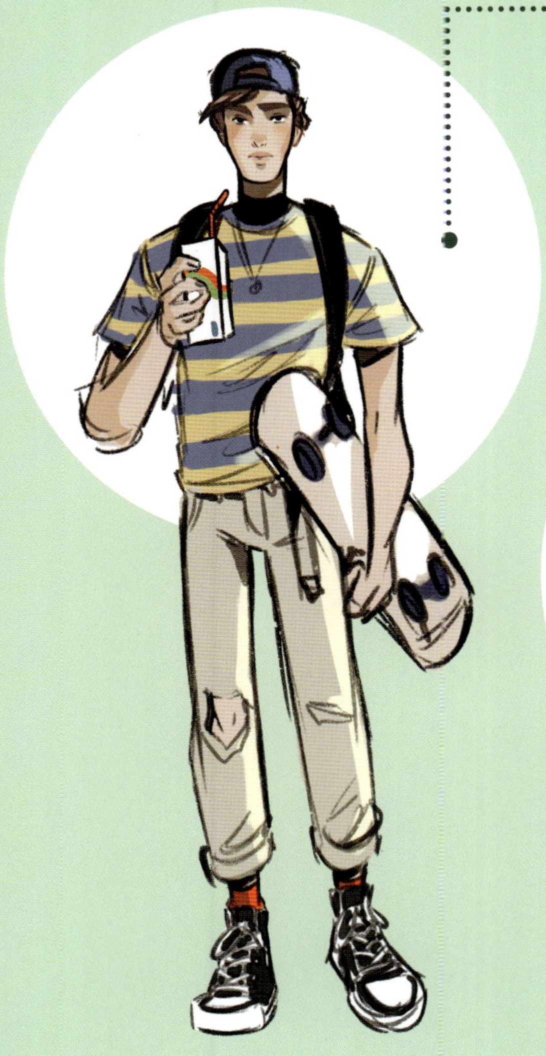

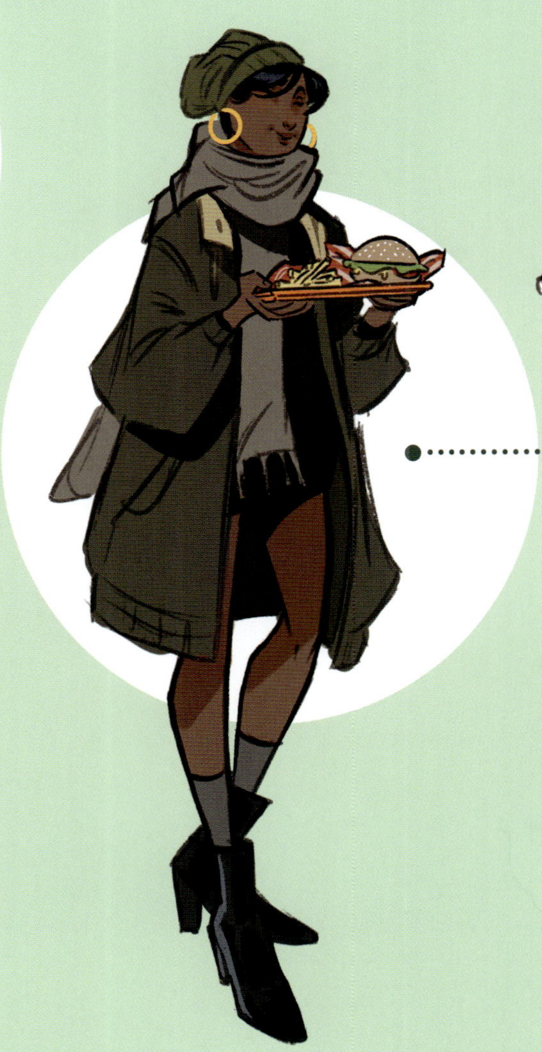

Here a fashionable character carries her takeout lunch on a tray, hinting at her fun, easy-going personality and love of comfort food.

Corah Louise

Personalizing a character's props and surrounding them with accessories suited to their nature can help their world feel more believable and genuine. You will already have given your character a style with how they dress and present themselves; this must extend to their belongings and surroundings to help widen their story. Each of your characters' homes will look different because they are drawn to different colors, interests, and styles, influenced by their story and personality. Try designing something like a cake or mug for each of your characters. If you had to buy them one as a present, what would it look like?

A professional and highly composed chef working at a stylish, affluent restaurant uses a decorated plate and pair of chopsticks. The extra detail on the objects suggests luxury.

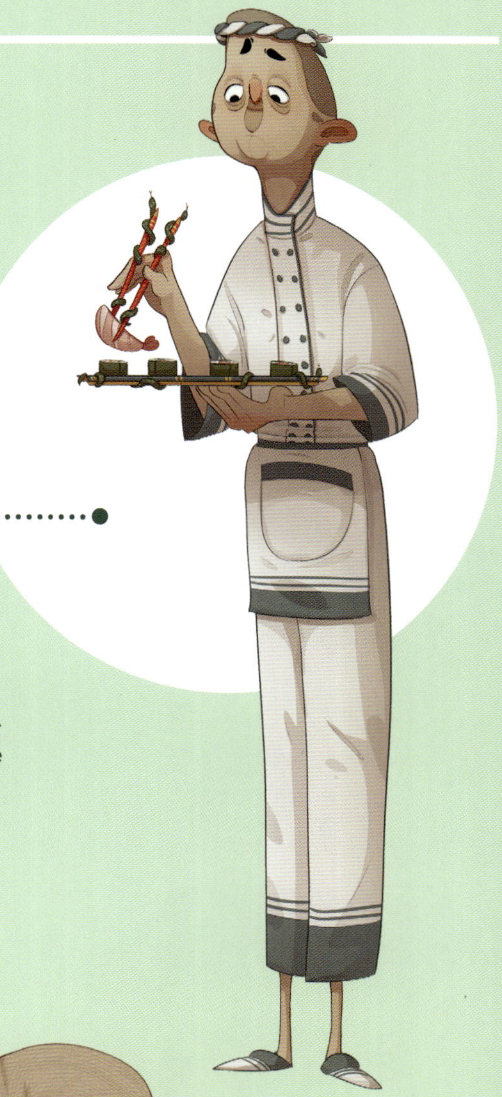

This character is 100 today! Her father designed, baked, and decorated this cake especially for her – the colors and shapes of the cake mirror her character and provide insight into her story.

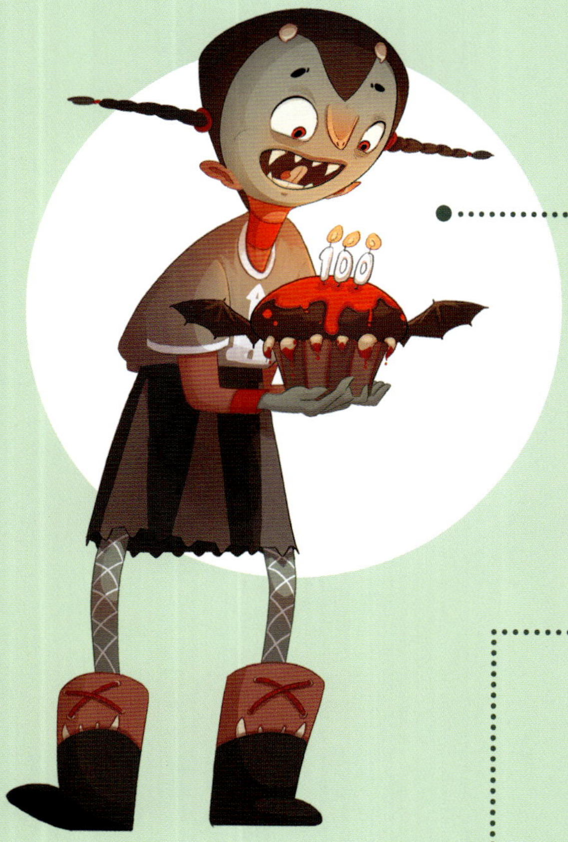

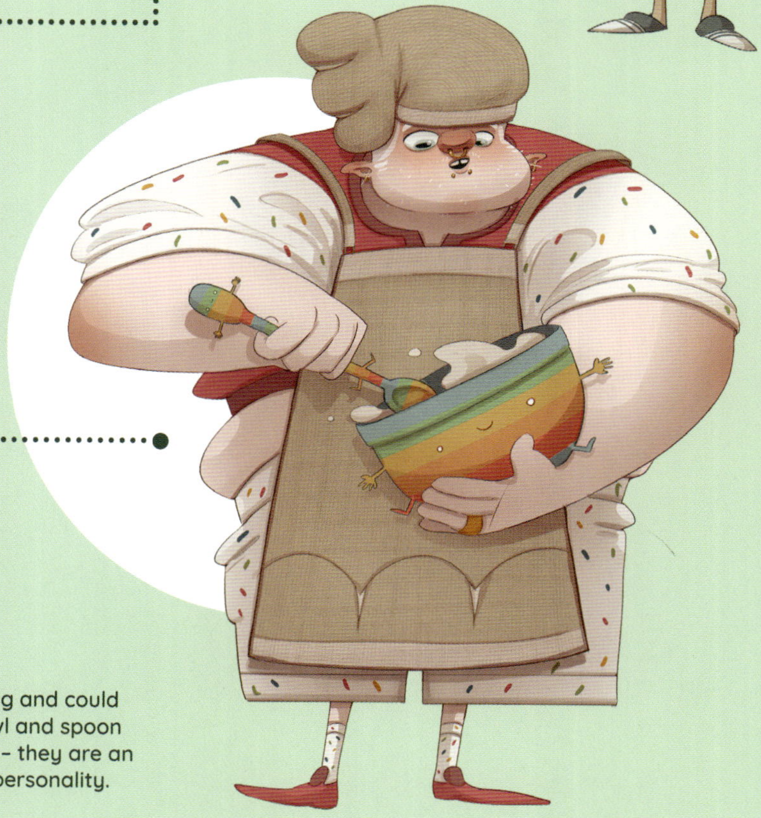

This character loves baking and could not resist this rainbow bowl and spoon duo to add to his collection – they are an extension of his colorful personality.

Olga Andriyenko

When designing props, it is important to keep their purpose and history in mind. Consider whether the item is old and well-loved, or shiny and brand new. Establish a connection to the character by reusing elements from their design, or a few colors from the same color scheme, in the design of the prop.

Gathering reference images is key when designing historic props. References will not only help your historical accuracy, but will often provide unexpected inspiration, too. When an item has been used a lot, especially in battle, it will show signs of wear and tear such as scratches, dents, dirt, and weathered paint.

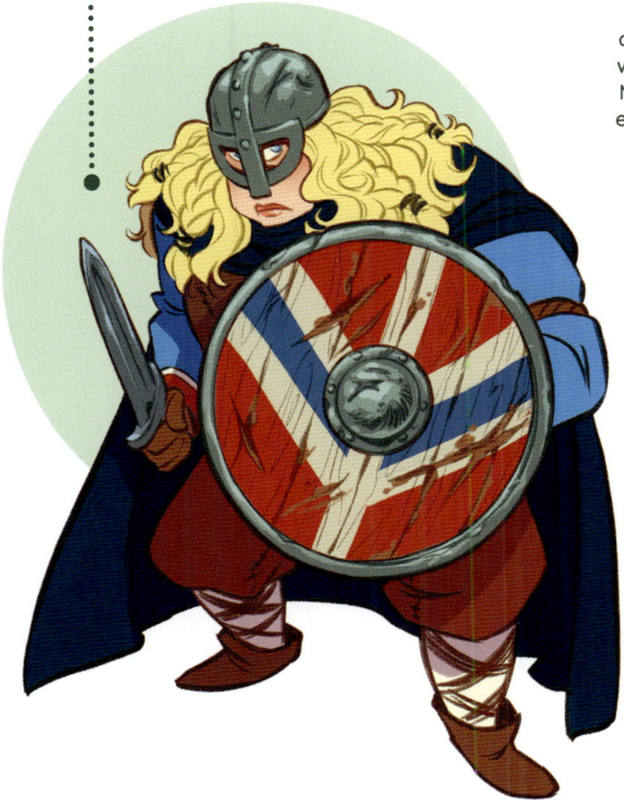

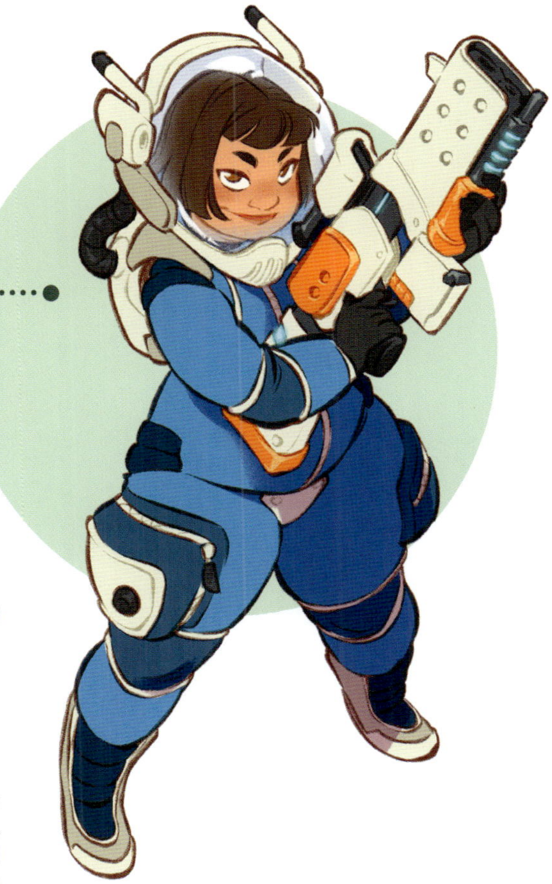

Sci-fi does not follow strict rules, so there are no limits to your creativity! When designing a space gun, start by studying the various elements that make up a real-life gun, and then try to recreate it with more unusual shapes. Make use of neon-colored elements and bright lights.

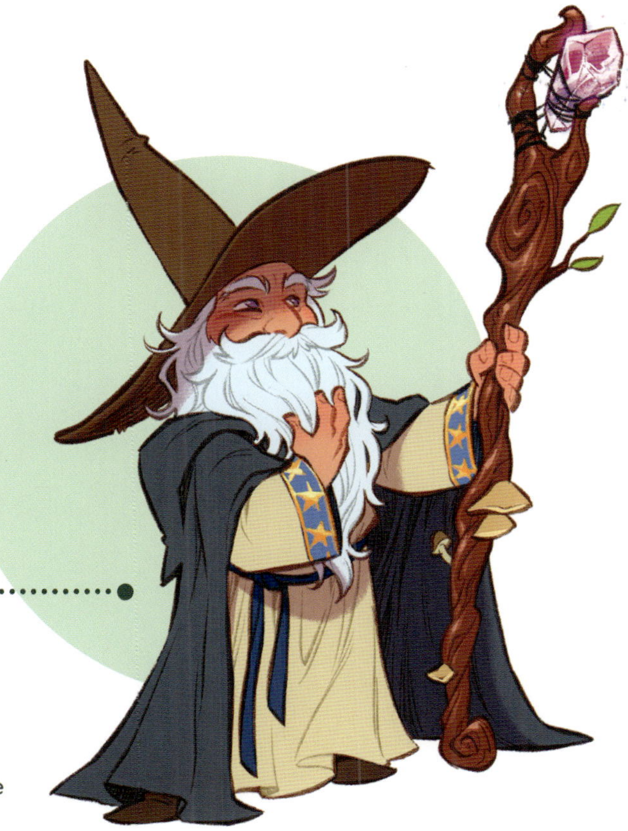

Create fantastical props by combining elements from nature with curious magical elements. This wizard's staff might once have been a regular tree branch, but its unusual shape and the decoration indicate the magic flowing through it.

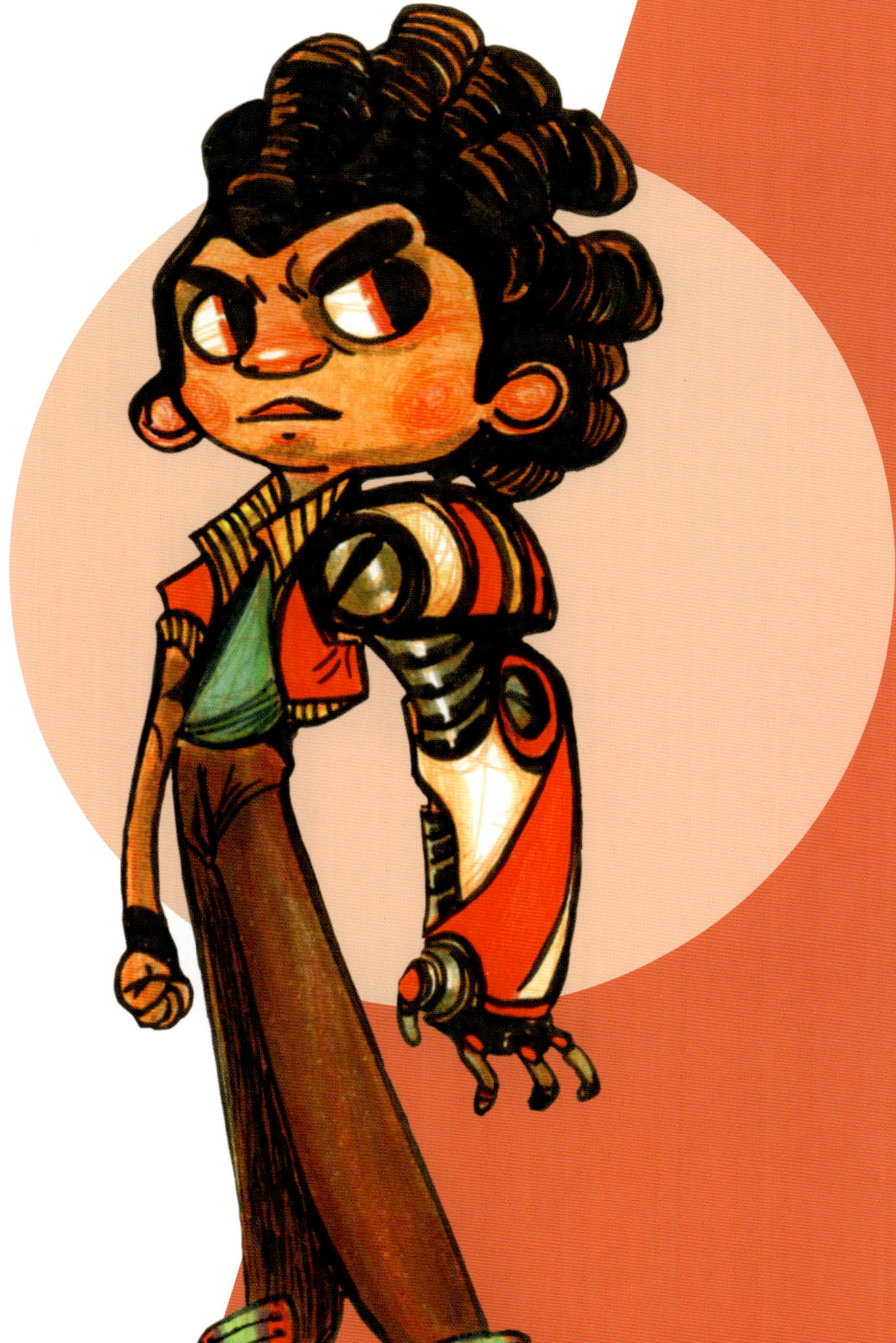

Image © Eduardo Vieira

PUTTING IT ALL TOGETHER

CREATING ENGAGING CHARACTERS
PAGE 242

HERO VERSUS VILLAIN
PAGE 244

CREATING ENGAGING CHARACTERS

Eduardo Vieira

Designing engaging characters is not an easy task. Character design is a process where you are basically creating life on paper. Every character artist wants to make a design that seems to live and breathe, ready to be the star of a game, movie, book series, or animation, but this can be an overwhelming task if you do not know how to conduct it. The process will vary from artist to artist, as each artist's approach is organic, tailored to answer a specific problem or need, and influenced by what they like and how they think. This section will show an example process for creating characters that engage the audience's emotions and attention, which you can experiment with to find your own unique way of working.

Before we begin, let's look at two designs and how they work in terms of audience engagement. Below, there are two versions of the same character. The first (below left) is very neutral, with a regular design and good colors, but it is lacking something. The second version (below right) has exaggerated features that strengthen the character's visual identity: a giant chest, thin legs, big arms with small hands, longer eyebrows, a minimal chin, and misaligned features. The audience will be more engaged by an irregular, imperfect character, because that is also how we are as human beings. We are not symmetrical and perfect in real life, so why should your character be? Use size variance and asymmetry to make your designs more interesting and unique.

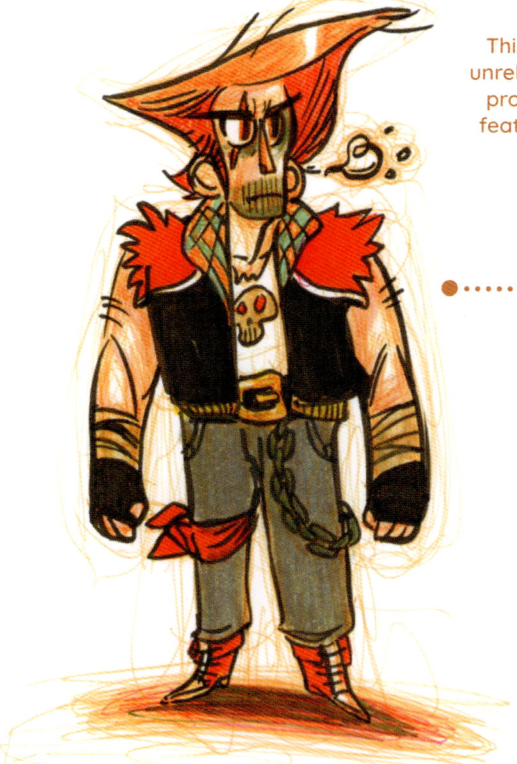

This character is neutral and unrelatable. The audience is not provided with any distinctive features, traits, or personality to fully engage with.

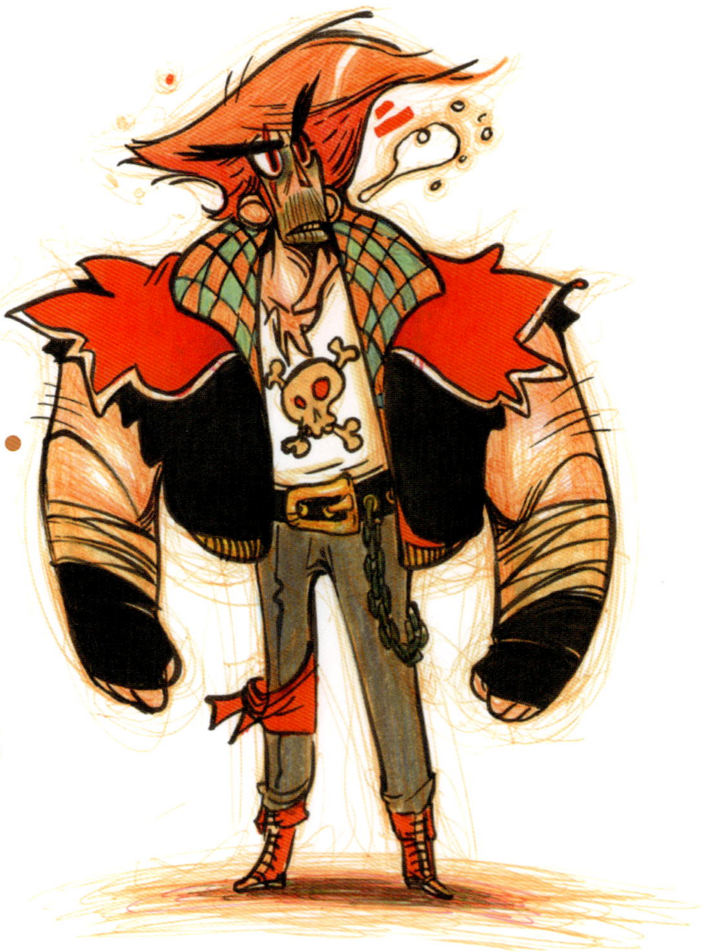

This version of the character is far more visually relatable and appealing, using irregularity, asymmetry, and exaggeration to give life to the design.

In the examples below, the emotional response is created by making the character's feelings clearer through the use of very exaggerated, stylized visuals. The character is already angry in the first pose (below), but it is possible to amplify her feelings further, making them immediately identifiable to the viewer. In the revised version (below right), her shoulders are more retracted, her head is angled lower, her eye is hidden by her hair, the colors are hotter and more saturated, and visual effects add some extra staging around her. The audience can relate more strongly to her because everybody has felt a burning anger like that at least once in their life!

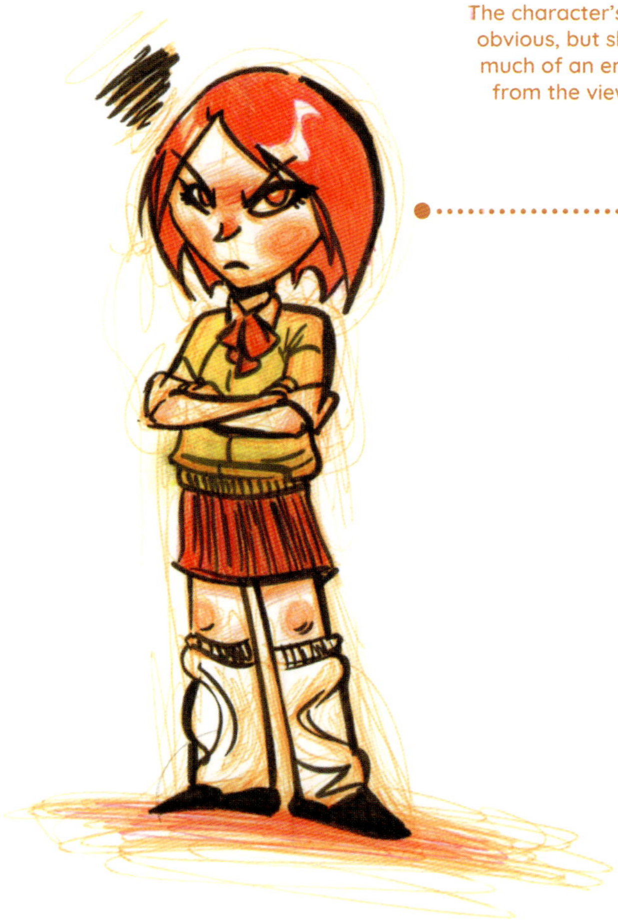

The character's emotional state is obvious, but she doesn't elicit as much of an emotional response from the viewer as she could.

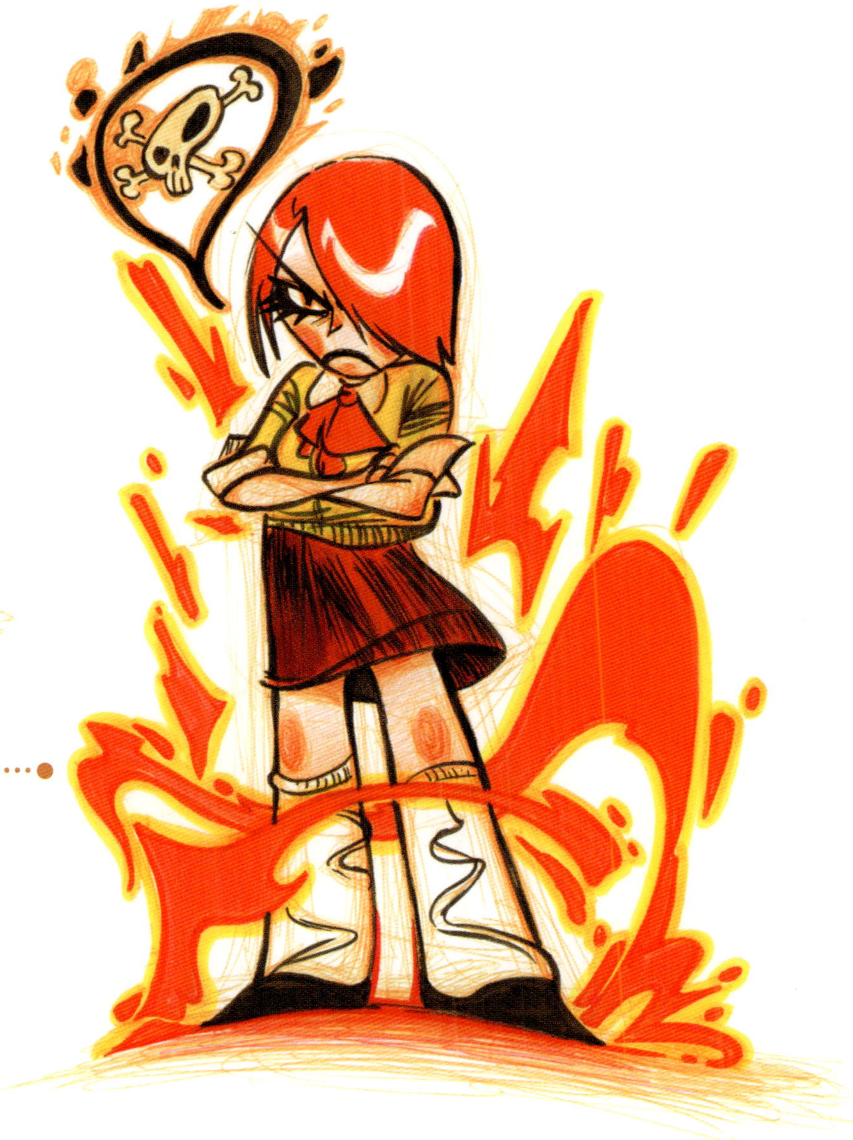

Exaggerating a pose, and even adding some staging and visual effects, can hugely help to set the mood and connect your character fully with the audience.

HERO VERSUS VILLAIN

Eduardo Vieira

In this section, we will look at the design process behind a contrasting pair of characters, developing them using some of the key skills and concepts covered in this book so far.

DAVID & GOLIATH

DYSTOPIAN, FUTURISTIC CYBERPUNK

HERO VERSUS VILLAIN

WHAT TO EXPLORE?
- Relatability
- Story
- Emotion
- Justice

SMALL, SLIM HERO
- Resilient
- Fast and agile
- Brave
- Street-style fighter
- Left arm detail

BIG, IMPOSING VILLAIN
- Oppressive
- Square
- King
- Heavy
- Right hand detail

Mind map & research

Starting with a mind map helps you organize the ideas you want to use. In this case, we will explore the contrast between two characters – a small protagonist against a giant adversary, a classic "David and Goliath" story. The brave and determined hero of the people is small and weaker than his foe, who is an oppressive, imposing, and powerful king. This contrast will instantly engage the audience's sympathy, because people generally identify with the battle between weak and strong. Using the mind map, you can research relevant information, such as different body types, weapons, and armor.

Initial thumbnails

Next, you can begin sketching very small thumbnails, working from the large outer silhouettes to the smaller interior details of the characters. This helps keep the initial ideas flowing without too much commitment to one drawing. It's a good idea to mark the sketches you like the most, so you can develop them further later on. The strongest thumbnails below are marked with a red exclamation point.

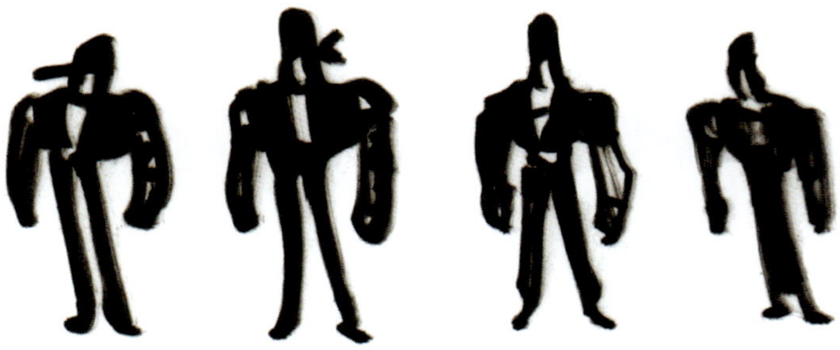

When making thumbnails, work from the outside in – from big shapes to small. Using silhouettes helps keep them quick and simple. Thumbnails are for exploring, not for rendering!

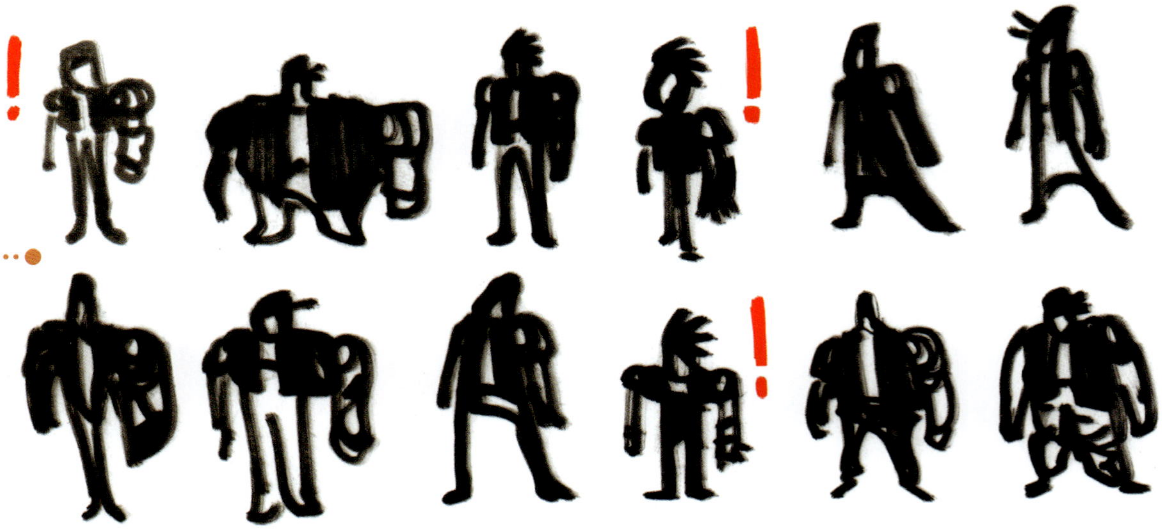

Further thumbnails

You can now make a second pass of bigger, slightly more detailed thumbnails. You should think about size variation and how to refine the shapes, but still avoid spending too much time on unnecessary details at this stage. Exploring a few different tools or brushes can sometimes help you stumble upon "happy accidents" that could improve your design.

Detail explorations

The thumbnail process can also be applied to important parts of a design. In this case, one of the defining features that will engage the audience's attention is the hero's mechanical arm. Using thumbnails, you can establish the design and size relationships of the arm and its parts, thinking about how its design and proportions can show how bold the hero is. This will save a lot of time on drawing later – if a feature does not work as a sketch, it will not work as a rendered image.

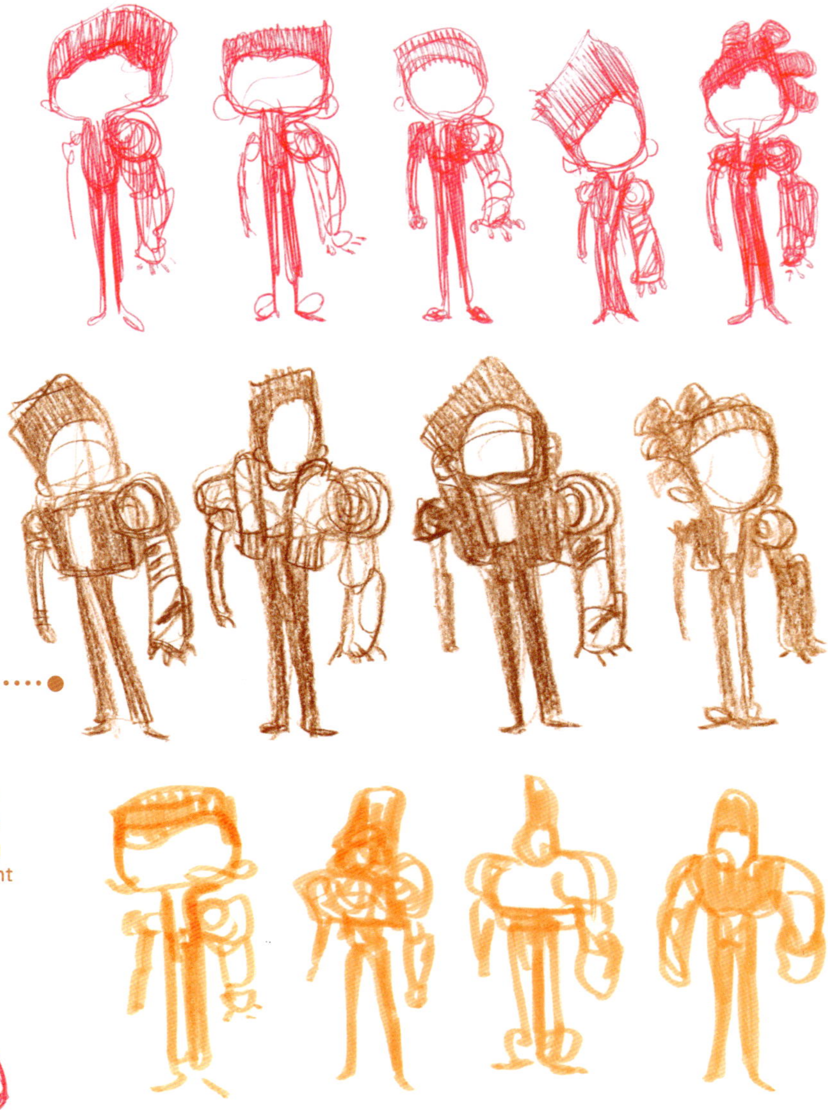

In the second pass of thumbnails, focus on shape and size variation. Try to find shapes that will visually engage the audience, using contrast and exaggeration. Exploring different drawing tools can be helpful for this.

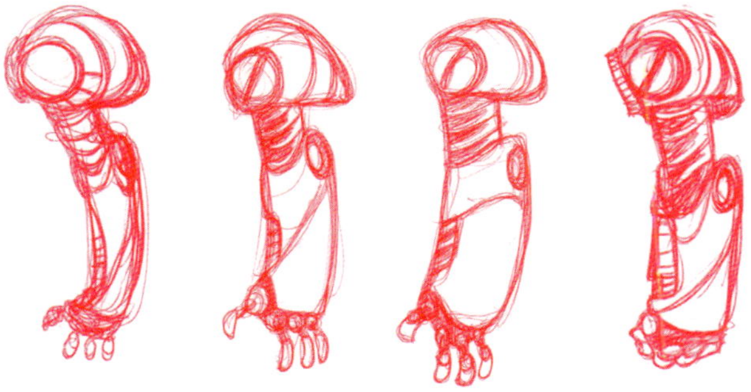

If something is going to be an important feature of the character, and a focal point for the viewer, it is a good idea to explore it on its own. Working out its design now will save second-guessing later. Keep thinking of shape, contrast, and proportion here.

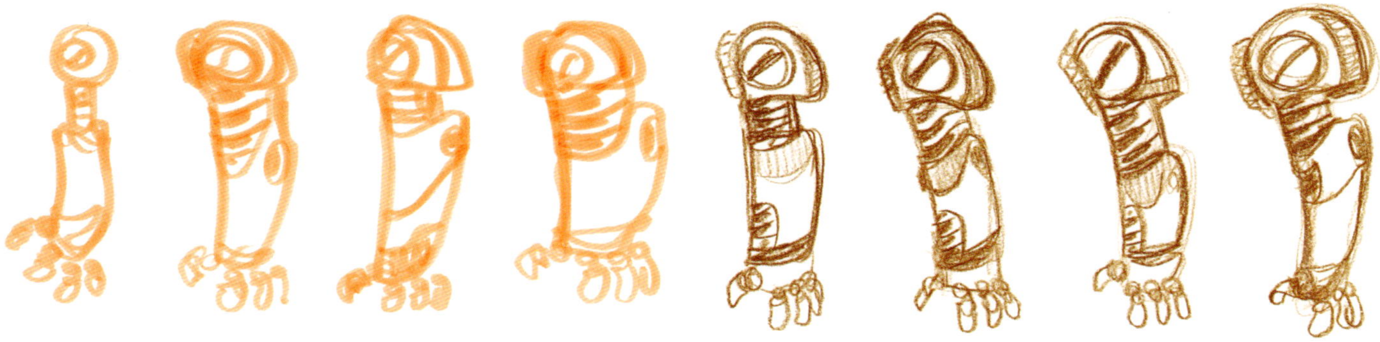

Rough sketches

With the thumbnails and important details set up, it is time to make bigger sketches, exploring the character's pose and gesture. Long rhythm lines should flow through the whole character to make his poses feel organic. Not only do these flow lines help make the design more visually fluid, but they help connect the body parts better, and show the character's personality. It is important to make the audience believe that he is a confident, agile fighter, capable of beating the villain – a hero the viewer can root for!

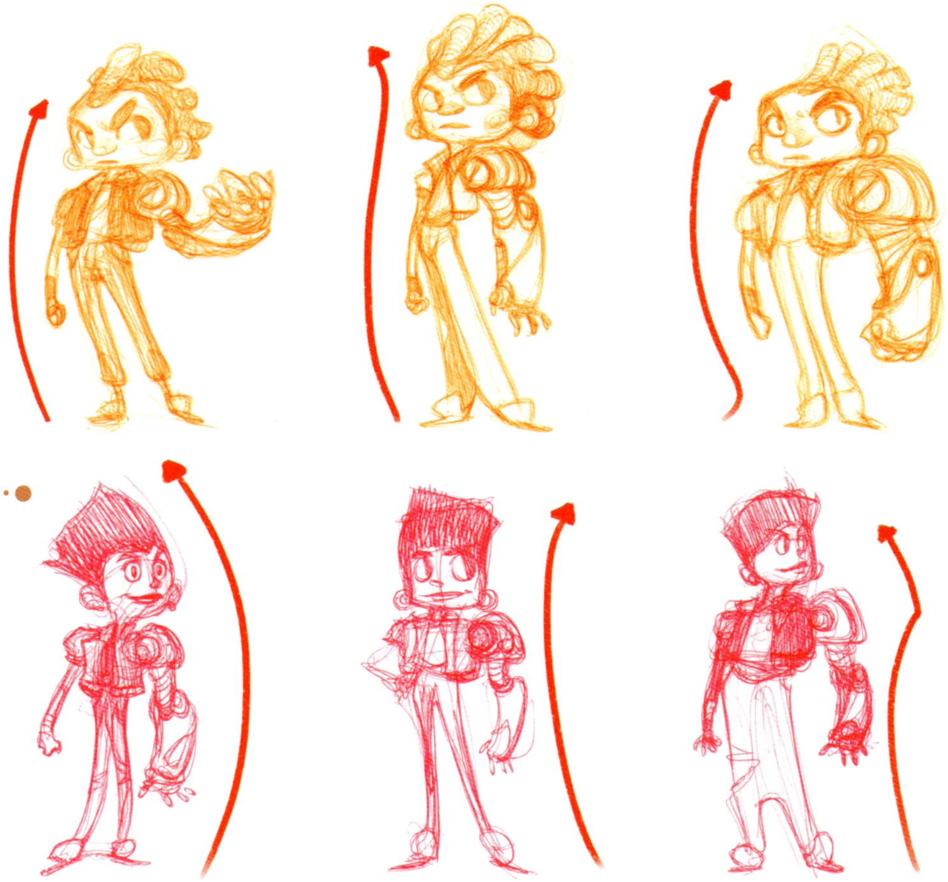

Good flow is key to drawing the audience in and giving attitude to your character's pose. Try to make your lines more fluid and visualize the rhythms of the character.

STAGING & EFFECTS

It is fun to explore a bit of staging for your character, graphically adapting the space around them in order to add some extra interest and excitement. These elements amazed me as a child when I saw them in fighting games like *Street Fighter* and *The King of Fighters*. They express so much about a character and make the world around them even more fun. By creating designs for things like puffs of breath, word balloons, action lines, and bursts of energy, you can transform invisible abstracts into eye-catching visuals for the audience. They make the space around the character more graphical, and easier to read and relate to. By using these to frame the character, it's as if we are seeing an exciting moment suspended in time, which adds tension and energy to the design.

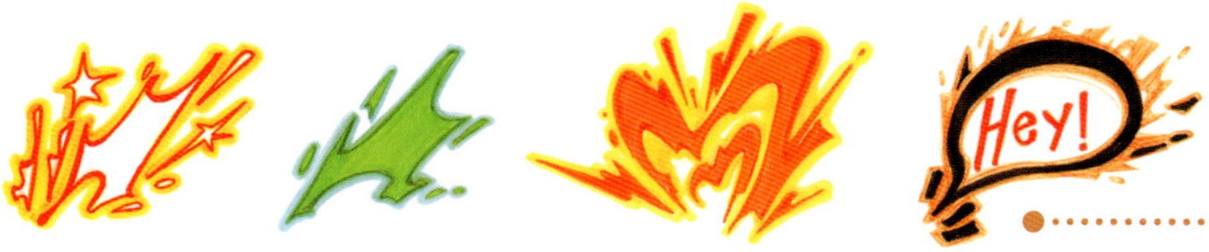

Staging and special effects can help set the mood for your character. Do not be afraid to tweak the reality and space around your design, and find visual ways to communicate emotional concepts.

Final character

Here is the final version of the hero character. A dynamic pose, determined expression, vibrant colors, intriguing details, and fun effects all work together to make an engaging design that speaks loudly to the audience. He looks and feels like a brave hero, and now the audience is primed to see what he might do next!

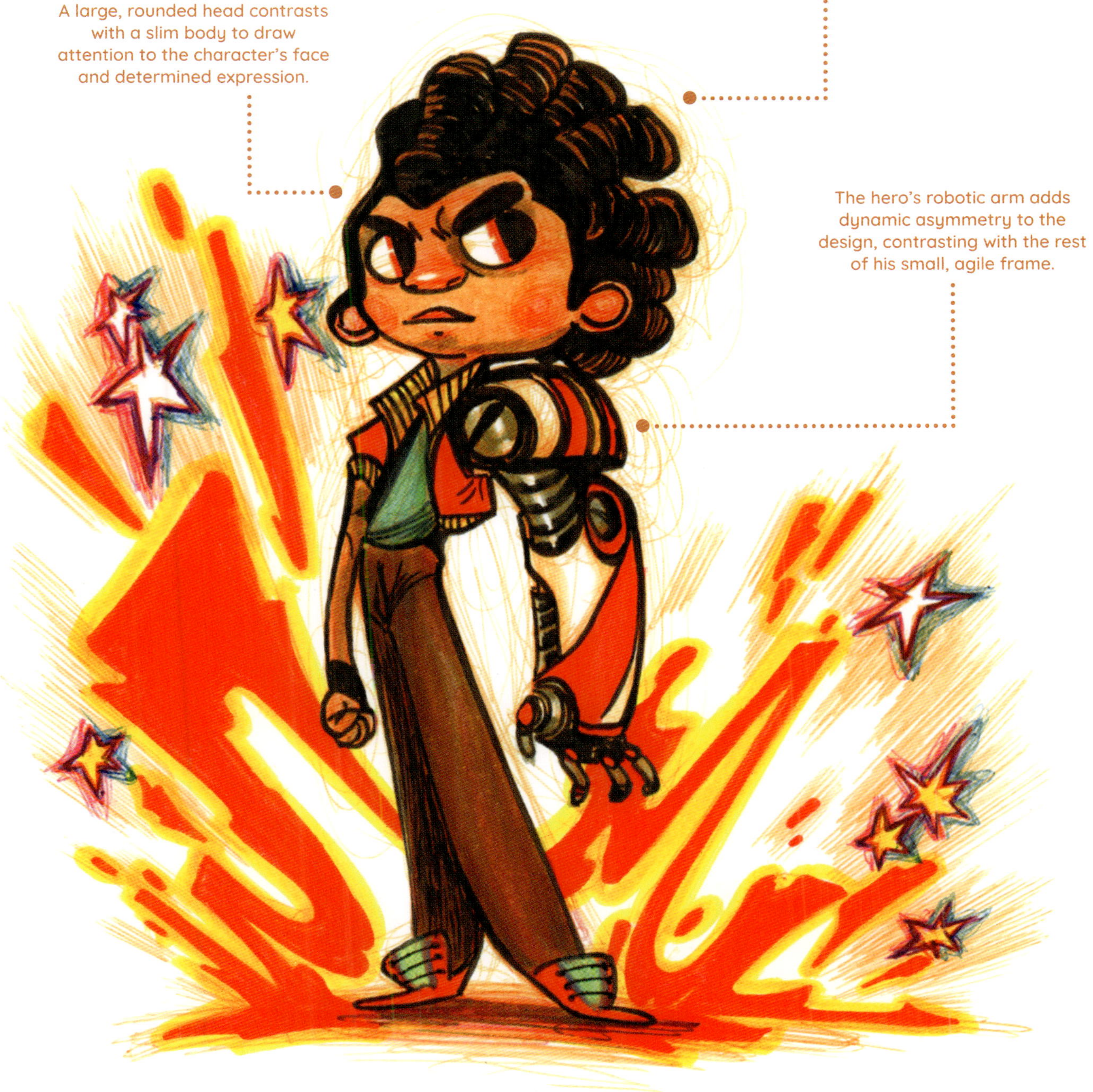

Image © Eduardo Vieira

The villain

The process on the last few pages works for all kinds of characters, including this villain – the counterpoint to the hero character. Here you can see the two stages of thumbnail development, from the very basic to the more focused. The thumbnails help determine the most efficient design for this antagonist – a strong, menacing villain, but one full of details and attitude that will engage the viewer. He is heavy and angular while the hero is rounded and slight. Like the hero, he has an intriguing, asymmetrical design, with a powerful mechanical arm, making the characters both opposites and alike.

Do not worry about the artistic quality of your thumbnail drawings. They are just a step in the process, and are meant to be rough and experimental.

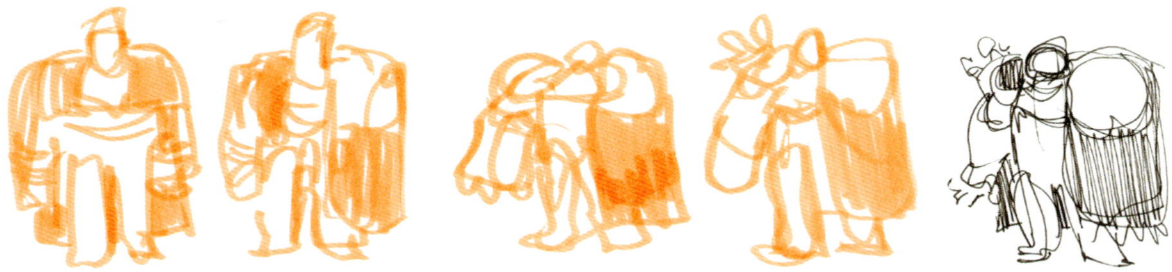

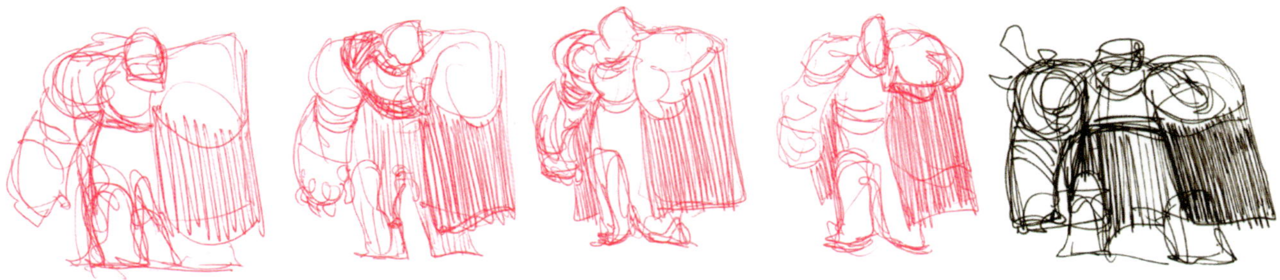

This character belongs to the same world and story as the hero, so you can spark the audience's interest by giving the two designs similarities and contrasts.

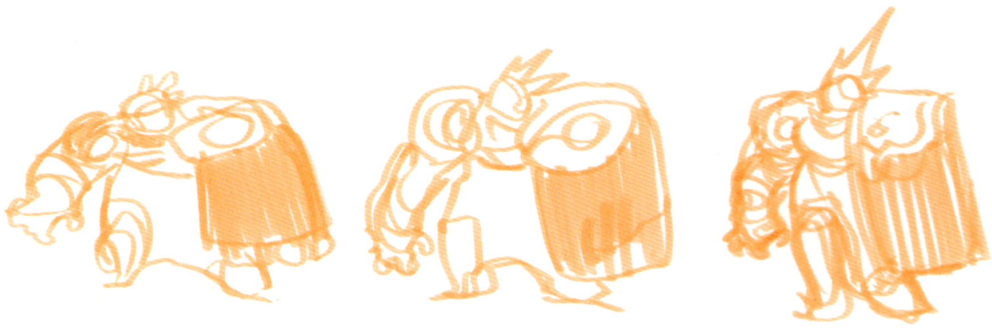

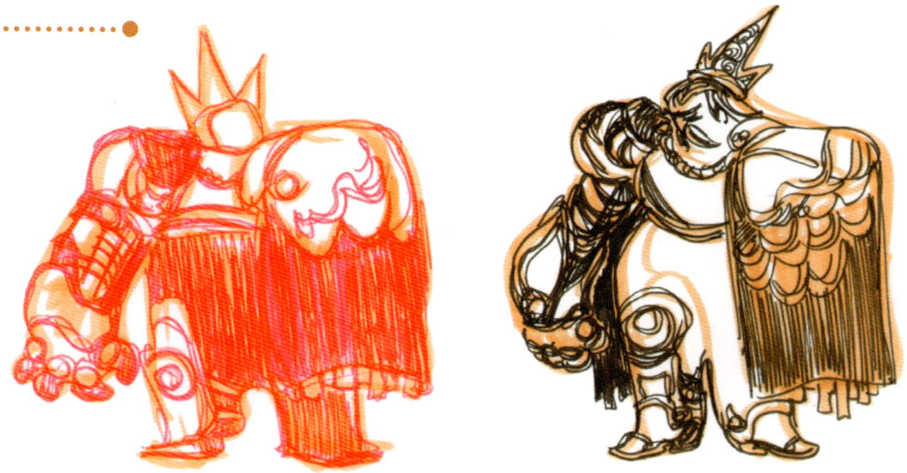

Patterns and textures add interest to the design, but are balanced out by zones of flat color and less detail. These areas of visual rest keep the viewer focused on the important details: the character's face, spiky crown, and metal arm.

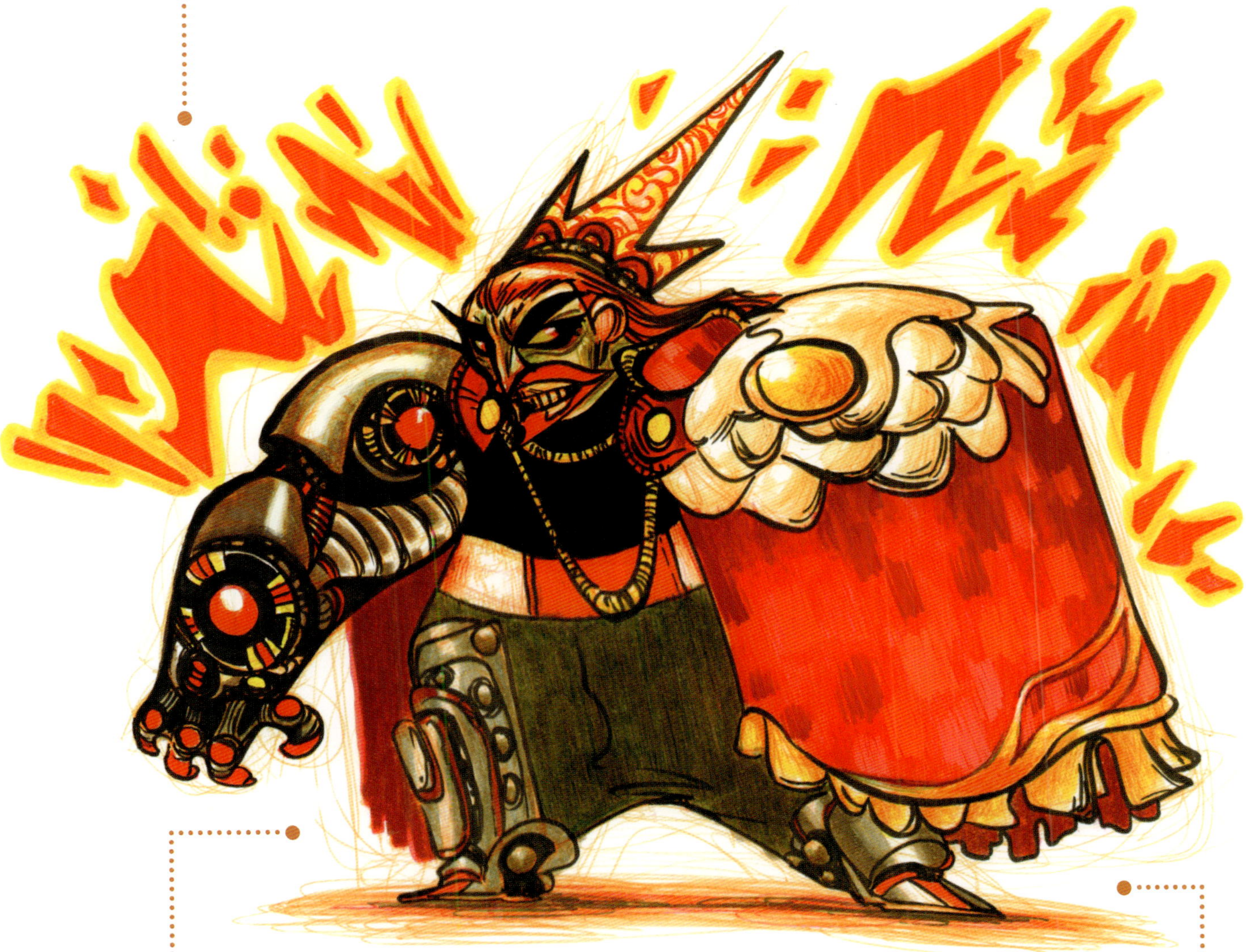

The villain design is simple yet efficient, with strong colors and a few visual effects to emphasize his attitude and dangerous nature. A good villain makes the hero look even better!

The villain's leaning pose adds some flow and action to his heavy, oblong shape, and shows that he is eager for combat.

An emphasis on fiery red hues makes the villain look powerful, angry, and dangerous. The dark green and black elements of his costume make the red cloak pop even more.

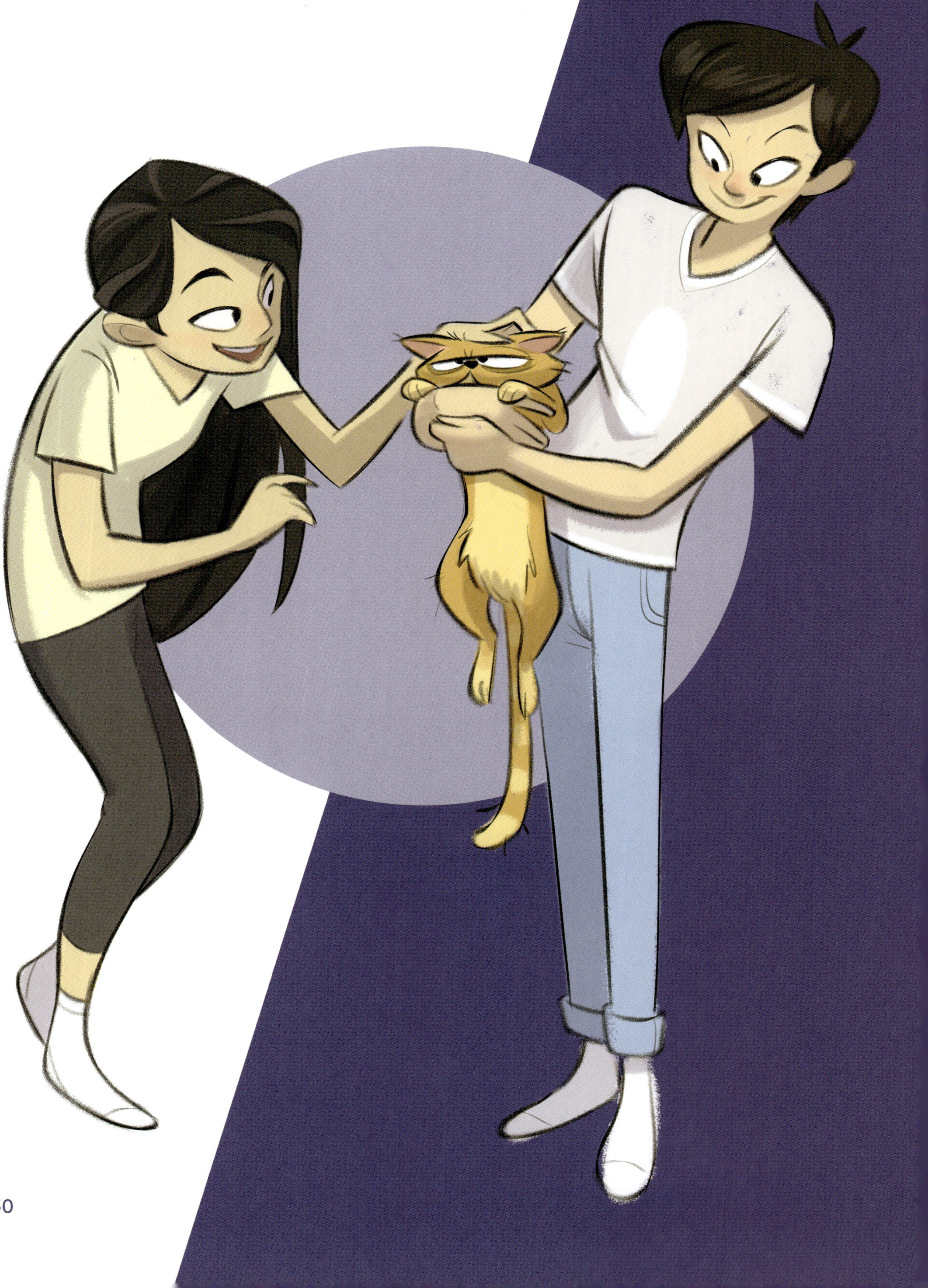

Image by Kenneth Anderson

WORKING WITH MULTIPLE CHARACTERS

OVERVIEW
PAGE 252

TWO CHARACTERS
PAGE 256

MAIN CHARACTER & SIDEKICK
PAGE 260

CLASSROOM
PAGE 264

BUS-STOP QUEUE
PAGE 268

FAMILY DINNER
PAGE 272

MUSIC BAND
PAGE 276

CROWD
PAGE 280

SPORTS TEAM
PAGE 284

OVERVIEW
Kenneth Anderson

Imagine a character that never interacts with another character. Sounds a bit dull, right? Characters rarely exist in isolation, in a bubble all of their own. Like us, their real-life counterparts, characters come to life when they are engaged with other characters, communicating and interacting with each other. Interactions can form the backbone of characters' conflicts and desires – how characters act through relationships with one another is fundamental to telling their stories. It is much harder (though not impossible) to fully reveal a character's story when they are alone in their universe.

Of course, sometimes in real life you have a situation where a group of people are in close proximity but are not interacting. Give it time, though, and throw in a little conflict, and interaction is inevitable. Picture a scene with a group of characters, perhaps waiting for a bus or queuing to enter a concert. If the bus is late, the group may start to vent their frustrations, while the excited concert attendees might start to bond over their love of the same music. This is where things get interesting, because now there is a story and personalities unfolding that an audience can engage with. If you design multiple characters all ignoring each other and not doing very much, it will not necessarily make for an interesting design, even if it is a scenario that sometimes plays out in real life.

Designing interacting characters can be challenging. Though you have full control over everything in the scene, it can be a little overwhelming when there are numerous characters involved. How can you arrange your characters so an interaction is visually interesting without being too complex? How can you make it feel like your characters are engaged in the interaction, while still having intentions of their own? And how can you give the scene visual appeal?

It can help to think about how you might capture a single moment in a story, and how you can engage all the characters in the unfolding event in some way.

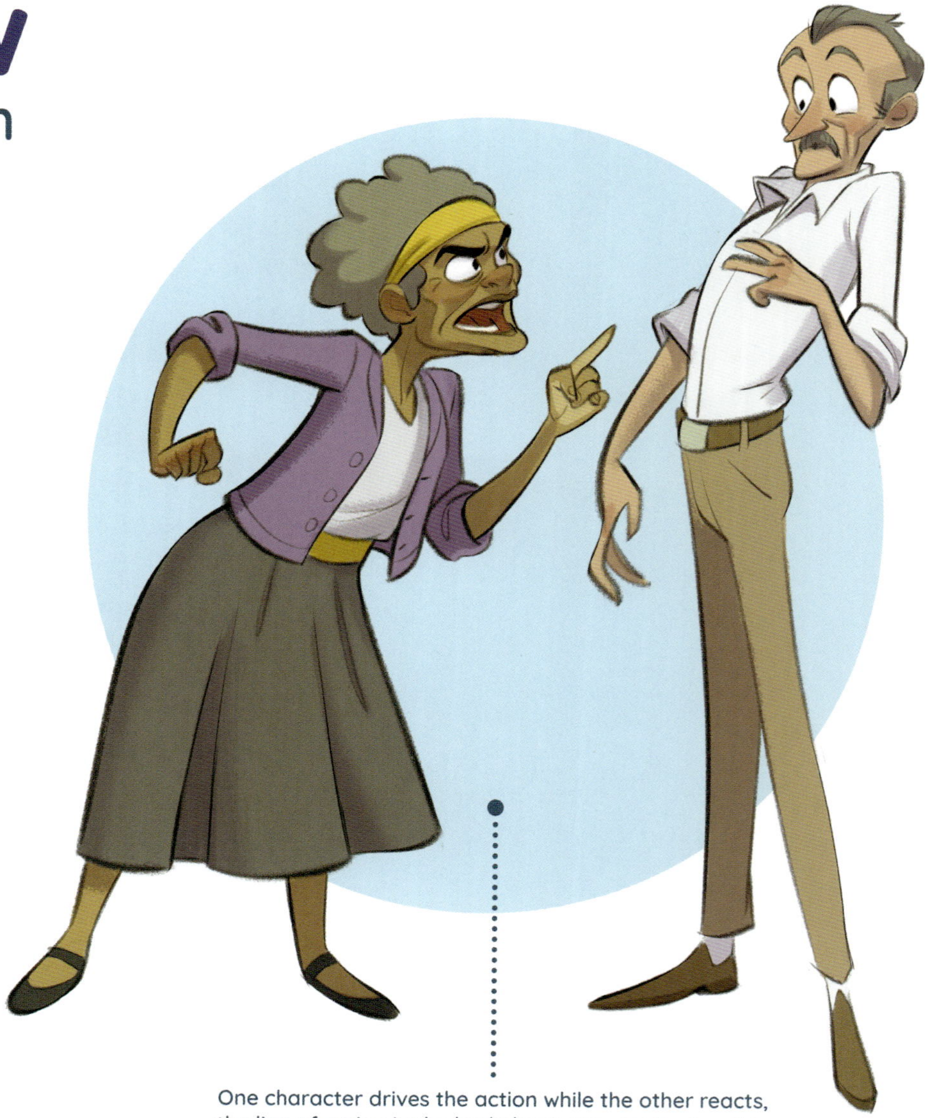

One character drives the action while the other reacts, the line of action in the body language reinforcing this.

This **story moment** glues the group together and provides an interaction with a unifying narrative. If there is more than one major story moment driving an interaction, things could get confusing, though some secondary story moments relating to the main one can add visual interest.

When designing multiple characters interacting in a large group, the challenge becomes trickier still. It helps to break a large group of characters down into smaller **groups** within a scene, thinking in terms of large, medium, and small, each dealing with their own mini drama within the context of the whole. The key concept to keep in mind is to create some **unity** in the action, with some **variety** too.

To make things **visually interesting**, use your design skills to ensure all the characters in an interaction or scene are different enough from each other – with different shape languages, silhouettes, proportions, and costumes – and then push these design choices to aid the overall composition and design of the piece as a whole. How you make your characters perform with each other will convey their different personalities, and ultimately reveal who they are. Such is the power of character interactions!

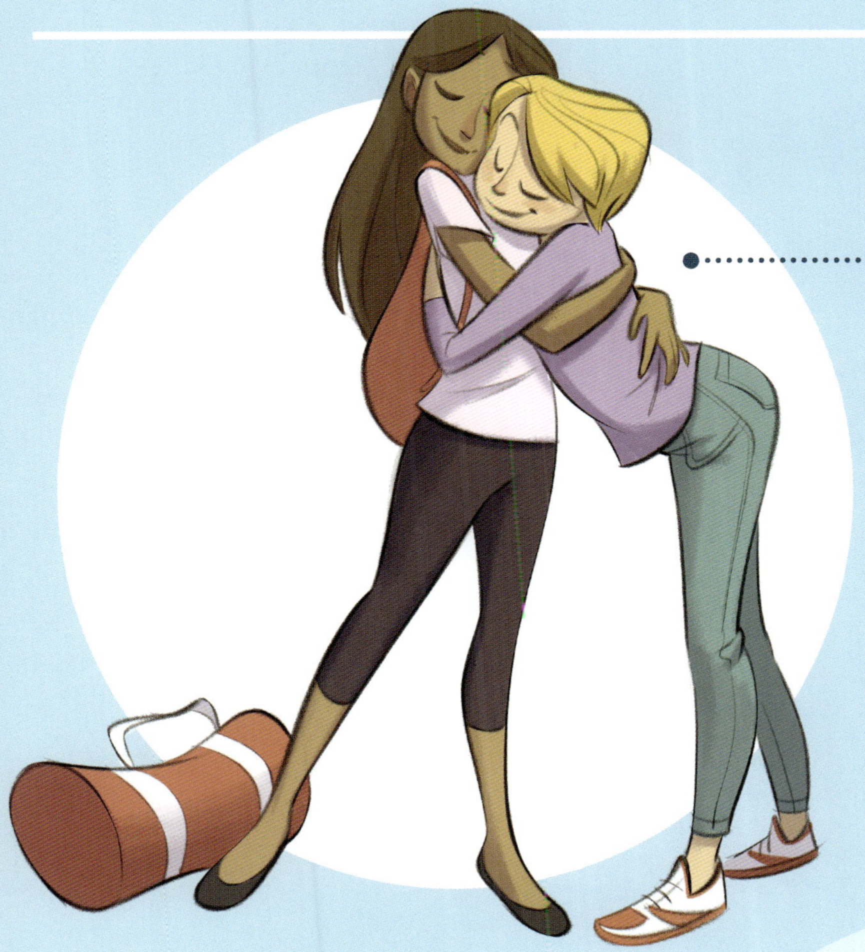

Two characters are engaged in a single mutual action together.

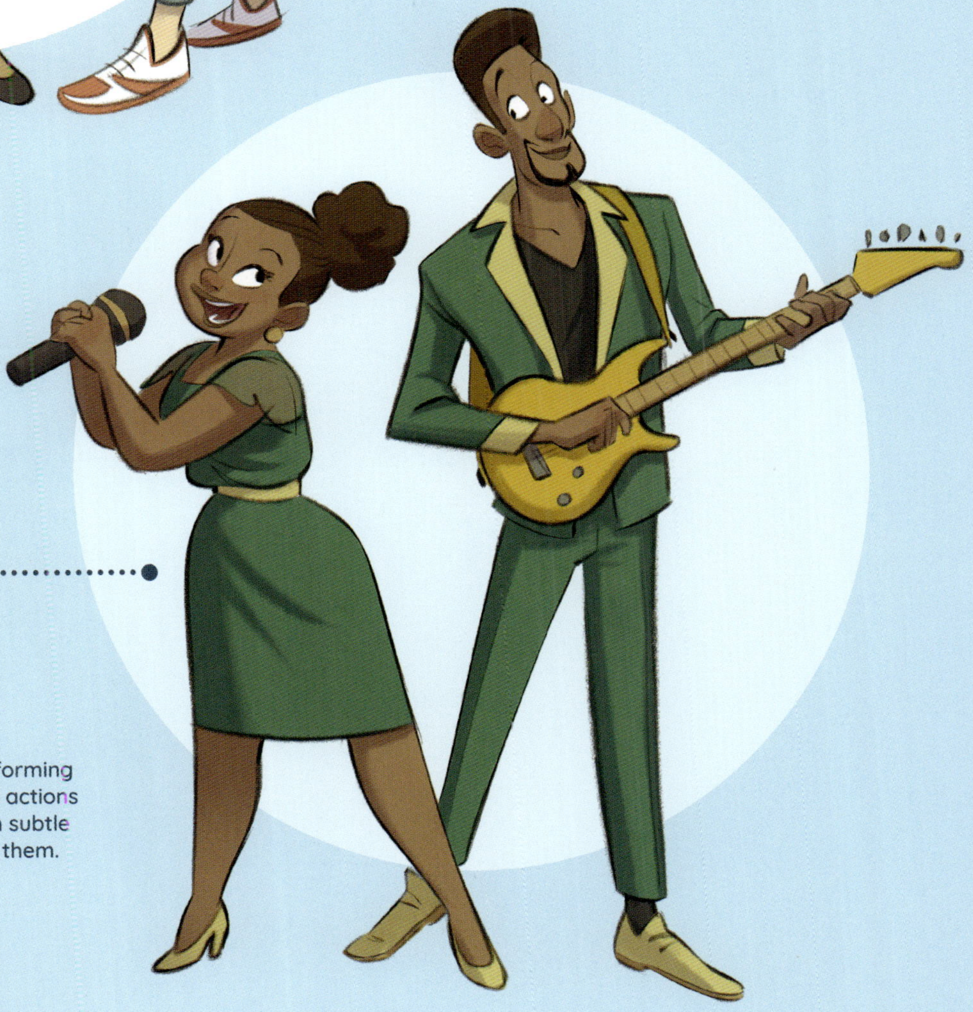

Two characters each performing their own action, but both actions relate to each other, with subtle eye contact connecting them.

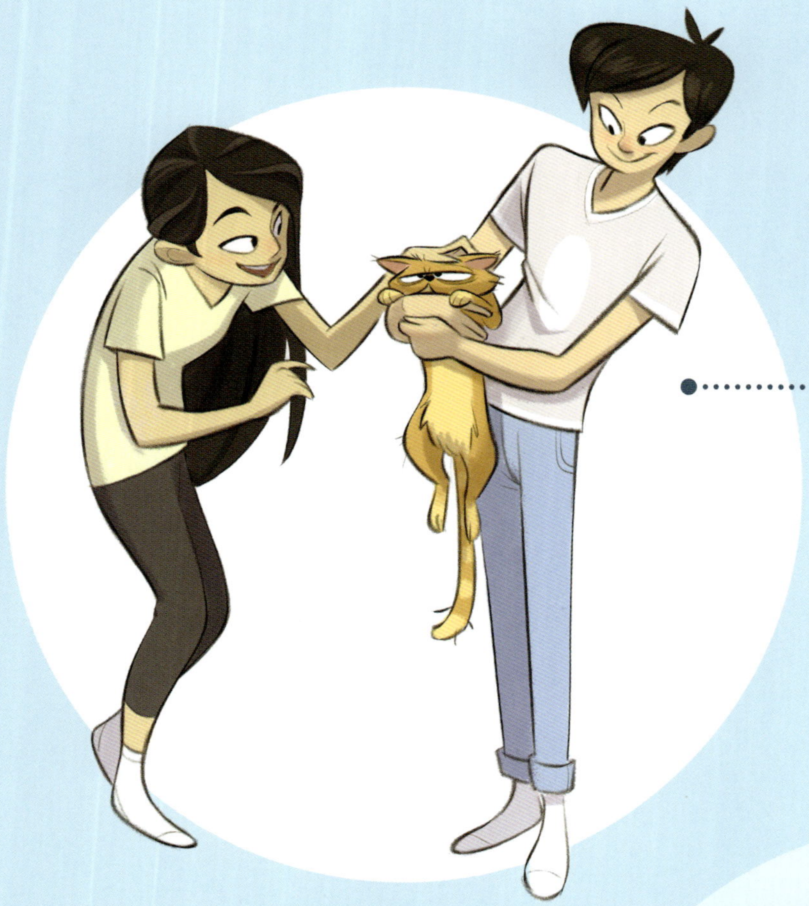

Character interactions can revolve around a conflict of action. Here two characters engage with a reluctant third character.

Multiple characters can play out different states of mind while all being tied together in pursuit of the same goal, reacting to each other as they go.

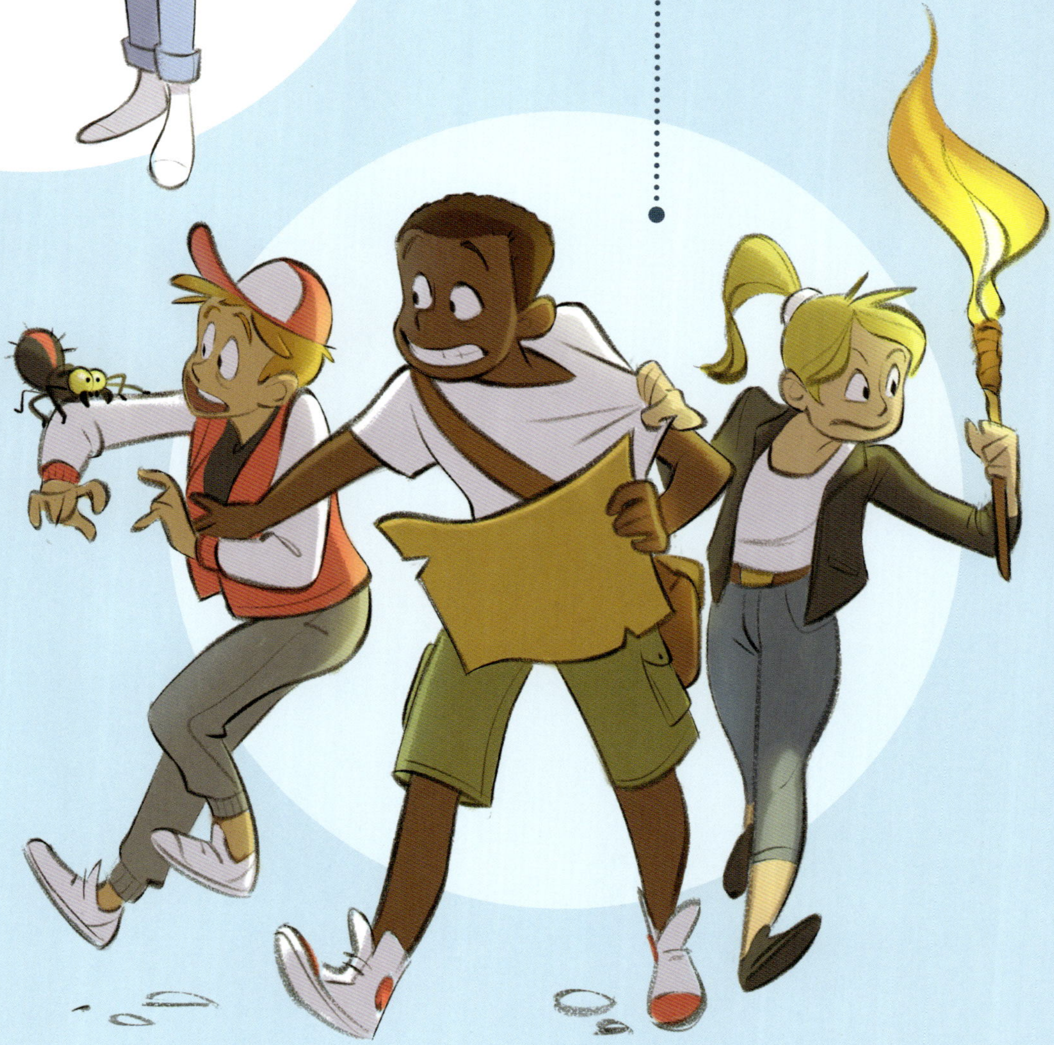

The character interaction does not quite work here – all three characters are doing their own thing while not engaging with or reacting to each other in any way.

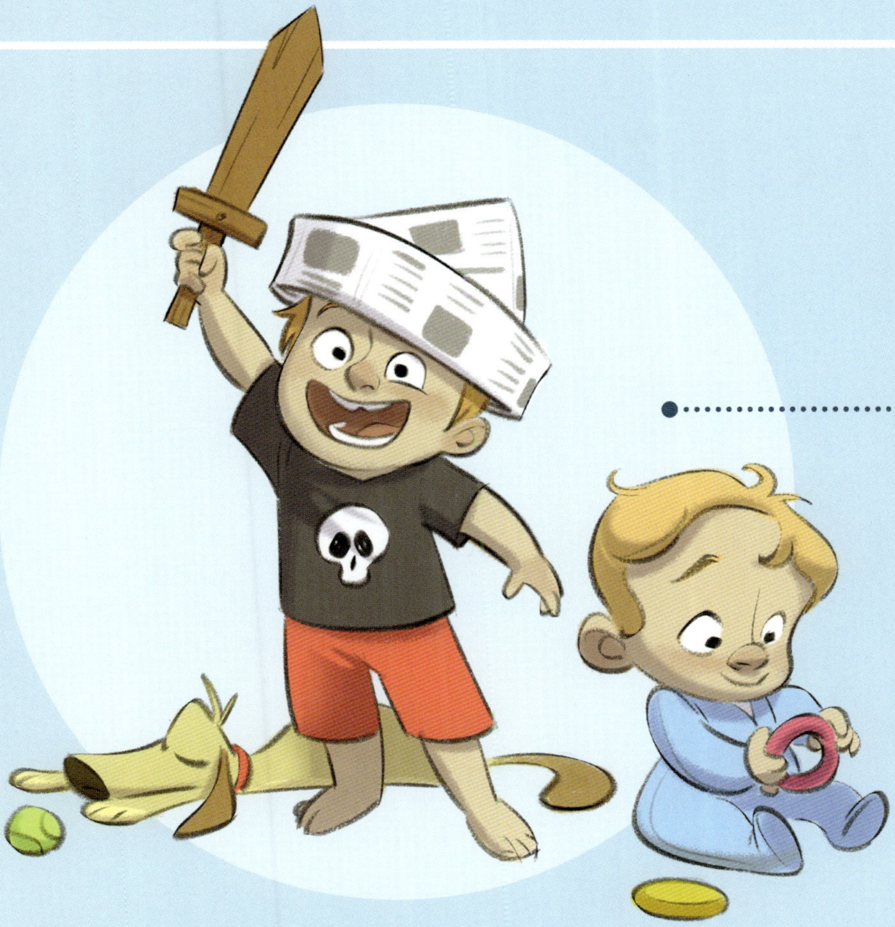

Character interactions can be subtle and personality-driven, or in this case, bold and purely action-driven.

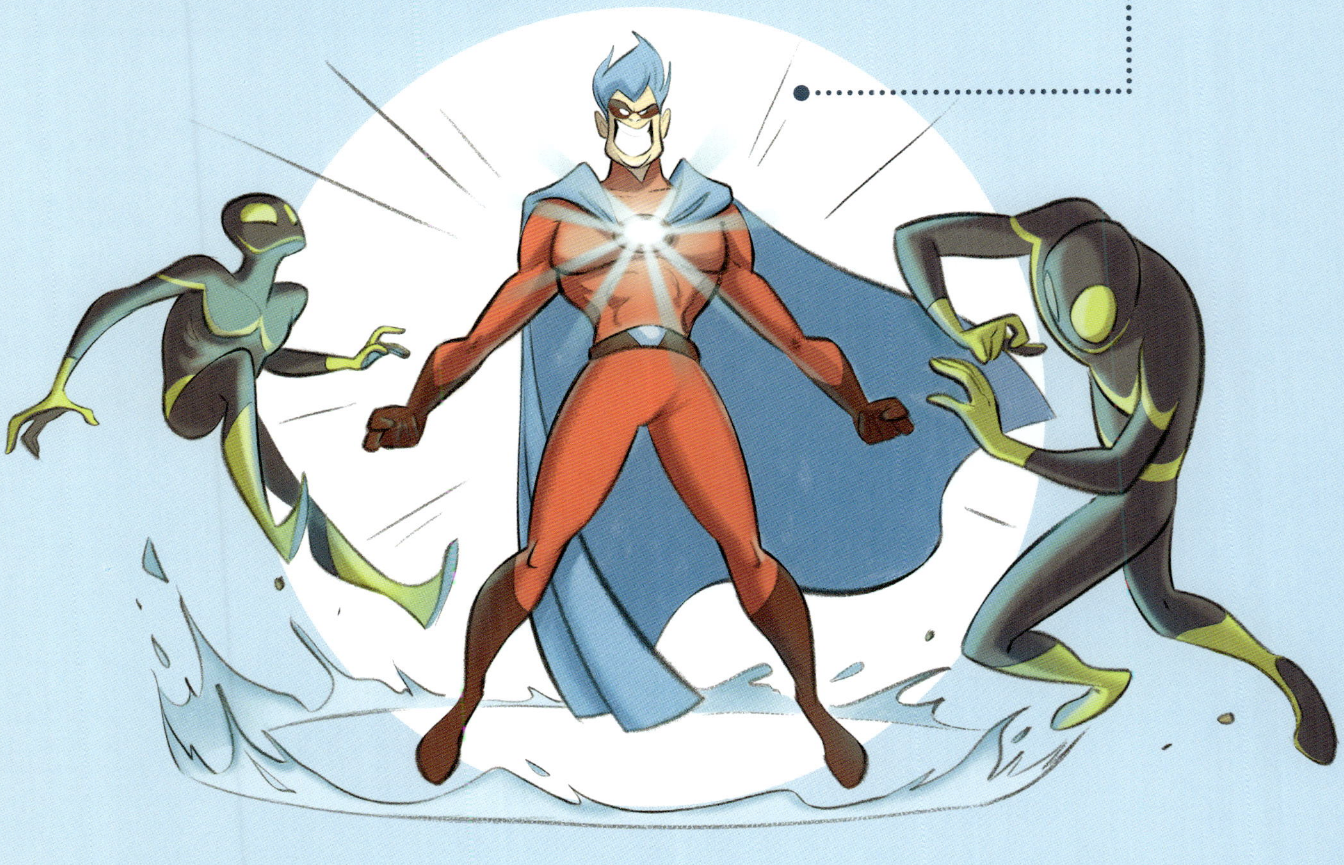

TWO CHARACTERS

Randy Bishop

Character design is about more than just appeal, silhouette, or technical skill. Your first thought when designing a character should be their role in the story you are trying to tell. Every character has a story and it is your job to bring that story out. One way to do this is by providing another character for them to interact with, whether that is a friend or, as in the project shown here, an enemy, to create a narrative or conflict.

GOOD
- Facing light
- Strong but rounded features

PREPARED
- Armor
- Sword

HEROINE

ADVENTUROUS
- Bag
- Cloak

STRONG
- Welcoming
- Defiant stance

WICKED
- Back to light
- Sharp features

SOMEWHAT INTELLIGENT
- Wears simple clothes

GOBLIN

BARBAROUS
- Sharp teeth, claws, and horns
- Loincloth

FERAL
- Aggressive stance
- Animalistic characteristics

When designing an antagonistic pair, or any interaction between two characters, start by sketching a variety of poses. These thumbnails explore different conflicts and size contrasts.

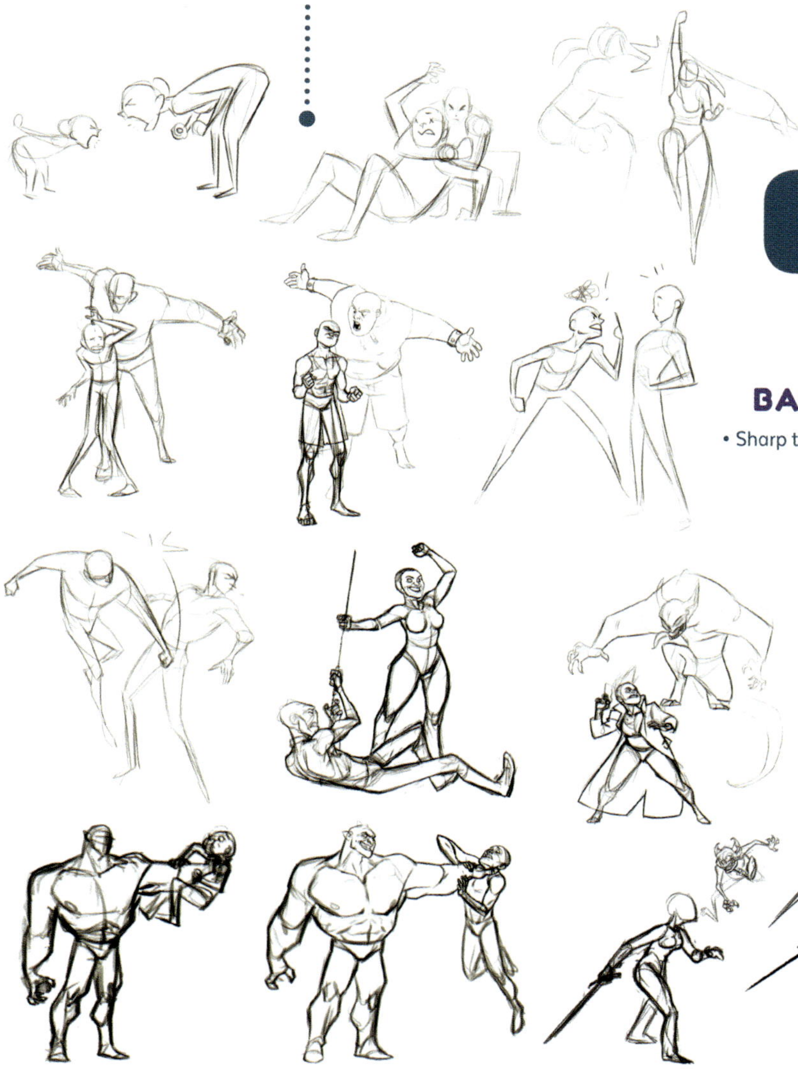

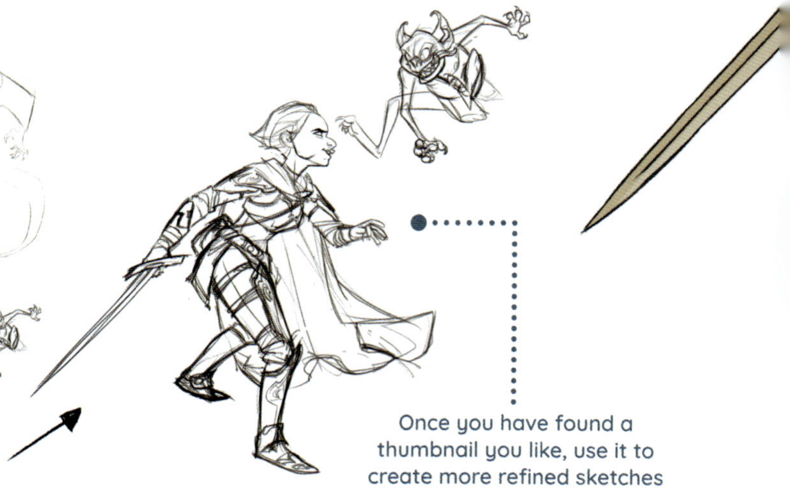

Once you have found a thumbnail you like, use it to create more refined sketches of the interaction, constantly rethinking the designs.

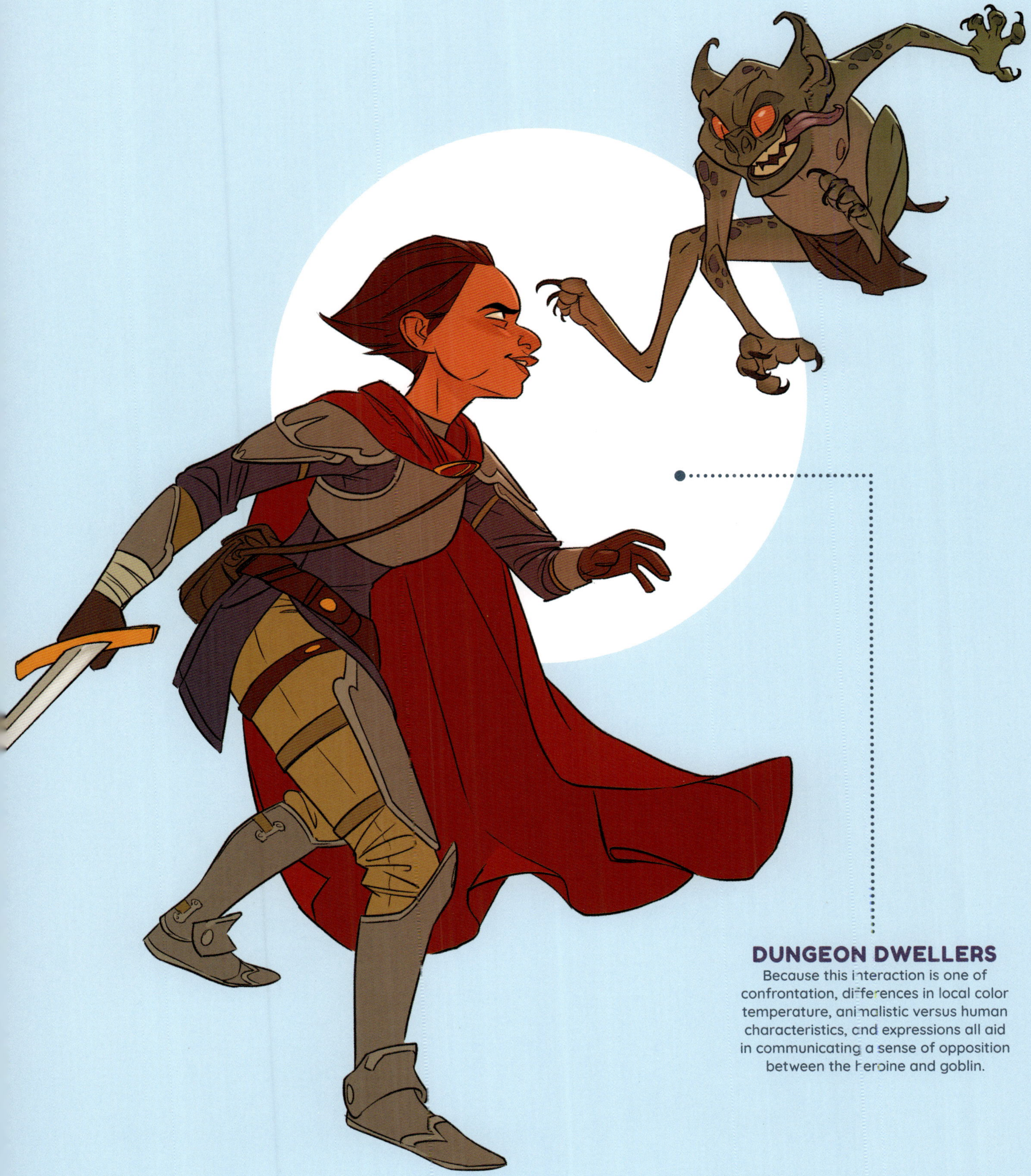

DUNGEON DWELLERS

Because this interaction is one of confrontation, differences in local color temperature, animalistic versus human characteristics, and expressions all aid in communicating a sense of opposition between the heroine and goblin.

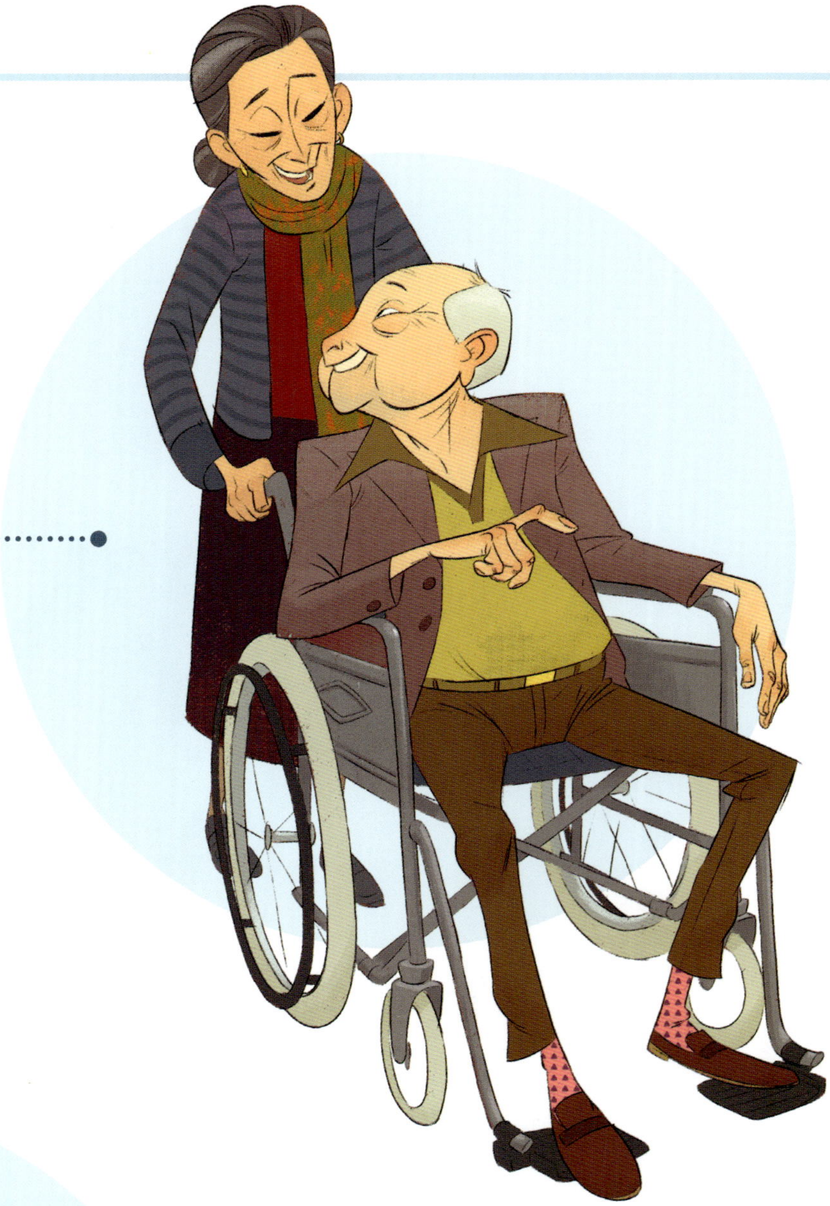

A STROLL IN THE PARK

It is always refreshing to see continued courtship in couples who have been together for decades. There is a lot that can be said in a familiar look between two people. The poses and expressions of this couple create a warm, affectionate interaction.

WATER FIGHT

Using a simplified style can help characters feel more youthful and happy. Capturing a moment like the water hitting the boy's face helps the audience feel like they are part of what's happening. The eye contact and water serve to visually connect the two characters.

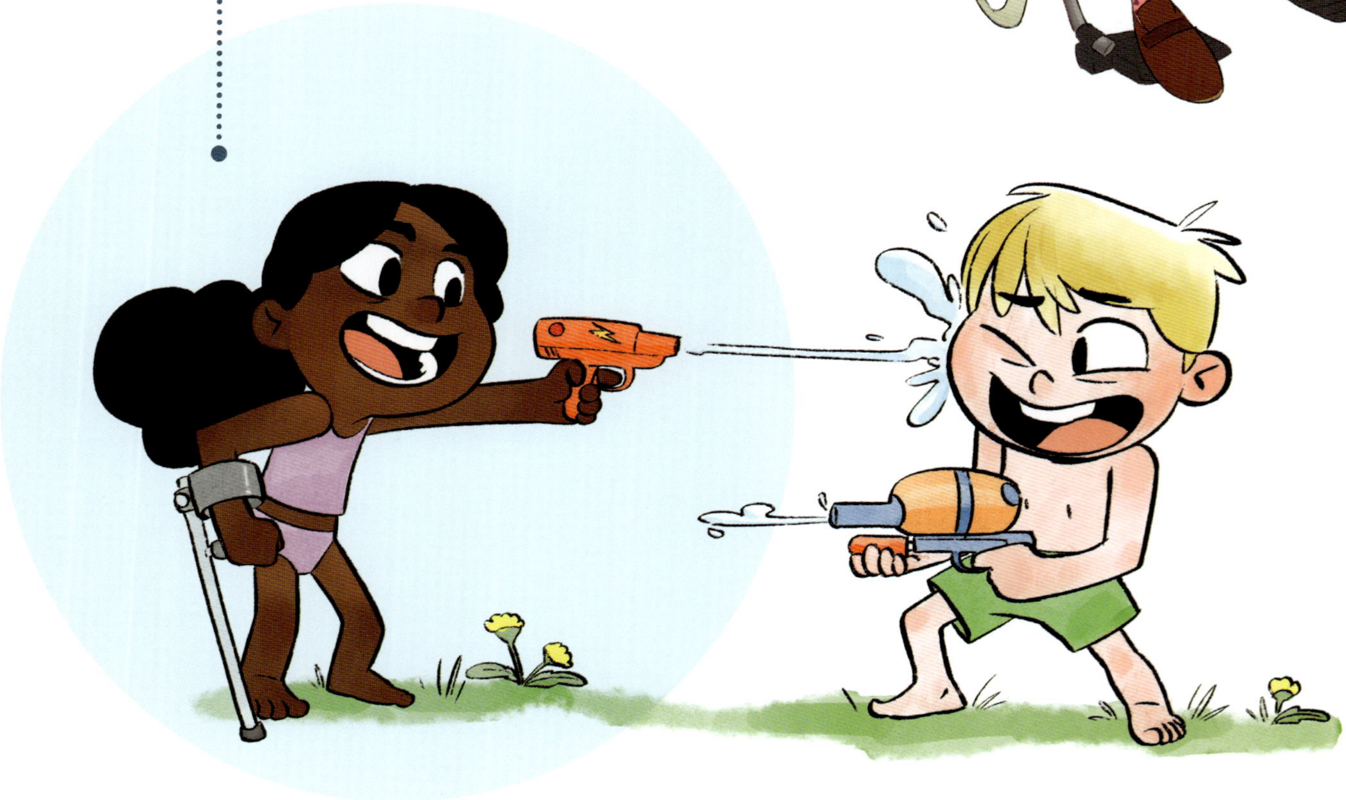

CURSED TOMB

You can highlight differences in your characters' personalities by showing how they react to the same situation. In this case, the man is full of wonder while the woman is full of apprehension.

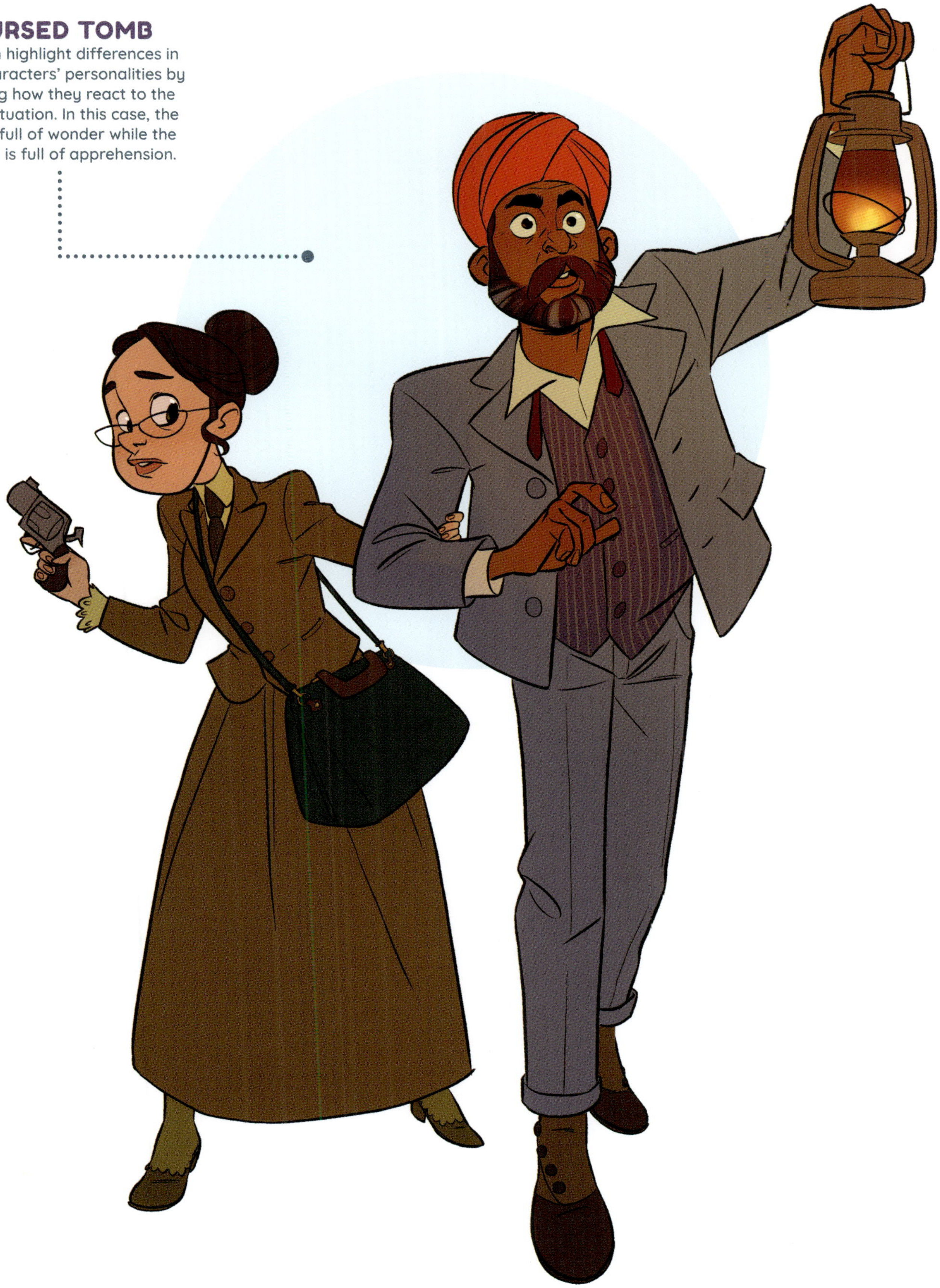

MAIN CHARACTER & SIDEKICK

Luis Gadea

When designing a main character and their sidekick, think about the story you wish to tell through their interaction. Gather ideas from your day-to-day experiences in your personal life and the outside world, observing people while taking the train, for example. Keep the idea simple - do not complicate it with too many details just yet. Start with small ideas, then begin to build on them. This will allow you to clearly depict an action, emotion, or even a silhouette for the composition. Though it might be easy to draw two characters standing side by side, when telling a story it is important to think beyond the default standing pose in order to add more value and visual interest to the piece. Your audience will love having a story to which they can relate.

DESIGN

- Colors
- Monochromatic
- Different silhouettes

ROLE

- What kind of team are they?
- Day-to-day team
- Person and pet?

MAIN CHARACTER & SIDEKICK

STORY

- Full-on action?
- More serious?
- Small gag

INTERACTION

- Movement
- Helping each other
- Smart and silly

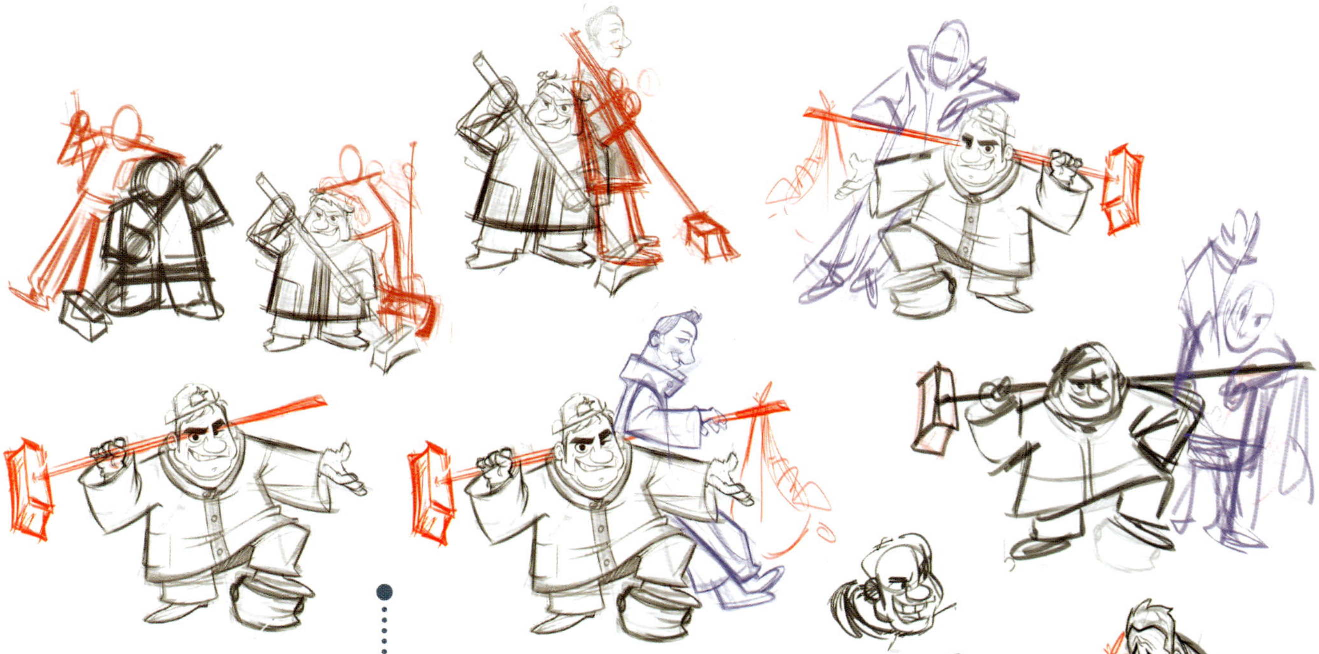

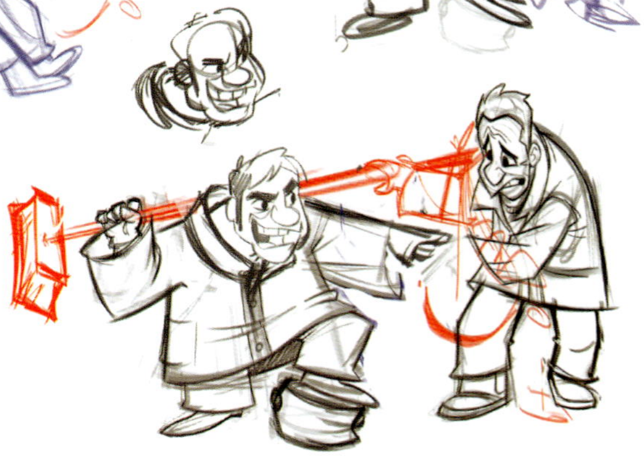

Create a selection of quick, rough sketches to explore your idea and the interaction between your characters. These thumbnails explore a comedic pair of garbage collectors with contrasting heights and personalities.

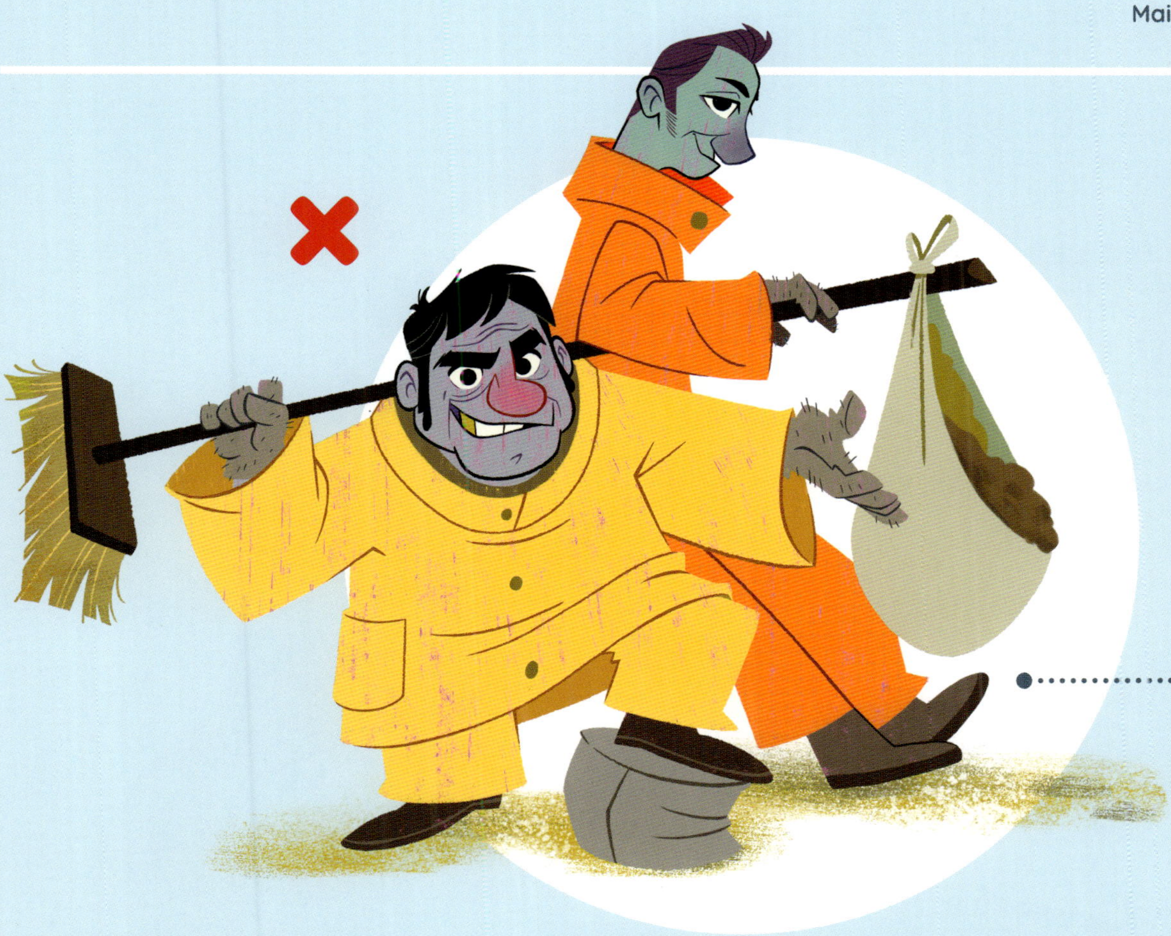

The idea was to portray two sweepers, proud of their job. The main character is clever and mischievous, and his sidekick is a little more nervous and insecure. Though this version was almost finished, it became clear the characters were not interacting much. They were not facing each other and the viewer gained no insight into their relationship.

Though you can save some elements from an earlier draft, sometimes you have to start over. In this new version, the main character's head has shifted to a three-quarter angle as he gives his sidekick an order. He also points to the garbage, instructing his partner to do as he says. The viewer gains an immediate impression of the personality dynamics at play.

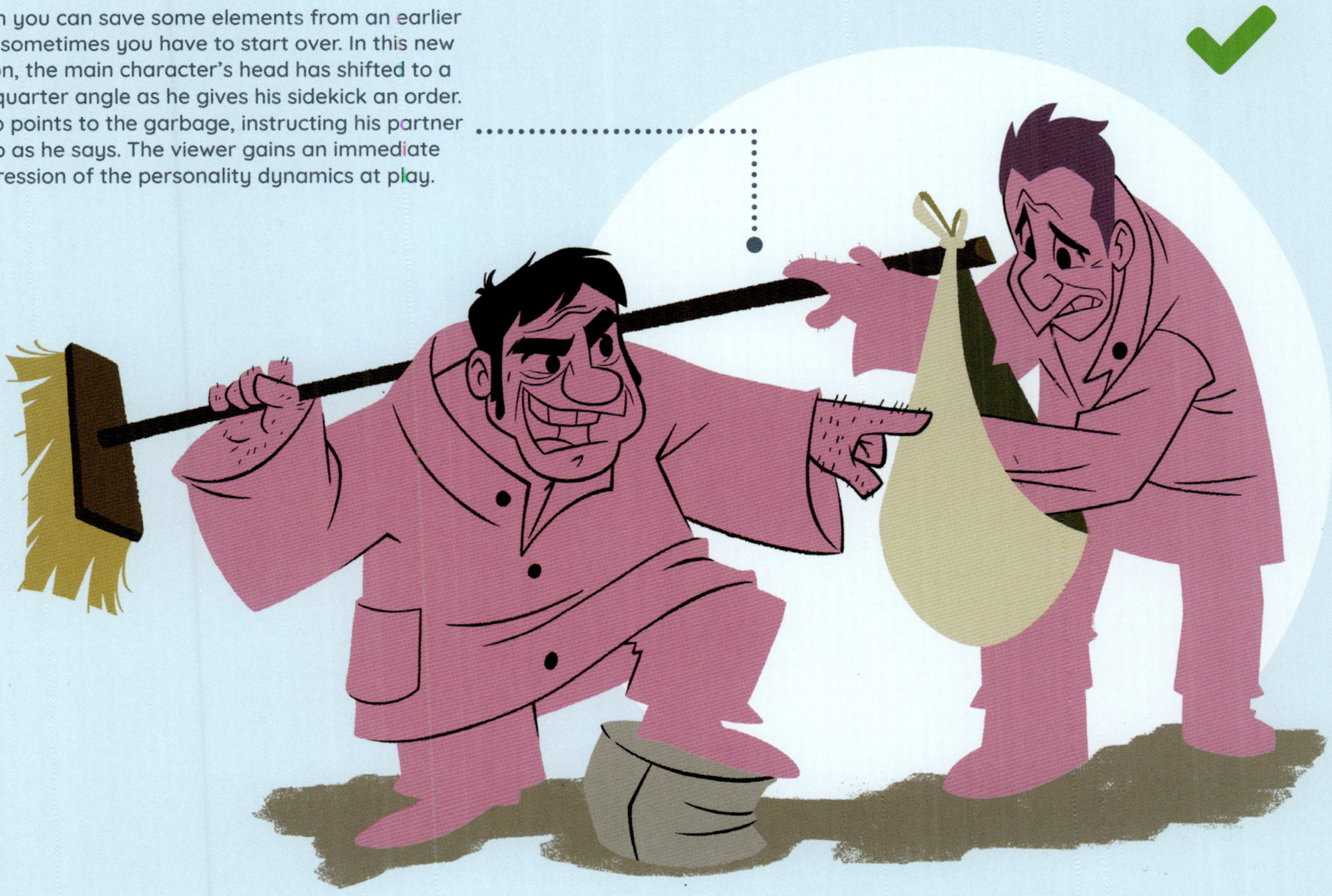

"WHAT DID WE GET TODAY?"

In the final version, the characters' uniforms have matching colors, which help to unite them as a pair. The sidekick is interacting not just with the main character, but also with the broom and the garbage bag – props that help to connect the characters, both visually and as part of the scene's narrative.

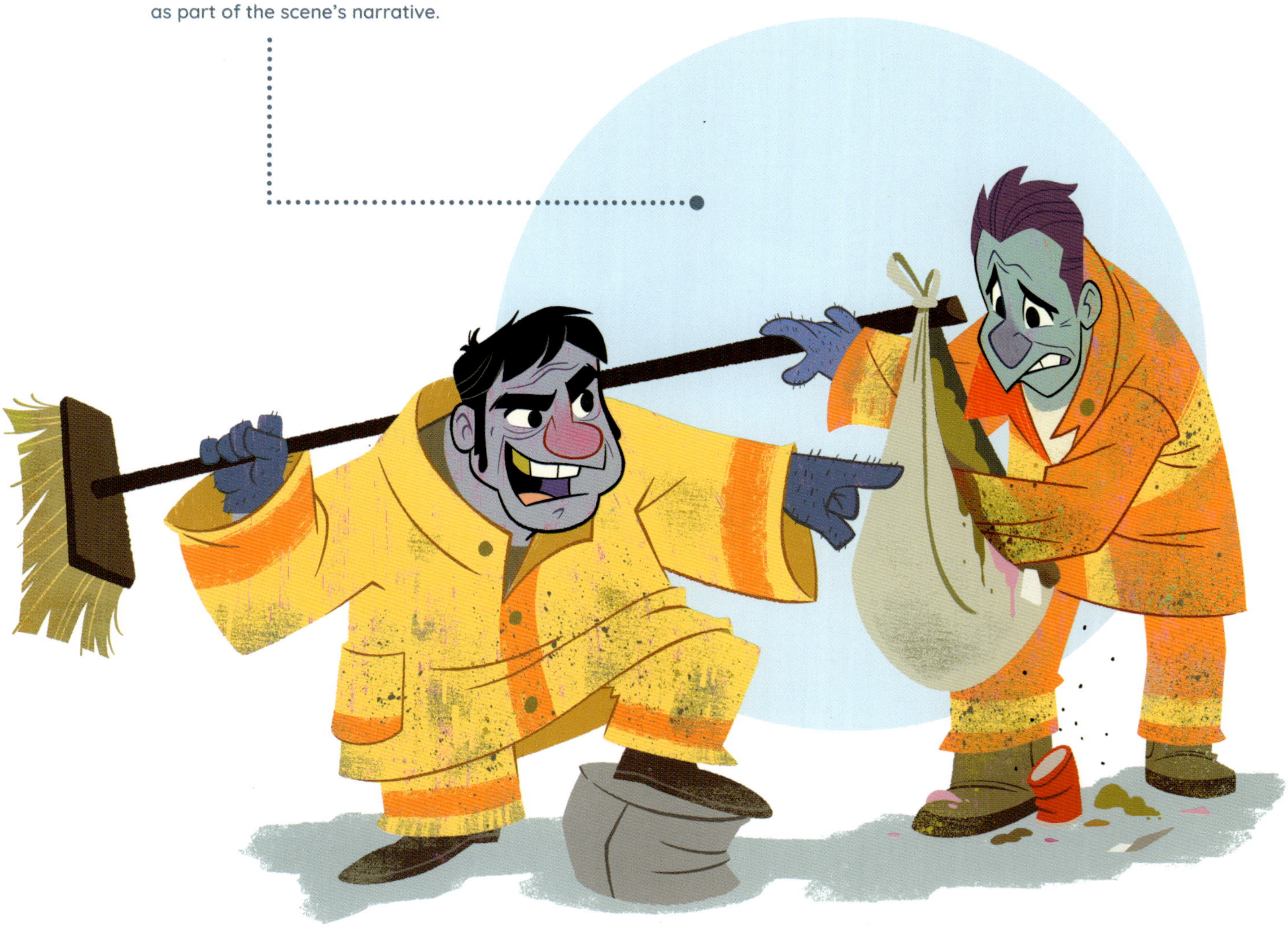

"HURRY WITH MY HAT!"

Here is another example of a main character and their sidekick. The idea behind this image was to create a more retro or vintage-looking pair. They are two circus performers, one being the main magician and conductor of the circus, while the other is a large yet quiet fellow who follows his boss's orders without ever complaining. The magician has a bolder color scheme and personality, looking cheerfully out at the viewer. His assistant has a duller palette, making him feel of lower rank and importance, and is fully focused on assisting his boss.

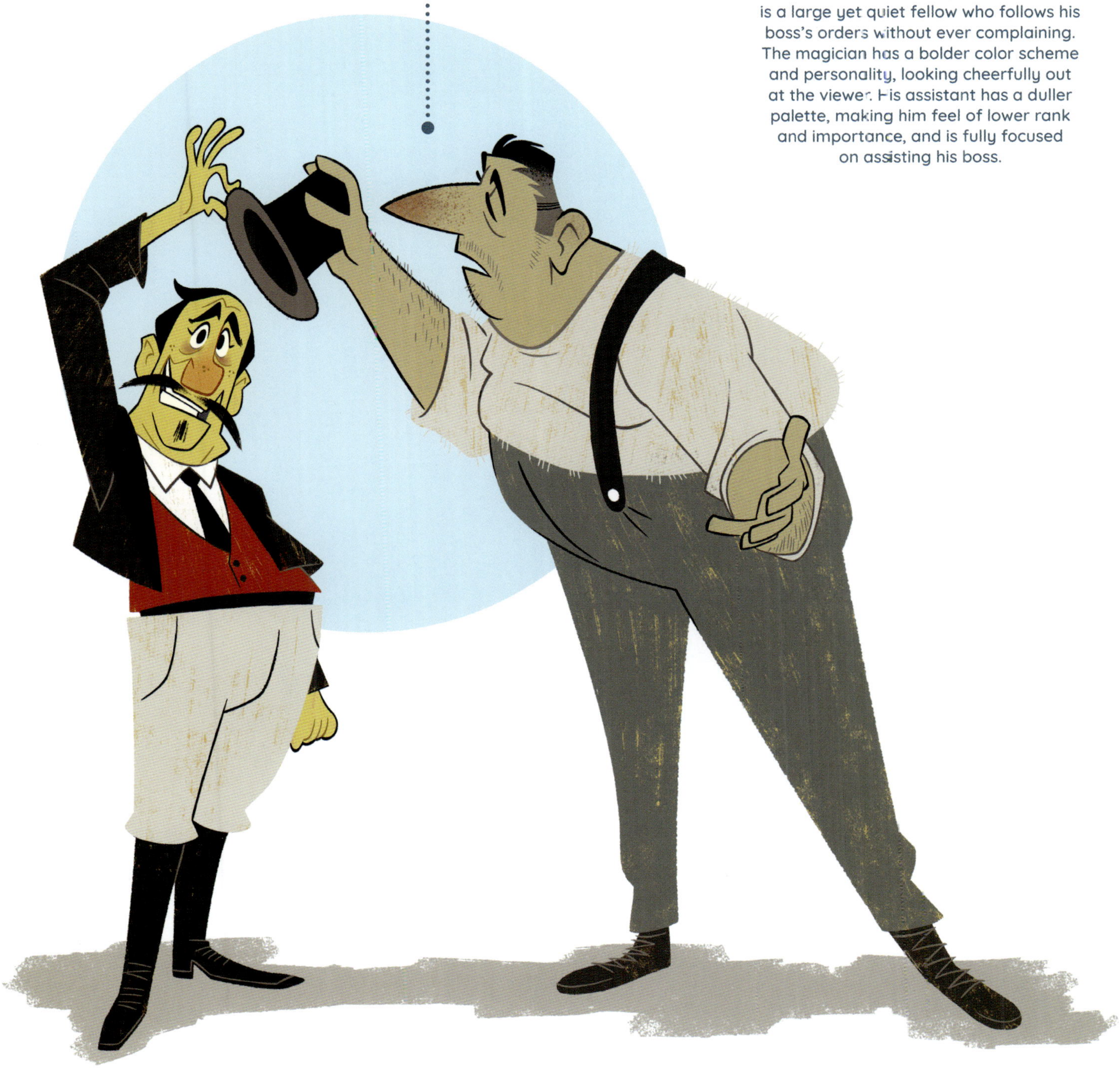

CLASSROOM

Meybis Ruiz Cruz

As you start drawing thumbnails, you must tackle two of the most critical elements of any illustration: the story and the composition. This is especially important for a scene with multiple characters, each with their own role and story to contribute. In just a few rough scribbles, it should be clear who is doing what, how they feel, and where they are in the frame. This stage is not about character design, style, or pose; all that comes later. This stage is about the ideas, situation, and story. Focus on three possible moments: what is about to happen, what is happening, or what has just happened.

SCHOOL

- Students
- Teacher
- Classroom equipment
- Class, exam, lunch break?

MUSIC CLASS

- Instruments
- Music stands
- Sheet music
- Band or choir rehearsal?

CLASSROOM

INTERCONNECTIVITY

- Everyone relates to each other
- Sitting in groups
- Paying attention or distracted?

SUBPLOT

- Romance subplot
- Opportunity for gossip
- Creates multiple stories
- Multiple character reactions

Avoid spending too much time on thumbnails; stick figures and notes are enough. Keep in mind what is important: idea and composition. Each character in the group should be legible and work as part of the whole scene.

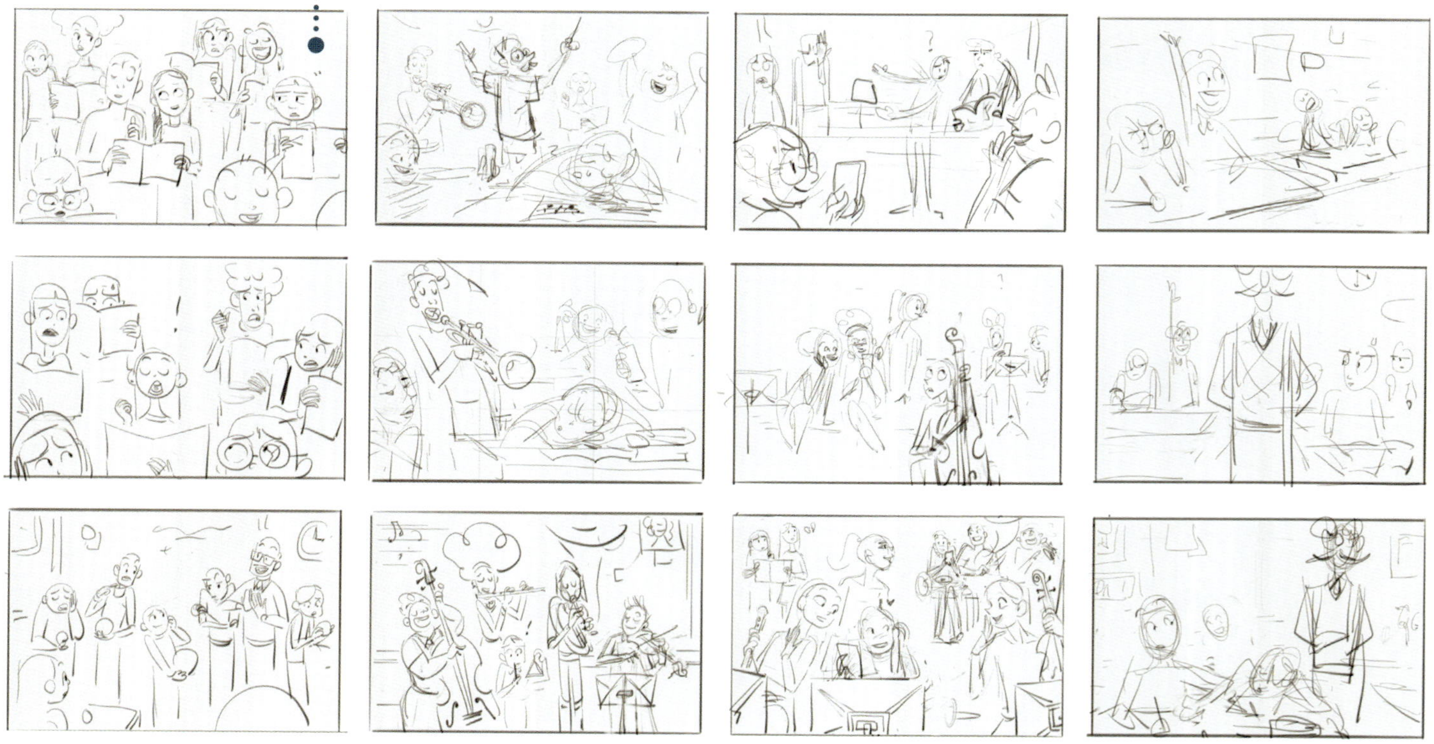

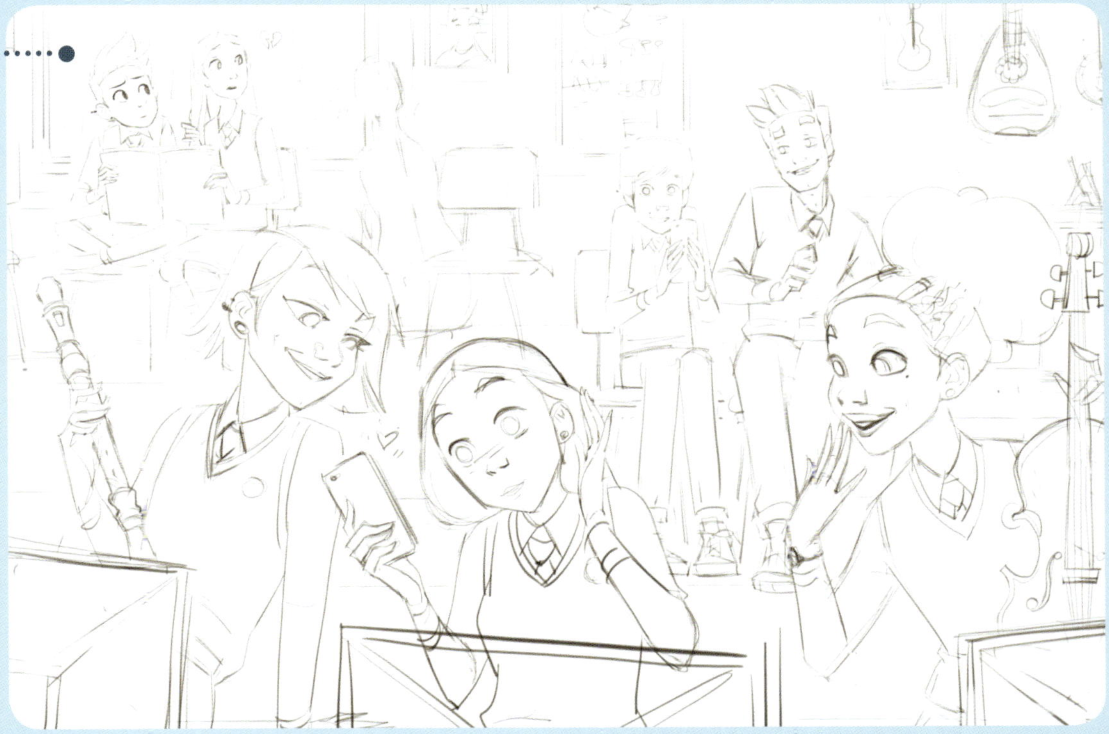

Choose your strongest concept and start working on the specifics of each character design and interaction, including the gestures, expressions, and environment. In this image, each group or pair of characters has an interconnected story.

When creating a basic color version, you can still adjust sizes and move things around to balance the composition and improve readability. Here, the actions and moods of each person are clearly discernible.

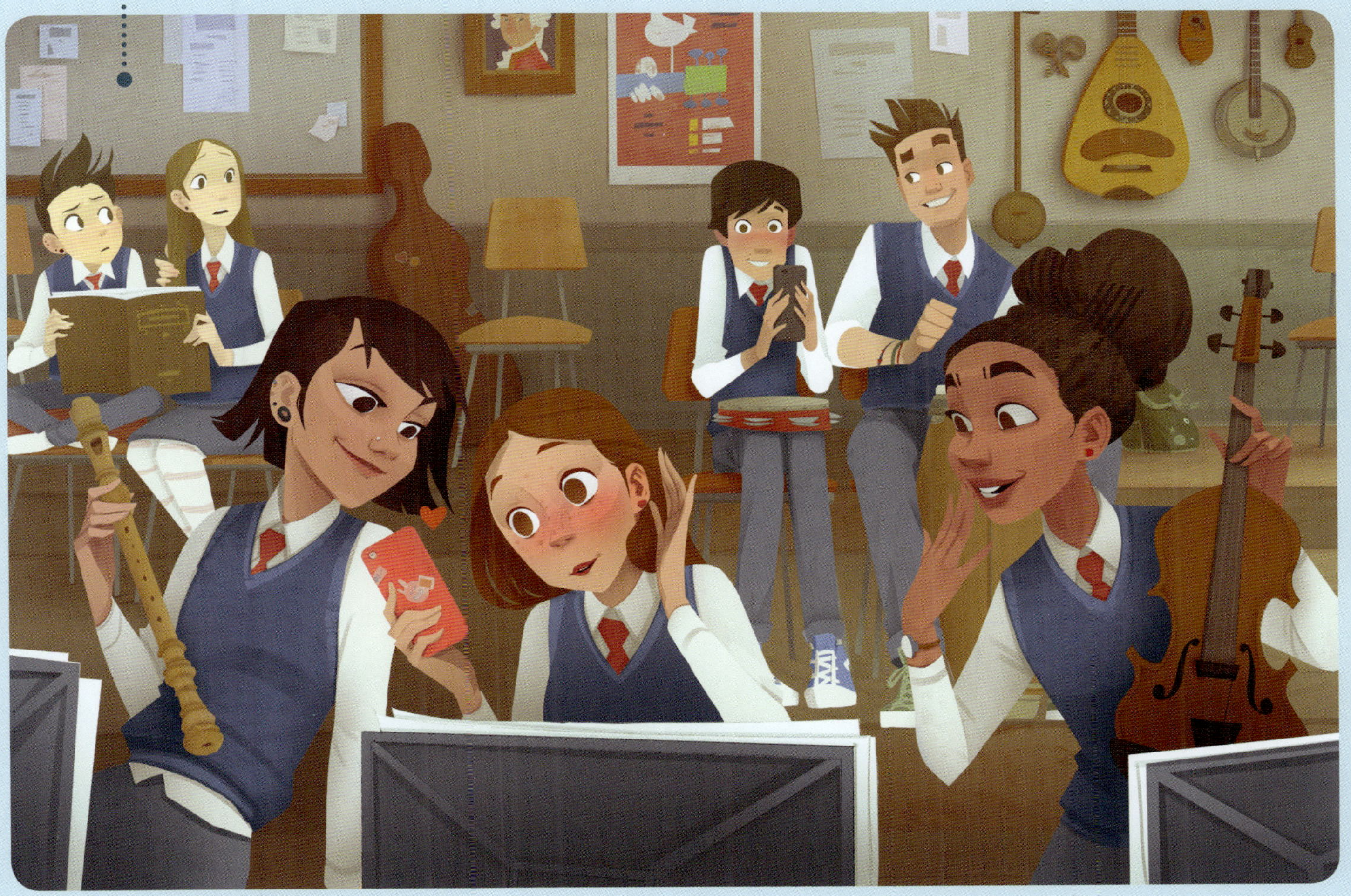

MUSIC CLASS

The final lighting adds a warm glow to this endearing classroom romance, highlighting the two key characters whose interaction drives the narrative and reactions of the whole scene.

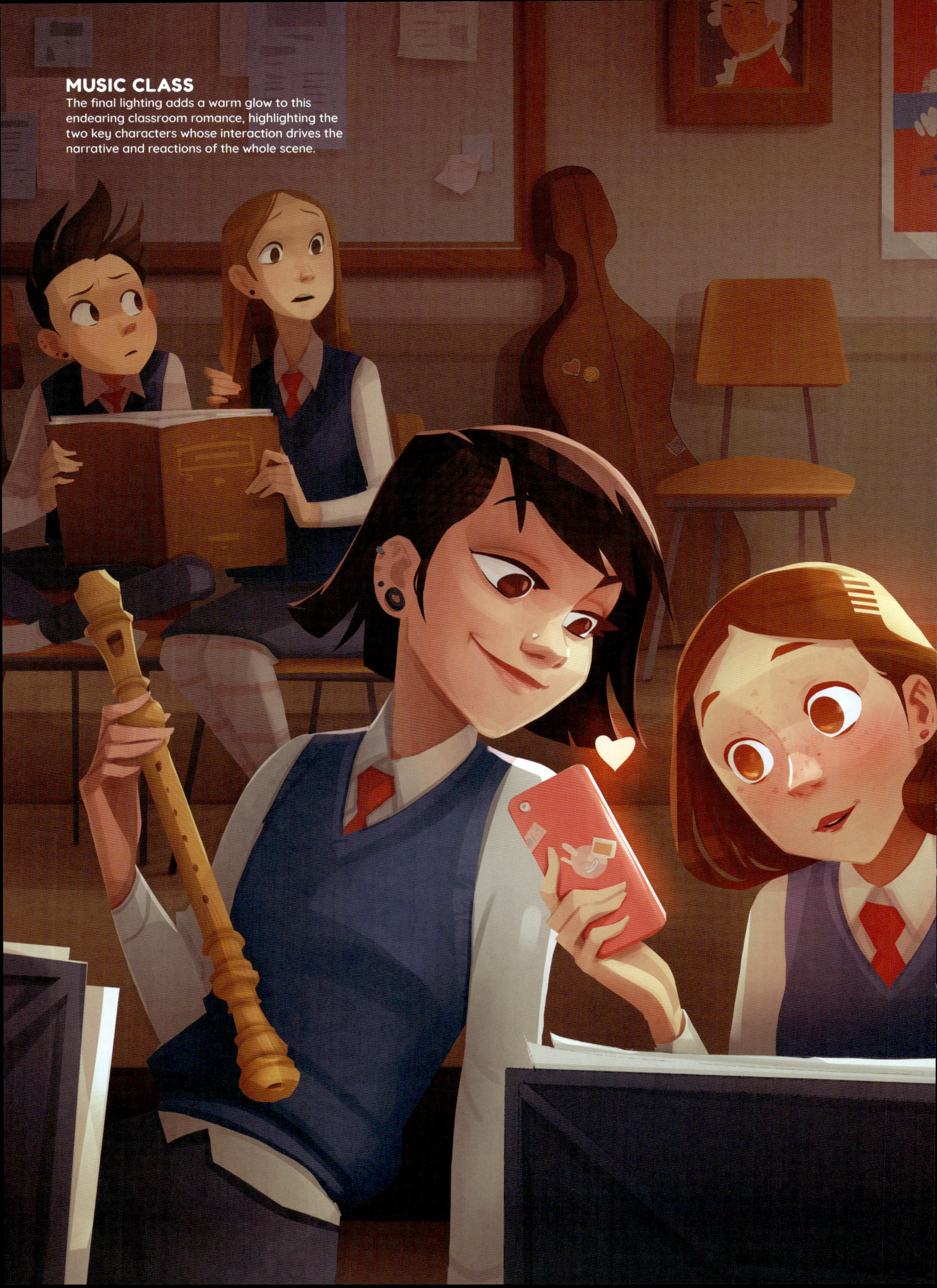

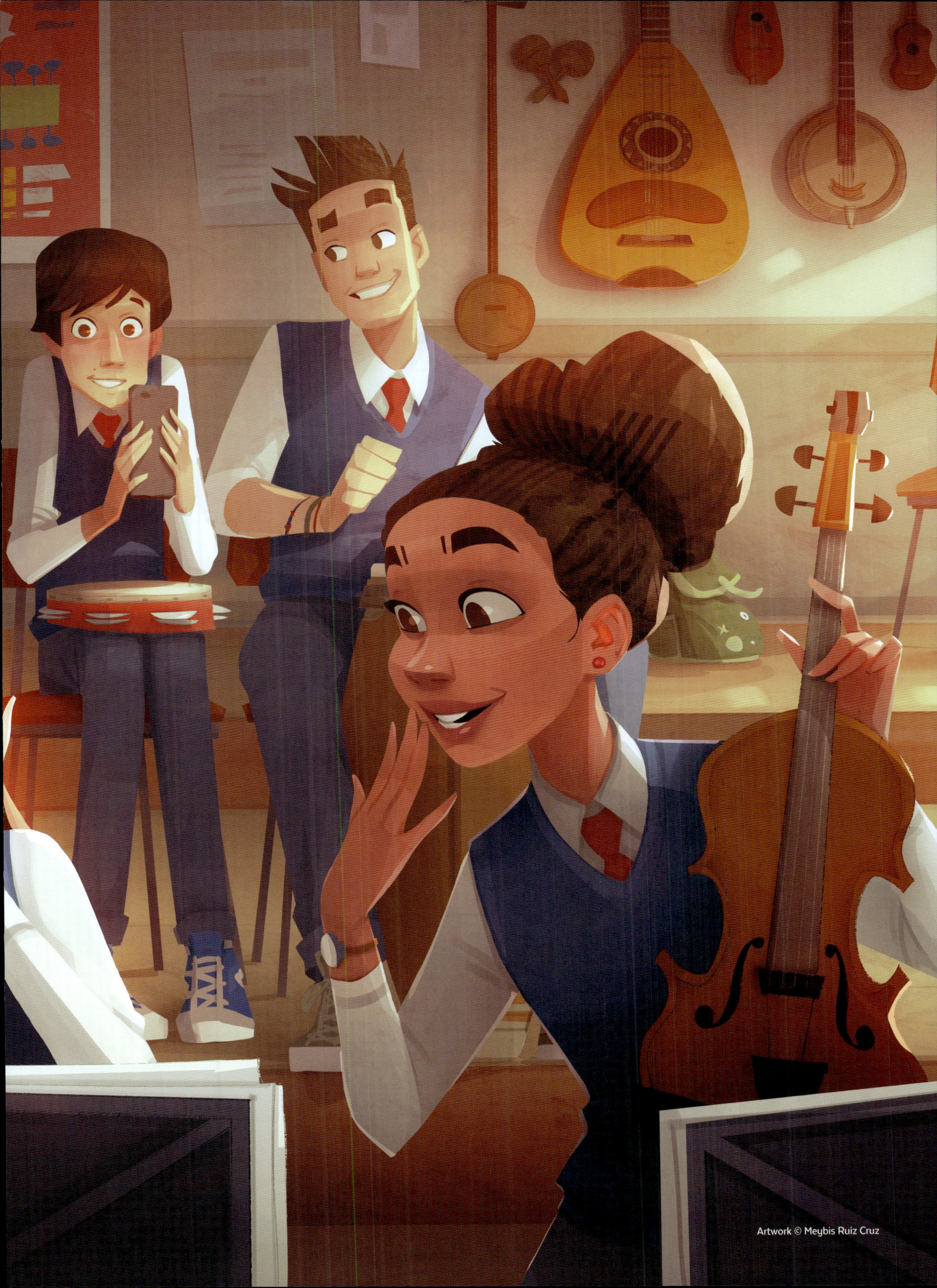

Artwork © Meybis Ruiz Cruz

BUS-STOP QUEUE

Olga Andriyenko

Scenes with multiple characters are always an exciting challenge. They work best when the featured characters are diverse in looks and personality. It is a good idea to start by brainstorming what kind of characters you want in your scene, placing them in a rough sketch and imagining their interactions. When portraying larger groups, it can be hard to make sure every character is interacting with another, so it can help to divide them into some smaller groups, like close friends or family members directly engaging with each other. Emphasizing different heights and body types will make each character unique and interesting. Take care to keep the clothing styles of the characters noticeably different, too. For example, teenagers usually have a different taste in clothes to elderly people.

BUS-STOP QUEUE

TYPICAL ACTIONS

- Waiting, bored
- Checking time or bus schedule
- Listening to music
- Scrolling on phone

SITUATION

- Everyday or dramatic?
- Bus is late
- Higher levels of stress
- Sunrise or sunset

MOODS

- Playful
- Tired
- Stressed
- Angry

CHARACTERS

- Toddlers/babies
- Teenagers
- Elderly couple
- Late for work

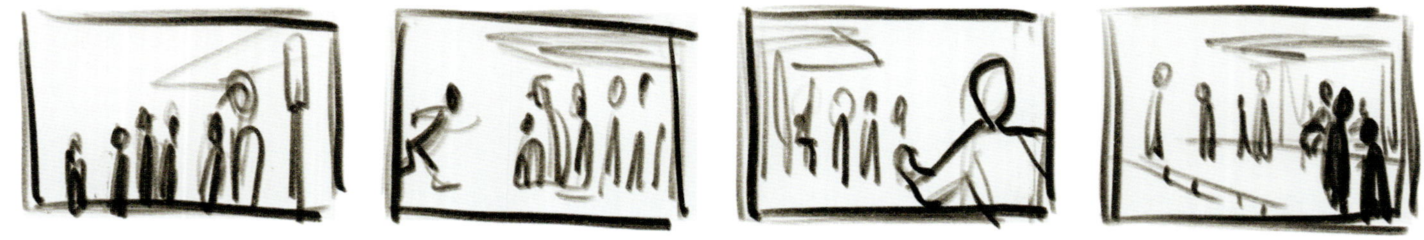

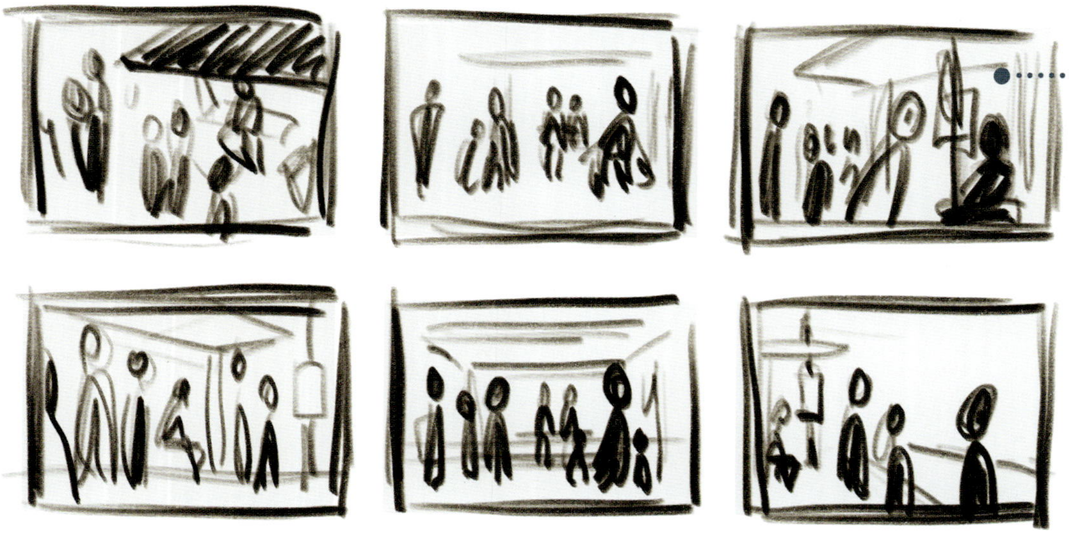

Use thumbnails to imagine your bus stop scene from different angles. While many of the options could be interesting, a couple work better in creating a cinematic story moment. As the focus should be on the characters, a simpler perspective works in giving them a proper "stage." Characters of different heights, some seated, some standing, will add dynamism and variation to the queue.

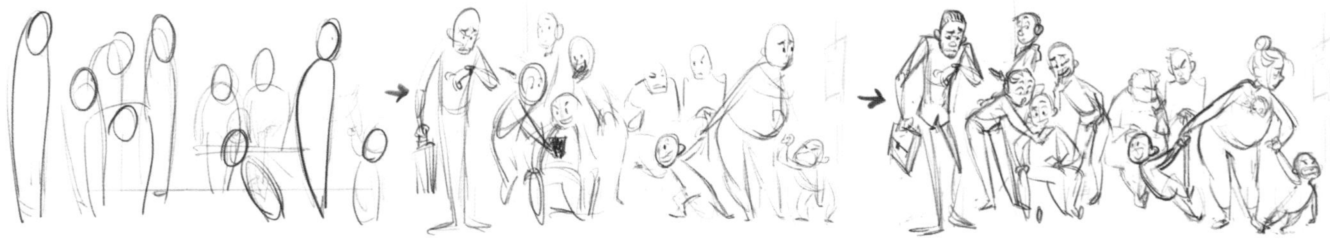

Roughly place the characters in the scene, starting to consider the different groups. Establish each character's pose and the direction they are facing. The excited little girl helps connect the family group on the right to the characters on the left; she is curious to know what the teenage girls are laughing about. The characters in the background are either intrigued or annoyed by those in the foreground.

Facial expressions and fine details, such as the unicorn on the little girl's dress and the print on the teenage girl's T-shirt, help distinguish each character and offer more for the audience to explore. As well as each looking unique, each character has their own role and reaction to the situation, ranging from distracted to distressed. Pigeons are added for relatability and comedic relief – nothing is more typical of a city bus stop than annoying pigeons!

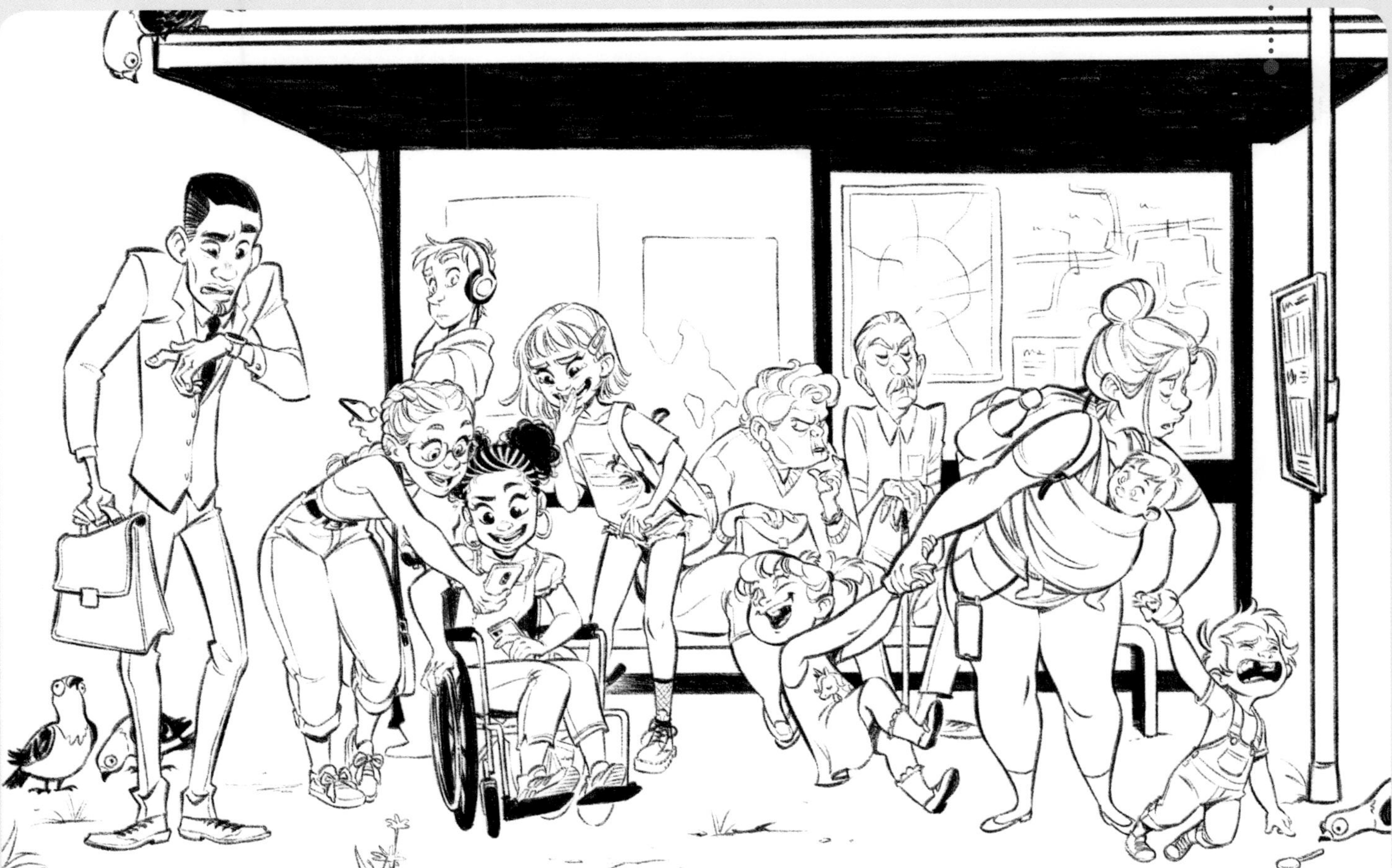

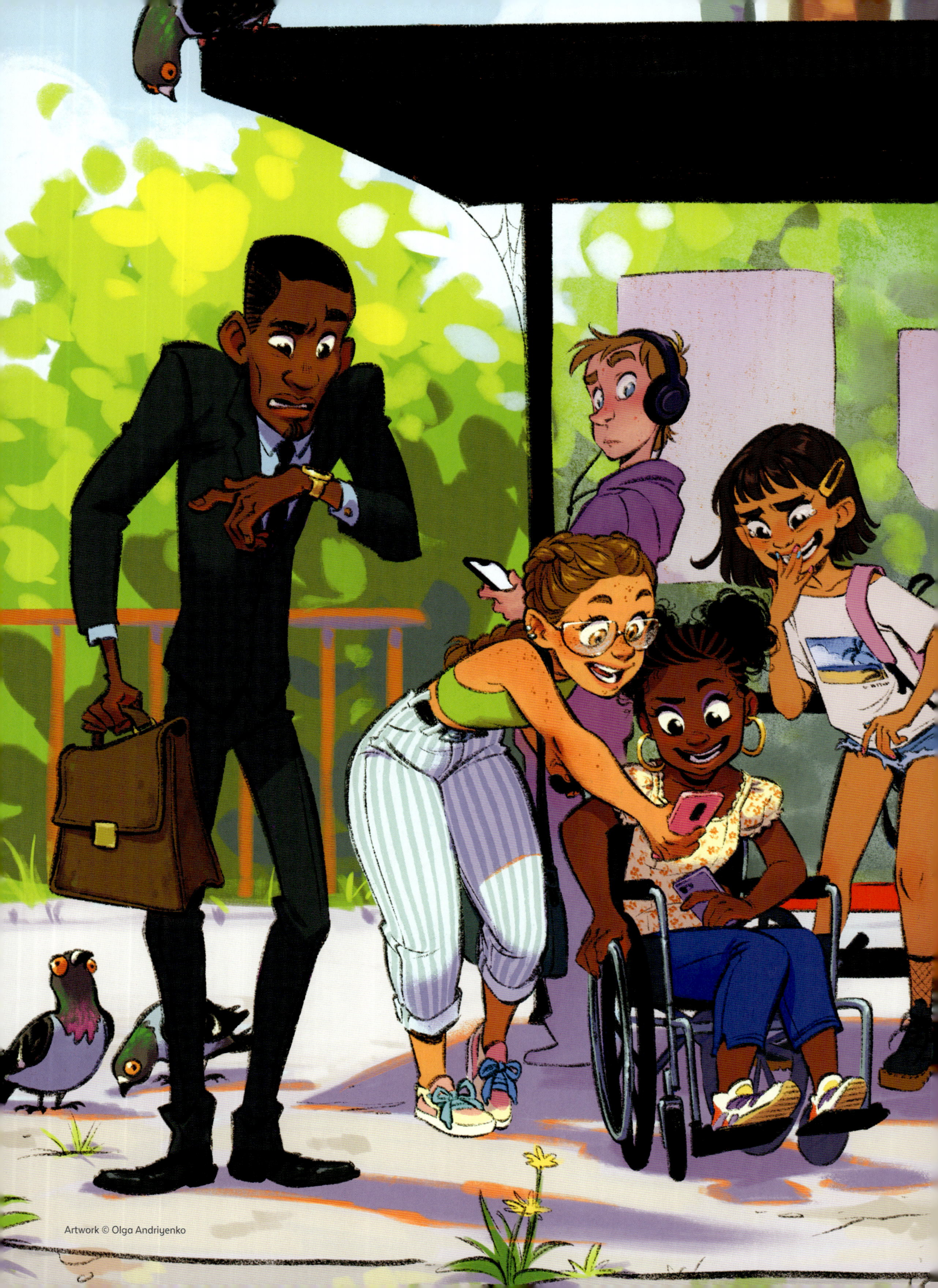

Artwork © Olga Andriyenko

FRIDAY MORNING

To keep the focus on the characters, the background and shadows are simplified just enough to indicate a warm, sunny day in the city. A variety of skin tones is helpful in making each character even more individual. Use your software's hue and saturation sliders to try out different skin undertones.

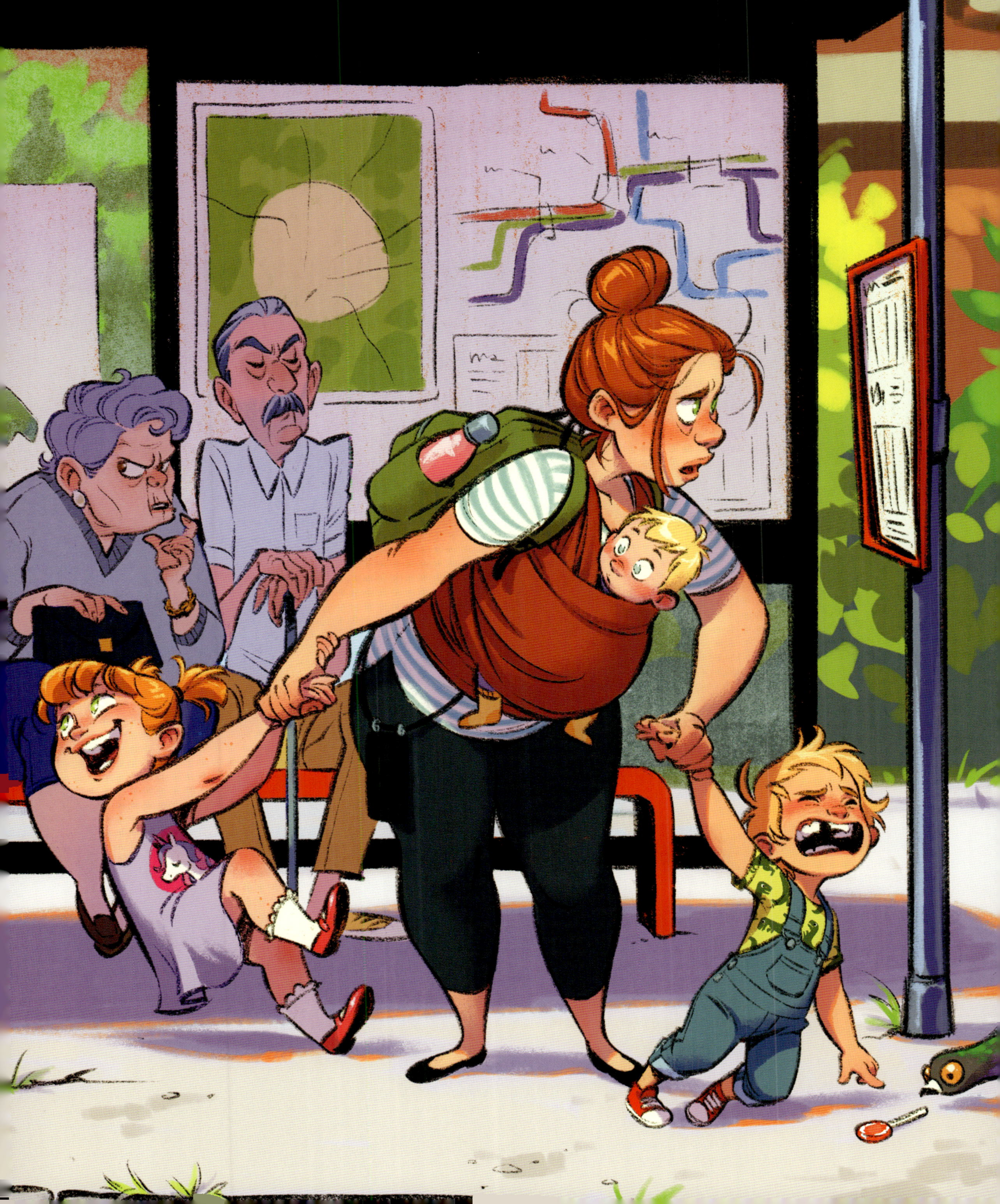

FAMILY DINNER

Noor Sofi

When designing a scene with multiple character interactions, consider the relationships between your characters and what story you want to tell in the overall image. Creating a clear story for your audience to understand will give them something to connect with. You might want to consider having a main story, with some additional side-stories in the details. This scene will show a celebratory family dinner, with all the happiness, excitement, and awkward tension that such a gathering often brings! When designing a scene where multiple characters are interacting, it is helpful to explore different ideas on how to best present your story. Think about each character's personality, motivations, and their relationships with the other characters, and how you will show these in your scene.

STORY

- Meet the parents
- Daughter brings fiancé home
- Misbehaving child
- Siblings look nervous

INTERACTIONS

- Father stares down fiancé
- Fiancé looks nervous
- Sister on phone
- Daughter shows off ring

FAMILY DINNER

COLOR

- Warm – loving atmosphere
- Cold – too sterile

SPECIFICS

- Culture – Indian family
- Indian food and tableware
- Modern time period
- Interracial couple

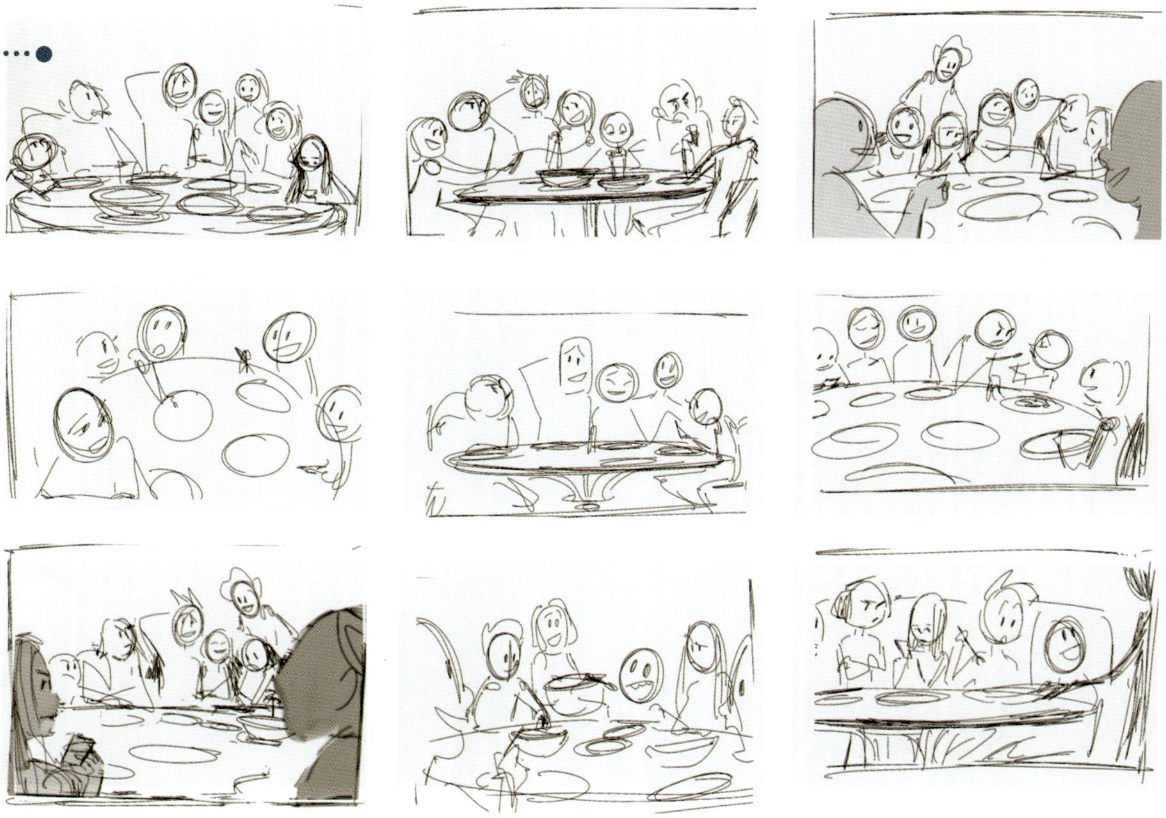

Sketching thumbnails is a great way to get out all of your visual ideas. Experiment with different compositions and character positions to help you figure out what you want your final image to look like. The challenge here is depicting a scene set around a table while still showing every character clearly.

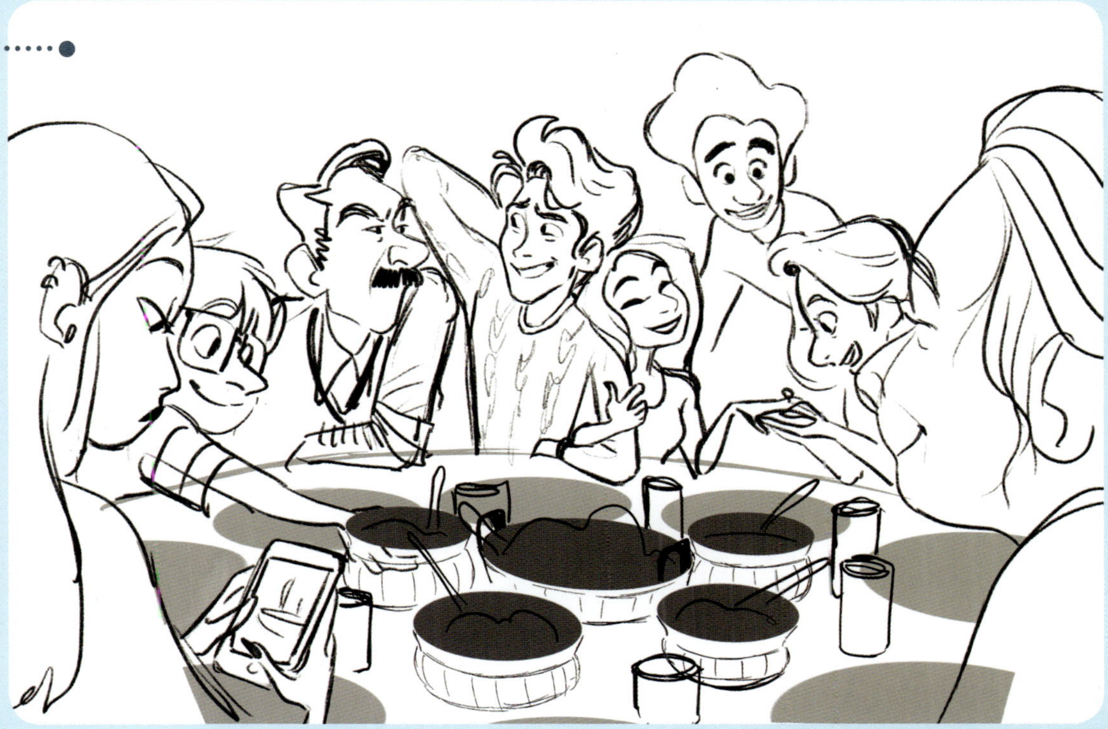

Once you have settled on an idea, draw out the fine details in your linework. This is where you can really capture the characters' personalities and expressions, and make sure the story is clear. Each character here has an interaction or reaction that shows their personality to the viewer.

This piece has an analogous color scheme with warm tones to bring a sense of warmth, home, and harmony.

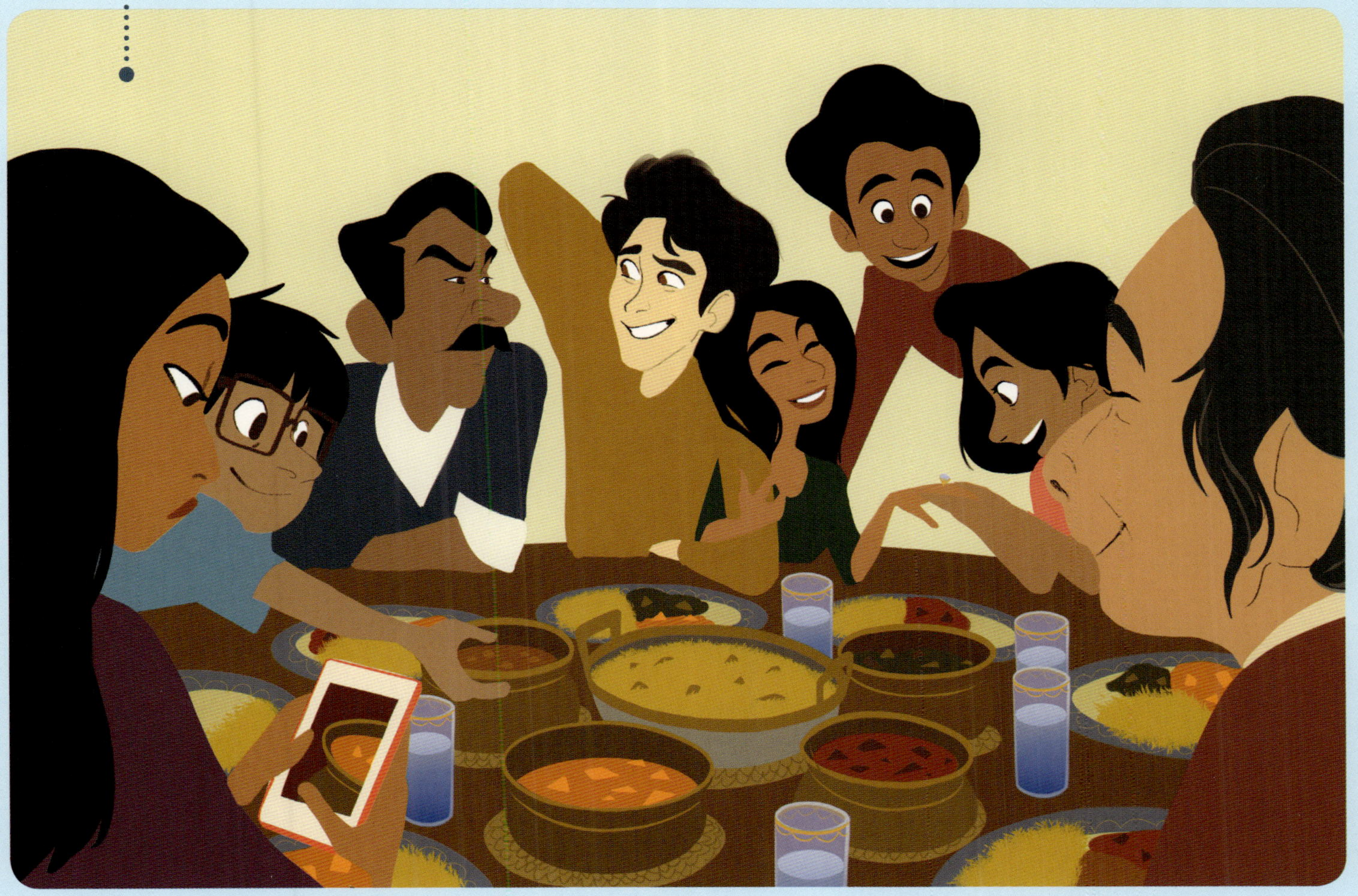

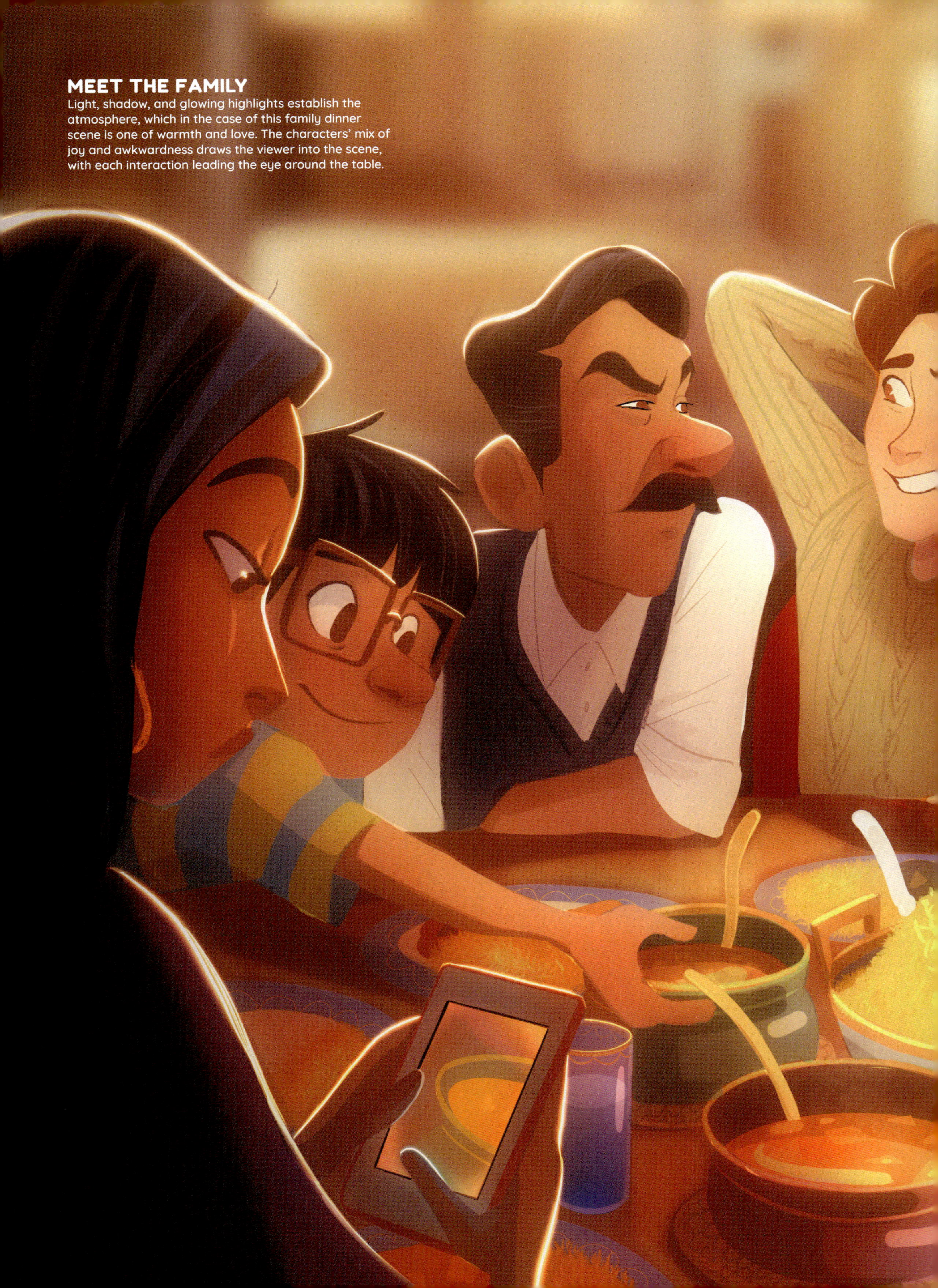

MEET THE FAMILY

Light, shadow, and glowing highlights establish the atmosphere, which in the case of this family dinner scene is one of warmth and love. The characters' mix of joy and awkwardness draws the viewer into the scene, with each interaction leading the eye around the table.

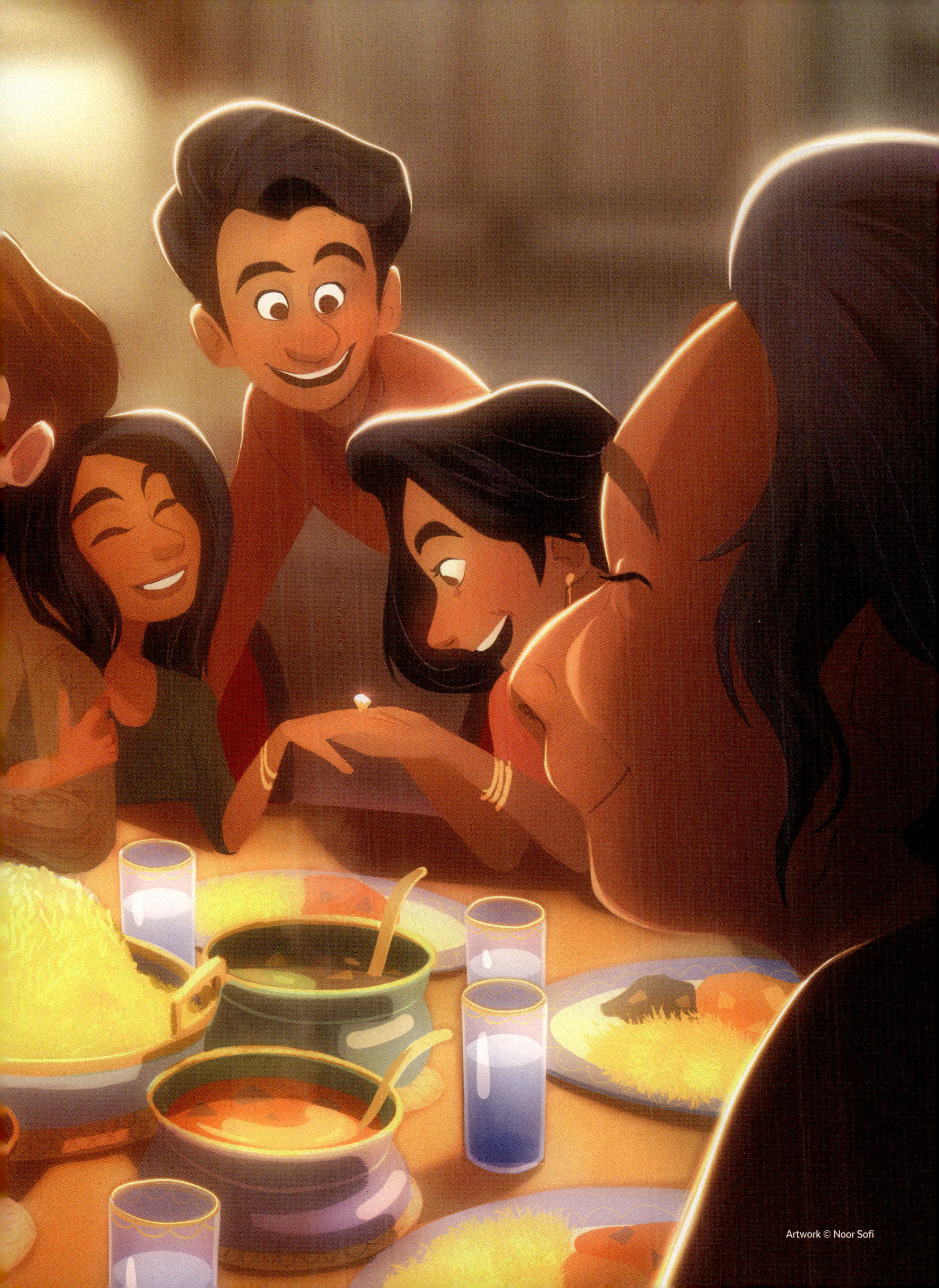

Artwork © Noor Sofi

MUSIC BAND

Corah Louise

This music band scene explores interactions between characters with a variety of different personalities as they practice in a small room together. The compact environment is strategic in forcing them to invade each other's space, enabling clashing temperaments to be explored. Pairing overly friendly characters with others who are easily annoyed creates visually interesting interactions that can be played out in the scene as they struggle to practice together. A flamboyant lead singer with a lack of awareness for personal space is perfect for annoying a character who is tense and easily angered. Using the instruments to create personalities and thinking about how they would work together in a band is a good exercise to explore how characters can interact.

MUSIC BAND

COLOR SCHEME
- Grayscale?
- Red and blue?
- Matching outfits

INSTRUMENTS
- Guitar
- Keyboard
- Brass
- Drums

STYLE
- Jazz?
- Country?
- Metal / 1980s rock?
- Marching band?

INTERACTION
- Tension
- Playing in a small space
- Annoying lead singer
- How would they clash?

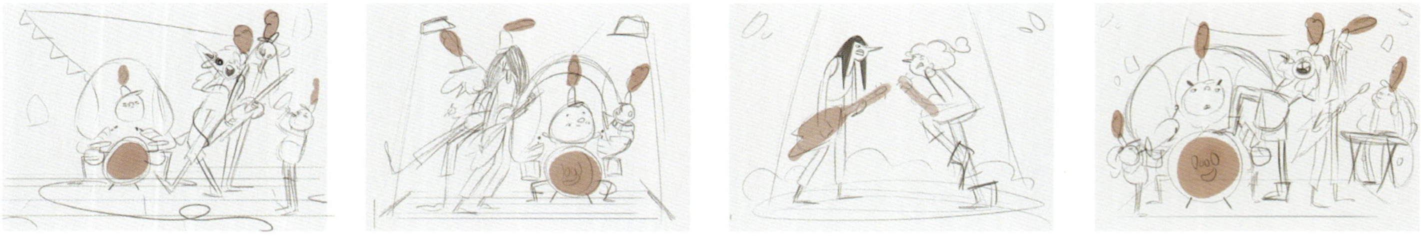

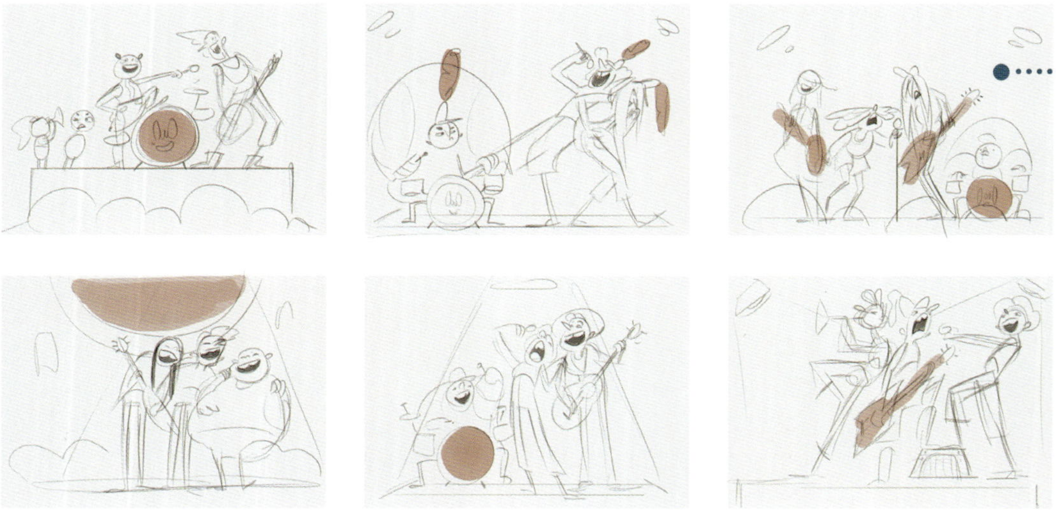

Use thumbnails to try out different compositions and consider how multiple characters could interact in one space, while keeping a balance across the piece. The composition needs to give each member of the band room to perform and show off their personality, while also showing the camaraderie or conflict between them.

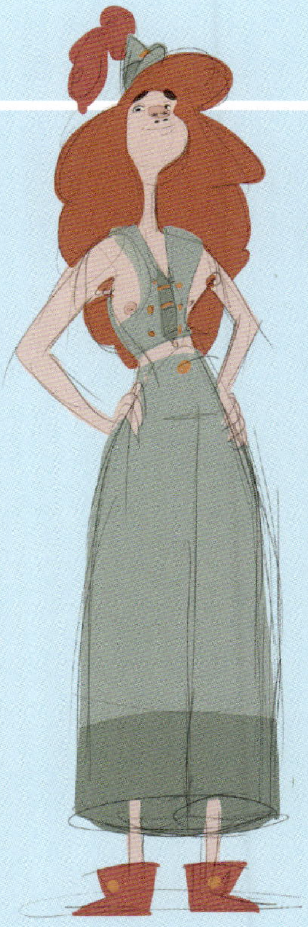

SINGER

- Leader
- Confident
- Overzealous
- Colorful
- Bouncy

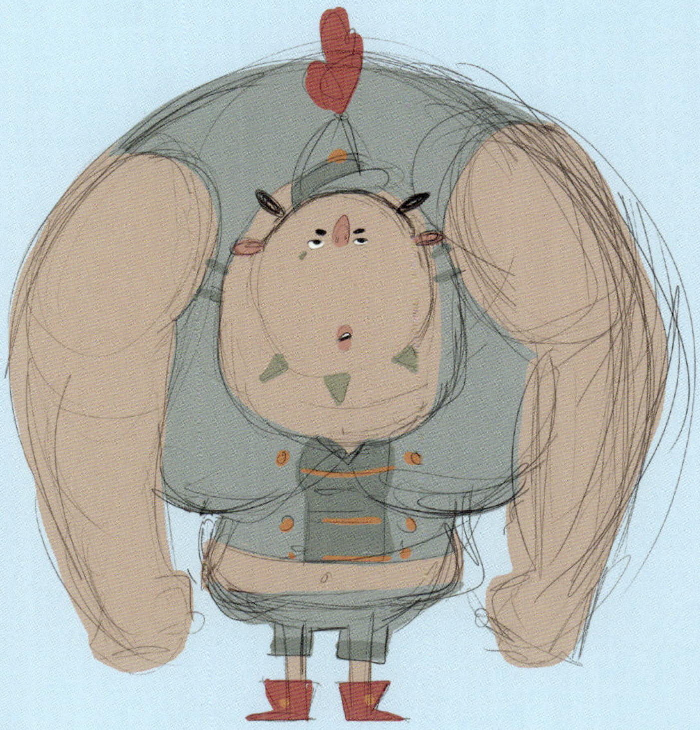

DRUMS

- Big shape
- Easily angered
- Fed up
- Overbearing

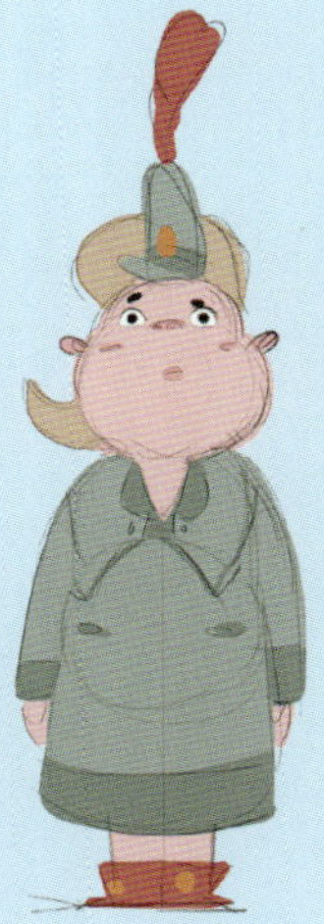

TRUMPET

- Cute
- Small
- Playful
- Round shapes

GUITAR

- Mysterious
- Introverted
- Aloof
- Head down

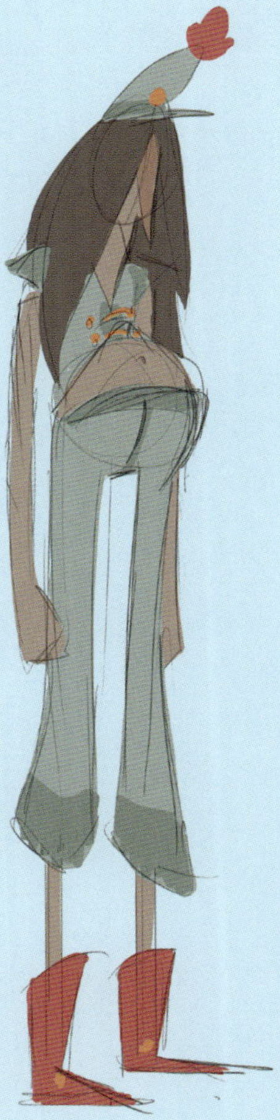

Roughly draft your characters' designs to see how they look together. Do their designs tell the story you want to tell, and can you imagine them interacting in the way you intend?

Note down details about your characters' personalities, thinking in depth about their designs and personas. Having a better understanding of each character will help you convey their relationships with each other.

KEYBOARD

- Sassy
- Unprofessional
- Mischievous
- Not focused

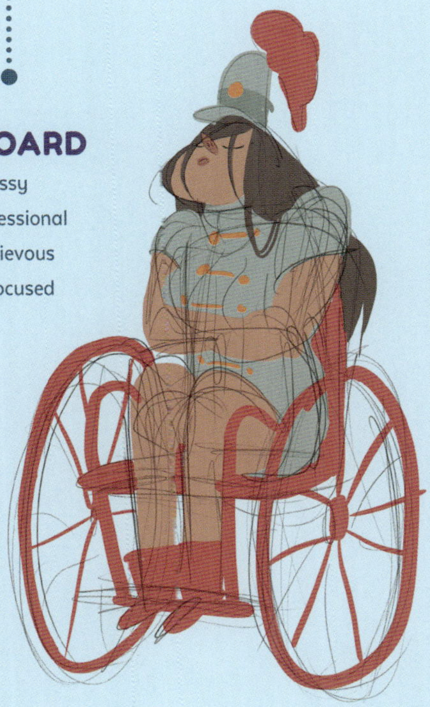

PRACTICE NIGHT

The final piece shows the band mid-practice, and the tension created from contrasting personalities forced to play together in such a tight space. Yet while they have contrasting personalities, keeping a consistent color scheme and band costume shows they are still a close family.

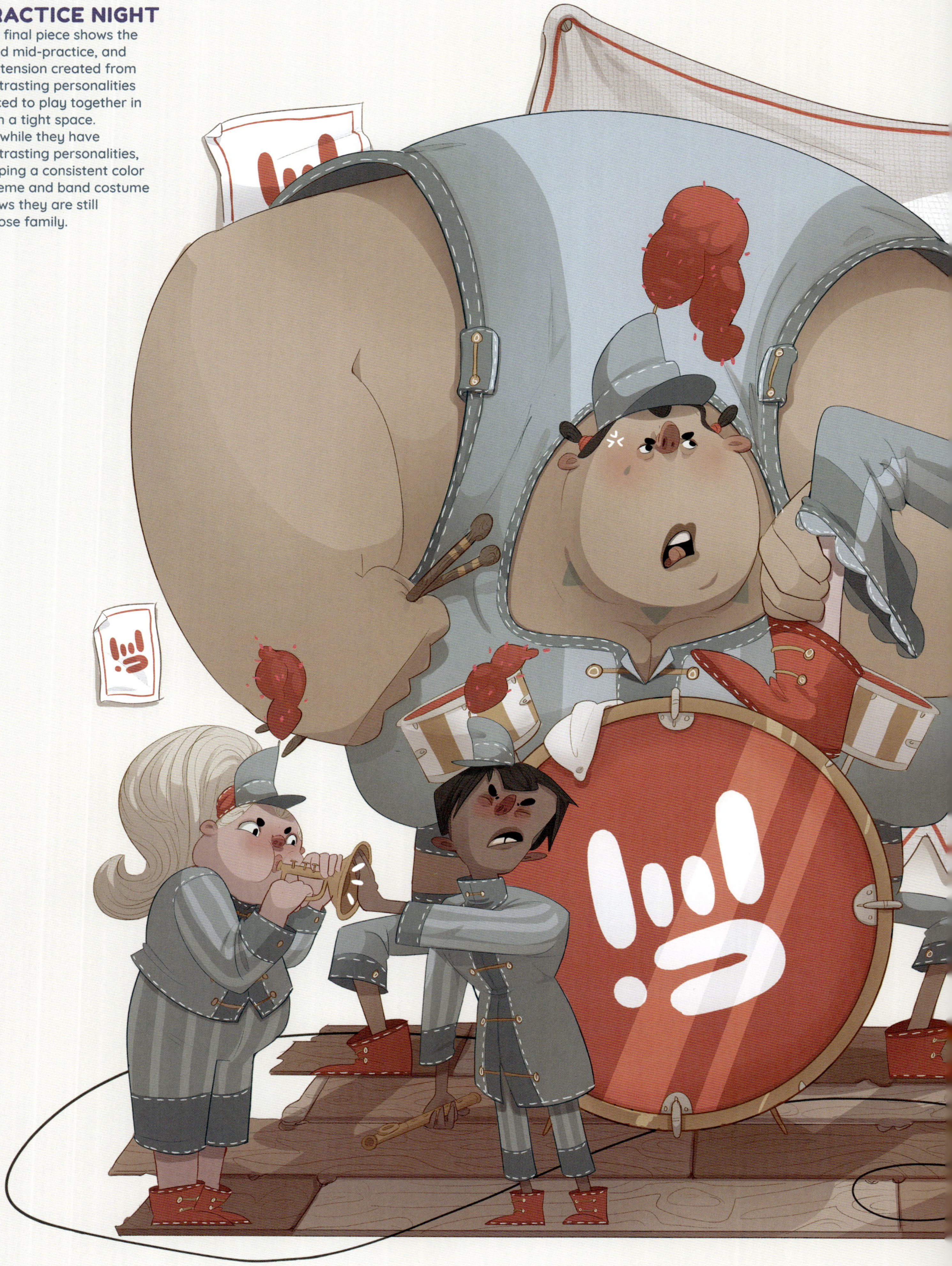

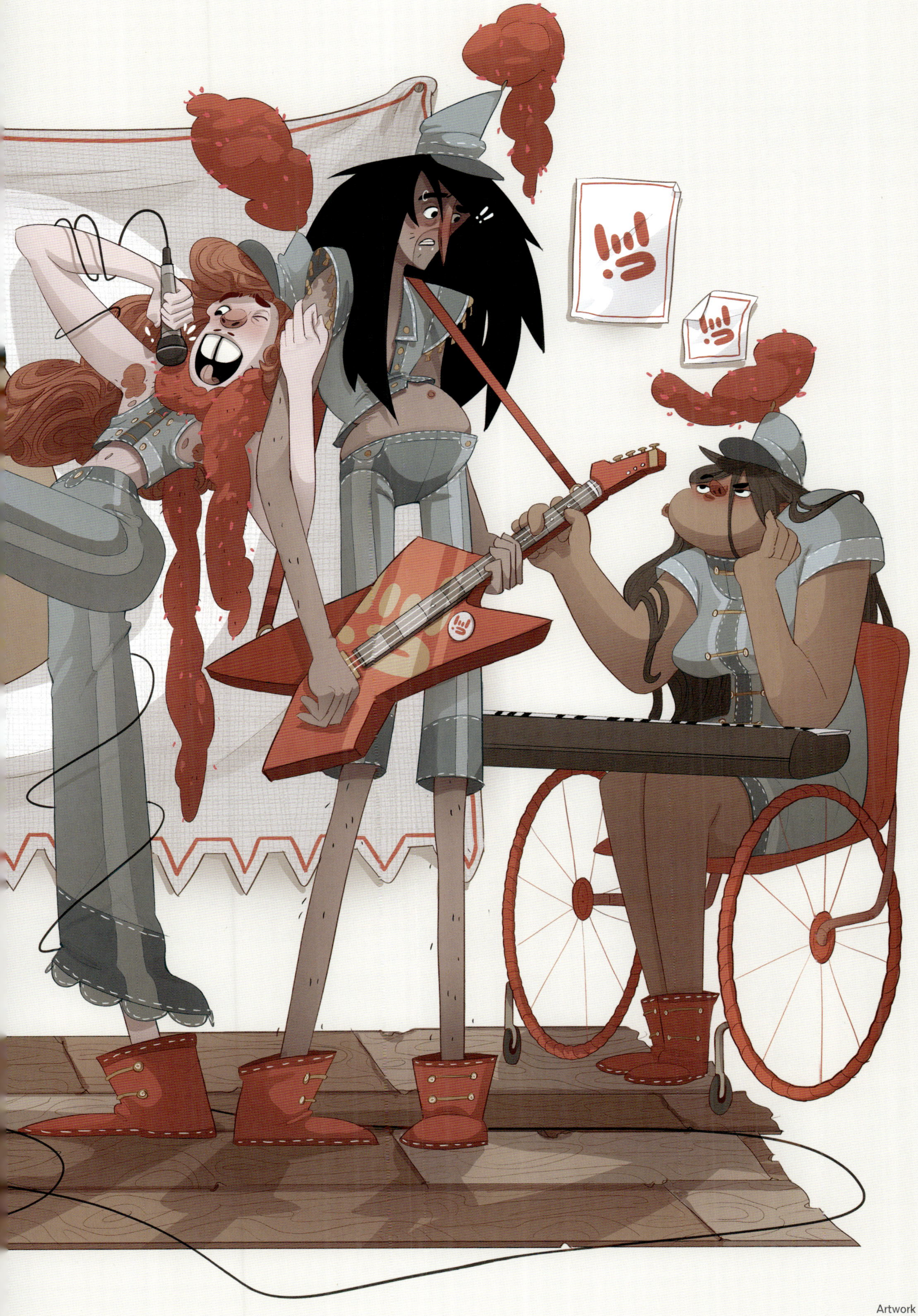

Artwork © Corah Louise

CROWD

Kenneth Anderson

Drawing a crowd scene might seem intimidating at first, so it can help to start with a simple story idea. Here the idea is a tour group exploring an Egyptian tomb and being taken by surprise when the ancient mummies start coming to life! This idea lends itself to many varied character interactions combined with high stakes. There are many ways to approach a crowd design – this example will be full of drama!

Consider the hierarchies in the scene's design: the main story event and the main characters' reactions to it, followed by secondary and tertiary character groups, reacting either to the main event or to other characters in the scene.

You can use the design of characters to aid composition and build interesting and varied character interactions. How the characters act will sell the narrative and build up an idea of who they all are, while forming the basis of the scene composition.

STORY

- An "act of God"
- On tour
- Field trip
- Magical event

INTERACTIONS

- Pointing
- Pushing out of the way
- Clinging together
- Taking selfies/photos

CROWD

CONFLICT

- Monsters
- Super-villains
- Aliens
- Characters fighting

LOCATIONS

- Tourist site
- Museum
- Egyptian tomb
- Haunted castle

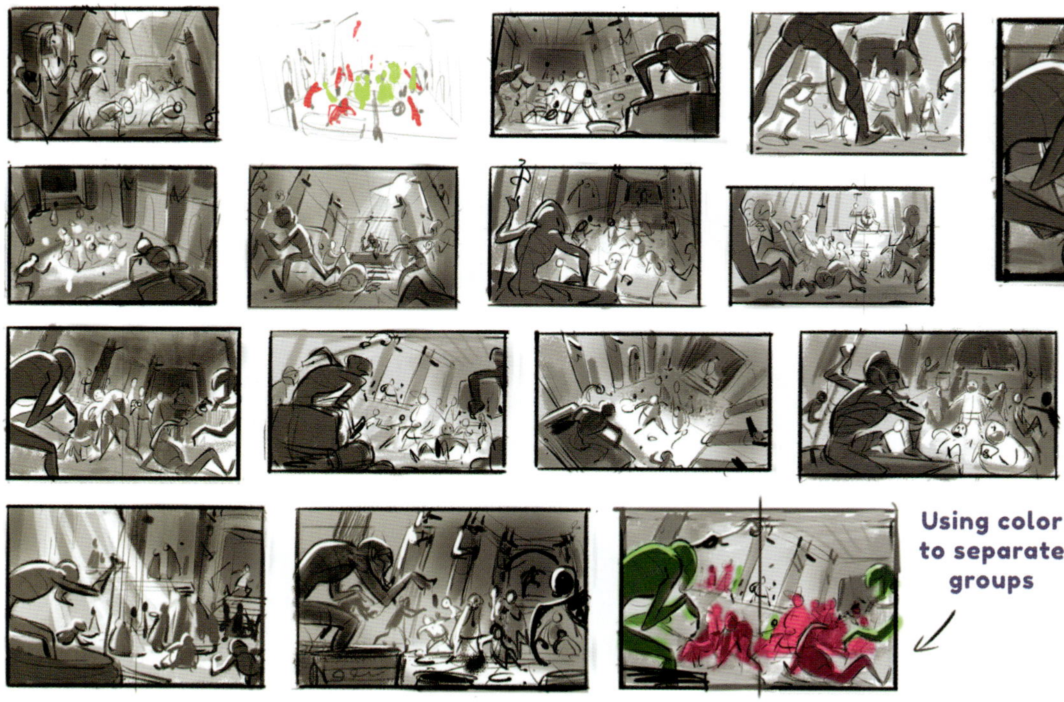

Using color to separate groups

Combined thumbnails into final direction

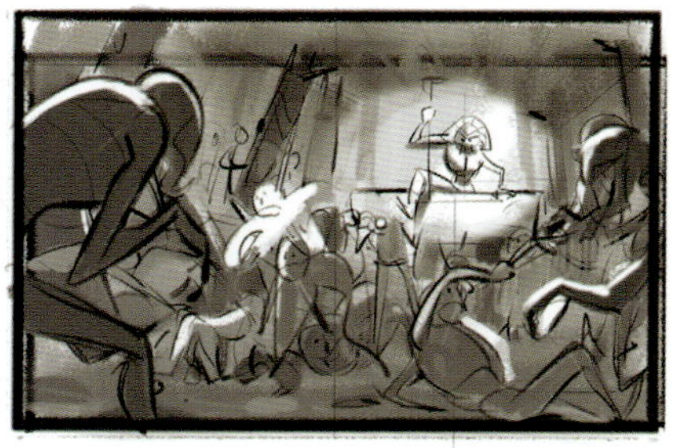

Figuring out the best composition for a crowd scene can be tricky, but creating thumbnail sketches can help problem-solve the best perspective and layout of characters, maximizing both the drama and space for the performance.

With complex scenes it can help to figure out where all the main characters will go early on, though this is just a placeholder and might change as you go. A perspective grid and basic backdrop can help.

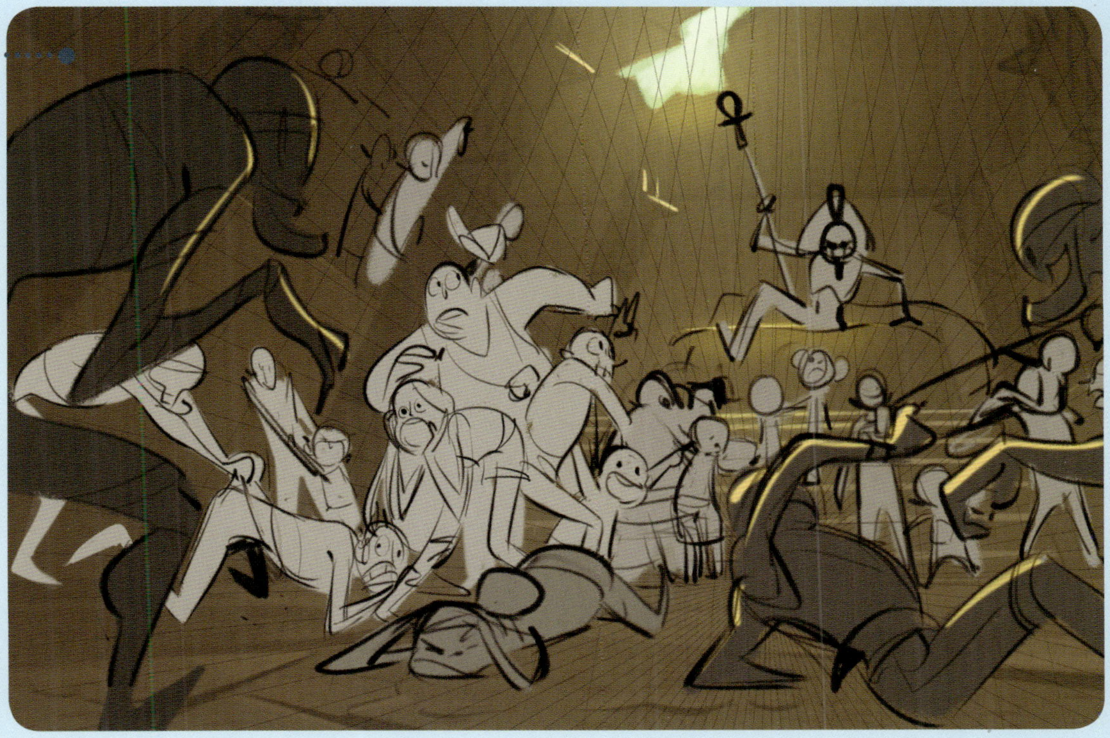

The problem-solving process in a complex image can continue well into the process, but strong foundations really help. Blocking out flat colors can be useful.

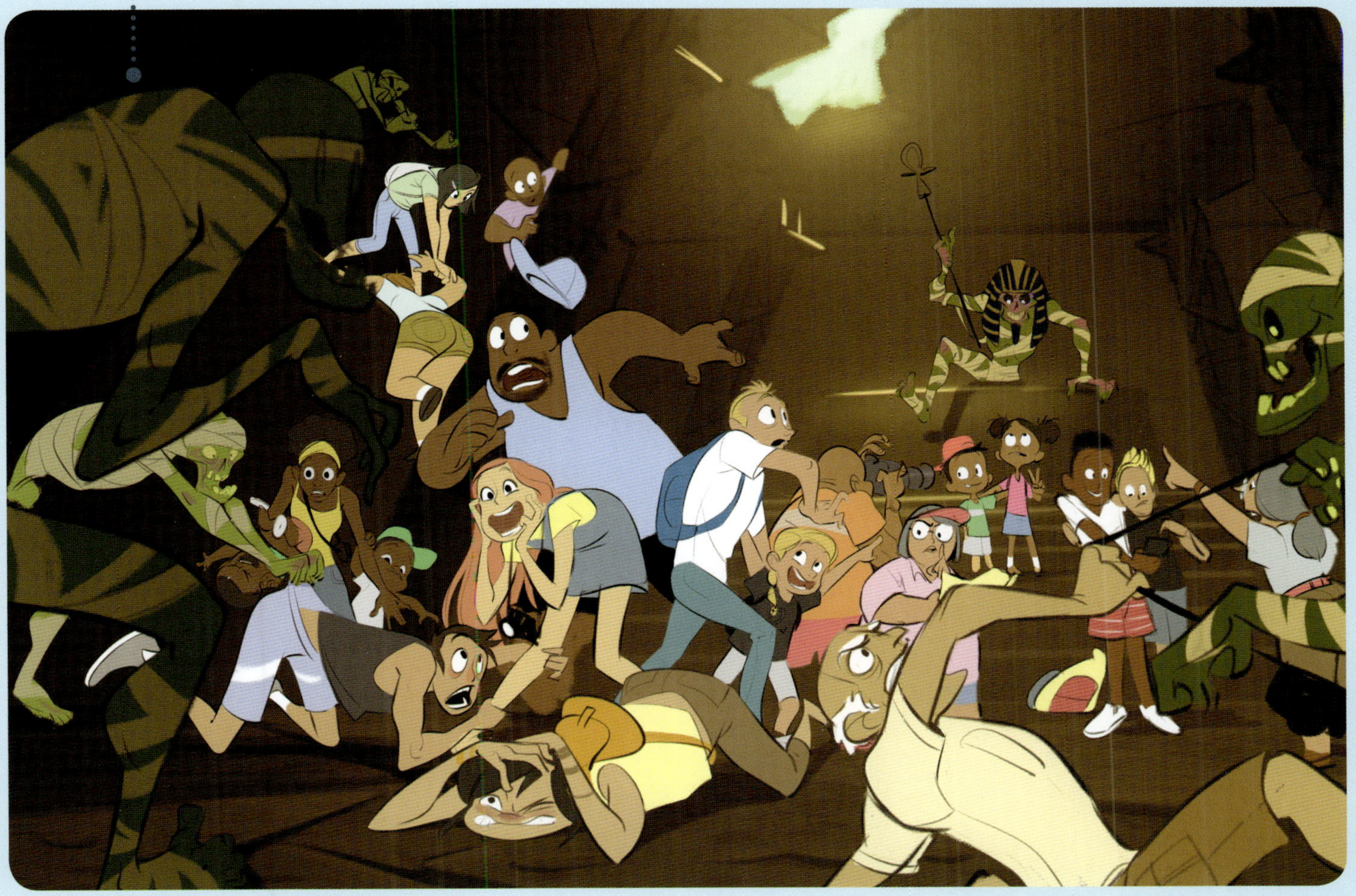

A DAY OUT AT THE MUMMIES' TOMB

The final crowd scene successfully balances high drama with multiple interactions by grouping characters together and guiding the viewer using color and lighting.

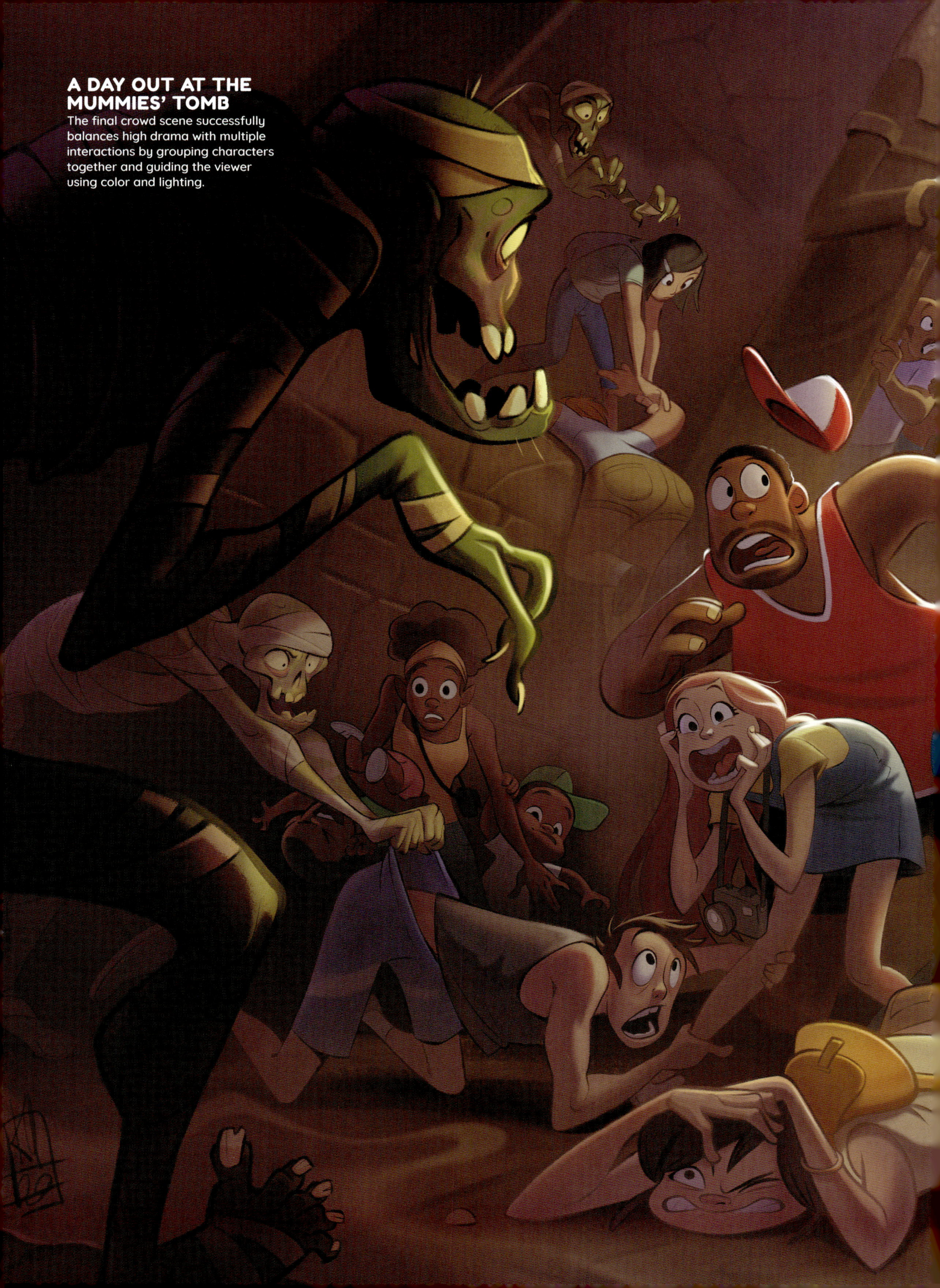

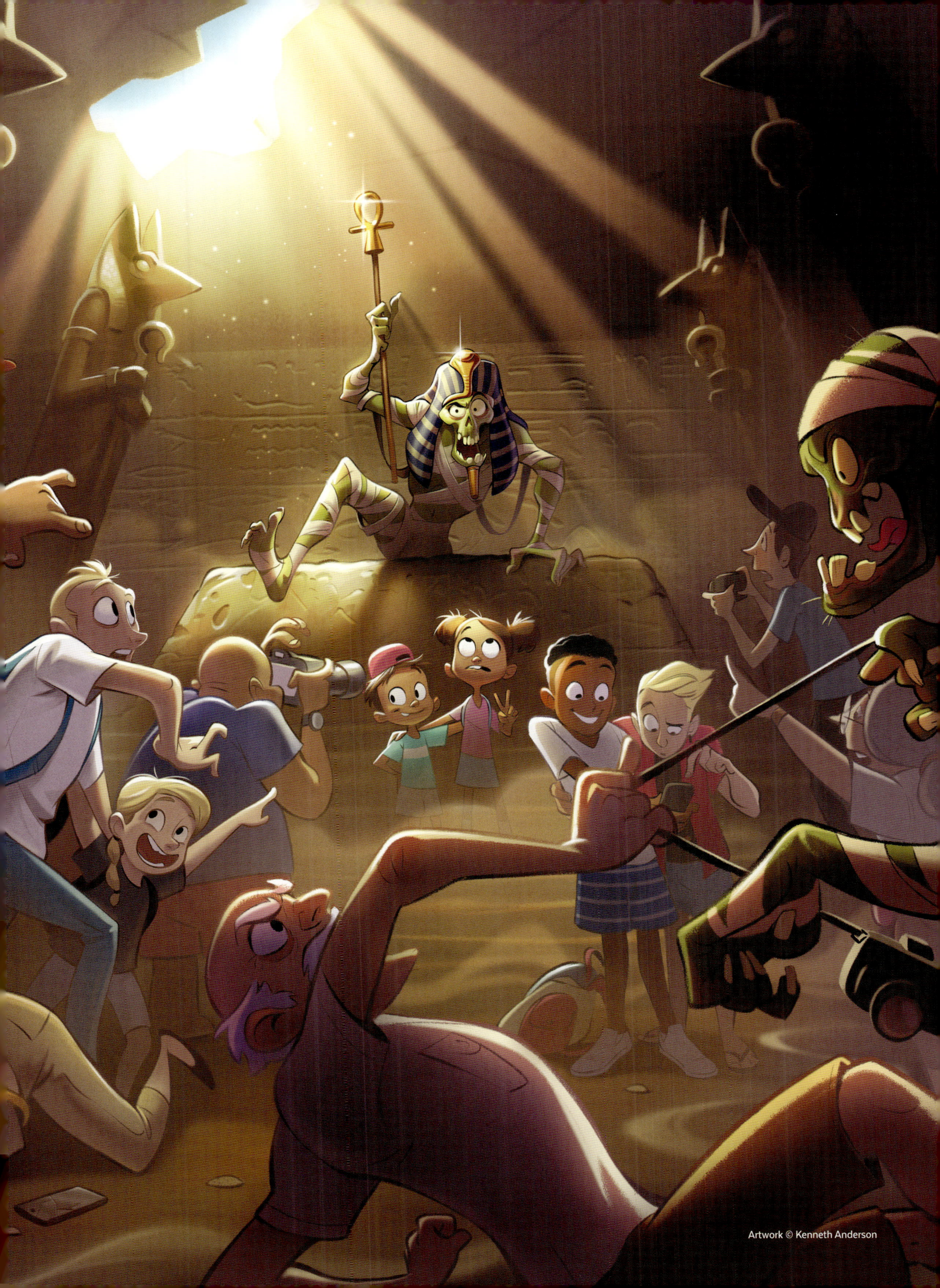

SPORTS TEAM

Sweeney Boo

When designing characters, it is important to have them performing an action, even if it is something simple like looking at their phone or sipping from a cup of coffee. Their action could also be in the form of an interaction with another character, such as a shared smile, a joke, or a hand placed on a shoulder. Such actions give characters a pinch of personality and help bring them to life, providing the audience with an immediate idea of who they are. This is demonstrated in this sports team, where the characters display a sense of pride, happiness, and team spirit as they celebrate together.

SPORTS TEAM

DIVERSITY
- Gender
- Body type
- Skin color

INTERACTION
- Team spirit
- Laughter
- Pride
- Smiles

COLORS
- Summer
- Joyful
- Pops of accent color

STYLE
- Not gender-defined
- Same uniform for all
- Retro style

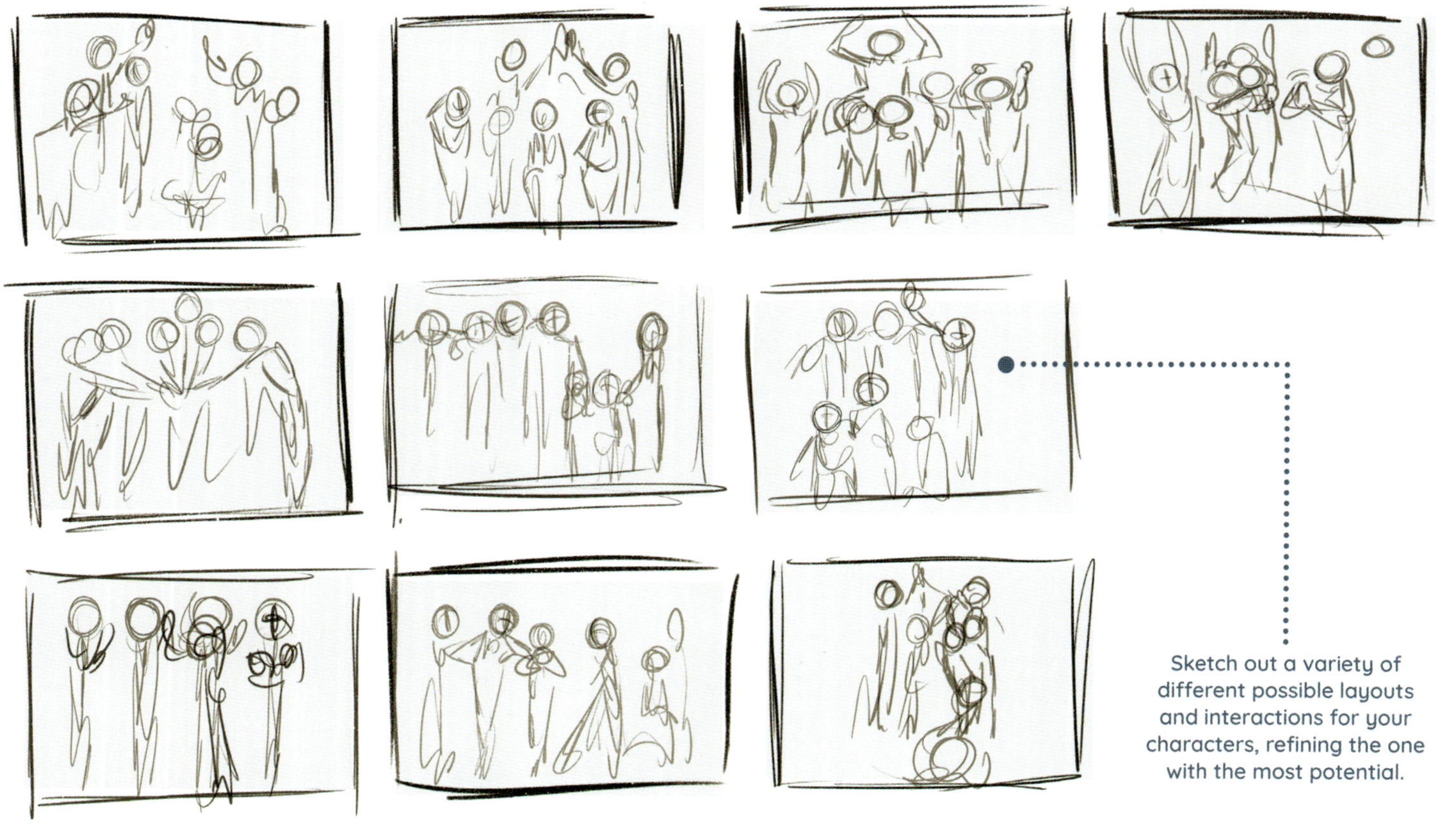

Sketch out a variety of different possible layouts and interactions for your characters, refining the one with the most potential.

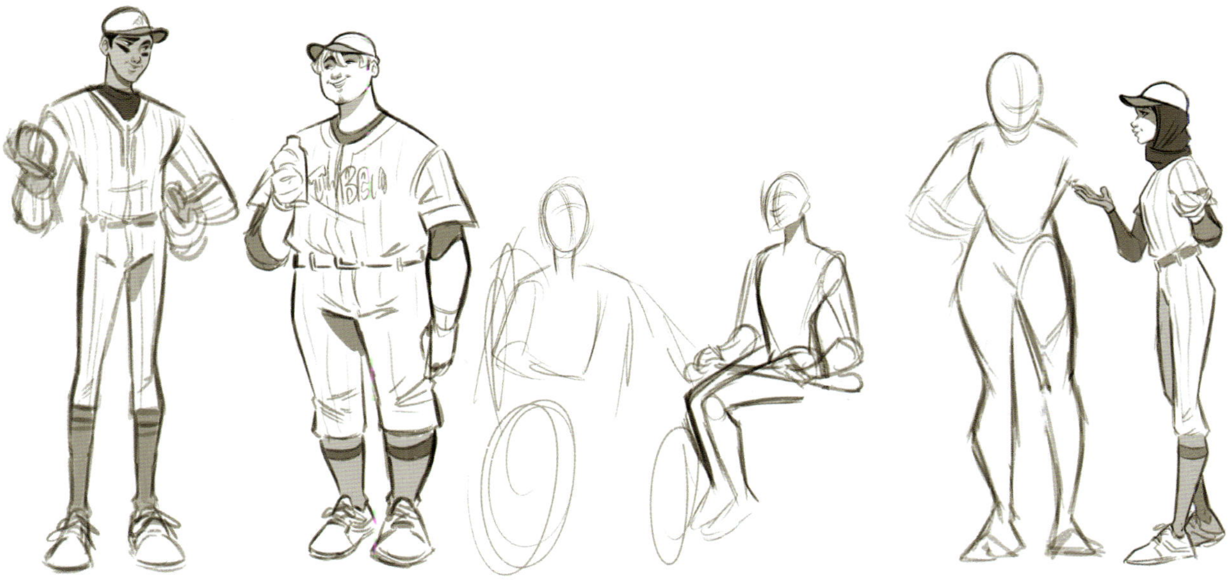

Sketch out your characters, exploring how they can interact with those around them.

Color in your characters and refine their expressions and emotions, but avoid a scene made up of only pairs – a team interacting as a whole makes for a more interesting image and tells more of a story.

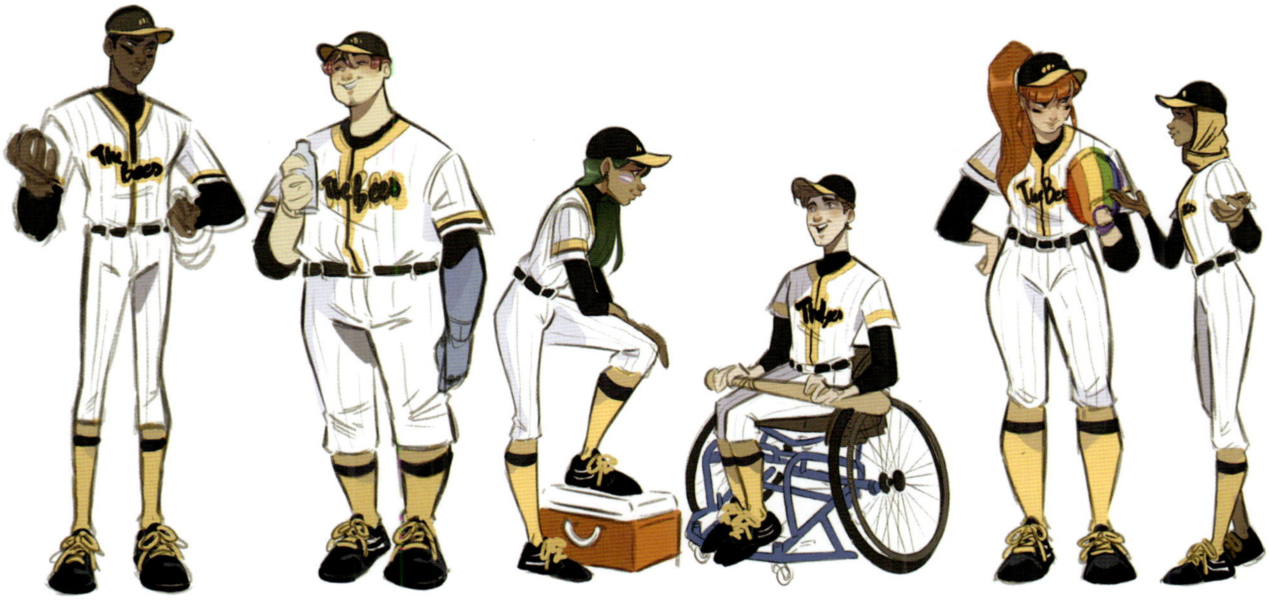

PRIDE

The final image provides a clearer idea of who the characters are as a team. Their body language is open and loose as they laugh together, high-five, and raise their drinks in celebration.

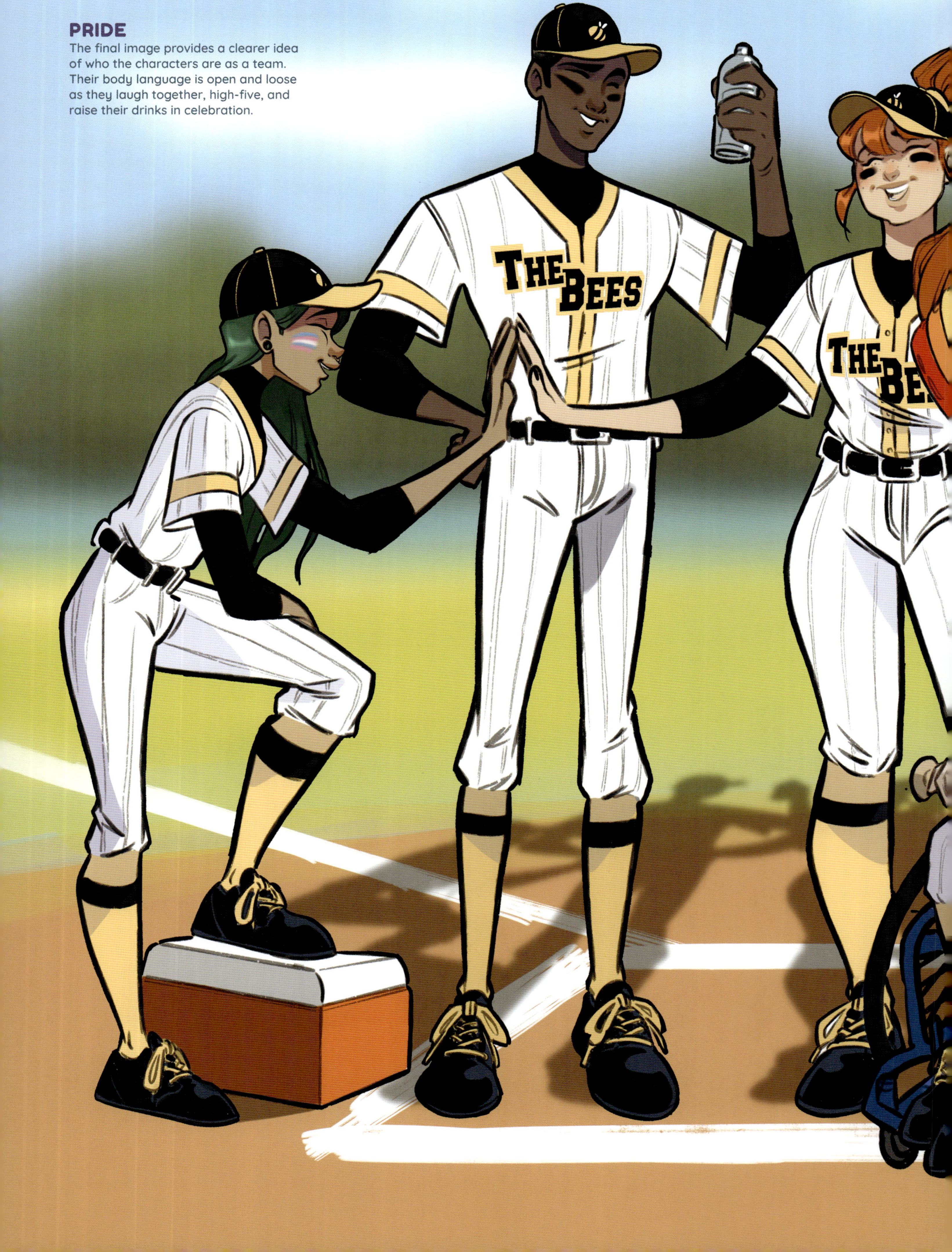

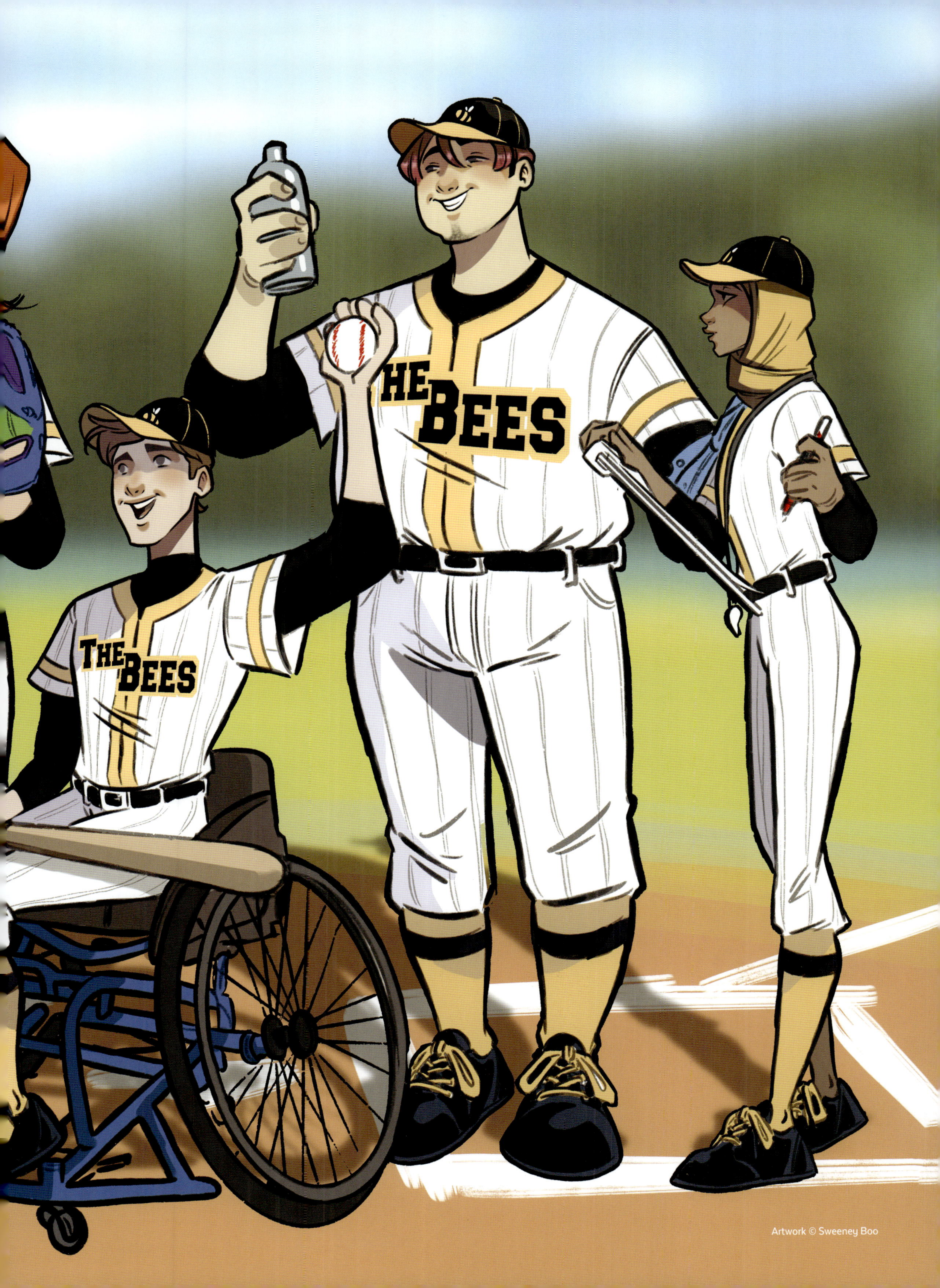
THE BEES
THE BEES

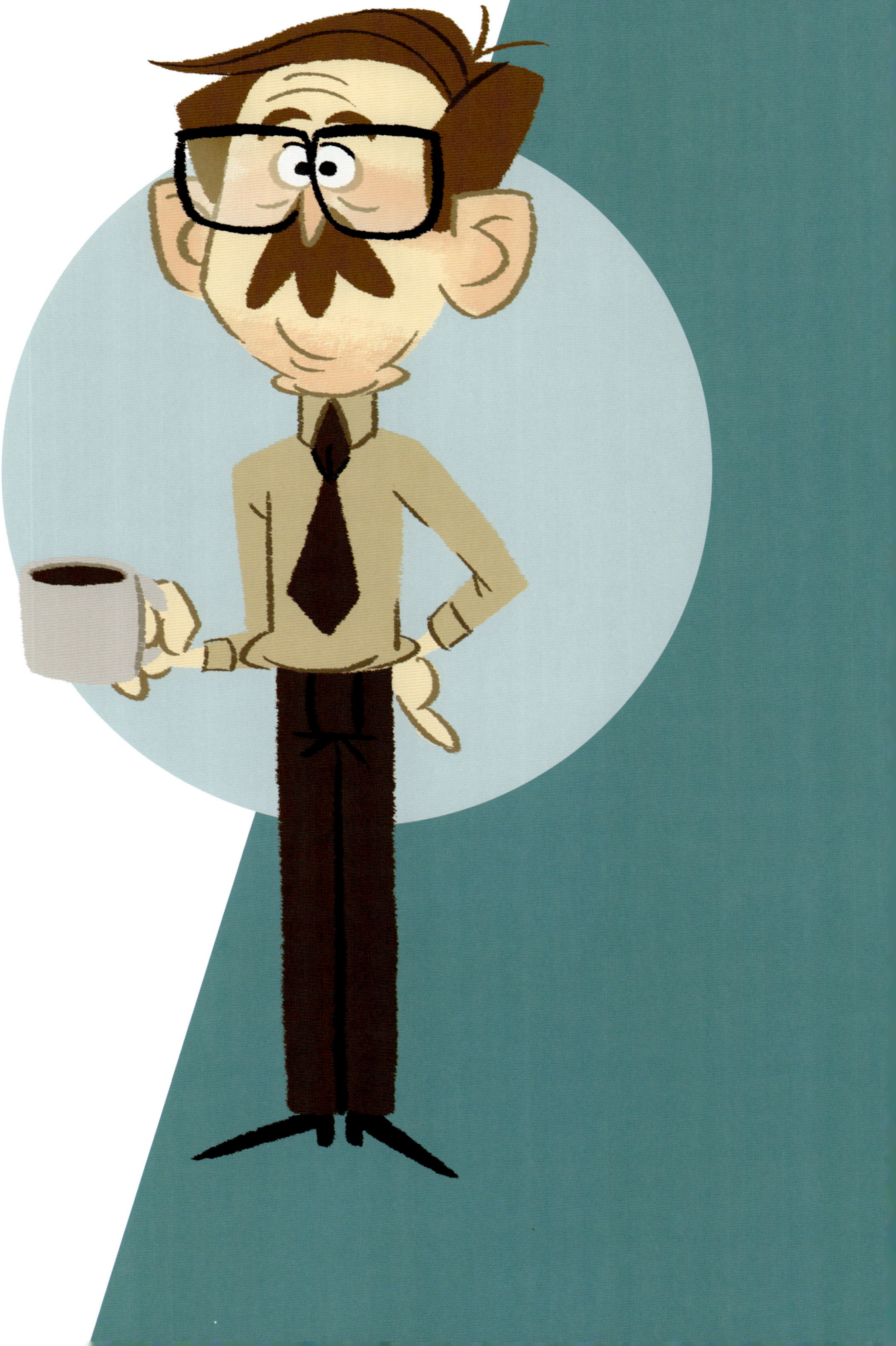

Image by Dom "Scruffy" Murphy

WORKING IN CHARACTER DESIGN

KEY CONSIDERATIONS
PAGE 290

PRESENTATION
PAGE 294

STYLE
PAGE 296

KEY CONSIDERATIONS

Dom "Scruffy" Murphy

When it comes to character design, assessing your time and budget for any given project is paramount and key to the quality of designs you can produce. For example, a project with a large budget may require a more polished and appealing look, but if the timeframe to complete the project is a tight one, the design quality may suffer. It is a matter of finding the right balance. It is your responsibility as a character designer to take all this into account and apply it to your work.

Before going forward with any project, big or small, find out from the client what the **budget** and **timeframe** will be, and **what the client is expecting** of the work and designs. With this information, you can safely and securely judge how much you will have to charge and how long the work will take you. This is why reading a brief closely is so important - just as every story is not the same, neither is every design project. For example, designs for a children's TV show might not have the same budget as designs for a CG feature film, nor will they have the same detail requirement. This would result in a very different workload needed for each, which would affect how long the project takes and what you would charge. Also take into account what revisions might be needed - as a rule of thumb, if you think a project will take "X" amount of time, add two or three extra days just as cushioning, allowing you to fine-tune everything that will be needed.

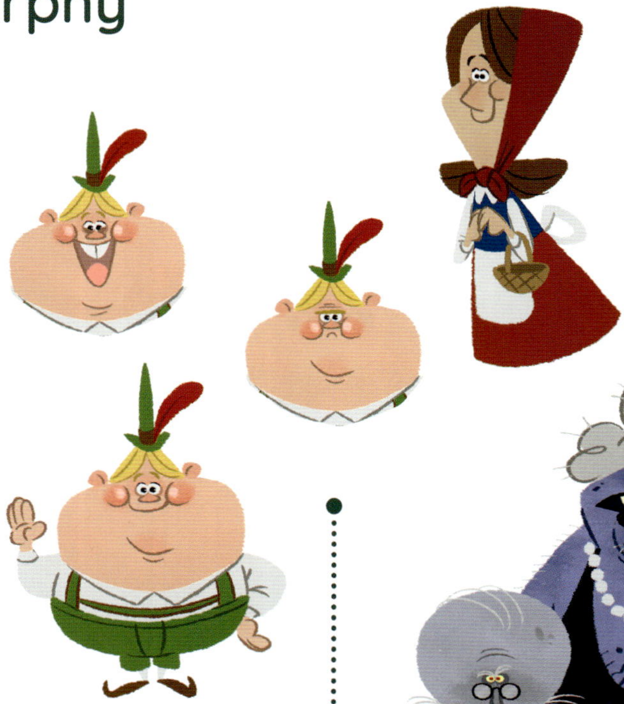

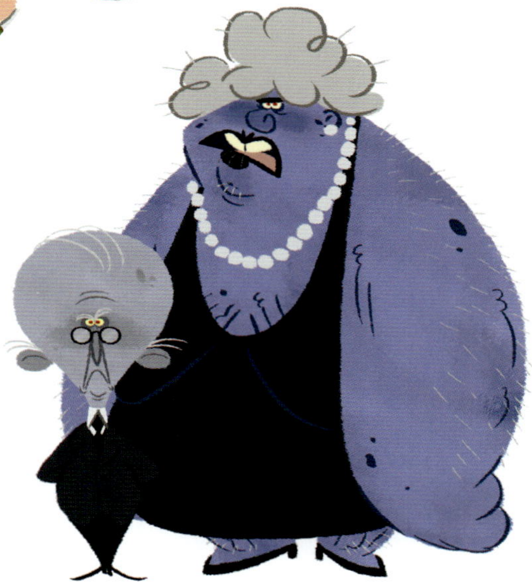

These designs would be suitable for illustrated books. Some are aimed at a more classic fairytale approach that stays true to the original tales, while the others are for a more niche project of a spooky family.

This leads us to when exactly character design is needed and what will be required of you as a professional designer. Character design is required in most, if not all, areas of modern entertainment, from games and cartoons to movies and books. All need character design and all come with their own specific requirements. It is important to know what a client wants for a project, **what that character will be designed for**, and what you will need to provide as the designer. A design for a video-game character or CG feature will be far more technical than that of one for a 2D animated show or illustrated book, needing assets such as detailed turnarounds, mouth and head charts, and many key poses to help bring the character to life. In contrast, you will need to know how far to push or when to stop on a project that requires less detail, such as a kids' show, to ensure that it works as a whole.

This is not to say that different categories do not overlap. It is not uncommon for TV-show characters to cross over into the realms of video games, toys, and feature films, but one thing to always keep in mind is that **what works in 2D will not always work in 3D**. Some shapes just will not translate well to a different format, and you will have to compromise, find a workaround, or "cheat" the shape to achieve the desired effect. Having a solid understanding of shapes and how they make up the form and volume of the character is key. Getting the shape and quality of your design correct from the start will help make it appeal in a number of genres, and will help it cross over and overlap effectively in different media.

This is where knowing your **target audience** comes into play. It is important to know what age group or audience the character is being designed for and what that demographic will need. A character designed for a preschool audience will not be as technical as one designed for a teen or more mature audience. Designing for preschoolers requires more meticulous design choices - knowing what to leave or what to add. Simplicity is essential in this case, as you want to catch and keep the childrens' attention, whereas for a teen or older audience you can present more complex character designs and add more story and detail.

This character would fit a 2D animated show with a slight horror theme. When designing for 2D animation, keep in mind how the finished product will look; offering multiple options, like dark lines versus colored lines, can help in development.

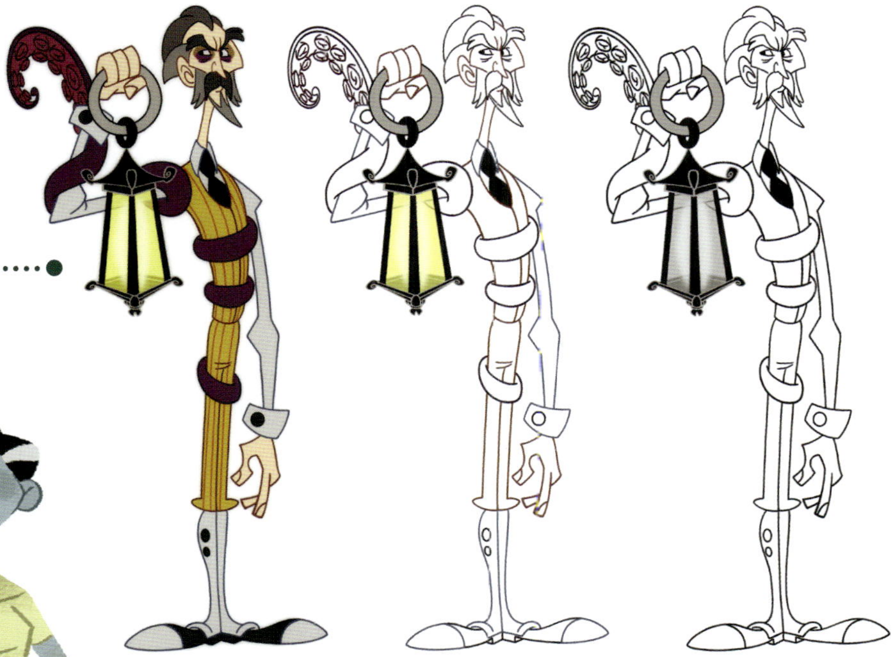

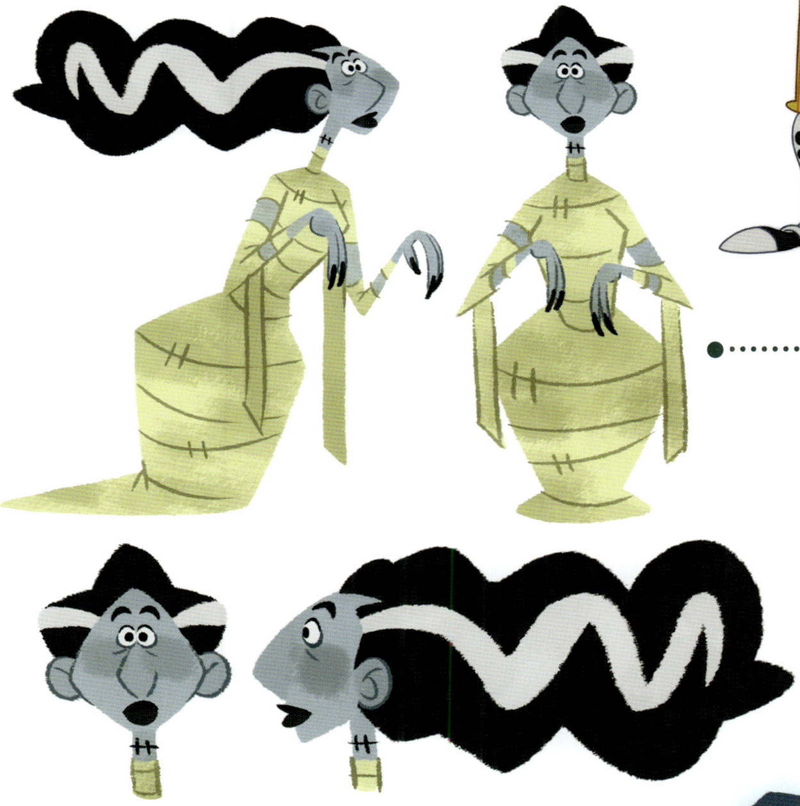

This type of monster character could appear in a 3D feature film, with the shapes and volumes explored from different angles.

Designs aimed at preschoolers can use simple shapes and bright colors to grab and keep children's attention.

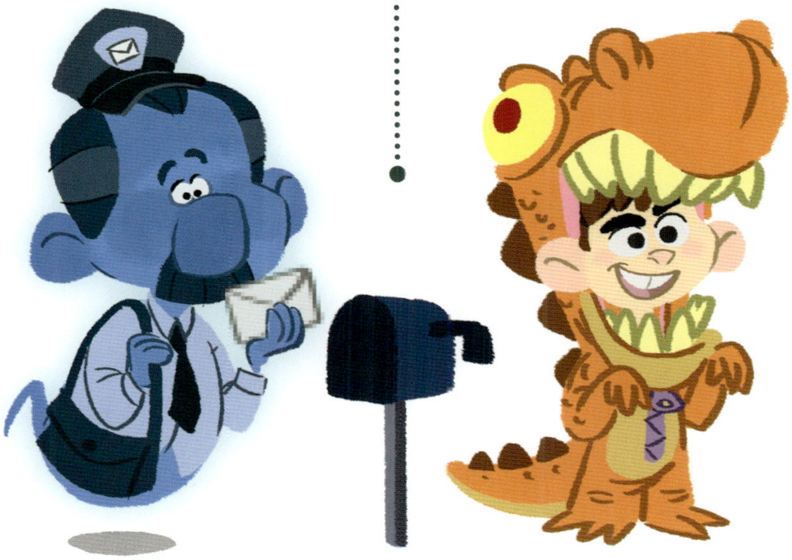

Reading the brief, and more importantly, **understanding the brief** is crucial. For example, if the client wanted you to design a character for a show aimed at girls, but to avoid stereotypes, you would fail to meet the brief if all your designs were cute, pink, and sweet. If the client wanted a more relatable or grounded design, avoiding those obvious stereotypes would be a better approach, leading to a unique design that stands out from the crowd and a more memorable project as a result.

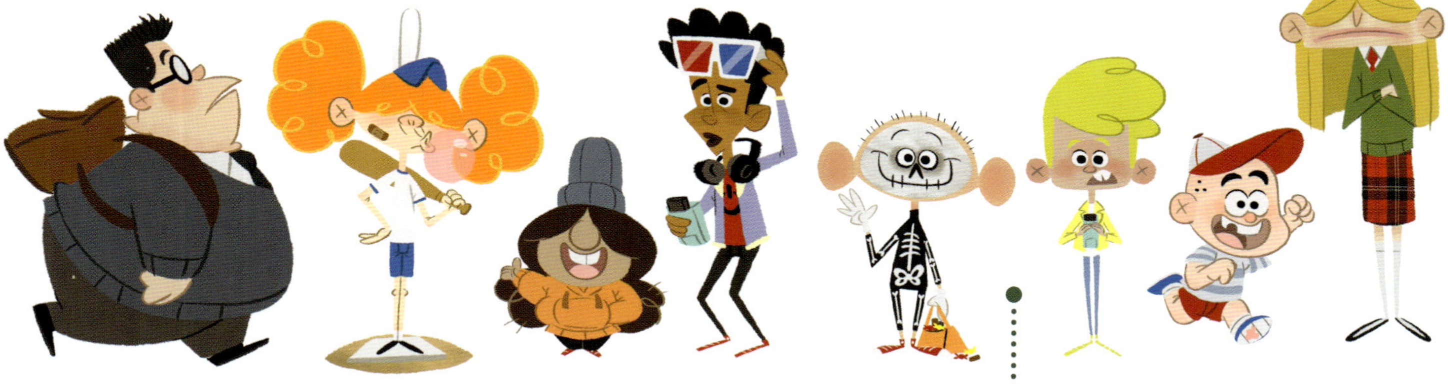

This lineup of characters could star in an animated show for preteens. They have a higher level of detail and complexity than designs for younger children.

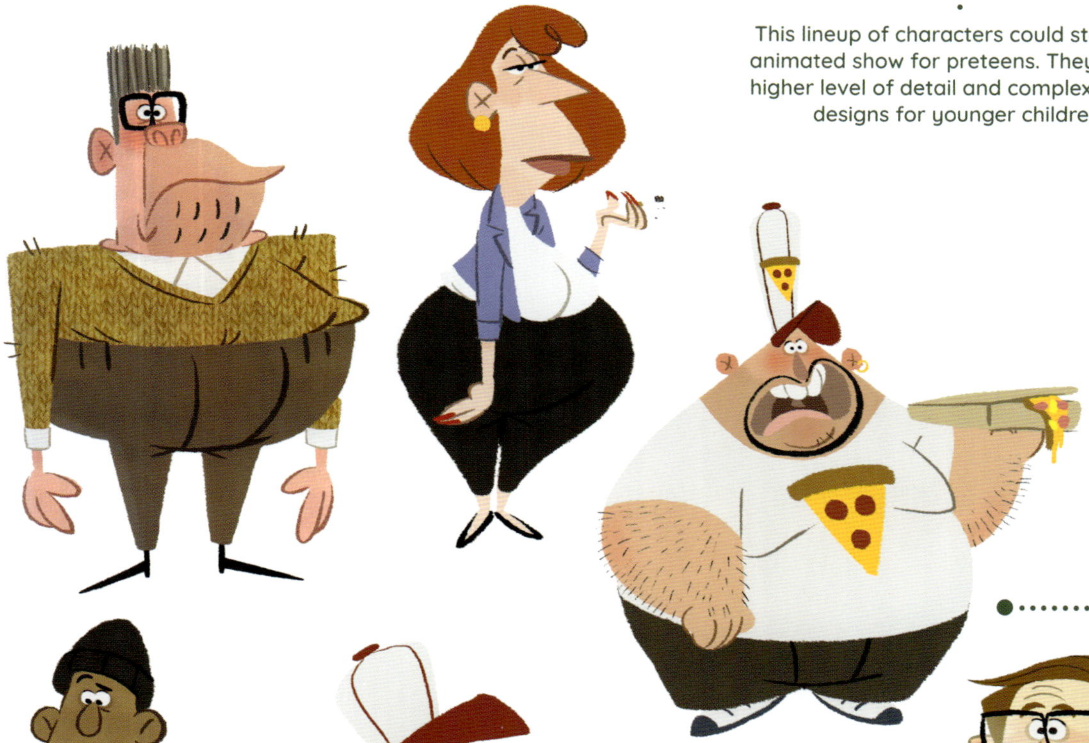

These characters would work well in a sitcom-type TV show aimed at older teens. When designing for this age group, leaning toward a mature look works best.

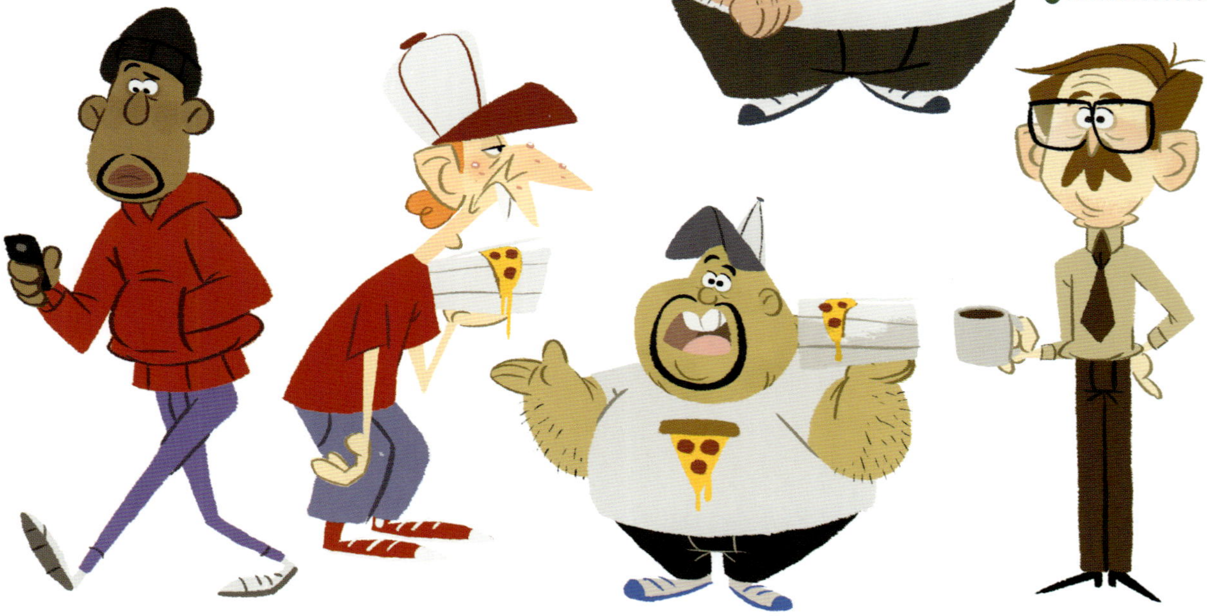

This yak character could appeal to an audience of boys and girls. When designing for all genders, a universal character or theme, such as animals, is often a strong choice.

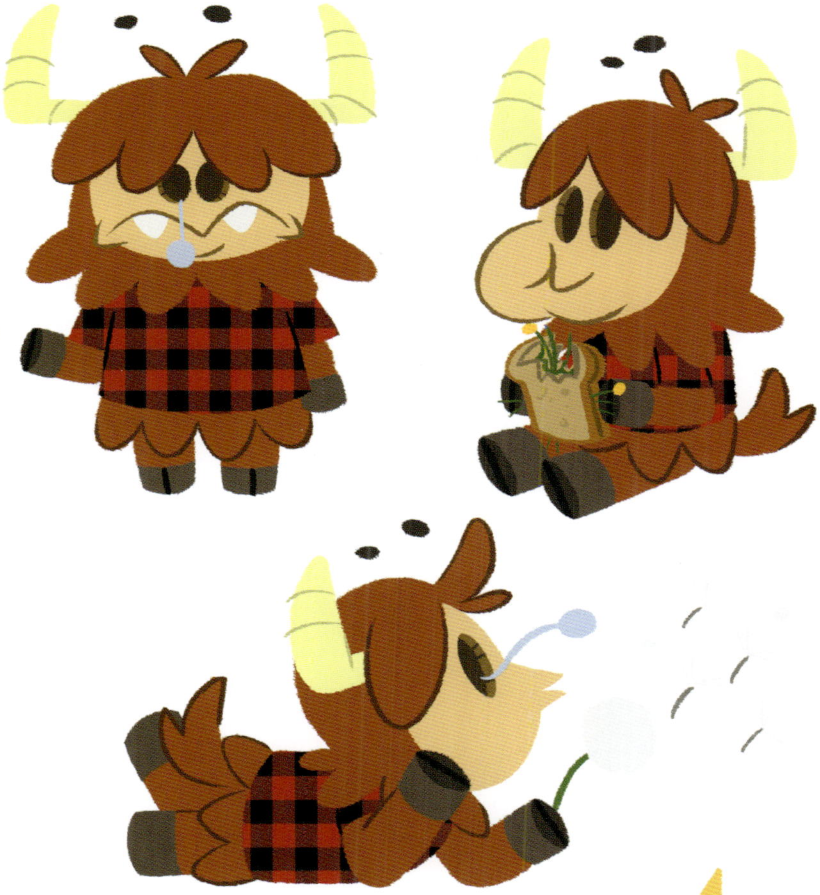

These characters are both designed for girls, but each is different. The design on the left is more grounded and relatable, while the design on the right is cute but stereotypical.

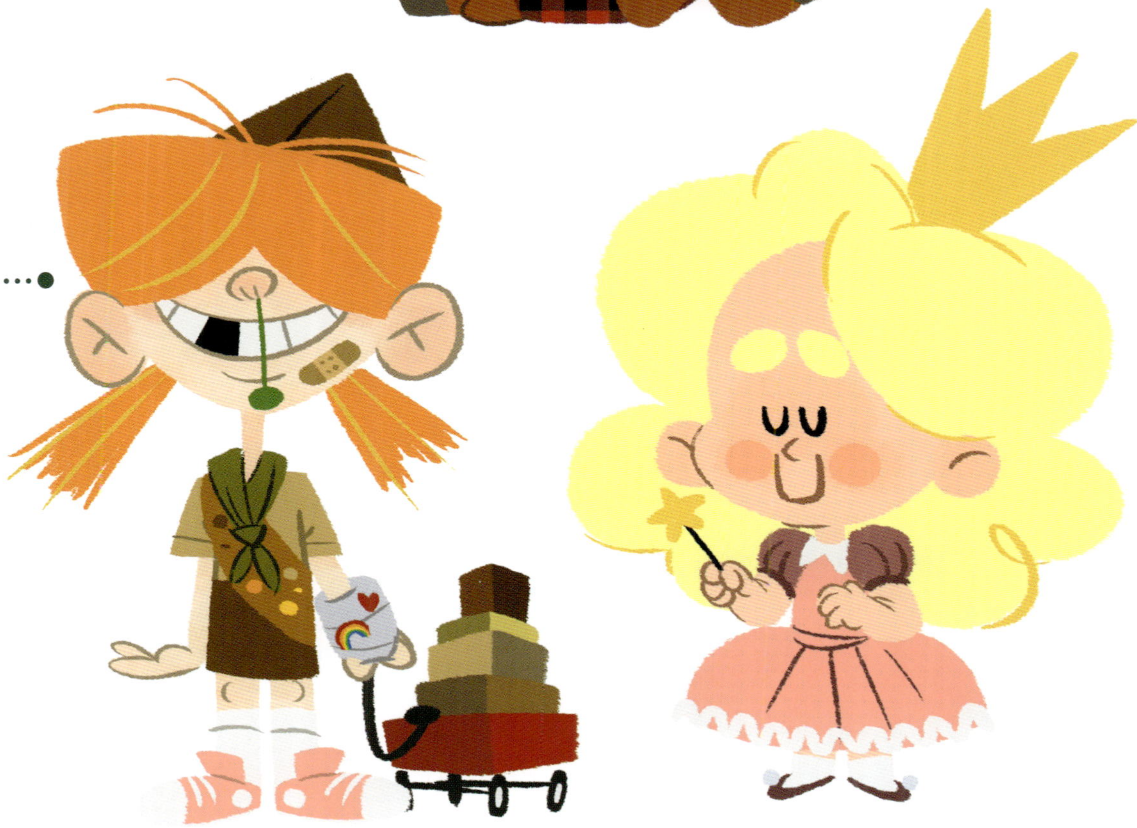

PRESENTATION
Dom "Scruffy" Murphy

Presentation is everything. It shows how you want your character to be seen and perceived by the client and ultimately the audience. Model sheets are a great help in achieving this – taking all the fine details and essence of a character and distilling them into a neat package. This information may include turnarounds, pose sheets, and hand and mouth charts that show how your character speaks and performs gestures.

Key pose sheets give the client an idea of how the character will act, their personality, and what they will look like in motion.

Turnarounds give the client an overview of what the character will look like from different angles. When creating a turnaround, always keep in mind what it is intended for, such as whether the final product is 2D or 3D, because each format comes with different needs. For a character that is to be used in 3D animation, for example, the most important aspects to show in the turnaround are the shape and form, and how the character's volume occupies those shapes from multiple angles. For a 2D character, a turnaround can be a bit different, as the design does not have to abide by the rules of three-dimensional space. This allows you to "cheat" certain shapes and proportions to make the character appear consistent from different angles, rather than following the physical constraints of a three-dimensional object, and gives a more stylized and unique look to the finished product.

This sketch turnaround starts off with basic shapes that lead to a rough design. This type of turnaround is best used in CG work, giving the sculptor an idea of shapes and volumes without being too technical.

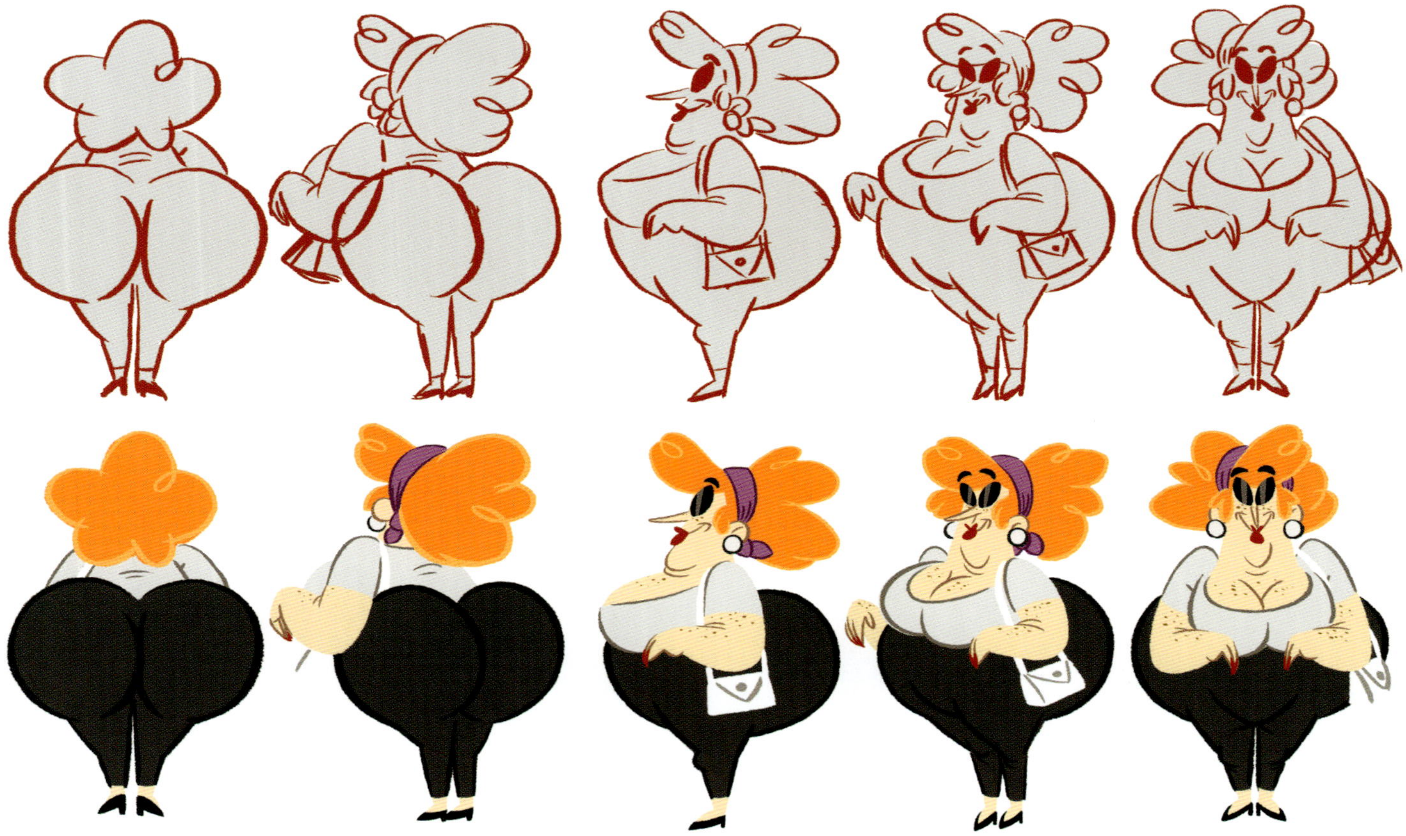

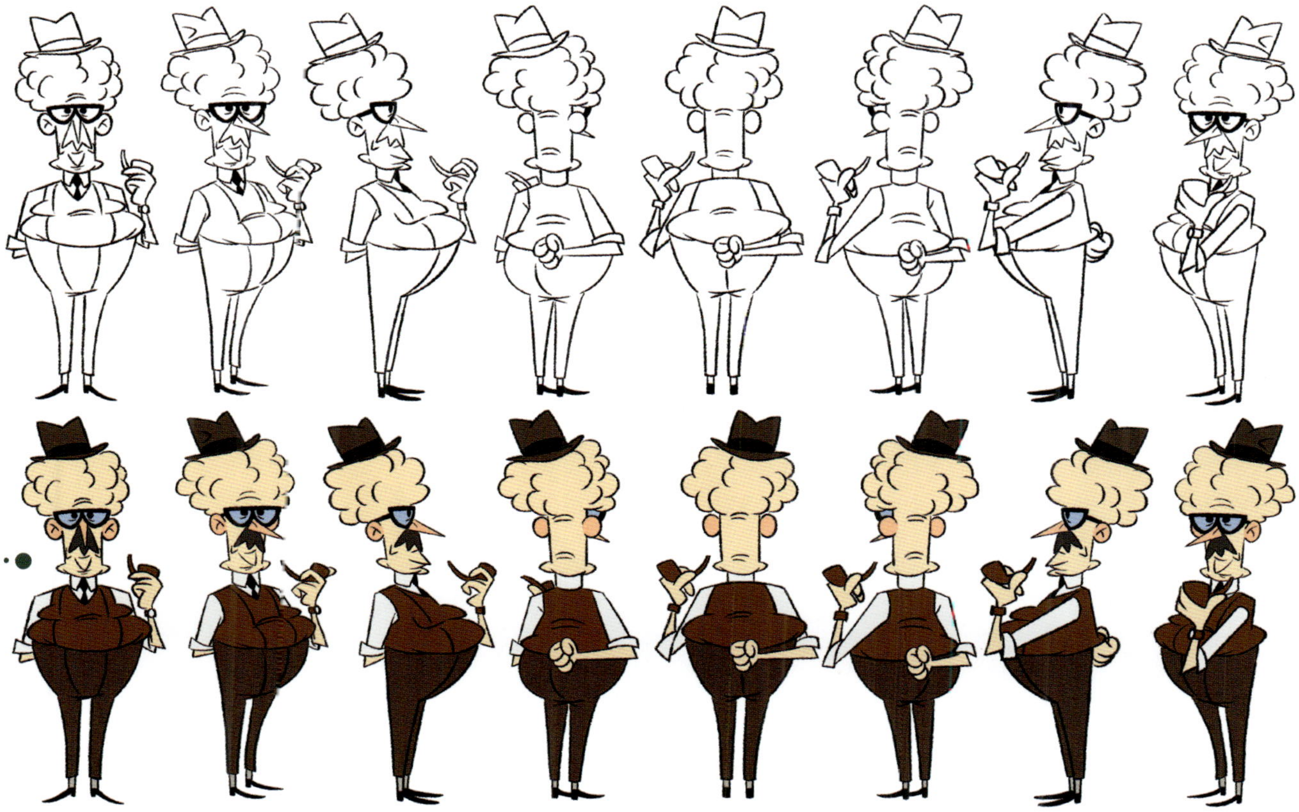

A turnaround intended for a 2D animated series must give the animators and designers a clear idea of how the character is portrayed and styled from multiple angles. This example starts with clean lines and leads to a more finished product.

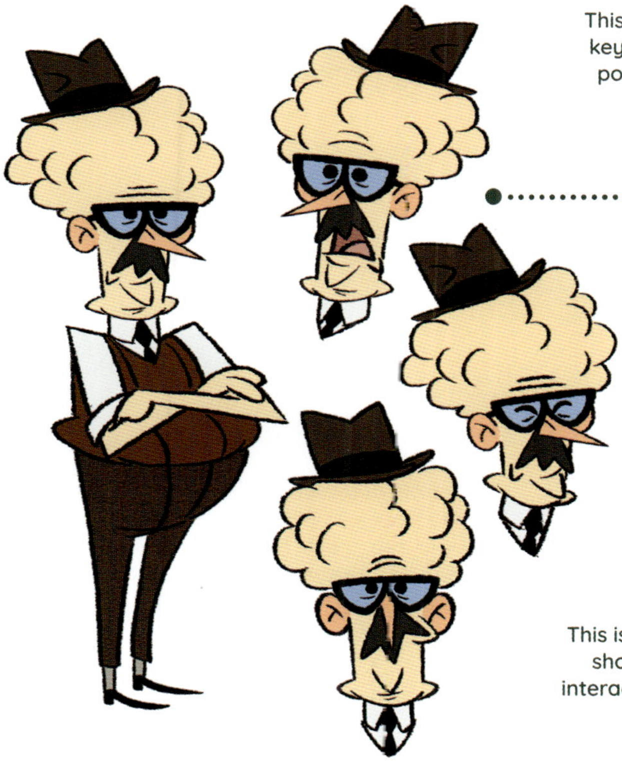

This is an example of a character in a key pose, with some additional head poses to provide more information about his facial expressions.

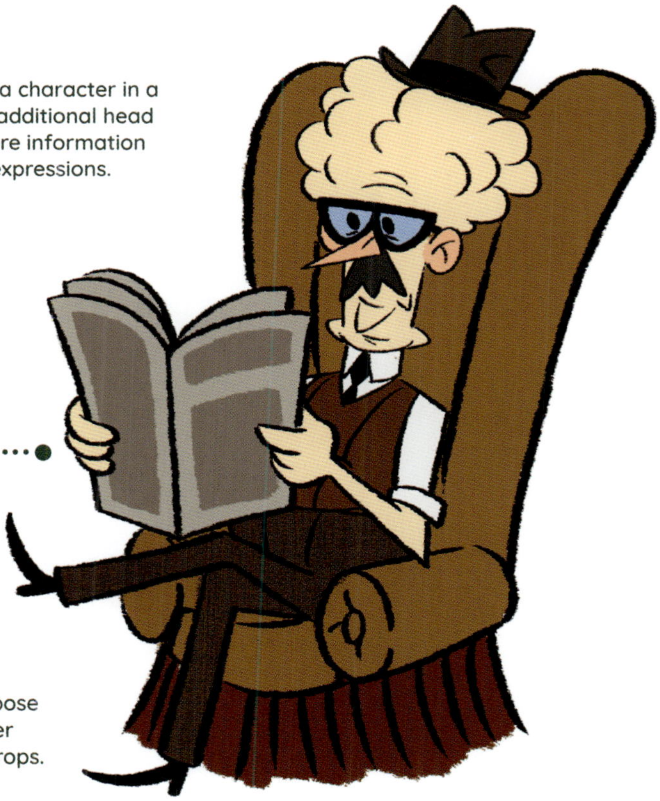

This is a more specific pose showing the character interacting with some props.

STYLE
Dom "Scruffy" Murphy

Style is a big factor in character design. It is what sets one project apart from another and makes it instantly recognizable, whether that style is a studio's "house style," such as Pixar's, or the personal style of an individual designer, such as Bruce Timm with his distinctive influence on *Batman: The Animated Series.*

This is why style can be so important in a design: it can be used to carve out one's own little corner of the industry and become memorable. From unusual artistic visions to more mainstream approaches, style can be used to set different tones for different projects. A cute style with simple shapes tends to work well for a younger audience, while a grittier or more graphical style, such as those based on well-known graphic novels, can work well for an older audience.

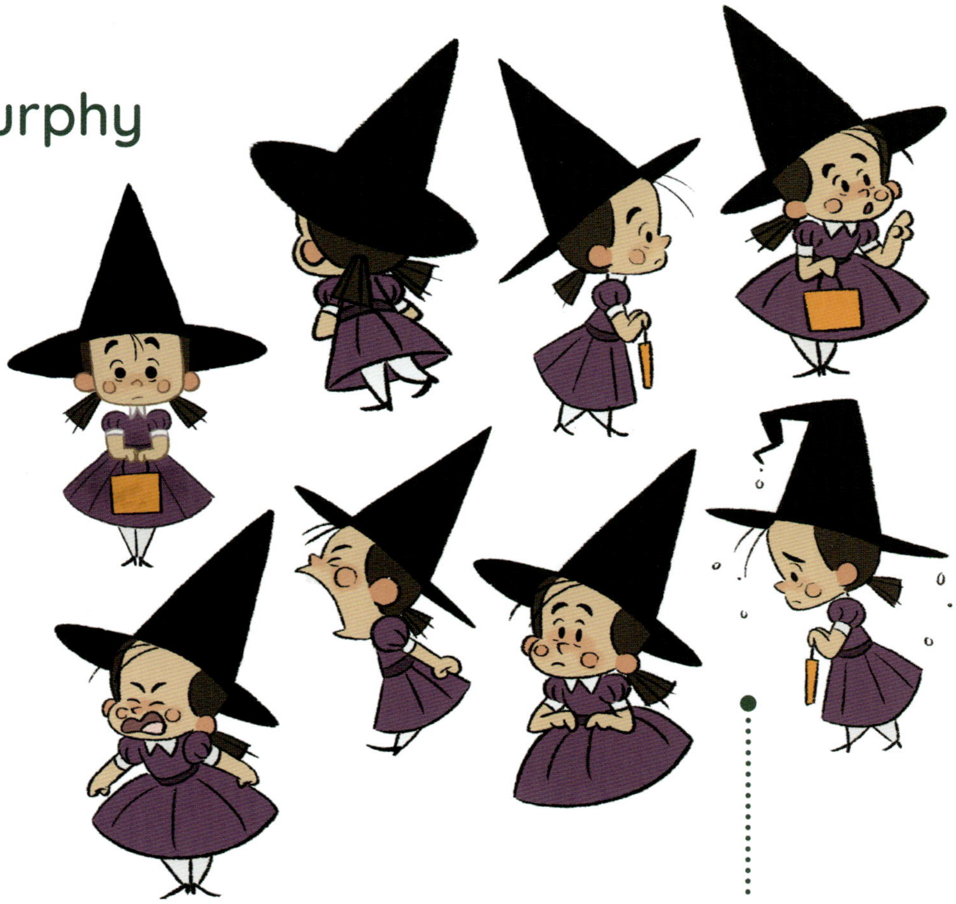

This little witch's style is ideal for a whimsical children's book series. The simplified design appeals to a young audience, while pushing shapes to get the most "acting" out of them.

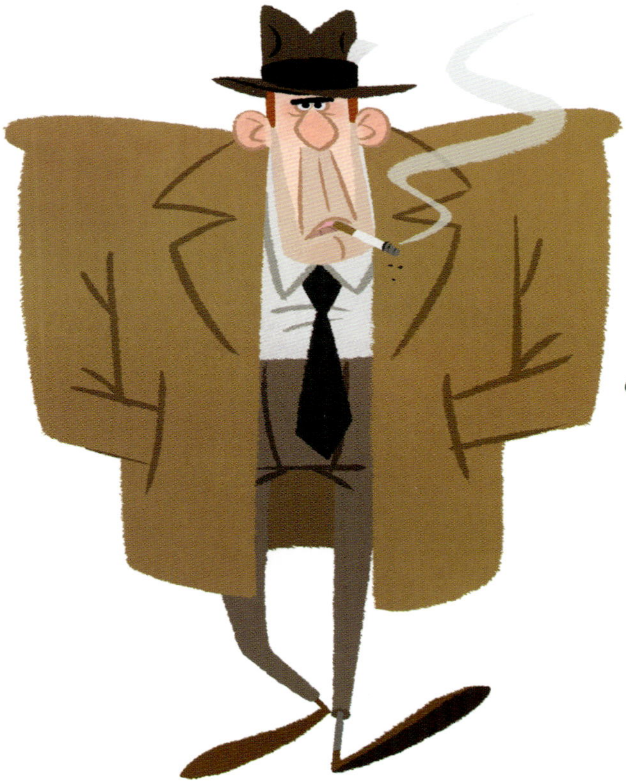

This private detective design would work well in a noir graphic novel for teens, with the exaggerated shapes creating a stylized, animated look.

These characters lean heavily toward an eccentric, fantastical genre, where interesting characters inhabit colorful worlds – such as in mainstream TV shows.

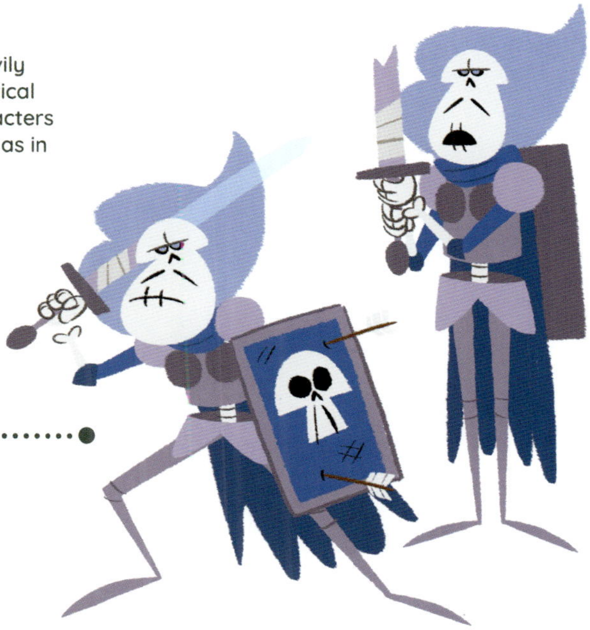

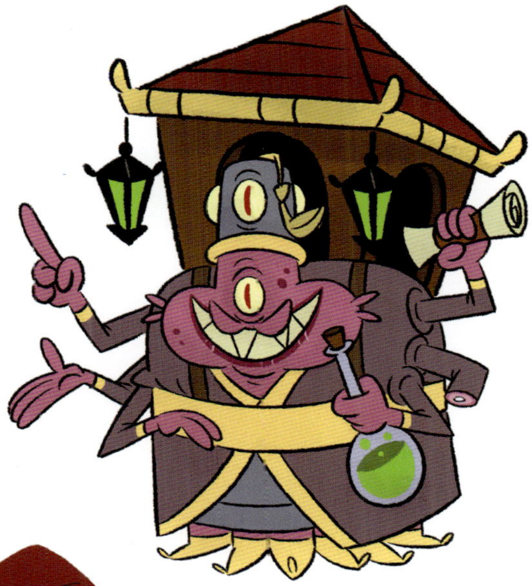

When designing for a resource such as a college textbook, a more graphic, mid-century look can work well. It doesn't distract from the information, but works as a visual aid to get the point across.

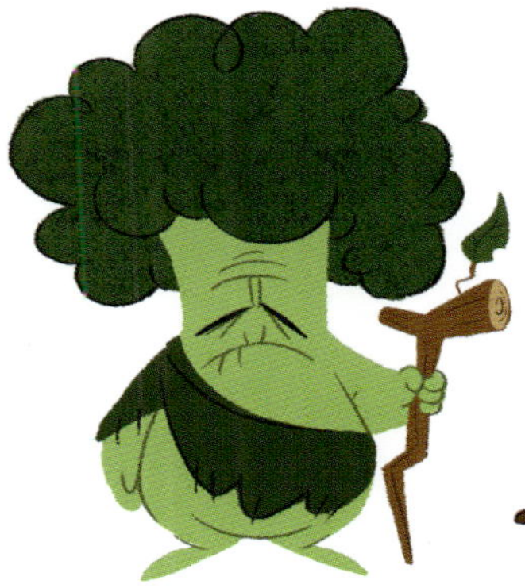

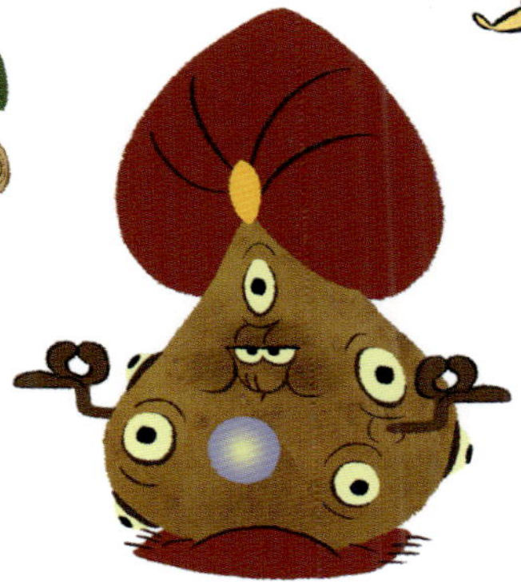

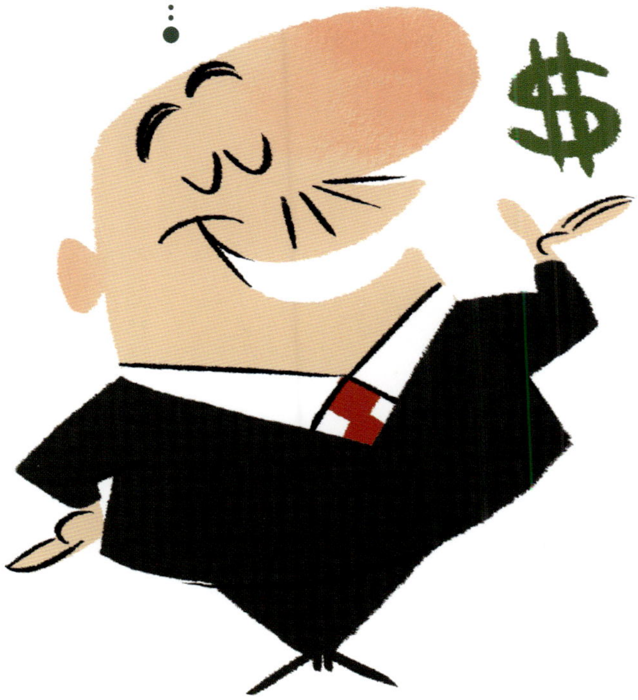

BE ADAPTABLE

A unique style can help you stand out in a sea of artists, but, ultimately, the key to being a good character designer is the absence of a set style – being able to be flexible and adapt to what a project needs. Knowing how, when, and where to do this is part of a character designer's job. A good way to practice this is to study life around you and the artists you admire, pick what you like from them, and use those inspirations to weave your own style with its own unique flair.

Top images © Dom "Scruffy" Murphy

IDEAS GRID

If you find yourself stuck for design ideas or would like to test your skills on a random project, you can use this section to create your own mix-and-match character briefs. Choose some themes from the columns and mash them together to generate a new character concept to research and draw!

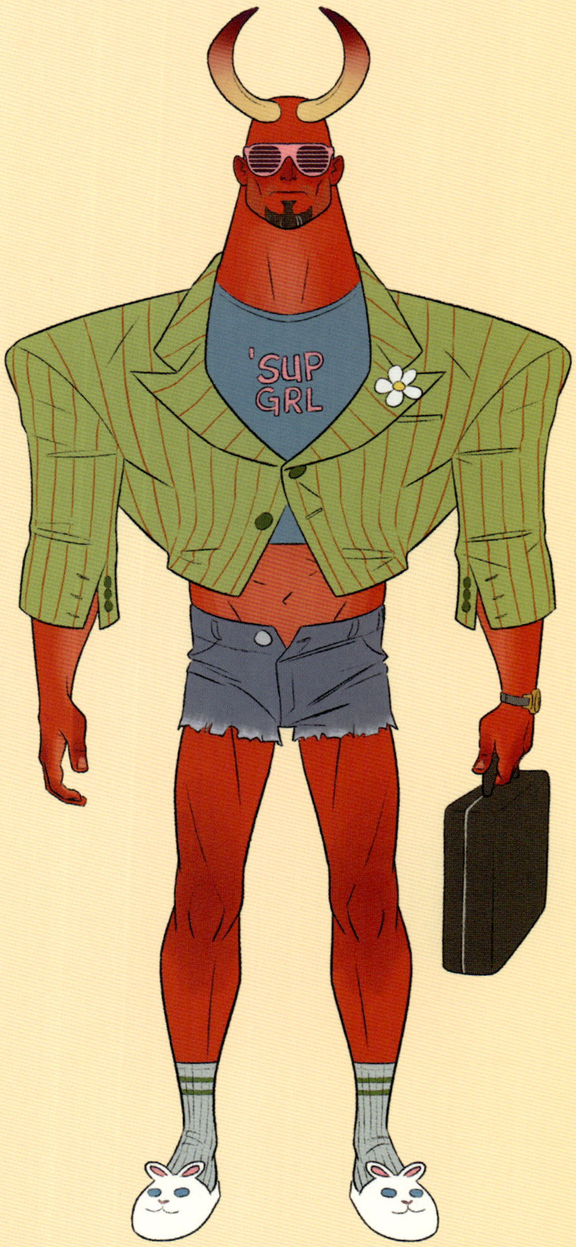

ANATOMY

- Tall
- Tiny
- Muscular
- Short
- Angular
- Soft
- Broad
- Adolescent
- Square
- Strong
- Slim
- Elderly
- Athletic
- Curvy
- Infant
- Petite
- Elongated
- Average
- Round
- Middle-aged

STYLE

- Colorful
- Plain
- Practical
- Severe
- Stylish
- Minimalist
- Eccentric
- Vintage
- Neat
- Sporty
- Mismatched
- Alternative
- Cozy
- Outdated
- Smart
- Messy
- Boring
- Comfortable
- Expensive
- Simple

EMOTION

- Cheerful
- Afraid
- Eager
- Sad
- Shy
- Annoyed
- Curious
- Worried
- Overjoyed
- Awkward
- Relaxed
- Disgusted
- Tired
- Surprised
- Wistful
- Bored
- Kind
- Awed
- Excited
- Furious

COLOR

- Warm
- Dark
- Vibrant
- Pale
- Cool
- Autumnal
- Contrasting
- Nocturnal
- Neutral
- Deep
- Faded
- Tropical
- Clashing
- Pastel
- Analogous
- Bright
- Natural
- Monochrome
- Neon
- Light

ROLE

- Hero
- Explorer
- Learner
- Entertainer
- Guardian
- Worker
- Villain
- Helper
- Troublemaker
- Fighter
- Parent
- Royalty
- Henchman
- Thinker
- Wanderer
- Rebel
- Companion
- Teacher
- Trickster
- Civilian

ITEM

- Book
- Hat
- Phone
- Scarf
- Weapon
- Necklace
- Cloak
- Spectacles
- Briefcase
- Artifact
- Torch
- Coat
- Spade
- Rucksack
- Cane
- Key
- Map
- Belt
- Glove
- Earring

SETTING

- Magical
- Modern
- Aquatic
- Castle
- Garden
- Vehicle
- Urban
- Historical
- Library
- Spooky
- Futuristic
- Beach
- School
- Forest
- Zoo
- Shop
- Dystopian
- Street
- Office
- Mountain

CONTRIBUTORS

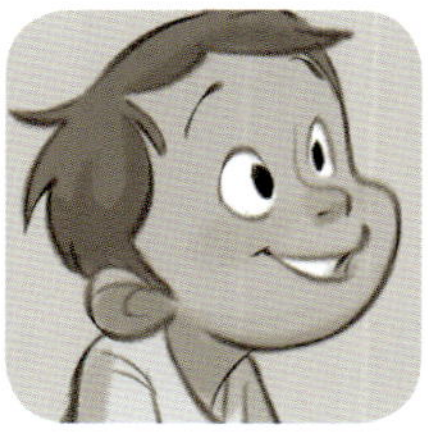
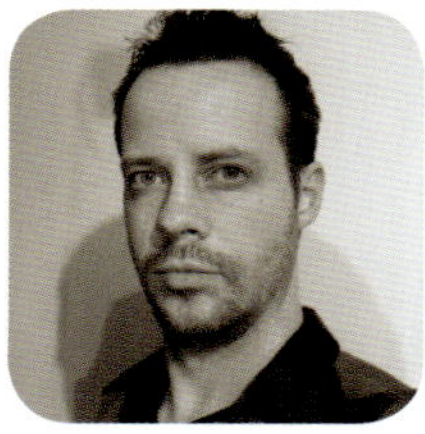

Kenneth Anderson

Character designer & illustrator | charactercube.com

Kenneth is a freelance artist from the UK, working on children's television production, illustration, and games.

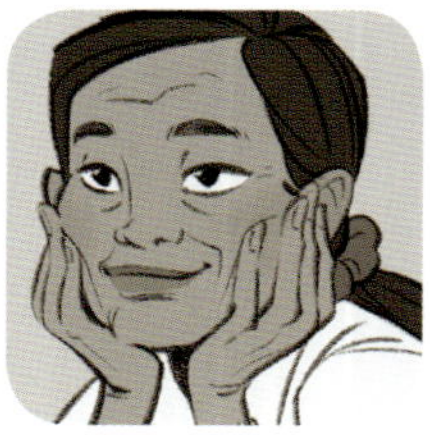
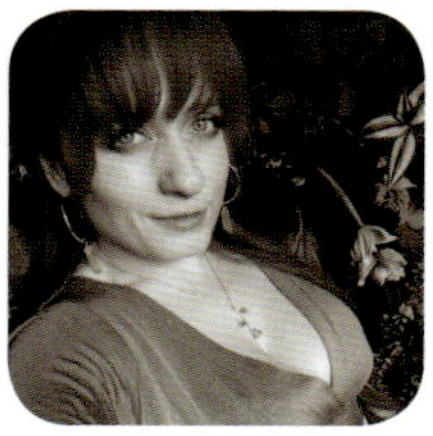

Olga "Asu Rocks" Andriyenko

Character designer & story artist | artstation.com/asurocks

Olga is an illustrator and published comic artist from Germany. Following a successful career in game design, she now works on animation projects and creates her own stories.

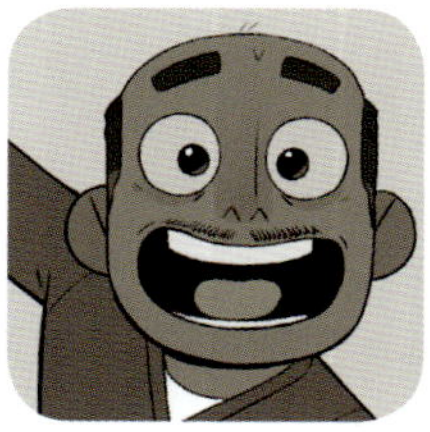
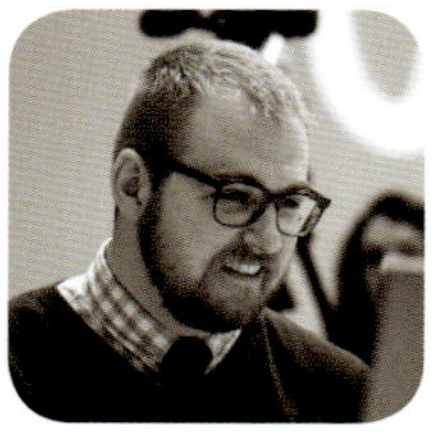

Randy Bishop

Character designer & art director | randybishopart.com

Randy is a character designer who works for various clients in the animation, gaming, and publishing industries.

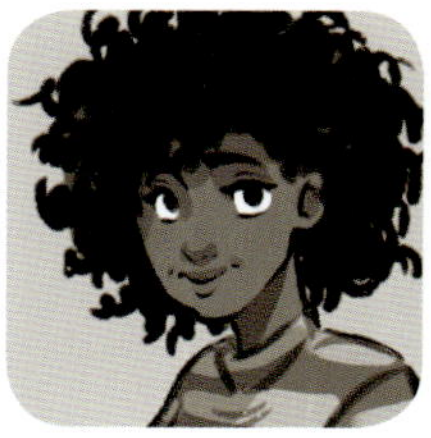
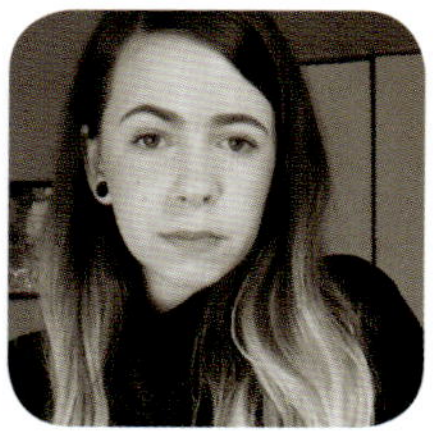

Sweeney Boo

Comic artist | sweeneyboo.com

Sweeney currently lives in Canada, where she is working on a Marvel project and a graphic novel called *Eat and Love Yourself.*

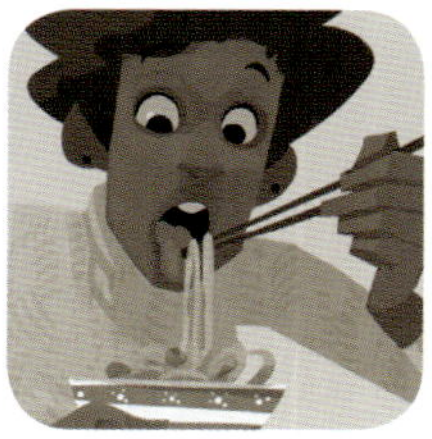
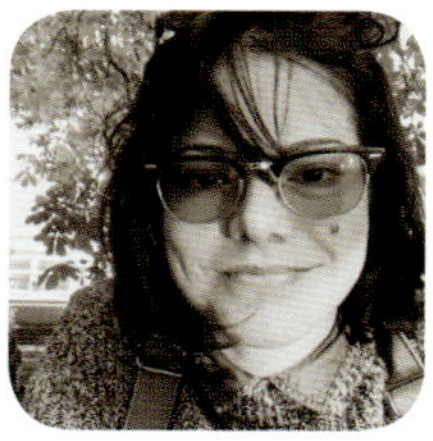

Meybis Ruiz Cruz

Lead illustrator | meybisruiz.com

Meybis is an illustrator and graphic designer based in Berlin. She mainly works on portraiture and character design.

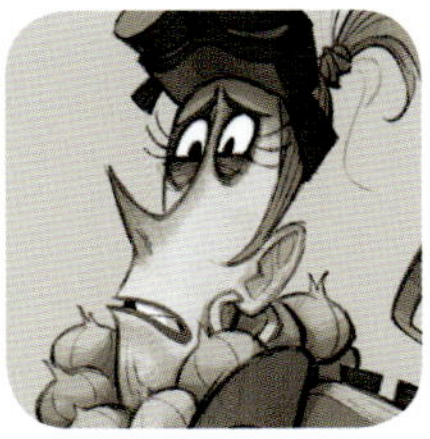

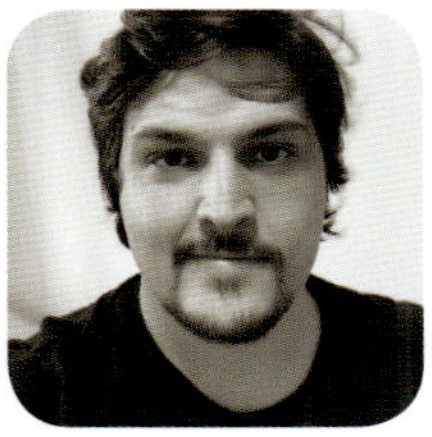

Guilherme Franco

Character designer & concept artist | guilhermefranco.com.br

Guilherme is a Brazilian artist who creates characters and environments for the animation and gaming industries.

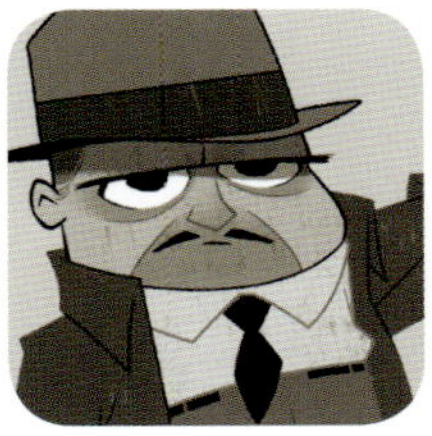

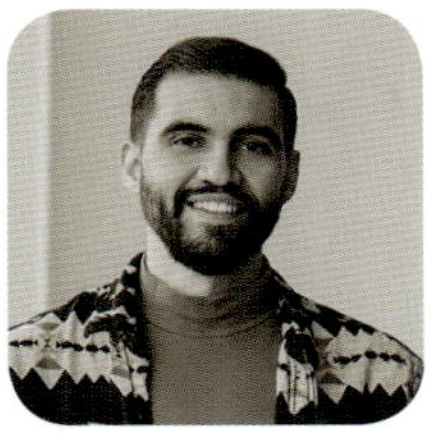

Luis Gadea

Character designer | luisgadea.com

Luis is a character designer and animator who has worked for Netflix, Dreamworks, and Warner Bros. He is happiest when he has a coffee, a pencil, and paper to hand.

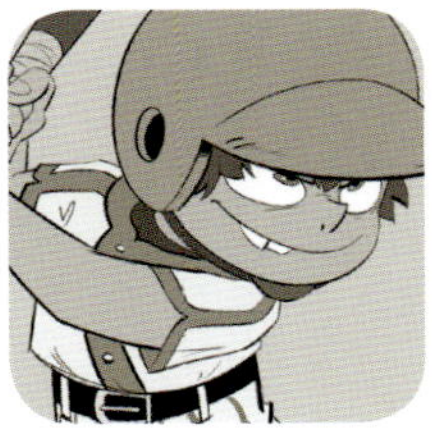

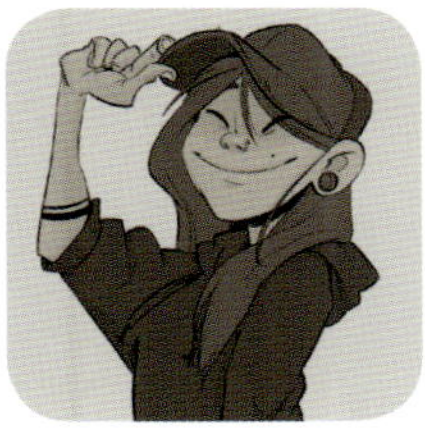

Ida Hem

Character designer | idahem.com

Ida is a character designer from Norway. She works within the Western animation industry and uses her free time to focus on personal projects.

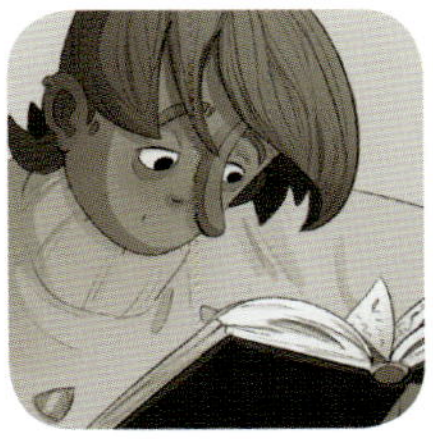

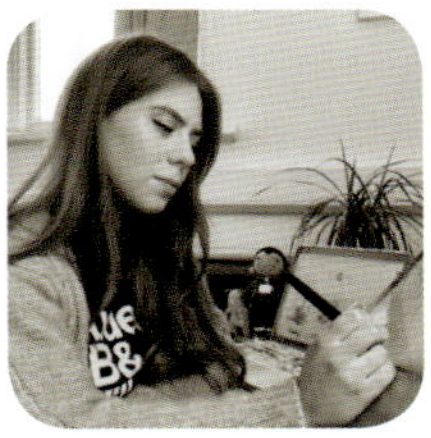

Corah Louise

Character designer & freelance illustrator | corahlouise.com

Corah is a freelance illustrator from the UK. She creates her characters and stories in an office above a library.

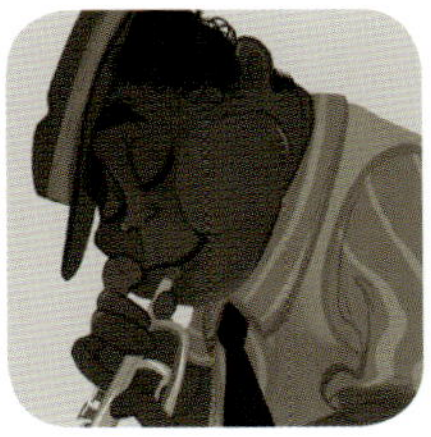

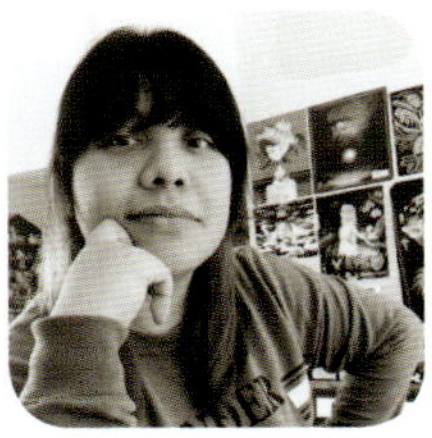

Vanessa Morales

Illustrator & concept artist | phonemova.carbonmade.com

Vanessa is a Mexican illustrator and fantasy enthusiast who has been working in the creative industry for five years.

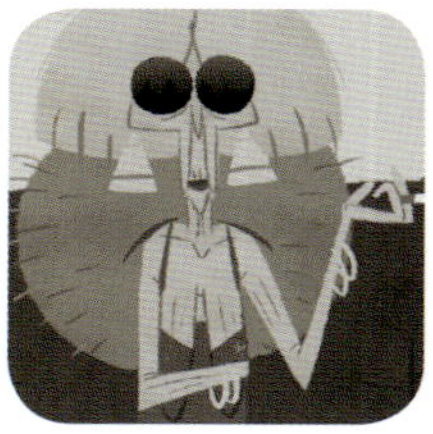

Dom "Scruffy" Murphy

Character designer | instagram.com/scruffyshenanigans

Dom works in animation and is a life-long sufferer of chronic "doodle-itis." He uses humor to soften the hard edges.

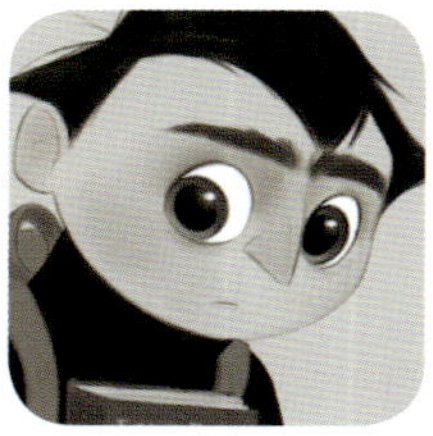
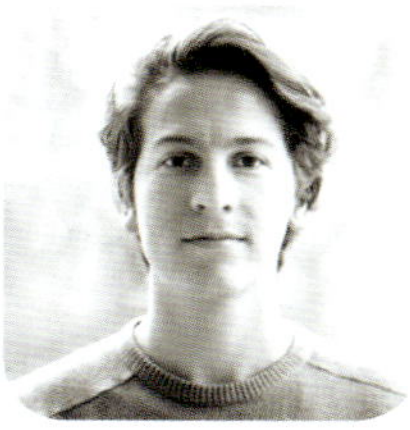

Tom van Rheenen

Character designer | tomvanrheenen.com

Tom is a character designer currently based in Amsterdam, and has worked for a variety of animation studios and production companies.

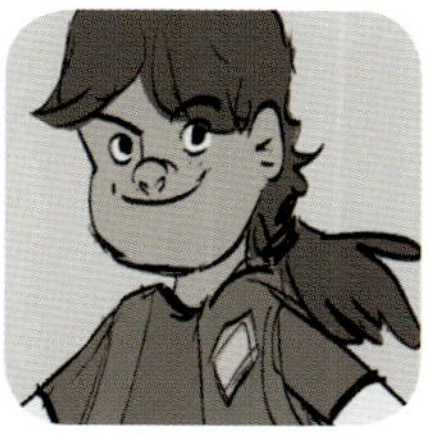
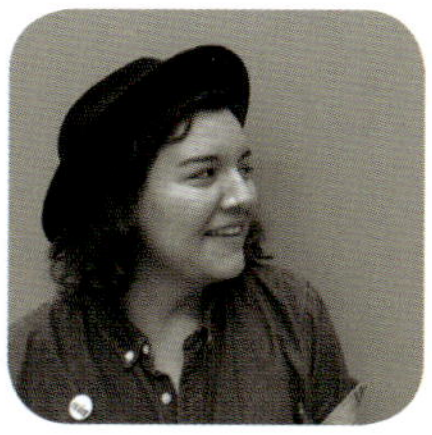

Stephanie Garcia Rizo

Character designer & storyboard artist | stephanierizo.com

Stephanie was born and raised in Southern California. She has worked with major studios such as Walt Disney Animation, Nickelodeon, and Sony Animation.

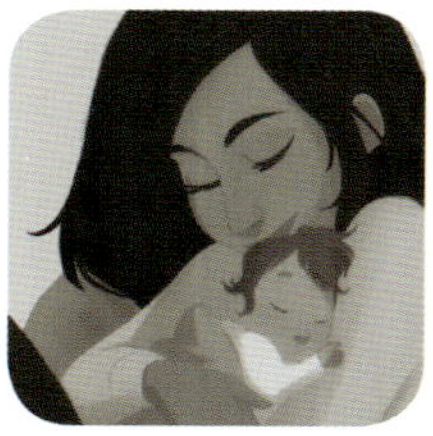
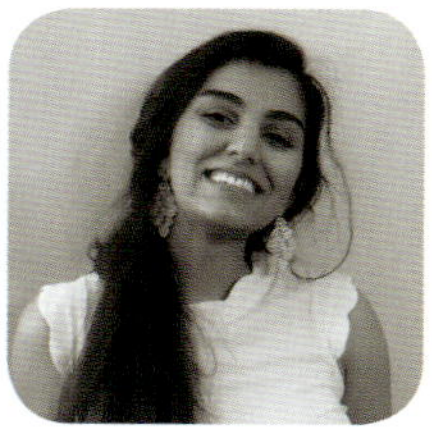

Noor Sofi

Visual development artist & illustrator | noorsofi.com

Noor lives and works in Los Angeles after gaining her degree in illustration from Brigham Young University-Idaho. Her clients include Taiko Animation Studios and Warner Bros.

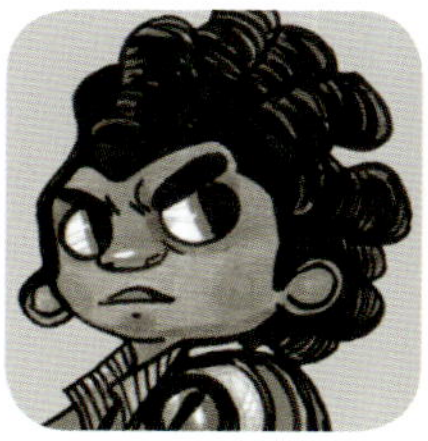
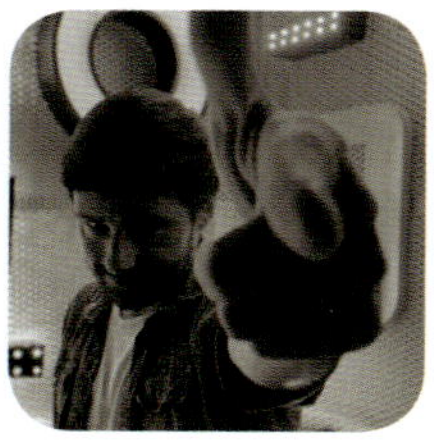

Eduardo Vieira

Character designer & illustrator | instagram.com/eduardovieirart

Eduardo produces work for animation and books, and provides expertise for tutorials and research. On the weekend you'll find him binge-watching Netflix series with a slice of pizza.

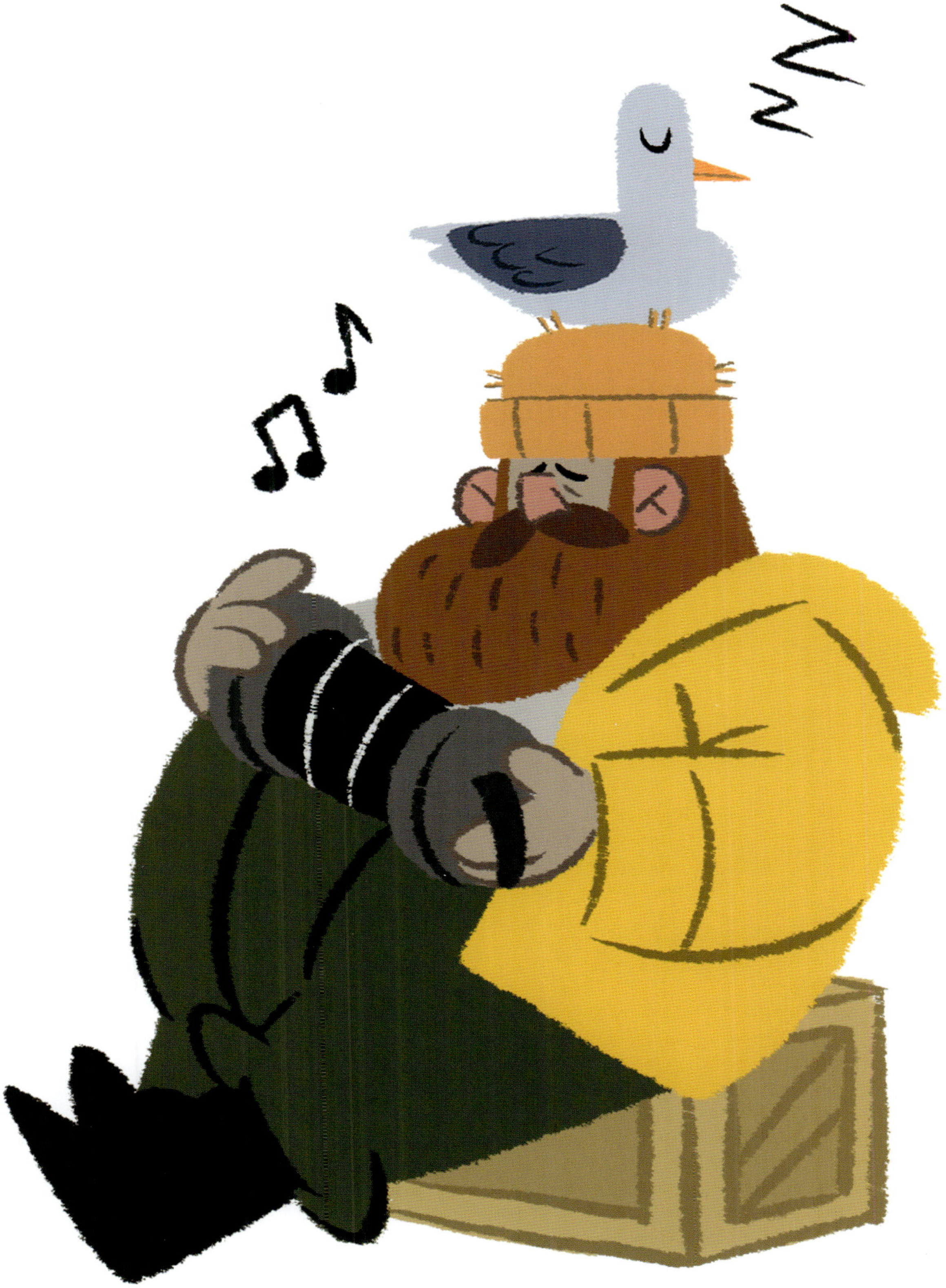

Image © Dom "Scruffy" Murphy

INDEX

A

accessories, 15, 23-24, 38, 43, 48, 60, 74, 138, 200, 212-215, 223, 238
acting, 49, 98, 166-167, 178, 182, 201, 296
action, 36, 71, 75, 80-82, 93, 98-99, 108-111, 113-114, 116-118, 120-121, 123, 127-128, 134-135, 137-138, 140-142, 145, 148-150, 170, 179-180, 213, 246, 249, 252-255, 260, 284
adult, 13, 24, 40, 48, 86, 97, 137-138, 159, 161, 193, 197, 202-204, 209, 235
age, 24, 32-33, 36, 47, 97, 120, 138, 158, 192-196, 198, 200, 202, 204-206, 208, 223, 225, 290, 292
anatomy, 80, 86-87, 89-93, 100, 114, 116, 174, 217
anger, 54, 56, 60, 136, 166, 171, 174, 177, 243
angular, 39-40, 58-59, 98, 100, 103, 155, 160, 162, 248
animal, 41, 48, 86, 197, 223, 293
animation, 13, 26, 29, 44, 99, 242, 291, 294
animator, 120, 157, 166, 295
anime, 13
appeal, 65, 78, 90, 170, 252, 256, 290, 293
arm, 75, 80-83, 109, 143-146, 151, 179, 244-245, 247-249
armor, 74, 217, 233, 244, 256
asleep, 125, 150, 180, 185
asymmetry, 70-71, 77, 175, 178, 181, 204, 218, 234, 242, 247-248
athletic, 95, 173, 203
atmosphere, 66-67, 236, 272, 274
attitude, 12, 49, 126, 163, 178, 200, 224, 230, 246-249
audience, 14-16, 22, 24-25, 50, 54, 60-63, 66-68, 70-72, 76, 80-82, 98, 101, 108, 119, 122, 125, 138-140, 162, 170, 176, 192, 196, 199, 207, 216, 225, 233, 236-237, 242-248, 252, 258, 260, 269, 272, 284, 290, 293-294, 296
axolotl, 41
aztec, 38

B

baby, 39, 137, 142, 193, 196-198, 207-208
background, 76, 143, 222, 269, 271
backlighting, 69
backstory, 17-18, 25, 48, 137-138
balance, 36-37, 43, 57, 59, 67-68, 70-75, 79, 101, 108-110, 112-113, 122, 124, 133, 145, 197, 207, 226, 265, 276, 290
bandit, 64, 71, 74
beard, 27, 203, 224
bone, 87, 96, 114, 155, 174, 195, 204
boy, 40, 46, 134-135, 141, 236, 258
brows, 166, 170-171, 175-176, 180-181, 184

C

cartoon, 13, 86, 89, 166, 170, 178, 180, 234, 290
character, 12-28, 30, 32-33, 36, 38, 40-51, 54, 56-78, 80-83, 86-94, 96, 98-102, 105, 108-110, 112-125, 127-151, 154-156, 158-168, 170-189, 192-194, 196, 198-199, 201, 203-208, 212-230, 232-239, 242-243, 245-249, 252, 254-256, 260-265, 268-269, 271-273, 276-277, 280, 284, 290-297
characteristics, 18, 23, 27, 36, 47, 94, 154, 207, 235, 256-257
cheeks, 135, 164, 166-167, 170, 176, 180, 184-185, 188, 196-198
chest, 90, 92, 94, 114-115, 118, 127, 133, 136, 194-195, 197, 202, 209, 242
child, 24-26, 97, 142, 146, 148, 197-200, 202, 208, 233, 237, 246, 272, 290-292, 296
chin, 89, 150, 154-157, 161, 164-165, 242
circle, 54, 56-57, 59, 78, 154-155, 163, 165, 189
classroom, 264-267
client, 290-291, 294
clothes, 42, 63, 73-74, 82, 114, 148-149, 198-199, 208, 212, 217, 222, 256, 268
clothing, 20, 48, 60, 72, 120, 192, 199, 203, 208, 212, 216-217, 219, 222-223, 229, 233, 268
color, 40, 44, 50, 54, 60-70, 78-80, 114, 142, 178, 207-208, 218-220, 222-223, 226, 231, 238-239, 242-243, 249, 257, 262-263, 265, 273, 278, 280-282, 284, 291
comics, 13, 86, 120, 221
complementary colors, 60
composition, 252, 260, 264-265, 276, 280
confidence, 19, 54, 57, 59-60, 108, 130, 132, 135, 138, 182-183, 192
conflict, 83, 252, 254, 256, 276
construction, 42, 114, 85, 90-91, 93, 154-157
contrast, 32, 40, 59-61, 68, 70-73, 75, 77, 90, 94, 98, 100, 102-105, 114-115, 123, 158, 162, 202, 208, 235, 244-245, 290
costume, 50, 60, 71, 74, 78-79, 100, 137, 212, 216-218, 220-221, 223-224, 249, 278
creativity, 36, 60, 230, 239
crowd, 15, 140, 280, 282, 291
culture, 13, 38, 40, 86, 216, 219, 272
curious, 12, 128, 208, 239, 269
curve, 80-81, 115, 123, 127, 154, 156-159
cute, 24, 110, 181, 197, 207, 217, 291, 293, 296

D

details, 18, 25, 36-39, 42-43, 48, 50, 54, 60, 65, 67, 71-72, 74, 76, 78, 81, 89-90, 92, 114, 138, 146, 154-155, 159, 180, 198, 201, 218, 226, 232-233, 244-249, 260, 269, 272-273, 277, 294
development, 14, 197, 248, 291
direction, 13, 16-17, 24, 27-28, 44, 108-110, 114, 118-119, 122, 148-149, 207, 226, 269, 280
drama, 67, 148, 252, 280, 282
drawing, 27, 36, 70, 72-74, 82, 89, 93-94, 99, 114, 116-118, 120, 128, 134, 139, 143, 151, 154-157, 160, 182-183, 188, 223, 226, 231, 236, 244-246, 248, 264
dynamic, 33, 55, 58-59, 65, 70-72, 74, 78, 126, 137, 165, 170, 193, 247

E

ears, 32, 71, 75, 97, 164, 200, 204, 222
edges, 114, 154, 156, 162-163, 222
elderly, 32, 47, 138, 193-194, 205, 268
embarrassment, 174, 201
emotion, 28, 32, 36, 60, 66, 73, 80, 120, 137, 146, 166, 170-172, 184, 186-188, 201, 260
enthusiasm, 70, 135, 138, 202
environment, 18, 44, 51, 206, 216, 265, 276

exaggeration, 12, 24, 27, 32-33, 49, 98-99, 104-105, 108, 114-115, 120, 138, 145, 158, 162, 164-165, 170-172, 176, 178-179, 184-185, 218, 242, 245
excitement, 54, 56, 68, 108, 246, 272
exhaustion, 129, 144, 184, 189
expressions, 28, 33, 45, 49, 142, 166, 169-171, 173-174, 176, 182, 184, 186, 188, 201, 214, 257-258, 265, 269, 273, 285, 295
eyebrows, 73, 116, 141, 157, 164, 167-172, 174-175, 177-184, 186-189, 197, 206, 209, 242
eyelids, 150, 157, 166-167, 170, 172, 179, 186-188
eyes, 27, 60-61, 63, 71, 76, 122, 135, 141, 154-162, 165-172, 174-189, 192, 196-198, 206, 230

F

face, 27, 32, 45, 51, 57-63, 66-67, 70, 73-74, 77-81, 89, 96, 99, 103, 114, 133, 135, 148, 154-166, 168-170, 172-174, 176-180, 182, 184, 186-188, 196-198, 200, 202, 206, 209, 221, 224, 226-228, 247, 249, 258
family, 149, 202, 215, 268-269, 272, 274, 278, 290
fashion, 16-17, 19-20, 203, 209, 221, 223, 230
fat, 87, 89, 91, 94-96, 195, 197-198, 202
fear, 98, 101, 111, 133, 149, 166, 168, 182
feeling, 54, 56-58, 60, 62, 67-69, 71-74, 86, 88, 98, 123, 136-137, 142, 166, 182, 209
feet, 33, 70-71, 77-78, 80-82, 86, 89-90, 92, 103, 108, 112-113, 132, 135, 147
female, 86-87, 92, 96, 154-155, 166, 202
feminine, 154, 202, 219, 222
figure, 12, 16, 54, 86-87, 90, 96, 98, 100, 140, 142, 162, 183, 272, 281
film, 13, 128, 290-291
flow, 70, 78, 80, 82, 202, 212, 246, 249
focal points, 60, 64, 66, 71, 74, 78, 213, 245
focus, 16, 60-61, 65, 70-71, 73, 79, 93, 120, 122-123, 126, 146, 154-155, 166, 168, 172, 184, 187, 202, 245, 268, 271
foot, 76, 82-83, 108, 113, 127, 135-136, 142, 148
forehead, 166, 169, 179, 182, 196-198
form, 13, 19, 26, 28, 75, 86, 98-99, 101, 103, 105, 108, 130, 154, 169-170, 179, 183, 188, 196, 198, 216, 231, 252, 284, 290, 294
friendly, 12, 24-25, 40, 47, 54, 60, 136, 163, 165, 222, 276
frown, 174, 180, 182, 188

G

gender, 195, 284, 293
gesture, 70, 80, 90, 93, 107-108, 110, 112, 114-128, 130, 132, 134, 136, 138, 140, 142, 144, 146, 148, 150, 194, 246
girl, 28, 36, 38, 41, 56, 59, 110, 135, 138, 140, 192, 228, 236, 269, 291, 293
glasses, 48, 80, 98, 139
gravity, 143, 150, 171-172, 204, 237
guide, 61, 73, 81, 108, 158, 165, 182, 198
guideline, 27, 32, 192-193

H

hair, 37-39, 42-43, 58, 70-74, 138, 144, 148-149, 163, 173, 182, 197-201, 203, 205-209, 212, 219, 221, 224-231, 243
hairstyle, 108, 173, 200, 207, 212, 218, 226-227, 229-231
hand, 14, 60-61, 71, 78-79, 81, 83, 89-90, 116, 118, 126-127, 133-136, 138, 141, 143, 146-147, 149-151, 170, 184, 188-189, 204, 218, 222, 234, 242, 244, 284, 294
happiness, 60, 166, 178, 196, 272, 284
happy, 108, 167, 169-170, 182, 231, 245, 258
hat, 15, 18, 43, 70-71, 77, 105, 116, 140, 218-219, 222
head, 27, 37, 56-58, 70-71, 73, 76, 78, 86-87, 90, 97-98, 102, 104-105, 114, 135-136, 141, 144, 146-148, 150-151, 154-157, 159-165, 171, 174, 176-178, 182, 184, 186-189, 193, 197, 207, 209, 224-225, 228-229, 231, 243, 247, 261, 290, 295
height, 86-87, 94, 222, 227
highlight, 98, 154, 162, 170, 226, 259
hips, 71, 87, 92, 109, 114-115, 122, 136, 195, 202
historical, 12, 36, 239
history, 86, 196, 239
horror, 24, 186, 291
hue, 60, 62, 218, 249, 271
human, 18-19, 36, 38-39, 48, 77, 86, 88-90, 94, 98-99, 114, 142, 154, 170, 182, 192-194, 197, 206, 242, 257
humor, 76-77, 183, 218

I

ideation, 36, 38, 40, 42, 44, 46, 48-51, 60
identity, 37, 39, 200, 242
illustration, 112, 139, 264
impact, 16, 60, 78, 142, 235
infant, 197, 207
inspiration, 13, 41, 47, 143, 218, 220, 223, 239
interaction, 76, 166, 209, 235, 252, 255-258, 260, 265-266, 272-274, 280, 282, 284
irritation, 136, 179
items, 18, 204, 212

J

jaw, 27, 59, 154-155, 174, 180, 193, 200
jawline, 200, 202, 209
jewelry, 38, 205, 219
job, 12, 24, 32, 108, 154, 174, 186, 192, 202, 212, 256, 261, 297
joy, 50, 141, 187, 202, 274
jumping, 75, 133

K

keywords, 38, 48, 108, 213
knees, 87, 108, 123, 151, 198, 204
knowledge, 86, 89-90, 128, 206

L

laugh, 176, 188-189, 286
leg, 70, 81-83, 109, 113, 134-136, 145
legs, 37, 71, 75, 88, 90, 102, 104, 108, 114, 130, 133, 143-144, 147, 197, 206, 242
lifestyle, 173, 198-199, 202-203
lighting, 60, 66-70, 266, 282
limbs, 59, 75, 90, 94, 96, 100, 108, 119, 122, 130-131, 142, 148, 193, 197-198, 200
line, 39, 49, 70, 72-73, 80-83, 90, 108-112, 114, 116-121, 123, 127-128, 140, 142, 150, 154-159, 161, 163, 179-180, 185, 188, 200, 212-213, 219, 226, 231, 246, 252, 291, 295
lip, 155, 166-167, 172, 174, 176-177, 180-181, 186-187, 189
love, 14, 36, 60, 142, 178, 223, 237, 252, 260, 274

M

male, 48, 86-87, 91-92, 95, 154-156, 166
medieval, 18, 197, 219
mirror, 36, 89, 92, 149, 166, 178, 181, 188, 238
model, 36, 99, 138, 157
modern, 13, 38, 48, 86, 212, 215, 290
mood, 66, 68, 80, 120, 130, 143, 180, 194, 202, 243, 246
moodboard, 44, 47-49
motion, 44, 75, 133, 144, 223, 294
moustache, 224
mouth, 75, 83, 144, 154, 156-158, 163, 165-172, 174-181, 183-189, 196, 198, 224, 290, 294
movement, 13, 36, 45, 54, 56, 58, 70, 73, 78, 89, 93, 108-114, 116, 118, 120, 122, 124, 126, 128, 130, 132, 134, 136, 138, 140, 142, 144-146, 148-150, 174, 187, 197, 204, 212, 219, 228
movie, 12, 36, 223, 242, 290
muscles, 86-88, 91, 94, 96, 99, 125, 166-169, 171, 174, 180-181, 185, 194-195, 200, 204
mystery, 12, 22, 60-61, 63

N

narrative, 252, 256, 262, 266, 280
nature, 25-27, 60, 69, 86, 89-90, 108, 116, 120, 179, 194, 206, 216, 220, 238-239, 249
neck, 67, 77, 89, 114, 155, 178, 196-198, 200, 206-207, 221
negative, 75, 137
nervous, 129, 135, 171, 178, 261, 272
neutral, 60, 63, 148, 166, 181, 242
nose, 32, 43, 77, 97, 116, 154-162, 165-167, 176, 180, 186, 188, 198-200, 202, 204, 206-207, 209
nostrils, 181, 186

O

observation, 89, 128, 212
old, 32-33, 43, 48, 114, 120-121, 139, 141, 179, 193, 198, 212, 233, 239
outfit, 12, 22-23, 203, 216-218, 220-222
oval, 56, 78, 154, 161, 163-164
overlap, 75, 82-83, 157, 290
overweight, 96, 195
owl, 206-207

P

palette, 40, 50, 60, 62-65, 67-69, 208, 263
parents, 181, 200-202, 272
patterns, 51, 70, 72, 100, 212, 219-220
people, 13-14, 17, 27, 30, 36, 44-45, 47-48, 86-87, 94, 96-97, 128, 131, 133, 139-141, 176, 180, 182, 195-196, 205-206, 209, 217, 219-220, 222, 227, 244, 252, 258, 260, 268
performance, 98, 180, 235, 280
personality, 12-18, 20-21, 23-24, 27, 32, 36, 38, 43, 54, 57, 66, 68, 72, 76, 78, 98, 105, 114, 119-121, 126, 131, 141, 143, 158, 163, 173, 199, 203, 207, 216, 218, 220, 222-223, 226-227, 230, 234-238, 242, 246, 255, 261, 263, 268, 272-273, 276, 284, 294
perspective, 112, 156, 268, 280-281
photo, 44, 48, 89, 128, 166, 232, 280
pink, 63-65, 69, 109, 200, 220, 291
playful, 148, 181, 187, 198, 202, 236
pose, 36, 50, 70-71, 75, 80-81, 83, 90, 93, 108-112, 114-115, 117, 119, 121-124, 127-128, 130-135, 137-138, 140-143, 146-147, 150, 156-157, 199, 205, 208, 213, 218, 220, 235, 243, 246-247, 249, 260, 264, 269, 294-295
posture, 32, 74, 80-81, 143, 146, 148, 192, 194, 197, 199, 201, 204-206, 208-209
preschool, 98, 290-291
presentation, 247, 294-295
proportion, 27, 32, 37, 41, 76, 86, 90, 94, 98, 143, 159, 197-199, 207, 232, 245, 252, 294
props, 23, 43, 46, 61, 71, 74, 76, 82, 138, 147, 199, 212, 218, 224, 233-234, 237-239, 262, 295
puberty, 202
pupils, 171-172, 178-179, 181, 189
purple, 64-65, 69

Q

queue, 268-269

R

rabbit, 73, 76
reaction, 264, 266, 269, 273, 280
readability, 41, 75, 138, 146, 212, 230, 235, 265
realistic, 27, 86, 89, 104, 158-159, 232
reality, 36, 48, 176, 183, 219, 228, 246
rectangle, 59, 163, 165
red, 60, 63-64, 79, 166, 244, 249
reference, 36, 39-40, 44, 46-50, 88-89, 94, 117, 128, 134, 138, 143, 166, 169, 174, 212, 218, 221, 239
reflection, 36, 66, 186, 206
relatable, 14, 50, 201, 242, 291, 293
relationship, 105, 148, 236, 245, 252, 261, 272, 277
relaxed, 129-130, 142-143, 146, 148, 175, 179-180, 182, 185, 219
repetition, 78-80, 220
research, 36-39, 41, 43-45, 47-50, 212, 220, 222, 244
rhythm, 80-82, 90, 246
role, 23-24, 48-49, 76, 166, 171, 178, 192, 201, 217, 234, 256, 264, 269

S

sad, 80, 120, 167, 171-172, 176
sadness, 60-61, 108, 144, 166, 176
saturation, 69, 271
scale, 76-77, 101
scenario, 66-67, 69, 82, 90, 125, 252
scene, 27, 66, 82, 252, 262, 264, 266, 268-269, 272, 274, 276, 280, 282, 285
school, 24, 43, 73, 136
sci-fi, 18, 220
setting, 24, 36, 38, 66, 216

shape, 13, 26-33, 40, 42, 44, 51, 54-57, 59, 61, 70-72, 75, 78, 80, 87-90, 92, 98-99, 105, 114, 116, 120, 134-135, 151, 154-156, 158-160, 162-165, 170-172, 175, 179, 188, 193-194, 206-207, 216, 218, 224, 226, 228, 230-231, 234, 239, 245, 249, 252, 277, 290, 294
shape language, 44, 53-58, 70, 78, 98, 114, 120, 154, 162, 193-194, 216, 252
sharp, 27, 54, 98, 162-163, 165, 197, 202, 206-207
shirt, 21, 50, 72, 75, 117, 198, 203, 219, 221, 269
shoulders, 13, 56-57, 59, 86-87, 90, 94, 109, 114, 130, 133, 144, 146-148, 174, 178, 182-184, 194-195, 230, 243
shy, 23, 48, 135, 143, 175, 192, 199, 206, 228, 230, 237
sidekick, 98, 236, 260-263
silhouette, 41, 69, 75, 82-83, 92, 96, 109, 119-121, 124-125, 127, 134, 137, 141, 146, 202, 206, 212-213, 216-219, 226, 228, 230, 234, 256, 260
simplify, 27-28, 87, 91, 149, 235
size, 36-37, 58, 76-77, 86-87, 90, 94, 97, 102, 105, 114, 135, 181, 189, 193, 235, 242, 245, 256
skeleton, 87-88, 91, 94
sketch, 44-46, 80-81, 90, 108, 120, 134, 146, 158, 173, 213, 245, 268, 294
skin, 19, 38, 72, 88, 97, 150, 166, 196, 204, 217, 231, 271
smile, 49, 141, 150, 162, 171, 174-176, 178, 180-183, 186-188, 201, 209, 284
space, 18, 47, 61, 74-75, 86, 91, 143, 154-156, 160, 162, 170, 198, 221, 239, 246, 276, 278, 280, 294
spine, 81, 87-88, 108-109, 117, 123, 127, 194, 205
square, 23, 27, 54-55, 57, 98, 117-118, 154, 158, 162-165
squash, 27, 32, 87, 99, 176, 196
stance, 71, 130-131, 148-149, 151, 256
standing, 70, 73, 77, 80-82, 108, 112-113, 134, 137, 171, 260, 268
stereotypes, 14-15, 43, 94, 138, 221, 291, 293
story, 12-19, 21-25, 27, 29, 31-33, 36, 44, 50, 54, 60, 65-66, 68, 72-73, 76, 94, 98, 108, 114, 116, 120, 122-123, 138-139, 146, 173, 178, 212, 216-218, 226, 230, 234, 236, 238, 244, 248, 252, 256, 260, 264-265, 268, 272-273, 277, 280, 285, 290
storytelling, 76, 80
stress, 132, 146, 189, 225, 268
stretch, 27, 32, 87, 99, 176
structure, 27, 33, 36, 44, 87-88, 96, 212
studio, 13, 296
study, 30, 44-45, 166, 180, 207, 209, 219, 297
style, 13, 24, 36, 72-73, 78, 98, 131, 159, 176, 197, 203, 205, 218-219, 226-229, 232, 234-235, 238, 244, 258, 264, 284, 296-297
stylized, 12-13, 27, 89, 98, 114, 218, 232, 235, 243, 294, 296
surprise, 166, 172, 176, 187, 280
symbolism, 54, 60-61
symmetry, 70-71, 242

T

tangents, 82-83, 121
teacher, 136, 165, 178, 180
team, 176, 260, 284-286
teenager, 159, 161, 200-202, 208-209, 269
teeth, 58, 83, 116, 179, 182-183, 186-189, 204, 256
tension, 54, 56, 129, 146, 149, 179, 181, 246, 272, 278
texture, 44, 72-73, 78-79, 231
theory, 120, 158, 198
thin, 94, 186, 204, 206, 242
thumbnails, 24, 43, 49, 55, 244-246, 248, 256, 260, 264, 268, 272, 276, 280
tired, 73, 128-129, 172, 192, 202
toddler, 138, 193, 235
tongue, 176-178, 181, 187
torso, 76, 108-109, 114, 127
triangle, 40, 54-57, 59, 78, 98-99, 100, 156, 162, 198
turnarounds, 131, 290, 294-295
TV, 12, 20, 24, 26, 36, 101, 128, 290, 292, 297

U

unbalanced, 148, 181, 186-187

V

value, 54, 60-65, 70, 78, 208, 218, 260
variation, 13, 27, 47, 73, 245, 268
villain, 14, 54, 56, 223, 245-249, 280
volume, 90, 110, 114, 202, 227, 231, 290, 294

W

waist, 94, 202, 221
walk, 14, 36, 80, 147-148, 192
warmth, 60, 142, 182, 273-274
warrior, 74, 77, 220
weapon, 74, 83, 232-233
weight, 16, 72-73, 96, 108-110, 112-113, 122, 124-125, 129-130, 134, 142-145, 150-151, 158, 160, 195, 202, 209, 212, 226, 234-235, 237
wizard, 63, 68, 223, 239
woman, 32, 40, 43, 81, 120, 142, 154, 218, 259
wrinkles, 158, 169, 176, 181, 188-189, 192, 196, 204, 234

Y

yawn, 185, 189
young, 16, 21, 24, 38-39, 141, 158, 160-161, 165, 186, 296

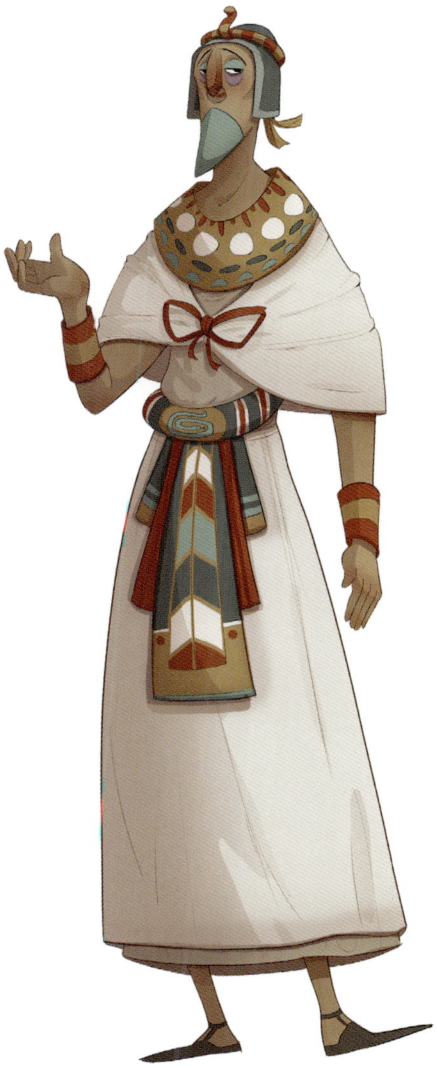

Image by Corah Louise

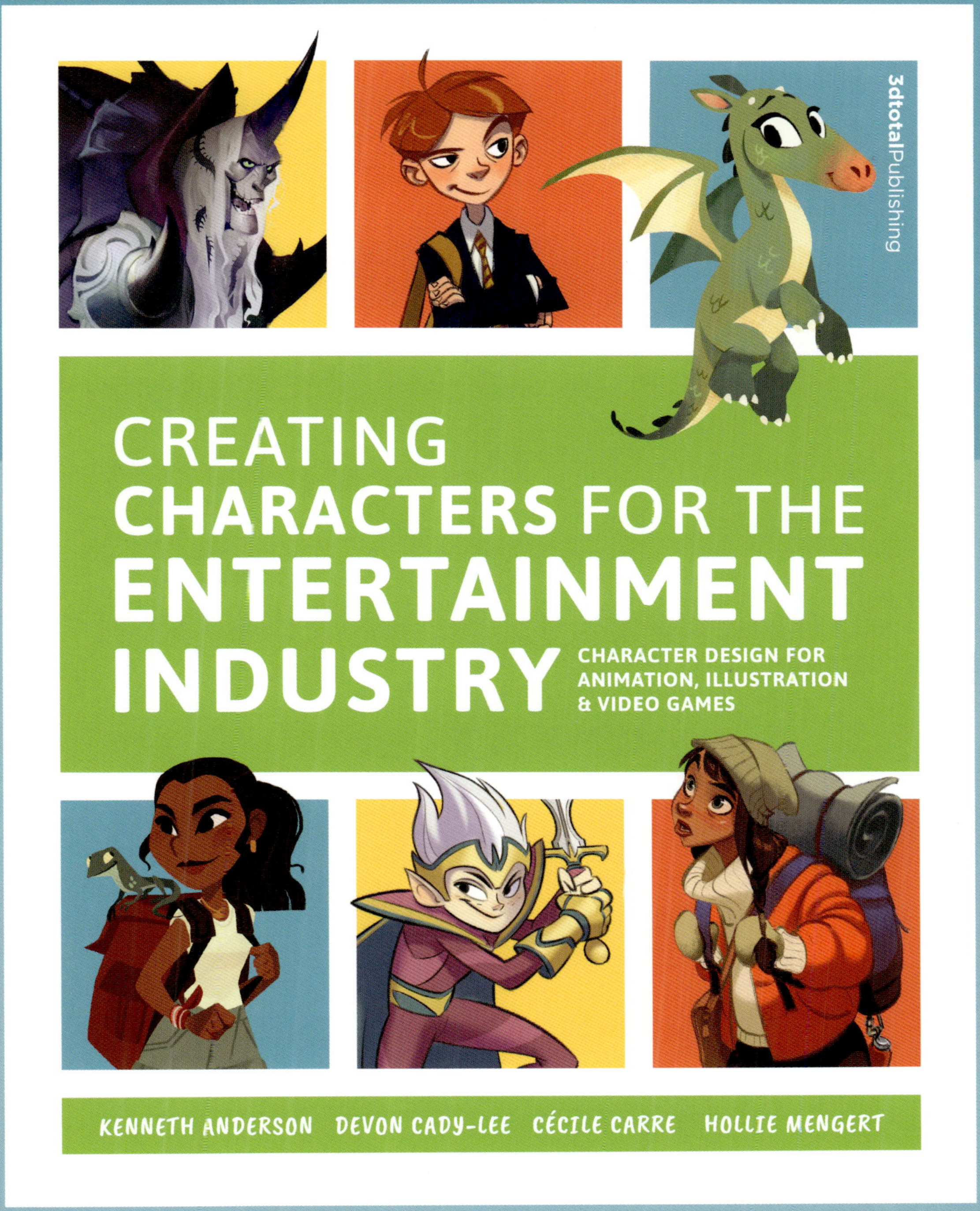
3dtotalPublishing
CREATING
CHARACTERS FOR THE
ENTERTAINMENT
INDUSTRY
CHARACTER DESIGN FOR
ANIMATION, ILLUSTRATION
& VIDEO GAMES
KENNETH ANDERSON DEVON CADY-LEE CÉCILE CARRE HOLLIE MENGERT

3dtotal Publishing

3dtotal Publishing is a trailblazing, creative publisher specializing in inspirational and educational resources for artists.

Our titles feature top industry professionals from around the globe who share their experience in skillfully written step-by-step tutorials and fascinating, detailed guides. Illustrated throughout with stunning artwork, these best-selling publications offer creative insight, expert advice, and essential motivation. Fans of digital art will enjoy our comprehensive volumes covering Adobe Photoshop, Procreate, and Blender, as well as our superb titles based around character design, including *Fundamentals of Character Design* and *Creating Characters for the Entertainment Industry*. The dedicated, high-quality blend of instruction and inspiration also extends to traditional art. Titles covering a range of techniques, genres, and abilities allow your creativity to flourish while building essential skills.

Well-established within the industry, we now offer over 100 titles and counting, many of which have been translated into multiple languages around the world. With something for every artist, we are proud to say that our books offer the 3dtotal package:

LEARN • CREATE • SHARE

Visit us at store.3dtotal.com

3dtotal Publishing is part of 3dtotal.com, a leading website for CG artists founded by Tom Greenway in 1999.